All the World Is Awry

All the World Is Awry

Al-Maʿarrī and the *Luzūmiyyāt*, Revisited

R. KEVIN LACEY

SUNY PRESS

Cover art: Original watercolor painting of al-Maʿarrī, by Melissa Coury.
Used with permission.

Published by State University of New York Press, Albany

Printed in the United States of America

Library of Congress Cataloging-in-Publication Data

Names: Lacey, R. Kevin, author
Title: All the world is awry / Al-Maʿarrī and the Luzūmiyyāt, revisited
Description: Albany : State University of New York Press, [2021] |
Includes bibliographical references and index.
Identifiers: ISBN 9781438479453 (hardcover : alk. paper) |
ISBN 9781438479460 (e-book) | ISBN 9781438479446 (paperback)
Library of Congress Control Number 2020937125
Further information is available at the Library of Congress.

10 9 8 7 6 5 4 3 2 1

CONTENTS

Acknowledgments vii

A Note on Transliteration ix

PART ONE

One The Man: A Bibliographical Sketch of Abū al-ʿAlāʾ al-Maʿarrī 3

Two The Milieu 39

PART TWO

Three The Medium: Reading and Interpreting *Luzūm Mā Lā Yalzam* in Light of Its Literary Character 139

Four The Message 177

Notes 353

Principle Works Cited or Consulted 443

Index 453

ACKNOWLEDGMENTS

I am indebted to a multitude of colleagues and former instructors of good will for helping me find the inspiration and resolve to have this project see the light of day. They are too numerous to name here, but I trust they are gracious enough not to be disquieted by this. In any event, the anonymity will serve to underscore that any infelicities or shortcomings are entirely my own. For extra special camaraderie in recent years, I owe an extra special word of thanks to Ralph and Melissa Coury. Ralph's scholarship has been extraordinarily helpful and influential. Melissa's insights have been valuable, and her art an inspiration. She provided the cover artwork. For their patience and understanding, my immediate family—wife, Gladys Maria Varona, and daughters, Alina and Alexa—as well as extended family deserve a heartfelt thank you.

Michael Abdelmessih helped in typing portions of the Arabic. Dr. Tayseer Gomaa helped with proofreading the Arabic, checking all citations, and in many instances drawing attention to enhanced understandings. Members of the Acquisitions Department of SUNY Press, especially directors James Peltz and Donna Dixon and editor Amanda Lanne-Camilli, SUNY Press promotional manager Kate R. Seyburyamo, and senior production editor Eileen Nizer have all been exceedingly patient and attentive in overseeing the final stages of production.

An earlier version of chapter 4, part 4 was published in *The Muslim World* (January–April 1995).

A NOTE ON TRANSLITERATION

For the most part, the system I followed is that used by the *International Journal of Middle East Studies* (*IJMES*). The most notable exceptions are (1) ة is represented by "ah" and not "a"; and (2) the elision of vowels preceding the hamzah (ء) that requires elision (همزة الوصل) is not represented with ' and the dropping of the following vowel. Thus, something like الفصول و الغايات, for example, will be transliterated as *al-Fuṣūl wa al-Ghāyāt* and not *al-Fuṣūl wa'l-Ghāyāt*. To give another example, في الشعر becomes *fī al-shi'r* and not *fi'l-shi'r*. Exceptions are made, however, in the case of citing authors whose approach to transliteration represents the elision preceding همزة الوصل with character ' and the dropping of the following vowel.

In some cases—for example, some technical terms or names of people, places, or book titles—both the Arabic and the English-language transliterations are given, essentially for the sake of assuring clarification.

Book or journal titles in transliterated Arabic follow the more conventional approach in English with respect to capitalization. Thus, all major words in a title are capitalized. Nouns (proper or otherwise) commonly found in English-language sources with standard English-language dictionary renderings (e.g., Baghdad, Mecca, Medina, Iraq) are left in those renderings (meaning first and foremost that they are without diacritics).

With only one or two exceptions, the names of Arabic authors that in English-language sources are commonly known in their Anglicized forms are kept in the Anglicized forms.

PART 1

CHAPTER ONE

The Man

A Bibliographical Sketch of Abū al-ʿAlāʾ al-Maʿarrī[1]

Abū al-ʿAlāʾ al-Maʿarrī/أبو العلاء المعري was born in 973 Common Era (363 Islamic Era) in the small Syrian town of Maʿarrat al-Nuʿmān (معرة النعمان), from which is derived his *laqab* (لقب) or *agnomen.* The town is situated in northern Syria about 20 miles south of the city of Aleppo. It lies in a semiarid region that is devoid of running water, although with the aid of cisterns and wells the population has long been able to sustain a fairly bountiful agriculture consisting of vineyards, orchards (olives, pistachios, almonds), and fields of wheat and barley. Writing in the fifth century of the Islamic Era, the Persian poet, philosopher, and traveler Nāṣir-i Khusraw (ناصر خسرو), passing through Maʿarrat al-Nuʿmān on a trip the principal destinations of which were Mecca and Cairo, could write of having seen the town's productive agriculture as well as flourishing bazaars: وبزارهاي او بسيار معمور ديدم . . . وكشاورزي ايشان همه گندمست وبسيار است ودرخت انجير وزيتون وبشته وبادام وانگور فراوان است.[2]

In the seventh century of the Islamic Era (hereafter IE), the Andalusian traveler and geographer Ibn Jubayr speaks of the town having arable land (سواد) devoted entirely to olive, fig, and pistachio trees, adding that he regarded Maʿarrat al-Nuʿmān as "one of God's most fertile and productive lands" (وهي من أخصب بلاد الله وأكثرها أرزاقاً). "It is a small, lovely city most of whose trees are pistachio and fig" (المعرة مدينة صغيرة أكثر شجرها التين والفستق), wrote the eighth-century (IE) Moroccan geographer Ibn Baṭṭūṭah/ابن بطوطة upon his visit.[3]

Maʿarrat al-Nuʿmān lies at strategic crossroads running both north and south and east and west. To the south lie the cities of Ḥamāh (حماة), Ḥimṣ (حمص), and, finally, Damascus. The road north leads to Antakya (Antioch) and İskenderun in present-day Turkey (الإسكندرونة and أنطاكية respectively in the Arabic). To the west lies Latakia (اللاذقية) on the Mediterranean, and to the east, the upper reaches of the Euphrates, which allow for riparian access to the heartlands of Iraq, including most notably Baghdad. In al-Maʿarrī's time, the area stretching on the south-to-north axis from Ḥamāh through Maʿarrat al-Nuʿmān and on to Aleppo was regarded as the locus for the frontier metropolitan strongholds (العواصم), the first line of defense against Byzantine Christian irredentism directed against Syria both as a valuable possession in and of itself and as an avenue of access to even more valuable territories of the Islamic commonwealth to the south (e.g., Palestine and Egypt). These frontier strongholds were also stepping stones for counteroffensives by organized Muslim armed forces. At the same time, in what amounted to a tripartite geopolitical dismemberment of Syria by rivals, the expansionist Ismāʿīlī Shīʿī (Fāṭimid persuasion) imām-caliphs in Cairo, and the semiautonomous Ḥamdānid/حمداني princes (who were Shīʿites but non-Fāṭimid, i.e., probably Ithnāʿasharī) centered in Aleppo, were active in promoting and protecting their own dynastic interests in the area. For the Fāṭimid imām-caliphs, this meant especially the attempt to establish suzerainty over Damascus if not areas to the north as well; for the Ḥāmdānids, this meant control of Aleppo if not as well Ḥamāh and Ḥimṣ and by extension Maʿarrat al-Nuʿmān (administratively regarded as falling under the suzerainty of Ḥimṣ or Ḥamāh the latter of which in turn was subject to the oversight of Aleppo).[4] Added to this mix of rivalries were (1) the growing political ambitions of the Banū Kilāb/بنو كلاب, Arab bedouins who had migrated to northern Syria from the Najd in the Arabian peninsula (eventually to establish their own dynasty centered in Aleppo), and (2) the ambitions of one or another slave page (غلام) or slave soldier (مملوك) and the troops at their disposal, who were of diverse ethnic backgrounds (e.g., Turkish, Kurdish, and Daylamī) with decidedly fluid loyalties.

All of these factors gave Maʿarrat al-Nuʿmān in the tenth and eleventh centuries of the Common Era a geopolitical importance most disproportionate to the town's size, an importance that was arguably its most remarkable feature. It lay in the way of the approach to Aleppo by invading forces moving on the city from south to north and in the way of the approach to Damascus by invading forces moving on the city from north to south. Maʿarrat al-Nuʿmān was close enough to Aleppo to be considered key to its defense. Several armed expeditions of the period, whether on behalf of a major or minor dynasty or a strongman with his own narrower interests at heart, laid siege to the town with the aim of taking it over permanently or occupying it merely as a temporary base from which to regroup in the midst of wider conflicts. (Specific examples of both cases, as well as the larger, more comprehensive political picture of which they were a part, will be given in chapter 2 of this study.)

In verses in his *dīwān* (collection) of poetry entitled *Saqṭ al-Zand* (سقط الزند) (*The Spark of the Fire Drill*), probably inspired while away from Maʿarrat al-Nuʿmān during his trip to Baghdad (undertaken in his late twenties), al-Maʿarrī could speak longingly of his homeland and particularly "the water of Maʿarrah [al-Nuʿmān]."[5] Around 400 (IE), in one of his many personal letters or epistles (الرسائل) that have been preserved, he vowed upon his return from Baghdad "to remain in the city [of Maʿarrat al-Nuʿmān] even though the inhabitants have fled through fear of the Greeks."[6]

In other letters, however—these coming from Maʿarrat al-Nuʿmān—al-Maʿarrī writes caustically that

> Maʿarrah [al-Nuʿmān] is like the two months called Spring, which originally were at the beginning of the year, but afterword shifted to the middle, and two others called Frost, which from the days of frozen water have shifted to those of windless heat . . . . And were it not that dust and stones are unable to assume the character of their neighbour, the squares of Maʿarrah would by now be devoted to learning, and the supplies of eloquence would be drawn from its inhabitants.[7]
>
> Were it not for the Ḳāḍi Abu Jaʿfar [أبو جعفر] his [the reference is to one Abū al-Ḥasan Muḥammad/أبو الحسن محمد] visit to this city would be like the vulture, who is a king and chieftain among birds, and from whose limbs there issues a musk-like odour, falling on a

> foul carcass. This is such an epithet as may be applied to Maʿarrah, which is the opposite of the Paradise described by the Koran. . . . Her very name "mischief" is ominous; God save us from it! The water-courses are blocked up, and the surface of its mould in summer is dry. It has no flowing water, and no rare trees can be planted there.[8]
>
> Then I was brought up in a city which contains no scholars, and the vine cannot grow without trellis-work to cling to.[9]

According to the thirteenth-century (CE) chronicler al-Qifṭī/القفطي, al-Maʿarrī bemoaned to his students that the affluent in Maʿarrat al-Nuʿmān were so miserly that they would not provide for the students studying under his supervision, he himself not having the means for this.[10]

Most of the families of Maʿarrat al-Nuʿmān in al-Maʿarrī's time were of the Banū Sāṭiʿ (بنو الساطع) division of the Tanūkh (تنوخ) tribal confederation, house of Sulaymān. Originally of south Arabian origin, the Tanūkh eventually migrated to al-Ḥīrah (الحيرة) in south central Iraq ("they were the first to build it and live therein" according to the thirteenth-century [CE] biographer and historian ابن العديم/Ibn al-ʿAdīm[11]), where, however, they were soon engaged in war by the Sassanian Persians and forced to move to central Mesopotamia, that is, the Sawād (السواد). Here, too, the Tanūkh were not free from wars and armed skirmishes initiated by the kings of Persia, although they managed to establish effective hegemony over, and flourish in, al-Ḥaḍr (الحضر), a small city in the vicinity of Takrīt (تكريت). When they allied themselves with the Byzantine emperor (ملك الروم), at his request, in response to Persian attacks on his territories, and when furthermore they provided the emperor with effective armies in confronting the Persians, they were rewarded with—among other things (including monetary remuneration)—"a feudal estate consisting of Syria and the surrounding lands, up to [the area of] al-Jazīrah" (الجزيرة)[12] (al-Jazīrah in this instance referring to the uplands and plains of northwestern Iraq, northeastern Syria, and southeastern Anatolia). They moved on to northern Syria (e.g., Qinnasrīn [قنسرين]; Ḥamāh; Maʿarrat al-Nuʿmān) in the early Islamic Era while advancing with the forces of ʿUbayd Allāh ibn al-Jarrāḥ/عبيد الله بن الجراح—this according to Ibn al-ʿAdīm. Shortly thereafter, some of the confederation, which at that time was Christian (*'alā dīn al-naṣrāniyyah*/على دين النصرانية), agreed, albeit not without protestations, to pay the land tax (*al-kharāj*/الخراج) as opposed to the poll or capital tax (*al-jizyah*/الجزية), the latter being the mark of non-Muslim subjects living under Islamic rule. These members of the Tanūkh tribal confederation settled in fixed homes; that is, they became sedentary. The ancestors of Abū al-ʿAlāʾ were among this group. Some embraced Islam. Others moved on to Byzantine-ruled territories, taking their Christian faith with them.

Once settled in Maʿarrat al-Nuʿmān, the House of Sulaymān of the Tanūkh confederation provided most of the judges (قضاة) of the town right up until the time of the Crusaders' attack on and occupation of it (492 IE; 1099 CE), a span of more than 200 years. The judges were often among the town's notable men of learning, a learning that included poetry and belle-lettres (*adab*/أدب). It was either Abū al-Ḥasan Sulaymān ibn Aḥmad ibn Sulaymān ibn Da'ūd ibn al-Muṭahhar who was the first of the house to assume the judgeship of Maʿarrat al-Nuʿmān— هوأول من تولى منهم قضاء معرة النعمان —or his son, al-Maʿarrī's great grandfather Abū Bakr Muḥammad ibn Sulaymān ibn Aḥmad.[13] This would have been around 290 IE. Abū Bakr has been described as a generous and beneficent head of the Tanūkh in whom could be found honorable distinction for those who sought it.[14] He was also a poet.[15] His son, grandfather of Abū al-ʿAlāʾ, Abū al-Ḥasan Sulaymān ibn Muḥammad ibn Sulaymān ibn Aḥmad, became judge (*qāḍī*/قاضي) of Maʿarrat al-Nuʿmān on or around 331 of the Islamic Era. Soon thereafter, he became judge of Ḥimṣ as well. He, too, was a poet; and an eloquent man of learning and refinement who was a transmitter of narrative reports (*aḥādīth*/أحاديث) about the Prophet Muḥammad. His son Abū Muḥammad ʿAbd Allāh and his grandchildren Abū al-ʿAlāʾ and Abū Ṣāliḥ Muḥammad Ibn al-Muhadhdhab—among others—transmitted *aḥādīth* on his authority. He died in Ḥimṣ in 377 IE (988 CE).

At this point in time, Abū al-ʿAlā's father, Abū Muḥammad ʿAbd Allāh ibn Sulaymān ibn Muḥammad ibn Sulaymān ibn Aḥmad ibn Sulaymān, became judge of Maʿarrat al-Nuʿmān. Like his father before him, he also composed verse and was noted for his overall literary and cultural refinement as well as expertise as a scholar of *aḥādīth*. As a new field of scholarly expertise in the family, language study is also associated with his name.[16]

Al-Maʿarrī's father had three sons: the eldest, Abū al-Majd Muḥammad ibn ʿAbd Allāh; Abū al-ʿAlāʾ, close to Abū al-Majd in age; and Abū al-Haytham ʿAbd al-Wāḥid ibn ʿAbd Allāh, the youngest. Abū al-Haytham was a poet with a *dīwān* reportedly transmitted to his son Zayd ibn ʿAbd Allāh by Abū al-ʿAlāʾ. A brother to Zayd, Munāfir, put down in writing some of what Abū al-ʿAlāʾ composed.

Abū al-Majd Muḥammad was also a poet with a *dīwān* to his credit. He had two sons, Abū Muḥammad ʿAbd Allāh ibn Muḥammad ibn ʿAbd Allāh ibn Sulaymān and Abū al-Ḥasan ʿAlī ibn Muḥammad ibn ʿAbd Allāh ibn Sulaymān, both of whom became judges in Maʿarrat al-Nuʿmān. Abū Muḥammad ʿAbd Allāh, like his cousin Munāfir, also wrote down some of Abū al-ʿAlāʾ's compositions and personally looked after him. In addition to being judge of Maʿarrat al-Nuʿmān, a poet, and an author of epistles, he delivered sermons for the congregational prayers on the Muslim sabbath and oversaw the administration of religious endowments (وله ديوان شعر ورسائل حسنة وتولى القضاء بمعرة النعمان وخطاباتها والوقوف بها).[17]

His son Abū Muslim al-Wādhiʿ (أبو مسلم الواذع) (the name and *agnomen* were chosen by Abū al-ʿAlāʾ, his father's uncle) was not only judge of Maʿarrat al-Nuʿmān immediately after him, but also reportedly a fine poet, the author of beautiful epistles, and overall a learned and refined man. Moreover, it has been recorded that he was the principal leader and elder of Maʿarrat al-Nuʿmān to whom general oversight or general superintendence of affairs was entrusted.[18]

The above-mentioned family members may not have constituted the trellis upon which al-Maʿarrī hoped to grow his learning, a trellis that he alleged was lacking in Maʿarrat al-Nuʿmān; but surely they would have allowed him an estimable stake for starters.

Al-Maʿarrī's mother was of the house of Sabīkah, and his maternal grandfather was from Aleppo (according to Ibn al-ʿAdīm, the most comprehensive of the medieval chroniclers).[19] Little else about her and her family can be gleaned from the medieval chronicles, although al-Maʿarrī wrote letters to her brother Abū al-Qāsim ʿAlī ibn Sabīkah in Aleppo on at least four occasions that have been documented,[20] one of which[21] was prompted by the death of a brother in Damascus (who is mentioned by name: Abū Ṭāhir), and another of which[22] was prompted when Abū al-ʿAlāʾ learned of his mother's death on his return to Maʿarrat al-Nuʿmān from Baghdad (400 IE/1010 CE). The letter prompted by his mother's death, one of his shorter and more accessible pieces of epistolary prose, is an expression of a son's grief and sorrow albeit coupled with a resolve not to overindulge in emotions.

> I can hope for no good after her death, nor can I do anything but plunge deeper and further into misery. . . . Were it not that the death days are fixed in writing, gladly should I have been killed for her sake in cold blood! Howbeit I tell her that I was bent on traveling, and that I was fully intent thereon, and she gave me leave. Maybe she thought it an idle fancy, the lightning of a cloud without water! However "the term of each is fixed in writing," and my grief over her loss is like the pleasures of Paradise, which are renewed so oft as they are consumed, and to dilate thereon would weary the hearer and be waste of time.[23]

In one short poem in *Saqṭ al-Zand,*[24] the mother's death is also lamented in more elusive and elliptical verse, notwithstanding the straightforward cathartic line "My mother has been summoned by God; would that I had been summoned before her, even if the warm middays were to become later afternoons"/(دعا الله أماً ليت أني أمامها / دُعيت ولو أنّ الهواجر آصال). Another (long) poem[25] expresses similar sentiments: "A mother has gone before me to the grave; it sorrows me that she has departed before I have" (وأمّتني الأجداث أم / يعز عليّ أن سارت أمامي). A long poem eulogizing the father is also among the poems of *Saqṭ al-Zand.*[26]

When not yet four years old, Abū al-ʿAlāʾ was stricken with smallpox. This left him with noticeable scars on his face, completely blind in his left eye, and almost completely blind in his right eye. It is doubtful that he was ever capable of seeing well enough to read. In one of his letters,[27] he speaks frankly of the limitations imposed upon him by his loss of sight: "How is it possible for me to be learned when I am blind,—a misfortune which it is sufficient to name?" According to Sibṭ ibn al-Jawzī, he referred to his blindness as one of his "prison houses," the other being self-imposed seclusion in his home.[28] However, he is also reported to have defiantly praised God for the loss of his eyesight "the way others praise Him for having it"/أنا أحمد الله تعالى على العمى كما يحمده غيري على البصر, remarking additionally:

People say that blindness is an ugly spectacle;
I say it's a trifle when losing sight of you all.

I swear to God, there's nothing in existence
losing sight of which eyes must need lament.

قالوا العمى منظر قبيح قلت بفقدانكم يهون
والله ما في الوجود شيء تأسى على فقده العيون[29]

Al-Maʿarrī's life was essentially one dedicated almost exclusively to learning. If his life may be spoken of as having been eventful or remarkable, it was so primarily in that sense. With respect to language and grammar, his education began at his father's knee but also with others in Maʿarrat al-Nuʿmān (قوم من بلده) such as members of the Kawthar clan (بنو كوثر), associates of Ibn Khaluwayh, a grammarian brought to the court of the Ḥamdānid Prince of Aleppo Sayf al-Dawlah, and the grammarian (النحوي) Abū Bakr Muḥammad ibn Saʿūd ibn Muḥammad ibn Yaḥyā ibn al-Faraj. On the authority of his father as well as his grandfather,[30] and also on the authority of fellow townsman Yaḥyā ibn Musʿar al-Tanūkhī,[31] al-Maʿarrī became a transmitter of *aḥādīth.* He learned the various styles of Qur'ān recitation from a number of learned men (*shuyūkh*/شيوخ) whom he sought out for that art.[32] *Al-Dhahabī*[33] recorded that al-Maʿarrī began to compose and dictate verse when he was eleven years old.

Between 987/988 and 994/995 of the Common Era, or when he was between fourteen and twenty-one years of age, Abū al-ʿAlā' according to several medieval biographers[34] continued his studies in Aleppo, the intellectual life of which must still have been quite remarkable if not as brilliant and scintillating when the city was the principal seat of authority for an essentially autonomous principality dominated by the potentate and patron of the arts and sciences Sayf al-Dawlah (d. 967 CE) of the Ḥamdānid dynasty. (The Ḥamdānids were a Shīʿite Muslim tribal grouping, originally nomadic, of northern Iraqi ascent.) It is said that in Aleppo, Abū al-ʿAlā' studied under the disciples of the grammarian and Qur'ān expert Ibn Khaluwayh, and with the grammarian Muḥammad ibn ʿAbd Allāh ibn Saʿd, who was also an expert transmitter (*rāwī*/راو) of the poetry of al-Mutanabbī. Perhaps al-Maʿarrī accompanied by an amanuensis also made use of Aleppo's libraries, one of which was supposed to have contained 20,000 volumes. Al-Qifṭī[35] has him going to Tripoli as well as Latakia and Antioch at some point between 987/8 and 994, this in order to augment his education. Al-Qifṭī reports that the people of means had endowed some libraries in Tripoli and that there stood a monastery (Pharos) (دير الفاروس) at Latakia with a monk who knew something about the "sciences of the ancients"; from the monk, al-Maʿarrī "heard the rudiments of the beliefs of the philosophers."[36] The other major classical biographical sources are at variance over the travels at this point in al-Maʿarrī's life. Al-Dhahabī records only the trip to Tripoli, whereas al-Ṣafadī and al-ʿAbbāsī record the trip to Tripoli and the visit to the monastery at Latakia.[37] Ibn al-ʿAdīm[38] makes no mention of the Tripoli and Latakia sojourns but observes that reports about a trip to Antioch cannot be true because the city was taken from the Muslims by the Byzantines by the time al-Maʿarrī turned twenty-one. (The suggestion seems to be that political realities, if nothing else, would have made the visit virtually impossible.)

In 994 CE, Abū al-ʿAlā' was back in Maʿarrat al-Nuʿmān. From that year until 1008, he occupied himself with the teaching of philology and literature. These years were also ones of considerable literary productivity on his part. Works produced during this period include a number of letters addressed to several contemporaneous men of letters (*udabā'*/أدباء); a collection (i.e., *dīwān)* of descriptive poetry on armor (entitled *al-Dir'iyyāt*/الدرعيات), most of which are included in the Beirut edition of *Saqṭ al-Zand*); much if not most of *Saqṭ al-Zand*, a *dīwān* of poems of various genres (including particularly poems of lament); and possibly *Mulqā al-Sabīl*/ملقى السبيل (*Cast Out on the Road*), a very small collection of short paragraphs interspersed with poetry, touching upon material of a predictable moral and pietistic nature that al-Maʿarrī was wont to weave into his works over the course of his lifetime.

In 1008, Abū al-ʿAlā' again took leave of Maʿarrat al-Nuʿmān. His travels this time took him to Baghdad. He was to stay in the city for approximately seventeen months. The primary reason for his quitting Maʿarrat al-Nuʿmān and going to Baghdad was probably a desire to enhance his literary and philological training and interact in more illustrious circles.

That all of this may have been, as Margoliouth has suggested, "the preparation for a lucrative career to which blindness was no obstacle" seems most plausible.

> In the Aghani we read of many blind poets, and indeed of one [ʿAlī ibn Jabalah] whose blindness was brought about by the same malady which deprived Abu 'l-ʿAlā of his sight. The custom of bestowing large sums of money in return for complimentary odes was inherited by the Caliphs from the pre-Islamic dynasties; and what the Caliphs did on a large scale was also done by their ministers, provincial governors, and in general by men of wealth and station in scarcely less lavish fashion.[39]

Baghdad at this time was still arguably the intellectual capital of the entire Islamicate world, the most vibrant place to be for someone interested in intellectual pursuits, although the ʿAbbāsid Caliph's authority and effective control were being frittered away by dynasties competing for power and authority as well as scientific, literary, and cultural preeminence. In early eleventh-century CE Baghdad, al-Maʿarrī would have found additional well-stocked libraries of the sort that (according to some) prompted his earlier travel to Aleppo. At the libraries as well as organized learned gatherings in homes or mosques or other public spaces (e.g., at the shops of book dealers or even city gates), he also would have had the opportunity to interact with many intellectuals and literary figures of considerable achievement and renown. Notwithstanding all of these compelling intellectual and career-driven reasons for leaving Maʿarrat al-Nuʿmān and going to Baghdad, it should not be discounted that al-Maʿarrī arranged for this relocation with the thought of escaping the escalating political turmoil in northern Syria. At this period in its history, northern Syria, and above all Aleppo, had become the arena for a major armed struggle for supremacy on the part of three competing ruling entities: to the south the expanding Shīʿite (Fāṭimid persuasion) dynasty centered in Cairo, Egypt; to the north the already well-established Byzantine Empire, never totally quiescent on it borders with Syria; and, in between, ensconced primarily in Aleppo, the remnants of the Ḥamdānids (Shīʿites but not of Fāṭimid orientation), who seemed determined to maintain a considerable degree of autonomy if not outright independence. To add to this regional tension and instability, an eventual fourth participant in the struggle for political and/or religious dominance in northern Syria—the Mirdāsid dynasty (of Syrian Arab semi-nomadic origin, possibly Shīʿite but non-Fāṭimid)—was beginning to make its presence and agenda felt. Like the Ḥamdānids, the Mirdāsids seemed to aspire to considerable independence in northern Syria, if not as well to the promotion of a nascent Syrian-focused Arab nationalism. As a consequence of all of the conflicting interests and competing dynasties, at the turn of the eleventh century of the Common Era, Aleppo and its environs including Maʿarrat al-Nuʿmān became more and more the targets of attacks and/or sieges and counter attacks, whether on the part of Fāṭimid or Byzantine armed forces and their allies or on the part of troops pledging loyalty to Ḥamdānid or Mirdāsid potentates.

In the very same letter to his maternal uncle Abū al-Qāsim ʿAlī in which he expresses his grief over hearing of his mother's death, al-Maʿarrī states that after turning twenty, he never had any thoughts about seeking out learning from either Syrians or Iraqis; it was the presence of the library in Baghdad that led him to the city (ومنذ فارقت العشرين من العمر ما حدّثت نفسي باجتداء علم من عراقي ولا شآمٍ . . . والذي أقدمني تلك البلد مكان دار الكتب بها).[40]

In the letter from roughly the same time, composed on route from Baghdad to Maʿarrat al-Nuʿmān once he had resolved to return to his home town, al-Maʿarrī relates that he did not go to Baghdad in order to gain materially or to make more acquaintances, but he went in order to take up residence "in a place of learning"; he found, he said, "the most precious of spots"/ وأحلف ما سافرت أستكثر من النشب ولا أتكثر بلقاء الرجال ولكن آثرت الإقامة بدار العلم فشاهدت أنفس مكان.[41]

Al-Qifṭī states that objections raised by officials in Aleppo over an endowed income of thirty dinars a year—al-Maʿarrī's sole source of income—is what compelled al-Maʿarrī to go to Baghdad; that is, he went there specifically in order to raise a complaint concerning said Aleppan officials.[42]

Al-Qifṭī notes[43] that al-Maʿarrī gained fame in Baghdad, particularly for the recitations of his *Saqṭ al-Zand*, and that among others he met with al-Sharīf al-Rāḍī and al-Sharīf al-Murtaḍā, the two renowned sons of Abū Aḥmad al-Mūsawī, *naqīb*/نقيب or head of the ʿAlids, that is, those supporting the descendants of ʿAlī as the rightful leader of the Islamic Commonwealth. He also visited the library that was under the custodianship of ʿAbd al-Salām al-Baṣrī, a.k.a. al-Wājikah, a savant of note, being an أديب (*adīb*) or man of letters, a transmitter of *aḥādīth*, and a Qur'ān reciter.

Ibn al-ʿAdīm[44] adds that al-Maʿarrī received instruction from Abū ʿAlī ʿAbd al-Karīm ibn al-Ḥusayn ibn al-Ḥākim al-Sukkarī, a linguist and grammarian; and, although he sought out one ʿAlī ibn ʿĪsā al-Rabaʿī for instruction in grammar, he refused to return to him after his first visit. Al-Rabaʿī angered him when he bid him to enter his home with the words "Let the blind man come in."

According to Ibn al-ʿAdīm, another insult was hurled at al-Maʿarrī when, on his very first day in Baghdad, he went to pay his condolences to al-Sharīf al-Rāḍī and al-Sharīf al-Murtaḍā, whose father (Abū Aḥmad al-Mūsawī, a.k.a. al-Sharīf al-Ṭāhir) had just died. As al-Maʿarrī tried to make his way through a room crowded with mourners, he stepped on people, causing someone to yell out, "Where are you going, dog?"/الى أين يا كلب؟. After responding with the words "The dog is anyone who does not know all of the various names for dog"/الكلب من لا يعرف للكلب كذا وكذا اسما, al-Maʿarrī proceeded to take a seat at the very back of the assemblage, until it came time for the recitation of poetry for the occasion, when he stood to recite a poem eulogizing Abū Aḥmad, after which al-Sharīf al-Rāḍī and al-Sharīf al-Murtaḍā showed him great honor and respect, having surmised his identity.[45]

Although already the *madrasah* (plural *madāris*) (مدرسة ؛ مدارس) or more formal institution for higher studies was in existence in the Islamic commonwealth, especially in Nīshābūr (Khurāsān), this period of time was slightly before the flourishing of Niẓām al-Mulk (1018–1092 CE), the minister of the Seljūk Turkish sulṭāns Alp Arslān and Malik Shāh who founded the *madrasah* in Baghdad that bears Niẓām's name (the Niẓāmiyyah; dedicated in 1067 CE), after which other *madāris* were established and soon became more commonplace as sites especially reserved and equipped for maintaining (i.e., boarding) as well providing instruction for students. Otherwise, "the circle, or the school, of a teacher in [this] period . . . must be understood in an informal sense. The school consisted of a teacher, his home, books, colleagues, pupils, and occasional visitors. The teacher sometimes met with individuals or small groups." As for scholarly discussions and exchanges among peers, there was the venerable institution of the *majālis* (sing. *majlis*)/مجالس؛ مجلس (meetings or gatherings), arranged by ministers or princes or scholars themselves. These could take place at a private residence or royal court. Scholarly discussions were also held in mosques; in gardens, markets, and commercial shops; at city gates; and in bookshops, "the most prominent of [the] less conventional academic forums" in Baghdad and found in great number. Teaching (as opposed to discussion) consisted of the recitation of texts as well as the teacher's commentary. Discussions followed a dialectical approach whereby theses and antitheses were advanced following the statement of an issue of concern or proposition to be considered *(mas'alah*/مسألة). Study and discussion of the religious sciences—for example, *aḥādīth*—typically occurred in mosques. Teachers' homes were sites for subjects such as speculative theology (*kalām*/كلام) and study of language and *adab*.[46]

Al-Sharīf al-Rāḍī (d. 1015 CE), a poet, student of Imāmī Shīʿite theology, scholar of the Qur'ān, and compiler of *Nahj al-Balāghah*/نهج البلاغة (*The Path of Eloquence*, the sayings and speeches of ʿAlī ibn Abī Ṭālib), organized an "academy," or house of learning, with a view to promoting and sponsoring the gathering of the learned. A more illustrious institution of this sort was established in the Karkh quarter of Baghdad in 993 CE by Abū Naṣr Sābūr ibn Ardashīr, minister (*wazīr*/وزير) to the sulṭān Bahā' al-Dawlah (ruled from 998 to 1012 CE), in whose family's hands (i.e., the Būyids, the tribal grouping of Shīʿite Muslims from Daylam on the southern shore of the Caspian Sea) belonged real as opposed to titular power in Baghdad and the surrounding district of al-ʿIrāq during the years 945 to 1055 CE. The minister

> dedicated this building to use by men of learning. Among the books collected, numbering 10,400, there were a hundred copies of the Qur'ān written by Banū Muqlah and many autographs of famous writers. Sābūr also prepared a catalogue of books in the library, entrusting it to the care of two members of the ʿAlid family and a Qāḍī and appointing the Shaykh Abū Bakr Muḥammad ibn Mūsā al-Khwārizmī supervisor of the establishment. . . . The Academy of Sābūr became a rendezvous for men engaged in literary pursuits.[47]

Abū al-ʿAlā' seems to have made use of this great public library-cum-academy founded by the Būyid minister Abū Naṣr Sābūr ibn Ardashīr. In the letter numbered XIX in Margoliouth's collection, he addresses one "Abū Manṣūr, Custodian of the Academy in Baghdad"/وكتب إلى أبي منصور خازن دار العلم ببغداد.[48] He proceeds in the letter to express his longing for "the Academy" (which incidentally may have been intended more specifically in the letter for which Margoliouth translates دار العلم as the generic "place of learning"; see above), for Baghdad, and, last but not least, for the companionship of his correspondent:

> Of truth I am fluttering more with anxiety than pleasure, so that those who would blame me say "Is thy passion for the 'House of Learning' from folly or sound sense?"
>
> My desire for you and the rest of my friends is like that of a ring-dove, full of learning with nothing to excite it. . . .
>
> Each time the raven says caw! I fancy it is a mounted messenger from Baghdad. . . . I ask of God's mercy that we may be brought together again. . . .[49]

In a line of verse attributed to al-Maʿarrī by Ibn Khallikān, there is specific reference to Sābūr, دار العلم, and an evening gathering that included a performance by a songstress, suggesting (if true) that music and song—and by women—could be part of a convocation (if not indeed the sole purpose) at a site associated with pursuit of scholarship.[50]

Abū al-ʿAlā' continued to compose while in Baghdad; principally for the collection of poems comprising *Saqṭ al-Zand* (judging from some of its eulogies), to a lesser extent for some of his other works, the vast majority of which, based on what the bio-bibliographical chronicles report in the way of the chronology of his compositions, were yet to come. Taking up residence in the city seemed the logical progression in his quest for learning and scholarly camaraderie during a period in the history of the Islamic commonwealth especially noted for the pursuit of knowledge. However, although there is evidence that he was not without a circle of friends and acquaintances in the great Iraqi metropolis—for example, Abū al-Salām al-Wājikah, Abū Manṣūr Muḥammad ibn ʿAlī (a curator at دار العلم), al-Sharīf al-Rāḍī and al-Sharīf al-Murtaḍā, the distinguished man of letters al-Qāḍī al-Tanūkhī, a second curator at Sābūr's library (ʿAbd al-Salām al-Baṣrī), and the grammarian Abū ʿAlī ibn Furrajah—he left never to return after a stay of approximately sixteen months.

He writes with considerable ambivalence about his decision to leave. In a passage of one of his letters, characteristically studded with proverbs and quotations from other poets, he speaks as though he has few regrets. There was a surfeit of knowledge in the city, it did not afford him a truly warm and rewarding reception, and hence it really offered him "nothing."

> 'Every occasion has its proper formula,' every season its
> fruit, every valley its acacia. I found Baghdad 'like a pie's wing,'
> fair, but carrying nothing.
> 'Truly Iraq is no home for my people. . . .
> So pile the carriage upon some powerful camel. . . .'
> 'It whined for far-off Nakhlah; but I said "Fie for shame!" Trouble
> is there; so make for Syria. For Iraq has no people that we love; its
> people are of proud looks.'"
>
> . . . and I found learning at a greater discount at Baghdad than gravel at the ʿAqabah heaps, cheaper than dates at Medinah, more common than palm-branches in Yemameh, more copious than water in the ocean. However, there is some obstacle in the way of every blessing.[51]

In the very same letter, however, al-Maʿarrī adds that

> The favor of God is upon all those whom you know in Baghdad; they treated me with singular courtesy, and spoke well of me in my absence, and honoured me above my equals and my peers. And when they learned that I was getting ready to leave them, and, indeed, on the point of going, they manifested great sorrow and said many kind words . . . .

> God reward them! If what they did was out of kindness, it was a great benefit; and if they did it for pretense, still it was an act of good fellowship; and so I left Baghdad, with my honor still in a vessel that did not leak; not one drop of it had I spilt in quest of either wealth or learning.[52]

Of similar gracious attitude toward the people of Baghdad is the closing to his letter addressing his townsfolk just prior to his arrival at Maʿarrat al-Nuʿmān after taking leave of Baghdad:

> . . . And may [God] give good recompense to the people of Baghdad, for they praised me more than I deserved, and testified to my merits before they knew them, and quite seriously offered me their goods. Albeit they found me not fond of praise, neither eager for other people's charity.[53]

But in verses in *Saqṭ al-Zand* that address his "brethren between the Euphrates and Damascus," al-Maʿarrī speaks of being distanced from supporters and what little income he had; hence, materially, somewhat deprived in fact. He also claims to have been "envied" merely because of his "superiority" (فأصبحت محسودا بفضلي وحده على بعد أنصاري وقلة مالي).[54]

His sense that in general he was the object of envy, irrespective of domicile, was allegedly repeated in the presence of a fellow poet. When the poet asked him, "What is there to all that is said and related about you?" (ما هذا الذي يروى عنك ويحكى؟), the reply was, "They have envied me and lied against me"[55] (حسدوني وكذبوا علي). Envy may have been suspected in an incident that Margoliouth believed "probably gives us the real reason why Abu 'l-ʿAlā left Baghdad; for such a humiliation was so likely to bring others in its train that it was unsafe for him to remain."[56] According to several traditionally cited sources that Margoliouth undoubtedly had in mind, while al-Maʿarrī was in the presence of al-Sharīf al-Murtaḍā one day, on the occasion of a *majlis*, mention was made of the poet al-Mutanabbī (d. 965 CE), whom al-Murtaḍā despised but whom al-Maʿarrī greatly admired, regarding him as the greatest Arab poet of the post-Jāhilī, post-Umayyad eras. Al-Murtaḍā began to detract from al-Mutanabbī and pursue his faults, to which al-Maʿarrī reacted with the words, "Had al-Mutanabbī composed no more than the poem with the words 'You have, O stations of the heart, many stations,' that alone would have sufficed to demonstrate his superiority." Upon hearing this, al-Murtaḍā was so angered that he ordered that al-Maʿarrī be dragged away by his feet. Someone else in attendance at the *majlis* was puzzled, wondering out loud what may have been the point of the rejoinder to al-Murtaḍā on the part of al-Maʿarrī, inasmuch as al-Mutanabbī composed better poems that al-Maʿarrī neglected to mention. Al-Murtaḍā answered the question by saying that al-Maʿarrī wanted to draw attention to another line in the al-Mutanabbī poem (which he [al-Murtaḍā] regarded as a personal insult), namely "And if disparagement of me comes to you from someone who is flawed, then that is proof that I am perfect." [57]

One needs to wonder to what extent this report may have been greatly embellished if not entirely fabricated. Margoliouth finds it "too circumstantial to be fictitious." One might reasonably counter that it is almost too outlandish to be true. Even if true, that it was probably "the real reason why Abū al-ʿAlā' left Baghdad" seems rather implausible. More likely—the more important point that the incident, even if apocryphal, seems designed to bring into sharper relief—is the considerable challenge that al-Maʿarrī faced in trying to secure patronage or remuneration for teaching and/or declaiming poetry in a large city that had no shortage of men of extraordinary erudition (literary and otherwise), as al-Maʿarrī himself conceded. At the same time, although Maʿarrat al-Nuʿmān was subject to certain troubling vicissitudes, particularly strife as a result of the armed conflicts resulting from dynasties competing for suzerainty over northern Syria (with one of the combatants representing non-Muslim rule), Baghdad was hardly immune from its own troubles because of (1) Shīʿite-Sunnī sectarian rivalries that often erupted into riots, (2) revolts on the part of recalcitrant and ambitious Turkish chieftains among the soldiery, and (3) urban gangs that engaged in banditry and thuggery. Baghdad at this time was already an enormous city. The urban unrest and turmoil there, and the resulting uncertainty that they imparted to life, would have been on an even larger scale than whatever in the way of similar such challenges may have been afoot in Maʿarrat al-Nuʿmān. As for the other reasons traditionally mentioned to explain Abū al-ʿAlā''s leaving Baghdad, these include the news of his mother's having fallen seriously ill (in point of fact, she died before he made it back to Maʿarrat al-Nuʿmān) and the disappearance of a small family estate that had been deposited for him in his country of birth.

The decision to leave Baghdad, writes al-Maʿarrī, was coupled with the resolve to remain isolated for the remainder of his life:

> Being unable then to remain in the spot I had chosen, I decided upon isolation such as should make me like an antelope in its lair, and should completely cut me off from mankind, except, indeed, those with whom God should join me as the arm is joined to the hand, or night to morrow.[58]

Such course of action was not determined precipitously, according to al-Maʿarrī, whose own account here certainly merits our regard before taking into consideration the speculation of others:

> I have found the best course for me to pursue in the days of my life is to go into retreat. . . . So I decided upon this course after asking God's help, and revealing my idea to a few friends on whose characters reliance could be placed, all of whom thought it was wise, and considered it could be carried out with prudence. And it is a matter "over which night-journeys have been undertaken. . . ." It is no offspring of the hour, no nursling of a month or a year; it is the child of past years and the product of reflection.[59]

According to the classical biographers, from the date of his return to Maʿarrat al-Nuʿmān in 1010 CE until his death forty-seven years later in 1057, Abū al-ʿAlāʾ, true to his own word, scarcely ventured beyond his home, let alone the town; although he was hardly the total recluse that some of his letters make him out to be. The very composition of the letters alone belies this. The letters were addressed to specific individuals. The collection translated by Margoliouth is but a small part of a collection made by al-Maʿarrī himself, "the lowest estimate [of which] would give us a work of 3,200 pages."[60]

Among the specific individuals addressed in the extant letters is Abū al-Qāsim al-Ḥusayn, a notable son of an even more notable father (ʿAlī ibn al-Ḥusayn al-Maghribī). Abū al-Qāsim (a.k.a *al-wazīr al-maghribī*, the North African minister) was a student of Ibn al-Qāriḥ, to whom al-Maʿarrī's *Epistle of Forgiveness*/رسالة الغفران was addressed. He enjoyed the patronage of Abū Ghālib Fakhr al-Mulk (appointed *'amīd al-juyūsh*—head of the armies—under the Būyid Prince Bahā' al-Dawlah [ruled 998–1012 CE], and as such was responsible not only for oversight of the armies but also the day-to-day administration of Baghdad). By 1023, Abū al-Qāsim *al-wazīr al-maghribī* was minister to Būyid prince Musharrif al-Dawlah (ruled as *amīr* of Baghdad 415–16 IE; 1024–25 CE), on the way to that post also having become secretary(*kātib*/كاتب) to Qirwash, the ʿUqaylid Arab leader whom the ʿAbbāsid caliph al-Qādir (ruled 991–1031 CE) officially granted possession of Mosul (entailing among other things revenue farming of the city).

In one of his rare poems of praise (*madḥ*/مدح; in *Saqṭ al-Zand*; poem in the rhyme *dimāmu*/ذماممه), al-Maʿarrī praised the father of Abū al-Qāsim (ʿAlī ibn al-Ḥusayn al-Maghribī) for his military skill and prowess. ʿAlī ibn al-Ḥusayn al-Maghribī was a confidante of the Ḥamdānid ruler of northern Syria Saʿd al-Dawlah (ruled 967–991 CE), and, for a brief period, his minister before becoming minister to Bakjūr, the Caucasian *mamlūk* army general in the employ of the Ḥamdānids but who revolted against Saʿd al-Dawlah from his base at Raqqah, with the approval of the Fāṭimid imām-caliph in Cairo (al-ʿAzīz) (although the revolt was at the instigation of ʿAlī ibn al-Ḥusayn al-Maghribī). Bakjūr was thwarted in an attempt to seize control of Aleppo (circa 990 CE) and captured and executed at the orders of Saʿd al-Dawlah, shortly after which ʿAlī ibn al-Ḥusayn al-Maghribī fled to Kufa and later to al-ʿAzīz's court in Cairo to become the imām-caliph's chancellor-secretary (*kātib*). In this capacity as well as his having been appointed *mudabbir al-jaysh*/مدبر الجيش (organizer of the army), the redoubtable ʿAlī ibn al-Ḥusayn al-Maghribī managed to have the imām-caliph appoint the Fāṭimid-approved governor of Damascus, the Turkish *mamlūk* Banjūtakīn, *amīr al-juyūsh*/أمير الجيوش (commander of the armies), in preparation for an expedition against Aleppo (991 CE) with the view to bringing northern Syria as well as southern Syria under the suzerainty of the Fāṭimids in Cairo. (ʿAlī was recalled from northern Syria by al-ʿAzīz after the initial expedition against Aleppo failed to conquer the city and led to several additional failed expeditions between 991 and 994 CE. He was executed circa 1009–10 CE by order of the Fāṭimid imām-caliph al-Ḥākim [ruled 996–1021 CE], at which point the son Abū al-Qāsim al-Ḥusayn sought refuge in Arabia; from there, before finding the patronage of Fakhr al-Mulk in Baghdad, he endeavored to support an attempt to overthrow al-Ḥākim.)

The "Sulṭān" in al-Maʿarrī's letter that is addressed to "some of the Sulṭān's ministers"[61] is according to Margoliouth "probably" ʿAzīz al-Dawlah. The letter to Abū Manṣūr is to the custodian of Abū Naṣr Sābūr's "Academy" in Baghdad (the site of which would have been Sābūr's home).[62]

The letter to Abū Naṣr Ṣadaqah ibn Yūsuf al-Fallāḥī[63] was written within the context of al-Fallāḥī's trying to bring al-Maʿarrī closer to the *amīr* ʿAzīz al-Dawlah, al-Ḥākim's governor in Aleppo. In *Saqṭ al-Zand* al-Maʿarrī has verses in praise of Banjūtakīn and ʿAlī ibn al-Ḥusayn al-Maghribī (see for the former the poem with rhyme *ḥimyaru*/حمير and for the latter the poem with rhyme *wiṣālu*/وصال; both discussed in detail by Pieter Smoor[64]). In the same collection of poems are verses of praise to Abū Aḥmad ʿAbd al-Salām al-Baṣrī (who was a custodian of Dār al-Kutub [the Library] in Baghdad; see poem with rhyme *arbuʿi*/أربع); to Abū Manṣūr, custodian of Sābūr's Academy library (see poem with rhyme *al-khaṭṭu*/الخط); and to Abū al-Qāsim ʿAlī ibn al-Muḥassin al-Tanūkhī (see poem with rhyme *bi-takrīta*/بتكريت), the son of the noted author of *Nishwār al-Muḥāḍarah wa Akhbār al-Mudhākarah (نشوار المحاضرة وأخبار المذاكرة)*, the Ḥanafī Judge (قاض) Abū ʿAlī al-Muḥassin ibn ʿAlī.[65]

According to Ibn al-ʿAdīm,[66] Abū Shujāʿ Fātik ibn ʿAbd Allāh al-Rūmī, a.k.a. ʿAzīz al-Dawlah, Banjūtakīn's emancipated Armenian slave who ruled the Citadel of Aleppo (with Fāṭimd caliph-imām al-Ḥākim's investiture), and eventually all of Aleppo and surrounding districts by dint of his own resolve and wiles (until 413 IE [1021–22 CE], when he was assassinated by one of his slave guards), "had a high regard for [al-Maʿarrī] and used to accede to his intercession. He even visited him in Maʿarrat al-Nuʿmān." Much of al-Maʿarrī's *Epistle of the Horse and the Mule* touches upon issues and events during the rule of *amīr* ʿAzīz al-Dawlah, and the work was dedicated to the *amīr* with a view to petitioning him with respect to a matter of taxes involving al-Maʿarrī and some of his family.[67] "Abū al-ʿAlāʾ must have been acquainted with life at [ʿAzīz al-Dawlah's]

Court, for Abū'l-Khayr al-Mufaḍḍal, an ex-pupil of his, had earned for himself a position as eulogist of the new master of Aleppo. The ex-pupil exchanged poems with his former teacher."[68]

Other prominent students of al-Maʿarrī include Ibn al-Sīd al-Baṭalyūsī, who wrote an exhaustive commentary on *Saqṭ al-Zand*, and Abū Zakariyyā' Yaḥyā ibn al-Khaṭīb al-Tibrīzī, who also wrote a commentary on *Saqṭ al-Zand* and became a professor at the Niẓāmiyyah in Baghdad. Abū Naṣr ibn Abī ʿImrān al-Mu'ayyad fī al-Dīn, by virtue of his being the chief proselytizer of Fāṭimid Ismāʿīlī Shīʿism and ensconced in Cairo, the capital of the Fāṭimid Ismāʿīlī Shīʿite state as well as home for an academy of higher studies (Dār al-ʿIlm) founded by al-Ḥākim, was a most distinguished correspondent. Al-Ḥākim's minister ʿAlī ibn Jaʿfar ibn Fallāḥ al-Kutāmī is reported to have issued an invitation to al-Maʿarrī to take up a teaching position at Dār al-ʿIlm, aware of al-Maʿarrī and his work; and ʿAzīz al-Dawlah allegedly paid a visit to al-Maʿarrī in Maʿarrat al-Nuʿmān in order to discuss al-Ḥākim's desire that al-Maʿarrī accept the offer of the teaching position in Cairo.[69]

During the reign of Ṣāliḥ ibn Mirdās (Asad al-Dawlah) in Aleppo (1025–29 CE), al-Maʿarrī in response to pleas from his town folk is reported to have agreed personally to intercede with Ṣāliḥ in order to have released seventy notables whom Ṣāliḥ had imprisoned in the wake of their uprising. The uprising, according to most if not all of the standard premodern historical-biographical sources, occurred after a riot (in 417 IE/circa 1026 CE) along sectarian (Christian/Muslim) lines, precipitated by molestation of a Muslim woman by a Christian tavern/brothel owner.[70]

An ʿAlid descendant by the name of Abū Ibrāhīm Muḥammad allegedly intervened in defense of al-Maʿarrī when one al-Miḥbarah al-ʿAbbāsī along with two experts in Islamic law tried to have the Mirdāsid prince Thimāl ibn Ṣāliḥ, who reigned in Aleppo and north Syria from 1041–58 CE (i.e., through al-Maʿarrī's very advanced years including the year of his death in 1057) pronounce al-Maʿarrī guilty of disbelief (*kufr*). The defense in the face of the charges took place in the presence of Thimāl. [71]

Pieter Smoor's painstaking, nuanced reading of *Saqṭ al-Zand* as well as key parts of *Risālat al-Ṣāhil wa al-Shājiḥ* (رسالة الصاهل و الشاحج) /*The Episitle of the Horse and the Mule* adduces evidence—from above and beyond al-Maʿarrī's more personal letter—for the considerable extent to which al-Maʿarrī kept abreast of, and commented upon (albeit often elliptically and allusively, as underscored by Smoor) the complicated and troubled politics of his day, particularly with respect to northern Syria and the reign of Abū Shujāʿ Fātik ʿAzīz al-Dawlah.[72] The latter part of *al-Ṣāhil wa al-Shājiḥ*, for example, amounts to a virtual running commentary—by way of the speaking animals whom al-Maʿarrī presents—on the political developments of northern Syria under ʿAzīz al-Dawlah up until a year or two before his death, involving not only the dynamics of Byzantine, Fāṭimid, and Arab (i.e., Kilābī Bedouin) rivalries and interactions at the military and diplomatic level—the ebb and flow of war and peace, in other words—but also the attendant socioeconomic consequences for the populace at large.

While continuing to compose poetry and various types of artful prose of the sort commonly associated with *adab* (of which his letters are examples), al-Maʿarrī taught grammar, philology, and literature. The most famous of his students was the grammarian and philologist Abū Zakariyyā' al-Tibrīzī. Al-Maʿarrī's voluminous correspondences were with family members, friends, fellow men of letters in various places in the Arabic-speaking world, and, as already observed, some notable potentates, such as Abū al-Qāsim al-Ḥusayn ibn al-Maghribī, Abū Naṣr Ṣadaqah ibn Yūsuf al-Fallāḥī, and last but not least the chief missionary (داعي الدعاة) of the Fāṭimid Ismāʿīlī Academy (دار العلم) in Cairo, Hibat Allāh ibn Mūsā al-Mu'ayyad fī al-Dīn, who because of his position enjoyed great political as well as intellectual importance in learned circles extending well beyond Cairo.[73]

On the basis of his letters if not as well the standard chronicles, it seems that al-Maʿarrī had proper, and sometimes even relatively close, relations with some of the governors of Aleppo, within whose governorship Maʿarrat al-Nuʿmān was situated and over which the Mirdāsids and Fāṭimids were the principal competitors for effective control during al-Maʿarrī's years of repose in Maʿarrat al-Nuʿmān after the return from Baghdad. In other respects, his life was relatively sedate but remarkable because of his enormous literary output, his often dissident religio-philosophical views, his dour pessimism and cynicism, and the extreme asceticism that he practiced as well as preached, an asceticism that included not only celibacy and vows of poverty but also vegetarianism (the vegetarianism ostensibly lay behind the exchange of letters with Hibat Allāh ibn Mūsā al-Mu'ayyad fī al-Dīn, who initiated the correspondence; the asceticism overall apparently prompted some questions from one Abū Naṣr Aḥmad ibn al-Munāz, a contemporary who was a poet and minister at Mayyāfārqīn[74]).

From 1010 to 1057 CE, Abū al-ʿAlā' composed most of his literary works, said by Ibn al-ʿAdīm to have added up to sixty-seven titles. Most of these pieces have not survived the ages. We have only references to the titles. Extant, however (above and beyond his several commentaries on the poetry of other poets), are the following: several poems that are included in the collection comprising *Saqṭ al-Zand*, which was begun before al-Maʿarrī's trip to Baghdad but completed subsequently; some of the relatively shorter epistles of the more personal type exemplified by Margoliouth's collection (although like all of his epistles, these, too, bristle with digressive displays of language erudition [e.g., points of rhetoric, philology, grammar [especially morphology and syntax], prosody, and proverbs and lore concerning the ancient Arabs[75]); the much-celebrated book-length epistle entitled *Risālat al-Ghufrān*/رسالة الغفران (*The Epistle of Forgiveness*); the book-length رسالة الصاهل والشاحج/*Risālat al-Ṣāhil wa al-Shājiḥ* (*Epistle of the Horse and Mule*); most of *al-Fuṣūl wa al-Ghāyāt fī Tamjīd Allāh wa al-Mawā'iẓ*/الفصول والغايات في تمجيد الله والمواعظ (*Paragraphs with End Rhymes on the Glorification of God and Moral Admonishments*); extracts from *Zajr al-Nābiḥ*/زجر النابح (*Driving Away the Barking Dog*); *Risālat al-Malā'ikah*/رسالة الملائكة (*Epistle of the Angels*); *Mulqā al-Sabīl*/ملقى السبيل (*The Castaway on the Road*); and *Luzūm Mā Lā Yalzam*/لزوم ما لا يلزم (*Necessitating the Unnecessary*).

Like *Saqṭ al-Zand*, *Luzūm Mā Lā Yalzam* (also commonly referred to as *al-Luzūmiyyāt*/اللزوميات) is a *dīwān* of poetry, although it is much larger than *Saqṭ al-Zand*. Most of *al-Fuṣūl wa al-Ghāyāt* and *Risālat al-Ghufrān* are written in rhymed prose, as are al-Maʿarrī's other letters (or, as it were, "epistles"), even those with the more personal messages that he wished to convey. (All of the letters in Margoliouth's collection are in rhymed prose.) In *Zajr al-Nābiḥ* (a very brief defense against criticism of some of some of his views expressed in *Luzūm Mā Lā Yalzam*), al-Maʿarrī wrote predominantly in nonrhymed prose; *Risālat al-Malā'ikah* (at one level a highly technical work revolving primarily around questions of morphology and etymology, but at another level not without occasional obvious sarcasm of broader ramifications), is a combination of rhymed and nonrhymed prose. *Mulqā al-Sabīl* is also written in rhymed prose.

In Europe and the Americas as well as the Arab-Islamic communities in the world, today the renown of Abū al-ʿAlā' and familiarity with him rest primarily on: (1) *Saqṭ al-Zand*; (2) the collection of the personal epistles that have been collected and translated by D. S. Margoliouth under the title *Dīwān al-Rasā'il* (*Collection of the Epistles*); (3) *Risālat al-Ghufrān*; and (4) *Luzūm Mā Lā Yalzam*. *Al-Fuṣūl wa al-Ghāyāt* could also arguably be bracketed with the above, especially in Europe in light of more modern research efforts, including in particular discreet articles by August Fischer and Josef Van Ess and the more recent exhaustive book-length overview, along with an Arabic–German glossary, by Christian Peltz, *Der Koran des Abū l-'Alā'*.[76]

Zajr al-Nābiḥ and *Mulqā al-Sabīl* are very short works. Only extracts have been retrieved from the former. Although both have attracted the attention of editors,[77] neither has proven quite remarkable enough, quantitatively or qualitatively, to sustain more than an incidental remark or two by scholars, or perhaps a short monograph here and there.[78]

Risālat al-Malā'ikah deals with much philological or morphological minutiae (e.g., how through metathesis [*qalb*/قلب] *ma'lak* [مألك] became *mal'ak* [ملأك]—and ultimately *malak* [ملك] for "angel"); an explanation for the meaning of grammarian Ibn Kaysān's utterance "*hādhā hādhā hadhā hadhā*/هذا هذا هذا هذا" which is the repetition of this one word—meaning "this"—four times in succession. However, even a cursory glance of the work reveals that embedded in the minutiae underscoring a point of morphology or philology, there can be found some not inconsiderable irreverence such as that in evidence with a discussion of the inhabitants of Paradise and the fruits thereof; al-Maʿarrī declares that it is not appropriate that the inhabitants eat of these fruits when they don't know the real facts about their names: for there are people in Paradise who do not know, for example, whether all of the consonants comprising the word for pear (كمثرى) are the original consonants; if asked the pattern of the word according to the teachings of the specialists in Arabic morphology, they would not know. Immediately following this is a discussion of similar thrust and tone concerning the Ṭūbā tree (شجرة طوبى) in Paradise.[79]

That there should be irreverence here and there in *Risālat al-Malā'ikah* should of course come as no great surprise to informed students of al-Ma'arrī.

Al-Fuṣūl wa al-Ghāyāt, according to Ibn al-'Adīm,[80] was the first composition that al-Ma'arrī undertook upon his return to Ma'arrat al-Nu'mān from Baghdad and upon his resolve to retreat to the seclusion of his home and isolate himself from the larger world. An edited version of all that has been retrieved of this work thus far was published by Maḥmūd Ḥasan Zanātī in 1977.[81] As already correctly observed by the medieval chronicler Ibn al-'Adīm, this composition is divided into "sections" (basically paragraphs of varying lengths; hence *al-fuṣūl*/الفصول in the title; plural for section or chapter of a composition), with each section following a rhyme (hence *al-ghāyāt*/الغايات of the title, "because [al-Ma'arrī] intended by *al-ghāyāt* the rhyme letters [used in the arrangement of the sections], inasmuch as the rhyme letter is the end-point of each line [in the sections]." Ibn al-'Adīm goes on to say that "this is the book on account of which al-Ma'arrī was slandered and said to have challenged [or opposed by seeking to emulate] the chapters and verses [of the Qur'ān]" (وهو الكتاب الذي افترى عليه بسببه وقيل إنه عارض به السور والآيات),[82] an assessment that in the Arabic chronicles was first recorded by al-Bākharzī (d. 1075 CE) although with a less spirited rebuttal of the critics of al-Ma'arrī in this respect, namely:

> We know the situation with respect to the vision of al-Ma'arrī's eyes. God knows best about the vision of his mind. Tongues have wagged with bad opinions of him with respect to the book allegedly intended as a challenge to the Qur'ān, that is to say the book that he titled *Chapters with End Rhymes and Imitation of Chapters and Verses* [of the Qur'ān]. He himself brought to light this offense, and hastened to the foolish fancies as the ass hastens to the Ṣilliyānah plant.
>
> عندنا خبر يضره والله أعلم ببصيرته . . . وإنما تحدثت الألسن بإساءته لكتابه الذي زعموا أنه عارض به القرآن وعنونه بالفصول والغايات ومحاذاة السور والآيات وأظهر من نفسه تلك الجيانة وجذّ تلك الهوسات كما يجذّ العير الصلّيانة.[83]

Ibn al-'Adīm rejected completely the proposition that *al-Fuṣūl wa al-Ghāyāt* was an example of *mu'āraḍah*/معارضة.[84] In his *Ma'a Abī al-'Alā' fī Sijnih*/مع أبي العلاء االمعري في سجنه (*With Abū al-'Alā' in his Prison*),[85] where he devoted much more careful attention to *al-Fuṣūl wa al-Ghāyāt* (indeed a whole chapter) than that in evidence in his *Tajdīd Dhikrā Abī al-'Alā'*/تجديد ذكرى أبي العلاء (*Recommemorating Abū al-'Alā'*) (where there are only a few remarks in passing), Ṭāhā Ḥusayn expressed the opinion that *al-Fuṣūl wa al-Ghāyāt* might more accurately be described as having been intended as a prose precursor to *Luzūm Mā Lā Yalzam*, with similar subject matter and philosophical orientation, and replete with a similar linguistic tour de force (i.e., the internal rhymes, with each *faṣl* always ending in a particular designated letter of the Arabic alphabet).[86] Ḥusayn notes (and correctly so) that al-Maʿarrī is certainly doubt-ridden and wavering over certain religio-philosophical questions broached in *al-Fuṣūl wa al-Ghāyāt* in the same manner that he is doubt-ridden and wavering in *Luzūm Mā Lā Yalzam*; but overall Ḥusayn regards the composition (here perhaps being too charitable by half) as an expression of genuine God-centered piety—in the sense of an act of "drawing nearer to God" (التقرب إلى الله)—regardless of the free-thinking process involved.[87] It is not a manifestation of *mu'āraḍah*/معارضة vis-à-vis the Qur'ān, insisted Ḥusayn; *unless* one is to understand by *mu'āraḍah*

> nothing more than following an example and trying to imitate (*muḥāwalat al-muḥākāh*/محاولة المحاكاة). . . , and [nothing more than] Abū al-ʿAlā''s having looked to the Qur'ān as an ideal for the art of literature, thus following its example and striving to imitate it (فتأثّره وجدّ في تقليده); just as every literary person follows the example of what he admires in the way of ideal artistic patterns.[88]

These words in *Ma'a Abī al-'Alā' fī Sijnih*, coming as they did over thirty years after Ṭāhā Ḥusayn's publication of *Tajdīd Dhikrā Abī al-'Alā'* (essentially his PhD dissertation that was completed in 1914), we might assume are meant to supersede Ḥusayn's statement in the latter on p. 288, namely, that al-Maʿarrī is "*al-faylasūf alladhī . . . 'āraḍ al-Qur'ān*"/الفيلسوف الذي عارض القرآن, which here quite strongly suggests the understanding that al-Maʿarrī is "the philosopher who . . . *challenged* [with "opposed" being inherent in the understanding of "challenged"] the Qur'ān";[89] although the question would still remain whether the challenge or opposition of which Ḥusayn at the time had in mind was in terms of challenge/opposition to the content of the Qur'ān or the style or both, since the debate over what came to be known in the history of Islamic thought as the "inimitability of the Qur'ān" (إعجاز القرآن)—by virtue of God's having made it thus—revolved around both content and form or style.

Redolent of the Ṭāhā Ḥusayn of *Ma'a Abī al-'Alā' fī Sijnih*, Josef Van Ess has pointed out on the topic of *mu'āraḍah* with respect to Ibn al-Muqaffaʿ, and on the basis of some few fragments that have been associated with him, that what one might loosely think of as an example of *mu'āraḍah* in terms of a challenge to Qur'ānic content may be—which Van Ess argues is the case with Ibn al-Muqaffaʿ's fragments—primarily "an experiment in rhetoric" and "calculated to demonstrate that . . . stylistically something comparable to the Qur'ān could be composed without, however, attracting the same acclaim for elegance of style and expression"; and not being a challenge in the sense of "a vehicle of anti-Qur'ānic, anti-Islamic rhetoric."[90]

With respect to the question of to what extent *al-Fuṣūl wa al-Ghāyāt* might be seriously regarded as an example of *mu'āraḍah* in the sense of a challenge to the *content* of the Qur'ān—a vehicle for anti-Qur'ānic rhetoric or polemic, in other words—although by the eleventh century CE already discussions by Muslim thinkers and litterateurs over whether the Qur'ān was inimitable/incomparable were in full swing, and although now as then a debate as it pertains to al-Maʿarrī—and specifically in terms of an anti-Islamic, anti-Qur'ānic challenge—might fall on attentive ears (and inquiring minds), a careful examination of the work makes Ḥusayn's argument in *Ma'a Abī al-'Alā' fī Sijnih* (leaving aside the charity with respect to tone and content) more plausible than the argument advanced in *Tajdīd Dhikrā Abī al-'Alā'*. The rhymed prose or سجع (*saj'*) and the carefully parsed cadences in *al-Fuṣūl wa al-Ghāyāt* are certainly redolent of the *saj'* and cadences in the Qur'ān, particularly when there is Maʿarrian moralizing or admonishing or seemingly sincere underscoring of God's majesty and might (of which there are indeed many examples); but the flights of supremely pedantic, archaic language (requiring the author's own commentary—*tafsīr*/تفسير—which in itself often requires commentary; see, e.g., Zanātī's edition], not to mention the abstruse references to people or places or proverbs or verses of poetry (for example), overall contribute to an almost tongue-in-cheek or parodic effect. But that of course could constitute the challenge. Drawing on a study by August Fischer,[91] Josef Van Ess has observed that *al-Fuṣūl wa al-Ghāyāt* "was of quite normal paraenetic content. Only its form, *saj'*, was reminiscent of the Qur'ān"; however, Van Ess wisely hastens to add in his short (but erudite) study of the phenomenon of *mu'āraḍah* with respect to Ibn al-Muqaffaʿ (d. 756 CE), "the step from a refutation to a parody is not very wide."[92] In the same article,[93] Van Ess concludes that although Ibn al-Muqaffaʿ did not wish "to replace the Qur'ān; he only wants to imitate it," and his intention was "experimental rather than polemical," at the same time he "wanted to show that *in his time* something similar to the Qur'ān could be created," and his use of *saj'* in that endeavor "was revolutionary and perhaps shocking" at the time.

The "revolutionary" and "shocking" nature of Ibn al-Muqaffaʿ's (alleged) *mu'āraḍah* must be seen as no less true, *mutatis mutandis*, of al-Maʿarrī's *al-Fuṣūl wa al-Ghāyāt,* given (1) its length and (2) the fact that a polemical intention, although inchoate and sporadic, seems quite in evidence.[94] Writing in 1918,[95] Ameen Rihani (Amīn Rīḥānī) minced no words in labeling *al-Fuṣūl wa al-Ghāyāt* "a work in which [al-Maʿarrī] parodied the Koran itself."

A copy of *Risālat al-Ṣāhil wa al-Shājiḥ* was discovered circa the early 1970s and made available in a critically edited form by Dr. ʿĀ'ishah ʿAbd al-Raḥmān "Bint al-Shāṭi.'"[96] One of the relatively few scholars who have directed serious and detailed critical attention to the contents of this work, Pieter Smoor[97] clearly illustrated how, through the means of speaking animals introduced (thus the title), here and there the epistle reveals information on the sociopolitical situation in and around Aleppo and northern Syria around the year 1020 CE; this is yet another instance of the author not being quite as aloof and detached from mundane affairs as his self-imposed and self-extolled withdrawal to his home suggests. However, the epistle tends more toward long and detailed disquisitions on metrics and rhyme, many references to verses that touch upon descriptions of animals, and the incorporation of learned proverbs, often even in the midst of the process of illustrating the sociopolitical observations that it has to offer.

Saqṭ al-Zand contains poems of lamentation (particularly over the decease of various individuals); panegyrics or praise (*madḥ*/مدح) poems;

poems of complaint (i.e., *shakwah*/شكوة); poems of romantic rhapsodizing (i.e., *ghazal*/غزل); poems in which vivid description (*waṣf*/وصف) is the chief goal; and poems of boasting (*fakhr*/فخر). Though occasionally there are pensive, moral-philosophical moments in this *dīwān*, especially with, but not limited to, the elegies (see particularly the fairly celebrated and often cited one to his father that rhymes in *shādī* /شادِ, opening with the hemistich *ghayru mujdin fī millatī wa-'tiqādī* /غير مُجدٍ في ملتي واعتقادي), on balance the poems contrast most noticeably, thematically and structurally, with *Luzūm Mā Lā Yalzam*.

Abū al-ʿAlā''s letters/epistles in *Dīwān al-Rasā'il*, although addressed to specific people (e.g,, friends and acquaintances) and thus in a sense personal, as previously mentioned, also incorporate many proverbs, verses of poetry, word-plays, subtle allusions, and elegant and pedantic turns of phrase, all the while never violating the *saj'* format, much in vogue by this time. In other words, *on balance*, these letters/epistles reveal less about the author's ideas or the social, political, religious developments of the day than they do the nature of the art and craft of *adab* and within that framework the epistolary style of the day. Art for art's sake more often than not inspires as well as propels the writing once an occasion seems appropriate.

Risālat al-Ghufrān, addressed to a contemporary of Abū al-ʿAlā', the philologist and *adīb* ʿAlī ibn Manṣūr ibn al-Qāriḥ, envisions the latter having died and been transported to both Paradise and Hell, whereat he converses with deceased poets, the jinn, and various other personalities. Rich in literary criticism and grammatical and philological erudition, *Risālat al-Ghufrān* also displays a noteworthy concern for religious issues and most particularly the Hereafter (which it arguably parodies to a greater or lesser degree; usually the former). As part of its response to Ibn al-Qāriḥ, the epistle also contains a long digressive passage that reads almost like a separate tract. Here there can be found many anecdotes or utterances relating to some reputed scandalous libertines or heretics (i.e., *zanādiq*/زنادق, singular *zindīq*/زنديق) over the course of Islamicate history up until that time (around 1032 CE), followed by Abū al-ʿAlā''s comments on them (although the comments, even when quite clearly *suggesting* disapproval, are often rather elliptical and enigmatic). Moreover, some of the clear or clearer expressions of disapproval are arguably—some might say indisputably—ironic. "What he thinks . . . or rather, what he says—[in this context]—while it cannot be regarded as finally significant of his real opinions, does at any rate afford the entertainment . . . of skating over thin ice."[98] In other words, this portion of *The Epistle of Forgiveness* should hardly be approached as a *bona fide* Islamic heresiography, but it does shed some light on the understanding of الزندقة (as defined by al-Maʿarrī, namely, the complete disavowal of prophecy and revelation). The *Epistle of Forgiveness* in its entirety was recently most masterfully translated into English, in two volumes, by Geert van Gelder and Gregor Schoeler.[99] The van Gelder and Schoeler English translation represents the first complete translation in any language.

Thematically, quite unlike *Saqṭ al-Zand, Luzūm Mā Lā Yalzam* departed from the at-the-time more or less well-defined genres of poetry such as panegyrics and elegies. Instead, it aspired to a more meditative, religio-philosophical and moralizing type of versification, quite often restricted to very short fragments that read like apothegms or even quatrains. (In fact, Ameen Rihani in 1918 published as quatrains English translations of portions of *Luzūm Mā Lā Yalzam* and furthermore maintained that "the skepticism and pessimism of Omar [al-Khayyām] are to a great extent imported from Ma'arrah."[100]) In chapter 3 of this study, I offer a fuller explanation of what precisely is meant by all of this, along with the more detailed description of *Luzūm Mā Lā Yalzam* overall. Here and now, it suffices to say that it is in this work where one is to find the most comprehensive and concentrated exposition of the key ideas or "doctrines" typically associated with the name Abū al-ʿAlā' al-Maʿarrī, and for which he is sometimes labeled not simply poet (*shā'ir*/شاعر) but also *faylasūf*/فيلسوف (philosopher), *ḥakīm*/حكيم (sage; philosopher), or *al-shā'ir al-faylasūf* (the philosopher-poet). It is primarily *Luzūm Mā Lā Yalzam*, too, that prompts the debates over the various appellations that one will find assigned to al-Maʿarrī as thinker.

From the late nineteenth or early twentieth century until close to the mid-twentieth century, outside of Arabic-speaking societies, if not within them as well, the best-known and appreciated of Abū al-ʿAlā''s surviving literary works was either *Saqṭ al-Zand* or *Risālat al-Ghufrān*, the latter particularly after the appearance of (1) R. A. Nicholson's partial translation plus commentary,[101] (2) Miguel Asin Palascio's linking of this work to Dante's *Divine Comedy*,[102] and (3) the publication of the more definitive and exhaustive critical edition, with notes, by ʿĀ'ishah ʿAbd al-Raḥmān.[103] In the Arab-Islamic world, *Saqṭ al-Zand* over the ages inspired at least several major commentaries including the imposing edition in 1945 (Cairo) that incorporates three of these commentaries over the course of five volumes. Arthur Wormhoudt translated parts of the *dīwān* into English in 1972.[104] Pieter Smoor referenced lines in his seminal work on al-Maʿarrī, *Kings and Bedouins in the Palace of Aleppo as Reflected in Maʿarrī's Works*,[105] a painstakingly detailed and learned study of instances where al-Maʿarrī's poetry may be seen to reflect the rather complicated and unstable political history of Aleppo and the northern Syria hinterlands in the early eleventh century of the Common Era.

Historically, *Luzūm Mā Lā Yalzam*—long; overwrought; repetitious; excessively clever technically; relentlessly pessimistic and skeptical where not absolutely cynical; misanthropic as well as misogynistic; often borderline if not egregiously sacrilegious—could never quite command the attraction and appeal of *Saqṭ al-Zand* or *Risālat al-Ghufrān* (for the latter, especially in Europe and the United States, undoubtedly because of the comparisons to Dante's *Divine Comedy,* with the at-times burlesque nature of the depiction of the Islamic eschaton being of no particular offense; in fact probably enhancing the work's appeal).

Through all of premodern times, no truly informed commentary on *Luzūm Mā Lā Yalzam* survived, perhaps as a reflection of its lack of appeal but also contributing to it. Today, however, one could plausibly argue that *Luzūm Mā Lā Yalzam* is just as recognizable as either *Saqṭ al-Zand* or *Risālat al-Ghufrān*, especially in the United States and Europe. In 1888, Alfred von Kremer brought some of its undeniably controversial contents but also poignancy and peculiar beauty and power to the attention especially of Europe, through his translations of key passages into rhymed German verse. The translations were accompanied by a long and thoughtful interpretative essay, "Ueber die philosophischen Gedichte des Abul-ʿalâ Maʿarry."[106] By 1895, there appeared a complete critical edition of *Luzūm Mā Lā Yalzam* with explanatory notes with respect to vocabulary and also occasional commentary.[107] Not long after this, Ṭāhā Ḥusayn's doctoral dissertation (published in 1914 with the title *Tajdīd Dhikrā Abī al-ʿAlā'*) contributed to a revival of an interest in Abū al-ʿAlā'’s *Luzūm Mā Lā Yalzam*, especially in the Arab-Islamic world. The first solid effort in the Arabic language at an open-minded, comprehensive, critical study, and one covering the life and thought of Abū al-ʿAlā' from a historian's and a comparatist's perspective, this work shed additional light on the so-called philosophy of *Luzūm Mā Lā Yalzam*. Ḥusayn's at-the-time (and place) quite ground-breaking study (nothing in Arabic along the lines of von Kremer's essay had yet to appear) served to prompt throughout the decades that followed scores of other works in Arabic on Abū al-ʿAlā's thought, in either book- or article-length, and all of which could hardly avoid taking into consideration *Luzūm Mā Lā Yalzam* (to one extent or another), especially given Ḥusayn's own reputation, even as a young student, as an undeniably formidable thinker and irrepressible contrarian.[108] Twenty-five years after publishing *Tajdīd Dhikrā Abī al-'Alā'*, Ṭāhā Ḥusayn revisited the thought of Abū al-ʿAlā' in another seminal work on the topic, *Ma'a Abī al-'Alā' fī Sijnih*.

Shortly before the appearance of Ṭāhā Ḥusayn's dissertation in published book form, R. A. Nicholson, in *Literary History of the Arabs*, which is still one of the more serviceable English-language accounts of the broad contours of the literary history of the Arabs, gave a brief but masterful description of *Luzūm Mā Lā Yalzam*'s contents.[109] Nicholson followed this up fourteen years later with a more in-depth study that incorporated translations of dozens of individual poems keyed to the original Arabic printed in an appendix. The piece appeared as a chapter ("The Meditations of Maʿarrí") in Nicholson's book *Studies in Islamic Poetry*,[110] also standard reading fare for serious students of the literature and thought of the premodern Arab-Islamic world. In 1945, Henri Laoust published his shorter but helpful "La vie et la philosophie d'Abū-l-ʿAlā' al-Maʿarrī,"[111] which included consideration of *Luzūm Mā Lā Yalzam*.

Thanks above all to the efforts of von Kremer, Ḥusayn, and Nicholson, whose longer and pioneering critical studies on al-Maʿarrī's *Luzūm Mā Lā Yalzam* have proven to be enduringly popular and useful, and thanks to the very nature of *Luzūm Mā Lā Yalzam* itself, today it would be unlikely for Euro-American students of Arabic literature and Arab-Islamic thought to speak of Abū al-ʿAlā' al-Maʿarrī without making more than a passing reference to *Luzūm Mā Lā Yalzam*; this regardless of whatever one might have to say about *Saqṭ al-Zand*, *Risālat al-Ghufrān*, or the other surviving works by al-Maʿarrī. The centrality of the *Luzūmiyyāt* within the framework of al-Maʿarrī's oeuvre has been well established.

That al-Maʿarrī today looms as a fairly important and intriguing *thinker* in Islam, and not simply a garrulous and prolific crank (whether in prose or poetry), is also scarcely in doubt because of the research efforts first and foremost of von Kremer, Ḥusayn, and Nicholson, but then too because of additional sober and carefully prepared studies that have followed in their wake. Among the more notable of these, roughly in chronological order, are *Ḥakīm al-Ma'arrah* (*The Sage of al-Ma'arrah*) by ʿUmar Farrūkh;[112] *Abū al-'Alā' al-Ma'arrī* by Aḥmad Taymūr;[113] *Abū al-'Alā Nāqid al-Mujtama'* (*Abū al-'Alā', Critic of Society*) by Zakī al-Maḥāsinī;[114] *al-Fikr al-Dīnī 'inda Abī al-'Alā' al-Ma'arrī* (*Abū al-'Alā' al-Ma'arrī's Religious Thought*) by ʿAṭā Bakrī;[115] "al-Jawānib al-Mītāfīzīqiyyah li al-Nafs wa Naẓariyyat al-Maʿrifah ʿinda Abī al-ʿAlā' al-Maʿarrī" ("The Metaphysical Dimensions of Self for Abū al-ʿAlā' al-Maʿarrī"),[116] "Makānat al-ʿAql fī al-Falsafah al-Khulqiyyah ʿinda Abī al-ʿAlā' al-Maʿarrī" ("The Place of Reason in Abū al-ʿAlā' al-Maʿarrī's Moral Philosophy"), and "Mītāfīzīqā al-ʿUlū wa al-Ṭabīʿah fī Falsafat Abī al-ʿAlā' al-Maʿarrī" ("The Metaphysics of Transcendence and Nature in the Philosophy of Abū al-ʿAlā' al-Maʿarrī")[117]—all by Saḥbān Khalīfāt; *Qaḍāyā al-'Aṣr fī Adab Abī al-'Alā' al-Ma'arrī* by ʿAbd al-Qādir Zaydān;[118] and *Abū al-'Alā' al-Ma'arrī al-Muntakhab min al-Luzūmiyyāt* (*Abū al-'Alā' al-Ma'arrī, Selections from the Luzūmiyyāt*) by Hādī al-ʿAlawī.[119] All of the above-mentioned works broaden the comparatist's perspective, often to include modern sociopolitical, historical, or philosophical developments. Zaydān's and Khalīfāt's efforts are especially remarkable for rigorous scrutiny and consideration squarely within the framework of philosophy, whether Islamic or otherwise, premodern or modern.

As long ago as 1970, one of the leading modern historians of Islamic philosophy, Majid Fakhry, went so far as to label al-Maʿarrī one of "the most fascinating Muslim thinkers. . . [who] fall outside the mainstream of thought in Islam. . . . The historian of Islamic thought cannot overlook [these thinkers] . . . without distorting the total picture."[120] Regrettably, and somewhat inexplicably, Fakhry did not proceed to include a discussion of al-Maʿarrī in his overview of the history of Islamic philosophy that he published in 1970, although in a subsequent abbreviated overview

(*Islamic Philosophy*) published in 2009,[121] he did devote several brief paragraphs to him, along with some quotations from *Luzūm Mā Lā Yalzam*.

Notwithstanding all of the more recent developments in the scholarship on al-Maʿarrī, considerable confusion or uncertainty can still adhere to an understanding of the exact nature of the man's thought. Atheism, deism, heresy, Epicurean materialism, free-thinking, Manichean dualism, Shīʿism, Sufism, Brahmanism, Islamism (albeit rethought and reformed)—these are just a few of the diverse, and sometimes mutually exclusive, systems of thought or religio-philosophical orientations with which one is apt to find the name of Abū al-ʿAlāʾ associated in the secondary literature that refers to him (especially that written in Arabic).[122]

What, then, did Abū al-ʿAlāʾ al-Maʿarrī really believe in, and intend to espouse, in full? How in the final analysis are we simply to *understand* him, regardless of whether we feel compelled to accept or reject, like or loathe, whatever confessional tendencies or life orientations he may or may not have exhibited? Which of the descriptive words or identifying phrases so frequently assigned him are actually appropriate or inappropriate and why?

After all of these years of our awareness of Abū al-ʿAlāʾ al-Maʿarrī, and notwithstanding the modern (i.e., the nineteenth and twentieth centuries) surge in interest that has amounted to a virtual rediscovery, these are really the most fundamental questions still likely to be raised with respect to the blind philosopher-poet from the relatively obscure, small Syrian town of Maʿarrat al-Nuʿmān; they are not the only questions, but they are the most basic and compelling. Accordingly, these questions first and foremost impel the present study. In search of the answers to the questions, the study concentrates on a critical analysis and interpretation of *Luzūm Mā Lā Yalzam*, foregrounding this before proceeding elsewhere (e.g., al-Maʿarrī's other extant works; or secondary sources) for possible elaboration, clarification, and qualifications. To repeat what has been observed previously in this chapter, based on our present knowledge, the *Luzūmiyyāt* is the *locus classicus* for most of the major ideas associated with Abū al-ʿAlāʾ, the sum of his teachings, opinions, or so-called philosophy over the course of his life.

Given a somewhat confusing and contradictory state of affairs in the secondary literature devoted to Abū al-ʿAlāʾ, I give thoughtful consideration first to what Abū al-ʿAlāʾ himself says in *Luzūm Mā Lā Yalzam* before turning to what his biographers, commentators, and interpreters—modern or premodern—have had to say about this collection of poems. My basic methodological approach, in other words, is akin to one advocated by Muhsin Mahdi in his study of Ibn Khaldūn:

> The object of this method is to ascertain the *deliberate intention* [Mahdi's emphasis] of the author . . . It concentrates on the text of the author and preserves its integrity. And its exclusive aim is the elucidation of what the author says and the way he says it. It does not challenge the possibility that a reader may have a deeper knowledge of the subject matter than the author he is reading. But it assumes that the reader can never know what the author deliberately meant to say better than the author himself, and that the full understanding of what the author intended to say must precede interpretations and judgments based on principles other than those accepted by the author.[123]

At the same time, I endorse the principal that interpretations (regardless of the provenance) that come after the elucidation of the fullest possible understanding of what an author himself says may be not only germane but also helpful *precisely in terms of the fullest possible understanding*, by suggesting genuine *possibilities* (including analogies, appropriations, or parallels) that might otherwise go unnoticed or remain inchoate.

To that end, among other things, I take into consideration works both in Arabic and various European languages that pertain to Islamic thought in general or to Abū al-ʿAlāʾs in particular. With respect to the scores of scholarly books or articles dealing specifically with one aspect or another of Abū al-ʿAlāʾs thought, references will be focused primarily on the above-described studies by von Kremer, Ḥusayn, and Nicholson and the handful of works in Arabic from the modern, post-Ḥusayn era. Many of the remaining works in the field—Maʿarrian studies, as it were—largely recapitulate in very brief synoptic fashion what von Kremer, Ḥusayn, and Nicholson, and/or the above-mentioned authors writing in Arabic have concluded by way of their more laborious and comprehensive scrutiny. Unfortunately, there is also the tendency to be rather fixated merely with arguing whether Abū al-ʿAlāʾ was, when all is said and done, still a Muslim (i.e., whether he more or less might be considered as falling within the pale of Islam as a مؤمن/*mu'min* [believer]); and, to that end, to summarily line up citations—but without much nuanced discussion—suggesting one side of the issue or the other. The tendency not so much to try to understand al-Maʿarrī, especially with respect to broader and deeper ramifications, as to summarily pigeonhole him with a religio-philosophical moniker, and particularly either the simple "Muslim"/"non-Muslim" or "believer" "nonbeliever/atheist" variety, is especially pronounced and determinative in premodern (i.e., medieval) Arabic source materials, but also in evidence in the more modern—at least until the appearance of Ṭāhā Ḥusayn's studies and those of the other above-mentioned authors (or their like, as few as they may be) writing in Arabic.

Concerning von Kremer's *Ueber die philosophische gedichte des Abul'alâ*, R. A. Nicholson wrote that

> [the] essay, for which in general I have nothing but praise, seems to me to suffer from want of proportion. It hails Maʻarrí as an original thinker . . . and discusses his theory and practice as though he were a philosopher writing in verse. Without denying that Maʻarrí was a pioneer of *Aufklarung* . . . I submit that Von Kremer has the cart before the horse. Maʻarrí is, first of all and essentially, a poet. His philosophy and ethics are only a background for his poetry. [124]

Nicholson expressed a similar sentiment[125] with respect to Ṭāhā Ḥusayn's approach to al-Maʿarrī in *Tajdīd Dhikrā Abī al-ʿAlāʾ*. Without wishing to debate here and now (there will be more on that later) the issue of whether al-Maʿarrī wished to speak primarily as a philosopher or primarily a poet in the *Luzūmiyyāt*, and fully aware of the invaluable contributions to the understanding of al-Maʿarrī's philosophy (or "thought," if that less technical term is preferred) made by Nicholson as well as von Kremer and Ḥusayn, I frankly acknowledge that I keep the cart where von Kremer and Ṭāhā Ḥusayn placed it. That is to say, the thinking of al-Maʿarrī in *Luzūm Mā Lā Yalzam* is foregrounded in the present study; the poetics are secondary.[126]

CHAPTER TWO

The Milieu

Part I. Political Developments: The Self-Assertion of the Provinces*

Al-Ma'arrī died in 1057 of the Common Era. He lived to be 84 years old. During his lifetime, the realm of the 'Abbāsid caliphs (750–1258 CE) in anything more than name was well on its way toward effective dissolution. The power and authority that used to radiate rather decisively and effectively from Baghdad and prevail over much of the Islamicate commonwealth was becoming more and more compromised in the major provincial military and administrative metropoli, which for long already had served as the seats of independent or quasi-independent dynastic, eponymous governments with governors who went by the title of prince (*amīr*) or *sulṭān*, or, in the case of the Ismā'īlī Fāṭimid dynasty centered in Cairo, imām-caliph.[1] Al-Ma'arrī's more immediate geopolitical environment was largely shaped by such regimens, the Fāṭimids in North Africa (with virtual suzerainty eventually over southern Syria/Palestine as well) and the Ḥamdānids and Mirdāsids in northern Syria (with the major locus of power and authority the city of Aleppo). At the same time, the Būyids and not the 'Abbāsid caliphs became the real governors of Baghdad as well as the surrounding province of al-'Irāq (i.e., lower Mesopotamia), and, with that, assumed suzerainty over the entire eastern expanse of the 'Abbāsid commonwealth of states/provinces. Meanwhile, a reinvigorated Byzantine Empire, through military campaigns as well as treaties, hastened to advance its own interests with respect to the realm of the 'Abbāsids, especially at the borders with northern Syria that were still being contested.

A. The Fāṭimids

The Fāṭimids were Shīʿites or ʿAlids (i.e., in the Arabic, علويون), which is to say those members of the Islamic community who believed that, after the Prophet Muḥammad, the supreme leader of the community or caliph ought to have been ʿAlī ibn Abī Ṭālib (the Prophet's nephew and son-in-law by way of marriage to his daughter Fāṭimah), and subsequently, someone from among the descendants of ʿAlī through transmission from father to son in a nomination process known as *naṣṣ*/نصّ. The nomination process was regarded as representing God's Will. The nominee's more common title was not caliph (successor to the successor of God, *viz.* the Prophet Muḥammad) but rather imām or leader par excellence of the entire community of Muslims, especially with respect to interpreting religious law or *Sharīʿah* (الشريعة). The imām was considered infallible (*maʿṣūm*/معصوم).

The Fāṭimid partisans of ʿAlī believed that after the sixth imām descended from ʿAlī and wife Fāṭimah (Jaʿfar al-Ṣādiq [d. 765 CE]), Ismāʿīl (Jaʿfar's eldest son; d. 760 CE) and *his* descendants, beginning particularly with his (Ismāʿīl's) son Muḥammad, were to be recognized as the rightful imāms—as opposed to Mūsā al-Kāẓim/موسى الكاظم (d. 799 CE; he was Ismāʿīl's brother and second son of Jaʿfar) and *his* descendants, whose line was recognized up through Muḥammad al-Muntaẓar (محمد المنتظر) (the fifth imām after Mūsā al-Kāẓim) by the faction of Shīʿites who became known as "Twelvers." For the Twelvers, Muḥammad al-Muntaẓar, the twelfth imām (in their reckoning) descended from ʿAlī and Fāṭimah by way of Mūsā al-Kāẓim, was the final imām. For the Twelvers, he did not die but rather concealed himself (around 878 CE) from his community by way of temporary "occultation" (*ghaybah*/غيبة). Twelver Shīʿites await his return in the flesh in order that he set things right throughout Islamdom, vanquish all of Islam's antagonists, and inaugurate an era of uprightness that will usher in the end of life on earth.

The Sevener Shīʿites (of ninth century CE Qarmaṭī [Carmathian] inspiration) recognized Ismāʿīl's son Muḥammad (grandson of Jaʿfar al-Ṣādiq) as the final imām, who, although he died as a mortal, is to return to life on the Last Day and usher in the end of life in the Here and Now. The Fāṭimid branch of Shīʿism, however, recognized as imām one of

Muḥammad's sons, and, thereafter, whomsoever was designated (by way of *naṣṣ*) his successor. These individuals, in other words, were regarded as the properly designated successor imām (by virtue of *naṣṣ*). This was the view of the majority of the Seveners. The son of Muḥammad and after him the series of imāms in occultation extended the imāmate, although the appellation "Ismāʿīliyyah"/إسماعيلية is nonetheless attached to this Shīʿite orientation (as well as to any other Seveners) because of the obvious affiliation with Jaʿfar al-Ṣādiq's son Ismāʿīl as opposed to son Mūsā al-Kāẓim (whom the Twelvers recognized as the rightful imām to have succeeded Jaʿfar al-Ṣādiq).

The foundation of the Fāṭimid dynastic state was laid by one of the professed descendants of Ismāʿīl's son Muḥammad, Saʿīd ibn Ḥusayn, who at the end of the tenth century CE lived in Salamiyyah, Syria, where Ismāʿīlī missionaries/*du'āh* (دعاة) had already been active. Saʿīd soon left Salamiyyah for al-Ramlah in Palestine and then Ifrīqiyah (present day Tunisia, approximately), where a major Ismāʿīlī missionary or *dā'ī* (داع), Abū ʿAbd Allāh al-Ḥusayn al-Shīʿī, originally propagating in Yemen, had been active among the Kutāmah Amāzīgh since 893 CE. Saʿīd ibn Ḥusayn was either imprisoned or arrested in Sijilmāsah by the governor (*amīr*/أمير) there, who ruled in the name of the Aghlabid dynasty. Abū ʿAbd Allāh eventually overthrew the *amīr* and summoned Saʿīd ibn al-Ḥusayn in 909 CE to join him at Raqqādah (in Ifrīqiyah). There in 910 he assumed first the title of *al-mahdī*/ المهدي (signifying "the rightly guided [imām])" and then the title of *amīr al-mu'minīn*/commander of the faithful. It was during this time that Saʿīd also became known by the name ʿUbayd Allāh.

Saʿīd/ʿUbayd Allāh eventually plotted to have Abū ʿAbd Allāh—heretofore the chief Ismāʿīlī missionary in North African—killed. At the same time, by force of arms, he and his supporters (including his son al-Qā'im, destined to become the second Fāṭimid imām-caliph) prevailed over recalcitrant Muslims (including various quasiautonomous dynastic rulers, particularly the Idrīsids in Morocco) who were not converted by the Ismāʿīlī missions. In Sicily Saʿīd/ʿUbayd Allāh managed to successfully repeal the suzerainty of the Byzantine Empire.

The murder of the missionary Abū ʿAbd Allāh prompted a revolt among the Kutāmah Amāzīgh of North Africa. They designated their own Mahdī. Another Amāzīgh faction, the Zanātah, revolted; but armed forces under the command of Maṣālah ibn Ḥabūs quelled the revolt, seizing in the process Tāhart (from the Rustamid governor) in 911 CE and then Fez and Sijilmāsah (from the Idrīsids; Fez falling in 920 and Sijilmāsah in 921). A lieutenant to Maṣālah ibn Ḥabūs, Mūsā ibn Abī al-ʿĀfiyah, subsequently pacified the entire Maghrib (i.e., the North African littoral), helped in the cause by the military campaigns of Saʿīd/ʿUbayd Allāh's son al-Qā'im; although the territory, including especially Fez, had to be virtually reconquered later under al-Qā'im when he assumed the Fāṭimid caliphate after his father's death in 934 CE. This territory was to be more effectively brought under Fāṭimid suzerainty during the reign of the imām-caliph al-Muʿizz (953–75), by virtue of military campaigns led by the general Jawhar al-Ṣiqillī.

Al-Qā'im led three military expeditions to Egypt during his father's lifetime, first in 934–935, then in 919–21, and finally in 925. His Fāṭimid armies penetrated as far as Fayyūm and al-Fusṭāṭ near Cairo, although they withdrew. Al-Qā'im's father, ʿUbayd Allāh, was more successful in challenging the Byzantines, specifically regarding rule in Sicily. In 916, after having put to death a Sicilian governor who declared his support for the ʿAbbāsid caliph in Baghdad, ʿUbayd Allāh appointed a new Fāṭimid-loyal governor to rule the island. Two years later, the Byzantine emperor entered into a treaty with the governor according to which the emperor agreed to pay an annual tribute, a virtual sign of acquiescence to Fāṭimid supremacy. At around the same time, Fāṭimid maritime forces were sent to Genoa, Sardinia, Corsica, Malta, and other islands in the Mediterranean, making clear the extent of their imperial ambitions and the wherewithal (including sea power) to realize them. In 920 CE. ʿUbayd Allāh founded a new city in Ifrīqiyah, al-Mahdiyyah, which he made his capital.

The third Fāṭimid imām-caliph, al-Manṣūr (ruled 946–53 CE), consolidated Fāṭimid suzerainty in Sicily by sending to the island in 948 a loyal governor who along with his scions were to usher in a rule of considerable stability. Closer to home in Ifrīqiyah, he inherited serious opposition; in fact, a virtual armed revolt that at one point led to a yearlong siege of the new Fāṭimid capital at al-Mahdiyyah. However, by 947 Fāṭimid-loyal forces had effectively subdued the dissidents.

Under the fourth imām-caliph al-Muʿizz (ruled 953–57 CE), in addition to advancing by land as far west as the Atlantic Ocean in a campaign (958 CE) to repacify the Maghrib, Fāṭimid armies defeated an offensive against them (953 CE) directed by the Umayyad caliph of Spain, ʿAbd al-Raḥmān III. In 956–57, al-Muʿizz dispatched a war fleet to attack the Byzantines in the Italian mainland. The expedition led to putting troops on the ground. This forced a truce at the behest of Byzantine emperor Nicepherous Phocas, with his agreeing to pay a tribute to the Fāṭimids. Shortly thereafter, when the Byzantine emperor refused to pay the tribute, and furthermore fomented resistance to Fāṭimid suzerainty in Sicily, the Fāṭimid armies and maritime forces defeated the Byzantines in two key battles (in 965 CE). This led to a peace treaty in 967.

These successes on the part of the Fāṭimids paved the way for their conquest of Egypt, a clear desideratum since the reign of ʿUbayd Allāh. In 969—just four years before al-Maʿarrī's birth—Jawhar al-Ṣiqillī and his Fāṭimid army marched victoriously to al-Fusṭāṭ and occupied it. With the taking of the city, Jawhar announced that mention of the ʿAbbāsid caliph's name in the sermon/*khuṭbah* (خطبة) of the Friday congregational prayers was to be stopped. At the same time, he began to plan a new city for his troops, al-Qāhirah (القاهرة) (Cairo), which signaled not only that the Fāṭimids were about to assume active rule over Egypt, but also that they were not going to rule merely from a distance with surrogates. By 975 CE, the Fāṭimid imām-caliphs would establish court not in al-Mahdiyyah but in al-Qāhirah.

Once firmly established in Cairo, Jawhar and the Fāṭimid imām-caliphs (the first of whom to begin rule from Cairo was al-ʿAzīz, in 975 CE) set out to extend their governance farther east, beginning with the Holy Cities of Mecca and Medina, Palestine, and Syria, all of which were dependencies of the Ikhshīdids (whom the Fāṭimids had overturned in Fusṭāṭ), and, as such, territories at least nominally subject to the ʿAbbāsid caliph in Baghdad. Mecca and Medina accepted Fāṭimid overlordship without resistance in 970–71 CE; they remained part of the Fāṭimid realm until the advent of the Seljūk Turks in the middle of the eleventh century CE. (The Seljūk Turks would restore to Mecca and Medina nominal ʿAbbāsid caliphal authority. They were Sunnī Muslims, as were the ʿAbbāsid caliphs; i.e., they were not partisans of ʿAlī and the

ʿAlid imāms as the rightful leaders of the Islamic Commonwealth [*al-ummah al-islāmiyyah*/الأمة الإسلامية] and from whom ultimate authority with respect to the religious law ought to be derived. They were, rather, followers of the customs [*sunnah*/سنة] of the Prophet Muḥammad and his close associates, customs that as idealized by consensus became the norm for the righteous behavior of the community of faithful Muslims, the bedrock with respect to determining the religious law.)

Expanding their rule into Syria, especially north of Damascus by land, proved more challenging for the Fāṭimids; and, although they made important gains in that endeavor—including the city of Damascus and the southern landward approaches thereto—they could never establish true suzerainty over the province of Syria. Jawhar al-Ṣiqillī's lieutenant (Jaʿfar) seized territory leading up to and including Damascus. This occurred shortly after the Fāṭimid conquest of Fusṭāṭ. However, the Qarmaṭī (Carmathian) Sevener Shīʿites in Syria under the leadership of al-Ḥasan al-Aṣmaʿī counterattacked and killed Jaʿfar in 971 CE. Al-Ḥasan seemed poised to advance as far as Cairo. Realizing this, Jawhar took to the battle field in 971 and forced al-Ḥasan to retreat, reoccupying in the process parts of Palestine, although by 974 al-Ḥasan and his forces re-grouped and attacked Cairo. Al-Ḥasan was eventually defeated, allowing the Fāṭimids to take Damascus again, but by 975 the governorship was in the hands of Alptekīn, a Turkish soldier of fortune with ambitions of his own. Alptekīn gained the support of the Syrian Carmathians, and, although under the Fāṭimid imām-caliph al-ʿAzīz the Fāṭimids reestablished their suzerainty over Damascus, a tribute had to be paid to the Carmathians in order to keep them acquiescent. Moreover, Fāṭimid attempts to take Aleppo (from the Ḥamdānid dynastic governors) in 983, 992–93, and 994–95 (CE) all failed.

Aleppo fell to Fāṭimid armies in 1015 during the reign of imām-caliph al-Ḥākim (ruled 996–1021 CE), al-ʿAzīz's successor. But by 1025 CE, during the reign of al-Ḥākim's successor (al-Ẓāhir; ruled 1021–36 CE), rule of Aleppo was in the hands of Ṣāliḥ ibn Mirdās, a chief of the Kilābī Bedouin tribe and founder of the short-lived eponymous dynasty (viz. the Mirdāsids).

The Byzantine Empire played a major role in thwarting Fāṭimid efforts to take and hold Aleppo, especially during the reign of al-ʿAzīz, when the emperor dispatched forces to fend off assaults, and, for all intents and purposes, in the process protected the quasiautonomy of the Ḥamdānid dynasty. The objective seemed to be the establishment of a buffer state between Byzantium's southern flank and the Fāṭimid Empire. Towards the end of the tenth century CE, the Byzantine emperors and the Fāṭimid imām-caliphs were prepared to negotiate significant truces and treaties, culminating in the thirty-year peace treaty of 1038. Some of the terms of the various truces and treaties aimed to promote mutual respect and prosperity and not merely peaceful co-existence. In 987–88, the emperor, Basil II, agreed to rescind Byzantine commercial restrictions on the Fāṭimids, while at the same allowing that the prayers at the mosque of Constantinople be led in the name of the imām-caliph. In the treaty of 1038, concluded during the reign of the the imām-caliph al-Mustanṣir (ruled 1036–94), the Byzantines were granted permission to rebuild the Church of the Holy Sepulchre in Jerusalem, which had been destroyed on the orders of the imām-caliph al-Ḥākim during his rule.

Under al-ʿAzīz, the Fāṭimid court in Cairo exchanged ambassadors with ʿAḍud al-Dawlah, the Būyid governor of Baghdad whose family members were the true overlords of the city from 945 CE to 1055, and furthermore overlords of whichever provinces of the ʿAbbāsid caliphate that they could manage to retain as vassal states; eclipsing the ʿAbbāsid caliphs' authority in all practical regards with the exception of the formality of the investiture ceremony by which the ʿAbbāsid caliphs bestowed upon the Būyid rulers the title of *amīr al-umarā'* or chief governor (literally, "the prince of princes"). However, the Būyid governors would not recognize the (anti-)caliphate of al-ʿAzīz. They continued to seek their legitimacy from the ʿAbbāsid caliphs. This was not simply a matter of *realpolitik* owing to the Būyids proximity to what remained of the ʿAbbāsid domains including especially Baghdad. Although Shīʿites, the Būyids were Twelvers and hence not in agreement with the Fāṭimids on the key issue of the rightful succession of the imāms after the sixth, Jaʿfar al-Ṣādiq. Moreover, they questioned the authenticity of the Fāṭimids' proclaimed genealogical link to ʿAlī ibn Abī Ṭālib.

In 1034 CE, the Fāṭimid imām-caliph, al-Ẓāhir (ruled 1021–36), sent Fāṭimid missionaries to Baghdad. By 1057 in Mosul and 1059 in Baghdad, just two years after Seljūk Turkish-led forces under Ṭughril Bey had stormed Baghdad, the Turkish military governor of Baghdad (although still under nominal Būyid suzerainty), al-Basāsīrī, had the sovereignty of the Fāṭimid imām-caliph al-Mustanṣir recognized. This took place while Ṭughril Bey—recognized as sulṭān of Baghdad in 1055 CE by ʿAbbāsid caliph al-Qā'im (ruled 1031–75 CE)—was absent from Baghdad on a military campaign to the north. When Ṭughril Bey returned to Baghdad in in 1060, he abrogated al-Basāsīrī's proclamation of recognition of the Fāṭimid imām-caliph al-Mustanṣir and, furthermore, had al-Basāsīrī executed. As Sunnī Muslims, the Seljūk Turks were not prepared to countenance the claims and aspirations of the Shīʿite Fāṭimids.

In 1070 CE, Nāṣir al-Dawlah al-Ḥamdānī, governor of Damascus under Fāṭimid suzerainty and with a Fāṭimid garrison at his disposal, resolved to seize control of Cairo and topple the Fāṭimid imām-caliph. To that end, he asked Alp Arslān, then sulṭān of Baghdad, to march on Egypt. Alp Arslān responded, and with his army, he got as far as Aleppo, intending to then head south to Egypt. The ruler of Aleppo at that time, Maḥmūd ibn Nāṣir (a scion of the Mirdāsids), had given his allegiance to the Fāṭimid imām-caliph al-Mustanṣir. But realizing his declining strength and influence in light of Seljūk ascendancy in the Near East, he sent an envoy to Baghdad announcing that he was ceasing to recognize the suzerainty of al-Mustanṣir and instead would acknowledge the overlordship of both the ʿAbbāsid caliph (al-Qā'im) and sulṭān Alp Arslān.

During its rule from Cairo, the Fāṭimid dynasty witnessed not a few periods of economic hardship and political instability. The occasions of economic hardship were typically linked to periods when the Nile river in Egypt—and Egypt was the Fāṭimid state's most bountiful and enriching domain—did not flood its banks, causing not merely decreased yields in agriculture that in turn led to a loss in state revenues but also famines that in turn led to general public malaise and disorder. In the eleventh century CE, there were at least three instances of failed flooding of this magnitude: in 1025, 1055, and, last but hardly least, 1065–73. Instability in the Fāṭimid state was more remarkably occasioned by persistent religio-political revolts and rebellions generally. Especially in the eleventh century, there were frequent eruptions of rivalries and quarrels within the army, the recruits for which increasingly included North African Amāzīgh, Turks, Daylamites, and Africans from the Sudan.

On the whole, however, the Fāṭimids' highly centralized and hierarchical administrative and financial institutions, with the imām-caliphs and their viziers or chief ministers (*wuzarā'*/وزراء) at the head, oversaw a reign of considerable economic efflorescence. Industry (textiles; glass and crystal; pottery; metalworking; paper; sugar) flourished, as did trade, especially through Mediterranean as well as Red Sea ports that allowed linking up with Cairo. Goods exported included textiles, spices, and wheat. Imported goods included iron, wood, and wool. Imports as well as exports were greatly stimulated by a large, elaborate, and opulent court culture, and the financial and administrative acumen of Fāṭimid Cairo.

Cultural developments under the Fāṭimids were remarkable; indeed extraordinary. "The Fatimid period is characterized by a burst of intellectual curiosity analogous to that of the 18th century in Europe."[2] Notable mathematicians, historians, geographers, physicians, legal scholars, astronomers, and philosophers flourished during the Fāṭimid period. The philosophers alone—e.g., Abū Ḥātim al-Rāzī, Ḥamīd al-Dīn al-Kirmānī, and al-Mu'ayyad fī al-Dīn al-Shīrāzī—are enough to attest to the intellectual vitality that has come to be associated with this period of history in the Islamicate commonwealth. The caliphs, who were also imāms and thus with religio-philosophical and religious law interests, were eager to support the propagation of the Fāṭimid Ismā'īlī doctrine, which in the hands of the philosophers as well as theologians or religious thinkers evolved into an elaborate esotericism replete with neo-Platonic overtones (i.e., Plotinian emanationism filtered through Muslim commentators-interpreters) and in a distinct cosmology that integrated the imāms and all prophets into a cyclical notion of time and historical development. Fāṭimid missionary activity *(al-da'wah*/الدعوة) was continuous, zealous, and highly organized. Missionaries traveled far and wide in order to make converts. The al-Azhar mosque in Cairo became a center for teaching, as did the دار الحكمة /*Dār al-Ḥikmah* (House of Wisdom) established by the imām-caliph al-Ḥākim (ruled 996–1021 CE), who otherwise is typically regarded as manifestly mercurial and mysterious. By his fiat, Jews and Christians in Cairo, for example, were subjected to discriminatory edicts with respect to their expected dress and demeanor in pubic. He also ordered the destruction of several Christian churches (in addition to that of the Holy Sepulchre in Jerusalem). This severe, even militant intolerance, however, is atypical for the Fāṭimid imām-caliphs; the exception underscoring the rule. Jews and Christians were not only generally tolerated under the Fāṭimid imām-caliphs but also on occasions appointed to the post of *al-wazīr*/الوزير or chief minister par excellence, the highest appointed office in the Fāṭimid government. With respect to administering the realm, many of the Fāṭimid ministers had as much real (as opposed to titular) power and authority as did the imām-caliphs themselves.

B. The Ḥamdānids and Mirdāsids

The founder of the Ḥamdānid dynasty was Ḥamdān ibn Ḥamdūn, of Taghlib Arab descent from northwestern Mesopotamia (al-Jazīrah). During the early years of the ʿAbbāsid caliphate of al-Muʿtaḍid (892–3 CE), Ḥamdān ruled over portions of al-Jazīrah in semiautonomous fashion. Al-Muʿtaḍid, in an attempt to reassert more effective caliphal suzerainty over the area, sent out forces in order to take Ḥamdān's strongholds. Ḥamdān fled rather than face armed forces loyal to the caliph and was later apprehended and imprisoned; but his son Ḥusayn, whom Ḥamdān had left in charge of his strongholds, did not resist al-Muʿtaḍid. Moreover, under ʿAbbāsid caliph al-Mutawakkil, he assisted in suppressing Carmathian insurgencies. By 910–11 CE—notwithstanding his participation in a failed plot to choose a new caliph in Baghdad—he was named a provincial governor (although later [918 CE] executed for opposing a chief minister). From 905 through 906 CE, Ḥusayn's brother ʿAbd Allāh Abū al-Hayjā' was appointed court governor of Mosul (Moṣul) by the ʿAbbāsid caliph. Subsequently dismissed for a period, he was reinstated in 914–15 and by 920 had been granted other territories to govern. From 920 until his death in 929, he played an important role in supporting the ʿAbbāsid caliphs' on-going campaign to at long last crush Carmathian insurgents centered in Syria. By 928, roving Carmathian armed bands had reached al-Anbār in central Mesopotamia. Abū al-Hayjā' and his three brothers served in the caliph-loyal armies that confronted the Carmathians, halted their advance along the Euphrates, and forced them to retreat.

Upon the death of Abū al-Hayjā', his son al-Ḥasan became governor (*amīr*) of Mosul by appointment of the 'Abbāsid caliph al-Rāḍī in 935 CE. By 936, with the help of his brother 'Alī, al-Ḥasan asserted his governorship over Diyār Bakr and with that effectively the whole of northwest Mesopotamia. By 942, he felt established enough to contest the post of chief minister in Baghdad under the aegis of caliph al-Rāḍī; he arranged the assassination of a rival (Rā'iq) in 942. With the rival removed, al-Ḥasan, who by that time had secured from the 'Abbāsid court the honorific title *nāṣir al-dawlah* (the state's victor), became the chief minister to the 'Abbāsid court. In that capacity, he was the de facto governor of Baghdad, by virtue of which also overlord (at least nominally) of all territories that recognized 'Abbāsid caliphal suzerainty. His ministering from Baghdad lasted for approximately one year. A revolt by one of his officers in Mosul prompted him to hasten to Mosul. By 944, he was able to reach a negotiated peace with the officer, reassuring him of continued governorship of all of northwest Mesopotamia.

By 946 CE, the Būyid strongman Mu'izz al-Dawlah had marched into Baghdad with supporting troops, taking effective control of the city from an embattled caliph who could scarcely maintain order in Baghdad and its environs, not to mention in the provinces farther afield that were nominally within the 'Abbāsid realm. The Ḥamdānid al-Ḥasan (Nāṣir al-Dawlah) recognized the overlordship of Mu'izz al-Dawlah. In exchange—although also with the agreement to payment of tribute—al-Ḥasan Nāṣir al-Dawlah's suzerainty over Mosul and al-Jazīrah (i.e., northwest Mesopotamia) was recognized.

Al-Ḥasan Nāṣir al-Dawlah's brother 'Alī, who also became better known by an honorary title conferred upon him by the 'Abbāsid caliph (*sayf al-dawlah* [the state's sword]), became the founder of the semiautonomous Ḥamdānid principality of Aleppo. This came about as follows.

In his attempt to gain control of northern Syria as well as Mosul and al-Jazīrah, al-Ḥasan Nāṣir al-Dawlah dispatched his lieutenants to northern Syria after arranging the assassination of Ibn Rā'iq and becoming himself chief governor (*amīr al-umarā'*) in Baghdad under the aegis of the caliph. Nāṣir al-Dawlah's lieutenants, however, felt compelled to cede to the authority of the Ikhshīdid ruler of Egypt at that time (Muḥammad ibn Ṭughj/محمد ابن طغج; reigned 935–46 CE), the Turkish Ikhshīdid dynastic rule in Egypt having become semiautonomous within the ʿAbbāsid caliphs' realm and determined to extend Ikhshīdid suzerainty northeastward as far as Syria. At that time (944 CE), the ʿAbbāsid caliph under Sayf al-Dawlah's protection traveled to Raqqah to meet with the Ikhshīdid ruler of Egypt. At Raqqah, the caliph agreed to approve of the Ikhshīdid Muḥammad ibn Ṭughj's governorship of Syria. But as the caliph was on his return to his court at Baghdad, Sayf al-Dawlah with the support of the Kilābī Bedouin tribe in northern Syria moved to assume rule of Aleppo. Muḥammad ibn Ṭughj opposed this; therefore, he went to war against Sayf al-Dawlah. By 947, a peace agreement was reached whereby Sayf al-Dawlah's right to rule northern Syria—including Aleppo, Ḥimṣ, Qinnasrīn, the territory comprising the northernmost fortresses on the frontier with Byzantium (*al-ʿawāṣim*/العواصم), and Diyār Bakr and Diyār Muḍar in al-Jazīrah—was recognized. Sayf al-Dawlah's principality was supposed to be subordinate not only to the nominal authority of the caliph in Baghdad but also to the authority of his brother Nāṣir al-Dawlah. Sayf al-Dawlah became virtually independent from both for the duration of a relatively long, uninterrupted governorship (944/5–67 CE) centered in Aleppo.

The rule of Sayf al-Dawlah is especially remarkable for the prince's patronage of a vibrant court culture, the leading lights of which include the esteemed Greco-Islamic philosopher and musicologist al-Fārābī (d. 950 CE), the court preacher Ibn Nubātah (d. 984), the renowned historian of music and literature al-Iṣfahānī, and the celebrated poets al-Mutanabbī (d. 965) and Abū Firās al-Ḥamdānī (d. 968), the former destined to achieve legendary status in the history of Arabic poetry, and whom al-Maʿarrī is said to have studied religiously and written commentaries upon.

Sayf al-Dawlah also gained fame for nearly annually dispatching armed expeditions into Byzantine territories that abutted the fortressed frontier territories under his authority. However, although some of the expeditions may have been successful in terms of treasure taken and destruction inflicted upon Byzantine-held territories, few led to actual expansion of the principality of Aleppo. In fact, by 961, five years before Sayf al-Dawlah's death, Byzantine counterinvasions under the command of Nicephorus led to Byzantium's capture of Aleppo. Byzantine troops occupied Aleppo for only eight or nine days, but they killed thousands of captives and destroyed Sayf al-Dawlah's palace before withdrawing to their own territories.

Sayf al-Dawlah's son Abū al-Maʿālī, a.k.a. Saʿd al-Dawlah (the state's support), succeeded his father as *amīr* of Aleppo. He ruled from 967 through 991, that is, from shortly before al-Maʿarrī's birth (973) until he was nineteen or twenty. During his reign, Abū al-Maʿālī Saʿd al-Dawlah had to contend not only with continuing Byzantine aggression from the north but also Fāṭimid territorial ambitions in Syria once the Fāṭimid state established its court and administrative center in the newly founded city of Cairo. At the same time, the Būyid governors in Baghdad, now firmly established in the capital of the ʿAbbāsid caliphs, were resolved to keep the territories that were nominally under ʿAbbāsid suzerainty more demonstrably subservient and loyal to the ʿAbbāsid caliphs. This state of affairs would continue to affect Syrian politics—particularly in the north—for the remainder of the Ḥamdānid rule of the principality (*imārah*/إمارة) of Aleppo (Ḥamdānid rule would last until 1001 CE) and for most of the eleventh-century rule of the Mirdāsids, who replaced the Ḥamdānids as governors of the principality of Aleppo.

Throughout this era the principality's independence was more apparent than real, with the Byzantine emperors tolerating it—indeed frequently sending expeditions to defend it—only so long as it (1) did not pose a serious threat to the interests of the Byzantine emperor and (2) served to foil Fāṭimid interests in conquering northern Syria and annexing its territories to the Fāṭimid state.

As early as 968 CE, only one year after his father's death, Saʿd al-Dawlah was forced to flee the city of Aleppo and not return until 977 because of a major Byzantine armed invasion from the north that led to the occupation of both Ḥimṣ and Tripoli. In 969, Peter the Stratopedarch and Michael Bourtzes forced Saʿd's chamberlain (*ḥājib*/حاجب), whom Saʿd had left in Aleppo to govern the city in his stead (but who subsequently rose in opposition to his master), a treaty that made Aleppo a Byzantine protectorate with Saʿd banished from the city.

He was able to return to Aleppo in 977 CE only after his chamberlain's rule was overturned by Bakjūr, a lieutenant of the chamberlain. Bakjūr had become governor of Ḥims, but instead of remaining loyal to Ḥamdānid suzerainty, he allied himself with the Fāṭimid imām-caliph in Cairo in order to lay the groundwork for the imām-caliph's plan to take hold of northern Syria in the name of the Fāṭimid state. Bakjūr actually laid siege to Aleppo, siege at the time being a standard modus operandi for armed forces bent on conquest of enemy cities; but Sa'd successfully arranged for the intervention of a Byzantine army that helped him repel Bakjūr. Nonetheless, because the Fāṭimid imām-caliph al-'Azīz (ruled 975–96 CE) appointed Bakjūr governor of Damascus (the city at the time more firmly under Fāṭimid suzerainty), and because the governorship of Damascus was a post considerably more consequential (i.e., imposing and intimidating) than the governorship of Ḥims, Sa'd al-Dawlah in 986 agreed to recognize Fāṭimid suzerainty over Aleppo. Five years later, when Bakjūr as a Fāṭimid-loyal governor mounted another armed assault on Aleppo, Sa'd, with the help of Byzantine forces, prevailed over Bakjūr, captured him, and had him executed.

When Sa'd al-Dawlah died in 991 CE, his son who became known as Sa'īd al-Dawlah (the state's felicitous one) succeeded him and ruled for a decade (991–1001/2 CE). Within three years of assuming the governorship of the principality of Aleppo, Sa'īd al-Dawlah faced three sieges of Aleppo led by Mangūtakīn, the Fāṭimid-loyal governor in Damascus who replaced Bakjūr. The first siege was short, lasting only several days before its being called off; the second and third were longer affairs. The third and final siege found Sa'īd better prepared to resist although not entirely through his own resources. Even during the first siege, he had to arrange for the intervention of a Byzantine army under the direction of the Byzantine governor/*magistros* of Antioch, in the Arabic sources known as al-Burjī, although this army Mangūtakīn managed to rout at the Battle of Jisr al-Ḥadīd. (In fact, Mangūtakīn pursued al-Burjī as he withdrew into Antioch itself). During the third siege (993 CE), al-Burjī again came to the aid of Sa'īd al-Dawlah and the inhabitants of Aleppo. With an army that allied itself with Ḥamdānid-loyal troops, he forced an open-field battle with Mangūtakīn. This forced the raising of the siege of the city of Aleppo. But the battle itself (Battle of the Ford [on the Orontes River]) (994 CE) ultimately led to another defeat of al-Burjī and the Ḥamdānid-loyal forces, which in turn freed Mangūtakīn to resume the siege of the city of Aleppo. During this siege, Sa'īd, with the help of his chamberlain, Lu'lu' al-Jarrāḥī, managed to persuade the Byzantine emperor himself to intervene with an expeditionary force. The troops reached the outskirts of Aleppo, Mangūtakīn retreated back to Damascus (995), and Saʿīd al-Dawlah's authority over Aleppo was reestablished.

Saʿīd al-Dawlah was murdered by Lu'lu' al-Jarrāḥī in 1002 CE. Lu'lu' was a special personal guard (*ghulām*/غلام) to Saʿīd's grandfather Sayf al-Dawlah. He had grown increasingly influential as a minister under Saʿīd. Saʿīd's death effectively marked the end of Ḥamdānid rule in Aleppo and the surrounding areas of northern Syria. Lu'lu' exiled to Egypt Saʿīd's two sons Abū al-Ḥasan ʿAlī and Abū al-Maʿālī Sharīf (in 1003/4 CE). A brother to Saʿīd, Abū al-Hayjā', fled to Byzantium where he was given asylum by Emperor Basil II. Abū al-Hayjā' would later attempt to reestablish the Ḥamdānid dynasty at Aleppo with support of Aleppine notables who arranged to have his father-in-law (then ruling Diyār Bakr and on good terms with the Byzantine emperor) win permission from Basil II to allow Abū al-Hayjā' to leave Byzantine territory and march on Aleppo. But the Kilābī Bedouins, whose armed support the Aleppines loyal to Abū al-Hayjā' thought they had secured, were persuaded by the son of Lu'lu', Manṣūr (the *amīr* of Aleppo; Lu'lu' had died in 1008/9 CE), to refrain from supporting the cause of Abū al-Hayjā'. Manṣūr also requested and received the backing of Fāṭimid-loyal troops stationed in Tripoli. These troops marched on Aleppo and the armed camp of Abū al-Hayjā', which they pillaged. In the wake of these developments, Manṣūr, son of Lu'lu' was in a position to negotiate successfully with Basil II to have Abū al-Hayjā' removed from Syria and kept confined in Constantinople, capital of the Byzantine Empire.

The aftermath of the Fāṭimid support for Manṣūr and his victory over Abū al-Hayjā' increased pressure on Manṣūr to acknowledge Fāṭimid suzerainty. This also brought al-Maʿarrī's birthplace, Maʿarrat al-Nuʿmān, closer to the theater of war. After storming and pillaging the military encampment of Abū al-Hayjā' outside the walls of Aleppo, the Fāṭimid troops from Tripoli attempted to storm the city proper. Manṣūr, however, had locked the city gates. Responding to this turn of events, the Fāṭimid caliph in Cairo, al-Ḥākim, dispatched fresh troops towards Aleppo by way of Maʿarrat al-Nuʿmān. One of Saʿīd al-Dawlah's two exiled sons—Abū Maʿālī Sharīf—accompanied the Fāṭimid forces. Bedouin forces in the area put up some resistance but, in the end, Manṣūr opted for a compromise. He recognized Fāṭimid suzerainty over Aleppo rather than that of the ʿAbbāsid caliph in Baghdad. He was the first governor of Aleppo to do such.

In 1015–16 CE, Manṣūr's rule over Aleppo was challenged on the battlefield by Ṣāliḥ ibn Mirdās, a chief of the Kilābī Bedouins who heretofore had given their allegiance to Manṣūr. Manṣūr was defeated on the battlefield by Ṣāliḥ and thus fled his palace in Aleppo and took refuge in Byzantium.

To fill this geo-political vacuum, in coordination with the Fāṭimid imām-caliph al-Ḥākim, indeed with his appointment that carried with it the honorary titles of *amīr al-umarā'* (chief governor) and *'azīz al-dawlah* (the state's powerful one), an emancipated Armenian slave of Mangūtakīn—Abū Shujāʿ Fātik ibn ʿAbd Allāh al-Rūmī—was soon granted governorship of the citadel of Aleppo. Rule of the city proper was entrusted to Abū al-Ḥasan ʿAlī ibn Aḥmad al-ʿAjamī, a.k.a. al-Ḍayf (الضيف), who was also given the honorific title of *sadīd al-dawlah* / سديد الدولة (the state's defender). Meanwhile Ṣāliḥ ibn Mirdās, bestowed with the title of *asad al-dawlah* (the state's lion), was expected to work cooperatively with the new Fāṭimid-appointed leaders and bring the Kilābī Bedouin into the alliance.

At this time, al-Maʿarrī's former student Abū al-Khayr al-Mufaḍḍal was the court eulogist for Abū Shujāʿ ʿAzīz al-Dawlah. Abū Naṣr Ṣadaqah ibn Yūsuf al-Fallāḥī, a minister to the caliph-imām in Cairo, wrote to al-Maʿarrī at the request of al-Mu'ayyad fī al-Dīn and with the latter's offer of some financial assistance. He tried at the same time to get al-Maʿarrī more closely involved with ʿAzīz al-Dawlah's court. Al-Maʿarrī refused the offer of financial assistance, and also kept his distance from ʿAzīz al-Dawlah's court.

ʿAzīz al-Dawlah ruled as Fāṭimid governor of Aleppo until 1022–23, when he was murdered by one of his slaves, reputedly through the machinations of al-Ḥākim's sister, Sayyidat al-Mulk (the First Lady of the Realm), who took over the affairs of the Fāṭimid state in Cairo when al-Ḥākim mysteriously disappeared, never to reappear, while walking in the hills surrounding Cairo in 1020.

Although a Fāṭimid governor, ʿAzīz endeavored to promote the independence of Aleppo. To that end, he embraced peaceful co-existence with both the Byzantine Empire and the Kilābī Bedouins led by Ṣāliḥ ibn

Mirdās. At the time of al-Ḥākim's death, however, ʿAzīz's policies were arousing the suspicions of both the Byzantines and the Fāṭimid regime in Cairo, leading to the likelihood of intervention by both parties and more armed conflict centered on Aleppo. Northern Syria at this time was especially rife with unease.

With the death of ʿAzīz al-Dawlah and, shortly thereafter, the death of Sanad al-Dawlah, who succeeded ʿAzīz as Fāṭimid-appointed governor of Aleppo, the Banū Kilāb under the leadership of Ṣāliḥ ibn Mirdās moved to fill the vacuum. With neighboring Bedouin Arab tribes, they united in an alliance that aspired to establish permanent Arab (i.e., of ethnic Arab stock) rule over greater Syria, albeit within a framework of accommodating the concerns of the more powerful states to the north and south (Byzantium and Fāṭimid Egypt respectively). In 1025 CE, Ṣāliḥ and his Kilābī army seized Aleppo from the Fāṭimid governor after a siege of the city that lasted fifty-six days.[3] This came on the heels of a victory in Palestine over Fāṭimid troops under the command of army officer al-Dizbirī (a manumitted Turkish slave who had been trained in affairs of state at al-Ḥākim's court in Cairo, eventually to become "the most distinguished Fāṭimid ruler" in Syria[4]), and, following that, Ṣāliḥ's laying siege to Damascus (although without bringing about the city's surrender).

Abandoning the siege of Damascus, Ṣāliḥ on the way to his return to Aleppo expanded what was rapidly becoming his own state; he sacked and then placed under his rule coastal cities of the Levant. It was Ṣāliḥ's secretary/chancellor (*kātib*) in Aleppo, along with Kilābī forces and the city's citizen-based militia (*aḥdāth*/أحداث), who actually captured the famed citadel of Aleppo, which is where Fāṭimid troops were garrisoned. The garrison, along with the governors of the citadel as well those of the city, were allowed to leave Aleppo. Ṣāliḥ had the citadel's former governor executed, exacted a payment from the former governor of the city, and had a former judge (*qāḍī*) buried alive. A Fāṭimid Ismāʿīlī missionary was released. By sending his chancellor/secretary to the Fāṭimid caliphal court in Cairo, Ṣāliḥ indicated that he did not deny Fāṭimid suzerainty. (Coins struck at the time under Ṣāliḥ's superintendence bear the Fāṭimid caliph's name as well as Ṣāliḥ's.) The caliph at the time (al-Ẓāhir) acknowledged Ṣāliḥ's authority over his newly expanded state.

Fāṭimid suzerainty may have been absolutely essential for even short-term survival of Ṣāliḥ's state, notwithstanding the considerable prowess shown by the allied forces under his command and the genuine court culture (including administrative protocol) that was evolving despite the nomadic origins of the Kilābī and allied tribes in the area. In any event, Ṣāliḥ's rule was over by 1029 CE. In that year the Fāṭimid-loyal and appointed governor of Damascus, al-Dizbirī, led an army into Palestine to challenge Ṣāliḥ. Ṣāliḥ responded to the challenge and engaged in battle, but his forces were defeated at Uqḥuwānah, and both he and his youngest son were killed on the battlefield.

Upon Ṣāliḥ's death, his eldest son, Nāṣir (with honorific title of *shibl al-dawlah*/شبل الدولة or the state's lion cub), assumed oversight of the administration of the city of Aleppo while his younger brother Abū 'Ulwān Thimāl Mu'izz al-Dawlah assumed control of the citadel, although Nāṣir soon (1030 CE) seized the citadel for himself when his brother temporarily left it for an excursion in the country. The Byzantine emperor at that time, Romanus III, demanded from the Mirdāsid brothers that they cede rule of Aleppo to him. Nāṣir offered a tribute instead. The emperor rejected this and with an army marched towards Antioch indicating his resolve to take Aleppo by force if necessary. At 'Azāz, however, Kilābī Bedouin warriors raided advance regiments of the Byzantine army in a show of force suggesting that they were prepared to resist Byzantines designs on taking control of Aleppo. With that, Romanus III decided to have his army retreat. Over the course of the next few years, he entered into negotiations with the Fāṭimid imām-caliph in Cairo and arranged for a truce and finally a treaty (1034–35 CE) that allowed for Byzantine oversight in the rule of the city.

Ṣāliḥ's son Nāṣir responded to this by currying favor with the Fāṭimid imām-caliph al-Ẓāhir in Cairo, sending him an envoy bearing treasure taken at the battle at 'Azāz. After several years of representation at the caliph's court, the envoy secured for Nāṣir a robe of honor and several new honorific titles, indicating Fāṭimid pleasure and the prospects for protection. But by 1037 CE, al-Dizbirī moved with an army to challenge Nāṣir at Ḥimṣ. In an ensuing battle there against Nāṣir and his army, al-Dizbirī prevailed. (Like his father before him, Nāṣir was killed on the battlefield.) Nāṣir's brother Thimāl tried to take control of Aleppo with the view to fending off al-Dizbirī, but the latter and his Fāṭimid-loyal army were able to enter the city in 1038 CE and seize it in the name of the Fāṭimd imām-caliph. Thimāl fled Aleppo. On route back to Damascus, al-Dizbirī passed through Maʿarrat al-Nuʿmān and while there inquired about Abū al-ʿAlāʾ.[5]

The redoubtable al-Dizbirī was to die in Aleppo's citadel in 1042 CE, not as governor but as a refugee from his own Damascus. His successes in 1038 caused the Fāṭimid imām-caliph al-Mustanṣir (ruled 1035–1094 CE) in Cairo to fear his growing renown and strength in Syria. The caliph arranged that al-Dizbirī's garrison in Damascus refuse to obey his command. At the same time, the caliph asked Thimāl to reoccupy Aleppo. With his garrison in Damascus turned against him, al-Dizbirī fled to Aleppo for refuge.

Upon al-Dizbirī's death in 1042 CE, Thimāl effectively reestablished rule of Aleppo in the name of the Mirdāsids. Thimāl's rule was to last until 1057/1058 or through the last year of al-Maʿarrī's life. It was characterized by yet more conflict and turmoil because of the on-going Byzantine and Fāṭimid rivalries in Syria, exacerbated at times by Thimāl's reluctance to be a docile subject of Fāṭimid overlordship and his eagerness to prevail upon the Byzantine emperor to intervene in Syrian affairs in order to promote Mirdāsid interests vis-à-vis the Fāṭimids. In 1048, al-Mustanṣir sent armed troops to confront Thimāl over his having refused to make his tribute payments. In 1049, al-Mustanṣir ordered a similar expedition. On this occasion as opposed to the former, Thimāl asked the Byzantine emperor Constantine to come to his aid, a request that the emperor honored with the dispatch of troops from Antioch in order to intimidate the Fāṭimid forces on the outskirts of Aleppo (which in fact contributed to Thimāl's being able to prevent a whole-scale Fāṭimid onslaught). After this face-off with the Fāṭimid imām-caliph's forces, Thimāl made peace with the caliph by agreeing to resume paying a tribute to him. The peace lasted until 1057, when Thimāl, faced with a rebellion in Aleppo, a combative brother, dissension among the Kilābīs, and a Fāṭimid army on the move in the south, abdicated in favor of a Fāṭimid general, al-Ḥasan ibn ʿAlī ibn Mulhim; although in exchange for abdicating he was allowed to become ruler over Beirut, Acre, and Jubayl.

During the first Fāṭimid expedition against Thimāl, the Fāṭimid armies took control of Maʿarrat al-Nuʿmān. This prompted Thimāl to send forth troops in order to recapture it (which he succeeded in doing). Thimāl with allied Kilābī tribal forces destroyed the town's citadel as well as walls once was there was notice of the second Fāṭimid expedition against Maʿarrat al-Nuʿmān. The destruction was ostensibly in order to allow for easier recapture should the town fall into the hands of the Fāṭimid army[6] and not an expression of enraged spite or nihilistic self-destruction.

Ethnic Arab tribal rule over Aleppo in the form of the Mirdāsid dynastic rule lasted until 1080 CE. At that time, Muḥammad ibn Nāṣir, son of Nāṣir (son of Ṣāliḥ) and a nephew of Thimāl, ceded authority to the Seljūk Turkish sulṭān Alp Arslān. The Mirdāsids, not surprisingly, were autocrats, but they typically took up residence in the citadel of Aleppo high above the city proper; and, save for taxation, defense, and security, they had little to do with the day-to-day affairs of the ordinary denizens. Under Ṣāliḥ, the position of head/chief of state (*shaykh al-dawlah*) was instituted. This functionary was second in command to the *amīr* (governor) as well as the chancellor/secretary and the representatives of embassies in Cairo and Constantinople.[7] Ṣāliḥ also appointed the leader or head (*ra'īs* or *muqaddam*/رئيس؛ مقدم) of the *aḥdāth*, a type of civil defense force comprised of young men of the city. Beneath the *shaykh al-dawlah* in the administrative hierarchy was the chief minister (*wazīr*). He was served by local professional bureaucrats; with the ascendance of the Kilābīs, Kilābī princes (*umarā'*) were also influential in "state" affairs.[8]

Trading and commerce were important to Aleppo of the tenth and eleventh centuries CE. When the Byzantine emperor effected a temporary reconciliation between Ṣāliḥ and Lu'lu', because of his displeasure over the prevailing feuding and turmoil, he enacted what amounted to punitive sanctions, namely, forbidding travel and commerce between Syria and the territories under the jurisdiction of the emperor; which prompted Ṣāliḥ to request that he be spared this specific proviso of the Byzantine-brokered peace.[9] In 1015 CE, while Manṣūr, son of Lu'lu', fled Aleppo fearing a revolt by the garrison in the citadel, and when al-Ḥākim in Cairo endeavored to bring peace to the city with the rule of Abū Shujāʿ Fātik (ʿAzīz al-Dawlah), al-Ḥākim promised the people of Aleppo an alleviation of their tax obligations, which included lifting certain customs duties and market taxes.[10] Aleppo lay at the crossroads of the important caravan route connecting the city through trade to both Egypt and Byzantium on a north-south axis and to Baghdad and (from there the rest of al-ʿIrāq) on an east-west axis. The Baghdad physician Ibn Baṭlān, who visited Aleppo in 1048, spoke of an important silk market.[11] Nāṣir-i Khusraw described the city as, inter alia, "a place where they levy customs on goods going to Syria and Byzantium and Diyār Bakr and Egypt and Iraq."[12] By the mid-eleventh century, when significant numbers of Turks were migrating to Byzantium as well as northern Syria, Aleppo became an important center for Turkish soldiers buying their provisions and selling treasure seized in armed conflicts. A large slave market was also part of the economy.[13]

The *aḥdāth* in Syrian cities of this period were instrumental in helping to maintain public order. Although not professional soldiers, they were salaried and among other things seemed to have control of city gates that allowed entrance to and exit from cities. They joined forces with one side or another side in the armed struggles over the governorship of Aleppo. They were instrumental, for example, in Ṣāliḥ ibn Mirdās's capture of Aleppo inclusive of the citadel, which was defended by Fāṭimid soldiers pledged (and also paid) to serve the interests of the imām-caliph in Cairo. The *aḥdāth* were a documented major urban phenomenon in Damascus as well as Aleppo through the tenth and twelfth centuries (CE). One might reasonably infer that they (or similar such groups) were also to be found in other, smaller Syrian cities or towns (e.g., Maʿarrat al-Nuʿmān, which, after all, was not so small that it did not have a citadel and gates).

The population of Aleppo in the tenth and eleventh centuries was comprised of non-Arabs as well as Arabs. Among others, the Tanūkh and the Quraysh represented the Arab tribes. Armenians were notable among the non-Arabs. Jews and Christians were in residence, but Muslims comprised the overwhelming majority of the population. The Christian community predated the arrival of Muslims. Its numbers were greatly augmented by the migration of Egyptian and Syrian Christians (the Syrians from south Syria) during the rule of the Fāṭimid imām-caliph al-Ḥākim, due to his discriminatory strictures against Christians and Jews. The Christians of Aleppo—especially the Armenians—were concentrated in particular quarters, namely, those in the north of the city. Ibn Baṭlān reported in 1048 that the city of Aleppo had six churches and the citadel two chapels.[14] Maʿarrat al-Nuʿmān and surrounding villages also had Christian populations.

The Syrian Christians, according to Suhayl Zakkar, often took up occupations that Muslims of Arab Bedouin stock considered inappropriate (either because of religion or culture), such as blacksmithing, working in gold and silver, and, last but no least "trading in wine and those trades akin to it, such as the keeping of public taverns and brothels. In the emirate of Aleppo during the eleventh century there were many public taverns and inns . . . where travellers with money could be provided with wine, women and song in addition to a night's lodging." At the same time, educated Christians were also clerks, tax farmers, physicians, and government ministers. Ṣāliḥ ibn Mirdās's chief minister, Tadharus ibn al-Ḥasan, was Christian and reportedly in charge of military as well as administrative affairs. Nāṣir, son of Ṣāliḥ, also appointed a Christian as chief minister, and this minister's brother was appointed governor of an outlying district of Aleppo.[15]

Relations between Christians and Muslims became palpably uneasy during the rule of Ṣāliḥ ibn Mirdās in 1026 because of an incident—alleged and highlighted in the medieval chronicles—in which a group of Muslims destroyed an inn/brothel at which the Christian owner allegedly tried to rape a Muslim woman. Ṣāliḥ, after imprisoning some Muslim suspects, was going to have them killed on the recommendation of his chief minister, Tadhurus. Al-Maʿarrī's plea for leniency led to Ṣāliḥ's fining the Muslims and releasing them otherwise unharmed. Around the same time, Tadharus's father-in-law, a priest, was murdered in a village close to Maʿrrat al-Nuʿmān. After Ṣāliḥ's death on the battlefield, Muslims from the area of Maʿarrat al-Nuʿmān attacked the Christian village of Kafar-Nubbu. When Ṣāliḥ's struggles with Lu'lu' led to the abdication of Manṣūr son of Lu'lu', Muslim gangs pillaged Jewish as well as Christian houses and businesses.[16] Ostensibly, these latter instances of sectarian strife were symptomatic of a general malaise coming to the fore on occasion.

The Muslim population of Aleppo in the tenth and eleventh centuries consisted mostly of Sunnīs and some Shīʿites. The Ḥamdānids and Mirdāsids were Twelver Shīʿites. The Twelvers became predominant among the Shīʿites in Aleppo. The Muslims of Maʿarrat al-Nuʿmān were Sunnīs. Sevener (specifically, Fāṭimid Ismāʿīlī) missionary activity seems to have been considerable in Aleppo. Imāmī missionary activity in support of al-Ḥākim's self-proclamation of being the incarnation of the Divine took on great zeal after al-Ḥākim's disappearance in 1021 CE. This was Drūzī propagation of faith, in other words (the sect taking its name from its first leading missionary, al-Darazī [d. 1019 CE]). In fact, in 1031 CE there was a Drūzī-inspired revolt in a region surrounding Aleppo, Jabal al-Summāq. During the course of the revolt, Drūzī faithful destroyed mosques and attacked neighboring villages, until finally being subdued by a combined force consisting of Byzantine troops from Antioch and Syrian troops from Aleppo.

That the majority of Aleppo's Shīʿites were Twelvers no doubt contributed to the history of Aleppo's governors opposing direct Fāṭimid rule, to their only reluctantly accepting Fāṭimid suzerainty when circumstances (i.e., *realpolitik*: either submission without struggle and resistance or submission by lethal force of arms) made this virtually unavoidable. At the same time, the Twelver orientation of Aleppo's governors would explain their reluctance to show strong support for the ʿAbbāsid caliphs, who were Sunnīs. In any event, by the late eleventh century, during the ascendance of the Seljūk Turks (also overwhelmingly if not entirely Sunnīs), there were open protests in Aleppo on the occasion of the first *khuṭbah* in the city to be delivered in the names of the ʿAbbāsid caliph al-Qā'im and the Seljūk Turkish sulṭān Alp Arslān.[17]

C. The Būyids (a.k.a. Buwayhids)

The Būyids were ninth century CE converts to Twelver Shīʿite Islam. Ethnically, they were Daylamites of origin hailing from the territories along the southern shores of the Caspian Sea. They first rose to prominence in the annals of Islam as free soldiers fighting on behalf of the Sammānid dynastic potentates (and their ally Mardawīj ibn Ziyār) in their confrontations with the Zaydī Shīʿite dynasty in Ṭabaristān, a semiautonomous province in the ʿAbbāsid realm during the early years of ʿAbbāsid rule. Mardawīj was to found his own dynastic rule (Ziyārid), the domains of which stretched across the central Iranian plateau to as far as the city of Rayy. Mardawīj appointed ʿAlī ibn Abū Shujāʿ Būyī as governor of

Karaj, but then he revoked the appointment. With that, ʿAlī moved to the province of Fārs, overturned the ʿAbbāsid-loyal governor there by force of arms, and himself assumed rule of the province (in 322 IE/934 CE). Ḥasan, ʿAlī's brother, upon Mardawīj's death by assassination, marched on Iṣfahān, the center of Mardawīj's government, and occupied the city. By 955 CE, he would be in possession of most of Ṭabaristān including the city of Rayy.

A third Būyid brother, Aḥmad, would win even greater renown for his exploits. It was he who would establish the Būyid dynasty of governors (*umarā'*) in Baghdad, who would assume virtually complete control over the army as well as the treasury of the ʿAbbāsid caliphs from 946 until 1055 CE (after which effective administration over the ʿAbbāsid realms would be appropriated by Seljūk Turkish governors).

A growing financial crisis in the ʿAbbāsid caliphate contributed to Aḥmad ibn Abū Shujāʿ's rise to power. So, too, did the ascendance of the Ḥamdānids of Mosul and Aleppo, and that of two brothers of the al-Barīdī family in Basra and Ahwāz. Faced with the ever-increasing de facto dissolution of the ʿAbbāsid commonwealth into smaller states with semi- if not complete autonomy, and particularly in districts or provinces such as Aleppo, Mosul, and Basra that were gateways to central Mesopotamia (i.e, al-ʿIrāq) and the ʿAbbāsid caliphal court; and, at the same time, losing revenues from the provinces (often precisely because of the de-facto independence or quasi-independence), the caliph al-Rāḍī in 936 CE (324 IE) appointed a tax farmer (Ibn Rā'iq) *amīr al-umarā'* with the authority to oversee not only the management of state revenues but also the army. Several years later, Ibn Rā'iq, as already noted, was to be ousted from his post by the Ḥamdānid rival Nāṣir al-Dawlah, and Nāṣir in turn was soon ousted by an officer of the caliph's Turkish troops, Tūzūn. When Tūzūn was on leave from Baghdad in his campaign to force Nāṣir al-Dawlah to retreat to Mosul, Aḥmad ibn Abū Shujāʿ advanced with an army to Wāsiṭ in 946 CE (334 IE) with the intention of proceeding on to enter Baghdad. Tūzūn with his forces would force Aḥmad to withdraw from Wāsiṭ on two occasions before he (Tūzūn) died in 946 CE (334 IE), but, upon his death, and after the rule of his replacement as *amīr al-umarā'* proved unpopular, Aḥmad was encouraged by Wāsiṭ's governor to enter Baghdad and proclaim himself *amīr al-umarā'*. In 946 CE, Aḥmad did such, facing little if any resistance in Baghdad.

As a sign of the times if ever there was one, the ʿAbbāsid caliph al-Mustakfī, the Turkish troops who remained loyal to him, and the incumbent *amīr al-umarā'* had all disappeared. The Turkish troops eventually headed for Mosul, at which point the caliph did appear in public, to recognize Aḥmad not only as the new *amīr al-umarā'* but also to confer upon him the title *mu'izz al-dawlah* (fortifier of the state). The caliph at the same time gave Aḥmad's brother ʿAlī the honorific title of *'imād al-dawlah*/عماد الدولة (pillar of the state), and upon brother Ḥasan, he conferred the title *rukn al-dawlah* (prop of the state); thereby recognizing the rising fortunes of the entire family and the need to cement alliances with them.

As the first Būyid *amīr* in Baghdad, a major preoccupation of Aḥmad Muʿizz al-Dawlah was curtailing the power of the Ḥamdānid Nāṣir al-Dawlah, whom Aḥmad wished to regard as under his authority but who challenged Būyid suzerainty repeatedly. Nāṣir broke various treaties that demanded paying tributes to the caliphs in Baghdad and the formal restriction of the borders of his effective rule. He also attempted to oust Aḥmad Muʿizz al-Dawlah, in the course of which he invaded Baghdad and occupied the Karkh quarter although eventually he was driven out.

In 960 CE (348 IE), Aḥmad Muʿizz al-Dawlah took the offensive against Nāṣir al-Dawlah. With armed forces under his command, he managed to occupy Mosul, Nāṣir's principal stronghold, and he forced Nāṣir to seek the protection of his brother Sayf al-Dawlah at Aleppo. It was at this time that Aḥmad Muʿizz al-Dawlah decreed that all of the territories under the suzerainty of Nāṣir were to be considered part of the principality of Aleppo ruled by his brother (Sayf al-Dawlah). The actual reconfiguration never took place, however, and four years later, a resolute Nāṣir al-Dawlah presented yet another challenge to Muʿizz al-Dawlah by demanding from the ʿAbbāsid caliph that he recognize Nāṣir's son (Abū Taghlib) as heir to Nāṣir's rule over Mosul and the surrounding areas that constituted a rather large Ḥamdānid principality. With this, Aḥmad Muʿizz al-Dawlah again took to the battlefields to confront Ḥamdānid ambitions and hold them in check. Abū Taghlib and forces loyal to him put up stiff resistance. Consequently, in what amounted to a compromise, Abū Taghlib was allowed to take the revenues of his father's territories in exchange for paying fixed sums of tribute to the caliphs in Baghdad.

Carmathian (i.e., Qarmaṭī) insurgents in the area of Basra, supported by allies from ʿUmān, proved as intractable to Muʿizz as the Ḥamdānids in Mosul. Although Muʿizz turned back a Carmathian attack on Basra in 952 CE (341 IE), at the time of his death fifteen years later, the Carmathians remained as combative and committed to their cause as ever.

Basra, virtually independent under the rule of the al-Barīdī family, gave in more easily to Būyid overlordship, putting up very little resistance to an expedition that Muʿizz al-Dawlah sent against the family in 948 CE (336 IE). But to the south where the Tigris and Euphrates converge to form large marshes and swamps, an insurgent (ʿImrān ibn Shāhīn) and a band of followers resisted subordination, to the extent that Muʿizz al-Dawlah felt compelled to accept ʿImrān's governorship under nominal Būyid suzerainty.

Before his death in 967 CE (356 IE), Muʿizz al-Dawlah had proclaimed his son Bakhtiyār ʿIzz al-Dawlah his successor as *amīr al-umarā'* to the ʿAbbāsid caliph in Baghdad, making clear that he sought a hereditary dynasty to follow in his lead. That lead included checking the proliferation of independent principalities or emirates, against which Muʿizz had fought. Nonetheless, at the time of his death, which came approximately two hundred years after the establishment of the ʿAbbāsid hereditary dynasty to succeed the Umayyads as the rightful holders of the caliphate to include all of Islamdom (Dār al-Islām), the ʿAbbāsid caliphs' domains in actuality looked like a checkerboard of dynastic holdings, the rulers of which—save perhaps some of the scions of Abū Shujāʿ the Būyī, depending upon time and place—put their own interests ahead of those of the central caliphal administration in Baghdad and ahead of an idealized monolithic, cohesive ʿAbbāsid empire. Bakhtiyār ʿIzz al-Dawlah was to take control of al-ʿIrāq (i.e., the province of lower Mesopotamia) and to the east Ahwāz. Fārs was under the governorship of ʿAḍud al-Dawlah, Bakhtiyār's cousin. (He was the son of Muʿizz al-Dawlah's brother Rukn al-Dawlah.) Rukn al-Dawlah governed Rayy, Iṣfahān, and Hamadān. Ṭabaristān was under the rule of the Ziyārid dynasty, Azerbayjān under the rule of the Salārids, Kirmān and Sijistān under the rule of various strongmen, and the vast expanses of Khurasān and Transoxiana in central

Asia under the rule of the Sāmānids (who nourished a proto-Iranian/Persian nationalism). To the northwest of Baghdad and al-ʿIrāq, al-Jazīrah (upper Mesopotamia) was in the hands of the Ḥamdānid Abū Taghlib, heir to his father Nāṣir al-Dawlah, and Aleppo and its environs in northern Syria were governed by Nāṣir's brother Sayf al-Dawlah. The two holy cities of Mecca and Medina were formally under the governorship of the Ikhshīdid rulers in Egypt, although within two years, they would be subordinate to the rule of the Fāṭimid state now centered in Cairo. Egypt and southern Syria were also under Ikhshīdid rule at the time of Bakhtiyār ʿIzz al-Dawlah's becoming *amīr al-umarā'* of Baghdad in 967 CE, but by 969 they also fell to the Fāṭimids. A branch of the Carmathians were virtually in control of Bahrain.

Bakhtiyār ʿIzz al-Dawlah was *amīr al-umarā'* for eleven years. His reign was plagued with palace intrigues among four ministers whom he appointed and with diminishing state revenues, occasioned to a large extent by his father's policy of paying the Turkish officers in the caliph's army by way of giving them entire provinces as fiefs, thereby reducing lands taxable directly at the state level with regular, fixed, and fairly predictable tax revenues. To make ends meet, extortion became more and more common, not to mention the outright seizing of treasure by force of arms. At the same time, growing hostilities between Daylamite soldiers, on the one hand, and, on the other hand, Turkish soldiers under the command of the Turkish chief Subtekīn, were impediments to peace and order, with armed altercations frequently erupting. This eventually led to ʿIzz al-Dawlah's adopting the draconian measure of quelling Turkish soldiers' recalcitrance by force of arms, relying on the aid of his brother Abū Isḥāq and Būyid-loyal Daylamite soldiers. However, in the armed confrontation, the Turkish soldiers got the better of the Daylamites, leading to general disorder in Baghdad. The caliph fled the city. Subektekīn forced him to return only to have him abdicate in favor of a son.

In what was developing into a battle for supremacy between Daylamite soldiers and the Turkish garrisons stationed in the city, the Sunnī population of Baghdad, in demonstration of their support for Subektekīn (a Sunnī Turk), set upon the Shīʿite quarter of al-Karkh and set fire to it. Al-Karkh, an important commercial center, had been attacked earlier (971–72 CE) by one of ʿIzz al-Dawlah's Turkish (ergo Sunnī) ministers in response to Shī'ite riots. The rioters were volunteers recruited to respond to the Byzantine raids into Muslim territories as far as Niṣībīn in northwest Mesopotamia (al-Jazīrah). Refugees from the territories fleeing the Byzantines armies had stormed mosques in Baghdad, interrupting prayer and demanding that the caliph mount a *jihād* to defend the territories regarded as Dār al-Islām.

'Izz al-Dawlah eventually lost the province of Ahwāz to rebellious Turkish soldiers. He therefore ensconced himself at Wāsiṭ and appealed for help from his uncle (Rukn al-Dawlah) in Rayy, who promised to send armed forces under the command of his cousin 'Aḍud al-Dawlah in Fārs. This appeal was to prove fatal for 'Izz al-Dawlah, for although 'Aḍud al-Dawlah would help him defeat the rebellious Turkish soldiers, who under the command of Alptekīn (freed former slave of Mu'izz al-Dawlah) had eventually managed to chase him from Wāsiṭ, 'Aḍud al-Dawlah forced his cousin 'Izz al-Dawlah to abdicate, and 'Aḍud then appropriated for himself the post of *amīr al-umarā'*. The caliph in Baghdad accepted this as a fait accompli and officially named 'Aḍud al-Dawlah the new *amīr al-umarā'* for Baghdad. 'Izz al-Dawlah was placed in his cousin's custody. He was later released upon the protestations of his uncle ('Aḍud al-Dawlah's father), who disapproved of his son's coup and induced various governors of the 'Abbāsid provinces not to support him. This encouraged 'Izz al-Dawlah to attempt a counter-coup with support of the Mosul Ḥamdānid Abū Taghlib. However, in a battle in Samarrā in 978 CE (367 IE), forces loyal to 'Aḍud defeated 'Izz al-Dawlah's army, captured 'Izz al-Dawlah and killed him (upon his cousin's orders).

'Aḍud al-Dawlah went on to reign as *amīr al-umarā'* of Baghdad for five years, from 978 through 983 CE. Already before usurping the post from cousin 'Izz al-Dawlah, he not only consolidated his governorship of the province of Fārs but also expanded his suzerainty through military conquest of Kirmān and 'Umān. Once established in Baghdad, he quickly moved to assert more effective control over the Ḥamdānid rulers, particularly Abū Taghlib at Mosul, who in al-Jazīrah now ruled over Diyār Rabī'ah, Diyār Bakr, and Diyār Muḍar just to the east of Aleppo. Abū Taghlib had allied himself with 'Izz al-Dawlah in the latter's countercoup against 'Aḍud al-Dawlah. 'Aḍud al-Dawlah marched with an army towards Mosul; Abū Taghlib fled, first from Mosul and then beyond al-Jazīrah entirely, seeking refuge first with a Byzantine rebel (Bardas Sclerus) in Byzantine territory and later in Syria. In Syria, he aimed to win the support of the Fāṭimid caliph al-ʿAzīz in Cairo; but this never materialized. Saʿd al-Dawlah at Aleppo, Abū Taghlib's cousin, had earlier pledged his support for ʿAḍud al-Dawlah's claim to the governorship of Baghdad, so he was of no help to Abū Taghlib. In fact, Saʿd al-Dawlah, at ʿAḍud al-Dawlah's urging, at this point assumed suzerainty over most of Diyār Muḍar (which encompassed Rahbah and Raqqah on the upper Euphrates), thus enhancing the Ḥamdāndid Emirate of Aleppo at the expense of the Ḥamdānids in Mosul and al-Jazīrah.

With his overrunning of al-Jazīrah completed in 979 CE, ʿAḍud al-Dawlah could claim overlordship of both lower and upper Mesopotamia and thus more effectively maintain order and security in Baghdad. The ʿAbbāsid caliph was compliant in recognizing the growing strength of ʿAḍud. He had his name added to the Friday *khuṭbah* in Baghdad. He also allowed ʿAḍud to have the music known as the *nawbah*/نوبة played at his palace gate for three of the five daily prayer times—the first time that any caliph had granted this honor to any of his functionaries.

With the central base of Būyid suzerainty legitimized with caliphal approval, ʿAḍud al-Dawlah next proceeded to organize armed expeditions into Jibāl (a semiautonomous Kurdish stronghold), into the marshes and swamps at the confluence of the Tigris and Euphrates, and into Hamadān, Rayy, and Iṣfahān (all in present-day Iran), which ʿAḍud's brothers Fakhr al-Dawlah and Mu'ayyad al-Dawlah had inherited upon the death of their father, Rukn al-Dawlah. Al-Mu'ayyad joined forces with ʿAḍud and supported his ambition—in opposition to Fakhr al-Dawlah—to have the Būyid-ruled provinces subordinate to his (ʿAḍud's) overlordship expanded as far east as Gurgān and Ṭabaristān. This induced Fakhr al-Dawlah to flee to Nīshāpūr, where he sought the protection of the quasi-independent Perso-Iranian Sāmānids.

ʿAḍud al-Dawlah died as his brother Mu'ayyad was about to invade Khurāsān. Upon his death, to the northeast of al-ʿIrāq, he held authority as far as the Caspian Sea; to the southeast, as far as the Persian Gulf; to the direct east, as far as the Great Desert of the Iranian plateau; and to the northwest, all of Mesopotamia, including al-Jazīrah. Fārs, Kirmān, ʿUmān, and lower and upper Mesopotamia he governed directly in his name. Rayy,

Iṣfahān, Hamadān, Nihāwand, Gurgān, and Ṭabaristān were under the supervision of his brother Mu'ayyad. Sijistān and Kirmān recognized his overlordship, as did the Ḥamdānids at Aleppo. The Fāṭimid imām-caliph al-ʿAzīz sent him an ambassador, hoping to form an alliance with him against the Byzantine Empire. The Byzantine emperor sent him an ambassador, hoping to win his support for bringing to heel the Byzantine rebel Bardas, who had been given sanctuary within the Islamic commonwealth at Mayyāfāriqīn. ʿAḍud sent two of his own ambassadors to Constantinople in 982 CE (371 IE). During the mission of one of the Fāṭimid ambassadors in Baghdad, ʿAḍud arranged for a regal investiture ceremony at the ʿAbbāsid caliph's court, during which the caliph bestowed upon ʿAḍud robes of honor and officially pronounced that by the caliph's fiat ʿAḍud was entrusted with the management of the ʿAbbāsid affairs of state with the exception of what concerned the caliph's private properties and domicile.

In the standard premodern sources that chronicle this time in the history of the Islamic commonwealth, ʿAḍud is credited with having undertaken many initiatives to bring stability, order, prosperity, and overall well-being to the ʿAbbāsid commonwealth and above all to its then-largest and most important city, Baghdad. All of the following is reported of him: he paid his troops regularly and avoided fomenting rivalries between the Turkish soldiers and the Daylamite soldiers; he had the pilgrimage routes to Mecca and Medina protected from highway robbers and extortionists and provided with wells and water wheels to assure adequate supplies of water for pilgrims; he arranged salary increases for prayer leaders and Qur'ān reciters in Mecca and Medina; he appointed a Christian as his chief minister and directed him to oversee the restoration of churches and monasteries that were in disrepair; under the direction of another appointee, the *naqīb* of the ʿAlids (who kept the genealogical records of descendants of ʿAlī in order to prove and preserve the pedigree), there was a restoration of mosques for which ʿAḍud assigned funds from religious endowments (*awqāf*/أوقاف); he also ordered the reconstruction of residential areas of Baghdad damaged by riots and armed conflicts that preceded his rise to power; in eastern Baghdad he arranged for the construction of Dār al-Mamlakah, a new palace complex for the Būyid governors replete with gardens, a royal court, and a hall for public audiences (replicating a palace complex he had undertaken at Shīrāz before his ascendancy to the governorship of Baghdad); he ordered the reconstruction and elaboration of the sanctuary for the martyr al-Ḥusayn at Karbalāʾ (the sanctuary had been destroyed by the ʿAbbāsid caliph al-Mutawakkil in 850 CE); he arranged to have ʿAlī ibn Abī Ṭālib's tomb at al-Najaf refurbished, with new buildings erected around the tombs of the seventh, ninth, tenth, and eleventh Shīʿite imāms of Twelver Shīʿism (respectively, Mūsā al-Kāẓim, Muḥammad al-Jawād, ʿAlī al-Hādī, and Ḥasan al-ʿAskarī); he had bridges and canals restored; and, finally, to promote law and order in Baghdad and bring about an end to sectarian strife along Shīʿite/Sunnī lines, he allowed only the police or paid infantry to bear arms, and he proscribed the public observance and celebration of religious acts of faith, whether by Sunnīs or Shīʿites. Preaching in public, which on the part of the Shīʿites during the reign of Muʿizz al-Dawlah and ʿIzz al-Dawlah (who countenanced such) had antagonized the Sunnī majority, was forbidden by ʿAḍud al-Dawlah. Although his rule was short, "at least during his reign in Baghdad, we hear of no further religious trouble."[18]

Upon ʿAḍud al-Dawlah's death, his son Abū Kalījār Marzubān was named heir apparent to the governorship of Baghdad by the ʿAbbāsid caliph, who bestowed upon his son the honorary title of *ṣamṣām al-dawlah*/ صمصام الدولة (the state's steadfast one). Abū Kalījār Marzubān Ṣamṣām al-Dawlah was not ʿAḍud al-Dawlah's eldest son. That was Abū al-Fawāris Shīrzīl (later to be given an honorific title by which he became better known, *viz.*, *sharaf al-dawlah* [the state's honor]). The latter, displeased that he had been passed over by the caliph when the caliph named his brother governor of Baghdad, was soon to contest his brother's authority, especially when his brother faced a mutiny of the Turkish troops and some of the various provincial governors who were prepared to challenge him as well. One from among the latter—Fakhr al-Dawlah—was a cousin to Ṣamṣām and Sharaf and with his own territorial ambitions (not to mention the caliph's blessings in the form of the honorary title of *falak al-ummah*/ فلك الأمة [the commonwealth's firmament]). Sharaf, however, remained the real challenge to Ṣamṣām's authority, not only because he was ʿAḍud's eldest son but also because of the proximity of the province that the father did appoint him governor over—Kirmān.

By 986 CE (at which time al-Maʿarrī would have been an adolescent thirteen years of age, but already allegedly composing verse), with the trouble of the rebellious Carmathian bands reasserting themselves around Basra, and with the Kurds of Diyār Bakr also in revolt, Ṣamṣām reached an agreement with Sharaf with the mediation of the ʿAbbāsid caliph. According to the agreement, Ṣamṣām would acknowledge Sharaf as his superior, and Sharaf's name would be mentioned in the Friday *khuṭbah* in Baghdad. In other words, Sharaf and not Ṣamṣām would be *amīr al-umarā'* or chief governor of Baghdad. To leave no questions about the matter, Sharaf marched to the gates of the Būyid palace complex in Baghdad (Dār al-Mamlakah) and had Ṣamṣām spirited away to Fārs, where he was confined to a fortress.

Sharaf would rule uncontested as chief governor until 989 CE, although without much distinction. In fact, he would lose control of much of Jibāl in northwestern Mesopotamia, where Kurds and Arab tribes of ʿUqayl and Numayr took to ruling semiautonomously.

Upon Sharaf's death (of natural causes; in 989 CE), his brother Abū Naṣr Fīrūz Khwāshād was recognized as his successor by the ʿAbbāsid caliph. Upon his investiture as governor, he was entitled *bahā' al-dawlah*/بهاء الدولة (the state's splendor) and *ḍiyā' al-millah*/ضياء الملة (the light of the creed). Bahā' al-Dawlah, as he was better known, ruled for twenty-four years, including during the brief period that al-Maʿarrī was in Baghdad. Only the first four of his years of rule were spent in Baghdad. He then set up his court in Wāsiṭ and Basra (for six years). For the remaining fourteen years of his tenure as governor of Baghdad, he took up residence even farther from the city, in Shīrāz, leaving day-to-day administrative affairs in the hands of subordinates in Baghdad.

For the first ten years of his governing, Bahā' al-Dawlah was greatly preoccupied with battling for control of Fārs with Ṣamṣām (who had escaped from the fortress to which he had been confined by Sharaf). The battle for suzerainty over Fārs lasted eight years and was not conclusively decided until Ṣamṣām's capture and execution. This strife as well as Bahā''s ruling from the distance of Shīrāz for fourteen years allowed for recalcitrant tribal-based regimes (e.g., the ʿUqaylids, the Marwānids, and the Mazyadids) to become independent in al-Jazīrah. One of these regimes, the Mazyadids under Ibn Mazyad, was so emboldened as to move on Baghdad itself in 1006 CE. This would have been only a few years after al-Maʿarrī chose to end his sojourn in the city. (Ibn Mazyad was persuaded to settle for other dominions to superintend, by means of a formal caliph's investiture with a title of honor.)

In the hands of Bahā' al-Dawlah's subordinate state functionaries, Baghdad during the early years of the governor's rule witnessed virtual anarchy. This was occasioned by intense Sunnī-Shī'ite sectarian strife, by rebellious Turkish army chiefs and soldiers, and by banditry and thuggery on the part of what amounted to urban gangs of discontented and alienated lumpenproletariat. In 1001/1002 CE, Bahā' temporarily checked the troubling state of affairs by appointing a Daylamite chief as commander of the armies in Baghdad (*amīr al-juyūsh*), and he—Abū 'Alī ibn Ustādhurmuz—moved to have law and order restored to Baghdad, arresting bandits and refractory Turkish army chiefs as well various other malcontents and trouble makers. He also reinstated 'Aḍud al-Dawlah's strictures against both Sunnī and Shī'ite public displays of sectarianism. This stricture included the public celebration of 'Āshūrā' or the holy day commemorating the martyrdom of al-Ḥusayn at Karbalā'.

When the *amīr al-juyūsh* Abū 'Alī ibn Ustādhurmuz died in 1010 CE, one of Bahā' al-Dawlah's ministers, Abū Ghālib ibn Khalaf Fakhr al-Mulk (a.k.a. Fakhr al-Mulk) succeeded him. Fakhr al-Mulk continued to oversee the repair work on Iraq's vital irrigation system and to reinforce the safety of the pilgrim routes to the Holy Cities of Mecca and Medina. He also provided relief for the indigent, and lessened the severity of judgments against prisoners whose misdeeds were relatively petty. In religious matters, however, he opened old wounds by allowing the Shī'ite population of Baghdad to revive the public celebration of Shī'ite ceremonies, including most notably 'Āshūrā'.

The new *amīr al-juyūsh* was a Daylamite. Like his Daylamite compatriots among the soldiery, he was a free soldier as opposed to slave soldier (although slave soldiers could, and often were, manumitted). The slave soldier was especially commonplace in the ranks of the ethnic Turks, many of whom served in the royal garrisons. Under Bahā' al-Dawlah, notwithstanding his Daylamite *amīr al-juyūsh*, the Turks in the state's soldiery would make gains in favor and prestige at the expense of the Daylamites. Bahā's victory over Ṣamṣām was tantamount to a victory of Turkish troops over Daylamite troops. The Baghdad garrison was largely Turkish, whereas the fighting forces in Fārs and Ahwāz were primarily

Daylamite. During a Daylamite revolt against Turkish elements in the Baghdad garrison in 986, the Turks had gotten the upper hand and killed many Daylamite soldiers. As early as 993, Ṣamṣām al-Dawlah started to purge the Daylamite elements from the forces at his command. More and more Turkish soldiers were compromising the armed forces during the reign of Bahā'.

It was at that time that Maḥmūd of Ghaznah overturned the independent Sāmānid ruler in Marw ('Abd al-Malik), bringing an end to the Sāmānid dynasty. Maḥmūd then seized Khurāsān from the Sāmānids and declared his allegiance to the 'Abbāsid caliph in Baghdad. This turn of events led shortly thereafter to a dynasty from Turkestan seizing the last major urban stronghold of the Sāmānids, Bukhara, and with that yet more Turkish tribes took to migrating westward and offering soldiers for armies of various governors.

Before his death in 403 IE/ 1012 CE, Bahā' had nominated his son Abū Shujā' (Sulṭān al-Dawlah) to succeed him as governor of Baghdad. The nomination was presented to Fakhr al-Mulk, who would continue to serve as *amīr al-juyūsh* in Baghdad until 1013 CE, the year that the caliph would formally pronounce Abū Shujā' Sulṭān al-Dawlah's investiture as governor (although at the time Abū Shujā' Sulṭān al-Dawlah was at court in Shīrāz).

Within three years, and while Abū Shujā' was still in Shīrāz, as a result of the influence of court functionaries in Baghdad and a minister to Bahā' (al-Muwaqqaf) who appropriated much of the authority of the governor of Baghdad, Fakhr al-Mulk was arrested and executed. With his demise a new wave of civilian unrest descended upon Baghdad. Shī'ite/Sunnī sectarian quarrels were once again a root cause. Abū Shujā' appointed one Ibn Sahlān to replace Fakhr al-Mulk as the *amīr al-juyūsh*, and to quell the outbreaks of violence in Baghdad. Ibn Sahlān moved with Daylamite soldiers to make a show of force in Karkh, the quarter of the Shī'ites, and also in Bāb al-Basra, a predominantly Sunnī district. But dissolute behavior on the part of the Daylamite soldiers angered Sunnīs and Shī'ites alike.

Abū Shujā' Sulṭān al-Dawlah had yet to enter Baghdad; and did not do so until 1018 CE, a full six years after having been proclaimed *amīr al-umarā'* by the 'Abbāsid caliph. The general urban disorder in the wake of

Ibn Sahlān's crackdown on violent Shīʿite and Sunnī disputants, and the anger over the general state of affairs on the part of the Turkish soldiers in the caliph's garrison, induced him to tarry. Abū Shujāʿ could not pay these Turkish soldiers. In 1020, consequently, they revolted and announced that they favored having Abū Shujāʿ's younger brother Abū ʿAlī (Musharrif al-Dawlah) governor of Baghdad. Abū Shujāʿ thereupon gave thought to exiling his brother Abū ʿAlī. Faced with stiff Turkish resistance to this move, he reached an agreement whereby Abū ʿAlī would govern Baghdad as deputy to Abū Shujāʿ (but with Abū Shujāʿ maintaining his sole governorship over Ahwāz and Fārs). Ibn Sahlān was to be precluded from the governing of Baghdad.

Abū Shujāʿ soon broke the agreement; not only by making Ibn Sahlān his chief minister, but also by conferring upon him honorary titles and privileges that made him nearly the equal of the governor of Baghdad. This revived the feud between the forces supporting Abū ʿAlī (Musharrif al-Dawlah), on the one hand, and, on the other hand, the forces supporting Abū Shujāʿ. Abū ʿAlī now insisted that he no longer be merely a deputy in the government of Baghdad but the sole *amīr al-umarā'* or chief governor—instead of his brother Abū Shujāʿ. To that end, with troops loyal to his cause he forced a pitched battle against Ibn Sahlān and troops loyal to him and Abū Shujāʿ. The battle was at Wāsiṭ. Abū ʿAlī's forces prevailed, arrested Ibn Sahlān (who was later executed), and by 1021 CE managed to have Abū ʿAlī's name instead of his brother's invoked during the *khuṭbah* of the Friday prayers in Baghdad.

Abū Shujāʿ opposed his brother's machinations but soon accepted the turn of events. Through intermediaries he made peace with the brother (by 1022 CE), allowing in fact that Abū ʿAlī be sole governor of al-ʿIrāq. This allowed for Abū ʿAlī to move from Wāsiṭ to Baghdad in 1023 and to take up residence at the Būyid palace complex [Dār al-Mamlakah]). He asked that the ʿAbbāsid caliph receive him on route to the palace. "The Caliph came accompanied by two of his sons, the Naqībs of the ʿAlids and ʿAbbāsids and the Chief Qāḍī. [Abū ʿAlī] Musharrif al-Dawlah kissed the ground before the Caliph and then entered the Dār al-Mamlakah."[19]

Abū Shujāʿ died a year later (1024 CE) at Shīrāz. The minister of the governorship of Baghdad that time, Abū al-Qāsim al-Maghribī, was a correspondent of al-Maʿarrī, as previously noted. He arranged a renewed pledge of allegiance to Abū ʿAlī Musharrif al-Dawlah, eliciting the support of both Turkish and Daylamite soldiers in the royal garrison, and then the support of the caliph.

Abū ʿAlī Musharrif al-Dawlah died in 1025 CE, one year after the investiture arranged by Minister Abū al-Qāsim al-Maghribī. By the time of his death, for all intents and purposes, the voice of the Turkish soldiers in Baghdad was now decisive in determining who would be governor, although in the case of Abū ʿAlī Musharrif al-Dawlah they were factionalized, some supporting a brother to Abū ʿAlī and Abū Shujāʿ (Abū Ṭāhir, a.k.a. Jalāl al-Dawlah) while others supported the son of Abū Shujāʿ, Abū Kālījār. Eventually Abū Kālījār, preoccupied as he was with a war against his uncle over Fārs, proved reluctant to accept a nomination from the Baghdad troops that supported him; and Abū Ṭāhir Jalāl al-Dawlah, although himself not very eager to assume the challenges of the governorship of Baghdad, was named governor in the Friday *khuṭbah* in 1027 CE, and he took up residence in the Būyid palace complex in Baghdad.

Between the time of Abū ʿAlī Musharrif al-Dawlah's death and Abū Ṭāhir Jalāl al-Dawlah's nomination, close to two years elapsed during which Baghdad was without a governor and on the brink of self-destructing. Bandits roamed freely in the streets. Troops from Wāsiṭ and Baghdad were needed to bring them to heel. In the process, and in the course of the general mayhem, Turkish soldiers wrought considerable havoc on the city, particularly the Karkh district. Already in Abū ʿAlī Musharrif's last days, anarchy and violence were commonplace. Mobs burned the house of al-Murtaḍā, the distinguished head (*naqīb*) of the ʿAlids, and in retaliation, ʿAlid mobs attacked Sunnī houses. The Turkish soldiers, unable to receive timely payment of their salaries, were in open revolt. On several occasions, Abū Ṭāhir Jalāl al-Dawlah had to flee Baghdad for his safety. Organized pillaging and plundering on the part of civilians soon became routine. *ʿAyyār* (عيار) groups—essentially armed urban gangs—became a permanent feature of urban life. One of their leaders, Abū ʿAlī al-Burjumī, became so powerful between 1030 and 1033 CE that he was able to extort protection money from state-appointed revenue collectors. He successfully resisted the attempts of state-ordered regiments to accost him. When at last a bounty was offered for his capture, he was seized in an ambush, taken to state authorities, and drowned in the Tigris (1033 CE).

Abū Ṭāhir Jalāl al-Dawlah's tumultuous years as governor of Baghdad ended with his death in 1043 CE. His eldest son, known as al-Malik al-ʿAzīz, was asked by the Turkish troops in Baghdad to come to the city in order to succeed his father as governor. Abū Kālījār, however, bribed the Turkish troops as well as the caliph, and in 1044 CE, his name was invoked in the Friday *khuṭbah.* Al-Malik al-ʿAzīz, deserted even by his own troops, never made it to Baghdad. Instead, he spent the remainder of his life (he died in 1049) serving at various provincial cities in the vast Būyid realm.

Abū Kālījār would rule as governor of Baghdad from 1044 CE to 1048 CE. His rule restored some order to Baghdad and also to some of the outlying provinces of the Būyid state whose administrators not to mention population at large nominally still owed allegiance to the ʿAbbāsid caliphs as well as the Būyid governors. Nonetheless, at this juncture in the history of the sprawling Islamic commonwealth, the Seljūk Turks had become so central to the sociopolitical dynamic that Abū Kālījār himself felt compelled to commit to making peace with Ṭughril Bey, the pre-eminent chief of the Seljūk Turkish tribes who by 1037 CE had taken Marw and Nīshāpūr from the Ghaznawid rulers and shortly thereafter Gurgān, Ṭabaristān, Khwārizm, Hamadān, Rayy, and Iṣfahān. As part of the pledge of peaceful coexistence, Abū Kālījār sought a cessation of Seljūk Turkish migrations into Būyid territories.

Abū Kālījār died in 1048 CE, nine years before al-Maʿarrī's death. He died in Kirmān where he had gone to confront the governor, who had allied himself with a Seljūk Turkish chief upon the latter's invasion of Kirmān and defeat of Būyid forces. Abū Kālījār's eldest son, Abū Naṣr Khusraw, was invested with the post of governor, with the honorific title of *al-malik al-raḥīm* (the compassionate king). Soon, however, Abū Kālījār's second son, Abū Manṣūr Fūlād Sulṭān, seized Fārs, and with that caused a civil war in which Abū Manṣūr and his uncle (Abū ʿAlī) allied themselves with the Seljūk Turks. By 1053 CE, Abū Manṣūr was invoking the name of Ṭughril Bey in the Friday *khuṭbah.* Two years later, after enduring a feud between the Turkish military governor in west Baghdad, al-Basāsīrī and Ibn al-Maslamah (whom the caliph had appointed as, respectively, his chief minister and secretary/chancellor) summoned Ṭughril Bey (then in Rayy) to come to Baghdad. The ʿAbbāsid caliph (al-Qā'im) at the same time ordered that Ṭughril Bey's name be mentioned in the Friday *khuṭbah* before mention of the name of Abū Naṣr Khusraw al-Malik al-Raḥīm. With the Seljūk Turkish army on the outskirts of Baghdad by 1055 CE, Ṭughril Bey asked permission to enter the city in peace. The caliph commanded his chief minister, Baghdad notables, and the city's religious officials to welcome Ṭughril Bey. Ṭughril entered the city, and within days, al-Malik al-Raḥīm was arrested and exiled. His name was dropped from the Friday *khuṭbah*. This marked the end of Būyid dynastic rule in Baghdad.

Politically, economically, and socially, life in Baghdad during the epoch of the Būyids, whose rule was contemporaneous with the life of al-Maʿarrī, was generally tumultuous and precarious. Hostile factionalism (e.g., Turkish vs. Daylamite) was rife in the armed forces; revolts over salaries were frequent. The many armed struggles among the Būyids themselves, one the one hand, and, on the other hand, between the Būyids and recalcitrant Būyid-appointed provincial governors and functionaries, consumed time, energy, and attention that were needed for better maintenance of Baghdad and al-ʿIrāq's infrastructure, above all (1) the canal system that provided water for agriculture and (2) safe and secure trade routes. The inadequate maintenance of irrigation and security on the trade routes led to a decline in agricultural production, trade, and commerce, which in turn led to periods of famine and decreased tax revenues for the state. The *iqṭāʿ*/إقطاع system of land management, whereby government functionaries as well as army officers were compensated for their services to the state with grants of land and the tax rights thereto—this instead of outright monetary payment—exacerbated the crisis in agriculture and the central treasury. The recipients of the land grants, whose numbers began to approach those of civilian landowners, did not own the lands assigned them. They merely used the land grants temporarily for the purpose of exacting income for themselves by way of collection of taxes. They had little interest in being good stewards of the land and overseeing maximum productivity. In making the land grants under the *iqṭāʿ* system, the state administration essentially conceded its control over management of the lands in question.

Frequent sectarian strife between Sunnīs and Shīʿites, replete with mob violence involving armed attacks, burning, and looting, characterized life in Baghdad during the late tenth and first half of the eleventh century CE, that is, during al-Maʿarrī's life span. Such strife predated the Būyids, and ʿAḍud al-Dawlah attempted to put an end to it once and for all with categorically restrictive measures applicable to Sunnī and Shīʿite devotional activities alike. But on balance over time, the Būyid governors seemed either unwilling or incapable of ridding Baghdad of this menace to peace, law, and order. The governors' sympathies for popular Shīʿite expressions of confessional loyalty (particularly the public celebration of ʿĀshūrāʾ, the impassioned commemoration of al-Ḥusayn's martyrdom), although quite natural given the Būyids' own religious orientation, did not help the situation.

The phenomenon of the *ʿayyār* groups may have reflected either a lapse in, or a willful disregard for, more normative top-down approaches to the maintenance of peace, law, and order; or the phenomenon may have represented making the best of decidedly less than ideal situations; but in any event one can easily envision how it could have contributed to the problem it probably sought to address. The *ʿayyār* groups may have provided order and defense for urban neighborhoods where other means of order and defense were not available, but it seems that they operated largely according to their own precepts and whims and not in the name of the judiciary or the state. In any event, they were of little comfort and reassurance when, for example, they were confronted with a crisis of the magnitude of the Byzantine capture of Niṣībīn in northern Mesopotamia in 972 CE. (Shortly thereafter [974–75 CE)], Byzantine imperial forces launched even more destructive armed attacks in northern Mesopotamia and northern Syria.)

Ambitious royal building projects on the part of the Būyids (e.g., the palace complex of Dār al-Mamlakah), and the reconstruction or refurbishing of bridges, dams, canals, mosques, churches, and residential and commercial districts, led to heavy taxation of the populace at a time when the tax base of the central treasury in Baghdad was shrinking. The population of the city was on the decline at this time.

In terms of culture, Būyid rule was accompanied by remarkable vitality. By the end of the tenth century of the Common Era and through the eleventh, learning throughout the Islamicate commonwealth was in full bloom. In all of the arts and sciences, there was boundless creative energy among those who sought knowledge and a keen interest in self-expression, particularly by way of putting pen to paper. (Paper making had been mastered by the second half of the eighth century CE.[20]) Many if not most of the Islamicate authors whose works are regarded as seminal, and typically included in any standard anthology or survey of Islamicate civilization, flourished during this timeframe. The translation of Greek scholarship was in full swing.

> [F]rom about the middle of the eighth century to the end of the tenth, almost *all* non-literary and non-historical secular Greek books that were available throughout the Eastern Byzantine Empire and the Near East were translated into Arabic . . . astrology and alchemy and the rest of the occult sciences; the subjects of the quadrivium: arithmetic, geometry, astronomy, and the theory of music; the entire field of Aristotelian philosophy through its history: metaphysics, ethics, physics, zoology, botany, and especially logic—the *Organon*; all the health sciences: medicine, pharmacology, and veterinary science; and various other marginal genres of writing, such as Byzantine handbooks on military science, popular collections of wisdom sayings, even books on falconry.[21]

The translation of Indian scientific writings (astronomy, astrology, mathematics) and Iranian science (e.g., astrology) as well as religio-philosophical, historical, and literary material (by way of Pahlavi [Middle Persian]) was also taken up by translators. The impetus for this was an innate thirst for knowledge—particularly science and philosophy—and the deliberate intent to retrieve and revive the learning of earlier civilizations.[22] The Būyid governors were not merely tolerant of the intellectual ethos of the day; they promoted and patronized it, and in their leading provincial metropoli (e.g., Basra, Rayy, Iṣfahān, Shīrāz) as well as in Baghdad. Learned ministers appointed by the governors—for example, Abū Muḥammad al-Muhallabī (d. 963 CE) by Muʿizz al-Dawlah, Abū Faḍl ibn al-ʿAmīd by Rukn al-Dawlah (d. 970 CE), Abū ʿAbd Allāh ibn Saʿdān (d. 984) by Ṣamṣām al-Dawlah, Ṣāḥib Ismāʿīl ibn ʿAbbād (d. 995) by Mu'ayyad al-Dawlah, and

Abū Naṣr ibn Sābūr Ardashīr (d. late tenth century or early eleventh) by Bahā' al-Dawlah—are emblematic of the Būyid era, as are the learned gatherings (*majālis*) that the chief ministers encouraged and that attracted scholars of diverse interests, such as science, math, medicine, philosophy, law, poetry, and music. Abū Ḥayyān al-Tawḥīdī (d. around 1024 CE), one of the major savants and litterateurs of the Būyid era, was secretary/chancellor to both Ṣāḥib Ismā'īl ibn 'Abbād and Abū 'Abd Allāh ibn Sa'dān. Historian and ethicist Abū 'Alī ibn Miskawayh (d. 1033 CE), another major figure in the intellectual development of the period, was secretary to al-Muhallabī and Ibn al-'Amīd before later serving Ibn al-'Amīd's son (Abū al-Fatḥ, who was minister for one year), 'Aḍud al-Dawlah, and Ṣamṣām.

Equally noteworthy in this context are the circles or societies that met for scholarly discussions or debate and that coalesced around the personalities and orientations of specific individuals, for example, the noted philosopher, theologian, editor, and translator Yaḥyā ibn 'Adī (d. 974); the philosopher and polymath Abū Sulaymān al-Sijistānī (d. 985); and the philosophers who comprised the Sincere Bretheren or Brethren of Purity, who were particularly active in the tenth century of the CE.[23]

Additional Geopolitical Groupings and States in the Islamicate World of the Ninth through the Tenth Centuries CE

The Carmathians (Qarāmiṭah/القرامطة)

The Carmathians represented a religio-political movement that evolved from the Sevener (or Ismā'īlī) Shī'ite ideology with respect to the imāmate. Like the Fāṭimids who embraced (read "captured" as far as Massignon was concerned[24]) much of their religio-philosophical thinking (although they were not in agreement over the imāmate post-Ismā'īl [son of Ja'far al-Ṣādiq]), they established a Shī'ite state that was anticaliphal (i.e., opposed to the Baghdad 'Abbāsid version of the caliphate). Both the state and the movement preceding its formation were bound up with socioeconomic causes as well (e.g., "justice based on equality"[25]); and the movement was associated with a veritable insurrection or revolt over wide areas of the Islamic commonwealth, with wide ramifications.

The origins of Carmathian religio-philosophical thought can be traced back to imāmī-driven speculative thought in the city of Kufa and its environs in the late eighth and early ninth centuries of the Common Era; the insurrection or revolt can be traced to the year 890 and to the personage of Ḥamdān Qarmaṭ, a Kufan Sevener Shīʿite who because of his propagating on behalf of the imāmī position that he embraced, and because of his identification with the revolt of 890, is commonly identified as the founder of Carmathianism (although he eventually took a position on the imām that represented a break with his original views, and thus a break from those who remained faithful to those views—i.e., the larger body of adepts that would found the state along the central and southern eastern littoral of the Arabian peninsula).

With respect to the imāmate, the Sevener or Ismāʿīlī Shīʿites were fairly united in accepting the line of the imāmate through Jaʿfar al-Ṣādiq's son Ismāʿīl (as opposed to brother Mūsā), whom they believed actually died (i.e., had not merely disappeared only to return at a later date). Similarly, they were fairly united in recognizing Ismāʿīl's son Muḥammad as the next legitimate imām, carrying on from Jaʿfar by way of descent from son Ismāʿīl (who predeceased his father). But when Muḥammad's death was reported in 809 CE, although the majority of the Sevener Shīʿites denied the death and maintained that he must be recognized as the Rightly Guided Imām who was destined to reappear, a minority maintained that Muḥammad, son of Ismāʿīl, was in fact dead and thus would not reappear/return as imām; hence the imām was to be found elsewhere, namely, in the personage of a purported descendant who emerged in the Syrian steppes in the vicinity of the small city of Salamiyyah. That purported descendant was one Saʿīd ibn al-Ḥusayn, who, once he relocated in Ifrīqiyah in the vicinity of al-Qayrawān, and with the support thereat of the Shīʿite *dāʿī* Abū ʿAbd Allāh al-Ḥusayn al-Shīʿī, was not only heralded in 909 CE as the imām ʿUbayd Allāh al-Mahdī but also accepted as a descendant of Ismāʿīl (and by way ultimately of ʿAlī ibn Abī Ṭālib and wife Fāṭimah; hence the birth of the "Fāṭimid" dynasty that by 969 would establish the new city of Cairo as its principal administrative, cultural, and intellectual center).

Although Ḥamdān ibn Qarmaṭ did not initially accept this turn of events in the Sevener Shīʿite understanding of the imāmate, that is, initially he did not accept the Fāṭimid dynasty founder's claim to be the descendant of Ismāʿīl and hence the rightful successor to the imāmate, eventually he did. Those Sevener Shīʿites who did not follow in Ḥamdān's footsteps, who denied the claims of the Fāṭimids and thus still awaited the return of Muḥammad son of Ismāʿīl as imām, nonetheless remained identified as Carmathian (i.e., partisans of Qarmaṭ; it was they who would coalesce to form the Carmathian state on the eastern coast of the Arabian peninsula).

Carmathian missionaries were especially active in the late ninth century CE in Yemen (e.g., Ṣanʿā' and Najrān), Khorāsān (e.g., Rayy and Merw), lower Mesopotamia (e.g., Wāsiṭ and Kufa), and the northeast Syrian steppe (e.g., Salamiyyah). They were also implicated in the black slave (Zanj) rebellion in the saltpeter mines in the marshes of the lower Euphrates area (868–83 CE). The insurrection associated with Ḥamdān ibn Qarmaṭ in the year 890 CE took place in Wāsiṭ where Ḥamdān founded for his followers a *dār al-hijrah*/دار الهجرة or retreat/refuge house, which also served as the center of a commune of shared wealth and possessions and secretive initiation rites bound up with Carmathian doctrine on the imāmate, a Sevener Shīʿite doctrine to be sure, but, in terms of the legitimacy of the imām, not as unequivocally ʿAlid as compared to Fāṭimid doctrine generally.[26]

In 900 CE, another initiate in the movement, Dhikrawayh al-Dindānī, called for another uprising, in the Syrian desert, announcing the leader to be one Abū ʿAbd Allāh Muḥammad. The latter would lead an armed force that would lay siege to Damascus in 901 CE, on the occasions of which Abū ʿAbd Allāh was killed. A brother replaced him as leader, but he was captured by forces loyal to the ʿAbbāsid caliph and executed in Baghdad in 903 CE.

With the death of Dhikrawayh al-Dindānī in 903 CE, Carmathian insurrectionary assertions subsided in lower Mesopotamia, but by 899 CE the faithful under the leadership of one Abū Saʿīd al-Ḥasan al-Jannābī had already formed an independent state centered in al-Aḥsā', "the bulwark of Carmathian power and the terror of the caliph in Baghdad."[27] Al-Jannābī conquered al-Yamāmah in 903. Abū Ṭāhir Sulaymān, his son who ruled as leader of the state at al-Aḥsā' from 914 to 943, systematically pillaged lower Mesopotamia, cut the pilgrim routes from al-ʿIrāq to Mecca, ambushed pilgrims, and with an armed force invaded Mecca in 930, during which he took possession of the Black Stone at the Kaʿbah and carried it off to al-Aḥsā', demanding a ransom sum for it (finally paid by the ʿAbbāsid caliph in 952) before returning it.

> The [Carmathian] revolution and desecration shocked the Muslim world and humiliated the Abbasids. But little could be done; for much of the tenth century the Qarmatians were the most powerful force in the Persian Gulf and Middle East, controlling the coast of Oman and collecting tribute from the caliph in Baghdad as well as from a rival Ismāʿīlī Imām in Cairo, whom they did not recognize.[28]

Carmathian military strength would wane by the early eleventh century CE. However, the imāmī propaganda and religio-political doctrines of the Carmathians remained influential. By 1030 CE, the administrative apparatus of the state at al-Aḥsā' was still extant and furthermore quasi-autonomous. The Druze religion that would arise after the disappearance of the Fāṭimid caliph-imām al-Ḥākim in 1021 CE, and which is anchored in the divination of the Fāṭimid caliph-imām al-Ḥākim, "is simply a Karmaṭian heresy" according to Massignon.[29]

Al-Zaydiyyah Shīʿites

Al-Zaydiyyah Shīʿites endorsed neither the teachings of the Seveners (al-Ismāʿīliyyah) nor those of the Twelvers nor those of the Carmathians with respect to the imāmate. Coalescing at first in Kufa around a grandson of al-Ḥusayn, Zayd ibn ʿAlī (d. 740 CE), whom they recognized as the rightful imām after al-Ḥusayn's son ʿAlī Zayn al-ʿĀbidīn (as opposed to Muḥammad al-Bāqir, recognized by both the Seveners and the Twelvers), by the ninth century CE they had evolved into enough of a community with respect to allegiance to their own religio-philosophical and political teachings, and with respect to their strength in numbers and influence, to establish a small semi-autonomous state in the area of the southern shores of the Caspian Sea. By the tenth century, they had established another state in Yemen. The Zaydiyyah did not endorse the doctrine of the concealed imām who would in time reappear, nor did they endorse automatic son-from-father inheritance of the imāmate (although they held that the imāms must be from the Prophet Muḥammad's family).

Instead, the imām among the Zaydiyyah had to earn his position by virtue of demonstrated leadership qualities and effectiveness and by demonstration of learning. Moreover, there could be more than one imām at the same time or occasionally no imām at all if no one came forth to demonstrate to the satisfaction of the community the requisite qualifications.

The ʿAlawiyyah (Alawites), a.k.a. al-Nuṣayriyyah (Nuṣayrīs)

Worth mentioning in this context—not because of their establishment of an anti-caliphate (nor even a smaller state, which in fact they never achieved) but because they are ʿAlids whose main strength in adherents during al-Maʿarrī's lifetime lay (where it has remained until this day) to the west of Aleppo and along the northwestern Syrian coast—are the community who, although sometimes referred to by others as al-Nuṣayriyyah (after one of their early theologians), themselves more recently self-identify as al-ʿAlawiyyah (i.e., the supporters of ʿAlī ibn Abī Ṭālib par excellence; hence the English appellation "Alawites"). Their theologian Muḥammad ibn Nuṣayr (d. 868 CE), from whom was derived the appellation al-Nuṣayriyyah, was a student and partisan of the Twelver line of Shīʿites, and particularly the tenth and eleventh imāms ʿAlī al-Hādī and al-Ḥasan al-ʿAskarī (respectively), who were his contemporaries (the former died in 868 CE and the latter in 874). Ḥusayn ibn Ḥamdān al-Khaṣībī, a later theologian and "initiator" into the doctrines of the somewhat secretive community, patronized by the Ḥamdānids and "the real founder of the Nuṣairīs,"[30] was active in Kufa and Aleppo (where he died in 957 or 968 CE). His disciple in north Syria, al-Ṭabarānī, whose theological writings form an important part of the written heritage of Nuṣayrī beliefs and practices, was a contemporary of al-Maʿarrī.

Although Twelvers in terms of recognition of the proper line of imāms, the Nuṣayrīs advanced a highly syncretistic, esoteric religio-philosophical system with Ismāʿīlī influences as well as Gnostic, neo-Platonic, Zoroastrian, and possibly Christian. Arguably the most arresting feature of this system is not just the subordination of the Prophet Muḥammad to ʿAlī ibn Abī Ṭālib in terms of ultimate significance to the adepts, but the apotheosis of ʿAlī or, what amounts to virtually the same thing, the teaching that the Divinity "in-dwells" with respect to ʿAlī; hence one of the acknowledgments of faith, historically according to some of the sources (for there is not absolute consistency or clarity), is the proclamation that "there is no God but ʿAlī."[31]

The Ṣaffārids

The Ṣaffārids were a Sunnī Perso-Iranian dynasty who established suzerainty over eastern Iran, Khorāsān, and Afghanistan from 861 to 1003 CE. The founder of the dynasty, Yaʿqūb ibn Layth, a rival to the ʿAbbāsid caliph al-Muʿtamad's candidate for the governorship of Transoxiana (Naṣr ibn Aḥmad, of Sāmānī descent), at one point extended his authority into western Iran nearly to Baghdad. By 900 CE, the state's territory was greatly reduced. In 875, al-Muʿtamad officially named Naṣr ibn Aḥmad governor of Transoxiana; in 900 a successor brother of Yaʿqūb ibn Layth, whose army was confronted and defeated by the Sāmānī Ismāʿīl ibn Aḥmad, was forced to be a vassal of the latter when the ʿAbbāsid caliph appointed Ismāʿīl ibn Aḥmad governor of Khorāsān, Ṭabaristān, Rayy, and Iṣfahān. By 1002, the last Ṣaffārid prince (*amīr*) was overthrown in the original Ṣaffārid homeland (Sīstān, in southern Afghanistan) by the Sunnī Turkish Maḥmūd of Ghaznah.

Of special note with respect to the Ṣaffārids is that they patronized Persian poets. This along with Sāmānid support for Persian language, literature, and scholarship at approximately the same time laid the foundation for the revival, efflorescence, and spread of Persian language culture within the Islamic commonwealth.

The Sāmānids

The Sāmānid state (819–999 CE) included Khorāsān, Afghanistan, and Transoxiana. The founder of the dynasty that took his name was Sāmān Khudā, allegedly a Zoroastrian convert to Islam, which among other things may help explain his and his successors being such strong patrons of the sciences and Perso-Islamic culture, above all Persian poetry. Ismāʿīl ibn Aḥmad, who successfully challenged Ṣaffārid suzerainty in Khorāsān, was a grandson of Sāmān Khudā, one of several who in exchange for their allegiance to the ʿAbbāsid caliph in Baghdad were allowed semi-autonomous rule over the vast provinces of the ʿAbbāsid state in southwest and central Asia. Bukhara, Samarqand, Balkh, and Herat were flourishing centers of culture and learning during this era.

> Bukhāra . . . and Samarqand . . . almost eclipsed Baghdad as centres of learning and art. Not only Arabic but Persian scholarship was protected and fostered. . . . [Physician and philosopher] al-Rāzī dedicated his book on medicine entitled *al-Manṣūrī* in honor of his patron [a Sāmānid prince of Sijistān]. . . . [Philosopher] Ibn-Sīnā, then living in Bukhāra and still in his teens, was accorded free access to the rich loyal library [founded by the Sāmānid ruler Nūḥ II (976–97 CE). . . . Firdawsi (934–1020) wrote his first poetry in this period and . . . Balʿami, the vizir of Manṣūr I (961–76) translated [into Persian] an abridgment of al-Ṭabari's history.[32]

The Ghaznavids (976–1186 CE)

With his invasion of Sīstān in 1002 CE and the overthrow of Yaʿqūb ibn Layth (who would be the last Ṣaffārid prince to rule in the name of a Ṣaffārid state), Maḥmūd, son of Subuktigīn (of Turkic slave soldier origin), from his base in the southern Afghani city of Ghaznah laid the foundation for even greater expansion of dynastic rule that assumed the name of the city of Ghaznah. Maḥmūd ruled as sulṭān from 999 to 1030 CE, expanding his state to the west (Rayy and Hamadan in Iran), the north (Oxus River), and the northeast (Indus River valley). He directed over a dozen expeditions through the northern and northwestern Indian subcontinent. Although the (Sunnī Muslim) Ghaznavids were ethnic Turks, they became Persianized in terms of language and high-culture orientation. The Ghaznavids patronized, for example, the great Persian-language poets Anṣārī, Farrokhī, Manucherī, and Sanā'ī. Maḥmud invited Firdawsi and Ibn Sīnā to his court in Ghaznah. It was during the Ghaznavid era that Abū Faḍl al-Bayhaqī wrote a comprehensive history in Persian. Due to the influence of the Ghaznavids, Perso-Islamic scholarship, and scientific, historical, and literary production in the Persian language, took even deeper hold not only in central and southwest Asia but also northwest India.

The Umayyads in Spain

The Umayyad dynastic rule in the Iberian Peninsula, established by ʿAbd al-Raḥmān ibn Muʿāwiyah (the grandson of the eleventh Umayyad caliph Hishām who ruled in Damascus) and superimposed upon an indigenous predominantly Christian population, lasted from 756 to 1031 CE. ʿAbd al-Raḥmān ibn Muʿāwiyah and his successors, up to ʿAbd al-Raḥmān III through the seventeenth year of his reign (which lasted 49 years from 912 to 961), ruled with the title of *amīr* (prince). Thereafter, beginning with ʿAbd al-Raḥmān III in 929 CE, the successors to Umayyad rule in Iberia ruled with the title of caliph, thereby constituting another anti-caliphate second only to the Ismāʿīlī Fāṭimid imām-caliph in terms of its rivalry to the caliphate of the ʿAbbāsids in the tenth and eleventh centuries CE.

By the time of the rule of Amīr ʿAbd al-Raḥmān II (822–852 CE), already a rich and diverse Arab and Islamic culture had taken hold in the Iberian peninsula; "the lure of the language, literature, religion and other institutions—including the harem system—had become so strong that a large number of urban Christians had become Arabized though not actually Islamized. Dazzled by the glamour of Arab civilization and conscious of their own inferiority in art, poetry, philosophy and science, native Christians soon began to ape the Arab way of living."[33] By the beginning of ʿAbd al-Raḥmān III's succession to Umayyad rule in Iberia, the Arab-Islamic state (al-Andalus) under effective Umayyad rule had been reduced to a small area centered around the city of Cordoba, due to, inter alia, the secession of various Muslim renegade princes or governors. But within twenty years ʿAbd al-Raḥmān III managed to reincorporate most of the lost territories through systematic reconquest.

Throughout the caliphate as well as emirate of the Umayyads in Spain, even during the declining years of the caliphate when central authority was weakened because of (1) sectarian strife (among Arabs, indigenous North Africans [Amāzīgh] and imported east European or central Asian slave soldiers in the royal guard), and, (2) more unified Christian military campaigns from the north aiming to overthrow Muslim rulers in Iberia, Cordoba was the capital city and a leading center of cultural activity. In this respect, it was nearly the equal of ʿAbbāsid Baghdad at its zenith, or Fāṭimid Cairo. By the time of the reign of ʿAbd al-Raḥmān III and his son al-Ḥakam II (961–76), Cordoba was one of the largest and most prosperous cities in all of Europe; and all of al-Andalus was flourishing commercially and agriculturally. "The caliph's court at that time was one of the most glamorous in all Europe. Accredited to it were envoys from the Byzantine emperor as well as from the monarchs of Germany, Italy and France. Its seat, Cordova, with half a million inhabitants . . . yielded in magnificence only to Baghdad and Constantinople."[34] ʿAbd al-Raḥmān III founded a university in Cordoba, in the main mosque, which predated the founding of al-Azhar in Cairo. Al-Ḥakam II al-Mustanṣir (ruled 961–76 CE) expanded the mosque and provided salaries for professors including those whom he invited from outside of al-Andalus. He also oversaw the expansion of the library of Cordoba, sending out agents to purchase or copy manuscripts from Alexandria, Baghdad, and Damascus. Al-Ḥakam was regarded as a scholar as well as statesman, with interests in literature, philosophy, and theology. Ibn Ḥazm (994–1064 CE), a celebrated and influential poet, theologian, historian of religion, and vizier, flourished in Umayyad al-Andalus. His *Ṭawq al-Ḥamāmah* (*The Ring of the Dove*), an anthology of chaste love poems, and *al-Faṣl fī al-Milal wa al-Ahwā' wa al-Niḥal*/الفصل في الملل والأهواء والنحل (*The Decisive Tract on Religious Sects, Heterodoxies, and Faiths*), a compendium of comparative religion extending to five volumes, are two of his more important extant works. As a theologian, Ibn Ḥazm was a celebrated literalist, eschewing esoteric interpretations by various exegetes and focusing instead almost exclusively on *aḥādīth* narratives.

In literary developments of note from the time, arguably the most remarkable was the production of *muwashshaḥāt*/موشحات or poetry with stanzas as a refrain and also the incorporation of colloquial Arabic and Andalusi romance. More conventional celebrated poetry from the same time and place is represented by that from the pen of Ibn Zaydūn (1003–71 CE). Ibn Masarrah (883–931 CE) was a noted religious philosopher from Cordova. Very much unlike Ibn Ḥazm, he was a proponent of esotericism in his interpretations of Islam. He had considerable influence on, among others, the celebrated Andalusian Muslim religious philosopher Ibn al-ʿArabī (d. 1240).

Part II. Major Socio-Intellectual Currents and Discourses in the Islamicate Community before and during the Age of al-Maʿarrī

Al-Maʿarrī remarked in *Luzūm Mā Lā Yalzam*, in the first hemistich of a poem among his poems with the rhyme consonant م , "I have become the son of my time" (غدوتُ ابن وقتي); certainly meaning, at one level, as Nicholson has noted in his *A Literary History of the Arabs*,[35] and, as al-Maʿarrī himself made clear in completing the verse ("I have forgotten what's past and I have no taste of what's "coming": ما تقضّى نسيتُهُ / وما هو آتٍ لا أُحسُّ له طعما), that he saw no need to live his life taking more than one moment at a time; but, at another level, in all likelihood meaning that he could not help but be a product of his times.

This would be cause enough for one's wanting to stop and consider the major constructs of the civilizational background out of which he emerged, at the time that he emerged. Even if al-Maʿarrī had not uttered the above words, the conscientious investigator of his thought would hardly be inclined to approach it without at the same time taking into consideration the intellectual trends and developments that may be fairly described as typical, influential, or noteworthy for his society and times. Finally, because the present study has already conceded that in many ways al-Maʿarrī quite noticeably departs from the mainstream of Islamicate thought, in order to be able to appreciate that divergence properly and fully, one needs to be reminded of what the mainstream consisted.

For all of these reasons, therefore, it would be good to turn to a brief outline of the more lasting and consequential socio-intellectual currents in the Islamicate societies of the Middle East just prior to and during the age of Abū al-ʿAlā', and which in one way or another contributed toward giving distinctive shape to what is commonly associated with the Islamicate world (or Islamicate civilization) in the period leading up to and concluding the first half of the eleventh century CE. At the same time, some key personalities in this civilizational growth and development ought to be highlighted.[36]

As we have just seen in the preceding section of this chapter, al-Maʿarrī came of age and flourished during centuries when the supremacy and might of an effectively centralized Islamic commonwealth, when real administrative authority that flowed from the office of the caliph and his imperial court and entourage, were well on their way to being seriously eroded. The rise and efflorescence of at least semi (if not completely) autonomous decentralized agents and institutions of power and prestige, a phenomenon that would become especially characteristic of Islamicate society in the years immediately leading up to the advent of Seljūk and then Ottoman Turkish dynastic rule, was becoming relatively commonplace. The previously mentioned ruling dynasties of the Mirdāsids (1023 to 1079 CE), Fāṭimids (909 to 1171 CE), Ḥamdānids (944 to 1003 CE), and Būyids (945 to 1055 CE) all exemplify this turn of events and, furthermore, represent only a numerically small part thereof. They are only the more illustrious or geo-politically relevant in terms of al-Maʿarrī's domicile and travels.

The establishment of effective Būyid rule in Baghdad—which is to say, in franker terms, the occupation of the ʿAbbāsid dynasty's capital city in 945 by the Būyid leader Muʿizz al-Dawlah, and his assuming the title *amīr al-umarā'* (supreme commander; literally,"prince of princes"), notwithstanding the Būyids acceptance in principle of the ʿAbbāsid Caliph's overlordship—is of course a pivotal chronological cut-off point in the history of the ʿAbbāsid caliphate. It signals a de facto end to true caliphal independence (as geographically limited as it may have been at times) during which "internal disturbances were relatively infrequent and generally localized" and "the leading social strata of the empire, of whatever background—even that minority that was not yet becoming Muslim—lived in a single vast society" of "common cultural patterns."[37]

As we have also underscored in part 1 of this chapter, accompanying the dissipation of centralized, caliph-based political power and authority—and in fact sometimes contributing to it, if not constituting essentially one and the same thing—was an especially acute fragmenting of religious authority and confessional allegiances. This development occurred most conspicuously along the lines of the divide between, on the one hand, the more mainstream, or normative, Muslims (which is to say, those who today would refer to themselves, in abbreviated form, as Sunnīs, those of "established practice" in dogma and ritual, as determined by the consensus the of the *'ulamā'* especially but also to a large extent by the consensus of the entire community of believers), and, on the other hand, the most important minority offshoot, that is, the Shīʿah (Shīʿite), the abbreviated reference for "the (Muslim people belonging to Caliph ʿAlī's) faction" (with respect to dogma and ritual).

At the same time, even within the Shīʿah orientation within Islam, there were the competing subdivisions of the Ismāʿīlī or Sevener faction, on the one hand, and, on the other hand, the Twelvers. To add to the centrifugal tendencies, within the Ismāʿīlī community, there arose the further major bifurcation of the "Nizārīs" (النزارية) as opposed to the "Mustaʿliqīn" (المستعلقين), this as a result of a disagreement over the proper Fāṭimid imām-caliph after the death of Mustanṣir in 1094 CE.

All told, the adherents of the Shīʿite variety of Islam remained a comparatively small minority prior to and during al-Maʿarrī's lifetime. But the tenth and first half of the eleventh centuries CE witnessed an overall ascendancy (socially, politically, economically, intellectually) of the Shīʿites in the Islamicate world, an ascendancy most disproportionate to the number of the rank-and-file followers and nothing short of extraordinary (especially on the part of the Ismāʿīlīs). The Būyids were Shīʿite Muslims (Twelvers), as were the Fāṭimids (Sevener [Ismāʿīlī] branch). The Būyid-ruled confederated domains comprised in addition to Baghdad vast territories to the East, which today would constitute most of Iran inclusive of the major urban centers of Rayy, Shiraz, and Merv. The Fāṭimids were architects of a systematic religio-political movement, replete with learned and skilled itinerant propagandists, that aimed ultimately at eliminating completely—i.e., dislodging and disempowering by force if necessary—the ʿAbbāsid dynasty of caliphs who ruled from Baghdad. The Fāṭimids scarcely concealed their hopes of replacing the ʿAbbāsid dynasty with one whose rulers descended from ʿAlī, whose significance derived not only from the fact that he served as the fourth caliph, but also because he was the son-in-law of Muḥammad by virtue of his marriage to Muḥammad's daughter Fāṭimah. The Ismāʿīlī Shīʿite leaders of the Fāṭimid dynasty were deliberate and self-conscious rivals not just to the ʿAbbāsid caliphs but also to any rulers whatsoever in the Islamic commonwealth—be they Sunnīs or Shīʿites (Twelvers)—who recognized the legitimacy of the ʿAbbāsid dynasty's hold on the caliphate.

At the zenith of its power in the second half of the tenth and eleventh centuries CE, the Cairo-based (Ismāʿīlī) Fāṭimid dynasty of Egypt effectively held dominion over an enormous expanse of the Islamicate world, from as far west as the Atlantic littoral of North Africa to as far east as the borders of Iraq in the Fertile Crescent area and—beyond that—the areas of Oman (ʿUmān) and Sind. To the northeast, Fāṭimid suzerainty was established (and to a greater as opposed to lesser degree) in the Levant and greater Syria as far as Aleppo and the frontiers with the Byzantine Empire. To the southeast, Ismāʿīlī minions could claim to have made noteworthy inroads in the Yemen. In other words—a fact that is not without specific intellectual/ideological dimensions as well—in the tenth century CE Shīʿite rulers, especially the followers of the Ismāʿīliyyah within the territories comprising the Fāṭimid state, were recognized in half of the predominantly Islamicate territories of North Africa, the Near East, the Middle East, and Southwest Asia; while Shīʿite missionaries were making converts, even among rulers, in the other half. Accompanying the decline of the authority of the ʿAbbāsid caliphate and the proliferation of autonomous or semi-autonomous dynastic centers of power and authority—some of which had only fairly local bases and relied primarily on overwhelming military might (e.g., aggressive warlords with sizable armed troops at their command) as the chief means of establishing rule—was a gradual but steady decline in the overall economic and social well-being of the Islamic commonwealth. This is not to deny that here and there certain socioeconomic classes of individuals, or dynastic courts, or cities and even broader regions, continued to prosper, perhaps for decades to come if not longer; and that, depending upon the place and era, periods or cycles of fat years could alternate with periods or cycles of lean years. Nor is it to suggest that by the tenth and eleventh centuries, already the once vaunted and impressive social and economic vigor of a veritable empire, based on surplus-generating agriculture and brisk and diverse urban-centered trade and commerce with sizable educated classes of landowners, merchants, and religious and political functionaries, was essentially completely sapped.

Rather, the point to be underscored, as a general principle only, and as might be expected, is that along with the weakening of the effective governing authority of ʿAbbāsid caliphate within Dār al-Islām, and along with the establishment of rival independent dynasties or warlords, came a drop in overall prosperity and in the amount and quality of goods and services expected of civic and administrative institutions. Something as elemental and yet crucial as day-to-day peace and security, for self and family as well as neighborhood or city or state, was also imperiled.

This situation was only exacerbated in certain parts of the wholly or partially Islamicate territories (e.g., and most noteworthy for the present study, northern Syria) when, contemporaneous with the decline of the strength of the caliphate in Baghdad, and with the decline of local rulers (which was sometimes the case), there occurred the major military incursions by Byzantine Christian forces (such as the one led by Nicepherous Phocas as early as 961 CE, which resulted in the brief but highly destructive occupation of the city of Aleppo and the slaughter of many captives).

In time, even the powerful and influential Cairene Fāṭimids fell prey to the same debilitating trends and tendencies that wracked the Islamic commonwealth as a whole, regardless of Sunnī or Shī'ite overlordship. The demise of this Ismā'īlī Shī'ite dynasty was nearly as meteoric as its rise. By the mid and latter parts of the eleventh century, the Ismā'īlī caliphate in Cairo fell victim to an injurious dispute over succession. Continuity and stability were maintained, but to a great degree only by virtue of the intervention of a strong military chief (e.g., Badr). The expansion beyond the lands of Egypt was over. Trade and urban prosperity declined. The management of land, taxes, and the military became more and more decentralized, falling into the hands of locally based governors and generals who were allowed to exercise nearly absolute control. While all of this was taking placee, Turkoman (Sunnī) Muslims descended from the chieftan Saljūk (of the Khirgiz region of Turkestan) were establishing their rival Islamic dynasty based in the central territories of the Islamicized (or rapidly Islamicizing) world. It was this dynasty that ultimately not only forced the absolute end of Būyid Shī'ite rule in Baghdad (1055 CE), but also effectively kept in check Fāṭimid irredentism. The Seljūks defeated the short-lived pro-Fāṭimid coup in Baghdad from 1058 through 1060.

By 1070, just thirteen years after al-Ma'arrī's death, the Seljūks had extended their authority into Aleppo. By 1094, all of the district of Syria was under Seljūk suzerainty, not to mention most of Asia Minor, the Islamicized territories of Central Asia including especially those of present-day Iran, and—last but not least—the province of al-'Irāq and the city of Baghdad where by 1091 the Seljūk sultanate had moved its seat of government (as opposed to one or another of the major cities farther east, e.g., Isfahan, Marw, or Rayy). The Seljūks allowed the still-surviving ʿAbbāsid caliphate *de jure* authority but themselves assumed actual rule.

In terms of intellectual and cultural developments, the same period of history in Islamicate territories, that is, approximately the tenth and eleventh centuries CE, was remarkably vibrant notwithstanding the decline in overall economic prosperity and the increasing social, political, and religious fragmentation.[38] One might rightfully argue that the more formative developments of premodern Islamicate civilization in the fields of (for example) literature, medicine, science, religious thought, and philosophical speculation, had preceded in the late seventh and then especially the eighth and ninth centuries CE; with the first waves of Muslim-led conquests and expansion, and when Hellenism, Judeo-Christian monotheism, and other even older religions or world-views from Arabia, the Near East, North Africa, and Central Asia (e.g., Zoroastrianism, Buddhism, and Confucianism; to a lesser extent perhaps Hinduism) were first more squarely encountered by the nascent Islamic community. Nevertheless, great creative impulses remained. Original contributions continued to be made. "The Arab warrior caste was deposed, and replaced by a ruling class of landowners and bureaucrats, professional soldiers and literati, merchants and men of learning . . . A diversified urban culture evolved."[39]

More important for the purposes of the present study, this was the time when one can speak of the maturation of Islamicate literature, art, theology, philosophy, and science.[40] And if one can at least in part explain the cultural efflorescence of one century with that of the preceding, Baghdad's role in this development looms large. "The full development of Arabic literature in the ninth century is inconceivable without Baghdad as the great melting-pot and crucible" of a vibrant culture, a culture which not only had the patronage of the ʿAbbāsid court but also the support of "a genuine bourgeoisie" grown wealthy from manufacturing as well as trade.[41]

By the time of al-Maʿarrī's maturation, the religion of Islam and Islamicate civilization, as well as the attendant "cultural patterns," had been articulated and configured along clearly recognized lines, lines that were proving to be definitive (even within the nonnormative trajectories, which after all had their mainstream corpus of ideas or principles). Although with various permutations, and possibly totally new and original ones superadded, the resulting patterns would endure for generations to come. Or, as Wolfhart Heinrichs has observed,

> One might say, albeit with a grain of salt, that it is in the fourth/tenth century that the various fields of intellectual pursuit within Islam come of age. The traditions that had steadily been growing during the preceding two centuries now begin to reflect upon themselves: commentaries, compilations, and handbooks make the available material accessible by clarifying or organizing it, *uṣūl*-works are being written to determine the underlying structure of several disciplines (*fiqh, naḥw, ḥadīth,* possibly *lugha*), the translation movement comes to an end and Islamic philosophy takes off in earnest. The various sciences (*'ulūm* or, with a vaguer term, *funūn* "branches"), thus, become conscious of themselves, their technical terms (*muṣṭalaḥāt*) and their topics (*abwāb*), including their problem sets (*masā'il*), become stabilized to be henceforth handed down through the centuries and thus ensure the identity of each science and the continuity of its tradition. In their totality, the *'ulūm* of the fourth century form a blueprint for the *universitatis litteratum Islamicarum* of all succeeding centuries which, up to the advent of modern times, is not subjected to radical revision.[42]

Within the network of constitutive elements, several strands are particularly remarkable, not only with respect to apprehending the defining sociopolitical and intellectual developments overall (at least for high culture), but also—and especially—with respect to understanding better how certain (if not all) aspects of al-Ma'arrī's life orientation and intellectual progression could have come about as a transparently logical, explicable outcome of place and time; of where he lived (in terms of the larger geography) and the contemporaneous prevailing interests and animating disposition(s). These strands may be said to include most notably the following: (1) informed discussion of theology and closely related topics (e.g., cosmology); (2) philosophy-centered discourse, especially that clearly informed by Greek and Hellenistic sources but as these were mingled with tenets central to Islam (whether normative Sunnī or Shīʿite or nonnormative offshoots); (3) the general learning and etiquette that emerged from and was associated with the more privileged and educated strata of urban Islamicate society; (4) ascetic and Sufistic approaches to Islam; and (5) the elaboration of ritual piety based more squarely on the letter as opposed to the spirit of the religious law. To use the standard corresponding Arabic terminology, the first four elements correspond to, respectively, *kalām*/كلام, *falsafah*/فلسفة, *adab*/أدب, and *taṣawwuf*/تصوف. The development of *al-sharīʿah*/الشريعة (literally "the way"; more specifically, to the religious law) and the parallel concern for its veneration, in the abstract if not as well in the meticulous application in real-life, day-to-day situations, constitute the fifth item. This state of affairs closely parallels the intellectual "compartmentalization" in the *universitatis litteratum Islamicarum* that Wolfhart Heinrichs speaks of: "If we simplify matters . . . we may distinguish between four different ideals of education, or four types of ideally trained men: the *faqīh* 'jurisprudent and religious scholar,' the *adīb* 'man of letters and language scholar,' the *ḥakīm* 'philosopher-scientist,' and the *faqīr* 'mystic.'"[43]

On-going remarkable developments in art, architecture, music, astronomy, astrology, medicine, mathematics, natural science, history, geography, or related intellectual endeavors or life-orientations, and that are not necessarily or readily associated with *adab* or *falsafah* or *kalām* (or whatever the case might be), are no less significant for the full appreciation of the Islamicate civilizational culture into which al-Maʿarrī was born and within the scope of which he flourished. Any standard survey of Arab and Islamic history and civilization would not fail to make mention of these accomplishments, many of the influences or effects of which are still relevant to this day, in both Arab and Islamicate societies and beyond (e.g., European and Euro-American).

However, with respect to al-Maʿarrī's thinking and writing, these fields had less—if indeed any—significant impact. Additionally, to the extent that one or another may have concerned or had some impact on him (which indeed is the case, for example—and as perhaps the most notable example—with respect to his knowledge of the names of the stars and constellations; or, for another example, geography and history, at least in the sense of a demonstrated awareness of the larger physical world around him), this would have resulted more as a natural outgrowth of his dedication to *adab* than a deep interest in the fields in and of themselves. That is to say, for the sake of completeness as an *adīb,* he may have occasionally taken into his purview, albeit relatively superficially compared to the true masters, one or another of these fields (such as, again, knowledge of the stars). The master of *adab* was expected to be capable of conversing and writing intelligently about as broad a spectrum of topics as possible in the arts and sciences; but breadth was accomplished at the expense of depth. If nothing else, or, more accurately perhaps, before all else and least incontrovertibly, al-Maʿarrī was an *adīb*, a master of *adab.*

That said, to close out this section of chapter 2, some of the broader intellectual activities that came to be compartmentalized unto themselves in Arab Islamicate civilization, those likelier to have had influence on al-Maʿarrī (especially as a thinker) to one degree or another, consciously or not, directly or indirectly, will be briefly discussed in terms of their state of development or major currents by the tenth and eleventh centuries CE.[44]

Kalām/كلام

Kalām in Islamicate civilization took shape as a result of contrasting or conflicting interfaith views or disquieting doubts over interpretation of religious doctrine and dogma. As well, based on the record of issues and topics taken up and treatise or monograph titles, to one degree or another, *kalām* gives indication of responding to all of the following: the various non-Islamic confessional orientations of the time (for example, Judaic, Christian, Mazdean, or Manichean; but above all Christian, the leading strand of monotheism at the time of the birth of Islam, and very much in its midst especially in its early years of diffusion); domestic political considerations (especially, for example, the question of whether the Umayyad dynastic rule absolved the rulers inclusive of the caliphs themselves of all excesses on the grounds that humankind's actions are, according to many passages in the Qur'ān, predetermined by God; the question of free will as opposed to absolute predetermination and the moral implications therefrom was one of the earliest points of contention among Muslim thinkers);

and the enduring influences of Greek/Hellenistic philosophy and speculative thought (for example, eastern—i.e., Jacobite or Nestorian-Christian—but above all Alexandrian Hellenistic, especially as represented by the Platonist orientations of (1) Plotinus [d. 270 CE], (2) his Syrian editor and protégé Porphyry [d. 303 CE], and (3) Proclus [d. 485], although also by such pre-Socratics as Pythagoras [d. 495 BCE] and Empedocles [d. 430 BCE].)[45]

Kalām at its outset (e.g., in the seventh and eighth centuries CE) involved argued theories or positions regarding specific theological points, with a resort to dialectics and other methods of rational argumentation (e.g., making comparisons or analogies) and resulting in independent judgment on matters (i.e., the discourse even at its outset represented more than merely a citation of statements—including especially verses from the Qur'ān or *aḥādīth*—as authoritative and conclusive). Over time, *kalām*-driven discourse became highly nuanced, variegated, and voluminous, all in an attempt by the learned specialists in the discourse, the *mutakallimūn*/متكلمون (plural of *mutakallim*), to demonstrate rationally (i.e., by appealing to human reason)—as opposed to asking simply for unequivocal acceptance on the basis of citations of revelation—the truth value of revealed words about God, man, and the world. At the very least, the aim seems to have been to render a transmitted and fixed revelation (the Word of God, which as is must be the truth because He is the Truth, the Real) as compatible as possible with human reason that is inclined to (and does) speculate about things irrespective of Revelation. In Arabic, this is typically thought of as the challenge of being confronted with two sources of knowledge, *al-naql*/النقل (the transmitted [by way of God's Word]) and *al-'aql*/العقل (the mind, intellect, reason), which do not always seem to be in perfect harmony. In simpler terms, although this eventually got lost in the detail, the overriding concern of the *mutakallimūn* was "to show that there was nothing in the Qur'ān which was repugnant to careful reasoning."[46] The complicating detail arose with the *mutakallimūn* because "in the course of disputes with non-Muslims as well as with Muslims . . . they had to decide standards of what should be considered repugnant to reason; this ultimately meant establishing an overall cosmology which they could claim was rational and with which they could show the Qur'ān to be in harmony."[47]

Kalām became a vast field of learning. Henry Austryn Wolfson's masterful canonical overview in *The Philosophy of The Kalam*[48] is over 700 pages long. Nevertheless, writing in the fourteenth century, Ibn Khaldūn, with the benefit of hindsight as well as his characteristic succinct acumen, declared that *kalām* in its considerable entirety consisted essentially of just six basic "articles of faith" (*'aqā'id īmāniyyah*/عقائد إيمانية), namely, belief in (1) God; (2) angels; (3) God's revealed word; (4) God's messengers or apostles (i.e., prophets, those chosen by Him to convey His Word/Law to specific communities, and to lead them); (5) the Last Day; and (6) divine predetermination (*al-qadar*/القدر).[49]

By the late eighth and early ninth centuries CE, on-going *kalām* discussions resulted in the rise of the Muʿtazilah/المعتزلة or "the party (or group) that has seceded (from the other Muslim theological parties, groups, or factions)." The Muʿtazilah loyalists represented the first major self-contained, self-conscious tendency or strand within the broader *kalām* movement with its own distinct tenets (e.g., God's absolute justice; the inevitability of whatever God decrees), the unequivocal embrace of which was the mark of the Muʿtazilī par excellence; it set him off from other *mutakallimūn*. The group had its master thinkers, writers, and disputants; such as Abū al-Hudhayl al-ʿAllāf/أبو الهذيل العلاف (d. 841 or 849 CE); Ibrāhīm al-Naẓẓām/إبراهيم النظام (d. 835 CE); Bishr ibn al-Muʿtamar/بشر بن المعتمر (d. 825 CE); and Thumāmah ibn Ashras/ثمامة بن أشرس (d. 828 CE). The leading personalities were predominantly active in either Basra or Baghdad, with differences of opinion to a greater or lesser degree on some secondary or tertiary matters, depending upon whether one participated in or aligned one's self with the Basra or Baghdad circle or "branch." Abū al-Hudhayl al-ʿAllāf, for example, is associated with the Basra branch, as is Ibrāhīm al-Naẓẓām; whereas Thumāmah ibn Ashras is associated with the Baghdad branch.

The Muʿtazilah of all stripes and regardless of branch were especially associated with five basic principles: God's complete and absolute justice and oneness; the certainty of the punishment He has threatened (for wrong-doing) and the reward He has promised (for doing right); God's commanding only what is right and prohibiting only what is wrong (which by extension humankind is obliged to emulate); and an intermediate position on the status of the grave sinner, i.e., such a sinner, notwithstanding the sins, is still a Muslim, albeit suspended between *īmān*/إيمان or holding to his/her belief in Islam, and *kufr*/كفر or no longer holding belief in Islam; i.e, no longer to be regarded as Muslim.

As a corollary to their belief in God's absolute justice, the Muʿtazilah opposed in particular Jahm ibn Ṣafwān/جهم بن صفوان (d. 745 CE) and his followers, *al-Jabariyyah*/الجبرية, a fairly vocal and vigorous religious faction that preached absolute predeterminism (*al-jabr*/الجبر); that is, they held that there is no such thing as human free will and agency. This of course vitiated the concept of God's justice—not to mention the meaningfulness of one's fulfilling one's duties according to Islam. The Muʿtazilah argued that *reason* dictated human free agency; that humankind is endowed with the ability to recognize right from wrong and to choose one as opposed to the other; that "good and evil are not conventional or arbitrary concepts whose validity is rooted in the dictates of God . . . but are rational categories which can be established through unaided reason."[50]

In order to reconcile human free agency with a Creator God's omnipotence, and, at the same time, not compromise His absolute, unimpeachable justice, some of the Muʿtazilah developed the theory of "generation" (*tawallud*/تولد) so as to explain the connection between cause and effect in the case of the doer or agent of an action and the action that is done. According to this theory, the action "done" is "generated" by the human actor; only in that sense "created" by him/her, not in the sense that the Creator creates (because only He truly creates). In the same vein, it would seem, and perhaps influenced (either indirectly or directly) by early Greek atomism, there was advanced among the Muʿtazilah a metaphysics of (1) indivisible particles (sing. *juz'*/جزء; pl. *ajzā'*/أجزاء; commonly translated into English, in fact (in this context at least) as "atoms"); and (2) accidents (*a'rāḍ*/أعراض), whereby everything other than God was regarded as consisting of the accidents superadded to the indivisible particles/atoms and utterly dependent upon God's will for both coming to be as well as perduring.[51] "Were He . . . to cease creating any accidents in the atom altogether, the atom itself would cease to exist. In this elaborate speculation . . . the Mutakallims are simply seeking to prove their grand theological thesis of God's absolute and exclusive efficacy."[52] The aim was to "show the inability of reason to vindicate the causal nexus and the subsequent necessity of ascribing every act in nature to the direct agency of God."[53]

By the late ninth century CE and thereafter, *kalām* developments came to be dominated not by the Muʿtazilah movement but by the adherents of a theological tendency—al-Ashʿariyyah (الأشعرية)—that owes its name to the theologian Abū al-Ḥasan al-Ashʿarī/أبو الحسن الأشعري of Basra (d. 935). Al-Ashʿarī is reputed to have studied under the direction of al-Jubāʾī/الجبائي (d. 933) of the Basra branch of the Muʿtazilah movement. It is reported that he broke with his master, and in fact with all of the Muʿtazilites, over several key issues, including especially the following: the nature of God's characteristics or attributes predicated of Him in the Qurʾān, which became extremely contentious as an almost inevitable extension of the Muʿtazilite concern for defending God's oneness and singularity (i.e., uniqueness as a being beyond comparison or likeness to anything human); the true extent of God's power and sovereignty, which in turn was bound up with the question of free will, human agency, and moral responsibility; and the explanation for evil in the world alongside the good, which in turn was bound up with the question of God's justice.

Al-Ashʿarī did not entirely repudiate either speculation—that is, using العقل as well as النقل—in matters theological, or (in of themselves) the rationalizing tendencies and methods of the Muʿtazilah, including deductions on the basis of analogies and empiricism.[54] And he could be as critical of the strict literalist opponents to rationalism in theological discussions—for example, those whose literalism with respect to divine attributes mentioned in the Qurʾān was tantamount to assigning unto God human corporeal characteristics—as he was of the Muʿtazilah. But the effect of his efforts, especially once they were taken up in turn by forceful thinkers of succeeding generations who shared his views and methods, led to a noticeable reinvigoration of the sharp critique of theological rationalism (particularly as represented by the Muʿtazilah), foreshadowed most remarkably by the ninth-century CE theologian Aḥmad ibn Ḥanbal/أحمد بن حنبل (d. 855), after whom was developed and institutionalized one of the four approaches (in Arabic, *madhhab*/مذهب) to religious law in Sunnī Islam. In one of his most important works, in a manner that suggests a nod to literalism or exotericism (*al-ẓāhiriyyah*/الظاهرية), al-Ashʿarī rejected rather unambiguously the Muʿtazilah believe in free will and, as a concomitant, the belief that good and evil can be rationally determined.

> [T]here is nothing good or evil on earth, except what God has ordained. We hold that everything is through God's will and . . . that the deeds of the creature are pre-ordained by God, as He said [in the Koran]. We believe that good and evil are the outcome of God's decree and preordination: good or evil, sweet or bitter.[55]

The extreme determinism evoked here, and all that it logically implies with respect to humankind's moral responsibility for their acts, was modulated, apparently somewhat later, by the doctrine known as *kasb*/كسب or acquisition; attributed (e.g., by the theologian al-Juwaynī/الجويني [d. 1085 CE]) to al-Ashʿarī although in his two most important extant works, *al-Ibānah*/الإبانة and *al-Maqālāt*/المقالات, *kasb* isn't mentioned.[56] According to this doctrine, God as sole Creator is the Creator of all action, always and everywhere, eternally. However, the human being acquires the action *morally* by virtue of his/her being the locus of the action. Only to this extent may one speak of human agency, although humans are fully responsible for their acquired actions.

With respect to attributes predicated of God in the Qur'ān (e.g., knowledge, power, speech, sight), although al-Ashʿarī could criticize the conceptualizations of crude anthropomorphism (*tashbīh*/تشبيه) (i.e., he could embrace *tanzīh*/تنزيه or the rejection of any human dimension to God), he could not accept the allegorizing or extreme abstractionism of the Muʿtazilah in this regard (which was their way of *not* denying God's Qur'ān-based predicates while at the same time denying His likeness to anything human), and, with respect to the abstractionism, especially not accept the view that attributes like knowledge and power inhere to God's essence, i.e., that they are one and the same.[57]

The theologian Ibn Ḥanbal (d. 855 CE), in opposing the Muʿtazilah during his lifetime, "taught that the Kuran and *sunna* must be taken in their literal sense, without asking questions, *bilā kaifa.* This rule should be applied to the anthropomorphic expressions in the Kuran, such as the face of Allah, His eyes and hands, His sitting on the throne, and His being seen by the faithful in Paradise."[58] In his own words, at least in *al-Ibānah*, al-Ashʿarī was very much influenced by Ibn Ḥanbal, notwithstanding his (al-Ashʿarī's) accepting at least a qualified version of rational speculation in theology.

> [A]l-Ashʿarī describes his position and method as "adhering to the book of our Lord, to the *sunna* of our Prophet, and to what is handed down on the authority of the Companions, the generation that succeeded them and the masters of *ḥadīth* (these are our binding authorities), and to the views of Abū ʿAbd Allāh Aḥmad ibn Ḥanbal. . . opposing that which opposes him."[59]

Al-Ashʿarī reinvigorated an orientation in theology toward vindicating and relying upon not just God's Word as revealed to the Prophet Muḥammad with the Qur'ān, but also upon the accumulated narrative reporting about the doings and sayings of the Prophet Muḥammad (i.e., the collection of *aḥādīth*), and above all upon taking God's revealed Word as it was literally received. Ideally the believer was expected to accept Qur'ān-based propositions or formulas in the literal or exoteric sense even if the propositions or formulas were not fully understood; to do otherwise, al-Ashʿarī flatly asserted, was forbidden.[60]

Al-Ashʿarī's tendencies in *kalām* over such key topics as free will, atomism, and God's attributes were reinforced, notwithstanding some differences here and there, by virtue of a host of noteworthy *kalām* adepts and expositors over succeeding generations; for example, and most notably, the Basrite Abū Bakr al-Bāqillānī/الباقلاني (d. 1013), the Baghdadī Abū Mansūr ʿAbd al-Qāhir ibn Ṭāhir/أبو منصور عبد القاهر ابن طاهر (a.k.a. ʿAbd al-Qāhir al-Baghdādī; d. 1037), and al-Juwaynī (d. 1085 in Nīshāpūr, but active in Baghdad around 1054 through 1059), all of whom took up with greater elaboration, refinement, and systematization al-Ashʿarī's major theological concerns. Al-Bāqillānī is especially noteworthy (in his *al-Tamhīd*/التمهيد for example) for expanding upon and refining the atomism of al-Ashʿarī and his ninth-century precursors in this regard (e.g., Abū al-Hudhayl and his own teacher al-Jubā'ī), and for revising the theory of acquisition, of great concern also to al-Juwaynī (who disapproved of al-Bāqillānī's revision and therefore offered his own counter-revision). ʿAbd al-Qāhir al-Baghdādī's *Uṣūl al-Dīn*/أصول

الدين (*The Roots of Religion*) is essentially an al-Ashʿarī-inspired treatise. His *al-Farq bayna al-Firaq*/الفرق بين الفرق (*The Difference between the Sects*), typically regarded as an early work in comparative religion, explains, among other things, the ways the various religious orientations *within* the broader Islamic community represented (in the author's eyes) errant or misguided views.

Al-Ashʿarī's influence extended well beyond these notable eleventh-century theologians to include also al-Ghazzālī (al-Ghazālī)/الغزالي (d. 1111), al-Shahrastānī/الشهرستاني (d. 1153), Fakhr al-Dīn al-Rāzī/فخر الدين الرازي (d. 1209), and al-Ījī/الإيجي (d. 1355), all of whom, in addition to al-Ashʿarī and his earlier minions, are to this day subjects of serious study among scholars of theology in Muslim societies.

Falsafah/فلسفة

At one time or another, Greek, Hellenic, Indic, Semitic, and Iranian intellectual lines of development all entered into the complex process that gave rise to philosophy in its Islamic garb. But it is "purely Greek" with respect to its origins.[61] That is to say, its point of departure over the course of the ninth and early tenth centuries was the Greek philosophical texts translated into Arabic (mostly by way of Syriac). Especially influential were the translations of Aristotle or pseudo-Aristotle and as filtered as well through Aristotle's commentators or interpreters (e.g., and especially, Galen with respect to logic, physics, and metaphysics).

> The Islamic *faylasuf* (pl. *falasifah*) received the Writ [of Aristotle] as piously as others before him. It had been worked over for centuries, modified in some areas and enlarged in others, argued, synthesized, and compacted into textbooks. It was an organized and impressive body of learning. By the time of its arrival in Islam the great body of sciences that rested on the bases of logic and was crowned by the "first philosophy," or metaphysics, had come together in a single unified curriculum whose parts were the various "foreign sciences" and whose acknowledged masters were Plato and Aristotle, Galen, Hippocrates, Euclid, and Ptolemy.[62]

Platonism and Aristotelianism became conflated particularly as refracted through Plotinus, Porphyry, and Proclus. The influential *Theology/Athūlūgiyā* [أثولوجيا] *of Aristotle,* a translation by ʿAbd al-Masīḥ ibn Nāʿimah/عبد المسيح بن ناعمة of Ḥimṣ in northern Syria (d. 835 CE), represented a paraphrase of the last three books of the *Enneads* by Plotinus (which in its entirety had been collected and edited by Porphyry); that is, authorship was incorrectly assigned to Aristotle. Another *Theology*, quite likely representing the *Elements of Theology* by Proclus (another leading Platonist redolent of Plotinus with respect to theology; d. 485 CE), as translated into Arabic and associated with Aristotle (referred to by the Scholastics of the thirteenth century with the Latin title of *Liber de Causis),* was not without its influence.

> There thus developed a neo-Platonic interpretation of Aristotelian metaphysics centered upon the doctrine of One and the emanation of the intellect and grades of being from it, a new synthesis which is not found with the same accent . . . in any school of Greek philosophy.[63]

Some of the Muslim philosophers—in what amounts to the grain of salt to which Wolfhart Heinrichs has referred—were extraordinary polymaths (Abū Bakr al-Rāzī/أبو بكر الرازي was also a physician, as was Ibn Sīnā/ابن سينا [Avicenna]; al-Fārābī/الفارابي was also a musicologist); and the most influential (e.g., al-Kindī/الكندي and al-Fārābī, to name but two) were certainly conversant with Greek logic, math, physics, ethics, and politics. In any event, "Plotinus' doctrine of the One and the emanationist manner by which it generates the whole order of being beneath it," specifically as this doctrine was transmitted by the *Theology of Aristotle* (i.e., Ibn Nāʿimah's paraphrase of three books of Plotinus's *Enneads* as redacted by Porphyry), and by Proclus's *Theology* (the Latin title of which became *Liber de Causis*), became "the cornerstone of almost the whole of [premodern] Arab philosophical thought."[64]

Plotinian emanationism alone would have been enough to make the philosophers quite anathema to a *mutakallim* as well as to a *faqīh* religious scholar and jurisprudent. The Creator God of the Qur'ān (16:40) has created the world and everything in it by saying "Be"; that said, it all came "to be." But there was much more to the quest of the philosophers that was cause for alarm among (and placed them at loggerheads with) theologians and religious scholars:

> What *falsafah* added to the accumulating pieces of the Greek sciences was an epistemological claim. It brought forth before the Muslims an alternative theory of wisdom that . . . set down in an inferior position the channel of revelation opened by the Prophet of Islam. As clearly as the Qur'ān itself, the *Posterior Analytics* proposed to tell wherein lay the truth. The *faylasuf* came to Islam bearing a new revelation, and he had necessarily to answer to the old.[65]

What is commonly regarded as the first era of systematic *falsafah* stretches from the ninth through the eleventh centuries CE; in other words, a century before al-Maʿarrī's birth and two centuries that include the years of his birth, maturation, and efflorescence. This period gave rise to the careers of four widely acknowledged seminal philosophers: Abū Yūsuf Yaʿqūb al-Kindī/أبو يوسف يعقوب الكندي (d. 866), Abū Bakr Muḥammad Zakariyyā' al-Rāzī/أبو بكر زكرياء الرازي (d. 925/935), Muḥammad ibn Tarkhān ibn Uzlagh al-Fārābī/محمد بن ترخان بن أزلغ الفارابي (d. 950), and Abū ʿAlī al-Ḥusayn ibn ʿAbd Allāh Ibn Sīnā/أبو علي الحسين عبد الله ابن سينا (d. 1037). Of equal importance during this period were the scholarly epistles of the Brethren of Purity or Sincere Brethren/إخوان الصفاء, the philosophical confraternity that was active as early as the tenth century CE and even more influential in the eleventh.

For the purposes of the present study, an overview of the abovementioned philosophers and the Brethren of Purity need only be relatively brief and concern itself primarily with very broad topics of metaphysical or theological import that constitute a sort of grand world view. Al-Maʿarrī may have touched upon directly or indirectly, explicitly or implicitly, *some* of the issues that the *falāsifah* touched upon (although the latter exhibiting greater technical specificity) when taking into consideration such broad topics as the nature of God, creation, man, the world, and so forth. But he was hardly a *faylasūf* in the strictest sense of the word, neither with respect to learning and method nor (a demonstrated) comprehensive knowledge of basic terms and definitions; and certainly he gives no indication of having been an adept of logic, not to mention the other hard Greek sciences (e.g., physics and math) that the Muslim philosophers proper, the *falāsifah*, so assiduously and expertly cultivated.

Al-Kindī (c. 801–73 CE)

As F. E. Peters has observed, "The [Hellenic] philosopher, whether Greek or Muslim, was an encylopaediast. His range was expected to cover everything from the propaedeutic logic, through the physical and mathematical sciences, to 'first philosophy,' theology or metaphysics."[66] Thus, with respect to al-Kindī, Peters could continue with the following: "All these sciences neatly ordered in their ranks along the path to theology are reflected in Kindi's own immense bibliography. The Mu'tazilite interested himself within the narrow confines of what constituted 'Islamic questions'; al-Kindi inherited an entire curriculum. The upwards of two hundred titles, only a fraction of which are actually preserved, attributed to al-Kindi by his bibliographer cover the ancient curriculum."[67]

Typically regarded as the first genuine systematic *faylasūf*, al-Kindī was nonetheless as much a theologian (with Muʿtazilite leanings) as he was *faylasūf*. Some of the titles attributed to him from among his many unrecovered works show a preoccupation with God's unity and justice, with free will, and with the denunciation of dualism and atheism (which would seem to indicate the extent to which these two tendencies were commonplace in the Islamic commonwealth of the ninth century CE). "[His] work indeed should be placed in the mainstream of the theological ideas we associate with the Muʿtazilah."[68] He upheld the Qur'ānic view of a Creator God who creates the world out of nothing (*ex nihilo*) (i.e., he was not an emanationist), the resurrection of the body, the finiteness of the world, and the truthfulness of prophetic revelation that encapsulates something other than the truth that philosophers seek. Prophetic wisdom is moreover superior to philosophical wisdom inasmuch as prophets are endowed with a representative or depictive (*muṣawwirah*/مصورة) faculty "developed to an extraordinary degree and conferred on the prophets as a divine favor."[69] Rational arguments, moreover, can demonstrate the truths of the Prophet Muḥammad, although to appreciate this one is sometimes required to go beyond merely the more exoteric, literal sense of passages of Qur'ānic revelation. Al-Kindī gives a basically Aristotelian definition of metaphysics in his *On First Philosophy,* which becomes his "divine science." "First Philosophy" is defined as metaphysics, a knowledge of the immaterial and immutable that explains the existence of objects and the "why?" or final purpose of their existence. Above all else, it is the knowledge of the first principle or cause of all things, which is the True One, the Eternal pure Being, necessary and uncaused, without predication. This is "being . . . *per se*, it cannot possibly cease to be, nor change into a more perfect being . . . or into a less perfect being. . . . Being necessarily perfect, it is in a state of permanent excellence."[70] Since it is not physical, it is beyond time and motion and space.

Advancing arguments for the illogic of the actual infinite with respect to a body (and thus with respect to bodily attributes such as motion and time, the latter being a measure of motion)[71]—which is to say that bodies have a specific beginning and end, a circumscribed or determinate temporality—al-Kindī makes the rational/logical argument for the existence of God on the basis of a necessary beginning and end, a determinate temporality (*ḥudūth*/حدوث) of the world, which can thus be said to be *muḥdath*/محدَث (generated or caused to appear in time) and therefore perforce having a *muḥdith*/محدِث or the One/the Agent who causes or generates it (the world) as a temporally determinate body (i.e., one with a beginning and end). For al-Kindī, this creative act by the creative One/creative Agent is out of no thing, nothing. "Contrary to Aristotle, al-Kindī consistently upheld the theory of creation out of nothing (*creatio ex nihilo*). God is the one, the Creator out of nothing (*al-mubdi'* [المبدع]) who maintains in existence what he has created out of nothing. He uses the word *ibdā'* [إبداع], unlike later philosophers [in Islam], to denote creation in time out of nothing."[72]

As Creator *ex nihilo*, the First Being, the ultimate Cause of everything, God is superior to all other created things and thus incomparable to these things. Cognition cannot be assigned God because cognition suggests mutability and motion (the self/soul being moved) and furthermore plurality (in embracing all universals). Therefore, God is not Reason or Intellect. Neither is He Soul. He is not the author of everything in the sense suggested by the neo-Platonic emanationists. He is an Agent (*fa''āl*/فعّال) of act (*fi'l*/فعل). He first brings forth being—out of no thing; out of nothingness—as an action. In this sense He is the ultimate cause of everything. Only He and no other is the author of actions in this sense; "creatures are sometimes referred to as agents," but "in reality they are mere recipients of the impact of God's sovereign action, who then pass it on successively."[73]

Causality in this sense—which is to say, secondary to that which is ultimate/primary—is admitted into al-Kindī's scheme of being. God is the ultimate cause of everything, but the proximate cause inheres in the outermost "sphere" of heaven, which is living and sentient and causes generation and corruption in the sublunar world. Heavenly bodies, which are animate and sentient and eternal, not only influence human character but also exercise supervision over earthly affairs as part of "the universal order and beauty of the whole creation,"[74] with humankind as a reflection of the order, harmony, and intelligence in God's creation. There is a certain amount of naturalism in this scheme of things, but ultimately determinism as well, although al-Kindī's Creator God, who superintends all of being and is all-knowing, all-powerful, and all-wise, orders and maintains the universe in intelligent, orderly, righteous fashion.

Soul for al-Kindī is described in neo-Platonic terms. It is an "entity" with "substance," but the substance is very fine, "analogous to the Creator's own substance, just as the light of the sun is analogous to the sun."[75] The soul is divine substance inasmuch as it derives from something analogous to God's substance. Its conjunction with body is accidental and temporary. It eventually leaves the body at the body's death and departs for the higher world of intelligibles. While cojoined with body, the soul (or more precisely, the rational faculty thereof) perpetually strives to restrain the urges of body. Passionate and vegetative (or nourishing) faculties are also part of the soul. They can, and do, tempt the body to commit foul deeds. The rational faculty of the soul must restrain them so that the soul overall can be rightly guided.

The soul once released from the human body may not immediately join the higher world (the world of intelligibles) wherein lies divine favor and illumination. Only the pure souls will be allowed to ascend directly and immediately to the higher world. Impure souls ascend only by way of moving through the spheres (starting with the lowest, the moon) where they tarry until purified in stages over time. Only when purified are they be able to enter the higher world of intelligibles.

In dealing with human cognition or knowledge, al-Kindī indirectly admits of a special knowledge superior to that of ordinary human thought processes; namely "prophetic knowledge, reserved by God for his chosen emissaries or apostles, who can dispense altogether with the human process of rationalization and partake directly of a supernatural light, which God imparts to whomsoever he pleases."[76] No ordinary human knowledge can rise to this level. Knowledge from revelation is superior to knowledge achieved through the ordinary processes of human intellection. Even philosophy, therefore, should be subordinated to, and in the service of, revelation.

Al-Rāzī (d. 935 CE)

Al-Rāzī was a physician (medical doctor) as well as a metaphysician; in fact, in his lifetime, he headed two hospitals, one in Rayy in Khurāsān (where he was born) and one in Baghdad. And his major medical work (*al-Hāwī*/الهاوي), a compendium of medicine, was in its Latin translation (1279 CE) consulted in European medical circles for close to three centuries. It was as a metaphysician, however, that he is best remembered in the Islamic historical sources—but also reviled as "an archheretic . . . who drank from every tainted spring emptying into Islam."[77] The "tainted springs" are variously associated with Manicheanism, Brahmanism, Pythagoreanism, Platonism, and the Sabians of Ḥarrān; and although one or several or all of these systems of thought may have provided general inspiration (as well as specificities), Platonism alone may have sufficed; more specifically, the trajectory of *Timaeus,* which al-Rāzī is reported to have written a commentary on.[78]

Al-Rāzī's cosmology involved five principles, all eternal: Matter, Place (Space), Time, Soul, and Creator God (al-Bāri' [البارى]). The Creator God creates, but hardly *ex nihilo,* and, therefore, "in an eternal time" since Matter is co-eternal with the Creator God. Soul—alive but at first without knowledge—became infatuated with Matter and wished to unite with it, but it (Soul) could not achieve the union because alone it was incapable of bringing about form from Matter. The Creator God's help was needed. "God was compelled to come to its assistance and to create this world, with its material forms, in order to enable the Soul to satisfy its vile urge to partake of material pleasures for a while. In the same manner, God created man and imparted Reason to him from 'the essence of His divinity,' so that Reason might eventually rouse the Soul from its earthly in man's body and remind it of its genuine destiny as a citizen of the higher (intelligible) world and of its duty to seek that world through the study of philosophy."[79] In other words, salvation for individual human souls (which are merely distributions of eternal Soul into human bodies when that Soul sought to be united to formed matter) comes about when souls in humans rid themselves of the attachment to the material bodies in the sublunar world and join the higher world of intelligibles.

Al-Rāzī believed in the transmigration/translocation of the soul, even to the extent of animal souls transmigrating/translocating to "superior bodies" (e.g., human)—and hence moving up the ladder of purification—upon the death of animals (which fact he cited as the best justification for the killing of animals, especially domestic).[80] He rejected revelation and prophecy. Humans are endowed by their Creator with Reason; Reason leads to the truth; prophets are unnecessary. Moreover, prophets have been the cause of strife. According to F. E. Peters "[Al-Rāzī] was unique [in pre-modern Islamicate philosophical thought] in announcing that revelation had no truths and that those who claimed to be prophets were in fact mere impostors. Plato was the only prophet and his revelation was *falsafah*."[81]

At the same time, as Peters has also insightfully pointed out, al-Rāzī's Platonism in one most crucial regard is not that which was so influential on other Muslim Platonists, which is to say the Platonism that was filtered through Plotinus or Proclus and pseudo-Aristotle. "Instead of a single transcendent and spiritual cause Razi posited five eternal coprinciples which are substantial hypostases but not emanations from a unique First Cause."[82]

Al-Fārābī (d. 950)

Al-Fārābī was an eminent logician as well as physicist, metaphysician, political philosopher, and musicologist. In his *Book of Letters* that was informed by Aristotle's *Metaphysics*, among the three divisions he assigns to metaphysics is that which concerns itself with the immaterial culminating in the "perfect being, nothing more perfect than which can exist."[83] This perfect being is elaborated upon in al-Fārābī's *Principles of the Opinions of the Inhabitants of the Virtuous City*, his most renowned work, which contains definitive views on politics as well as metaphysics. The perfect being is First Cause of all else that exists. He is eternal, perfect, and His only purpose is to be, to perdure. He is both intellect in act and the object of that intellection, or thought thinking about itself (which is pure thought). He emanates because of his surfeit of goodness, and through His emanation everything else in the phenomenal world exists, is. Inasmuch as He is nothing but Being, everything else that is, is by way of extension of His Being. The first emanation to come forth in a series of emanations that ultimately allows for the being of life here on earth, is the first intellect. In recognizing the First Cause/Being (from which it is emanated), the first intellect brings forth a second intellect; in recognizing itself, the first intellect leads to the coming-to-be of Soul and body (Matter) and the outermost heaven. Emanations of this sort continue, in descending order of perfection, with separate intellects and heavenly bodies in their own spheres, from Saturn to Jupiter to Mars to the Sun to Venus to Mercury, and finally to the Moon. There are ten intellects all told. The tenth superintends the sublunar world, wherein life evolves or is generated from matter according to the process of generation and corruption. Divine intelligence trickles down, diffusing through the series of intellects and eventually reaching human intelligence. At the tenth intellect level, human intelligence is capable of being "illuminated" by the downward descending divine intelligence. The tenth intellect is the Active Intellect (of Aristotle). By virtue of contact (*ittiṣāl*/اتصال) with this, humans can reach the highest level of cognition possible for them.

Prophets as well as philosophers know what they know by way of contact with the Active Intellect, which allows for intelligibles to be activated and thereby constitute Acquired Intellect. Philosophers' knowledge derives from well-developed intelligence; their contact with the Active Intellect leads to Acquired Intellect obtaining intelligible forms directly, just as they are. It is by way of imaginative powers, albeit extraordinary ones, that prophets make contact with the Active Intellect. In revelation they reformulate the intelligibles in language that ordinary people can more readily understand, language that includes, for example, symbols and metaphors. The reformulation of intelligibles in this manner becomes the stuff for laws that are in the best interests of society and ordinary mortals. Prophetic knowledge thus is basically quite human; i.e., it can be explained rationally in terms of the dynamic of human cognition overall (by which al-Fārābī, deliberately or not, is allowing for one's taking philosophical knowledge to be at least the equal of prophetic knowledge *in terms of the acquisition of intelligibles*). For humans other than prophets, philosophy best embodies wisdom; and it is wisdom (*ḥikmah*/حكمة) which often connotes the wisdom associated with philosophy; *ḥakīm*/حكيم in Arabic can mean wise man or philosopher) that humans should try to acquire in order to fulfill their highest potential.

It is the rational faculty of the human soul (as opposed to the nutritive and passionate; al-Fārābī follows the standard neo-Platonic tripartite constitution with respect to the soul's faculties) that desires happiness. The highest degree of happiness for humans occurs when the soul leaves the body upon body's death and moves to join the world of intelligibles. But the degree to which the migrated, body-less human soul finds happiness depends upon the soul's proclivities while cojoined with body in the lower world. Virtuous souls whose rational faculty keeps the nutritive and passionate faculties in check, so that crude carnal pleasures are eschewed, can hope for higher degrees of happiness in the nether world of intellibles. Nonvirtuous souls, since the bodies to which they are bound in the lower world indulge in fulfillment of sensual pleasures, will never be able to partake of the happiness that can be attained by the virtuous souls because they will never be freed from being bound to matter, either in human or nonhuman form. Rather, they "will appear in one material condition, then another, either endlessly, if they are fated to be reincarnated in human form, or until such time as they have degenerated by degrees to the bestial level, whereupon they would simply perish."[84]

Humans at the same time desire happiness here on earth, and humans are communal by nature. Thus, happiness on earth entails, indeed requires, the formation of societies; in other words, city-states. But it is only the virtuous city-state that allows for the development of virtuous souls, and the virtuous city-state among other things requires both revealed (religious) prophetic wisdom and philosophical wisdom. Ideally, this is provided in one and the same person as head of the city-state, the philosopher-prophet, who assures through his person that the truths of speculative knowledge as well as the truths of religion can and should coexist, with the latter being embodied in the former, although the latter figuratively and symbolically expresses the truths of the former.

Ibn Sīnā

Ibn Sīnā acknowledged his assiduous study of al-Fārābī, especially his metaphysics. Thus, his views on God, man, soul, world, and cosmos have strong resemblances to al-Fārābī's thinking, excluding the realm of politics, which Ibn Sīnā did not take up to any appreciable degree.

In addressing the nature of being/existence (*wujūd*/وجود), which he took as the principle subject of metaphysics, Ibn Sīnā distinguished between necessary being/existence and contingent being/existence. The contingent needs a dependent cause, and a series of contingencies must by necessity have an end point or terminus after which there is no other entity in the series (i.e., said end point or terminus is a cause beyond which there is no other cause), because an infinite regress of contingencies is irrational; if there is no end to a contingent series it is not actually contingent. The world is contingent; its nonexistence can be grasped, and there is in it observable generable and corruptible entities. The world, therefore, requires a causative agent beyond which there is no other causative agent; such causative agent is necessary, in other words. This cause is the First Cause and thus simultaneously First Being, the ultimate cause of all existing things, whom Ibn Sīnā equates with God (although here there is somewhat of a leap of faith; God for Ibn Sīnā—who was a Muslim—was an *a priori* something; it already existed in his mind).

The world issues forth or emanates from the Necessary Being Who is also eternal; the world is not a temporarily determined creation out of nothing. The emanation is due to the surfeit of the Necessary Being's generosity in contemplating Himself, and the emanation gives rise to First Intellect, which in thinking about itself gives rise to the Second Intellect and Soul (Soul is not preexistent), which in this instance is soul first and foremost of the outermost heaven. In a similar fashion, and in consonance for the most part with al-Fārābī's neo-Platonism, for Ibn Sīnā, all of the remaining intellects, with their corresponding souls and spheres, numbering ten in total, emanate or issue forth, in descending order of perfection in terms of intellection. The series ends with the tenth intellect, abode of the Active Intellect beneath which is the terrestrial world. Ibn Sīnā identifies specific angels with the intellects (and also with the heavenly bodies). They are spirits possessing both intellect and will and "ontological intermediaries between God and lesser orders of being . . . , executors of High God's providence."[85]

The First Cause is pure Being; only Being is His essence. His Being consists of pure intelligence or thought thinking only (His own) thought. He cannot be imagined as having position or time or equal or even likeness (but neither can He be demonstrated with "apodeictic proof"[86]). Because He is pure thought, His thinking is the ultimate origin/cause of all contingencies in the world, which in the terrestrial world consists of observable generable and corruptible entities that give form from matter—once matter is predisposed to become form because of the principles of motion and growth in the world that proceed from the locomotive processes of the heavenly bodies.

As was the case with the psychology of al-Fārābī, that of Ibn Sīnā was well-developed and with wide implications for metaphysics, cosmology, and cognition including that of prophets (i.e., revelation). The rational faculty of the soul—as opposed to the "animal" (i.e., that which gives rise to lust and passion) or vegetative (i.e., that which superintends nutrition)—is the highest level of the soul's development. The rational soul includes a theoretical component. Through it, universal intelligibles are grasped, as when contact is made with the Active Intellect that leads to Acquired Intellect. This amounts to the perfection of humans and the destiny truly intended for them.

Ibn Sīnā does not deny bodily resurrection, on the basis of the teachings of his faith's Revelation (the Qur'ān). But his doctrines on soul would seem to undercut that. The greater the soul's exercise of its rational faculty and the acquisition of intelligibles while conjoined to body, the sooner after its absolute release from body (upon death) it can be absorbed into the world of eternal ethereal intelligibles that are absolute good and beauty. In other words, the more that the soul while conjoined to body exercises appetitive and animal faculties over and against the rational, the longer the wait after release from body (upon death) before the soul can be integrated into the world of intelligibles. Souls after death may continue to long for pleasures associated with body, that is, physical pleasures. To this extent, they will suffer after death, although not permanently. Eventually, the soul in this state can be purged of all associations with body and allowed admission to the world of intelligibles and with that attain absolute and true happiness.

A soul's acquisition of intelligibles is more readily and perfectly accomplished by humans who have a special rational power, that which Ibn Sīnā refers to as Holy Reason/Intellection. This is "a divine favor for the very few."[87] Philosophers as well as prophets have Holy Reason. It allows for contact with Active Intellect that leads to an instantaneous intuitive apprehension of universals without the need for the normal human reasoning processes (e.g., those depending on logical reasoning). Prophecy (revelation) comes about in this manner. Prophets can also have "contact" with celestial souls and acquire knowledge even of particulars. But whereas philosophers convey their knowledge/truths by way of intelligibles *qua* intelligibles, prophets use their special imaginative faculty to convey their knowledge/truths; they convey their truths by way of symbols or images, which resonate more completely and effectively among ordinary humans.

In treatises employing more figurative language, particularly allegorical (e.g., *Ode on the Soul*; *The Bird*), Ibn Sīnā expanded upon his more strictly formal philosophical speculations on God, man, soul, and world, emphasizing especially that human souls long to be freed from the material world that comes about through attachment to body. Human souls long to apprehend the ultimate truth/reality of the world, which involves a beatific vision of the Divine. Love of the Divine (God) and a metaphysics of light evolved from this. The soul's perfection entails passionate love (*'ishq*/عشق) of God. He has a luminous brilliance that nearly blinds those as they attempt to apprehend Him. God becomes nearly synonymous with beauty. The soul that develops passionate love of Him therefore naturally seeks consummation of the love through spiritual union with Him.

The Brethren of Purity or Sincere Brethren (إخوان الصفاء)

The Brethren of Purity or Sincere Brethren comprised a quasi-secretive intellectual society, replete with initiatory rites and grades of ascendancy, that first took shape in Basra, Iraq, but later attracted adherents in the surrounding districts of the Islamic commonwealth including as far off as the predominantly Islamic regions of the Spanish peninsula (al-Andalus). The society was bound up with Isma'īlī Shī'ī religio-political thinking and Ismā'īlī missionary activity, particularly with respect to one of the more fundamental methods of Ismā'īlī thinkers overall, namely, esotericism or the search for the deeper, more authentic truths that they believed lay behind revelation as literally expressed. The fifty-one extant epistles of the Brethren, compiled over the tenth century CE, represent an overview of the philosophy, politics, and science of their society. Mathematics and numbers were given great attention because of a self-confessed affinity for Pythagoreanism. The Brethren proclaimed that they embraced all sciences, books, and religions because the world view of their society or association, their "creed," "encompasses all the others. . . . This creed is the consideration of all existing things, both sensible and intelligible . . . from beginning to end . . . in so far as they all derive from a single principle, a single cause, a single world, and a single Soul."[88] The Brethren drew on Indian, Hellenic, Iranian, and Judeo-Christian strands of thought, committed as they were, as just indicated, to a monistic oneness of truth. They considered that differences in religion result from "accidentals" such as place and time and race but that these differences in religion do not vitiate the oneness of truth.

In Pythagorean fashion, numbers for the Brethren were imbued with esoteric metaphysical significance revealing the deeper understanding of God and the world. The number 4 was especially significant in this regard. It represents the four realities undergirding the world: Creator, universal intellect/reason, universal soul, and simple prime matter. God (Creator) in His oneness is the first principle behind all existing entities, analogous in the science of numbers to 1, which is the beginning and source for all other numbers. The entire physical world emanates from God through the intermediary agency of reason and soul, creations of God that reside in the heavenly spheres. Reason is given a luminous quality, and it is from this light that soul is brought into existence. In the terrestrial world, prime matter is the stuff out of which existing entities are given form by virtue of the creative agencies of reason and soul.

Numbers adhere even to the human soul. Thus, one's understanding numerical properties helps one understand the soul, and in knowing the soul better one knows God better. Knowledge of God is the highest level of knowledge that humankind can have. The soul can be refined and purified through philosophy. In this manner there is the potential for the soul ultimately to learn that its true destiny is spirit, rid of material (corporeal) affinities, in an original spiritual domicile—that of the intelligibles in the higher world. The ascent thereto can only be achieved when the soul is purified through philosophical wisdom (if not purified, the soul will return to body and remain imprisoned there, tormented by the pains attendant upon the world of generation and corruption). Muḥammad and Pythagoras are credited with affirming this truth as well as Hermes, Aristotle, and Jesus Christ.

Hence, there is a common truth, or unity of truth, irrespective of religious or philosophical groundings. There is a difference, however, in the manner of conveying the truth. Philosophy allows one to get to the deeper meaning of revelation, the esoteric meaning as opposed to the exoteric. The exoteric is the end point of comprehension for common folk, but in fact it is defective, imperfect. True understanding of revelation requires that many revealed pronouncements need to be understood allegorically. Although even allegorical interpretations have their limits. Human intellection, even that which is refined by way of the study of philosophy, simply cannot grasp certain things; God's essence and the origin of the universe, for example. In instances of this nature, one must accept prophetic revelations, which after all are God-given inspirations.

The unity of truth advanced by the tolerant and ecumenical Brethren was rejected by two of the more illustrious and influential thinkers at around the time of the Brethren's full flowering, who were familiar with the society's religio-philosophical orientation: the philosopher Abū Sulaymān al-Sijistānī/أبو سليمان السجستاني (d. 1000 CE) and his minion Abū Ḥayyān al-Tawḥīdī/أبو حيان التوحيدي (d. 1024 CE) who although not a trained *faylasūf* kept abreast of the philosophical discussions of his day, many of which were dutifully recorded in his *al-Imtāʿ wa al-Muʾānasah*/الإمتاع

والمؤانسة (*The Book of Entertainment and Conviviality,* which notwithstanding the title was also intended as serious edification). Al-Tawḥīdī as well as al-Sijistānī held that religion was one thing, and philosophy, something else. The two could not be reconciled. Religion is a matter of belief, specifically, in what is laid down in divinely revealed scripture. Philosophy is based on reason, on logic.

Taṣawwuf/تصوف

The first Muslims to be associated retroactively with the rubric *taṣawwuf*/تصوف or the notion of adopting the life orientation of a Ṣūfī/صوفي (Sufi in its most common English rendering) drew their inspiration primarily from the scrupulous piety and otherworldliness of the Prophet Muḥammad and his early close associates, including especially the first four caliphs, all of whom traditional sources regard as being especially pious and abstemious. Focusing one's thoughts on God, prayer, and similar such religious obligations, while at the same time eschewing worldly pleasures and comforts, were the hallmarks of early *taṣawwuf*; which can be said to have begun to coalesce as a particular approach to piety in Islam, setting it off from others to a greater or lesser degree, as early as the seventh century CE. Originally a minoritarian movement with roots in lower Mesopotamia (especially Basra), by the end of the tenth century CE it was widespread throughout the Islamic commonwealth, and there was superadded to its embrace of rather simple and straightforward piety and world-renunciation a metaphysics, cosmology, and psychology as well as systematized praxis. It also had its pantheon of celebrated theoreticians, chroniclers, biographers, and individuals regarded as having so exemplified the Sufi ideal that they were to be given the special designation of *awliyā' Allāh*/أولياء الله, "those close to, and following, God" (often rendered in English-language source materials on Sufism as "the friends of God").

In the chain of authentication that was eventually established for *taṣawwuf*, the early piety joined with asceticism and world renunciation (to the extent that the world is to be hated, even, particularly since God himself "has created nothing more hateful to Him than this world"[89]) are associated with the postprophetic, post–first four caliphs era, and more specifically with Ḥasan al-Baṣrī حسن البصري (d. 728 CE). One of his disciples, Rabī'ah al-'Adawiyyah/ربيعة العدوية (d. 801 CE), became more memorable for intense yearning for God out of overwhelming love, a feature that subsequent to Rabī'ah would remain central to *taṣawwuf.* With her also are the early glimmers of *fanā'*/فناء or the doctrine of psychically transcending the phenomenological world and totally effacing or annihilating one's self or ego and existing only "in" God, that is, achieving psychical transubstantiation that amounts to being merely one with God's Oneness, being with His Being that is all Being. The doctrine of *fanā'* would become more fully developed by the Persian Abū Yazīd Bisṭāmī/أبو يزيد بسطامي (d. 875), who went so far as to proclaim that with the annihilation of human self (i.e., self-identity) and existing only in God, human self became one with God in the sense of in-dwelling as the result of the culmination of divinization. An extension of this logic led Bisṭāmī to become known for ecstatic outbursts of self-glorification (as the Divine by virtue of being one with Him), which at the literal level could only suggest blasphemy and antinomianism, trajectories in fact already adopted by the Malāmātiyyah/ملاماتية (The Blameworthy) strand of *taṣawwuf* in Khurāsān under the influence of Bishr ibn al-Ḥārith al-Ḥāfī/بشر بن الحارث الحافي (d. 841), who promoted radical indifference to outward manifestations of religious rectitude. Bishr was at the same time a pronounced pessimist.

Abū al-Qāsim al-Junayd/أبو القاسم الجنيد (d. 910 CE), within the context of *taṣawwuf* that for him meant especially the notion that "God should cause thee to die from thyself and to live in Him,"[90] elaborated upon *fanā'* as well as *tawḥīd* and Being. Al-Junayd (Iranian by birth but domiciled in Baghdad) was "the undisputed master of the Sufis of Baghdad . . .; the representatives of divergent . . . schools and modes of thought could refer to him as their master, so that the initiation chains of of later Sufi orders almost invariably go back to him."[91] For al-Junayd, dying from self (i.e., from self-identity, self-recognition) is equated with *fanā'*, and *fanā'* leads to what he terms *baqā'*/بقاء (perduring or continuing in God). *Fanā'* does not not mean for him, however, that one can truly transcend one's existence; in leading to *baqā'*, *fanā'* also returns one to existence although one's identity as an individual simultaneously becomes "transmuted and eternalized through God and in God."[92] *Baqā'* should be the ultimate objective of the

Sufi. Al-Junayd also taught that God "covenanted" with humans when they did not actually exist other than in Him as spirit; later He willed their formal individual existence, which came about as "the outpouring of His own Being."[93] Thus, the soul's ardent longing for God. It longs to return to it its original place of origin.

A generation before al-Junayd, the Iraqi al-Muḥāsibī/المحاسبي (d. 857) as a Sufi theoretician stressed the importance of rigorous soul-searching on the part of the Sufi, this for the purpose of purifying the self. This entailed "a personal 'holy war' against the passions with the intent not of extirpating them but of bringing them under control." Also, in upholding the Qur'ān and *sunnah*, intent was all important for al-Muḥāsibī: "[T]his focusing upon the morality of intention was the foundation stone upon which a true Islamic conscience could be built."[94] A contemporary of al-Muḥāsibī, the Egyptian Dhū al-Nūn al-Miṣrī/ذو النون المصري (d. 859 CE), introduced a gnostic dimension (*ma'rifah*/معرفة) to *taṣawwuf*, that is, a knowledge that comes about intuitively and not through systematic formal study and reflection. Hence, he who has معرفة (i.e., the *'ārif*/العارف) can "see without knowledge, without sight, without information received, and without observation." The gnostics "are not themselves . . . in so far as they exist at all they exist in God."[95]

Al-Tirmidhī/الترمذي (d. ca. 932 CE), who studied in Balkh (northern Afghanistan) before taking up residence in Iraq and eventually Mecca, made the importance of gnosis even more explicit in his theoretical writings on *taṣawwuf*. His gnosis also became bound up with a metaphysics of light and cosmology connected with the idea of al-Awliyā' or those Close to God. The gnosis of the Awliyā'—an "experiencing" of God—allows them a special, privileged illuminated understanding of the Divine. There is a hierarchy of the Awliyā' that corresponds to the level of gnosis and illumination attained. All of the Awliyā' assist in maintaining order in the world, but at the top of the hierarchy is situated one referred to with the honorific nomenclature of "pole"/قطب. And just as Muḥammad's prophecy was the final in a series of prophecies, the "seal" to all previous prophets, the "pole" of the Awliyā' is the "seal" on the subordinate ranks or grades of the Awliyā'. By the eleventh century, the theory of the special spiritual status of the Awliyā' was so central to *taṣawwuf* that the Persian chronicler al-Hujwīrī/الهجويري (d. 1071) could write that "the principle and foundation of Sufism and knowledge of God rest on saintship [i.e., on the notion of *al-awliyā'*]."[96] In time, there would evolve from the metaphysics of light the notion of Muḥammadan Light or the Muḥammad of Light, who preceded the existence of the Muḥammad of flesh and blood, the mortal who lived and died on earth as a historical reality. The Awliyā' by virture of their gnosis could share in the primordial Muḥammadan Light, virtually as "beneficiaries of ongoing revelation."[97]

Al-Ḥallāj/الحلاج, the Iranian-born Sufi executed in Baghdad (922 CE) for his beliefs and practices, like Bisṭāmī embraced the doctrine of *fanā'*, although an even more extreme version, suggesting that it led to a true man-in-God dwelling, a true unification (albeit not corporeally with respect to the two essences involved, the human and the divine). This was most notoriously exemplified in his remark "If ye do not recognize God, at least recognize His signs. I am that sign, I am the Creative Truth (*ana'l-ḥaqq*) [أنا الحق], because through the Truth I am truth eternally,"[98] *al-ḥaqq* being one of God's ninety-nine attributes according to Islam. This frenzied strand of *taṣawwuf* would continue in certain quarters, as would the antinomianism of the sort that can be traced back at least as far as Abū Yazīd Bisṭāmī (indeed the Khurāsānian Abū Sa'īd ibn Abī al-Khayr/أبو سعيد بن أبي الخير, who died in 1049 CE, was renowned for his antinomianism, allegedly once boasting, for example, that he gave no thought to performing the pilgrimage to Mecca because the Ka'bah was merely a house of stone, and, furthermore, *it* virtually performed the pilgrimage to *him*, so perfectly spiritually illuminated he was[99]). Nonetheless, by the end of the eleventh century CE, the extreme antinomian and frenzied strand of *taṣawwuf* was overshadowed by the more sober approaches that were less anathema to mainstream Islamic piety as professed by the upholders of the exoteric understanding of the Qur'ān and the *aḥādīth, sunnah*, and *sharī'ah*. *Taṣawwuf* in its more sober manifestations came to be regarded as one of the "Islamic sciences." Even Abū Sa'īd ibn Abī al-Khayr composed impassioned but otherwise rather chaste expressions of love of God, which along with similar such literature (in Persian) by 'Abdallāh-i Anṣārī of Herat/عبد الله أنصاري (d. 1089) became "the prototype of all devotional literature in Persian Sufism."[100] Finally, the consummate theoretician Abū al-Qāsim al-Qushayrī/القشيري (of Nīshāpūr; d. 1072 CE), in his *Epistle* on *taṣawwuf* was influential in distancing the movement from antinomianism and keeping it closer to the more widely acceptable fundaments of Islamic piety, an effort more perfectly realized by the theologian al-Ghazzālī (d. 1111), although both of these men were anticipated to an extent by Ibn Baṭṭah/ابن بطة as early as the late tenth century CE. Ibn Baṭṭah as a legal scholar (of Ḥanbalī persuasion) proclaimed that world renunciation was perfectly acceptable for Muslims, but otherwise the *Sharī'ah* had to be observed by the Muslim faithful, and the frenzied form of *taṣawwuf,* especially if entailing trance-like swooning when recollecting God, or a perceived vision of union with God, was impermissible.[101]

Sharī'ah-Driven Ritual Piety/*Ahl al-Sunnah wa al-Jamā'ah*/أهل السنة والجماعة

The impetus for the new social and political order embodied in the establishment of the Islamic commonwealth was God's revelation to the Prophet Muḥammad, the Qur'ān. Eventually, this revelation was put down in writing in a standardized redaction. To the conscientious, meticulously observant Muslims, their faith meant first and foremost commitment to the message of the Qur'ān. Relating this message to the practical concerns or needs of day-to-day living, especially as the Islamic commonwealth grew into an ever larger and more complex sociopolitical entity, called for the formulation of a common body of law and customs, more detailed and situation-specific, which outlined "the way" by which pious Muslims could be said to regulate or observe correctly—that is, quintessentially Islamically—their lives. In order to work toward this desideratum, the learned pious from within the community resorted to citing reports (the *aḥādīth*) of the Prophet Muḥammad's sayings and doings in his lifetime. This helped to bring the Qur'ān to bear on practical specifics. *Aḥādīth* coupled with revelation became the basis for a detailed exposition of correct Islamic comportment in virtually every human situation imaginable, individually and collectively. This correct way of bringing to bear on the mundane world God's revealed word came to be known as "the way" (the literal meaning of the Arabic *al-sharī'ah*/الشريعة). Inasmuch as veneration of the words of the Qur'ān lay at the center of this concern—although along with (second only to the Qur'ān in sanctity) the veneration of the Prophet's *sunnah*—there was engendered among the pious learned a keen concern for studies in grammar, lexicography, the life of the Prophet, and gathering *aḥādīth* and establishing their authenticity and degree of importance.

Within the broader contours of the Islamic ideal—for example, belief in the Prophet Muḥammad's mission; belief in resurrection and divine reward and punishment—a *Sharī'ah*-driven view of life evolved, an awareness of a specifically Islamic world view and way of ordering and living one's life, spelled out by the religious scholars drawing upon what soon became recognized as the "foundations" or "roots" (*uṣūl*/أصول) of the mastery of the *Sharī'ah*: the Qur'ān, the *sunnah* of the Prophet (which is expressed by *aḥādīth*), use of analogy (*qiyās*/قياس) when the Qur'ān and *sunnah* cannot provide clear-cut principles or directives, and consensus (*ijmā'*/إجماع), especially of the religious scholars but also not without regard for consensus of the community of believers as a whole.

The evolution of the *Sharī'ah,* from loose and disparate pronouncements (at times representing merely freely expressed individual points of view) into something much more systematic with a transparent modus operandi and body of canonical rulings, was a gradual process. However, by the end of the ninth century CE, the process culminated in four recognizable "ways of proceeding" (i.e., approaches) (*madhāhib*; sing. *madhhab*/مذهب ؛ مذاهب) to addressing legal questions or problems, with each approach associated with a specific, revered theoretician, including most significantly al-Shāfi'ī/الشافعي (d. 819), who "must be credited with establishing the overruling authority of decisions based directly on alleged prophetic action over those based on on *ra'y* [رأي or an individual's considered opinion], *istiḥsān* [استحسان, deeming preferable], or *ijtihād* [اجتهاد, personal studious investigation]; from his time dates the exclusive definition of the four *uṣūl,* "foundations," of *fiqh*."[102] The three other major *madhāhib* that emerged before the end of the ninth century CE, and that along with al-Shāfi'ī's are followed to this day, are the Mālikī (after Mālik ibn Anas/مالك بن أنس, d. 795 CE, author of *al-Muwaṭṭa'*/الموطأ [*The Levelled Path*], the oldest work of *fiqh*); the Ḥanafī (after Abū Ḥanīfah/أبو حنيفة, d. 768 CE), and the Ḥanbalī (after Aḥmad ibn Ḥanbal/أحمد بن حنبل, d. 855 CE).[103]

The major collections of *aḥādīth* and the "science" for determining their authenticity (and, closely bound up with that, gradations in importance) were brought to completion by the end of the ninth century CE. The two most highly regarded collections of *aḥādīth*, commonly referred to as *al-Ṣaḥīḥān*/الصحيحان (*The Two Sound Works*), represent the efforts of al-Bukhārī/البخاري and Muslim/مسلم (the former died in 870 CE; the latter in 875). Four additional collections considered acceptably authoritative (if not as esteemed as *al-Saḥiḥān*) were arranged by Ibn Mājā/ابن ماجا (d. 886 CE), Abū Dā'ūd /أبو داؤود (d. 888 CE), al-Tirmidhī/الترمذي (d. 892 CE), and al-Nasā'ī/النسائي (d. 915 CE). The Shī'ites, while accepting the importance of *aḥādīth* for *fiqh*, later compiled collections that they accorded preeminence in the discipline. Although dealing with similar situations and topics, these collections contained only *aḥādīth* that could be connected to 'Alī and his descendants (particularly the imāms) and with chains of transmitters who were known to be Shī'ites. The earliest were *al-Kāfī fī 'Ilm al-Dīn*/الكافي في علم الدين (*The Sufficient Book on Religion*) by al-Kulīnī/الكليني (d. 939 CE) and *Kitāb Man Lā Yastaḥdiruhu al-Faqīh*/كتاب من لا يستحضره الفقيه (*The Book of Non-Conjectural Jurisprudence*) by Ibn Bābawayh al-Qummī /بابَوَيْه القُمّي (d. 991). "Yet except as regards the special role of 'Alī and the imâms, their ḥadîth were often almost identical with those of the Sunnīs. What gave them their vitality was a special mood of devotion superadded to the common Shar'ism."[104]

Thus the supremacy of the *Sharī'ah* was accepted, on the one hand, by *ahl al-shī'ah*, the people of the faction of 'Alī who rejected the authority of their coreligionists who would not accord 'Alī (and his descendants) the sole and indisputable right to the caliphate, and at the same time by *ahl al-sunnah wa al-jamā'ah*/أهل السنة و الجماعة, "the people of the *sunnah* and the unity of the community," the fuller and more revealing sobriquet for the Sunnīs, the Muslims who rejected the Shī'ite-inspired position with respect to loyalty to 'Alī, endorsing instead legitimacy of *all* of Muḥammad's close associates in determining the *sunnah* and the paramount importance of maintaining the unity and solidarity of the community of believers.

It was around this time that, not totally coincidentally, Twelver Shī'ite theology (or, if you will, religio-political philosophy) began to emerge as a distinctive orientation within overall 'Alid loyalism. Theologians who in the last half of the eighth century CE rejected the legitimacy of the three caliphs prior to ʿAlī, and who insisted that the Prophet Muḥammad had specifically chosen ʿAlī as his *immediate* successor as supreme leader (imām) of the entire Islamic community, to be succeeded in subsequent generations only by ʿAlī's descendants (by a process of formal, father-to-son designation), prevailed among the largest body of ʿAlid loyalists in winning support for the notion that (1) at any time there was only one authoritative imām (as religious teacher-guide and savior of true Islam); (2) commencing with the imamate of ʿAlī, each succeeding imām from ʿAlī's descendants was specifically designated to be imām by his predecessor; and (3) there was a clearly recognized line of properly designated imāms. Including ʿAlī as the first imām, there were twelve properly designated imāms, the last of whom was Muḥammad, who disappeared shortly after the death of his father (Ḥasan al-ʿAskarī/حسن العسكري) in 874 CE (in Samarra, Iraq). This marked the beginning of Muḥammad's designation as the hidden imām and the "guided one"/*al-mahdī* (المهدي), who will reappear in the flesh only on the Last Day, until which time, contact with him will not be possible.

In reflecting on this development, F. E. Peters noted,

> Nothing new or startling was introduced into the complex of Shi'ite ideas; almost all the motifs were present in one or another group of Shi'ites from the beginning: the adulation of 'Ali, the conviction that the Imamate was somehow connected with an 'Alid genealogy, and last of all perhaps, the twin themes of the *Imam* as a teacher, already much in evidence among the early Zaydis, and of the *Imam* as the restorer . . . of a true Islam. Crucial to this latter was acceptance of the once scorned view of the "extremists" that the last *Imam* was also the *Mahdi*, who would surely return.[105]

However, Peters added,

> The consequences . . . were enormous. At a stroke the Shi'ite premise undercut both the claims of the speculative theologians [the *mutakallimūn*] and the authority of the lawyers [the *fuqahā'*]. For the first time, it substituted recourse to the authority (*taqlid*) of the *Imam* or his surrogate as the only source of authentic teaching. And in law the Shi'ah denied in effect the entire structure of

> *hadith* that rested upon the simple witness of the Companions of the Prophet, men whose authority was compromised in Shi'ite eyes by their failure to recognize the Imamate of 'Ali . . . they were insisting that all valid *hadith* went back through the infallible Husaynid *Imams*.[106]

Al-Kulīnī's pioneering *al-Kāfī* contained 16,000 such *ḥadīth* reports. Al-Kulīnī was born in Rayy. He spent the later years of his life (he died in 939 CE) in Baghdad, which soon attracted a cluster of especially notable Shī'ī jurisprudents and learned advocates for the Shī'ī cause, arguably to a large extent because of the arrival and ascendancy of the Būyids. Among these notables were al-Mufīd/المفيد (d. 1022) and al-Sharīf al-Rāḍī/الشريف الراضي (d. 1015). Al-Sharīf al-Rāḍī was the official head (*naqīb*/نقيب) of the descendants of 'Alī and the compiler of reported sayings of 'Alī (under the title *Nahj al-Balāghah*/نهج البلاغة [*The Path of Eloquence*]). The theologian (i.e., *mutakallim*) al-Murtaḍā/المرتضى (d. 1044), al-Sharīf's brother, succeeded him as *naqīb*. One of al-Sharīf's and al-Murtaḍā's students, Abū Ja'far al-Ṭūsī/أبو جعفر الطوسي, was a commentator on his teachers' teachings as well as the compiler of a catalogue of important Shī'ī books. Abū al-Faraj al-Iṣfahānī/أبو فرج الإصفهاني (d. 967), perhaps best known for his anthology of poetry accompanied by observations and comments on the poets, *Kitāb al-Aghānī*/كتاب الأغاني (*The Book of Songs*), was also the author of *The Martyrs of the House of 'Alī* (*Maqātil al-Ṭālibiyyīn*/مقاتل الطالبيين).

Adab

Adab assumed the cultivation of a broad range of fields of study, the broader the range the better, although knowing a little about a great deal of subjects, as opposed to achieving real depth in one or two areas of inquiry, seemed to be paramount, as was the secular as opposed to the religious. Nothing should be beyond the scope of interest of the dedicated and conscientious master of *adab*, except perhaps fictional compositions designed primarily to entertain the unlettered without providing any significant edification. The ideal master of *adab* or the *adīb* (أديب) was expected to be at least conversant in, for example, history, geography, science, the religious law and *aḥādīth*, ancedotes, proverbs, and, last but hardly least, poetry. Poetry and anecdotes were to be memorized and liberally cited as suggested by particular situations and contexts. In writing (as in conversation), the good representative of *adab* training was expected to display all of his erudition, linguistic (i.e., vocabulary and idioms) included, in language that was not only meticulously correct in terms of the grammar and syntax of high literary Arabic (with an official "chancellory" style especially paradigmatic) but also witty, urbane, and entertaining.

The composition of poetry (*shi'r*/شعر) was central to Arab Islamic *adab* culture. It was considered pre-eminent in verbal expression. The legacy predated the revelation of the Qur'ān and the establishment of Islam, along with which came the flowering of literary Arabic and Arabic learning and letters. In its most revered and common pre-Islamic stage of development, the basic format of *shi'r* consisted of two syllabically equivalent hemistichs that taken together form what is considered a single verse. At the end of each verse and throughout the entire poem regardless of length, the rhyming letter remains the same. The metrical system was quantitative, being based on the number of syllables in a verse. A *shi'r* composition could be written/recited in one of several of the recognized meters. The main contents or topics were expressive especially of Arabian tribal and nomadic society: praising one's tribe or oneself; denigrating a tribal or individual rival or opponent; expressing sorrow over death of acquaintances or loved ones; descriptions of desert nature and life, particularly the breaking of camp and the camel ride; and the joy and sorrow attendant upon romantic liaisons that are all too frequently disrupted and thus all too ephemeral. Once the main purpose of the poem was established—e.g., praise of someone, which was very typical—it was pursued, for the duration of the poem, albeit at times somewhat loosely or indirectly and opaquely, for the duration of the poem without a switch to another topic or purpose.

The most celebrated pre-Islamic type of poetry contained more than one topic, although these became stock and furthermore followed a set sequence: pining over a beloved who can no longer be met and over the remnants of her tribe's campsite; a camel ride through the desert with descriptions of the camel, the surrounding landscape, and the rigors of the ride; and, finally, praise of a generous and powerful patron and perhaps some self-adulation. This example of *shi'r* is thought of as the model *qaṣīdah*/قصيدة, although the nomenclature *qaṣīdah* (an adjective derived from the verb meaning "to aspire to, to intend") is sometimes also used, rather loosely, for longer poems that don't exactly follow the same format in terms of topics and their sequencing. Shorter pieces more circumscribed in purpose (although observing the monorhyme and one of the recognized meters)—for example, the description of something or lampooning, praising, or eulogizing someone—were also part of the canon of *shi'r*. That is to say, they were thought of, designated as, *shi'r* although at the same time assigned a generic categorization (e.g., praise poem, poem of description, lampoon) that called attention to the main topic.

The most celebrated of the longer, pre-Islamic *qaṣīdah* poems that follow the formula of regretful reflections over a lost love and her abandoned campsite, the description of the camel ride through the desert, and the intrepid poet and/or gracious patron were included in the *Mu'allaqāt*/المعلقات, the seven poems that according to tradition were awarded prizes in annual poetry contests near Mecca. These and other examples of pre-Islamic and early Islamic-era poetry, which for the most part were transmitted orally from generation to generation by professional reciters (the writing of poetry did not begin to take place until around 700 CE), were collected and anthologized by linguists, grammarians, or poets of the early 'Abbāsid era—Mufaḍḍal al-Ḍabbī/مفضل الضبي (d. 786 CE); Abū Tammām/أبو تمام (d. 850 CE); and al-Buḥturī/البحتري (d. 897 CE). Abū Tammām's chapter headings, although referring in some instances merely to fragments taken from longer poems, reflect the range of topics typically taken up, either to the exclusion of other topics (in shorter poems) or (in longer poems) most likely accompanied by other topics or themes. His anthology, titled *Kitāb al-Ḥamāsah*/كتاب الحماسة (*The Book of Courage*; the reference was to the verses contained in the first section) included, to mention a few examples, sections on good manners and upbringing (*adab*/أدب), dirges (*marāthī*/مراثي), the romantic prelude (*naṣīb*/نصيب) of longer poems, lampooning or invective (*hijā'*/هجاء), praise (*madḥ*/مدح), and description (*ṣifah*/صفة). Women poets, at least those of renown, seem to have gravitated toward declaiming dirges.

Poems attributed to an individual poet or to individuals from the same tribe were compiled in collections called *dawāwīn*/دواوين (sing. *dīwān*/ديوان). One of the more famous was, and remains, that of Imru' al-Qays/ إمرؤ القيس, one of whose poems is also numbered among the Muʿallaqāt and who may be regarded as especially evocative of "the Bedouin way of life [that] was thoroughly hedonistic . . . Love, wine, gambling, hunting, the pleasures of song and romance, the brief, pointed, and elegant expression of wit and wisdom—these things he knew to be good. Beyond them he saw only the grave."[107]

R. A. Nicholson gives a fine English-language rendition of one of the poems in Imru' al-Qays's *Dīwān*:

Roast meat and wine: the swinging ride
On a camel sure and tried.
Which her master speeds amain
O'er low dale and level plain:
Women marble-white and fair
Trailing gold-fringed raiment rare:
Opulence, luxurious ease,
With the lute's soft melodies—
Such delights hath our brief span;
Time is Change, Time's fool is Man.
Wealth or want, great store or small,
All is one since Death's are all.[108]

During the Umayyad caliphal era, poets composed both the shorter fragmented or occasional poem and the imitation of the exemplary desert *qaṣīdah*. Praise poems and invectives were also part of the canon. Both are exemplified in the compositions of three preeminent poets of the era: Jarīr/جرير (d.728), al-Farazdaq/الفرزدق (d. 728), and al-Akhṭal/ الأخطل. "All these poets, like their Post-islamic brethren generally, were professional encomiasts, greedy, venal, and ready to revile any one who would not purchase their praise."[109] Al-Akhṭal, although Christian, was much in favor at the Umayyad caliphal court in Damascus because of his verses in praise of the Umayyads. Jarīr was the encomiast at the court of al-Ḥajjāj, the governor of al-ʿIrāq during the caliphate of ʿAbd al-Malik.

At Mecca and Medina towards the end of the seventh century CE, love poetry as an independent genre—that is, not as fragments intended for the introduction to the long desert- and Bedouin-inspired *qaṣīdah*s—was composed, most notably by the Meccan ʿUmar ibn Abī Rabīʿah/عمر بن أبي ربيعة (d. 719 CE), but also anonymously with respect to the celebrated romance of Jamīl and Buthaynah and Majnūn and Layla. "The shifting of the Islamicate political and cultural focus from Mecca and Medina to the urban centers of Syrian and Iraq" was underway in *adab* culture generally and *shi'r* specifically by late Umayyad times, so that "Bedouin refinement yielded to urban refinement."[110] This process was accelerated in the ninth and tenth centuries CE of the ʿAbbāsid caliphal era, when urbanization extended well beyond greater Syria and even Iraq, to include the entire Islamicate commonwealth that stretched in North Africa as far west as present-day Morocco, in Umayyad Spain as far as both the central and southern parts of the Spanish peninsula, in the east as far as the Indus River and the Punjab, and in the northeast as far as the shores of the Aral Sea and well beyond the Oxus River. The urbanization was accompanied by, among other things, urban-based and, more specifically, court-based, patronization. "[W]e have to bear in mind that from first to last (with very few exceptions) [poetry during the ʿAbbāsid caliphate] flourished under the patronage of the court. There was no organized book trade, no wealthy publishers, so that poets were usually dependent for their livelihood on the capricious bounty of the caliphs and his favourites whom they belauded."[111] Poetry less and less emulated the old desert-*qaṣīdah* masterpieces (although these were hardly dislodged from the canon), whether with respect to images and contents and/or the stock arrangement thereof, and more and more represented more circumscribed approaches to topics or themes (especially in the case of the shorter compositions that often resemble occasional poetry of a more personal nature), with some new content along with new sentiment, new thought, new imagery.

In terms of form, the court-supported and urban-based poetry of the ʿAbbāsid caliphal era did not abandon the (mono)rhyme scheme of the pre-Islamic and Umayyad-era poets, nor the meters and the division of each line of verse into two hemistichs. Otherwise, however, added to the concern for the metaphor, simile, or turn of phrase that might resonate especially well with the listener and prove memorable in terms of sense and sound was the special concern for frequent use of figures of speech such as *jinās*/جناس (the clustering of two or more words that have the same or nearly the same spelling but different meanings), *ṭibāq*/طباق (the pairing of words of contrasting meaning in the same line), *tarṣīʿ*/ترصيع (internal rhymes that have the same or similar cadences), *tajāhul al-ʿārif*/تجاهل العارف (the rhetorical question; literally "the knower pretending not to know"), *mubālaghah*/مبالغة (exaggeration; hyperbole), and *īhām*/إيهام (the use of a word that has multiple meanings depending upon the context, but the more common meaning not being intended).[112] In terms of topics and tone, "Every change of many-coloured life is depicted in the brilliant pages of these modern poets, where the reader may find, according to his mood, the maddest gaiety and the shamefullest frivolity; strains of lofty meditation mingled with world-weary pessimism; delicate sentiment, unforced pathos, and glowing rhetoric; but seldom the manly self-reliance, the wild, invigorating freedom and inimitable freshness of Bedouin song."[113]

One might submit that the (in)famous Abū Nuwās/أبو نواس (from Basra; d. 810), closely associated with the caliphal court in Baghdad (caliphs Hārūn al-Rashīd and Amīn), alone encapsulated nearly all of these tendencies in the poems in his *dīwān*. The *dīwān* includes praise poems, invectives, dirges, poems on wine and love (both rather scandalously addressed with near complete abandon), and perfectly pious meditative verses of remorse and world renunciation.

Abū al-ʿAtāhiyyah/أبو العتاهية (from Kufa; d. 828), a well-known contemporary of Abū Nuwās and an associate of the Baghdad caliphal court, became renowned (and in some circles reviled) for somber and decidedly bleak reflections on the meaning of life and death, in this respect remarkably redolent of al-Maʿarrī in terms of tone and topics, although virtually the polar opposite in manner of expression and on this score quite unique for all of Arabic poetry and not merely that of the ʿAbbāsid era. "He showed for the first and perhaps for the last time in the history of classical Arabic literature that it was possible to use perfectly plain and ordinary language without ceasing to be a poet."[114] Before taking up the writing of poems expressing his pessimistic reflections on humankind and the world, Abū al-ʿAtāhiyyah composed customary praise poems and some romantic verse.

Al-Mutanabbī/المتنبي (from Kufa; d. 965), arguably the most popular of the ʿAbbāsid poets as well as the most revered for his style (in his time as well as that of subsequent generations up through the present), enjoyed the patronage of both the court of Sayf al-Dawlah in Aleppo (for the years 948–957 CE) and subsequent to that the Ikhshīdite court in Cairo under the control of the Abysinnian strongman Kāfūr (who ruled the province of Egypt independently from 966 to 968 CE). Consequently, he was primarily an encomiast for both Sayf al-Dawlah and Kāfūr. In truth, some of the "invigorating freedom and inimitable freshness of Bedouin song" can be found in the poetry of al-Mutanabbī, alongside the posturing as hero and self-serving, excessive flattery directed to his patrons. However, a thousand years after the death of al-Mutanabbī, Philip Hitti felt compelled to write that his "bombastic and ornate style with its flowery rhetoric and improbable metaphors" is what "renders him to the present day the most popular and widely quoted poet in the Moslem world."[115]

A generation removed from that of al-Mutanabbī, the anthologist and critic al-Thaʿālibī/الثعالبي (of Nīshāpūr; d. 1038 CE) seems to suggest that superiority in "elegant expression, subtile combination of words, fanciful image, witty conceits, and a striking use of rhetorical figures" are what set al-Mutanabbī head and shoulders above other poets,[116] although al-Thaʿālabī was admittedly favorably disposed to the style of the ʿAbbāsid-era poets to begin with.

Al-Maʿarrī is reported to have admired the poetry of al-Mutanabbī. He is said to have studied it assiduously. If not in themes, in terms of technical virtuosity in frequently deploying the by-then most fashionable figures of speech associated with "the moderns," and in terms also of the overall striving to show more than anything else erudition and cleverness in the use of language, resulting in the frequent overreaching and over-ripeness ("in the contest between *ars* and *igenium* it was often the first that won out in the soul of the Arabic literary artist"[117]), there are undeniable similarities between the two poets.

Iranian cultural identities (Abū Nuwās's mother was Iranian; the noted poet Bashshār ibn Burd [d. 784], an encomiast for Umayyad governors and also a favorite of the ʿAbbāsid caliph al-Manṣūr, was of Iranian descent) probably contributed to the break with the old standards, at least in the sense that the ties with the Bedouin desert-*qaṣīdah* would not have been so inviolable. The Iranian/Persian cultural assertion movement (*al-shu'ūbiyyah*/الشعوبية) was very much in the ascendancy in the ninth and tenth centuries CE. Bound up with this, coming as it did with the maturation of Shīʿite religious philosophy and particularly imāmism, were notable poets who expressed their Shīʿite loyalties in verse—al-Sharīf al-Rāḍī and Miḥyār al-Daylamī/محيار الديلمي, for example.

"In the fifth century [1000–1100 CE] the dogma of the unattainable perfection of the heathen poets may be regarded as utterly demolished."[118] "By the time al-Thaʿālibī (d. 1038) put together his *The Unique Epoch* [يتيمة الدهر], an anthology of contemporary poets, the love of ornamentation that characterized Arabic poetry from the beginning had begun to generate into unbridled lust. Rhetoric ran riot among the poets, as it did among almost all the literary men of the day."[119] In fact, as early as the late eighth and ninth century CE, the poets Bashshār ibn Burd and Abū Tammām were manifestly representative of this trajectory, the so-called *badīʿ*/بديع ("original"; "unique") style; and the caliph poet Ibn al-Muʿtazz (d. 908) devoted an entire treatise on the topic: *Kitāb al-Badīʿ*/كتاب البديع.

By the tenth century CE, nonspecialized (i.e., nondiscipline-based) prose in Arabic, the development of which originally was closely bound up with the utilitarian needs of government courts (more specifically, official letters or documents emanating from secretaries, scribes [*kuttāb*/كتاب], or judges), took the general fondness for ornamentation that characterized prose as well as poetry to a new level with the special obsession for frequent use of *sajʿ*/سجع or rhymed clauses and phrases. The Basrite al-Jāḥiẓ/الجاحظ (d. 869 CE), who became very influential at (among other places) the caliphal court in Baghdad and who was renowned for his encyclopedic erudition (which helped make him the quintessential *adīb*), and Abū Ḥayyān al-Tawḥīdī/أبو حيان التوحيدي who was equally influential in Būyid court circles as an accomplished *adīb*, did much in their writing style to make respectable and acceptable less ornate, pompous, artificial, and opaque forms of prose. But their examples could not carry the day, especially after the popularity of the *maqāmāt*/مقامات of al-Hamadhānī/الهمذاني (d. 1007 CE), which were a collection of vignettes involving a roguish character. All of the vignettes are studded with *sajʿ*.

The back story to all of this in terms of the history of Arabic language and literature was the transition from an earlier stage—a stage of collection of material, of determining correct recensions, of compiling anthologies of poetry, and of investigations of grammar, syntax, and patterns of prosody—to a stage of "research, reflection, personal independent interpretation and putting the human mind to its proper use" with respect to materials previously compiled.[120] There emerged out of this the formal disciplines of literary criticism (النقد), eloquence (البلاغة), purity of language (الفصاحة), and clarity of expression (البيان); the last along with eloquence—with which it was almost exactly equated, and ironically long before the remonstrations of al-Tawḥīdī or ʿAbd al-Qādir al-Jurjānī (d. 1078 CE) against affectation or figurative speech—implying directness and lack of artifice.[121] In the course of arguments between, on the one hand, the literati who preferred the poetry of the early ʿAbbāsid poets or those whose compositions preceded the advent of Islam, and, on the other hand, the literati who preferred the poetry of the second and especially third centuries CE of the ʿAbbāsid era with its surfeit of *badīʿ*-style embellishments in poetry, there arose in the tenth and eleventh centuries CE works of literary criticism such as Qudāmah ibn Jaʿfar's *Naqd al-Shi'r*/ نقد الشعر (*The Criticism of Poetry*); al-Āmidī's *al-Muwāzanah bayna al-Ṭā'iyyayn* /الموازنة بين الطائيّين (*Comparing Abū Tammām to al-Buḥturī*); ʿAbd al-Qādir al-Jurjānī's *Al-Wiṣaṭah bayna al-Mutanabbī wa Khuṣūmih*/الوساطة بين المتنبي وخصومه (*Mediating between al-Mutanabbī and His Adversaries*); and Abū Hilāl al-ʿAskarī's *Kitāb al-Ṣinā'atayn*/ كتاب الصناعتين (*The Book on the Two Crafts*), a treatise analyzing both poetry and prose.

Central to the debates and arguments over language and literature, eloquence and rhetoric was the debate over whether the Qur'ān rendered impossible another verbal production of its equal. Al-Jāhiẓ and al-Naẓẓām took up the issue, as did al-Bāqillānī (d. 1013 CE) and al-Jurjānī. Al-Jāhiẓ suggested that no one dared to take up the challenge (implying that Arab poets or orators nonetheless possessed the "eloquence" and "outstanding aptitude for fine language" requisite for this).[122] Al-Naẓẓām's argument was similar; the eloquence and rhetoric of the Qur'ān do not explain its inimitable quality; the Arabs have the ability to produce something that is its equal; but God turned them away from that in order to confirm the truth of the Prophet Muḥammad. The Qur'ān in and of itself does not render impossible the production of anything like it. The impossibility such as it is results from people being diverted from imitating it.[123] Al-Bāqillānī in upholding the inimitability of the Qur'ān emphasized the newness of the form of expression; whereas al-Jurjānī argued that the special eloquence of the Qur'ān with respect to words, their meaning, and how they were arranged simply could not be achieved by humans; that is, humans simply did not have the ability.[124]

PART 2

CHAPTER THREE

The Medium

Reading and Interpreting *Luzūm Mā Lā Yalzam* in Light of Its Literary Character

Luzūm Mā Lā Yalzam (لزوم ما لا يلزم)[1] is usually referred to as, and indeed essentially is, a volume of poetry. However, it begins not with a poem straightforward but instead a rather sizable (approximately thirty-five pages in a standard typescript version) prose introduction—rather surprising and arresting for both its presence and its length (although for something else as well). The first thing, therefore, that ought not be neglected in a discussion of the structure of *Luzūm* is underscoring how, strictly speaking, this work consists of two very distinct parts: the more celebrated text proper comprising the poems and the lesser known prose introduction. It is the text of *Luzūm* that is of primary concern to us in this study, although the introduction practically begs to be reflected upon.

The introduction deals with essentially two topics: (1) the overall literary nature of the poems in *Luzūm* as seen by al-Maʿarrī himself; and (2) the rules of rhyme in Arabic, particularly those employed in the poems of *Luzūm*. The second of the two topics occupies by far the greatest share of al-Maʿarrī's attention. It fills thirty-three of thirty-five pages of the Zand typescript edition. That is to say, al-Maʿarrī's introduction to *Luzūm* opens with some remarks on the literary nature of the poems in *Luzūm*; then, the introduction digresses for thirty-three pages with the disquisition on rhymes, only to resume on the last page the discussion of the very same topic it began with on the first page.

Among other things, the page that opens the introduction states what the book's poems are about. An English translation of the Arabic would read along the lines of the following:

> Among the events fated in the past is the fact that I have composed structures of meters in which I have pursued the truth and eliminated lying and deviation. I do not claim that these structures are like the seized pearl string, but at the same time I hope that they are not deemed like a range of bricks. Among them, then, is that which glorifies God, who transcends glorification and hangs blessings around each neck; while some of them remind the forgetful, awaken the heedless, and warn against our greater mother [i.e., the world], who has acted treacherously with [our] forefathers. . . . And I have added to what I have [here] described some moral admonitions and various sorts [of other things] in accordance with what natural impulse grants; so, if I have gone beyond that which is required [of me to write] in favor of something else, then what I have attained is discourse stripped of falsehood. All of this I have collected in a book that I have titled *Luzūm Mā Lā Yalzam.*
>
> كانَ من سوالف الأقضية أني أَنشأْتُ ابنية أوزان[2] توخَّيتُ فيها صدقَ الكلمةِ ونزَّهتُها عن الكذب والميطِ ولا أزعمها كالسمطِ المتخذِ وأَرجو أن لا تحسب منَ السميطِ فمنها ما هوَ تمجيدٌ للهِ الذي شَرُفَ عن التمجيد ووَضَعَ المِنَنَ في كلّ جِيدٍ وبعضها تذكيرٌ للناسين وتنبيهٌ للرَقَدَة الغافلين وتحذيرٌ من والدتنا[3] الكبرى التي غدرت[4] بالأُوَلِ[5] . . . . وأضفتُ إلى ما وصفتُ[6] أشياءَ من العظةِ و أفانين على حسب ما تسمحُ به الغريزةُ فإن جاوزتُ المشترطَ إلى سِواهُ فأنّ الذي جاوزتُ إليه قولاً عُرّيَ من المين وجمعتُ ذلك كله في كتابٍ لقبتهُ لزوم ما لا يلزم.
>
> (L I.9.1–5, 8–11)

One will find that indeed among the topics of *Luzūm* are God's glory, the heedlessness of man, and the treachery of the world. However, to the extent that the above remarks taken from the introduction to the work imply that these topics are the really salient topics, and the "various sorts of other things" are merely incidental, the remarks are considerably less than accurate. A concise yet more revealing glimpse of the range of the book's contents was first most remarkably provided by Alfred von Kremer writing in 1888:

> [Al-Maʿarrī] hat in diesen Gedichten seine Selbstbekenntnisse und seine Ansichten über die hochsten Fragen der philosophischen Geistesarbeit niedergelegt, über Tod und Unsterblichkeit, über Glauben und Unglauben, über Gott und Welt, die Menschen und ihre Leidenschaften, über Willensfreiheit und Vorherbestimmung; dann aber auch über sociale Fragen wie: über die sittlichen Pflichten, die Ehe und Polygamie, die Kindererziehung, den Sklavenhandel u.s.w, ebenso auch über die religiösen und politischen Probleme: den Ursprung und die Berechtigung der Religionen, die Ansichten der verschiedenen Secten und Religionsparteien. Man kann im allgemeinen sagen, dass er alles was in jener Zeit die Gemüther bewegte und die Geister der gebildeten Classe beschäftigte, in den Kreis seiner Betrachtung zieht.[7]

In the part of his introduction dealing with rhyme, which follows immediately after his mention of the title of *Luzūm*, al-Maʿarrī sets out with the rather limited objective of mentioning the technical terms of the rhymes he employs in *Luzūm*. He undertakes this, he says, "out of fear that this book come to someone unfamiliar with those terms" (مخافة أن يقعَ هذا الكتابُ إلى قليل المعرفة بتلك الأسماء ; L I.9.10–13); a stroke of *adīb*-like playful one-upmanship. It is more than just the above-mentioned technical terms that he ends up elucidating. He also identifies all of the possible letter combinations in Arabic rhyme generally speaking, tells where these letters may be situated in the rhyme syllables and what they are called in these positions, and gives ample illustrations of many of the various types of rhyme other than the ones employed in *Luzūm*. What results is in effect a short but very comprehensive treatise on Arabic rhyme technique. This part of the introduction is of a highly technical nature and deals with a complex subject, although it is worth noting how remarkably clear, coherent, and methodical it is.

On the last page of his introduction, al-Maʿarrī returns to the notion that his poetry is free from lies, adding that this explains an old remark of his[8] to the effect that he does not, in fact, write poetry (شعر) at all. Whoever follows his style of writing, he continues, is going to write verse deemed deficient; for a maxim of Arabic literary tradition holds that true poetry does not aim for anything other than falsehood,[9] and Arab poets strive for beautiful speech by "lying"[10] and by adorning their compositions with descriptions of things such as wine, women, camels, horses, and the hardships of treks in the desert and going to war (see L I.41.12–14, 42). As R. A. Nicholson intimated long ago—and rightly so—these remarks taken in conjunction with those of the opening page of the introduction amount to nothing less than an apology for a new poetics in *Luzūm* that al-Maʿarrī feels is very likely to upset the aesthetic sensibilities of his readers.[11]

Al-Maʿarrī then begins the text proper of *Luzūm*. Altogether, this consists of approximately 1,600 poems, or between 12,000 and 13,000 lines.[12] The length of these poems varies, the shortest being no more than two lines, and the longest, ninety-six; but relatively few are longer than twenty or so, and most are considerably shorter, as a quick division of poems into lines makes obvious. The poems have no titles. They are arranged solely according to the alphabetical sequence of the rhyming letters.[13]

As we have just had occasion to remark, al-Maʿarrī considered his poems in *Luzūm* so different that he felt obliged in effect to apologize for them. In point of fact, he scrupulously avoided calling them *shiʿr*/شعر, the Arabic word for poetry regardless of provenance or genre, referring to his compositions instead literally as "structures of meters" (perhaps "metered structures" would be a more felicitous translation for أبنية أوزان) and "discourse stripped of falsehood." Yet except for their subject matter, they largely adhere to the basic, time-honored conventions of premodern Arabic prosody; and, technically, they look and read very much like ordinary (i.e., standard) premodern Arabic poetry. They all follow an end monorhyme scheme, scrupulously avoid violations in the rules of rhyme,[14] are written in the traditional meters, have each line consisting of two hemistichs with a caesura between them, and *in general* avoid *taḍmīn*/تضمين or the completion of a thought in two or more lines (although this is not to say that that there is not extension or elaboration of a thought—sometimes clearly, other times more opaquely—that extends beyond a line; there is, but more on that below).

An additional feature to the rhymes of the poems—highly unconventional if not unique—explains the title of the collection (at least at one level of meaning). According to the traditional rules of Arabic versification, rhyming is ordinarily achieved through the repetition of a syllable (very commonly a consonant-vowel or vowel-consonant sequence) at the end of every line of a poem. This is the monorhyme so commonly associated with premodern (and still in many instances modern) Arabic poetry. Provided that the consonant in this sequence remains the same throughout the poem, and provided that its accompanying vowel, if not also invariable, is at least only made variable by means of vowels that the poet might use indifferently, the basic requirements of rhyming are fulfilled.

In the following lines that begin a celebrated poem by Ibn al-Fāriḍ (ابن الفارض), for example,

شربنا على ذكر الحبيب مدامةً　　سكرنا بها من قبل أن يُخْلَق الكرمُ
لها البدر كأسٌ وهي شمسٌ يديرها　　هلالٌ وكم يبدو إذا مجزت نجمُ

> We drank upon the remembrance of the Beloved a wine wherewith we were drunken before even the vine was created.
> The full moon was a cup for it, itself being the sun that a crescent moon passes round; and how many a star shows forth when it is mingled.[15]

rhyming is achieved by the repetition of the consonant-vowel sequence of Arabic *mīm* (م)-*ḍammah* (ضمة) (i.e.: مُ) at the end of each line. In this particular rhyme structure, so long as the *mīm*/م is repeated at the end of each line thereafter, along with the *ḍammah*/ضمة (ُ) vowel, then the poem would be said to meet the requirements of rhyme. An additional invariable consonant preceding the *mīm-ḍammah* (مُ) sequence, although permissible, would be considered superfluous.

Similarly, in the lines from the following poem that ends in a vowel-consonant sequence,

لَيْتَ هِنْداً أنجزتْنا ما تَعِدْ　　وشفتْ أَنْفُسَنا مِمّا تَجِد
واسْتبدَّتْ مرَّةً واحدةً　　إنَّما العاجزُ مَنْ لا يستبد

> Would that Hind had fulfilled to us her promise, and healed our souls of their suffering!
> Would that she had acted independently for once! It is the weakling who does not act independently.[16]

it is the repetition of the Arabic *kasrah*/كسرة (short *i* vowel)-*dāl*/دال (consonant *d*) sequence (i.e., together constituting the sound of "id") that constitutes the rhyme. Provided that the consonant *dāl*/د is repeated every line thereafter *and* is preceded by a short *i* vowel or one of the other two short vowels in Arabic (*a* or *u*), then the poem needs nothing else in order to rhyme.

In the poems of *Luzūm*, al-Maʿarrī goes beyond these basic and ordinary requirements of rhyme. For each poem, he incorporates into the end word of each line one or more identical consonants preceding the basic rhyming syllable. Consequently, his poems rhyme not only through the repetition of said syllables but also through the repetition of one or more identical consonants immediately preceding them.

To better illustrate what is meant here, citation of an actual poem from *Luzūm* is in order:

أخبرتَ عن كُتبكَ أعجوبةً   ورُبَّ مَيْن ضمنتْهُ الكتبْ
تُواصلُ الغيَّ ولو لم يكن   فيكَ حجى ما عَتَبتْكَ العُتُبْ[17]
وطبعك الشرُّ فإن أمكنتْ   توبةُ ليلٍ من سوادٍ فَتُبْ
ويطلبُ النقلةَ عن خِيمهم   ناسٌ على كلِّ قبيح رُتُبْ

> You've told of a wondrous thing through your books;
> but many a lie has been contained by books.
> You continue to go astray; had you no mind
> the fault finders would not have reproved you.
> Your nature is evil; so if the night can repent
> for her blackness, then you, too, go and repent.
> It's a people firmly fixed in every vice
> who seek to move away from their innate nature.
> (L I.153.4–7)

In this poem, the basic rhyme is that of the short *u* vowel + *b* sound ("ub"; in Arabic the sequence of the ب preceded by the ضمة) repeated at the end of each line (although in this particular rhyme structure, the short *u* and short *i* could be interchanged without any violation of the rules of prosody). Had al-Maʿarrī repeated *only* this sound in this position, he would have fulfilled all the necessary rules of rhyme. However, in addition to the "ub" sound sequence, he also repeated the consonant that immediately precedes it—the letter *t* (Arabic *tāʾ*/تاء)—thereby increasing the rhyme sound from "ub" to "tub."

In the poems of *Luzūm* in which the basic rhyme is found in the repetition of a consonant-vowel sequence at the end of each line, an "additional" rhyme (i.e., one above and beyond the only one absolutely necessary according to the rules of prosody) would look somewhat like the following:

ثلاثُ مراتبٍ ملكٌ رفيعُ   وإنسانٌ وجيلٌ غير إنسِ
فان فعل الفتىَ خيراً تعالى   إلى قِنسِ الملائكِ خَيرِ جنس[18]
وإن خفَضتْهُ شيمتُهُ[19] تهاوَى   إلى قنسِ[20] البهائم شرِّ قنسِ[21]

There are three classes [of creation]: sublime angels,
humans, and those people who are inhuman.
If the human being does good, then he rises
to the genus of angels, the best genus;
but if his character abases him, he sinks
to the lineage of the beasts, the worst lineage.
(L II.35.15; 36.1–2)

Here the Arabic consonant *nūn*/نون (*n* sound) is repeated at the end of each line immediately before the Arabic consonant *sīn*/سين (*s* sound), and the vowel *kasrah*/كسرة (here read as long *i* because it ends the line). Thus, the rhyme sound is increased from simply "sī" to (vowel plus) "-nsī." Again, only the "sī" sound would have been sufficient for the rhyme, *ordinarily*; the consonant *n* could have been replaced by any other consonant.

The two poems just cited are rather simple examples of how al-Maʿarrī went beyond the minimum that he made obligatory in his rhyme patterns in *Luzūm*. In each case, he added only one extra consonant to the basic rhyme. Often, he added two, as in the following poem, where Arabic ر (*r* sound) and *hamzah*/ء (glottal stop) followed by short vowel *i* invariably precede the rhyme syllable “rī”, so that the full rhyme formula is “-rā’irī”:

إذا كُنتَ ذا ثنتين فٱغْدُ محارباً   عدوَّينِ وٱحذرْ من ثلاثِ ضرائرِ
فإن[22] هنَّ أَبدين المودَّة والرضا   فكم من حقُود غُيِّبَتْ في السرائرِ
قرائك ما بين النساءِ أذيَّةٌ   لَهنَّ فلا تحملْ أذاةَ الحرائرِ
وإن كنتَ غرًّا بالزمانِ وأهلهِ   فتكفيك إحدى الآنساتِ الغرائرِ
لقد ودَّ أصحابُ الكبائرِ لو رأوْا   جرائرهم مقذوفةً في الجرائر

If it is two wives you have, be prepared to do battle
with two enemies; and beware of taking on a third.
For though they display love and good will, how many
an ill-feeling is concealed in their consciences?
Marrying more than one woman is also harmful to women;
so don’t take up this harming of the noble ladies.
If you are inexperienced with the times and its people,
then one young beguiled miss will be enough for you.
If the perpetrators of great sins could only see their crimes
they would wish to have them all cast down the bottom of wells.
(L I.376.17; 377.1–4)

To take this enhanced rhyming process one step further, al-Maʿarrī often increases his rhymes not only by the addition of consonants that are not strictly speaking necessary, but also by the addition of vowels that are not necessary in more conventional *shi'r* or by keeping a certain vowel constant although ordinarily it could—and indeed would—alternate with another vowel.

Thus, in the following poem taken from *Luzūm*, there is superimposed upon the basic, rather simple rhyme syllable of the sound “um” (ضمة or short vowel *u* followed by consonant م) the Arabic letters *rā'*/ر, *alif*/ا, *hamzah*/ء, and *kāf*/ك, so that the full rhyme then becomes (with the English *x* here standing for any consonant in the Arabic alphabet) *x+arā'irikum.*

يا أُمة في التراب هامدةً   تجاوز الله عن سرائِرِكُمْ
يا ليتكُمْ لم تَطوا إماءَكُمُ   ولا دنوْتُمْ إلى حرائِرِكُمْ

إن استرحتُم مما نكابدُهُ   فنحنُ من بعدُ في جرائِرِكُمْ
قد خطبَ الخاطبون نِسوتكم   وأُسكتَ الحسّ مِن ضرائِرِكُمْ
ذرَّ البِلى فوقَكم رمادتَهُ   ولم تَعودُوا إلى ذرائِرِكُمْ
لو شاءَ ربي أمرَّ مقتدِراً   ما نقضَ الموتُ مِن مرائِرِكُمْ

O nation that is slumbering beneath the earth!
May God overlook your deepest secrets!
If only you had not harbored your slave girls,
and also not approached your free-born ladies.
If *you've* found rest from what *we* now endure,
we still remain in the thick of your sins.
The suitors have courted your women; all feeling
in your multiple partners has been silenced.
Decay has spread its ashes over all of you;
and you have not returned to your perfumes.
Had my Lord willed as much, in His omnipotence
He'd have twisted from your ropes what death has frayed.
(L II.326.5–9)

In the following poem, which has a *qāfiyah murdafah*/قافية مردفة or a rhyme a portion of which consists of one of the Arabic letters of prolongation (*alif*/ا, *wāw*/و, *or yā'*/ي —and in this particular case *wāw*/و), al-Maʿarrī keeps the *wāw*/و (i.e., ū) letter of prolongation constant throughout *along with* the *hā'*/ه (i.e., h sound) immediately preceding it; although according to the rules of rhyme, he could have alternated the long *wāw*/و with long *yā'*/ي.

لَهْفِي على ليلة ويوم   تألفت منهما الشهورُ
وأُلفيا عنصرَيْ زمان   ليس لِأسْرارهِ ظهورُ
قد أصبح الدينُ مضمحلاً   وغيَّرَتْ آيَهُ الدهورُ
فلا زكاةٌ ولا رمادته   ولا صلاةٌ ولا طُهورُ
وٱعتاضَ حِلَّ النكاح قومٌ   بنسوة ما لها مُهورُ

O how I regret day and night
from which the months are composed,
and which are as two elements of time

whose mysteries aren't to be revealed.
For religion has has been rendered barren,
its miraculous signs altered by the ages.
There's no paying of the alms tax, no fasting;
no prayer and no purification.
And a people forfeit lawful marriage
for taking women who have no dowries.
(L I.322.11–15)

In other words, the rhyme in the poem just cited is made more complex than necessary by the inclusion of the consonant *hā'*/ه as well as by the invariable use of *wāw*/و as a long vowel immediately preceding the basic rhyme syllable/sound of "rū," the enhanced rhyme sound thus being "hūrū."

The *invariable* use of either *yā'*/ي or *wāw*/و as a long vowel (whichever the case might be) in the poems of *Luzūm*—when they are used in a *qāfiyah murdafah*/قافية مردفة, in other words—is an especially common practice by al-Maʿarrī. Yohanan Friedmann found no deviation from the formula whatsoever whenever al-Maʿarrī employed it in *Luzūm*. This, Friedmann adds, makes al-Maʿarrī somewhat unique as a writer of poems containing *qāfiyah murdafah*.[23]

The use of enriched or supererogatory rhymes throughout the entire *Luzūm*—poem for poem and line for line—was an extraordinary technical accomplishment on the part of al-Maʿarrī, giving this volume of poetry an intricate texture of rhyme sounds[24] virtually unparalleled in Arabic poetry.[25] On the other hand, carried on for so long without interruption, the technique becomes decidedly monotonous over the course of the entire *Luzūm* (although Arabic poetry, like most if not all poetry, is meant primarily to be listened to as it is recited; ordinarily one would hardly recite for listeners anything remotely close to an entire volume of poetry, even if a comparatively short volume). Further, the enhanced rhymes sometimes dictate the use of a rare or relatively unfamiliar choice of words—the forced *bon mot*—at the expense of clarity, precision, and, finally—the truth be told—sense. At the end of each line of his poems, al-Maʿarrī had to use words or particular forms of words (to take but one example: one of a variety of allowable broken plurals, and not necessarily the most commonly used) that before all else met the requirements of his rigid, more complex rhyme patterns.

In any event, it was within this framework of short, multiple-rhymed poems, in the final version that has come down to us (beginning with a poem ending in *hamzah*/ء and concluding thousands of lines later with a poem ending in *yā'*/ي), that al-Maʿarrī chose to lay down his thoughts in *Luzūm*, his "speech stripped of falsehoods." To paraphrase the long paragraph by von Kremer recently quoted, these thoughts indeed very often revolve around social, political, religious, and moral-philosophical questions; and it is with the elucidation of these and only these that this study is ultimately concerned. It can't be denied, however, that *Luzūm* does have its more mundane side. In it al-Maʿarrī relates many sundry and incidental facts pertaining to history, geography, grammar, etymology, prosody, fellow poets, folklore, astrology, and other branches of learning typically canvassed by the learned class of his era, especially the masters of *adab*/أدب. Also, notwithstanding his remarks to the contrary in the introduction to *Luzūm*, al-Maʿarrī devotes considerable attention, albeit as asides, to rather florid descriptions of people, places, objects or events, or a conceit, the main purpose of which seems to be the exhibition of his immense vocabulary and formidable rhetorical (i.e., بديع) skills (although to an extent quite appropriate—because expected—for the master of *adab*/أدب).

In short, *Luzūm* is likely to strike many as a strange combination of thoughts both profound and commonplace; of the philosophical, as von Kremer and Ṭāhā Ḥusayn, for example, would have it, but also the decidedly unphilosophical and even trite, as has been stressed, for example, by R. A. Nicholson and Ṭāhā Ḥusayn himself; and both of whom were admirers of al-Maʿarrī.[26] Although there is often a *loose* logical relationship or affinity between many of the various ideas and topics of *Luzūm*, including especially those described by von Kremer, the ideas or topics are rarely arranged in a logically ordered sequence. On balance, the *Luzūm* is as disorderly and incoherent thematically as it is orderly, methodical, and coherent structurally. Often, no sooner does al-Maʿarrī broach one subject than he moves on to another quite unrelated one, seemingly unconcerned with the lack of transition and the (at least on the surface) juxtaposition of dissimilar thoughts and ideas. This occurs not only between poems but also within them. The following short individual poems, which are contiguous in L II.202; 203, 1–7, should serve to make this clear:

طلبَ الخسائسَ وارتقى في منبر   يَصِفُ الحسابَ لِأمَّةٍ ليهولَهَا
ويكون غيرَ مُصدِّقٍ بقيامةٍ   أمْسَى يُمثِّلُ في النفوسِ ذُهولَهَا
ووجدْتُ ليل الغَيِّ ألبسَ مُرْدَها   وشيوُخَها وشبابَها وكُهولَها
لو قامَ أَمْوات العواصم وحدها   مَلأُوا البلادَ حُزونَهَا وسُهولَهَا
فَخُذِ الذي قالَ اللبيبُ وَعِشْ بهِ   ودعِ الغواة كذوبها وجَهولَهَا

اِفْهَمْ عن الأيامِ فَهْيَ نواطقٌ   مازالَ يَضربُ صرفُها لأمْثالا
لم يمضِ في دنياك أمرٌ معجِبٌ   إلّا أَرَتْكَ لِما مضى تِمْثالا

حديثٌ جاءَ عن هابيـــــلَ   فـي الدهـر وقابيلا
وطيرٌ عكَفَتْ يوماً   على الجيشِ أبابيلا
مَتَى تَرحلُ عن دنياً   تزيدُ الأهل تَخبيلا
سِواهُمْ نَخَلَ النُصّحَ   ولاقَوْكَ غرابيلا
لَبِسْنَا مِن مَدَى الأَيا   مِ للغيِّ سرابيلا
وقضَّيتُ زمانَ الشَرْ   خِ تقييداً وتكبيلا
وزارَ الطَّيفُ في النومِ   فلم تسألْهُ تقبيلا
ففَرِّقْ مالَكَ الجمَّ   وخلِّ الأرضَ تسبيلا
ولا[27] تستزْرِ بالقومِ   إذا كانوا تنابيلا
فما كنتَ من الرهط   يُعَدّونَ مقابيلا
ولا يبقى على الساعا   تِ أغفارٌ بإشبيلا

أَيا شيعةَ إسماعيلَ   إنَّ الصبرَ قد عِيلا
كذاك الدهرُ والأيّا   مُ يَفْعلْنَ الأَفاعيلا
أَرى الأمصارَ لا تملـ   كُ للحافرِ تنعيلا
وقد غَيَّرَ معناها   أذًى يأتي أَراعيلا
كما جُزِّئَ بيتُ الشِعـ   رِ تقطيعاً وتفعيلا

He has pursued the wicked and yet mounted a pulpit
describing Judgment Day so as to terrify a community.
Not himself a believer in resurrection,
he's taken to depicting its fright to others.
I've found the night of seduction enveloping the young
as well as the old; the boys as well as the men.

If the dead of our frontiers alone were to arise,
they would fill both the hill and the dale of the country.
Take what the intelligent man says. Live by *that.*
Ignore the seducers, be they fools or liars.

Understand the passing of the days, for they speak.
Their misfortunes continue to provide parables.
A strange event never occurs in your world without
showing you its likeness from the days gone by.

Over time a story came down
concerning Cain and Abel;
And once too there were the birds
that clove to the army in swarms!
When will you depart from a world
that adds to peoples' misery?
Others have sifted good advice;
they've found *you* like sieves.
With the passing of the days we've
robed ourselves in misguidance,
and I've spent my youth bound; fettered.
The specter has visited during sleep—
yet you did not ask it for a kiss.
So disperse your possessions;
leave the earth charitably.
And don't slight people if of small stature;
for you're not of stock to be accepted.
And neither will the goats in Ishbil
survive the passing of the hours.

O followers of Ismāʿīl!
Truly, steadfastness has been lost.
Such is the course of fate
when the days work their ways.
I see that the frontier cities
are no longer shodding the hoof.

And their meaning has been changed
by harm coming like blasts of wind—
a change just like when a line of verse
is parsed into segments and feet.

The above section is actually an example of one of the thematically less desultory moments in *Luzūm.* Despite the sudden switch in topics or themes between poems, the individual poems themselves, with the possible exception of the third, may be said to cling to an idea or two and hang together reasonably well. To a large extent, this is because the poems are short, necessarily limiting the number of topics al-Maʿarrī could address in them. To see the most extreme manifestations of the disjointed thematic nature of some of the poems of *Luzūm,* one needs to turn to the longer specimens (as comparatively few as they may be), where al-Maʿarrī could—and often would—touch upon and abandon with dizzying abruptness a myriad of topics. Despite its length, at least one poem of this sort should be quoted from start to finish in order to illustrate adequately the point being underscored here. Hence the lines below.

قد أصبحت ونُعاتُها نُعَّاتُها   وكذلك الدنيا تَعيبُ[28] سُعاتُها
كَرّارةٌ أحزانها ضَرّارةٌ   سكانُها مَرّارةٌ ساعاتُها
نامت دعاةُ الدولتين فضاعتا   وهي المنيةُ لا تنامُ[29] دُعاتُها
ذَرْها وتلك نصيحةٌ معروفةٌ   عَظُمَت منافعها وقَلَّ وُعاتُها
لا تَتْبعَنَّ الغانياتِ مُماشياً   إنّ الغوانيَ جَمَّةٌ تَبِعاتُها
واْحْذَرْ اطّلعْنَ من المناظر فالهُدى   أَن لا تراكَ الدهرَ مُطّلِعاتُها
وآحْذَرْ مقالَ الناسِ إنّك بينَها   سرحانُ ضأْنٍ حين غابَ رُعاتُها
ودَعِ القراءةَ إن ظننتَ جهيرها   ذَكَرتْ بهِ الحاجاتِ مستمعاتُها
فالصوتُ هَدرُ الفحلِ تُؤْنِسُ رِكزَهُ   أُلافُهُ فتُجيبُ مُمتنِعاتُها
أَوْلى من البيضِ الأوانسِ بالعُلا   قُلُصٌ تجوبُ الليلَ مُدَّرعاتُها
جُمِعتْ جسومٌ من غرائزَ أربعٍ   وتفرّقت من بعدُ مُجْتَمِعاتُها
وهي النفوسُ إذا تُميّزُ بينها   فأعزُّها في العيشِ مُقتنِعاتُها
ومتى طَرَدْتَ أُمورَها بقياسها   فأَحقُّها بمذَلّةٍ طَمِعاتُها[30]
وكأَنَّ آمال الفتى وحُتُوفُهُ   فِئتانِ تهزأُ منه مصطَرِعاتُها
أوقاتُ عاجلةٍ كأَنَّ مُضيَّها   ومضُ البروقِ خواطفاً لَمَعاتُها
وتخالُفُ الأيامِ[31] حُكمٌ واقعٌ   فيها ومثلُ سُبُوتها جُمُعاتُها

كم أُوقِدَتْ لِشموعِها صُبْحيّةٌ   في الليلِ ثُمَّتَ أُطفئَت شَمعاتُها
فَمَتى يُنَبَّهُ من رُقادٍ مُهلِكٍ   من قد أَضرَّ بعينِهِ هَجَعاتُها
وترادفتْ هذي الجُدُوبُ ولم تلحْ   غرَّاءُ تبغي الروضَ منتَجِعاتُها
وكأَنَّ تسبيحاً هديلُ حمامةٍ   في مجدِ ربِّكَ أَلِفَتْ سَجَعاتُها
من يغتبطْ بمعيشةٍ فأَمامهُ   نُوَبٌ تطيلُ عناءَهُ فَجَعاتُها
وإِذا رَجَعْتَ الى النهى فذواهب   الأيامِ غيرَ مُؤَمَّلٍ رَجَعَاتُها
تَهْوَى السلامةَ والقُبورُ مَضاجعٌ   سَلِبَتْ[32] عن اليقظاتِ مضْطَجِعاتُها
دنياكَ مُشبِهَةُ السَرابِ فلا تَزُلْ   برَزينِ حلمِكَ مُوشِكاً خُدَعاتُها
رقشاءُ فيها ليلها ونهارها   تلك الضئيلةُ شأنها لَسَعاتُها
وتَرِثُّ أغراضُ الشبابِ وينطوي   إبّانُها فتُنيبُ مُرتدعاتُها
ويُنهْنِهُ الرجلُ الحصيفُ بِسِنِّهِ   أوْطارَهُ فتَضيقُ مُتّسعاتُها
وتقارعتْ شُوسُ الخُطوبِ فَكُشِّفَتْ   عن مَهْلكِ الحيوانِ مقترعاتُها
تستعذِبُ المُهَجَاتُ وِرْدَ بقائِها   فَتَلَذُّهُ وتُغِصُّها جُرَعاتُها
وتَظَلُّ حَبّاتُ القُلوبِ زَرَائِعاً   كالأرضِ والشهواتُ مُزدَرِعاتُها
إن كان قد عَتَمَ الظَلامُ فطالما   مَتَعَ النهارُ فما وَنَتْ مُتَعاتُها
نُظِمَتْ قصائدُ مِن أذىً مُثُلاتُها   أَمثَالُها فأَتَتْكَ منتزعاتُها
وتُعينُ أسبابُ الحياةِ وينتَهي   أَمَدٌ لها فَتَخونُ مُنقطِعَاتُها
فاخْفِضْ حديثَكَ للمحدِّثِ جاهداً   فذَميمةُ الاصواتِ مُرتفعاتُها
مُهَجٌ تخافُ من الردى ولعلهُ   إن جاء تأْمَنُ صَوْلةً هَلِعاتُها[33]
أَو ما تُفيقُ من الغرامِ بفاركٍ   مشهورةٍ مع غيرنا وَقَعَاتُها
نفسٌ تُرَقِّعُ أَمرَها حتى إذا   أَجَلٌ تَوَرَّدَ أُعجزتْ رُقَعَاتُها
وترى الصلاةَ على الغويِّ ثقيلةً   مثلَ الهضابِ تؤُودُهُ[34] رَكَعَاتُها
وتُضِلُّ أَفعالُ الشرورِ جُناتَها   وتفوزُ بالخيراتِ مصطنِعاتُها
ومحاسنُ الدوَلِ التي غُرَّت بها   حالت فقيلَ حِسانُها شَنِعاتُها
والنارُ إن قَرَّبتَ كفَّكَ مرةً   منها ثنت عن قبضها لَذَعاتُها
ولعلَّ عكساً في الليالي كائنٌ   فتعودَ في الشُرُفاتِ متَّضعاتُها

She has become as though her announcers of death are her praisers
Such is the world. Those who run after her find fault with her.
Many are her sorrows, evil her inhabitants, and fleeting her hours.
The propagandists of the two regimes have slept, and thus are lost;
but as for the propagandists of death, they never sleep.
Leave her. This is good and familiar advice.
Its benefits are great though those aware of it few.
Do not follow the beautiful ladies while walking;
many are the evil consequences of this.

If they should look down from their balconies,
it would be best that they never catch sight of you.
You should take caution lest people say about you
you're a wolf among sheep whose pastors are absent.
And avoid reciting the Qur'ān if you think that
its declamation has listening women think of desires.
Its sound is the stallion's neigh (for those intimate with it);
they sense the softness; thus though denied it they accede to it.
More worthy of being exalted than the pleasant white ladies
are the camels traveling at night trudging through the darkness.
Bodies are put together as a whole from four natures;
their aggregates are later to become separated.
As for souls, if you were to distinguish among them
the most glorious in life are the self-contented.
And when you follow their affairs by comparison,
the most contemptible are those that are covetous.
It would seem that man's fates and hopes are two
factions whose struggles with each other mock him.
They are rapidly fleeting moments whose passing by
is like the flicker of lightning whose flashes are brief.
The succession of the days is an established edict,
and the Fridays among them are just like the Saturdays.
How often a beauty is inflamed at night out of joy—
but only to have her candles of joy extinguished!
So when is there awakening from deadly slumber
for the one who has gone astray with his sleepy eyes?
These dry years come one after another; yet to appear
is a rain cloud for the followers who seek meadows.
It's as if there is divine praise in the pigeon coo,
with the coos being composed in praise of your Lord.
He elated by life has before him misfortunes
whose afflictions will only prolong his suffering.
And if you resort to intelligent reasoning,
it follows that the days pass with no hope of return.
You crave well-being but the graves are beds and those
who sleep therein are unaware of the awakening.

Your world is like a mirage; and thus her deceptions
don't leave your strong resolve to accomplish something.
She's a serpent speckled with her days and her nights,
and it is the concern of this thin snake to bite.
The aspirations of youth grow shabby as time passes,
and as the obstacles come one after another.
Whereas the man grown judicious by age checks his desires,
so that the comforts that they can provide become curtailed.
The head-strong fates have cast their lots among themselves;
what they draw is revealed in the destruction of life.
Souls find sweet the water of their long duration;
savor it; but their draughts from this water choke them.
And, just like the earth, the seeds of the heart remain
prepared for cultivation; the passions are the crops.
If the night has grown very dark, well then the day
for long has been bright and its joys unremitting.
Harm has been fashioned into long poems; the proverbs
are harm's punishments—and the citations have reached you.
The ropes of life give support until their end is reached,
and then the severed pieces of the rope forsake you.
Lower your speech to the person who addresses you;
for the blameworthy voices are the raised voices.
Souls fear their ruination, yet if it comes, perhaps
the anxious among them will be safe from tyranny.
Or they never recover from passion for a wench
who has become well known for her affairs with others.
A soul patches up her concerns—until such time as,
death having come, her patches are no longer effective.
You see that prayers weigh heavy on the misguided one.
The prostrations weigh upon him like mountain tops.
Evil deeds lead astray those who commit them
while those who do good deeds will obtain them.
The good qualities that distinguish nations have changed;
now it's said that their abominations are good deeds.
And the burn of fire deters you from grabbing it—
if merely one time you draw your hand close to it.

Perhaps with nights' passing there will be a reversal
so that the once lowly rise among the crenellations.
(L I.170–72;173.1–4)

The above poem as a whole could hardly be considered as an example of al-Maʿarrī at one of his profounder moments in *Luzūm,* when he is the man of lofty thoughts as described by von Kremer or as portrayed by Nicholson in his carefully selected and exquisitely cadenced "Meditations," or as portrayed by Ameen Rihani in his equally masterful *The Luzumiyat of Abu'l-Ala,* or, for that matter, as envisioned by anyone who facilely refers to al-Maʿarrī as "philosopher" with comparisons in the same breath to Lucretius, Milton, or Dante. And yet a good portion of *Luzūm* reads precisely like the last cited poem insofar as the topical meanderings (not to mention the level of the discourse) are concerned.

In other words, it can be quite taxing, to say the least, to follow and comprehend al-Maʿarrī for the longer stretches in *Luzūm* because of the rambling approach to his many thoughts, especially when the concern for sense is quite obviously at least *compromised* by the need to meet the rigors of the self-imposed enhanced rhyme format.

At the same time, as the long poem just cited should have made clear, even in places other than the end-rhyme words in al-Maʿarrī's verses in *Luzūm*, the language is no easy matter. Occasionally, al-Maʿarrī composed in relatively simple and unaffected speech, of which the shorter poems just cited above might be taken as examples. But more often than not, he chose to make his poems as florid and erudite as possible—much like the long one just cited. Extraordinarily learned in grammar and philology, even by the formidable standards of the Arabic *adab*/أدب culture, he lost no opportunity to display his immense vocabulary and knowledge of rare and doubtful words. Further, like virtually all of the poets of his time, his aesthetic standards in the main were those of the *badīʿ*/بديع orientation in Arabic poetry. Al-Maʿarrī employed the more common of these devices quite liberally. Examples include *jinās*/جناس (punning involving words of similar if not identical letters/sounds), *ṭibāq*/طباق (the mentioning of words of opposite meaning in the same line), *tarṣīʿ*/ترصيع (internal rhymes corresponding in rhythm), *ighrāq*/إغراق (hyperbole), *taḍmīn*/تضمين (quoting from the Qur'ān, a *ḥadīth*/حديث report, or a fellow poet), *talmīḥ*/تلميح (allusion without direct quotation), *īhām*/إيهام/(double entendre), and *radd al-'ajuz 'alā al-ṣadr*/ رد العجز على الصدر (making a line end with the same word with which it begins).

Most of these figures just named have already appeared in the few selections of *Luzūm* cited thus far. In the last selection cited, for example, the very first line has the pun *nu'ātuhā-nu''ātuhā*/نُعاتُها نُعّاتُها; the second line has an example of *tarṣī' (karrāratun aḥzānuhā ḍarrāratun sukkānuhā marrāratun sā'ātuhā*/ كرّارةٌ أحزانها ضرّارةٌ / سكانُها مرّارةٌ ساعاتها); line three has *talmīḥ*/تلميح (*ad-dawlatayn*/الدولتين proabably refers to the ʿAbbāsid and Umayyad dynasties of the Islamic commonwealth, although maybe the dynasties of the Fāṭimids and Mirdāsids); line eleven has an example of *ṭibāq* (*jumi'at . . . tafarraqat*/تفرقت . . . جمعت ["put together . . . dispersed"]); and line twenty-eight has a double entendre (*taqāra'at*/تقارعت can mean either "to clash" or "to cast lots with one another"; and thus *muqtari'āt*/ مقترعات, the participle derived from this verb, means either "clashing" or "casting lots"). In the second line of the poem quoted above that begins with حديث جاء عن هابيل في الدهر وقابيلا, there is a good example of *taḍmīn*/تضمين in the line that follows it: وطير عكفت يوما على الجيش أبابيلا. This line is taken in part from the Qur'ān 105:3, which reads: *wa-arsala 'alayhim ṭayran abābīla* /وأرسل عليهم طيراً أبابيل ("And he sent against them birds in swarms").

Of all these rhetorical embellishments, *jinās*/جناس, or punning, was arguably al-Ma'arrī's favorite. His use of it is unrelenting. The reader of Arabic will have noticed that the last poem cited from *Luzūm* above has many plays on words other than *nu'ātuhā/nu''ātuhā*/نُعاتها نُعّاتها. It is not an exception in this respect. The following passages from *Luzūm,* where the plays on words are underlined, are comparable in terms of frequency of *jinās*. Many similar examples could be cited.

عذيري من الدنيا عَرتني بظُلْمِها   فتمنحني قوتي لتأخذَ قُوَّتي
وَجدْتُ بها ديني دَنيّاً فَضرَّني   وأَضللتُ منها في مُروتٍ مُروَّتي
أخوتُ كما خاتت عُقَابٌ لو أنني   قدَرْتُ على أَمرٍ فَعَدِّ أُخُوَّتي
وأصبحتُ في تيهِ الحياة منادياً   بأَرفع صوْتي أَين أطلبُ صُوَّتي
وما زال حوتي راصدي وهو آخذي   فما لمتابي ليس يَغسلُ حُوَّتي
رآنيَ ربُّ الناس فيها مُتَابعاً   هَوايَ فويحي يَومَ أسكنُ هُوَّتي
وما بَرِحتْ لي أَلْوةٌ حَرَجيَّةٌ   تُصَيّرُ مِن رَطْبِ العَضاةِ أَلُوَّتي
أَبَوْتُكَ يا إثمي ومَن لي بأنني   أَتيتُكَ فاشكُرْ لا شكرتَ أُبُوَّتي

واودوا إلى الله ما أُدٌّ ومفخرها　　شيءٌ يُعَدُّ ولا أَوْدٌ ولا أُودُ
طوبى لموؤُودةٍ في حالِ مولدها　　ظلماً فليتَ أباها الفظَّ موؤُودُ
يا ربِّ هل أنا بالغفرانِ في ظعني　　مزوَّدٌ إنَّ قلبي منك مزؤُودُ
والناس كالأيْكِ مخبوءٌ[35] لعاضدهِ　　إلى اليَبوسِ وماضٍ وهو يموُودُ

Who will excuse me if I avenge the world? It has stricken me.
She gives me my sustenance only to take my strength away.
I have found my religion weak with her, and this has harmed me;
I have lost in her in a desert my manly qualities.
I'd pounce on my prey like an eagle—were I able.
Therefore you can give up on my brotherliness.
In the wasteland of life I've come to shout, calling out
in my loudest voice, "Where do I seek my guiding light?"
My Pisces still lies waiting for me; it is my captor.
Thus why repent? It does not wash out the black of my sins.
The Lord of humankind has seen me pursuing my whims,
so woe unto me on the day I go to dwell in my grave.
And I still have for myself the coffin's aloes wood,
which from the soft acacia tree is what forms aloes for me.
I fathered you, O sin, and who could have helped me bring you forth?
So be grateful for my fatherhood if you really must.
(L I.179.8–10; 180.1–5)

Turn to God; for the tribe of Udd and their boasting
are of no worth; nor are the tribe of Awd or Ūd.
Blessed is the baby girl buried alive at her birth
unjustly; would that the cruel father were buried too!
O Lord, is it with forgiveness that, upon my departure,
I will be provided? My heart is frightened of you.
People are like a thicket of trees: hidden from pruning
until stiff and dry yet also cut when soft and tender.
(L I.254.4–7)

At its most excessive, *jinās* in *Luzūm* could look very much like the following (of course virtually inimitable in the English, as is the case even in the previous examples):

نوائبُ إن جَلَّتْ تَجلَّتْ سريعةً   وإمّا توالت في الزمان تولَّتِ
ودنياكَ إن قلَّت أَقلَّتْ وإن قَلَتْ   فَمِن قَلَتٍ في الدين نجَّتْ وعلَّتِ
غَلَتْ وأَغالتْ ثم غَالتْ وأَوحشت   وحَشَّتْ وحاشت واستمال وملَّتِ
وصلَّت بنيرانٍ وصلَّتْ سُيُوفُهَا   وسلَّتْ حساماً من أداةٍ وسلَّتِ
أَزالتْ وزلَّتْ بالفتى عَن مقامِه   وحلَّتْ فلَمّا أُحِكْمَ العِقدُ[36] حلَّتِ

If misfortunes become great, they reveal themselves quickly;
if over time they come uninterrupted, they also pass on.
If your world has become small, it also elevates;
if it hates, through faith it raises and saves from doom.
It transgresses and suckles, kills and causes loneliness;
it kindles and hinders, wins affection and grows weary.
It causes conflagrations, and its swords clink and clash;
it draws a sharp-edged blade but it also gives solace.
It eliminates, causing man to slip from his domicile;
and it adorns, but when the necklace is fast it undoes it.
(L I.180. 9–11;181.1–2)

Word plays as complicated as these can eventually be made reasonably comprehensible. But it is a long and tedious process, particularly when the words being played upon are not very familiar to begin with: yet one more formidable challenge to the reader and interpreter of *Luzūm.*

Adding to this list of challenges, and more formidable still at first sight, is perhaps the single most arresting (and celebrated) feature of al-Maʿarrī's writing in *Luzūm*, at least in the context of reconstructing the man's thought: the contradictions. These are both obvious and frequent. "These stars are not eternal, not to my mind. / By my life! Rather they are created in time" (وليست بالقدائم في ضميري / لعمركَ بل حوادثُ مُوجَدَات) al-Maʿarrī says at one moment (L I.167.1) in one of his poems that touches upon the eternity of matter and the creation of the world; and, in the same vein elsewhere, "My belief is not in the eternity of the stars, nor my school of thought the eternity of the world" (وليس اعتقادي خلود النجوم/ ولا مذهبي قدم العالم) (L II.320.11). Yet elsewhere (L II.169. 10–ll) he says, "If what the philosopher says is true, then my time / has never been free from me, and never will be. I'm split up at one moment but recombined another" (i.e., the matter of bodies is subject to composition and decomposition but not total annihilation) إذا كان ما قال الحكيمُ فما خلا / زماني مني منذُ كان ولا يخلو/ أُفَرَّق طورا ثم أُجْمَع تارة; and then, with reference to the sun, moon, and stars

They run their course within the celestial sphere turned
by God's will, with no fear of being breathless.
Praise be their Creator! I do not profess that
the stars are something that exists only in time.

يجرين في الفلك المُدار بإذ   نِ الله لا يخشَيْنَ مِن بُهْرِ
سبحانَ خالقهنَّ لستُ أقو   ل الشهبُ كائنةٌ[37] مع الدهرِ

(L I.415.3, 6)

With regard to bodily resurrection after death, in one line al-Maʿarrī states وإنما الجسمُ تُرْبٌ خير حالاتِهِ سُقْيا الغمائم (L I.415.3) ("The body is only dust whose best state is being watered by the rain clouds") and in another (L I.106.3), نُوَدَّعُ بالصلاةِ وَدَاعَ يأْسٍ / ونُتْرَكُ في التراب فلا نهادُ ("We are bid a sad farewell with prayer, and then left in the earth where we are unmoved"); his implication in this instance being that there is no bodily resurrection. Elsewhere (L I.185.14) he implies the very opposite: وقُدْرةُ اللهِ ليس يُعْجزُها / حَشَرٌ لخلقٍ ولابعثٌ لأمواتِ ("God's omnipotence is a real fact; it is not incapable of assembling Creation [on the Day of Judgment] nor of resurrecting the dead). L I.391.13 is similar: بحكمة خالقي طيّي ونشري / وليس بمُعْجِزِ الخلّاقِ حشري ("My being folded under [i.e., buried] and unfolded [i.e., resurrected] are by way of my Creator's wisdom; it is not beyond the power of God the Creator to gather me up with others on the Day of Resurrection"). Al-Maʿarrī seems to question the credibility and worth of religion when he says, "Whenever you fall back on religion, assaulting it / are concepts that work to conspire against good conscience. And the mind is made to marvel as all religious laws / are but a story blindly followed, unjudged by logic."

ومتى ركبتَ إلى الديانةِ غالَها   فِكَرٌ على حُسن الضمير دسائسُ
والعقل يَعجَب والشرائعُ كُلُّها   خبرٌ يُقلَّد لم يَقِسْهُ قائسُ

(L II.20.13–14)

Yet he seems to defend religion at a moment such as L II.99.10, where he says خاب الذي سارعن دُنياهُ مُرتحِلا / وليس في كفّهِ مِن دينِه طَرَفُ ("He who departs from his world comes to naught if he does not have in his hand a share of his religion"). Similar in L I.304.3 are the words نبذتمُ الأديان مِن خلفكُمْ / وليس في الحِكمةِ أن تُنْبَذا): "You have thrown religions behind you yet it is not wise that they be rejected." Contradictions like these—usually pertaining to some of the more important social, political, and religio-philosophical issues of concern to Islamdom during al-Maʿarrī's day—run throughout *Luzūm*.

A careful and thorough reading of *Luzūm* reveals that some of these contradictions are perhaps more apparent than real. Over the course of his poems, al-Maʿarrī rewords, expands, or modifies his thoughts and themes in a way that sometimes allows for a plausible resolution of seemingly inconsistent lines of argument. Fatalism and belief in predetermination, for example, are absolute in many instances (see, e.g., L I.84.13; 160.7–9; 325.6; L II.124.4; 234.14; 309.10–11). And just as absolute in many instances is his conviction that humans should strive to do good and eschew evil, the assumption in this case being that humans are in fact capable of freely determining their behavior with respect to good and evil, and thus to an extent capable of determining the course of human events in the world (L I.174.8; 266.13; 434.4–5; L II.87.7; 115.4; 314.4–5). These two positions as such are irreconcilable. How can humans choose a course of action if fate, or a predetermined divine decree, governs all? Elsewhere, however, al-Maʿarrī rather straightforwardly—almost prosaically—states that he adheres neither to a belief in predetermination nor to free will (L I.351.1); tells humans not to live according to one of these doctrines or the other but according to a doctrine somewhere between the two (L II.358.9); and asserts that human beings have not been created as creatures of fate to the extent that they must sin just because others do (L II.388.16). On balance, then, one can plausibly advance that he was neither a strict predeterminist nor a strict believer in free will, but part one and part the other. That is to say, he felt that God set in motion in the world certain forces over which humankind has little or no control; but he would not go so far as to say that humankind is *absolutely* incapable of deciding his own destiny. At the very least, humans have enough free will to choose to do good and try to live the just and righteous life.

In similar fashion, one might plausibly argue for a resolution of some of al-Maʿarrī's apparently contradictory (and fairly infamous) statements concerning religion. As has just been illustrated by way of citation (in one instance at least), he both criticized religion as being illogical and incredulous yet insisted that humans not dismiss religion, not leave this world without having partaken of it. But he defines what he means by religion in a way that would allow him to hold these views with no real contradiction. "True religion," he says, "is man's obligingly renouncing sensuous pleasures with his power and might for as long as he lives" (L I.361.14; الدِينُ هَجرُ الفتى اللذاتِ عن يُسُرٍ / في صحَّةٍ واقتدارٍ منهُ ما عَمِرا); it is "sincerity always coupled with chasteness" (L I.438.5; الدينُ نصح الجيوبِ مقترناً / مدَى الليالي بعِفَّةِ الحُجَز) and "your treating justly *all* people" (الدين إنصافُكَ الأقوامَ كُلَّهُم) (L I.103.9). Religious piety is not merely—and perhaps not at all—a matter of adhering to particular prescribed rituals.

وتحسبُ أَنّ التقيَّ الذي تُشاهدهُ راكعاً ساجدا
تَنَبَّهْ فأنتَ على غِرَّةٍ أخالُكَ مستيقظاً هاجدا

You think that the pious is the one whom
you see prostrating and bowing in prayer.
But take notice. You are being deceived.
I fancy you awake yet as though asleep.
(L I.277.5–6)

In light of these remarks, one could reasonably suggest that when al-Maʿarrī criticized religion and/or religious piety, he had in mind the formal teachings and ritual-oriented practices of a faith; and when he encouraged humankind to be religious, what he intended by that was that people simply lead a just and morally upright life, altogether and indiscriminately, without consideration for the differences in formal religious systems.

Unfortunately, a great many of the other contradictions in *Luzūm* do not allow themselves to be ironed out in this fashion. Certain sentiments or thoughts in al-Maʿarrī's verses seem absolutely incompatible with one another, no matter how many different ways he expresses them and we "read" them. No amount of dictionary work—unlike the case with his puns and erudite vocabulary—nor cross-referencing—unlike the case with his topical meanderings and abrupt subject-jumping—are of help here.

Shortly, it will be underscored how the contradictions of this nature are to be made comprehensible; nearly predictably so. Before turning to that, however, there are other features to al-Maʿarrī's composition style in *Luzūm* that deserve mention. In addition to the contradictions, these, too, are frequently manifested and render his thoughts—especially on matters social, political, and religio-philosophical—considerably less than unconditioned or unambiguous. Examples follow.

As the first, mention ought to be made of a reluctance to identify clearly and fully a school of thought, religio-philosophical sect, or individual being commented upon. The following short poem illustrates this tendency.

لقد جاء قومٌ يدَّعونَ فضيلةً　　وكُلُّهُم يبغي لِمُهْجَتهِ نَفْعا
وما انخفضوا كي يرفعوكم وإنما　　رأَوْا خُفْضَكم طولَ الحياةِ لهم رَفْعا
وما ثبَّتوا مِن شاهدٍ يُهتَدى بهِ　　فإن لزموا دَعْواهم فالْزَموا الدَفْعا

A people have come claiming that they have virtue,
but they all desire what's of advantage to them.
They do not lower themselves so as to uplift you; rather,
they find that lowering you is always uplifting to them.
Nor have they established a witness for right guidance.
So hold fast to your defense if *they* hold fast to their claims.
(L II.85.8–10)

Given the undeniable religious overtones of the words *daʿwā*/دعوى, *yaddaʿūna*/يدّعون, *shāhid*/شاهد, and *yuhtadā* يهتدى it is rather obvious that al-Maʿarrī is attacking in these lines the proselytizers of religion, and within that broad framework, in all likelihood the Fāṭimid Ismāʿīlīs in particular, casting aspersions on their sincerity and the demonstrability of the truth of their doctrines (especially belief in *al-mahdī*/المهدي, i.e., the [divinely] rightly-guided as the one quintessentially from whom one finds right guidance). Yet *qawm*/قوم hardly provides much certainty. *Qawm* can be "a people" or "a group of people" and also "a nation." The *qawm* in this context might be "generic" clerics or religious scholars but also the trained and proactive Ismāʿīlī missionaries (i.e., the *du'āh*/الدعاة); the rank-and-file members of a faith; or all of the above. Then again, the *qawm* in question could be adherents of a particular religion—such as Judaism, Christianity, or Islam—or adherents of religion in general. Quite simply put, one cannot immediately determine upon whom, exactly, al-Maʿarrī is casting aspersions in these lines. Elsewhere, he might very well clarify this; but he might not.

Qawm is but one of the vague terms of reference al-Maʿarrī employs in *Luzūm* when attributing to a person or persons certain practices or beliefs with which he agrees or disagrees. He also uses words like *ma'shar*/معشر, (among other things, a community, a group or association of people, a society, company); *nās*/ناس (a people, some people, humankind); *ummah*/أمة (among other things, a secular community or nation but also a community or nation possessing, and being associated with, a prophet); *madhhab*/مذهب (among other things, a school of thought, an ideological trend or orientation, a movement); *rijāl*/رجال (men); *ṭā'ifa*/طائفة (among other things, a group, a band, a faction); see, for example, L I.130.1; 140.1; 159.3; L II.79.7; 129.2,8; 385.12; 416.2. It is also characteristic of al-Maʿarrī to say "they" or "you" (you singular [masculine or feminine] or you common gender plural) "believe," "assert," "claim" or "do" such and such, after which he gives his opinion on the matter under consideration (see, e.g., L I.129.12; 173.10–11; 185.4–7; L II.179.1–3, 9–10; 408.13–15; 430.11–14). Regardless, the effect is the same. The reader or listener is denied the privilege of being able to identify quickly and surely whom or what al-Maʿarrī is expounding upon at moments like these, with what specific school or trend of thought he might be associated or disassociated. This can be most vexing, to say the least. A perfect example to quote word for word is L I.185.4–7, where, for added measure, unspecified جماعات ("gangs," "groups," "parties," "factions") are the antecedents to the "theys" that in turn are followed by "we" and "us":

إن شئتَ إبليس أن تلقاهُ منصلتاً بالسيفِ يضربُ فاغمِدْ للجماعاتِ
تجدهم في أقاويل مخالفةٍ وَجْهَ الصوابِ وأسرارٍ مذاعاتِ
يباكرونَ بألبابٍ وإن خلصتْ معصيَّةٍ وبأهواء مطاعاتِ
قالوا وقلنا دعاوٍ ما تفيدُ لنا إلا الأَذى واختصاماً في المداعاتِ

If you want Iblīs, to meet him as he is striking
with his sword drawn, proceed to the assembled factions.
You will find them engaged in incorrect teachings,
and with mysteries that are widely proclaimed.
They go forth early in the morning with their minds that
even if clear are refractory and subject to whims.
They allege their things, and we ours; but which profit us
nothing save damages and conflict in counterclaims.

There is a good deal of questioning in *Luzūm*, the use of interrogatives, another stylistic feature that leaves room for doubt over what precisely is being advanced, what is being accepted or rejected in the way of an article of faith or sociopolitical or philosophical position. A few typical specimens appear below.

وكيف أُقَضّي ساعةً بمسرَّةٍ   وأَعلُم أن الموت من غُرَمائي

How can I spend a moment of joy in life,
knowing that death is one of my creditors?
(L I. 64.11)

فهل قامَ مـن جدثٍ ميتٌ   فيُخبر عـن مسمعٍ أو مَـرا

Has a dead person ever arisen from the grave,
to give news of something he has heard or seen?
(L I.75.11)

جاءَ النبيُّ بحقٍّ كي يُهذِّبكُمْ   فهل أحسَّ لكم طـبعٌ بـتهذيبِ

The Prophet came with a truth in order to refine you,
but did you have the character to perceive refinement?
(L I.134.8)

هل الأُمراءُ إلاَّ في خسارٍ   أَو الـوزراءُ إلّا أهلُ وِزرِ

Are the princes anything other than at a loss?
The ministers anything but masters of vice?
(L I.389.8)

Only after one has perused the entire (or at least considerable contiguous portions of) *Luzūm* and become wise to al-Maʿarrī's ways will one not hesitate to take the above examples as anything other than rhetorical questions and thus seize upon the direct statements (and the fuller ramifications) for which they are a substitute. No, it is impossible for al-Maʿarrī (and by implication all of humankind) to lead a happy life knowing that life leads ultimately to death. No, a dead person has never arisen from the grave to give sure proof that there is a resurrection and life in a hereafter for our bodies as we know them. No, humankind's character is not naturally disposed to recognizing and accepting from the Prophet Muḥammad (and thus by extension all would-be reformers) truths that might improve it. No, princes, viziers, and other heads of state are nothing more than miscreants who perpetrate crimes against their subjects. All of this is not so transparent without a full (or fuller) reading of *Luzūm*. And intimation by way of rhetorical questions does not leave one on as solid a footing as that offered up by way of straightforward positive declarations. Further, many questions may not be rhetorical, but, rather, representative of genuine wonder, of al-Maʿarrī turning over in his mind various possibilities to thoughts and issues that he raises, asking questions that perhaps in his mind really have no clear answers.

The use of irony is very common in *Luzūm*. In the lines below, for example, the context in which the italicized words occur suggests that the intended meaning of these words can only be the exact opposite of what their expressed meaning would seem to signify (at first sight). (Italics are superimposed, of course, inasmuch as before as before the advent of printing Arabic had no such thing):

الحمد للهِ ما في الأرضِ وادعةٌ كلُّ البريةِ في همٍ وتعذيب

Praise be to God! There's not a tranquil soul on earth;
all of humankind is anxious and tormented.
(L I.134.7)

اللهُ صوَّرني ولستُ بعالمٍ لِمَ ذالك سبحانَ القدير الواحد

God created me and yet I know not why.

Glory be to the the One and the Almighty!
(L I.296.1)

عجبتُ لآمرِنا[38] لم يُطعْ　　　وللخُلدِ عَزَّ فلم يُستَطعْ

I marvel at our Lord's not having been submitted to;
and at Eternity, glorious yet unfeasible!
(L II.94.7)

Even here it is really only within the larger context—the entire *Luzūm*—that the irony is more assuredly recognized. Lines in isolation can mean almost anything. (In any event, many a past reader, including some of the more informed and perspicacious—Ṭāhā Ḥusayn, Alfred von Kremer, R. A. Nicholson, ʿAbd al-Qādir Zaydān—wished to maintain that in many [if not all] instances of the expressions along the lines of "Praise be to God," "God is a reality," "God's omnipotence is a fact," and so forth, absolutely no irony was intended notwithstanding the overall scathing skepticism of al-Maʿarrī's world view.)

To conclude this section here, an additional few words are in order with respect to the *Luzūm*'s overall generic character. In view of what has been said above in regard to its contents, the *Luzūm* overall can quite fairly be regarded a philosophical poetry according to the following observations:

> A poem may be philosophical in either of two main senses. It may serve as a vehicle of some philosophical teaching which is essentially independent of the poem itself and therefore could be paraphrased in a set of logically developed statements without loss or distortion of meaning. . . . Or on the other hand, and by a more deeply characteristic procedure, it may employ its full linguistic, rhythmic, and associational resources to open up new insights into values, relationships, and significant possibilities such as could not be adequately restated, except without gross distortion, outside the particular poem that has succeeded in expressing them.[39]

The *Luzūm* is at times philosophical in the first sense described above; but it is predominately so in the second sense. That is to say, it is no less poetic even when it addresses questions of a philosophical nature; and it is far from being a collection of thoughts or ideas that if divested of their rhyme and meter might be just as accurately expressed in prose. On the contrary. The work is exactly what we might expect of poetry in the fullest sense of the word. It is elliptical. It is highly condensed. It is full of metaphor, simile, symbolism, and imagery. It is rich in words with ambiguities and many associative meanings. In many places, just beneath an enigmatic (to a lesser or greater degree) surface meaning, *Luzūm Mā Lā Yalzam* practically begs to be considered as allegory or suggested analogy, what Wolfhart Heinrichs once referred to, in an observation shared with the author of this study, as the phenomenon of al-Maʿarrī's nearly unremitting predilection for "suppressed analogical thinking." There is almost always a subtext to his poetry. He was not so much interested in "going beyond the line" as in writing between the lines.

All of this, among other things, is what allows *Luzūm, when it is philosophical*, to transcend mere jingling didacticism (although not entirely without justification, the *Luzūm*'s severest critics—especially philosophical purists—might sometimes be inclined to think of it in these terms). As a necessary consequence, therefore, and even without such features as the contradictions, disarray in topics, erudite vocabulary, irony, and vague referents, the work is less than crystal clear and explicit in communicating its thought or "philosophy" (as modest as some might think it is). In a word, because of its very generic nature, often *Luzūm* at best is no more than an adumbration of its author's thoughts, and the thoughts are often difficult to restate in any way other than that by which the author originally expressed them.[40] Meaning is lost not only (as the cliché has it) in translation but also in any *transformation*, whether from characteristically poetic expression to more technical prosaic paraphrase (whether in Arabic or another language), or from characteristically poetic expression to characteristically poetic expression *but* involving a second language whose poetic structures and features cannot easily replicate those of the original Arabic, particularly the plays on words of similar sounds and etymologies and the double entendres.

Transcending the Contradictions and Other Challenging Features of *Luzūm*

Intellectual historian Majid Fakhry has remarked that giving an account of al-Maʿarrī's thought "with any degree of completeness" is difficult in part because of its "nonconformist character."[41] This to an extent cannot be denied. What the preceding pages have attempted to underscore, however, is that in *Luzūm* at least (although this observation applies to nearly all of his works) it is not so much *what* al-Maʿarrī says, nonconformist or otherwise (and in terms of what most would consider mainstream or normative Sunnī Islam, he indulges in advancing both), but *how* he says it that poses problems for his interpreters. The voluminosity of *Luzūm*; its topical disarray; its lack of internal titles or subject headings; the fact that its really meaningful philosophical utterances have to be sifted out from many decidedly unphilosophical (even playfully, almost perversely trivial) ones; and, finally, the fact that its language, not particularly transparent and explicit to begin with because it is highly poetic, is made even less so by certain aspects of style characteristic of al-Maʿarrī (the uncommonly erudite vocabulary even by the standards of Arabic *shi'r*, the excessive punning, irony, rhetorical questions, vague references, contradictions both apparent and real, and so forth)—these are the features of *Luzūm* that, as much as if not more than the nonconformity, make the understanding of al-Maʿarrī's thought therein, with any degree of final certainty, such an arduous task.

Yet while the formidability of these obstacles cannot be denied, especially in the aggregate, it is really only one among them that ordinarily would seem so serious as to seem insurmountable and demand more than painstaking labor and patience; namely, the pronouncements that appear to be bald contradictions, especially when a radical change of mind, a change in thinking, is involved. If readers can make sense out of the contradictions as such, they can make giant strides toward achieving a more certain understanding of *Luzūm* as a whole. Fortunately, there is a way that allows readers to make sense out of the contradictions, *on the whole*, and by which, furthermore, the reader can more fully appreciate what, ultimately and overall, al-Maʿarrī was attempting in *Luzūm* regardless of the extent to which the project may be seen to fall short of similar such undertakings by others. This understanding in turn allows for acquiring a few helpful rules of thumb for dealing with some of the other problematic features of *Luzūm,* so that although the difficulties do not dissipate completely, neither do they remain quite so intimidating and baffling.

As long ago as 1914, Ṭāhā Ḥusayn unequivocally pronounced the *Luzūm* as an example of *taqiyyah*/تقيّة ("dissimulation," and particularly of one's religious beliefs when one is under duress or fears the prospect of facing duress);[42] although Ḥusayn hardly had the intent of invoking a *shī'ī* allegiance or sympathy when using an Arabic word for "dissimulation" that is especially associated with *shī'ī*-oriented Islam as a technical term, an allegiance or sympathy that should not automatically be suggested with al-Maʿarrī, and maybe not at all (depending on how one wants to interpret al-Maʿarrī with respect to views that may be seen as touching upon Shīʿite doctrine or trajectories of religio-philosophical speculation).

To a greater or lesser degree, although more tentatively and not using the same technical term, von Kremer before Ḥusayn leaned in this same hermeneutical direction, as did Nicholson after Ḥusayn, to a greater degree than von Kremer, and, precisely like Ḥusayn, describing al-Maʿarrī's method of writing (in *Luzūm* in particular) as being basically a manifestation of *taqiyyah* that has a long tradition in Islamicate writing. The more discreet and probing more modern Arabic-language studies of al-Maʿarrī's thought in *Luzūm* also unequivocally acknowledge the need to appreciate al-Maʿarrī's dissimulation, especially as concern the contradictions.[43]

The most compelling reason for the argument along these lines is al-Maʿarrī's own rather frank—and not infrequent—acknowledgment of such, scattered over the course of *Luzūm,* buried in the detail to be sure, but to be found nonetheless. Some of the more revealing examples are the following:

أُرائيكَ فليغفِرْ لي اللهُ زلَّتي   بذلك ودينُ العالميـنَ رِيئَآءُ

I dissimulate with you. May God forgive me my lapse.
But then religion everywhere is mere dissimulation.
(L I.47.9)

كلمتُ باللحنِ أهلَ اللحنِ أُونسهم   لأنَّ عيبيَ عند القومِ إعرابي

I’ve used garbled speech to those given to garbles, amusing them.
Because it is the people’s opinion that frankness is my fault.
(L I.132.11)

بني زمني هل تعلمون سرائراً   علمتُ ولكني بها غير بائحِ

O people of my time! Are you aware of secrets
that I that have learned (although I am not divulging)?
(L I.233.2)

ولديَّ سرٌّ ليس يمكنُ ذكرهُ   يخفى على البُصراءِ وهو نهار

I have a secret that cannot be mentioned;
it’s hidden from the keen-sighted (yet clear as day).
(L I.339.8)

لا تُقَيّدْ عليَّ لفظي فإني   مثلُ غيري تكلُّمي بالمجازِ

Do not hold me to that which I pronounce upon.
My speech, like others’, is by way of metaphor.
(L I.437.7)

وليس على الحقائقِ كلُّ قولي   ولكن فيهِ أصنافُ المجازِ

The true state of affairs isn’t found in all that I say,
which contains a variety of figurative speech.
(L I.435.12)

آهِ لأسرارِ الفؤاد غواليا   في الصدر أستُرُ دونَها وأُجمجم

Woe to secrets of the heart boiling up in the chest!
I conceal them there and express indistinctly.
(L II.270.1)

Here and there, too, al-Maʿarrī in his own words unveils why as an *adīb* he chose to express himself the way he did.

أُجامل الناس ولو أنني   كاشفتُ ما في السرّ أخزاني
أسيتُ من نقصي ولكنَّ ما   يَظْهرُ من غيري عزّاني

I ingratiate myself with people; for were I
to bare what is in my heart, it would disgrace me.
I grieve over my shortcomings; but those that
are apparent in others console me.
(L II.383.1-2)

رريدَكَ لو كشّفتَ ما أنا مضمرٌ   مِن الأمر ما سميتني أَبداً بأسمي

Easy! If you were to lay bare what I am concealing
about things you would never have named me as you did.
[i.e. Aḥmad, al-Maʿarrī's first name, which means "the most praiseworthy"]
(L II.293.8)

ضحكوا أليك وقد أتيتَ بباطلٍ   ومتى صدقتَ فَهُمْ غِضابٌ رُجَّمُ

They laugh at you when you come with a falsehood.
When you speak the truth, they stone you angrily.
(L II.270.7)

لا تُخْبرَنَّ بكُنْهِ دينكَ معشراً   شُطُراً وإن تفعلْ فانت مغرّر

Never report the essence of your faith to groups
who are cunning; if you do such you're imperiled.
(L I.326.14)

غدا الحقُّ في دارٍ تحرَّر أَهلُها   وطُفتَ بهم كالسارقِ المتُلصِّصِ

The truth has come into a land whose people are wary of it;
thus you have circled around them like the pilfering thief.

[Al-Maʿarrī is referring to himself here]
(L II.56.5)

أُكاشِرُ من لقيتُ على حذارٍ   وليس على اعتقادي من عريبِ

I give a cautious grin to whomever I meet
when there's no one who shares my belief.[44]
(L I.150.1)

Inasmuch as al-Maʿarrī in his search for the truth as he saw it, in his own inquiry into the nature of things, was developing views egregiously not in consonance with the prevailing consensus (إجماع) of the community of believers (especially the religious scholars [علماء] and governing authorities) into which he was born, raised, and lived (Muslims of the أهل السنة والجماعة orientation), his contradictions need to be seen as deliberate, as a means by which—above and beyond, for example, figurative and metaphorical speech, symbolism, irony, elaborate word plays, double entendres, and erudite vocabulary, and notwithstanding the infrequent formulaic expressions of orthodox religiosity and God-fearing piety—he could advance his views but at the same time make it less likely that he be censored, ostracized or, worse, even formally condemned for apostasy, disbelief, or one heresy or another and thus put to death.[45] To avoid suffering such serious consequences and yet at the same time conduct his search for the truth—knowing or anticipating that that truth would contain contrarian confessions—he exploited techniques of writing that made it more problematic for would-be adversaries and critics to uncover and make cohesive sense out of his thoughts in any attempt to prove conclusively what he seriously espoused.[46]

In other words, with respect to contradictions, when considering which of the palpably contradictory elements in his thoughts al-Maʿarrī in all likelihood really hoped to advance as representing his real views, one ought to accept that it was the maverick, the nonconforming, the heterodox (compared to mainstream or more normative Sunnī-oriented Islam on the basis of إجماع). The contrary, the aura of orthodox religiosity and piety, *in general* one needs to see as being advanced primarily to frustrate and befuddle the potential coreligionist critics, to "restrain the barking dogs," as al-Maʿarrī's زجر النابح (itself a remarkable example of cleverly professing innocence in the face of arguably offensive lines of verse) rather uncharitably terms the process.

It would be rather naïve seriously to suggest that al-Maʿarrī was simply forgetful or confused in most instances of such stark contradictions, particularly given his legendary prodigious memory.[47] For the erstwhile doubting Thomases, theoretically a radical change of mind is possible; a momentary flight from, but then a final unequivocal return to, orthodoxy; although inasmuch as there is nothing on al-Maʿarrī's part even remotely indicating as much, this really can't be seriously entertained. In any event, with respect to the *Luzūm*, to quote Yohanan Friedmann,

> the *Luzūmiyyāt* are arranged solely on the basis of formal considerations. Consequently, they cannot be used as a source for the study of the development of al-Maʿarrī's thought. . . . [They] were written over a long period of time and it is possible that some of the contradictions found in them could be satisfactorily explained if earlier poems could be distinguished from later ones. Alas, the method of arrangement effectively precludes any such attempt and there is every probability that we shall never know what changes, if any, occurred in the thought of al-Maʿarrī during the fifty years in which he composed the *Luzūmiyyāt*.[48]

Could al-Maʿarrī with his contradictions have been writing half in jest with respect to his heterodoxy or dissidence, especially since he never explicitly renounced his faith? Perhaps. Such a comportment vis-à-vis inherited religion and received opinions was not uncommon, indeed almost an affected fad, among some notable Muslim poets who flourished a couple of centuries before al-Maʿarrī's time, the most celebrated of whom was أبو نواس/Abū Nuwās.[49] However, what might be said of Abū Nuwās and his ilk might be said of al-Maʿarrī: something that he composed half in jest was by definition half serious.

Could al-Maʿarrī in his obvious (indeed almost perverse) joy in baffling have intended neither his blamelessly orthodox (i.e., mainstream

Sunnī) meditations *nor* his views to the contrary? That is, both were a type of hoax? Neither can be taken seriously? Perhaps. But accepting that is of little heuristic value. Peter Avery has noted the following:

> Life is lived very publicly in the East. As a result, though the heart is much talked of, men have learnt how to conceal what is really in it and, while verses might beguile a moment of leisure among friends and win applause for the poet's skill, they very rarely, as any student of Persian lyrical poetry knows, reveal precisely what the poet believed or did not believe.[50]

But where does this leave us?

Anyone who reads large segments of the *Luzūm* can't help but notice how al-Maʿarrī's persistent use of the enhanced end rhymes, which places even greater than normal demands on the sounds of words as opposed to sense, in fact often dictates (1) that sound be given priority, and, consequently—lest there be excessive repetition (i.e., excessive recycling of the same words)—(2) that uncommonly rarified, opaque, ambiguous words be employed. In other words, artificial (as in "forced," exactly one of the connotations of *luzūm*/لزوم) rhyme and meter schemes frequently lead to artificial word choices, which can explain some of the confusion, ambiguity, and contradictions. Al-Maʿarrī, in being mesmerized by the medium, often loses sight of meaning and emerges as a supremely formidable yet frenzied poet swept away by his own sonority.[51]

These are the "chains" on al-Maʿarrī that both Ṭāhā Ḥusayn and R. A. Nicholson have written candidly about (and the former at times in especially perplexed terms as he discusses al-Maʿarrī's brilliance and creative breakthrough as a poet of sober thought who seems to have aspired to move beyond the merely epigrammatic or gnomic, not to mention the merely sonorous and clever).

Nonetheless, many of al-Maʿarrī's most consequential and incendiary contradictions of received opinions in *Luzūm, especially as they pertain to revealed, scripture-based religion,* are in remarkably straightforward, plain Arabic. In any event, as for "the chains," Nicholson's carefully considered opinion—"Take it all in all, the work is shaped by the artist, not by the mould which it fills. . . . No doubt he is apt to be dragged down by his chains, but often . . . they appear rather an ornament than a hindrance"[52]—is quite accurate.

To some, all of this may well appear as overstating the obvious; beating a horse already quite dead. That can be conceded by the present study—on the one hand. On the other hand, quite surprisingly, up until comparatively recent times, and notwithstanding the seminal studies of von Kremer, Ḥusayn, and Nicholson, in other circles, there have been lingering doubts as to how seriously one should take al-Maʿarrī's moments of irreligion, impiety, and transgression in *Luzūm* that are contradicted by tendencies of the exact opposite nature.[53] Thus, if to some the obvious is being overstated by this present study, it is only for the sake of emphasizing that the main quandary that investigations of al-Maʿarrī's thought need to contemplate is not *whether* he really intended his contrarian or dissident (or 'un-Islamic' if you will) ideas, but *what these ideas are more precisely, what are the broader and deeper implications, and exactly how might we best characterize them*—above and beyond simply noting that they are free thought or nonconformist or un-Islamic or heterodox or unorthodox (which can be problematic to begin with; for example, when "orthodox" Islam is invoked, is it always clear what is meant by the term?). Further, what are some of the inferential leaps, extrapolations, or parallels that may be justifiable and elucidating?

All this of course needs to be on the basis of a reading of the entire *Luzūm,* the shallow and tedious or initially hopelessly enigmatic along with the more profound, arresting, and unambiguous. Al-Maʿarrī's scattering of his thoughts pell mell over the long course of the *Luzūm*, his mixing of the philosophically or ideationally significant with the insignificant, makes this imperative.

CHAPTER FOUR

The Message

I. Humankind as Viewed in the *Luzūm*

Al-Maʿarrī's "philosophy"—or *Weltanshauung* if one prefers the slightly less elevated and distinguishing term—is diffuse as well as heterodox. To attempt to encapsulate it in a word or two is no easy task. Von Kremer discovered this over one hundred years ago; and perhaps in the end only a good, robust German sentence like his quoted earlier can do the *Luzūm* real justice. As a point of departure, however, this study would like to stress that when all is said and done, anthropocentrism fairly describes the trajectory of al-Maʿarrī's meditative verse; which is to say, in simpler terms, that if there is a pivotal point or axis around which the many and diverse poems of *Luzūm* may be said to revolve, something that serves to center this very lengthy and topically diverse and fragmented work, it is humanity or humankind. All *Luzūm*'s major concerns are ultimately human concerns. Hardly a page of the work goes by without one concrete reference or another to man (or woman). As R. A. Nicholson remarked in his "The Meditations" (p. 141), "Maʿarrí stands for the largest humanistic culture of his time."

To begin the more comprehensive consideration of what al-Maʿarrī has to say in *Luzūm*, therefore, this study will look first at al-Maʿarrī's views on humankind. Or, to be more specific, inasmuch as the ensuing sections of this chapter can be thought of as revisiting and interrogating al-Maʿarrī's thoughts on humankind in a variety of manifestly qualified senses—the religious human being, the social and political human being, human beings as they confront the universe, and human beings as they ought to behave toward their fellow human beings—it would be good to precede all of this with a consideration of al-Maʿarrī's views on the individuated human being stripped down to his or her most elemental.

A latter-day Spanish philosopher has remarked that this being always and everywhere is no more than—although also no less than—"the person of flesh and bone; who is born, suffers, and dies—above all, who dies; who eats and drinks and plays and sleeps and wills"; not *homo religiosus*, nor *homo economicus*, nor *homo politicus*.[1] Nor *homo Islamicus*, we might add; at least not for al-Maʿarrī. Geography and centuries of time separate the philosopher from al-Maʿarrī. There is hardly a question of an influence here. Yet al-Maʿarrī in his own way was attempting to come to terms with and articulate the same phenomenon, and above all the centrality of mortality to (what he would regard) as *the* human "predicament," namely, the incredible heaviness of being.

But to back up here and start at the beginning: the Maʿarrīan human being of flesh and bone consists first and foremost of a body (*jasad*/جسد; *jism*/جسم) with four "natures" or "instincts (*arbaʿ ṭabāʾiʿ*/أربع طبائع; *arbaʿ gharāʾiz*/أربع غرائز[2])—most likely a reference to blood, phlegm, black bile, and yellow bile the four "humors," or main physiological constituents of humans according to early Arabo-European science. The four natures are "brought together" or "united" in a human being (L I.170.11; 148.3–4; 91.2). God is quite frequently, and rather matter-of-factly, acknowledged as Creator God (الخالق) and in that capacity the Creator of humankind, Who has created (خلق) and formed (صوّر /صاغ) the human being and given him/her life (see, e.g., L I.99.10; 111.9; 173.9–11; 186.9; 241.7; L II.124.12; II.288.3; 383.3). Ostensibly, therefore, ultimately it is He who is the agent behind the bringing together of the four natures—the *Luzūm* says by implication. Or, to put it in other, more precise terms that seem to be implied, at least on occasion, God is the efficient cause of man's corporeality while the four humors appear as the material cause, although the body in its primordial state as matter derives from earth (i.e., it is earthlike matter), earth being one of the four natural elements (the others being air, water, and fire; L II.424.4) to which all being or life can trace its origin, says al-Maʿarrī (L I.91.6).

The body is essentially "earthlike," "earthy," or "of terrestrial origins" (*arḍī*/أرضي[3]) in al-Maʿarrī's poetic-philosophical lexicon[4] (but by which he also means that its final modality or end state, as well as its beginning, is earth or earthlike matter: "dust unto dust"; as we shall see later, and with materialism intended in both its narrower and broader sense).

Into this body is "deposited" (*ustudi'at*/استدعت), or made to be in a state of "incarnation" or "bodily in-dwelling" (i.e., *ḥulūl*/حلول), the soul (usually *nafs*/نفس in al-Maʿarrī's Arabic,[5] although sometimes *rūḥ*/روح; L I.287.1; L II.294.5). Unlike the body, soul as described by al-Maʿarrī is a very fine or delicate material if not immaterial altogether. The soul is "something subtle"; "no mind can perceive it" (L I.211.5: *al-rūḥ shay' laṭīf laysa yudrikuhu 'aqlun* /الروح شيء لطيف ليس يدركه عقل). Apparently—and also unlike the body—the soul if indeed material is not composite. At least there's no mention in *Luzūm* of it being as such.[6]

With respect to where soul comes from, al-Maʿarrī is equivocal. In one poem he speaks of it as having a "center" or "fixed station" in the "transcendent [or higher] world." *Al-nafs fī al-'ālam al-'ulwī markazuhā* (النفس في العالم العلوي مركزها) (L II.82.5). But by this he could mean that either soul's ultimate origin or soul's ultimate end is in the transcendent world or that even *both* ultimate origin *and* ultimate end are in the transcendent or higher world. In a fashion very typical for him in *Luzūm,* in another poem, he reports a divergence of opinion over the origin of the soul but then gives no indication of his own position on the matter (without giving as well the identity of those whose views he is reporting). ("It is said that they [the referent is human souls] come to it [body] from an earth nearby; and it is also said that they fall unto it from their places on high" (*fa-qīl jā'athu min arḍ 'alā kathab wa-qīl kharrat ilayhi min ma'ālīhā* /[7] فقيل جاءته من أرض على كثب / وقيل خرت عليه من معاليها). The "fall" may be with conscious reference to Pythagorean, Platonic, or Gnostic "descent of the soul" teachings (all of which would have been familiar to the Muslim philosophers), especially as filtered through one such as Abū Bakr al-Rāzī (854–925 CE). Al-Maʿarrī makes absolutely no mention of the soul being a direct creation of God, nor even implies as much, although this is a view traditionally embraced by normative Islam.[8]

Whether soul falls/comes to body acting on its own accord—as implied in the line just quoted from *Luzūm,* through use of the active verbs *jā'at*/

جاءت and *kharrat*/خرت —or by virtue of an extraneous force or power or agent—as implied in the passive verb *ustudi'at*/استدعت, also used to describe how soul comes to have its connection with body—al-Maʿarrī also leaves open to question. As if to incline to the latter view, he uses in addition to *ustudi'at*/استدعت other passive verbs or adjectives when he describes the conjunction of soul and body (L II.11.5; 92.10–11). As if to give support to the former view, he speaks of the soul as having itself (i.e., on its own accord) "settled in" (*istaqarrat*/استقرت; L I.283.11), and itself "occupied" (or "taken up dwelling in"), body (law lam *taḥullīh* . . . لو لم تحلّيه (L II.22.10); although in the poem in which he says that the soul settled into the body, he adds that it did such "by virtue of God's verdict/judgement (*bi-ḥukm Allāh*/بحكم الله), maintaining a divine causal nexus. In a poem addressed directly to soul (and from which comes L II.22.10; the conditional clause is answered in the poem), al-Maʿarrī will go no further than suggesting that soul either comes to body on its own powers ("if you chose to inhabit it"; *in ātharti suknāh*/إن آثرت سكناه) or it is in/with body because of compulsion or coercion (*jabr*/جبر; L II.22–8–9; although in this context "determination" is perhaps closer to the intended significance), and on the part of another agent; which, given the choice of words, not to mention the standard teachings of Islam, one might assume is compulsion or coercion that is constituted by the predetermined divine decree of the Creator God.[9]

Precisely when soul comes to body—whether prior to, or simultaneous with, or after, the creation of body (all of which finer points were a question of considerable concern to Islamicate philosophers[10] if not so much to the theologians[11])—al-Maʿarrī never explicitly discusses in *Luzūm*. In one line, however, he does imply that both body and soul may have had some type of existence (and a calm or peaceable—وديع—one) prior to their coming into union (اجتماعهما); that is, they were both simultaneously preexistent but then simultaneously became existent (L II.286.11).

One may not feel compelled to read a great deal of import into al-Maʿarrī's equivocation and reticence concerning the above-mentioned finer points on the origin of the soul and its nature while cojoined to body, notwithstanding some of the caveats in the preceding chapter with respect to how to interpret him generally in instances of this nature (i.e., some serious nonconformism or dissidence is apt to be afoot). For Islam and Muslims as a whole, the real issue of concern with regard to the soul was what became of soul (as well as body) after a person's death; al-Maʿarrī too may have had that in mind first and foremost in addressing the matters pertaining to soul.[12] The equivocation and silence over origin of soul may be (most likely are) attributable to this, although also to other reasons that have nothing to do with the concealing of something offensively nonconformist or heretical.

The first of these reasons of course, one the reader of al-Maʿarrī must always keep in mind before all else, is that all the evidence suggests that al-Maʿarrī was by no stretch of the imagination a philosopher in the strictest sense of the word, in the manner of, say, al-Kindī, Ibn Sīnā, or al-Fārābī, possessing and drawing upon not only a *thorough* acquaintance with the corpus of Greek and Islamic philosophical texts, but also the whole intellectual tradition and orientation of *falsafah*/فلسفة with respect to method as well as range, level and sophistication of discourse (inclusive of idiom).

Second, as we shall see shortly, al-Maʿarrī advanced an epistemology that included not merely skepticism but also a resolute "know-nothing" dimension (in the Ashʿarian sense; i.e., that he plead agnosticism about many matters, and especially the more rarified ones such as the origin and final destiny of the soul; this agnosticism—commonly لاأدرية in Arabic—is to be distinguished from the حيرة that one often finds attributed to al-Maʿarrī in Arabic language sources, in the context of which the intended meaning of the latter word [i.e., حيرة] is typically "perplexed" or "baffled" or "conflicted").

Third, irrespective of his educational background and interactions, al-Maʿarrī's central concern in *Luzūm* with respect to soul seems to have been less a matter of the more rarified, abstract, and theoretical issues that would have occupied the mind of a *bona fide* scientific philosopher (Is the soul material or immaterial? When does it come into existence? How and why does it become attached to the body?, questions that someone of the philosophical stature of Ibn Sīnā, for example, sought to resolve and sum up systematically and in great detail [13]), than a matter of the day-to-day, practical issues of how the soul is predisposed or how it behaves once it is in the body, and *the consequences* of this for humankind (which fact could also go a long way toward explaining, incidentally, al-Maʿarrī's rather brief and unsophisticated physiological analysis of the body; here, too, all the evidence suggests that his main preoccupation was *how the body functions or behaves* as a consequence of its having soul and what its destiny is upon its [the body's] demise). Concerning how soul is predisposed or behaves *once* it is joined to body, al-Maʿarrī is much more expansive in *Luzūm*. He is also much less equivocal.

As was just noted, in his view, soul and body were both calm and at peace (*wadīʿayn*/وديعين) before their coming into existence as a tandem; not in a state of anxiety (*hamm*/هم), neither diseased nor sickly (*saqīm*/سقيم) (II.286.11). But once soul and body are together, for each, the blissful state of affairs comes to an end. Soul becomes damaged, tarnished, demeaned because of its contact with body (L I.48.8; 194.10–11; L II.215.6). This happens because although the body originates in, or derives from, good and pure elements in and of themselves (L I.148.3;II.351.6), the body becomes evil and polluted once it becomes the composite of the four humors that are brought together or united in it (L II.11.5;148.4). Above and beyond being damaged and sickly once in-dwelling in body, the soul is also both dumb (*warhāʾ*/ورهاء) and corrupting (*mufsidah*/مفسدة[14]) (L I.368.5)—or at least so long as it remains in contact with body.

From this fundamental starting point to al-Maʿarrī's psychology, a long litany of negative consequences ensues. The human soul renders acceptable or palatable a person's abominable deeds (L I.368.4). It disrespects the shunning of evil/sinning (L I.430.6). In fact, it commands evil (L I.289.15), every abomination (II.354.9). It is like an evil mount the reins of which cannot keep it in check (L II.353.9), and it loves being deluded (L I.153.8); it pays no heed to reason or intellect (*ʿaql*/عقل), although it is by means of *ʿaql* that it might find its right or proper course (L II.22.11).

This leads al-Maʿarrī to conclude that the human soul/self is always an adversary at war against a human being (L II.10.10). It is a human being's greatest and most evil enemy (L II.129.12; 354.8). The soul is diseased (L II.410.2). Its in-dwelling in the human body is always a veritable disaster (*nakbah*/نكبة) (L II.294.5: وكان حلول الروح في الجسم نكبة). By provoking a human being into doing evil, the soul's in-dwelling causes him/her pain and distress, which afflict not just the human body but, ironically, also the soul itself (L I.283.12).[15] Without being aware of it, the soul is its own worst enemy, not merely enemy of body and mind. It carries the seeds of its own remorse and suffering.

Above and beyond body and soul, mind or intellect/reason (usually designated by *'aql*/عقل but sometimes by *ḥijan*/حجا or *lubb*/لب) is the other component of the individual human being with which al-Maʻarrī is greatly preoccupied in *Luzūm*. *'Aql* he likens to a lamp the God-given light of which is a "bestowal" to the soul (L II.22.11).[16] It is that part of the individual that strives for and reveals the proper course of behavior. It is an individual's moral compass, making intelligible the vast and complex array of affairs that confront humankind here on earth:

The *mind* shows a way to piety.
Therefore follow its example.
For a heart is not darkened
if it has an ember of reason.

العقلُ يوضح للنُسْــكِ منهجاً فاْحذُ حَذْوَهْ
وليس يُظلم قلبٌ وفيه للُّبِ جذْوَهْ

(L II.424.8–9)

The mind works for the best interests of my soul . . .

والعقلُ يسعى لنفسي في مصالحها

(L I.132.4)

Set out on the road of reason and you'll be rightly guided by it . . .

خذوا في سبيلِ العقلِ تُهْدَوْا بهَدْيِهِ . . .

(L I.214.10)

I consider *reason* the wise man's mirror; whoever has
his brethren as mirrors is given both lies and truths.

أَرى اللبَّ مرآةَ اللبيبِ ومن يكن مرائيهُ الإخوانُ يُصدَق ويُكذَب

(L I.120.15)

The mind is an axis; its concerns are a millstone.
On the axis the concerns are ordered and made to turn.

اللب قُطبٌ والأمورُ لهُ رَحًى فيهِ تُدَبَّرُ كُلُّها وتُدارُ

(L I.331.8)

Because of its potential to rightly guide humankind, arrange humanity's concerns in orderly fashion, and reflect the truth, al-Maʿarrī reserves for the mind and reasoning some of his highest praise. A strong rationalism pervades the *Luzūm*; in fact, it drives much of the skepticism or agnosticism; العقل supplants النقل or the received ideas and teachings of revelation or *aḥādīth* or the law (i.e., the *Sharī'ah*). The mind or intellect is described as beautiful (L I.322.2), the most precious thing that a human being is endowed with (L I.151.1). In two quite notoriously assertive and laudatory verses, it is nearly apotheosized, the ramifications of which for al-Maʿarrī's co-religionists (whether *Sunnī*- or *Shī'ī*-oriented), and for his own philosophy and theodicy or deistic tendencies, should be quite transparent: "There is no imām other than reason" (*lā imām siwā al-'aql*/ لا إمام سوى العقل) (L I.65.6); "Every mind is a prophet" (*fa-kull 'aql nabī*/ فكلّ عقل نبيّ) (L II.428.5). (Had these two verses been placed cheek to jowl, or at least much closer than the thousands of lines that separate them, following logic as an ordering principle as opposed to rhyme schemes, one can well imagine the even more serious opprobrium al-Maʿarrī might have earned for himself as a thinker.) Neither prophets nor imāms can lay claim to being endowed with a superhuman reasoning faculty that puts them in a possession of having a special type of unassailable, infallible knowledge. As a corollary to all of this, the positive power of thinking or reasoning is exalted in *Luzūm*. Man before all else is exhorted to think or reason, to be *homo intellectus*:

O misguided one! If you're distinguished with a mind,
consult it . . .

أيُّها الغِرُّ إن خصصت بعقلٍ فاسألنهُ . . .

(L II.428.5)

Thinking is a rope; whenever an end is held onto
that end is suspended as far as the Pleiades.
And the intellect is like the sea whose highest reaches
do not recede one bit; thus the world-wise dip from it.

الفِكرُ حبلٌ مَتَى يُمسكْ على طَرَفٍ   مِنهُ يُنطْ بالثريّا ذلكَ الطرفُ
والعقلُ كالبحرِ ما غِيضَتْ غواربُهُ   شيئاً ومنه بَنُو الأيام تغترفُ

(L II.98.13–14)

There is no distance reached in time, ever,
that is as far as what man reaches by thinking.

وما أمدٌ في الدهر يبلغُ مرّةً   بأبعدَ مما نالهُ المرء بالفكر

(L I.376.7)

O deceived one! Be intelligent by means of the mind . . .

يا أيها المغرورُ لَبَّ من الحجى . . .

(L I.150.2)

There is an obverse side to this coin in *Luzūm*, however. Up against the mind or intellect is fate (L I.322.2) or the decrees/determinations of God that are hidden from humankind, concealed and inaccessible somewhere in the celestial sphere that revolves overhead (L I.48.3). In other words, despite its great potential for providing enlightenment, truth, and moral propriety, the mind/reason has certain inherent limitations. Most significant of these is an inability to fathom intangibles, things not observable to the eye ("The unseen is unknown"; *al-ghayb majhūl*/الغيب مجهول (L II.124.13); but of course, intangibles are precisely what questions of truth and morality amount to. Further, even with the obvious or transparent (البيان), reason or intellect is sometimes merely not self-satisfied or content (L I.197.10), that is, not self-assured in its intellection.

All of this leads al-Maʿarrī to pronounce that even though the mind/reason may strive for the best interests of the soul, and even though a human being might belabor his or her thoughts in attempting to be reasonable/rational and morally upright, on balance these efforts are to no avail in terms of imparting wisdom and knowledge to the human race, to inducing humankind to be good on the whole (L I.132.4; II.245.17). Humans on balance continually confront life with error until the day they die, at which point they leave life not knowing what the real purpose was (L I.178.4; 253.1). Absolute certainty about matters (*al-yaqīn*/اليقين) is nonexistent; at best there is only conjecture (*al-taẓannī*/التظني (L II.375.4). The greatest mysteries in life, the things unseen, are absolutely impenetrable. In the struggle between the potentially wise and good mind and the stupid and corrupting soul/self, the soul/self typically prevails. It is reluctant to accept pronouncements of good (L I.47.2) and listen to loving counsel and advice (L I.66.2). Its طبع or natural instinct "gravitates toward evil" (إلى الآفات جذّاب) (L I.132.4).

At bottom, therefore, is the suggestion by al-Maʿarrī that the individuated human—and so by extension all humankind—is more often than not essentially an ignorant creature and furthermore irretrievably evil. These two positions, the latter especially, are firmly established time and again in *Luzūm*. Al-Maʿarrī relentlessly advances the cynical proposition that humankind on balance is, has been, and always will be evil:

We are all treacherous and inclined to evil
(as the unsullied days tend toward the sullied);
and the men among humans precisely like the women;
save the grammar distinction of feminine and masculine.

كلُّنا غادرٌ يميلُ إلى الظُّلْـــــم وصَفْوُ الأيامِ للتعكير
ورجالُ الأنامِ مثلُ الغواني غير فرْقِ التأنيثِ والتذكير

(L I.418.10–11)

Men have not ascertained the good. On the contrary.
They have been formed with a propensity for evil.
What fault of *theirs*, therefore, that they've been made evil?

لم يفطنوا للجميلِ بل جُبِلوا على قبيحٍ فما لهم قُبِحوا

(L I.229.1)

Evil was an instinct in the ancient forefather [i.e., Adam];
in each person pulses an artery that stems from it.

والشرُّ في الجدِّ القديم غريزةٌ   في كلِّ نفسٍ منهُ عِرقٌ ضاربُ

(L I.94.3)

The inborn nature of each generation is damnable;
no one on earth is predisposed to noble character.

فالطبعُ في كُلِ جيلٍ طبعُ ملأمةٍ   وليسَ في الأرض مطبوع[17]على الكرمِ

(L II.306.2)

Evil's an inborn nature for humans; it never leaves.
So gauge this among the wide-eyed as well as the narrow.

والشرُّ في الخلقِ طبعٌ لا يُزايلهُ   فقِسْ على خزَرٍ في العين أو نجلِ

(L II.221.1)

In effect, al-Maʿarrī occasionally retreats from this extreme position with respect to evil in the world and also from the view that humankind is basically ignorant and incapable of obtaining certain knowledge about things. He has his contradictions in this regard. Reason can beget good, he can sometimes concede; although, unlike evil, good is something that has to be acquired over time, not being a part of man's inherited make-up (L I.241.2; II.306.2). And sound thinking coupled with experience can, in fact, bring about knowledge, sometimes even of hidden and mysterious things (L I.128.6). Thus, too, humans can be—and some indeed are—good:

In truth the morals of mankind are like its time:
thus some are black to the eye and some white.

ألا إنَّ أَخلاقَ الفتى كزمانِهِ   فمنهنَّ بيضٌ في العيونِ وسودُ

(L I.243.12)

> Talk, like creation, consists of both the good and bad;
> and people, like eternal time, consist of light and darkness
> [i.e., good and bad].
>
> والقولُ كالخَلقِ من سيئٍ ومن حَسَنٍ   والناسُ كالدهرِ من نورٍ وظلمآءِ
>
> (L I.66.8)

Similarly, proffers al-Maʿarrī (at least in his moments as the irreproachable *mu'min*/مؤمن [believer]), humankind can agree that there is a Creator and know that He is wise, Omnipotent (L I.403.17; L II.252.15), Eternal (L I.339.4). The bulk of humanity can also know with certainty that there needs be a place in life for good, for virtue (*faḍl*/فضل) (L II.252.16).

Here one is confronted with one of the many major contradictions of *Luzūm* that begs to be resolved (so long as one wishes to hold that the contradictions are not a manifestation of carelessness or confusion, and given that contradictions can't be dated if in fact they reflect a change of mind). Does al-Maʿarrī truly mean to advance, as so overwhelmingly suggested by *Luzūm*, that the human intellect can know nothing with real certainty save God's existence and His wisdom, might, and eternal nature; that therefore humans cannot distinguish between good and evil so that they might choose the former as a course of behavior over the latter; and that hence, too, humanity is eternally condemned—by virtue of predetermination—to wicked and evil actions because, by law of nature or divine decree (which in any event might amount to the same thing), it has been predetermined that such is the state of affairs in the world, always and everywhere? Or is al-Maʿarrī truly such an advocate of reason and the power of the intellect, unrestricted by (and not in need of) holy scriptures and their tradition-bound exegetes, that he believes that the mind and the mind alone can truly help humankind discover and appreciate the good, eschew evil, and freely choose to opt for a virtuous life, despite the evil predisposition of the soul? Is humankind notwithstanding the bestowal of reason condemned to be absolutely and permanently evil and ignorant or only partially and sometimes so? Although to a very great degree related, as just suggested, there are two separate questions to be addressed here: (1) How much *can* and *does* a human being know with certainty; that is, what are the limitations of human intellect, of reason; and, (2) Do humans have a free will to the extent that once (and if) they know the good, they can do the good, actually having the agency for such?

If one were to keep strictly to the basic hermeneutical approach advocated at the outset of this study for resolving the contradictions in *Luzūm*, for that reason alone one would have good reason to conclude that al-Maʿarrī did not seriously espouse a determinism so thorough as to preclude the possibility of humankind's having the power to choose to do good and lead the virtuous life. That view would have meshed precisely with the view upheld by the early mainstream theologians of Islam:

> The early traditionist view, which culminated in the thoroughgoing determinism of Jahm Ṣafwān and his followers, simply confirmed the view implicit in the Traditions [i.e., *ḥadīth* reports] that man can have no part in determining his action, in any real sense. Indeed, argued Jahm, a man's life is so thoroughly predestined that we can only impute his actions to him figuratively, in the very same way as we impute "the bearing of fruit to the tree, flowing to the stream, motion to the stone, rising or setting to the sun—blooming and vegetating to the earth." God creates the actions of both animate and inanimate beings, and man, like other creatures, has neither power, will, nor choice.[18]

What is sometimes referred to as the "new Traditionism or orthodoxy" in the medieval Islamic community, the development of which is associated especially with the theologian Abū al-Ḥasan al-Ashʿarī/أبو الحسن الأشعري (d 935 AD),[19] also upheld God's absolute omnipotence in the world and denied man any part in choosing or doing moral acts.[20]

This being the mainstream (or, if one wills, normative) position taken by the masters of religious studies by the time that al-Maʿarrī flourished, for that reason alone what al-Maʿarrī must have really meant by his determinist versus nondeterminist contradictions (the present study would seem obliged to argue, following the rule of thumb for resolving the contradictions) is that humankind in fact has free will, absolutely, can absolutely discern between good and evil using reason, and can act accordingly. This was a position first advocated in Islam by the

Qadariyyah/قدرية, the loose group of theologians or speculative religious thinkers who in opposition to Jahm and his adherents believed in free will; later, the belief in free will became a basic tenet of the Muʿtazilah, in fact was one of the central points of dogma by which they set themselves apart from the traditionalists or orthodox.[21]

This ought to be this study's conclusion almost automatically if it strictly follows the general rule of thumb for resolving contradictions in *Luzūm* (viz., when al-Maʿarrī contradicted a more mainstream or normative matter of dogma in Islam with a more unorthodox or nonconformist one, he probably seriously intended the latter). In other words, on the issue of free will, al-Maʿarrī was probably more Muʿtazilī than Ashʿarī, even though this conclusion goes against the grain of the vast majority of al-Maʿarrī's explicit remarks concerning the issue of free will versus determinism, which Ṭāhā Ḥusayn has so meticulously added up. Moreover, the conclusion could be construed as being consistent with what al-Maʿarrī says implicitly about the issue by way of his contradictions. Despite his many deterministic pronouncements with respect to human agency in choosing one course of action as opposed to another, and his often repeated contention that a human being's *ṭabʿ*/طبع or inborn nature is evil through and through, he devotes a large part of *Luzūm*—as he promised he would in his prefatory remark to the work—to moral admonitions;[22] to encouraging humans to eschew evil and lead the good and virtuous life. An underlying assumption of the *Luzūm* would seem to be that humans can freely determine their actions with respect to good and evil. They have agency in this respect.

In one line of *Luzūm*, al-Maʿarrī says in no uncertain terms that he is neither a believer in the doctrine of a free will nor a believer in divine predeterminism: "And if they ask me about my school of thought it's fear of God; I affirm neither free will nor predeterminism" وإن سألوا عن مذهبي خشيَةٌ / من اللهِ لا طوقاً أبثُّ ولا جبرا (I.351.1).

Later in *Luzūm*, toward the end of the work (which fact is itself not insignificant if the poems ending with the last letter of the Arabic alphabet were composed after all preceding poems; a distinct possibility), al-Maʿarrī commands his reader to live neither as a believer in divine predetermination nor as a believer in a free will, but instead as someone who adopts a position between these two extremes ("Don't live believing in predeterminism *or* free will; strive for a middle position between the two"; لا تَعِشْ

مُجبراً ولا قَدَريًّا / وٱجتهِدْ في تَوسُّطٍ بينَ بينا [L II.358.9]). What these two lines propose is that in the final analysis, al-Maʿarrī wishes to be regarded as in part a believer in divine predeterminism and in part a believer in free will.

This might seem to raise as many questions as it answers; or maybe not answer anything at all. It becomes less enigmatic or cryptic if there is again called to mind that an undeniable underlying assumption of *Luzūm* is that, with respect to their agency, humans can at least choose and lead a morally upright life, to effect at least that much freely (and on their own) if not more intractable things as well. By operating under this assumption, at the same time in many verses coming down overwhelmingly on the side of predeterminism as opposed to free will, and then finally suggesting that he is neither a strict believer in divine predeterminism nor a strict upholder of the belief in free will, al-Maʿarrī in effect seems to be saying that he will not allow himself to advance his belief in divine predeterminism, his cynicism with respect to the issue of free will versus determinism, so far as to preclude humankind's having the power to choose good over evil. As he himself expressed it in one poem, although all things considered he *may* have had very good cause to subscribe to a belief in absolute and total divine predeterminism (cynic at times that he was), he would not extend that belief into the realm of morality and thereby advocate moral complacency or ambivalence:

> Some groups of people have said that everyone is impotent and weak,
> that humans in and of themselves have neither slowness nor speed;
> rather, they are *caused* to be disposed one way or another,
> and thus not to be scolded if they sin nor praised if they do good.
> Indeed I have found evidence for this doctrine in my time;
> but god-fearing piety has forbidden me from holding it.[23]

قالت معاشِرُ كلٌّ عاجزٌ ضَرَعٌ   ما للخلائقِ لا بطءٌ ولا سِرَعُ
مُدَبَّرُونَ فلا عتبٌ إذا خطئوا   على المُسيءِ ولا حَمدٌ إذا بَرعُوا
وقد وجدْتُ لهذا القولِ في زَمَني   شواهداً ونهاني دونهُ الوَرَعُ

(L II.79.7–9)

Further support for the interpretation being advanced at the moment can be found if one revisits the gist of al-Maʿarrī's remarks concerning the human intellect and knowledge. It needs to be recalled that despite his at times certainly cynical if not nihilistic epistemology ("there is no absolute certainty; there is only conjecture; the unseen is the unknown"), al-Maʿarrī allows for humans to be able to reach certain knowledge about at least a few things. The most noteworthy example is the knowledge that *there needs be a place for good in life, for virtue.* Otherwise, life truly is an indecent abomination. Good and virtuous acts are not only achievable in al-Maʿarrī's eyes, and furthermore through *ordinary human* agency, but also—the *sine qua non* for their being effected—subject to ordinary human apprehension, that is, knowable or recognizable by way of the human reason, the use of the intellect.

With this, and in conjunction with his praise of the human intellect and rationalism, on the one hand, and with the denial of the possibility of acquiring certain knowledge (اليقين), on the other, al-Maʿarrī also allows for a plausible resolution to what seem to be irreconcilable views with respect to العقل. The resolution is not an either-or proposition, of his having *absolute* trust in the power of reason to acquire certain truth or absolutely no truth whatsoever. It is a position in between these two extremes, analogous to his resolution with respect to the issue of free will as opposed to divine predeterminism. By exalting the mind or intellect and then saying that certain truth about matters is impossible, but finally mitigating the latter opinion by conceding that *in some instances* humans can know things for certain, al-Maʿarrī in effect suggests that reason generally is to be valued for what it is capable of apprehending and that a human being should aspire to be *homo sapien*; *homo intellectus*; although at the same time the human mind or intellect must be regarded as having very severe limitations. There is only so much that it can apprehend with certainty. (Later, I discuss al-Maʿarrī's views on reason and its limitations, including a description of his epistemology.)

So far, it has been observed that al-Maʿarrī's human being of flesh and bone consists preeminently of body, soul, and intellect; that body, although originally from a clean material element (earthlike raw matter), becomes sullied or impure in its composite form; that soul, once cojoined to body, becomes tarnished and diseased, inclining to command evil; that humankind's inborn character, if not unalterably predisposed to bad or evil, is at least firmly disposed to such; that intellect, although it *attempts* to work in the best interests of the soul and can produce the certain knowledge that good and virtue ought to be pursued, otherwise has very severe limitations and in any case often is not heeded. Last, although a human being, notwithstanding the challenges, might be able to choose or determine freely his or her moral course of behavior, set straight his or her moral compass, at the same time he or she is not really the master of his or her lot in life in other respects.

Taking all of these as basic premises, al-Maʿarrī's *Luzūm* on balance regards each human being as primarily an impotent and confused creature of enormous inner conflict. Reason and rationality may pull in one direction—toward the good, the proper direction in life—but soul beckons to follow another direction—the way of evil, the wrong direction in life. In this eternal struggle, the evil-commanding soul usually emerges victorious. Although humans potentially can come to know the good, and freely act to effect it, all too often (actually for the cynical al-Maʿarrī, *on the whole*) they behave as if ignorant of the good; as if powerless to effect it; as if their character in fact is innately and permanently evil. Metaphorically speaking, the human being is said to be enveloped in darkness (L I.403.17); the confluence of two agitated seas (L II.388.7); at war against his or her own self (L II.373.14); crippled and defiled (i.e., a bird whose wings are broken [L I.424.11–13] and that furthermore is forever black (which is to say, sullied; impure [L I.311.7]).

Above and beyond all of this, a human being is also a creature who dies. More than anything else, he surely does this. Human mortality is one of the great recurrent themes of *Luzūm*. As Adonis has remarked about al-Maʿarrī, "He creates the world—if creates is the right word—with death at his starting point. Death is the one elixir, the redeemer. Life itself is only a death running its course."[24] With cruel irony, al-Maʿarrī hammers home that death is one of the few things in life that humankind *can* know with absolute certainty (L I.387.15). It is the truest of all phenomena (L II.275.4); an aspect of the human predicament as obvious as life itself (L I.200.9). It is a fate delivered to all living creatures by divine decree (L I.98.8), not only arising with life itself (L I.126.6) but also representing the fruition of life (L I.342.4). Every human being will experience death just as surely as all of his or her forefathers have (L I.76.12).

In several fairly celebrated passages of *Luzūm*, al-Maʿarrī implies that man's death is a final, once-and-for-all experience, a total cessation of being not to be followed by a resurrection and a renewed life in a hereafter:

My sleep is death with looming resurrection,
while my death is a sleep of a long slumber.

ونومي موتٌ قريبُ النُّشور   وموتي نومٌ طويلُ الكرا

(L I.75.6)

Once we were non-existent, and God's decree gave us existence.
And then we chance upon a second state of non-existence.

في العُدمِ كُنّا وحُكمُ اللهِ أوجدنَا   ثم اتَّفقْنا على ثانٍ مِن العدَمِ

(L II.303.9)

Death is a long sleep that has no end . . .

والموتُ نومٌ طويلٌ ما لهُ أمدٌ . . .

(L I.87.6)

With prayer we are bid a sad farewell,
deposited in the earth but then not moved.

نُوَدَّعُ بالصلاةِ ودَاعَ يأسٍ   ونُتْرَكُ في التراب فلا نهادُ

(L I.260.8)

The grave is my final home; and that of others, too.
And we've seen no one to have risen from it.

والتُّربُ مثوايَ ومثواهُمُ   وما رأينا أحداً منهُ قامْ

(L II.324.6)

We have laughed although our laughter has been stupid.
It's fitting for the earth's inhabitants to weep.

The vagaries of time smash us as though we were glass
—but glass that is never to be melted and remolded.

ضَحِكْنا وكانَ الضحِكُ منا سفاهةً   وحُقَّ لسُكأَّنِ البسيطةِ أَن يبكُوا
يُحطمنا ريبُ الزمانِ كأنّنــــــــــا   زُجاجٌ ولكن لا يُعاد له سَبْكُ

(L II.143.4–5)

Elsewhere in *Luzūm,* this position is refined somewhat. That there is a final and permanent demise of a human being's body on earth al-Maʿarrī never denies nor contradicts. The body's composite form is split up, he says (L I.170.11), when the appointed time of a human being's life is over. Then the body decays and decomposes into dust/dirt, in which state it remains for all time (L I.398.6–7; 175.4; 248.4). Human corporeal form is ultimately completely erased (L I.160.3). It passes from being to nonbeing and ends up as though it never had a soul or animating spirit in the first place (L II.234.9). It leaves nothing behind to be sensed (L I.212.2) when it reaches this final state or condition, and itself senses nothing (L I.285.7). This state or condition is comparable to numbness according to L I.379.8.

As for the final end of the human soul, al-Maʿarrī seems to leave open the possibility that it survives after the death of the body. He remarks once or twice that some "communities," "societies," or "groups" (*maʿāshir*) profess that the soul stays with the corpse (i.e., it does not leave, and hence co-perishes with, the corpse), but other "people" (*nās*/ناس) profess that the soul ascends (L I.212.1). Several times, he vaguely implies that he might believe in souls' perishability.[25] But more frequently—and considerably so—he speaks in terms of the human soul as "moving at a distance," or "going," or "journeying," or "ascending," from the body at the time of death (see, e.g., L I.68.6; 112.6; 140.4; 212.1; 225.6; 248.4; 268.9; 285.7; L II.148.10; 158.11, 262.4).

Where the soul goes after it has gone from the body, al-Maʿarrī does not clearly resolve. On the one hand, In *Luzūm* I.225.6; 248.4, and II.148.10, for example, he says (in so many words) that neither he nor anyone else can ever truly know. In *Luzūm* I.268.9; II.158.11; 262.4, on the other hand, he gives as the final locus of the ascended soul (respectively) "the atmosphere" (or "the air"/*al-hawā'*/الهواء), "the celestial sphere" (*al-falak*/الفلك), or the "higher (or celestial) world" (*al-'ālam al-'ulwī*/العالم

العلوي). In at least two places in *Luzūm,* al-Maʿarrī says that the soul never returns to the body after having left it (I.427.5; 287.1); in at least one place (I.423.4–5), he implies that it "can" return (this is a possibility), arguing (although with an unconvincing example) that its reestablishment in the body is analogous to people abandoning an abode for a day and then reinhabiting it on another. In this last-mentioned citation, however (and above and beyond the ingenuousness), al-Maʿarrī only goes so far as to say that the soul *can* return to the body; he does not say that it does or that it will. Moreover, these particular lines are from a poem addressed to an imaginary adversarial heretic, specifically one who disbelieves in God (a *mulḥid*/ملحد or atheist) whom al-Maʿarrī is beckoning to reconsider his ways. Thus, the real purpose is probably not so much to give al-Maʿarrī's sincere belief as it is to give one that he would want *to appear* to uphold for the sake of properly conforming Islamic piety. What better straw man as an imaginary adversary or interlocutor than a ملحد, especially since al-Maʿarrī himself was undoubtedly accused of this by some of his contemporaries (and not just posthumously by biographers/commentators)?

Over and against this backdrop, al-Maʿarrī in *Luzūm* never denies *the possibility* of resurrection, whether bodily or spiritual.

Resurrection could be possible if the Sovereign calls for it. . . .

قد يُمكنُ البعثُ إن نادى[26] المليك به . . .

(L II.334.8)

God's power is a real fact. Neither the assembling of creation on Judgment Day nor the resurrection of the dead is beyond it.

وقُدْرةُ اللهِ حَقٌ ليس يُعْجزُها   حَشرٌ لخلقٍ ولا بعثٌ لأمواتِ

(L I.185.14)

How powerful God is that His creatures be called from their graves so that they might become again what they were before!

ما أقدرَ اللهَ أن تُدعَى بريَّتُهُ   من تُربهم فيعودُوا كالذي كانوا

(L II.334.4)

Whenever my bones are to turn into dust,
God won't be unable to recombine me.

إذا ما أعظُمي كانَتْ هَبآءً فإن الله لا يعييهِ جَمْعي

(L II.92.6)

The sum and substance of the foregoing and similar such remarks about death strongly suggest that al-Maʿarrī came ever so close to absolutely disavowing the mainstream Islamic teaching on death and resurrection, which posits that there is a death of body at which time the soul separates from the body; that on Judgment Day God restores soul to body; and that man's resurrection is most certainly bodily as well as spiritual.[27] Al-Maʿarrī does not deny the possibility of resurrection, bodily or spiritual; but, by stating clearly and unequivocally that the body in fact meets a final fate of permanent decomposition (to the extent that the body simply returns to the raw earthly matter from which it originated), whereas the soul might survive the demise of the body (in one modality or another), he virtually says that *if* there is a resurrection it will only be of soul and not of body. Bodily resurrection is rejected; not acknowledged.

This being the case, it is tempting not to conclude that in coming so close to denying *completely* the normative Islamic understanding of death and resurrection, al-Maʿarrī in fact intended just that; perhaps even his allowing the possibility of a resurrection of the soul should not to be taken seriously, but, rather, regarded as having been put forth only in order to save him from being facilely, convincingly labeled as a total disbeliever in the doctrine of resurrection as understood by mainstream Islam.

Taking the argument that far, however, is problematic, notwithstanding the deep despair, pessimism, skepticism (if not outright cynicism), and heterodoxy that pervade al-Maʿarrī's thought as a whole. Allowing for the possibility of a resurrection of soul or spirit while not believing in a resurrection of body would still have left al-Maʿarrī vulnerable to the wrath of the orthodox Muslim believers. It was one of the views that the celebrated, authoritative (to this day) theologian al-Ghazzālī (al-Ghazālī), for example, considered heretical and thus felt compelled to refute in his famous assault on Islamic philosophers (e.g., al-Fārābī and Ibn Sīnā), *The Incoherence of the Philosophers*.[28] Why the need to advance it as subterfuge, so to speak, if already there is a commitment to a doctrine that within the framework of Islam is so intolerably nonconformist, in fact, heretical?

Some segments of the medieval Islamic intellectual community, including most notably the more influential philosophers of neo-Platonic persuasion or sensibility, believed in the transmigration of the human soul after death[29] (transmigration in the sense of translocation and in-dwelling in another human body or *locus* outside of human body; metempsychosis would be the more accurate term for the soul's moving after death specifically into another *body*, whether human or animal), a doctrine that was decidedly not the norm for Islam.[30] Al-Maʿarrī briefly touches upon the topic in *Luzūm*. True to form, he is not entirely clear as to his own beliefs as opposed to what others profess, although the latter he hardly makes attractive when he elaborates (to the extent that he elaborates). In *Luzūm* II.166.14–16, he ridicules the more extreme forms of transmigration, making appear especially absurd or unreasonable (indeed comical) some of the possible logical implications of metempsychosis:

> O you there eating the apple! Don't run off on
> your day of death, nor let the mourners stand.
> For the Nuṣayrī[31] (although not I) has thus spoken
> (so listen, and hearten the weak on that Day of Din)
> "You, too, have been an apple in your time;
> and that apple of yours was once eating *you*."

يا آكل التفاَّح لا تبعدَنْ ولا يقم يومُ ردى ثاكِلكْ
قال النصيري وما قُلتهُ فاسمعْ وشَجِّعْ في الوَغى ناكلكْ
قد كنتَ في دهرِكَ تفاحةً وكان تفاحُكَ ذا آكلَكْ

In L II.166.14–16, even the less extreme or less irreverent forms of transmigration—such as metempsychosis where a human soul goes merely from one human body to another—appear to be rejected, on the grounds that such is either intrinsically unreasonable or unverifiable:

> They say that the body's soul is to be transported
> to another body so that this might purify it.

But do not mistakenly accept what they tell you
if reason doesn't confirm what thereby they bring you.

يقولونَ إنَّ الجسم يُنقلُ روحُهُ　　إلى غيرهِ حتى يهذبَها النقلُ
فلا تقبلنْ ما يُخْبرونَكَ ضلَّةٌ　　إذا لم يؤيدْ ما أتَوْكَ بهِ العقلُ

(L II.171.7–8)

L I.239.1–3 takes up reincarnation of human souls into animals (*maskh*/مسخ) as well as in innate matter, i.e., minerals (*faskh*/فسخ) or plants (*raskh*/رسخ). Line 1 of L I.239.1–3 can be interpreted as an outright acceptance of the transmigration of souls from one human body to another (metempsychosis, in other words, more strictly speaking; in Arabic نسخ) if the line is translated along the lines of what appears below:

We've found following the Divine Law firm among the wise;
and that those tested over time do not deny *naskh*.
So what's wrong with this era that there's no sign of *maskh*
if the Jews have witnessed an instance of *maskh* ?[32]
A group of people who uphold the principles of *naskh*
have gone to extremes with this and allow for *faskh* and *raskh*.

وجدنا اَتِّباعَ الشرعِ حزماً لذي[33] النهى　　ومن جرَّب الأَيامَ لم ينكر النسخا
فما بال هذا العصر ما فيه آيةٌ　　مِن المسخ إن كانت يهودُ رأت مسخا
وقال بأحكامِ التناسخِ معشَرٌ　　غلَوْا فأجازوا الفسخَ[34] في ذاك والرسخا

Naskh/نسخ is a *double entendre*. It can also mean "abrogation" or "invalidation." This creates a problem for interpretation. Reading the word as "abrogation" or "invalidation" rather than "transmigration" forces the following remarkably changed significance to L I.239.1:

We have found that the following of the Divine Law is unwavering for the wise, and that those tested by time have not denied [i.e., repudiated] the [the doctrine of] invalidation [of the Divine Law; i.e., in certain instances one pronouncement may be superseded, replaced, by another].

That is to say, here the idea would be that people of reason are unwavering in following the Divine Law, and, therefore, those among them who have long experience and thus are world-wise do not oppose the legal position that allows for a legal pronouncement to be superseded and replaced by another. Al-Maʿarrī in this instance is speaking *somewhat* like a conforming Sunnī Muslim true believer with respect to الشرع or the Divine Law (although his real intent may have been to say that the Divine Law *in its entirety* is susceptible to invalidation and replacement; not a thought that slipped his mind, as will be seen later); that is, نسخ in this context has nothing to do with transmigration. (The deployment of the double entendre wherein a possibly very transgressive, heterodox signification may be understood is commonplace in *Luzūm*, underscoring just one of the challenges to interpreting the work.)

Although the double entendre is certainly deliberate, it is difficult to advance categorically that the latter reading of نسخ (i.e., as the legal principle) should be the preferred one. The broader context of I.239.1–3 suggests that in this fragment from *Luzūm* al-Maʿarrī more than likely truly wishes to make some clarifying remarks on the various types of transmigration, that is, نسخ ، مسخ، رسخ (although ever the clever contrarian and devil's advocate, he does not let the true wish stand in the way of playful indulgence in ambiguity). Still, the nature of the ambiguity with respect to نسخ, and to the whole hemistich in which it appears when نسخ is understood in terms of a legal principle—that is, if it is perfectly innocuous (nay, properly pious and indignant) from a مؤمن (Muslim believer's) point of view on one level of interpretation but not so on another—remains consequential. The ambiguity is not over a trifle.

The most plausible conclusion from all of this with respect to transmigration or metempsychosis? Al-Maʿarrī might have rejected the more extreme forms of the doctrine of transmigration/reincarnation of the soul; but he did not flatly deny, and even seems to have accepted the possibility of, نسخ (the movement of the soul from one human being to another) as opposed to مسخ or فسخ —for example.[35]

In al-Maʿarrī's musings on the origin, composition, nature, and final destiny of soul, Khalīfāt[36] underscores the Platonic, Pythagorean, and Heraclitean elements; for example, with respect to the Pythagorean and Platonic: the transmigration of soul; with respect to the Platonic more specifically:

the images in the *Luzūm* such as body as prison for soul whose destiny is to be released, or the images of body as cage for soul that is like a bird whose destiny is to fly free, or the body described as garment over soul that is eventually shed, and the "transcendent world" to which it returns upon demise of body mirroring Plato's transcendent world of Ideal Forms; with respect to the Heraclitean element: the verses in *Luzūm* in which there are descriptions of soul as fire or ember that flames in body while body is alive, with body "corrupting" (i.e., decomposing; dying) when the heat of fire is lost, and soul ascending. (Khalīfāt cites the relevant supportive verses in the *Luzūm*.) ʿAbd al-Qādir Zaydān[37] sees similar such filiations, as well an Indian (Hindi) one. With respect to the Platonic, both Khalīfāt and Zaydān underscore that the Phaedon, familiar to the Islamic *falsafah* tradition, was obviously the likeliest font. Zaydān[38] cites a passage in al-Maʿarrī's *Risālat al-Ṣāhil wa al-Shājiḥ* that makes it very clear that al-Maʿarrī was familiar with even some of the more recondite details of the Phaedon.

Because al-Maʿarrī was so bold as to refuse to endorse the more normative Islamic understanding of death and resurrection (or at least the most important component thereof), it is not a total surprise that he extended his logic so as to question and reevaluate other closely related tenets of Islamic eschatology; for example, that there is a Judgment Day for resurrected humankind, when God gives out reward and punishment; that the righteous among the resurrected will be rewarded with eternal dwelling in the gardens of Paradise and the evildoers punished with eternal residence in the fires of Hell; that the bliss of life in Paradise and the pain of life in Hell are actual experiences that humankind will be conscious of. But all this is more the area of concern of part 3 of this chapter. To stay closer to the topic at hand, there are enormous existential consequences attendant upon the Maʿarrian man/woman because of the type of death that awaits him/her. These merit some discussion.

Because he/she lives for the most part ignorant, evil, and subject to a power or powers beyond his/her control and is not resurrected after death, the Maʿarrīan man/woman has an existence that amounts to a series of unavoidable unmitigated disasters; a largely joyless experience that is brutish and painful. The Maʿarrīan human being of bone and flesh does not so much eat and drink, love and laugh, and otherwise enjoy life's pleasures, as it does stumble through life in confusion, struggling futilely against its evil inclinations, suffering immensely, and finally perishing, with a renewed life of bone and flesh forever unrealizable. The extreme agony of life in view of all the afflictions and uncertainty that adhere to it, and in view of the absolute finality (i.e., eternal cessation) that adheres to it, is emphasized throughout *Luzūm*. It is expressed in some of the work's more powerful and haunting lines. Many of these have been cited and masterfully rendered into English poetry by Nicholson.[39] These can be consulted for the fuller and more artistic English-language treatment of al-Maʿarrī's negative assessment of life as expressed in his poetry. However, since the topic represents such a significant part of the upwards of 13,000 lines of verse in *Luzūm* so inextricably linked with the name of al-Maʿarrī, it would be appropriate for this study, too, to give its own brief overview. The following fragments have been assembled with that end in mind. In tone as well as religio-philosophical orientation, they can be considered typical for the *Luzūm*.

When fate of death overtakes me, obliterating my form
and my deeds, my whole life amounts only to an affliction.

إذا أَتاني حِمامي ماحياً شَبَحي   وما صنعتُ فعيشي كُلُّه عَنَتُ

(L I.160.3)

I swear my body will not be rid of hurt
until it returns to the eternal element.

آليتُ لا ينفكُّ جسمي في أَذًى   حتى يعودَ إلى قديمِ العنصرِ

(L I.398.6)

Life is war; only by death its weapons laid down.
All of it amounts to no more than burdens.

والعيشُ حربٌ لم يضعْ أَوزارَها   إلّا الحِمامُ وكلُّها [40] أَوزارُ

(L I.338.1)

Every human being hopes to continue living;
yet if you live you only experience time's horrors.

يُؤمِّلُ كلٌّ أن يَعيشَ وإنما تُمارِسُ أهوالَ الزمانِ إذا عِشتا

(L I.175.3)

The happy one shouldn't be envied for his blessings.
Wretched is the life that's a life followed by perdition.

لا يُغْبطَنَّ أخو نعمى بنعمتِهِ بئسَ الحياةُ حياةٌ بعدها الشَجَبُ

(L I.84.9)

I reckon the coming-to-be and corruption of my time
a boy dawdling with the dust of the earth, amusing himself.

أظنُّ زماني كونَهُ وفسادهُ وليداً بتربِ الأرضِ يلهو ويعبث

(L I.199.7)

How can I spend a single hour of joy
knowing that death is among my creditors?

وكيفَ أُقَضِّي ساعةً بمسرَّةٍ وأعلمُ ان الموتَ من غُرَمائي

(L I.64.11)

We pass quickly from one nullity to another:
like crossing a bridge, for us there's no stopover.

نمرُّ سراعاً بين عدْمَيْن ما لَنَا لباثٌ كأنا عابرونَ على جسر

(L I.376.14)

Life is a bridge between two deaths, a first and second.
The body is lost so that the bridge can be crossed.

حياةٌ كَجسر بينَ موْتينِ أوَّلٍ وثان وفقدُ الشخص أن يُعبرَ الجسرُ

(L I.308.11)

Life is no more than a disease, the only cure death.
So leave me and I'll proceed to my destiny.

وما العيش إلا علّةً بُرءُها الردى　　فخلِّي سبيلي أنصرف لطياتي

(L I.182.2)

The misfortune of life the living envelops,
and earth's denizens are vile; dishonorable.
So away with living; it has led me to ruin;
and with youthfulness; it has led to senility.

نحسُ الحياةِ على الأحياءِ مُشتمِلٌ　　وساكنُو الأرضِ مِن لُؤمٍ بلا كَرَمِ
فالبعدُ للعيشِ أدّاني إلى تَلَفٍ　　وللشبيبةِ قادتْني إلى الهرَمِ

(L II.300.14–15)

We fell into life through no choice of ours;
and our Creator hastens our demise.
We have ridden above dark night's mounts;
and O how speedy these camels are.
As the arrows of fortune pierce each shield
and penetrate the layers of armor.

وقعنا في الحياة بلا ٱختيار　　وخالقنا يعجّل بالخلاصِ
ركبنا فوق أكتاد الليالي　　فواهاً ما أَخبَّك من قِلاصِ
ونبلُ الدهرِ تنفُذ كل تُرْسٍ　　وتسلُك بين أثناء الدلاصِ

(L II.57.4–6)

The soul has told me, "I am in pain and torment."
"You need be patient and submissive," I replied;
"The like of what you face can't be avoided."

قالت ليَ النفسُ إني في أذًى وقذًى　　فقلتُ صبْراً وتسليماً كذا يجبُ

(L I.85.2)

We all want life; so if our inner thoughts resolve upon
what is better, the soul's desire says "Hold off on this."
We don't awake from the intoxication around us
until it is said that death at last has come to us.

نرجو الحيوة فإنْ همَّتْ هواجسنُا　　　بالخيرِ قال رجاءُ النفس إرْجآءَ
وما نفيقُ من السُّكرِ المحيطِ بنا　　　إلا إذا قيل هذا الموت قد جآءَ

(L I.62.1–2)

The collar of time is buttoned around all kinds of harm.
Only the unlucky and disadvantaged are in it.

جَيْبُ الزمانِ على الآفاتِ مزرورُ　　　ما فيهِ إلّا شقيُّ الجدِّ مضرورُ

(L I.321.1)

Irredeemable evil has surrounded us.
If ever a reformer stands out, it's a rarity.
Though our morals are not corrupted by choice,
it is a fateful decree that has determined this.
There's fraud at the root, the effects in the branches.
And so how can son be true when father is false?

حوتنا شرورٌ لا صلاحَ لمثلها　　　فإن شذَّ منا صالحٌ فهو نادرُ
وما فسدتْ أخلاقنا بٱختيارنا　　　ولكن بأمرٍ سبَّبتْه المقادرُ
وفي الأصل غشٌّ والفروع توابعٌ　　　وكيف وفآءُ النجل والأبُ غادرُ

(L I.311.3–5)

People have been struggling in the darkness of doubts,
never having gotten a glimpse of a splendid day.
We move on leaving behind us the land broad,
the morning resplendent, the stars shining in the sky.
Live as you may, you'll only see a fixed lifespan
ending as it always has; that and endless time.

والناس في ظُلَم الشكوك تنازعوا　　　فيها وما لمحوا نهاراً باهرا
نمضي ونتَّرك البلادَ عريضةً　　　والصبحَ أنور والنجوم زواهرا
عش ما بدا لك لن ترى إلا مدًى　　　يطوى كعادته ودهراً داهرا

(L I.366.10–12)

Knowledge and denial take possession of the soul;
every concept can be both negated and affirmed.

ويعترى النفسَ إنكارٌ و معرفةٌ   وكلُّ معنًى له نَفْيٌ وإيجاب

(L I.87.5)

Man is in a fog, not clarifying by thinking
anything other than the Almighty's wisdom.

والإنسُ في غَمَّاءَ لم يتبيَّنوا   بالفكر إلا حكمةِ القهَّار

(L I.403.17)

We've willed things but what we've wanted has never been . . .

نحن شئنا فلم يكن ما أردناه . . .

(L II.433.11)

The nature that is mixed into the souls of humans
is at war with their reason and therefore dulls it.
Reason continues to see its radiance as useless,
like the sun enveloped by clouds and their shadows;
until the fate of death arrives and humans see
that all of what they have accomplished is folly.

يتحارب الطبعُ الذي مُزجتْ به   مُهَج الأنامِ وعقلُهُمْ فيفلُّهُ
ويظلُّ ينظرُ ما سناهُ بنافعٍ   كالشمسِ يسترُها الغمامُ وظِلُّهُ
حتى إذا حضر الحمامُ تبيَّنوا   أن الذي فعلوهُ جهلٌ كلُّهُ

(L II.183.3–5)

Over the course of the remainder of this study, it will be seen that al-Maʿarrī found many reasons other than the fate of death for holding his bitterly negative assessment of life. Most of these reasons automatically ensue from his low esteem of humankind as described above (and elsewhere in *Luzūm*). It is the fate of a death without bodily resurrection, however, that emerges as the greatest single cause for his finding life little more than a vale of tears, fairly meaningless and absurd. "[Al-Maʿarrī's poetry] is often weighed down by a sort of cold intellectualism, overlaid by its nightmarish qualities . . . [I]t holds its reader constantly over a chasm of absurdity and nothingness."[41] For al-Maʿarrī, a human being's mortality makes everything over the course of his or her life seem absolutely pointless; and death is not only physically painful ("a morrow of dripping sweat"/غد من عرق نازل [L I.68.6]), but it is also psychologically so. It can scarcely be spoken of openly (L II.275.4). The thought of death is something we flee albeit unsuccessfully (L I.50.5). Death elicits fear (L I.90.2), anxiety (L II.121.4), hatred (L I.53.4), wariness, and dread (L I.161.4–7). In a word, it remains a brooding, disturbing omnipresence in the history of humankind.

But paradoxically this same painful death that inspires such fear and loathing holds a blessing, according to al-Maʿarrī. Because life entails the physical and psychic misery and despair that he so graphically portrays in his poetry, because it is a disease, death is the deliverance from the hapless adventure that is life (L I.200.4; 139.7; 232.4), the antidote to the disease (L I.182.2; II.280.11; 324.6). The human body decomposed is without sense perception (L I.285.7) and hence undisturbed by disasters (L I.175.4). Comfort and peace of mind (راحة) are what a person finds when the body and soul are finally sundered (L II.234.7). He or she has no grief (L I.115.13) and escapes the torment (L I.139.7), tyranny (L I.172.10), diseases (L I.232.4–5), and clamor and tumult (L I.97.10) that are attendant upon life. He or she is finally rid of the indignities of old age: physical infirmities (faltering steps, L II.49.8–10; shaking and drooling, L II.52.3) as well as mental ones (e.g., senility, L II.300.15).

Therefore, although al-Maʿarrī can depict the thought of death and its advent as extraordinarily frightful and terrifying, and the moment of its actual occurrence as painful, he also exhorts humankind to welcome it (L I.119.7; II.94.1), to try not to be anxious over its onset (L I.199.3; II.267.13).

Approaching mortality from this vantage point, he proclaims death a virtuous thing (L I.79.5; 399.7), even an enriching experience (L I.361.4). It is better than a continued long life that in the end is going to be without gain (L I.213.2; II.265.5). To die fearlessly is to be considered an act of wisdom (L I.417.8). Conversely, that there should be sadness in the face of death should be regarded as repulsive (L I.136.5) and stupid (L I.91.7).

Despite the many verses of *Luzūm* in which al-Maʿarrī speaks of the desirability of death—and yet precisely because of their abundance—conspicuous by virtue of absence (particularly since there are Epicurean overtones to al-Maʿarrī's world view, to be discussed later in this study) is any explicit mention and/or discussion of death by one's own hand. Practically begged is the question "Why not?" and, from there, the question, "Might not this be an instance of a Maʿarrīan silence pregnant with meaning, where in fact it is the unspoken that resonates as much as—if not more than—the spoken?"

Or, to rephrase all of this, given the many verses in *Luzūm* that speak of the desirability of death because of the supreme comfort and peace that it provides, inasmuch as al-Maʿarrī saw human existence as essentially a painful, evil-ridden, and purposeless affair that leads to an eternally final عدم (nullity, nonbeing, nonexistence, Adonis's "nothingness") with respect to human life as we know it, is it not fairly legitimate to assume that while composing *Luzūm* al-Maʿarrī at one time or another must have given thoughtful and extended consideration to suicide as a panacea for one's woes, and, *in not explicitly rejecting* death by one's own hand, he must have been sympathetic to the notion, notwithstanding the lack of any specific reference to suicide, including one or another of the technical terms in Arabic (e.g., قتل النفس؛ انتحار)?

In truth, it probably should be concluded from the many passages of *Luzūm* in which al-Maʿarrī suggests that death is preferable to life as he knows it that implicitly he is indicating that he *did* give careful thought to the issue of suicide, and he *did* accept the principle that one's voluntarily ending one's life is a sure, attractive, and acceptable antidote to the disease that is life. Although one might consider this interpretation an example of stretching the boundaries of this study's hermeneutics to an unacceptable extreme, it is almost inconceivable that the case could have been otherwise, given the overall orientation of *Luzūm* and the trajectory of al-Maʿarrī's entire life and body of thought. It's hard to imagine that suicide for al-Maʿarrī (especially during his maturer years) became no less than what it was for a leading modern investigator of the subject: the one and only "truly philosophical problem."[42]

Explicitly to broach and embrace suicide in *Luzūm*, not to keep it as a more esoteric dimension to his thinking in arguably his most "philosophical" work, his *Summa*, al-Maʿarrī probably did not dare.[43] Well before his time, it had been determined in Islam (and—very significant for this discussion—largely on the basis of Qur'ānic authority) that suicide was to be regarded as a very serious wrong-doing; an act tantamount to a sin, in other words, something unequivocally forbidden;[44] and, although apparently some segments of the Islamic intellectual or clerical community came to condone it (under certain circumstances) by the time al-Maʿarrī was born and flourished, the majority still held that it was forbidden by the religion of Islam.[45] (Only so many transgressive or subversive lines could be crossed in *Luzūm*, even for such a celebrated and often self-confessed contrarian as al-Maʿarrī.)

But, if we *are* to conclude that while composing the *Luzūm,* especially the many verses expressing the desirability of death, al-Maʿarrī must have given serious thought to suicide as an attractive antidote to the disease of life, we must also conclude that in the end he rejected it on principle, so that for him, too, notwithstanding its appeal and a justification he could offer, and notwithstanding that at times it may have been no less than *his* only truly philosophical problem, in the end it must have remained no more than what another celebrated modern thinker on the topic termed it: "the *thought* . . . that helps one through many a dreadful night."[46] Al-Maʿarrī died of natural causes after having lived to a very ripe old age.

In discussing later in this study al-Maʿarrī's ethics, we will have an opportunity see what surely must have been one of the main reasons for his refraining from suicide. The taking of any form of life, even animal, was abhorrent to him. In his own mind he may also have condemned suicide as an act of cowardice more reprehensible than the anguish or evil that it effectively eliminates. Despite his many negative pronouncements on life and his praise of the desirability of death, al-Maʿarrī says in at least one line of *Luzūm* that to chose to live (i.e., not to opt for the choice of death, a choice that humans can freely exercise) is the act of the courageous (L I.399.6).

It is well known, however, that al-Maʿarrī advocated what one could argue is an attenuated form of societal or communal suicide, namely, celibacy and sexual abstinence. Moreover, by all accounts—including his own of course—he practiced these. (Apparently, he made a distinction between preventing life and taking it and did not find the former morally unacceptable.) Through his promotion of celibacy and sexual abstinence, which he did in relatively open and unencrypted (i.e., exoteric) fashion, perhaps al-Maʿarrī was trying to eat his cake and keep it too? That is to say, was he not thinking of a *type* of self-destruction for humankind (i.e., self-applied practices that would unquestionably lead to the end of the human race if scrupulously followed), but one that could be squared with his own personal ethics regarding the taking of life, *and, at the same time,* not expose him to the same degree of condemnation and reprisals that a call for suicide proper would have?

This can never be proven conclusively. But what is hard to deny with respect to al-Maʿarrī's many praises of, and longings for, death, is that they must be treated for what they truly are: considerably more than figurative expressions, false bravado, or formulaic, heroic posturing of the sort that might be considered quite expected from many of his peers in شعر (especially those who strove to uphold the older bardic legacy). The many morose or lugubrious passions in *Luzūm* are expressions of a genuine, deep-rooted religio-philosophical malaise—and maybe more. Whether natural or self-inflicted, and whether with regard to an individual or a whole community, death in al-Maʿarrī's thinking quite seriously was a welcome deliverance from a life that is pain, evil, and misery, unavoidable for sure, as we have just seen, because of the individual human being's own constitution and the nature necessarily ensuing from that constitution, but also because of al-Maʿarrī's conception of the nature and constitution of God, society, and world, which is what the present study will turn to consider next.

II. Humankind and God: Al-Maʿarrī's Religious Philosophy

If it is fair to say that humankind is the pivotal point in *Luzūm*, it is also fair to say that God is never far removed from that point. No sooner is there mention of the nature or fate of man or woman in the *dīwān*'s poems than there is mention of God and His nature. This in turn occasions scattered reflections on how humanity binds itself to God in worship—in religious practice and beliefs, in other words. It is primarily the Islamic orientation thereof with which al-Maʿarrī is concerned, but he also has remarks on Judaism and Christianity, not to mention Zoroastrianism. Pieced together, his thoughts along these lines constitute what might loosely be called an attempt at a religious philosophy including a theology and theodicy. The concerns of this part of chapter 4 are isolating and elucidating the key components of this philosophy.

To open the discussion and connect to some of the very last points taken up in the previous part, at the apex of this philosophy, on the surface at least and more often than not if one is calculating quantitatively, there appears to be the unwavering belief that indeed there is a transcendent god to whom al-Maʿarrī might give thought in the first place; that is to say, God exists. That this *might* be the actual situation, however, is only as certain as one can be. True, al-Maʿarrī flatly asserts in *Luzūm* (e.g., I.94.10; 141.6; II.399.5) that God is a truth/reality (حق). "There is no doubt that He is a truth/reality" (لا ريب أن الله حق), reads L I.141.6. Similar such pronouncements are to be found in *Luzūm*. Nowhere does al-Maʿarrī explicitly contradict this. However, one is obliged to question whether this is yet another example of a perfectly acceptable orthodox remark intended only to placate those in his society (be they Muslims, Jews, or Christians; but of course especially Muslims) who would hardly have seriously entertained anything to the contrary (at least not openly, nor even semitransparently as far as that goes). At the very least, as von Kremer has quite plausibly suggested with regard to some of al-Maʿarrī's other perfectly reverential and rather predictable faith- (Islamic) based utterances and sentiments, his assertion that God is a reality/truth could very well be an empty formulaic statement uttered more out of a culturally induced force of habit than true conviction and thus as inconsequential in its real religious implications as parallels in old Western Christendom like "By Jove!" or "To the Devil!"[47]

When turning to God's nature, at his perfectly pious and conforming moments in *Luzūm* as a would-be believer, al-Maʿarrī describes it exactly as one might expect from a properly pious and reverential Muslim. He proclaims God's uniqueness and oneness (L I.111.8; 251.10; 257.2); His eternity (I.111.8; II.247.10; 267.11–12); His omniscience (I.290.15); His mercy and forgiveness (I.91.8; II.160.6; 425.4); His justice (I.121.1; II.312.1); His omnipotence (L I.118.1–3; 52.9; 99.10; II.62.3; 5.5); and His complete sovereignty over all things in the world (L I.57.10–12; 58.1). As we have already had occasion to mention, al-Maʿarrī also regards God as Creator of heaven and earth (I.57.10–13; 345.11; II.158.6) as well as humankind. He is the sustainer of all living things (L I.52.9).

But which of *these* expressions are also purely perfunctory or formulaic? Of dubious sincerity? (Indeed, many seem almost tongue-in-cheek or sardonic—because of the formulaic nature—when contrasted to expressions of opposite sentiment; similar in tone and spirit, for example, to L I.121.1 "I should fear God's torment, He being just? Having already lived the life of the oppressed and tormented?" أأخشى عذابَ اللهِ واللهُ عادلٌ/ وقد عشتُ عيشَ المستضامِ المعذَّبِ.) Which can we hope to take seriously, if any?

Hardly the notion that God is kind and merciful. This al-Maʿarrī clearly, frequently, and vigorously undercuts in *Luzūm* by accentuating the terrible and terrifying side to the omnipotent God. With His awesome power to will whatever He pleases, omnipotent God is portrayed as having (pre)determined that a human being must follow misfortune after misfortune in life until the day he/she dies (L I.366.5), profiting absolutely nothing for having lived (L I.409.1) (with the suggestion of course that there is no resurrection and divine reward for doing good). It is God who makes a man or woman the ignorant and weak creature that he or she is, either forever unaware of the proper course that should be followed through life or incapable of achieving it because restrained by predertimination (see, e.g., L I.420.16; II.62.3–4).

It is by virtue of God's divine decree that human souls are imbued with corruption (L II.206.4). Thus, the entire human race can never be cleansed of its dishonor (L I.110.8). Nor can there be the hope of self-improvement (L I.110.2; 121.2). God has no pity either for those who deserve to suffer the world's sorrows (i.e., persons who bring these sorrows on themselves by pursuing worldly pleasures) or for those who do not deserve such a fate (i.e., persons who shun the world and its evils). Yet it is God who sanctions these sorrows, who first makes humankind liable to them by bringing men and women into the world through His act of creation (L I.142.9; II.158.6: تباركتَ يا ربّ أنت صُغتها /فليتَك في أرزائها لم تبارك "Blessed are You, O Lord! You created her [the world]! If only You had not blessed her calamities!"). An individual *might* find some well-being in life, concedes al-Maʿarrī; but even if the well-being is achieved, it is at best only temporary. Ultimately, God takes His revenge (L II.265.6), the most obvious and painful example of which is that humans must die and come to naught despite all wishes to the contrary (L II.62.3–4):

ما يشأْ ربكَ يفعلْ قادراً　　جلَّ عن كل مقالٍ وٱعتراضِ
قد تجمَّعْنا على غير هُدًى　　و تفرَّقْنا على غير تراضي

Whatever God wills, He does, fully able.
He is above all reproach or doctrine.
We have all come together aimlessly.
We all depart discontentedly.

Because this state of affairs is every person's fate in life, always and everywhere, it casts a deep and troubling shadow of doubt on God's supposed wisdom and justice. Why should all humankind be condemned to such ill fortune? Where is the wisdom and justice in this? These are the questions begged by al-Maʿarrī's description of the terrible side to God's omnipotence, even if there is no explicit indictment of divine injustice. In the same vein, al-Maʿarrī explicitly asks: Why is it that God wills punishment upon people who are just if it is for *misdeeds* that people are supposed to be punished (L I.110.2–4)? and, Why is it that humans must suffer death solely because God wills it (L I.425.11)? Going more directly to the point is L I.121.1, already cited, where al-Maʿarrī wonders why, even though he considers himself as having already lived the life of the oppressed and tormented here on earth, he is nonetheless expected to fear one final punishment from God. He proclaims in L I.296.1–2 that he can find no reason for why God created him: الله صوَّرني ولستُ بعالمٍ / لما ذاك سبحانَ القدير الواحد / فلتشهد الساعات والأنفاسُ لي/ أني برئتُ من الغويّ الجاحد "God created me although I know not why. Glory is to the One, the Omnipotent; so let the passing hours and my breaths bear witness: I've nothing to do with the misguided denier").

The present study takes "Glory be to the One, the Omnipotent" in L I.296.1 as being ironic. It also takes as ironic the first hemistich of L II.264.4 (quoted beneath), so that the purport of the second hemistich, for all intents and purposes, is that al-Maʿarrī is saying that creation as a whole *is* لَمَم (madness) on God's part:

Were it not for the marvels proving that our Creator
knows better, is wiser, we'd say our creation is madness.

لولا بدائعُ دلَّتْ أَنّ خالقَنَا   أَدْرى وأَحْكمُ قُلنَا خَلقُنا لَمَمُ

(L II.264.4)

At his more absolutely fatalistic moments in *Luzūm,* when insinuating (as he does on occasion) that if there is posited an omnipotent Creator God, He is the one Who (by virtue of predeterminism) ought to be regarded as the ultimate cause of humans doing the evil that is so pandemic among them (thereby taking "the fates" off the hook—in these instances), al-Maʿarrī even more strongly implies that he questions whether God in all seriousness should be regarded as just:

If he who commits grave sins is compelled to do so,
punishing him for whatever he does is wrongful.
God was fully aware when He created mines that
glistening white sword blades would be fashioned from them,
with which men on bridled and iron-shod horses spill blood.

إن كان مَن فعل الكبائر مجبراً   فَعقابهُ ظلمٌ على ما يفعلُ
واللهُ إذ خَلقَ المعادنَ عالمٌ   أَنَّ الجِداد البيضَ منها تُجعلُ
سفكَ الدماءَ بها رِجالٌ أَعصمُوا   بالخيلِ تُلجَمُ بالحديدِ وتُنعلُ

(L II.181.3–6)

The young man yonder did not act treacherously.
Someone other than he encouraged the treachery.

ما خانَ ذاك الفتى ولكنْ   حثَّ سواهُ على الخيانَهْ

(L II.348.4)

Whom do you blame for the crime that is past?
The bell doesn't move until caused to move.

لمن تُؤَاخِذُ بالجرَّى التي سَلَفتْ   وما تحرَّكَ حتى حُرِّكَ الجرَسُ

(L II.12.9)

The same notion is more brazenly expressed in the verse beneath. By al-Maʿarrī's time, the condition posited with respect to divine predeterminism was virtually the one embraced by mainstream (i.e., Ashʿarī-oriented) Islam's understanding of determinism as opposed to free will (which fact perhaps explains why the line is not to be found in Zand's edition of *Luzūm* nor in the Beirut edition; it can be found in the Leyden ms., p. 107):

If it is by virtue of compulsion that humankind is unjust,
He who created him that he ill-treat creation is more unjust.

وإن يكن الإنسانُ بالجبر ظالماً   فخالِقُهُ كي يَظلم الخَلْقَ أظلمُ

What al-Maʿarrī is arguing here, virtually, is that inasmuch as humanity acts unjustly by virtue of compulsion, that is, divine predeterminism (again according to the Ashʿarī-oriented normative teaching of his inherited faith, Sunnī Islam, inasmuch as according to this teaching all meaningful causality or agency is denied humans), logically it must follow (according to that same faith-based orientation) that God is even more unjust for having created humanity as He did.[48]

Aside from on occasion simply perfunctorily declaring God to be just, notwithstanding the surfeit of references to the obvious and undeniable prevalence of evil and suffering in the world that is His creation (صنعته ؛ خلقه) and His alone, al-Maʿarrī at times attempts to uphold God's justice by arguing that blind, inanimate forces of fate (e.g., *aqdār*/أقدار; *maqādīr*/مقادير) as separate hypostases are directly responsible for humankind's evil ways and the misery the individual encounters in life on earth. The following lines from the *Luzūm*, for example, speak to this position:

Your Lord does not give you to drink for your good deed,
just as bad acts don't keep you from the life-giving rain cloud.
All of this is only a matter of fates, which are arranged
so as to be unrelated to doing good or bad.
Proof of this is a noble free man in need of food
while someone to the contrary has obtained wealth.
Many a person confined to home gets his sustenance,
while those who roam with horse and camel are denied it.

لم يَسقِكم رَبُّكُمْ عن حسن فِعلِكُم　　ولا حماكُم غماماً سُوءُ أعمالِ
وإنما هي أقدارٌ مُرتَّبةٌ　　ما علِّقتْ بإسآتٍ وإجمالِ
دليلُ ذلكَ أنَّ الحُرَّ أعوزَهُ　　قُوتٌ وأنَّ سواه فازَ بالمالِ
كم جُدَّ بالرزقِ ثاوٍ في منزِلِهِ　　وحُدَّ سارٍ بأفراسٍ وأجمالِ

(L II.223.12–15)

Our morals didn't become evil by our free choice,
but because of a dictum occasioned by the fates.

وما فسدتْ اخلاقنا باختيارنا　　ولكن بأمرٍ سبّبتهُ المقادرُ

(L I 311.4)

In a similar vein, al-Maʿarrī assures that it is inexorable eternal time, eternal perdurance (الدهر, a word whose connotation is often tantamount to fate) that is unjust (see, e.g., L I.104.1).

Passages of this sort in *Luzūm* somewhat serve to take the burden for the world's evil or injustice off of God's shoulders. However, al-Maʿarrī is quick to intimate that over and above fate or time stands a transcendent, superior driving or superintending force. It is hardly benign.

Suppose that man gets the most of what he hopes for;
is not the fates' shepherd still behind him, unmerciful?

هب الفتى نال أَقْصى ما يُؤَمِّلُهُ　　أَليس راعي المنايا خلفهُ حُطَم[49]

(L II.267.8)

It's as though you are chattels in the hands of time;
and by dint of fate all chattels are plagued by murrain.
I also reckon that we are haggard camels;
behind which labors a firm and despotic driver.

كأنك في يد الأيامِ مالٌ　　وكل المال عن قَدر يسوُفُ
وأحسبُ أننا إبلٌ رذايا　　أجدّ وراءَها حاد عسوفُ

(L II.102.8–9)

People are like a herd of dumb beasts off to pasture
led to the fate of death by a merciless shepherd.

والناسُ مثلُ سوامٍ لا حُلومَ لهمْ   يسوقُهُ للمنايا سائقٌ حُطَمُ

(L II.266.6)[50]

If al-Maʿarrī's many references (including especially the mordant ones) to God's complete sovereignty and power over all creation are not indication enough that he holds God to be the superior, transcendent force that superintends the fates (الدهر), the lines in which he more explicitly and with greater elaboration states that fate is arranged ultimately by God (e.g., L II.75.10; 174.11–12; 181.3–5; 261.3), are.

There is the occasional suggestion in *Luzūm* that the conjunctions or alignments of the planets and stars determine the evil nature of man and his life (I.129.2–3; 174.3; II.267–6), much like, if not indeed precisely the same thing as, the fates or الدهر. But above and beyond the heavenly bodies too, al-Maʿarrī opines, stands God. He is their sovereign (L II.373.7). It is He who causes them to move as they do (II.219.13). The bell does not move until caused to move.

In what might be construed as one final attempt to mitigate against all that is so strongly intimated in this aspect of his thought, al-Maʿarrī does some hair splitting. He says in L II.280.5 that God's creation of injustice, which here he openly concedes, perhaps so as not to compromise His omnipotence (and possibly avoid more transparent Mazdean affinities or intimations?), *cannot be equated with His actually being unjust.*

Nicholson has insightfully noted[51] that this might be seen as an effort on al-Maʿarrī's part to signal endorsement of the later mainstream Islamic (which is to say, Ashʿarite) solution to the knotty theological problem of preserving God's complete power and superintendence over all human deeds, good *and* bad, while at the same time maintaining His perfect justness, extricating Him from any involvement in evil. That is to say, this might suggest al-Maʿarrī's endorsement of the doctrine of *kasb* (كسب), the contention that indeed God creates all human deeds, but He endows humans with the ability or capacity to appropriate or acquire them,[52] so that in that sense *they* are culpable for any evil actions.

However, not only would there be reason to doubt the sincerity of al-Maʿarrī's subscribing to كسب—if in fact he did subscribe to it—because of the doctrine's decidedly normative or orthodox nature; there is also good cause to concur with Nicholson's final conclusion that "it would be rash to infer" al-Maʿarrī really gave *kasb* serious consideration at all.[53] By the time of *Luzūm*'s composition, the followers of al-Ashʿarī and the doctrine of *kasb*[54] would have been known by name to any Muslim thinker as preoccupied with the issue of determinism versus free will as al-Maʿarrī was. If al-Maʿarrī had seriously wanted to invoke *kasb*, it seems inexplicable that he didn't do so explicitly.

Even if al-Maʿarrī's contemporaneous readers of *Luzūm* erroneously *had* inferred that al-Maʿarrī did mean to suggest, as well as seriously subscribe to, the Ashʿarī doctrine of *kasb* for explaining how God can be just and at the same time the Creator of bad human deeds (Creator in the sense of ultimate Agent of all actions in the world), this understanding could not have effectively gotten al-Maʿarrī off the horns of his dilemma; not so much, as Nicholson believes, because *kasb* "really explains nothing"[55] (in actually it does, and rather ingeniously[56]) but because *kasb* explains or rationalizes in much too subtle and rarified fashion. It needs to be recalled that not even all Muslim theologians could be won over by the teaching. The Muʿtazilites, for example, on the whole rejected it. Thus it was that, in order to underscore further how in their eyes God could in no way whatsoever be implicated in the doing of something unjust, instead of endorsing *kasb,* they (1) advocated a more absolutist or totalizing doctrine of free will, by which they held human beings, and human beings alone, totally responsible for their actions; and (2) referred to themselves as the "people of justice"; that is, believers in God's absolute justness at all times. He is in no way whatsoever involved in, or responsible, for the injustices of the world.[57]

Should one conclude, therefore, that al-Maʿarrī in *Luzūm* is more than just disquieted by, and at a loss to explain, the presence of evil or injustice in a world over which according to normative Islam stands an omnipotent and just Creator? Does he really mean to advance, implicitly—as is so strongly suggested in *Luzūm* —that if God exists, then the God about Whom he was taught (the God of all the Abrahamic faiths, and not just Islam) is unjust?

This would seem to be a real possibility, regardless of the ramifications.[58] If al-Maʿarrī does not hold an Omnipotent Creator God directly responsible for causing humankind on the whole to behave unjustly, at the very least, he holds Him—if one is to posit His existence—indirectly responsible because of His human creation being so morally weak and flawed that humans are on the whole typically inclined to evil, innately incapable of listening to reason and pursuing the good and righteous. And if al-Maʿarrī does not suggest to believing monotheists that they must hold God directly responsible for the world's misfortunes, because of a role therein on the part of fate or the stars, they (the believers) are almost logically bound to hold Him indirectly responsible because it is He and He alone who ultimately superintends "the fates" and "the stars." That is to say, the fates or the stars may be proximate causes of all that transpires in the sublunar world, but the Creator God, if one posits His existence, His reality, must be regarded as the ultimate cause.

Khalīfāt[59] argues that "the fates" is Maʿarrīan vernacular for the mechanistic working of the universe according to laws of necessity of nature, a view that, as will be seen later, the *Luzūm* provides considerable textual support for. However, unless this view is somehow completely dissociated from a creation in time by a Creator God, it does not let God completely off the hook in terms of ultimate culpability (to one degree or another) for humanity's woes.

Aside from the frequent depiction of God as exercising His omnipotence rather tyrannically, mercilessly, so that His ways hardly seem wise, just, and compassionate, most of the other aspects of al-Maʿarrī's thoughts on God in *Luzūm* can be more meaningfully discussed either within the context of verses on Islam and religion in general, which are taken up later in this part of chapter 4, or within the context of part 4's examination of al-Maʿarrī's views on inter alia, space, time, matter, and creation. There are two exceptions to this, however. The first is what al-Maʿarrī has to say about a human being's capability of knowing God. The second involves an implication about God as Creator. The former has considerable bearing on al-Maʿarrī's sense of God's injustice. The latter seems to compromise, if not totally contradict, the sole God-centered assertions in *Luzūm* (from among all of those enumerated earlier, and similar such pronouncements scattered throughout the work) upon which al-Maʿarrī *does not* cast aspersions (directly or indirectly; indiscreetly or discreetly) when he evokes the philosophically (i.e., morally) problematic side to God's omnipotence: God's oneness and His eternity. These two items can be taken up best here and now.

To turn to the latter first: in keeping strictly to his view that, although the powers of reason are great, they nonetheless prove ineffectual and unconvincing when trying to fathom intangibles or things metaphysical, al-Maʿarrī submits in so many words that a human being has no hope of ever being able to truly know and thus truly understand God. He/she may conceive of God but not really know or understand Him. This is clearly the import of the following lines from *Luzūm*:

We have no knowledge of the mystery of our God.
So does the sun know it? Is it perceived by the stars?

وليس لنا عِلمٌ بسرِّ إلهِنا   فهلْ علمتْهُ الشمسُ أو شَعَرَ النجمُ

(L II.252.7)

They inform you lyingly about the Lord Most High
whereas no human knows the affairs of God.

يُخبِّرونكَ عن ربِّ العلى كذباً   وما درى بشؤن اللهِ إنسانُ

(L II.334.9)

As for God, He is a matter you don't understand;
so beware angering your people here on earth.[60]

أَما الإلهُ فأَمرٌ لست مُدركَهُ   فٱحذَرْ لجيلِكَ فوقَ الأَرض إسخاطا

(L II.69.7)

Misguided is an adjuring denier of God;
or whosoever defines Him. *Can* God be defined?

ضلُّوا عن الرشدِ منهم جاحدٌ جَحِدٌ   أو مَن يَحُدُّ وهل للهِ تحديدُ

(L I.256.4)

Although this aspect of al-Maʿarrī's theology is fraught with other significations (e.g., another possible confession of agnosticism, if not atheism as well?[61]), the first that comes to mind is that *if* one is to believe in the existence of God, there can be absolutely no rational explanation for God's ways (including the palpably capricious or despotic), such as they are. They must be accepted for what they are, even if inexplicably constituting harsh and unfair realities of life, and, what is more (and more morally problematic), an admixture of good *and* evil. Omnipotent God is not—cannot be—beyond good *and* evil.

As for the implication about God as Creator that seems to compromise His eternity and oneness, this is bound up with al-Maʿarrī's suggestion that earth is a sort of indestructible and eternal material element (i.e., elemental raw matter) from which the three other natural elements—and hence all creation—ultimately derive. The fuller ramifications of this view will be discussed in part 4 of this chapter. But one such that should be stressed here is that although al-Maʿarrī does not explicitly deny God's oneness and eternity, and actually quite explicitly confirms such in several instances, at the same time he implicitly proposes that there at least co-exists with Him in eternity something else, an "other"; and that other would be indestructible (though mutable) primordial matter of an earthly nature, the ultimate source of all creation, the material cause.

In what has been examined thus far of al-Maʿarrī's thoughts on God, there are ample reasons for one's wholeheartedly endorsing the statement with which Nicholson opened his study of the poet over seventy-five years ago: "The name of Abu 'l-ʿAlá al-Maʿarrí is not one of those which any body of educated Moslems would be likely to receive with placid approbation or polite indifference."[62] If one turns to a consideration of al-Maʿarrī's remarks on religion in general, and Islam specifically, there is even greater cause for concurring with Nicholson.

Al-Maʿarrī's fundamental starting point with respect to Islam and all revealed, scripture-based religions is that they do not represent truths made manifest by God. Nor are their core teachings or narratives verifiable by human reason. Rather, they are human fabrications that have little (if anything) to do with actual (i.e., empirically verifiable) historical actualities. They are blindly followed by one generation after another primarily because of the weight of tradition:

Instinct has an aversion to right guidance.
And the holy books are compiled upon vanities.

بَيْنَ الغريزةِ والرشادِ نفارُ   وعلى الزخارفِ ضُمَّت الأسفارُ

(L I.338.2)

The adolescent among us grows up based on
what his father has made him accustomed to.
The young man isn't religious out of reason;
it's his relatives who teach him religion.
And thus the Persian child has his guardians
who train him in the rites of Mazdeanism.

وينشأُ ناشيءُ الفتيانِ منّا   على ما كان عَوَّدَهُ أبوهُ
وما دانَ الفتى بحجاً ولكن   يعلّمه التديُّنَ أقربوهُ
وطفلُ الفارسي له ولاةٌ   بأفعالِ التمجُّس درَّبوهُ

(L II.403.12–14)

In all your concerns there's blind tradition with which you're content,
including your proclamation "My Lord is One, Unique."
We have been directed to think about God's marvels;
but if a community thus thinks, it apostatizes.
People of every argument disclaim what they hold
once they've seen the light of manifest truth.

في كلّ أمرِكَ تقليدٌ رضيتَ بهِ   حتى مقالكَ ربّي واحدٌ أحدُ
وقد أُمرنا بفكرٍ في بدائعهِ   وإن تفكَّر فيهِ معشرٌ لحدوا
وأهلُ كلِّ جدالٍ يمسكون به   إذا رأوْا نورَ حقٍ ظاهرٍ جحدوا

(L I.252.1–3)

People have lived just like their fathers who preceded them,
and bequeathed religion just as they found it: blind tradition.

They don't mindfully observe what they've said and what they've heard;
nor pay any concern to whom they prostrate, being misled.

عاشوا كما عاش آباءٌ لهم سلفوا　　وأورثوا الدين تقليداً كما وجدوا
فما يُراعونَ ما قالوا وما سمعوا　　ولا يبالون من غَيٍّ لمن سجدوا

(L I.248.10–11)

Religion versus irreligion; reports narrated;
a Qur'ān,[63] a Torah, a Gospel laid down in writing.
Every age has its absurd things that are believed in.
Has any generation stood alone with right guidance?[64]

دِينٌ وكُفرٌ وأنباءٌ تُقصُّ وفرْ　　قانٌ يُنصُّ وتوراةٌ وانجيلُ
في كُلِّ جيلٍ أَباطيلٌ يُدانُ بها　　فهل تفرَّدَ يوماً بالهُدَى جيلُ

(L II.177.7–8)

Above and beyond tradition, that is, the weight of received opinion as it concerns revelation, it is also fear that induces people to profess religion and piety, according to al-Maʿarrī (see, e.g., L I.139.9; and also II.266.12–14, which contains an especially strong condemnation of the legacy of *ḥadīth* scholars) or the hope of procuring monetary and other worldly gains (L I.64.8; 279.1; II.85.8–10; 249.8).

In speaking more specifically of the faith into which he was born, al-Maʿarrī in *Luzūm* shows the same degree of skepticism or cynicism as that which he directs toward the general phenomenon of religion (especially as institutionalized and ritualized). There is little in Islam's major doctrines or cult aspects that escapes his criticism. He advises women, and especially virgins, not to make the pilgrimage to Mecca because the holy city's custodians are in truth debauched, fallacious hypocrites. Their real concern is not protecting pilgrims but instead making as much money as possible by taking bribes in exchange for escort services to the Holy Sanctuary (L I.70.1–5). There is little reason for any Muslim, male or female, to attach meaningful religious importance to the pilgrimage. The Kaʿbah, al-Maʿarrī says, is a vestige of idolatrous worship (L I.130.1;

he adds that this is "the opinion of people whom I shall not mention"—the type of feigned horror and disapproval in his writing that actually signals endorsement; a hemistich of the preceding line reads: "People have not established the foundation of their religion according to any logic"/ (لم يُثبتوا بقياسٍ أصلَ دينِهم). The wearing of the special pilgrim's dress at Mecca he labeled an act of feeble-mindedness (L I.127.1; this is quite obviously the intent of ثياب سليب at the end of the line, especially if one follows the Leyden manuscript redaction of *Luzūm* as opposed to Zand's, which has ثياب سليبي). The *ḥajj*/الحج in its entirety is *riḥlat jāhilī*/رحلة جاهليّ, that is, a journey that is the vestige of someone still mired in the age of barbarism and paganism in Arabia (see L I.391.1, where there is little ambiguity over this pronouncement and its assignation). In several verses in *Luzūm,* al-Maʿarrī openly boasts of never having himself made the pilgrimage to Mecca (I.177.5; 209.1; 219.2; 330.8; II 2.4; 192.13; 417.1; although there is no dearth of transgressive lines in *Luzūm*—overt as well as covert—I.177.5 has to be one of the most egregious, underscored as it is by the jarring imagery: لم تَشْفِ ذنبي المكتان وإنَّ شَفَتَيْنِ / لي أَخْلافَ المعيشة مكّتا or "Neither Mecca nor Medina has ever cleansed my sins, although I have two lips that have sucked dry the teats of life").[65] He speaks dismissively and even derisively of those who have undertaken the pilgrimage to Mecca. They are said to bribe their way into the Holy Sanctuary (as just referenced with I.70.1–5; but cf. II.222.8). They do not become any more pious for having circumambulated the Kaʿbah (L II.160.1). Once they have made the *ḥajj,* they return to their erring ways (L I.321.5) and remain as recalcitrant as ever (L II.327.9). They are not even convinced that the *ḥajj* is a blessed act to begin with (L I.321.5). What truly motivates the pilgrims to undertake this religious duty, argues al-Maʿarrī, is an excess of insolence and mirth (وما يحجّون من دين ولا نُسُكٍ / وإنما ذاك إفراطٌ من الأَشَرِ) (L I.382.2). At Mecca they drink wine and commit other abominable and dissolute acts (L II.416.16; 417.1–2).

Obligatory prayers, fasting, and paying the alms tax (زكاة) are enjoined in L II.349.4–6. However, elsewhere they are criticized by al-Maʿarrī. Just as he openly boasts of never having made the pilgrimage in his lifetime, he states clearly and unequivocally that he also had no desire to observe the Friday congregational prayers; he believed there was no virtue in such when it amounts only to being jostled around with worshippers whose very best are no better than mangy camels (يقولون هلا تشهدُ الجُمَعَ التي / رجونا بها عفواً من الله أو قربا / وهل لي خيرٌ في الحضورِ وإنما / أزاحمُ من أخيارهم إبلاً جُرْبا) (L I.100.7–8).[66] They do not pray because they are genuinely pious (L I.277.5–6). They perform the prayers out of fear (L I.251.13). (It is fear, too, that compels Muslims to pay the *zakāh* [L I.251.13] and reinforces the influence of the *ḥadīth* scholars.) Even the God-fearing, Qur'ān-invoking supplicants in the mosques may be no more estimable than merry revelers in taverns (لعلَّ أُناساً في المحاريب خوَّفوا / بآيٍ كَناسٍ في المشارب أطربوا) (L I.81.10). If the one who prays hopes thereby to deceive or double-cross, says al-Maʿarrī (suggesting therein that this in fact occurs), he/she in fact would become closer to God by deliberately *eschewing* prayer (L I.81.11: إذا رام كيداً بالصلاة مقيمُها / فتاركُها عمداً إلى الله أقرب).

As for fasting during the month of Ramadan, al-Maʿarrī cynically remarks that those who do such avoid what is otherwise legally permitted while at the same time indulging in what is not (L II.347.6). He records in *Luzūm* that he "never took delight" in the religious holiday marking the end of the fast, *'īd al-fiṭr*/عيد الفطر (II.310.1), by which we might assume that he meant that he paid no attention either to the holiday itself or to the Ramadan fast preceding it. He never praised the Ramadan fast, he proclaims (see L I.351.5; although this contradicts L II.349.6, at least to the extent that there he enjoins fasting during Ramadan [وصُمْ رمضانَ مختاراً مطيعاً]). Elsewhere, he says that in his opinion more important than conventional fasting (*in any month*) is the abstention from doing evil (L I.103.11) because *real* religion in his eyes is simply a matter of treating people (*all* people; al-Maʿarrī's emphasis) justly (L I.103.9: الدينُ إنصافُكَ الأقوامَ كلَّهُم). Ignoring "the obliged fast" is not as deserving of punishment as are the evil deeds effected with money (L II.294.8).

What amounts to al-Maʿarrī's most basic criticism of the Qur'ān in *Luzūm* has already been indicated. He considered all religious scriptures human compilations and thus subject to falsehoods or incredulities. He hardly needed to have said anything more than this to indicate his dismissal of the truth value or efficacy of what those who believe in scripture uphold as God's literal revealed word. But he does. He goes on to add that reading the Qur'ān does not in and of itself keep one from following one's innate (i.e., evil) nature over the course of time (L II.397.3–4). Nor does it necessarily induce piety (L II.393.1). The Qur'ān can be used by hypocritical evil-doers who pray with it one moment but thereafter turn to pursue their sinning (L I.381.11–12). The Qur'ān can be something that people market, like any other potentially profit-making commercial commodity (II.186.2).[67]

Of course, all this arguably has less to do with the Qur'ān itself than the character of some of those who profess to believe in it and abide by it. But al-Maʿarrī did not exactly say this in the *Luzūm*.

Quite conspicuously, nowhere in *Luzūm* does al-Maʿarrī directly impugn the character of the Prophet Muḥammad or explicitly deny Muḥammad's prophetic mission, the belief that lies at the very heart of a Muslim's confirmation of faith, of what it means to be a Muslim in addition to being a *mu'min*/مؤمن (believer in God and His Divine word). لا إله إلا الله ومحمد رسول الله ("There is no god other than the One God, and Muḥammad is the Prophet of God") is the Muslim's *shahādah*/شهادة or testament of faith. But as Ṭāhā Ḥusayn noted in *Ma'a Abī al-'Alā' fī Sijnih*,[68] "[Al-Maʿarrī] does not openly enjoin the first of the pillars of Islam, which is the declaration 'There is no god but God and Muḥammad is the Prophet of God.'" Additionally, al-Maʿarrī says in L I.379.11, "I have not said that he was made to undertake his nightly ascension for a task that God directed from before the stars had revolved" (ما قلتُ أُسريَ في ليلٍ على عملٍ / أدارَهُ اللهُ والأفلاكُ لم تَدُرِ). The reference of course is to the Prophet Muḥammad and Qur'ān 17:1's account of the occasion of an ascension to heaven during the course of his prophetic mission. Inasmuch as the nightly ascension or *isrā'* (إسراء), especially if understood as a physical (i.e., bodily) translocation (as opposed to merely spiritual and consisting of a "vision"), is considered a proof not only of Muḥammad's prophetic mission but also of the initiation to his entire prophetic career,[69] one might be inclined to take L I.379.11 as having implications wider than a denial merely of Muḥammad's celebrated *ascension* (whether merely spiritual or bodily).

A similar temptation, for rather obvious reasons, occurs with L II.386.9–10, which reads / زعمَ الناسُ أنَّ قوماً من الأبر / ار عولوا في الجوّ بالطيران ومَشَوْا فوقَ صفحةِ الماء هذا الإ / فكُ هيهاتَ ما جرى العصران / ما مشى فوق لجة الماء لا السعد / دان فيما مضى ولا العُمران ("People claim that among the godly there are those who have been risen by flight into the air, and also have walked upon water. How preposterous is this falsehood, and for as long as the days and nights pass. Not even the two Saʿds nor the two ʿUmars ever walked upon water in days gone by.") Obviously, all such alleged evidentiary miracles, regardless of the faith, are being rejected here.

In L II.221.11–12, in a poem addressed to an imagined shepherd bereft over the to-be-expected adverse fate of his flock, one will find يا صاحبَ الضأنِ سَلِّمْ حَقَّ مُعْدِمِها / ولا تَقُلْ ضَلَّ إنساني بإنسالي/ وآرقُبْ إلَهكَ في عُسْرٍ ويُسْرٍ/ وآتْرُكْ في بعْثٍ وإرسال which translates "O herder of sheep, yield to the right of He who wipes them out, and don't say 'My personage is damaged with my perdition.' Fear God through difficult as well as easy times, and put aside your arguing over resurrection and prophecy." As for the admonition in the last hemistich, to connect it to one line of logic in the *Luzūm* (see, e.g., L I.52.2–8), prophets, after all, not to mention other religious moralizers (الواعظون), come and go; humanity's affliction, however, its incurable disease of inveterate evil and ignorance, remains.

As Bakrī (for example) has underscored,[70] the Prophet Muḥammad in the *Luzūm* is praised primarily in terms of being a *social* reformer (مصلح اجتماعي). But even if ones allows for the sincerity of that view, the *Luzūm* stresses that humans are so innately, irredeemably morally depraved that even with a truth-bearing social/moral reformer like the Prophet Muḥammad, and notwithstanding his reputed appeal that honor be accorded to the honorable (وقال لكم نبيكم إذا ما / كريمُ القوم جاءَ فأكرموهُ) regardless of their religious pedigree (L II.407.10–13; in this instance Christians are specifically referenced), the practical moral—and thus by extension social—impact is negligible; the prophetic mission, therefore, is misguided (L I.134.8–9; 139–140.7; 1–2).[71]

With the notion of "reform" lying behind the use of the word تهذيب in L.134.8, al-Maʿarrī composed جاءَ النبيُّ بحقٍّ كي يُهَذِّبُكُمْ / فهل أحسَّ لكم طبعٌ بتهذيب ("The Prophet came with a truth in order to set you right; but do you have a nature that can sense being set right?"); which in this and similar such instances (although far and few between) takes *the* Prophet as well as *prophets* off the hook with respect to humanity's woes. Paradoxically, L I.110.2 has as God's will that He "did not ordain that our world be set right; so don't hold out hope for it for people" (لم يَقْدُرِ اللهُ تهذيبا لِعالَمِنا / فلا ترومنّ للأقوامِ تهذيبا).

Above and beyond its argument for the inefficacy of prophets because of the ordinary human moral depravity and obtuseness that prophets are up against, and notwithstanding its acceptance of the historicity of the prophecy of Muḥammad (and others such as, and above all, Jesus and Moses; the historicity is never rejected), the *Luzūm* when touching upon the topic of prophethood in very general terms discredits prophets because it finds them nonrational or disingenuous (in this respect they are no worse—but also no better—than the rank-and-file devotees of institutionalized and organized religion i.e., أصحاب الدين.

ومالي لا أَكونُ وَصيَّ نفسي　　ولاتعصِي أموري الأَوْصياءُ
وقد فتَّشْتُ عن أصحابِ دينٍ　　لهم نُسْكٌ وليسَ لهم رياءُ
فألفيتُ البهائمَ لا عقولٌ　　تقيمُ لها الدليلَ ولا ضِياءُ
وإخوانُ الفطانة في اختيالٍ　　كأَنهم لقومٍ أنبياءُ
فأَمّا هؤلاء فأهلُ مكرٍ　　وأَمّا الأَوّلونَ فأَغبياءُ

(L I.52.12–15)

Why can't I be my own guardian?
Without others resisting my concerns?
I have scrutinized those who are religious—
the ones who are devout, not hypocritical.
What I have found are beasts who have neither minds
nor enlightenment to give solid proof of things;
while the brotherhood of the shrewdly arrogant
act as if they are prophets to a nation.
As for the latter group, they are impostors;
and as for the former, well, they are idiots.

What prophets legislate causes hatred and aggression among people (L I.186.2). Moreover, in the final analysis, they are superfluous. This has to be regarded as one of the intended meanings of al-Maʿarrī's dictum "Every mind is a prophet." The human intellect, or rationality, does not, and should not attempt to, confirm, verify, or mirror the prophetic experience; it needs to supersede it. To the extent that humankind might come to know something with certainty—as comparatively minuscule as that certain knowledge is—it comes to know it by virtue of the power of reasoning.[72]

Having essentially denied a belief in bodily resurrection, al-Maʿarrī also denied, or at least adopted an agnostic position toward, two other very important and related principles of the Islamic eschaton as expressed in the prophetic revelation. These are (1) the belief in a final day of recompense when good will be rewarded and evil punished, and (2) the existence of a heaven and hell. This seems to be the import of all the following passages of the *Luzūm,* although some are metaphoric to one degree or another.

Does my mount come to a stop or is she destined
a vale of lofty gardens with endless vegetation?
A word spoken about the sanctuary excites her.
But that is talk by one who hasn't any proof.

أَخبَّتْ ركابي أَم أُتيحَ لها خَبْتُ   عميمُ رياضٍ ما يَزالُ به نَبْتُ
وهيَّجها قولٌ يقالُ عن الحِمَى   وذاك حديثٌ ما محدِّثُهُ ثَبْتُ

(L I.157.2, 4)

At life's end we shall return to places for dwelling.
I've no knowledge of affairs after this return.

سَنَؤُوبُ في عقبي الحياة مساكنا   لا عِلم لي بالأمر بعد مآبِها

(L I.141.2)

Perhaps there are a people to whom their Lord gives reward
if they face Him with what they've shunned and what they've
obeyed.

لعلَّ قوماً يجازيهم مليكهم   إذا لقوهُ بما صاموا وما قنتوا

(L I.160.4)

It's said there's no hope for resurrection as recompense,
what you've heard about it is the claim of a stupid jester.
And how *can* the human body be summoned to bliss
after it rots in the earth or therein is imprisoned?

وقيل لا بعث يُرجَى للثوابِ وما   سمعْتَ في ذاكَ دعوى مبطل هَزَلا
وكيف للجسمِ أن يُدعى الى رَغدٍ   من بعدِ ما رُمَّ في الغبرآء او أُزِلا

(L II.195.2–3)

Seek out a good deed and do it because of its own goodness;
don't rule that God is to give a reward for doing this.
That's up to Him. If He wills as much, well, His domain is vast.
If He doesn't will as much, death will serve us in its stead.

تَوخّي جميلاً وٱفعليهِ لحسنِهِ   ولا تحكُمِي أن المليكَ بهِ يجزِي
فذاك إليهِ إن أراد فمُلكُهُ   عظيمٌ وإلّا فالحِمامُ لنا مُجْزِي

(L I.434.4–5)

Al-Maʿarrī in *Luzūm* fairly discredits the intellectual superstructure which sprang up around Islam. He vigorously dismisses the value of some of the major so-called Islamic sciences, which evolved subsequent to the revelation of God's word via the Qur'ān and which sought to interpret, define more clearly, and defend that word for the sake of the community of believers. The discipline of study and analysis of *aḥādīth,* for example, he accused of relying upon weak or totally falsified chains of transmission (L I.288.6–7; II.244.12; 346.9–10). It falsifies and deceives, he says (L II.201.13). Thus, he refused to believe in its findings (L II.199.9). "The *Ṣaḥīh*" (الصحيح) he adds in L I.209.1, in reference to one of the six great canonical *aḥādīth* compilations in Islam,[73] "falsifies, without doubt" (وقد كذب الصحيح بلا ٱرتياب).

Turning his attention to jurisprudence (*fiqh*/فقه), al-Maʿarrī accused this discipline of failing to produce any genuine knowledge of religion (L II. 419.1). The corpus of laws in Islam is denied any meaningful classification; the compilation is like a *rajaz* (رجز) poem (i.e., the short, occasional piece in premodern Arabic that allowed for enjambment) that has fallen apart; that is, there is no clear-cut indication of where various parts fit in relation to a comprehensible whole (L II.103.10). People when dealing with legal matters content themselves with referring to whichever one of the legal schools meets their fancy. Yet since one school permits something that another forbids, this approach cannot give genuine right guidance (L I.432.5–6). All religious laws are promulgated and arranged very subjectively, contends al-Maʿarrī (see, e.g., L II.404.2). They only produce hatred and animosity among people (L I.186.2). They enslave humankind; it is reasoned thinking (*al-qiyās*/القياس; more literally, "thinking by analogy") that liberates us (L I.326.12). Being "sick" (i.e., infirm) to begin with, religious laws can never be set right by way of rational processes (L II.349.14).[74] What good is "consensus" (إجماع)—one of the foundations of Islamic Law—if there is not even consensus with respect to God? (L II.422.7; although the lack of consensus here probably extends to all humankind and not merely Muslims).

Kalām/كلام or debate of theological dogma and positions is debunked in *Luzūm*. Al-Maʿarrī's critical remarks on this field of intellectual endeavor go fairly to the heart of the matter by including direct reference to some key technical concerns. The basic foundations or principles (*uṣūl*/أصول) of revealed religion al-Maʿarrī deemed as having no fixed moorings. Being themselves unfit or without integrity (*ghayr zākin*/غير زاكٍ), ipso facto so, too, are the *furū'*/فروع or derivative principles (L I.84.7). Hence, the disputations of *kalām* are meaningless verbal acrobatics: they are like the ripples on a pool of water that quickly become enmeshed and then disintegrate (L II.349.17).

In the final analysis, in all likelihood, the greatest cause for al-Maʿarrī's criticism of all religions (including the faith into which he was born and raised), and for his criticism of the major sciences or disciplines devoted to defending his inherited faith, was his inclination toward a pure skepticism (as opposed to mere incredulity) or what the present study would term a nearly nihilistic epistemology in many respects. However, the extent to which he was clearly more a rationalist (with even his skepticism being based on observation, on reflection, on weighing observable actualities over and against received and venerated teachings, on questioning the ultimate reality of things) than a revelationist (*if* a revelationist at all; and it would seem that he was not), also played a part in this process. It is when discussing what a person is enjoined to believe by his or her faith, and then commenting upon the individuals who dedicate their lives to expounding and defending faith, that al-Maʿarrī makes his greatest argument for the power of reason or intellect and the good that can result from it as opposed to the confusion, conflict, and unhappiness that typically ensue from formal institutionalized religion. Whatever its limitations, reason remains a more accurate source of information about the true nature of things than revelation. It is also a surer guide for humanity in its odyssey here on earth.

These ideas have in part already been expressed in some of *Luzūm*'s lines recently cited in this section of chapter 4, not to mention in those cited previously where al-Maʿarrī suggests that he resorts neither to imām nor to prophet for explanations of things, but only to his mind or intellect. Below are several from among the many verses in *Luzūm* to the same effect. They should leave little doubt as to which side of the divide al-Maʿarrī stands on in the great human debate over reason versus revelation.

Aḥādīth have appeared. If true they'd have import.
But their chain of transmission is weak.
So consult reason; leave all else for naught.
Reason is the best guide the seeker has embraced.

جاءَتْ أَحاديثُ إن صحّتْ فإنَّ لها   شأْناً ولكنَّ فيها ضعفُ إسنادِ
فشاوِر العقلَ واْتْرك غيرهُ هدَراً   فالعقلُ خيرُ مشيرٍ ضمَّهُ النادي

(L I.288.6–7)

Expose to your logic the *aḥādīth* a people bring
and you will swear that these people are liars.

واْعرِضْ أَحاديثَ مِن قومٍ أَتوْكَ بها   على قِياسِكَ تحلِفْ أَنَّهُمْ ولَعهْ

(L II.87.3)

When the sound-minded man resorts to reason
he berates religious schools of thought, reviles them.
Take from them that which reason has confirmed;
don't let ignorance plunge you in their stagnant pool.
Peoples' religions are weak in all aspects.
And are they firmed up by any intellect?

اذا رجع الحصيفُ إلى حجاهُ   تهاون بالمذاهب وازدراها
فخذْ منها بما أَدَّاهُ لبٌّ   ولا يغمِسنْكَ جهلٌ في لبٍّ
وهَتْ أَديانُهُم مِن كل وجْهٍ   فهل عقلٌ يُشَدُّ بها عُراها

(L II.416.2–4)

Let the intelligent be wary of the call to faith.
It ruins virtue, and is a calamity most grave.

وليَحْذَرِ الدعوى اللبيبُ فإنّها   للفضلِ مهلكةٌ وخطبٌ موبقُ

(L II.124.8)

You've rejected all but falsehood, breach of promise, and coarseness.
Thus, there's nothing to your promise to do that which is good.
Surely that which you tell us cannot be possible.
It's the exact opposite, logically, that is.

أَبيتُمْ سوى مَيْنٍ وخُلْفٍ وغلظةٍ   فليس لوعدٍ في الجميل نُجُوزُ
وإِنَّ الذي تحكونَ ليس بجائزٍ   ولكن سواهُ في القياسِ يجوزُ

(L I.430.14; 431.1)

The mind finds strange the religious laws,
be they Mazdean, Islamic, Judaic or Christian.
Thus, beware, and do not leave matters neglected;
examine with the heart of a clear-sighted thinker.

والعقلُ يعجبُ للشروعِ تمجُّسٍ   وتحنُّفٍ وتهوُّدٍ وتنصُّرِ
فاْحذرْ ولا تدع الأمور مُضاعةً   وٱنظرْ بقلبٍ مُفكرٍ متبصِّرِ

(L I.398.11–12)

I asked my mind, but it didn't inform; and I said to it "Ask the men."
But they didn't know, and they haven't rendered a decision.
They spoke and lied; when I urged them to be logical
they were incapable—and acknowledged as much.

سأَلتُ عَقِلي فلم يُخبِرْ وقلتُ لهُ   ســـــــل الرجالَ فما أَفتَوْا ولا عَرَفوا
قالُوا فَمانوا فلمّا أَن حَدَوْتُهُمُ   إلى القياس أبانوا العجز وٱعترفوا

(L II.100.1–2)

When humanity gives thought to the matter of its religion,
there emerges information that repels reason and is stifling.

إذا ٱفتكر الإنسان في أمر دينهِ   بدا نباءٌ يثنى الحجى وبه كبثُ

(L I.158.5)

I've questioned those differing with me in faith;
lacking was the informer who was not a liar.
They constantly propagate with no sound proof,
with everyone pulling for one's own side.

سأَلتُ من خالف عن دينهِ   فأَعوز المُخبرُ لا يكذبُ
وأكثروا الدعوى بلا حُجةٍ   كلٌّ إلى حيّزه يجذبُ

(L I.95.6–7)

Many a community's fools have dallied with it.
They have become skilled in meeting out punishment.
Fear compels their people into believing them.
But reason prompts them into disavowing them.

كم أُمةٍ لعِبتْ بها جُهّالُها   فتَنَطَّستْ مِن قبلُ في تعذيبها
الخوفُ يُلجئها إلى تصديقها   والعقلُ يحملها على تكذيبها

(L I.138.8–9)

What's with humankind? In their ignorance of religion
I've found them resembling grazing sheep or ostriches.
The disputant continues with his disputation,
yet he knows that the truth isn't as he claims it is.
The keen-eyed knows that our powers to discern have gone blind.
Thus, how often certainty is unknown; obscurely rendered.
Were a wolf in the woods to say "I am sent with a religion,
by way of my Lord!" Some would reply "Yes! Indeed you have!"

ما للأَنامِ وجدْتُهم من جهلهمْ   بالدين أَشباهَ النعامِ أَو النَّعمْ
فمجادلٌ وصلَ الجدالَ وقد درى   أَنَ الحقيقة فيهِ ليس كما زعمْ
علم الفتى النظَّارُ أَنَّ بصائراً   عميَتْ فكم يُخفَى اليقين وكم يُعَمّْ
لو قال سيِدُ غضاً بُعِثتُ بملَّةٍ   من عِندِ ربي قال بعضُهُمُ نعمْ

(L II.321.11–14)

Insofar as al-Maʿarrī's philosophy rejects (or is radically skeptical about) prophecy, divine revelation, scripture, and divine religious law, Ṭāhā Ḥusayn was one of the earliest modern biographer/commentators to have seen clear similarities between it and Indian as well as Greek philosophy in their general contours, speculating that the similarities, at least in part, were attributable to al-Maʿarrī's actually having studied Greek and Indian philosophy in their Arabic-language iterations and filters.[75] As a result of that study, in other words (according to Ḥusayn), there must have been a conscious direct borrowing from the teachings of these two traditions. This is especially the case with respect to Lucretian/Epicurean materialism, Ḥusayn quite compellingly underscored in *Ma'a Abī al-'Alā' fī Sijnih,* elaborating upon some specificities not taken up in his earlier book (i.e., his published dissertation) on al-Maʿarrī (although arguing—see, e.g., p. 36—that al-Maʿarrī did not take his materialism to the extreme that the Epicureans did, which would be to proffer that there are neither gods nor God). Von Kremer and Nicholson saw both Greek and Indian overtones in aspects of al-Maʿarrī's philosophy (with respect to the Indian, beyond merely the obvious veganism and disapproval of killing of animals), but without arguing that there must have been direct borrowing. Among post-Ḥusayn Arabic language commentators/biographers, Zakī al-Maḥāsinī[76] briefly notes some of the same affinities, mentioning for the Greek—among others—the Stoic. Al-Maḥāsinī fairly assumes conscious borrowing either indirectly or directly.

ʿAbd al-Qādir Zaydān[77] gives a broader, more detailed picture of very plausible Greco-Arabic and Indian borrowings, particularly in his discussion of the Epicurean parallels.

That said, if one is to engage in speculation in this regard, one could just as plausibly—if not more so—suggest that al-Maʿarrī may have gotten his nonconformist views on prophecy, revelation, and religious law (not to mention a few other aspects of his religious philosophy) by way of study of (1) the original teachings of the philosopher-physician Abū Bakr al-Rāzī (d. 925 or 932 CE) (as Nicholson, for example, has suggested) or (2) the original teachings of the iconoclastic Ibn al-Rāwandī (d. ca. 910 CE). Both men in premodern as well as modern commentaries/studies on their thought (for the latter, see, e.g., Stroumsa)[78] are typically regarded as boldly contra-prophecy, contra-revealed religion. As well, al-Maʿarrī may have appropriated some of these two men's ideas as filtered through the writings of others (e.g., commentators or biobibliographical chroniclers). Both men flourished just a few decades before al-Maʿarrī's birth. Certainly, the affinities are there:

> If we are to trust the undoubtedly hostile sources through which a very scant amount of information about Ibn al-Rāwandī's heterodox teaching has filtered down to us, this free thinker appears to have repudiated the grand supernatural themes of revelation and miracle, as well as the very possibility, according to one authority, of a satisfactory rational answer to the question of God's existence and the rationality of his ways. . . . According to a less hostile source, Ibn al-Rāwandī denounced the whole fabric of revelation as superfluous. He is reported to have argued that human reason was sufficient to determine the knowledge of God and the distinction between good and evil, a view in keeping with the Muʿtazilah to whom he was originally affiliated; revelation therefore was altogether unnecessary, and miracles, upon which the claims of prophecy are alleged to rest, were altogether absurd.[79]

> Al-Rāzī . . . rejected outright the concept of revelation and the role of prophets as mediators between God and man. He reasoned that prophecy was either superfluous, since the God-given light of Reason was sufficient for the knowledge of the truth; or obnoxious, since it has been the cause of so much bloodshed and warfare between the one people (presumably, the Arabs) who believed itself to be favored with divine revelation and the other less fortunate peoples.[80]

There is no clear-cut reference in *Luzūm* either to al-Rāzī or to Ibn al-Rāwandī (although the latter *is* mentioned—not surprisingly, usually in terms of revulsion and disapproval—in al-Maʿarrī's *Risālat al-Ghufrān*).[81] But it is almost inconceivable that the ideas of both men were not still very much "in the air" during the years when the *Luzūm* was being composed. It cannot be proven conclusively that they were a source of influence for al-Maʿarrī's thinking, but neither can this connection be ruled out.

The Islam that al-Maʿarrī is critical of in *Luzūm* was in his day, no less that today, hardly a uniform, monolithic faith. Aside from its basic Sunnī-Shīʿite split, already by the eleventh century CE it had experienced a number of additional (though historically less consequential) schisms. Al-Maʿarrī makes it clear that his harsh criticism toward Islam, especially as he observed it practiced, is meant to be all-inclusive, without exception to Sunnism or Shīʿism and the additional but smaller offshoots of the faith. With respect to Shīʿism, in another context the present study has already called attention to a verse in *Luzūm* obviously meant to be extremely critical—to say the least. It is foundationally critical. Whatever else the line might represent, "There is no imām other than reason" is first and foremost an unflinching dismissal of the Shīʿite belief in the centrality of the imāmate to Shīʿism. In the very same poem from which this line comes, al-Maʿarrī states outright that the theory of the imāmate is a lie (L I.65.6). The stick of a blind person is a better guide than an imām, he adds later (L II.193.13). *Luzūm* I.408.8 proclaims the Shīʿites to be in opposition to "the truth." In *Luzūm* II.297.14, al-Maʿarrī says that he remained indifferent whenever others in his community opted to glorify either Shīʿism or Sunnism.[82] ʿAlī, the Imām *par excellence* for the Shīʿites although also revered by Sunnīs, seems to be rather uncharitably denied his special religio-political status in *Luzūm* I.421.10, where al-Maʿarrī remarked that he is no better than his client-slave (Qanbar). L II.92.14 suggests that the prime *kāfir* (disbeliever; infidel) is whosoever harbors allegiance to ʿAlī.

As revealing as all of this is with respect to ʿAlī, arguably more telling still, notwithstanding the relatively circumspect or even enigmatic language (especially L II.92.14; the Zand edition of *Luzūm* offers no commentary; the Beirut edition only acknowledges that "*al-Imām al-Rābiʿ*" is ʿAlī ibn Abī Ṭālib), and given al-Maʿarrī's broaching the topic of Shīʿism in *Luzūm* in the first place, is his reticence to take ʿAlī personally into serious consideration, that is, in more extended discourse within the framework of the *Luzūm*'s musings on religious beliefs. While hardly being greatly and extensively criticized personally, neither is ʿAlī effusively defended or celebrated. In any event, the reticence should hardly be taken as dissimulation in order to conceal crypto-Shīʿī sentiments. Al-Maʿarrī's irreverence for and distrust of all organized religious movements is as broad as it is deep.

Touching specifically upon some additional schismatics of mainstream Sunnī Islam, al-Maʿarrī labels the Khārijites[83] extremists who are opposed to "right guidance" (L I.408.8). The Ḥashwiyyah[84] he regards as deceitful and heedless (L I.176.5–6), and the Carmathian Ismāʿīlīs,[85] licentious sinners who are no better than the crude and unenlightened during the pre-civilized (i.e., Jāhilī/جاهلي) era in Arabia (L I.182.3–9; 183.1–8; 384.3–7). In what seems to be a reference to the الباطنية (Bāṭinites or esotericists) in general as well as the Carmathians more specifically,[86] he submits while projecting the image of a true مؤمن that those who alter the simple, literal meaning of Islam (*ẓāhir al-islām*/ظاهر الإسلام) want to "prune and prick it" (i.e., damage it). What they teach, that is, their esotericism, is equated with the amorous rhapsodizing of poets (L II.404.5–6).

Although not properly speaking forming a quasi-autonomous, heterodox sect of Islam as opposed to a tendency or orientation (depending in some instances upon the particular "order" and its master), the *mutaṣawwifūn*/متصوفون or Sufis, too, should here be mentioned as meeting with al-Maʿarrī's broadsides. Playing on the etymology of the Arabic word by which the mystical religious outlook is designated, *al-ṣūfiyyah*/الصوفية; and, at the same time, employing a *double entendre,* al-Maʿarrī declares that although mystics claim that they have been sincere to God (*ṣafaw*/صَفَوْا), they lie. They have not been sincere but instead have deviated from their alleged goal (*ṣāfū* /صافُوا) (L II.103.6).[87] Al-Maʿarrī accuses the Islamic mystics of wandering from country to country out of greed and the desire to sate their appetite for sex and rather sumptuous sustenance (L I.104.10; II.384.11). He derides their rapturous displays of love for God (i.e., the ذكر/*dhikr* ceremony) for which they became especially recognizable. They dance in adulation, he says, as though they are drunk on wine rather than on the thought or recollection of God, Whom in actuality they do not have in mind at all (L I.195.4–5). What they really desire is the forbidden (L I.195.5). They may claim piety but God knows in what ways they are actually deficient (L II.54.5).[88]

Rounding out what amounts to a sweeping assault on specific revealed religions, al-Maʿarrī in *Luzūm* belittles Christianity and Judaism.[89] As was the case with his denunciation of Muslim mystics and the various schismatics of mainstream Sunnī Islam that he reflects upon, his critical remarks in this domain rarely if ever touch upon subtle, more rarified, or esoteric matters of dogma. Nor do they go into great detail. The point al-Maʿarrī seems content to make is that, taken on the whole, Christianity and Judaism are no more credible than any other religion in terms of teachings, and their practitioners and clerical representatives are unprincipled, hypocritical, misled. Thus, with respect to Christianity, he says simply and bluntly that what it professes are lies; their teachings cannot be proven (L I.174.11–12; II.409.9). Events that Christianity speaks of are hardly to be taken as certain (L I.158.11). Christian priests have recorded things for which ink and paper have been wasted (L I.313.5). Monks are seditious hypocrites (L II.382.3). They amass great wealth—whether in gold tender or other material goods—in secret (L II.130.6), and they turn their backs on normal social intercourse not for the sake of devotion to God but because their world has betrayed them (L II.408.9–11). Though churches might be established in the name of the Christian faith, could they speak they would have good cause to be reproachful of those who frequent them (L I.141.9). What really holds them together as houses of worship, al-Maʿarrī quite cynically suggests, is the opportunity they offer for the men and women to have close physical contact with one another (L II.381.12). Al-Maʿarrī alleges sexual misconduct on the part of priests and monks with their female devotees, although he does not neglect to reproach the Christian women themselves for this misdeed, as well as the Christian community as a whole inasmuch as Christianity condones women visiting their clergy in the first place (L II.381.12–14; 382.1–3).

While nowhere denying that Jesus Christ in actuality lived and thus is a historically verifiable figure, al-Maʿarrī in *Luzūm* does reject both Jesus's immaculate conception and his divinity (L II.406.1–3; 409.2–9).[90] In two instances, it would seem that *Luzūm* is prepared to allow for Christ's prophetic nature:

> Praise is God's. I've come to some watery depths
> and suffered an oceanful of time's adversities.
> Communities have said your God didn't send

either Jesus *or* Moses to humankind.
They made the Merciful One a thing to be gained from;
made their faith a divine law with which to dominate.
Were I capable, I would punish those who've transgressed
until the erring person becomes a buried person!

الحمدُ للهِ قد أَصبحتُ في لججٍ مُكابداً مِن هُمومِ الدهر قاموسا
قالتْ معاشرُ لم يَبعَثْ إلهكُمُ إلى البريةِ عيساها ولا موسَى
وإنما جَعلوا الرحمان[91] مأْكلةً وصيَّرُوا دينَهم للملك[92] ناموسا
ولو قدرَتُ لعاقبتُ الذينَ طغَوْا حتى يَعودَ حليفُ الغيِّ مَرموسا

(L II.22.12–13; 23.1–2)

Do not begin on *me* with your enmity;
to me your Messiah is Muḥammad's equal.
Will morning light aid a night traveler's eye,
or are we all in an eternal darkness?

لا تبدؤُني بالعداوةِ منكُمُ فمسيحكمْ عندي نظيرُ محمَّدِ
أَيُغيثُ ضوءُ الصبحِ ناظِرَ مدلجٍ أم نحن أَجمعُ في ظلامٍ سَرْمَدِ

(L I.295.1–2)

But Nicholson plausibly notes[93] that these two passages can be interpreted in quite a contrary manner. In the second, al-Maʿarrī could be suggesting that *all* humans, prophets included, are "in eternal darkness," so that if Christ in al-Maʿarrī's mind can be equated with the Prophet Muḥammad, it is in terms of his being no less unconvincing than Muḥammad with respect to claims of being supernaturally rightly guided by prophetic inspiration.

To turn back to the first passage:

> [R]eaders familiar with [al-Maʿarrī's] style will remark that the tag "some people say" is often used by him to introduce rationalistic judgments for which he declines to be held accountable. Further, "they" in the second verse is equivocal: we can refer it, as we please, either to the disbelievers in prophecy or to the prophets themselves; and the latter reference is suggested by the rhyme-word

> *nāmūs,* which in this context would naturally be taken as the Arabicised form of *nomos*.[94]

Thus, according to the thrust of Nicholson's argument, one can understand al-Maʿarrī as meaning in the lines of the second passage just quoted above either (1): he would have put to death, had he been capable, people who say that God did not send Jesus and Moses as prophets, because these people say what they say only to profit from their God and to use their religion to gain power; or (2) he would have worked to see the demise, had he been capable, of Jesus and Moses (and by extension, all prophets) because they were not in reality messengers of God sent by God to humankind, but only claimants of such for the sake of self-aggrandizement; that is, it is *they* who seek to profit from their God and religion.

The second option admittedly sounds scandalously extreme, even with respect to someone like al-Maʿarrī. But Nicholson's only point is alerting one to the type of Maʿarrian ambiguity that opens the door to scandalous inferences.[95] Having ample examples elsewhere of al-Maʿarrī's criticism of prophets, prophecy, and revelation, and knowing in general what to make of his seemingly unorthodox or blasphemous remarks, especially when expressed through innuendo-laden metaphor or enigmatic allusions, discreet readers of *Luzūm* other than Nicholson may feel that they can't totally dismiss his interpretation as the real meaning intended by al-Maʿarrī in L II.22.12–13; 23.1–2 (accepting, that is, the Leyden manuscript wording of these lines as opposed to the Zand's redaction).

As for Judaism as viewed by al-Maʿarrī, briefly, it, too, is accused of relating historical events that are highly improbable (L I.158.11). Its adherents are accused of being incapable of arguing convincingly for their articles of faith (L I.174.11–12). More bluntly put, the Jews are said to be confused falsifiers who are just as much in error as the adherents of other religions (e.g., Christians, Mazdeans, and Muslims [in this instance Muslims are designated by "*al-ḥanīfah*"/الحنيفة]) (L I.260.14–15; II.201.5; the latter line is followed by that more commonly cited instance of al-Maʿarrī's verdict on the reason vs. revelation debate: اثنان أهلُ الأرضِ ذو عقلٍ / بلا دين وآخر دَيّنٌ لا عقل له: "There are two types of people in the world: the rational without religion and the religious who are not rational"). Jewish religious scholars (*aḥbār*/أحبار) are said to make a science out of studying the Torah (denominated by al-Maʿarrī as a complete fabrication, and—rather infelicitously, perhaps dictated more by required sound than sense—a "disease of the liver"; L I.288.12) only for the sake of making a handsome living (L II.241.6–9). The hoped-for Jewish Messiah is a preposterous idea promulgated by people who have been "beguiled" (L I.105.3–5). Al-Maʿarrī declares in L I.108.7 that in fact the Messiah will never come; this is a false promise.

To what has been cited above in the way of al-Maʿarrī's hostile and critical attitude toward Islam, Christianity, Judaism, and religion in general, obviously there are exceptions. Otherwise, centuries ago it would have been a foregone conclusion among most commentators that the poet was manifestly, unquestionably, heretical, absolutely without belief in or respect for revelation, prophecy, and revealed religion, and possibly a genuine atheist (the notion of which, as indicated earlier, did not escape the minds of some of the premodern Arab biographers/chroniclers). And he probably would not have been so successful at avoiding a flogger's lashes (not to mention executioner's sword). Here and there, he certainly tempers his criticism of Christianity and Judaism. He says in *Luzūm* I.304.3–5 that it is God's wish that they as well as the other revealed religions (i.e., Islam and Mazdeanism [i.e., Zoroastrianism]) be accepted and obeyed by their adherents. In L I.324.10–11, he intimates that divine scripture would be fine if only obeyed. In L I.141.11, he affirms that Islam is in fact a "divinely" revealed religion and later (L I.279.10) adds that it is superior to all others. He speaks most approvingly, even reverentially, of the Prophet Muḥammad in II.214.3–9 (although there is scarcely anything else like this in *Luzūm*, and this is the praise that Bakrī regards as solely with respect to Muḥammad as a social reformer):

> Muḥammad summoned you to the best of matters,
> and the tip of a lance is hardly like the shaft.
> He guided you to glorify the Creator of dawn
> and the meteors of night in their rising and falling.
> He imposed on the weak as obligatory or beyond
> only that which is capable of being assumed.
> He urged cleanliness in both body and clothing,
> and he chastised the slandering of wayward women.

He forbad wine, whose drinkers' minds I imagine to be,
in light-headedness, like the minds of alarmed ostriches;
they drag their royal robes as women of the Bedouin do
when they are songstresses dressed in long and trailing skirts.
God pray for Muḥammad for as long as there's a rising star,
for as long as his name diffuses musk in gatherings.

دعاكم إلى خيرِ الأمور مُحمَّدٌ   وليس العوالي في القنا كالسوافلِ
حداكُمْ على تعظيمِ مَن خلَقَ الضُّحى   وشهبَ الدُّجَى مِن طالعاتٍ وآفلِ
وألزَمَكُمْ ما ليسَ يُعْجزُ حملُهُ   أخا الضَّعْفِ مِن فرضٍ له ونوافلِ
وحثَّ على تطهير جسمٍ وملبسٍ   وعاقَبَ في قَذْفِ النساء الغوافلِ
وحرَّم خمراً خِلْتُ ألبابَ شَرْبَها   من الطَّيش ألبابَ النعام الجوافلِ
يجرُّون ثوب المُلكِ جرَّ أوانسٍ   لدَى البَدْوِ أذيالَ الغواني الروافلِ
فصَلّى عليهِ اللهُ ما ذرَّ شارقٌ   وما فتَّ مسكاً ذكرُهُ في المحافلِ

One *can* find in *Luzūm* occasional solemn praise for the Qur'ān (e.g., L I.324.10–11; II. 152.12–13), for prayer (e.g., I.184.4), and for the *Sharī'ah* (e.g., L I.240.9). Al-Maʿarrī speaks frequently of the Creator God who is capable of reward as well as punishment on Judgment Day (e.g., in I.102.2; I.422.9–10; 434.4–5; II.74.9; 76.6–9; 307.3, 8, 11–12; although in L I.434.4–5, he exhorts one to do good for its own sake and not because of God's final reward or punishment: توخّي جميلا وأفعليه لحسنه / ولا تحكُمي أن المليكَ بهِ يجزي / فذاك إليهِ إن أرادَ فَمُلكُهُ / عظيمٌ وإلا فالحمام لنا مُجْزي). He also occasionally speaks matter-of-factly about the horrors of a fiery hell and the bliss of a heavenly, paradisal hereafter (e.g., in L I.79.1–2; 153.9; 154.1–7; 388.2; II.28.6). As we had cause to emphasize previously, *Luzūm* seems to allow (if only by not closing the door on it, or as hedging one's bet in a Pascalian manner) for a spiritual resurrection of man; and the possibility of a bodily one is never *categorically* ruled out. Finally, and most significantly, on top of all this, al-Maʿarrī constantly urges man to be righteous and God-fearing, and he was renowned for his own morally upright life, notwithstanding the doubts and recriminations in some of the Arabic chronicles regarding his 'orthodoxy' as a Muslim and the less commonly encountered or countenanced dimensions to his moral code.

However, with the exception perhaps of the instances where al-Maʿarrī professes a belief in the existence of God, it would be quite naive to take seriously these unassailably conformist, normative, and even assertively Islamic moments in *Luzūm.* What appears as the decidedly skeptical, and often angry, bitter, and dismissive trajectory to al-Maʿarrī's religious thinking sketched in this section of chapter 4 is essentially the one that should be associated with the poet's name. Nicholson was on quite solid ground to suggest close to one hundred years ago that although one *might* take al-Maʿarrī to be a deist, beyond that, "he would not be described accurately by any designation which connotes belief in a divine Word revealed through prophecy or in a religious code deriving its authority from tradition."[96] To be included among these designations, of course, is "Islamic," even though the influence of Islam and Islamicate civilization determined much if not most of the framework and contours (or, if you will, points of departure) for al-Maʿarrī's religio-philosophical speculations.[97]

At this juncture in the present study, the basic reason for emphatically affirming this conclusion, despite what on the surface seem to be some palpable examples of evidence to the contrary, should be quite clear. Al-Maʿarrī's verses in *Luzūm* that support a belief in the doctrines and rituals of Islam are comparatively infrequent, and, when such verses do occur, they are often expressed in a compromising manner; irony and even sarcasm are often intended. *Luzūm*'s arguably conformist or orthodox verses on rituals and dogma are hardly more numerous than what has just been indicated (again save for the matter-of-fact references to God and the perfunctory exhortations to his readers to be God-fearing and pious). The verses to the contrary are conspicuously more abundant. The arguably conformist verses are hardly unqualified, ringing endorsements even if one ignores the fact that they are sometimes flatly contradicted elsewhere. When al-Maʿarrī proclaims the superiority of Islam in L I.297.10, for example, in the very same line, he conceives a day when Islam will be superseded by another religion and lose its prestige, as though this is a natural progression in the history of *every* religion (i.e., rise, decline, fall, and supersession by another).[98] Where he affirms Islam's divinely revealed nature and infallibility (done so only rhetorically in the first place), the sequel to this line begins with the words أين الهدى, which in this context should be understood as "But where is the *real* right guidance to be found?" (L I.141.12). In one of the two places cited above as indications of al-Maʿarrī's embrace of the Prophet Muḥammad (i.e., L I.148.8), what al-Maʿarrī says precisely is جاء النبي بحق; ("the Prophet came with a truth"), which is considerably different from "the Prophet came with *the* truth". In the other verses of *Luzūm* that speak most approvingly of Muḥammad, specifically L II.214.3–9, al-Maʿarrī is irreproachably reverential and respectful of both him and his message to humankind. There is little if any doubt about that. But there is scarcely any other passage like this, not even remotely, in the entire approximately 900 pages that comprise the Zand edition of *Luzūm*. God's ways were subjected to rigorous questioning and speculation in *Luzūm*; arguably, His existence too. But He was scarcely ever out of sight, out of mind. Precisely the opposite is the case for the Prophet Muḥammad.

When al-Maʿarrī stresses the importance of prayers in L I.184.4, he does so only in relative terms; he says that *for him* they are more important than amassing great personal wealth. Where there are praises for the Divine Law in *Luzūm* I.240.9, the context allows, and indeed suggests, that al-Maʿarrī is being ironic. Where al-Maʿarrī speaks approvingly of the Qur'ān in *Luzūm* II.152.12–13, this is limited to أم الكتاب, which designates the first chapter. The chapter consists of only several short verses, and is perhaps the most ecumenical passage of the Qur'ān. Its main message is the affirmation of belief in a merciful Creator God. Further, reciting or upholding simply this chapter (as opposed to the whole Qur'ān), provided its soundness is appreciated (al-Maʿarrī goes on to say), is all that a Muslim needs to do in the way of fulfilling his or her religious obligations (أم الكتاب إذا قَوّمْتَ مُحكَمَها / وجدْتَها لأداء الفَرْضِ تَكْفيكا). And no sooner does he say this than he adds لم يَشْفِ قلبَكَ فرقانٌ ولا عِظَةٌ / وآيةٌ لو أطعتَ الله تشفيكا ("An entire Qur'ān cannot cure your heart, nor moral sermonizing; but just one verse can—*if* you obey God").

Because al-Maʿarrī repeatedly enjoins reverence for and devotion to God, denounces hypocrisy, bemoans the dereliction of religious duty (regardless of the denomination), and occasionally raises his voice in favor of Islam—in one respect or another, and to one degree or another—one might care to argue that perhaps the un- or anti-Islamic dimension to *Luzūm* is directed not so much at Islam *per se* as at what al-Maʿarrī perceived in his lifetime as a corrupt and degenerate form thereof; an

Islam no longer properly practiced and interpreted an Islam corrupted or debased by misguided latter-day practitioners and clerics.

To a certain extent, this can't be denied. Both Ṭāhā Ḥusayn and Alfred von Kremer (not to mention several of the more modern Arabic language sources consulted for this study) have capably shown in their writings on al-Maʿarrī how the tumultuous socioeconomic and religio-political developments in the Near East prior to and during his lifetime—developments that he regarded as deplorable because corrosive and destructive—must have prompted such a critique of Islam within the framework of his cynicism and pessimism in general.

Still, it must not be forgotten that al-Maʿarrī's fundamental point of departure in his criticism of all revealed religions is that in and of themselves, regardless of how practiced and interpreted by their adherents (which in itself is troubling), they are misleading, inadequate as the building blocks or organizing principles for society; inasmuch as they are based on divine scripture the authority of which is unverifiable (i.e., it is a matter of faith as opposed to certain knowledge) and the interpretation and application of which, the human record shows, has led to hatred and enmity among peoples.

Although paradoxically al-Maʿarrī at times seems to bemoan humanity's loss of religion, the only religion he might thereby be considered as seriously, sincerely defending is the one he defines and configures in his own terms: one based on sincerity, chasteness, and treating all humans justly (L I.103.9; 361.14; 438.6)—for example; and *perhaps*, too, one based on a belief in, if not certain knowledge of, a First Cause Creator God, or a God as Prime Mover or a God of deism or theism; but no more, and certainly not elaborate rituals and doctrines extrapolated from the authority of divine revelation by (mostly) men of religion claiming special interpretative and governing privileges.

In L II.242.11, al-Maʿarrī says in lean, clear Arabic, "God the Lord of perfection is aware of my paucity of religion as well as my paucity of knowledge and wealth" (لقد عَلِمَ الله ربُّ الكمالِ/ بِقلّة علْمي وديني ومالي). Sarah Stroumsa has noted, "In [medieval heresiographer] Shahrastānī's view the freethinkers par excellence, in whose case this title requires no further qualification, were those who rejected all revealed religions (*al-mustabiddūna bi'l-ra'y hum al-munkirūna li'l-nubuwwāt*." [99]

Al-Maʿarrī's self-confessed "paucity of religion" (L II.242.11) was at its core freethinking as defined by Shahrastānī. It was no doubt what Ḥusayn had in mind when invoking the attribute "revolutionary" in his discussion of al-Maʿarrī in *Ma'a Abī al-'Alā' fī Sijnih*; because as Stroumsa has pointed out (and Ḥusayn unquestionably knew) "the danger presented by freethinkers was felt by Muslims as profound and pressing. . . . The few people who really deserved to be called freethinkers remained individualists and did not establish any sect. But they embodied the idea that one can wish to establish a personal ethical system, organize a human society, or even worship God without relying on the authority of revealed scriptures. This very idea was perceived by Muslims as an abomination, a radical revolt against Islam." [100]

Part III. Humankind Interacting with Humankind: Al-Maʿarrī's Social and Political Views in *Luzūm*

In addition to his views on the physio-psychological nature of the individuated human being, and on human beings as they bind themselves to God in worship, al-Maʿarrī in *Luzūm* reveals his thinking on human beings as they live with their fellow human beings. His own immediate society and predominant culture—the Arab-Islamic as of the late tenth century and first half of the eleventh (CE)—serve as the basic frame of reference; although to a lesser extent he also reveals an interest in the more influential societal subcultures (e.g., Jewish and Christian), as well as society in general. The *Luzūm* was intended as a statement of universal validity transcending particular time and place.

Nearly all the verses of dealing with society at large are scathingly critical and condemnatory. The Arab Islamicate polis, and the typical Arab Islamic social patterns or institutional configurations, offer neither rescue nor relief for humankind's wọes, according to al-Maʿarrī. Christian and Jewish counterparts are no less inadequate or unsatisfactory. All human beings in and of themselves are basically evil and ignorant, runs al-Maʿarrī's argument in *Luzūm*; ignorance and evil are thus only compounded when men and women attempt to live, work, worship, and govern themselves collectively as societies, states, and, last but hardly least, confessional (faith-based) communities. This state of affairs results irrespective of confessional orientation and affiliation.

All of this has been foreshadowed in the preceding two sections of the present study. Al-Maʿarrī's low estimation of humanity at the level of the character of individuated men and women can hardly be expected not to apply to the character of men and women when living together in groups, whether with regard to immediate families, extended families, and societies and states wherein a certain rigid hierarchy of governing/governed is in force. The *Luzūm*'s especially severe critique of religion speaks ill of a very fundamental institutional as well as intellectual and emotional phenomenon in nearly all human societies, not merely al-Maʿarrī's own.

What follows beneath is a fuller and sharper picture of al-Maʿarrī as a critic of society at large: what he thinks about the family, the basic building block of his and all societies, will be reviewed first; then some additional remarks of his on men and women in general as he sees them characteristically interacting with one another; and, finally, his comments about a number of typically influential or powerful members of the society of his time and place whom he occasionally singles out for special observation.

The Family

As the ultimate solution to all humanity's afflictions and miseries, al-Maʿarrī in *Luzūm* advocates a cessation of life through celibacy and a halt in procreation. Arguably the most infamous and astonishing aspect of the poet's thought, it is urged time and again with little attempt to conceal the severity of the proposal (e.g., L I.366.13; 373.9; II.120.16; 187.9; 236.3), and with no expressed concern over the religious or theological implications for Muslim believers (not to mention other believing monotheists) to be told that the life that God gives is not worth preserving. In reference to his own historically verifiable bachelorhood and childlessness, al-Maʿarrī proudly proclaims in *Luzūm* (I.44.6):

> The chain of procreation is linked from Adam
> until me, but for me there's been no wedlock.

تواصل حبلُ ما بين آدمٍ   وبيني ولم يوصَلْ بلاميَ باءُ

In L II.236.4–5 is to be found the most compelling rationale for the celibacy and sexual abstinence. In denying life to children, al-Maʿarrī argues, one prevents perpetuation of suffering. Nonexistence (*al-'adam*/العدم) is a bliss (*ni'mah*/نعمة) that transcends any that one might experience in life here on earth. In nonexistence lies comfort.

> I've given *my* children comfort, for they're in the bliss
> of nonexistence which is better than this world's blessings.
> Had they come to be, they would have suffered a misfortune
> casting them into the destructive tracts of barren deserts.

وأرحْتُ أولادي فهمْ في نعمةِ الـ   عدَمِ التي فضلَتْ نَعيمَ العاجلِ
ولو أنهُمْ ظهروا لعانوا شدّةً   ترميهُم في مُتلفات هواجلِ

Because he is opposed to the very idea of the family, al-Maʿarrī in *Luzūm* considers marriage coupled with procreation madness (L II.51.8). It is evil, sinful, even criminal (L I.45.3–5; II.299.3; 211.7; 421.7).

In addition to the fact that marriage and procreation allow for the continuation of human life, there are three other major reasons for al-Maʿarrī's taking a dim view of the human family and arguing against the formation of such. In the first place, he holds in low esteem all would-be wives and mothers, which is to say women in general. Second, he has an equally mordant view of the intrinsic nature and behavior of children. Third, as a logical consequence of his views on women and children, he views the typical family life as one that engenders needless pain, hardship, and discord.

Al-Maʿarrī's remarks on women are so condemnatory and spiteful that, in the eyes of at least one modern Arabic language study of his thought, they make him the harshest critic of the female sex in the entire history of Arabic literature.[101] This is one dimension to his thought that would hardly allow him to be heralded as being uncommonly enlightened, humane, "modern." The misogyny can be found throughout the *Luzūm*. It is especially concentrated, however, in two long poems rhyming (interestingly enough) in the sound feminine plural. The first begins on page 163, vol. I of the Zand edition of *Luzūm*. It consists of 54 lines. The second begins 25 pages later. It has 94 lines, making it one of the longest poems in *Luzūm*. Both of these poems occasionally touch upon subjects other than women, but for all intents and purposes, they are rather straightforward, matter-of-fact listings of what al-Maʿarrī sees as damnable female traits.

In the first, to follow more or less al-Maʿarrī's own train of thought, women are said to ridicule the man of true understanding and reason (*al-ḥalīm*/الحليم), although they themselves are totally devoid of intellect (163.5). They might adorn themselves with jewelry, but behind this facade of beauty is the urge to sin (163.7). Women are weak and irresolute to the point that they cannot heed the censorship of their wrong-doing; although paradoxically they have enough resolve to talk incessantly, to render the steadfast man weak, and never to shun the type of sins that the God-fearing man guards against (163.8–10). Although with all of their gaudy clothes and jewelry they flit about like so many birds, they are less pure than the ostriches that scrounge for their sustenance among colocynth seeds fallen in the desert (164.3). They speak unfavorably of men who are pious (164.4). They hasten to do vile acts with those who would seek them out as a source of refuge or protection (164.5). They are absolutely shameless; it is with joy that they fall short of all that is morally proper for them (164.5). Their flamboyant, swinging gait diverts men from a tranquil and composed frame of mind (165.1), and even when they are veiled, they direct furtive side glances, destructive as drawn swords, toward men (165.6). As mates of men who are past the prime of their lives, they "give little water at the time of drinking" (165.8); that is, they don't provide for their older husbands' well-being and conjugal satisfaction. They may be attentive and obedient at bedtime but while awake they are refractory and aloof (165.9; which is to say, they may be valued only when and if fulfilling the sexual needs of husbands; in a further caustic reference to their being inadequate and ungrateful as conjugal partners, al-Maʿarrī says that they never lose sleep over being separated from their husbands, whereas husbands do lose sleep when separation occurs [165.10]).

In the *Luzūm*'s second long poem rhyming in the sound feminine plural that deals primarily with women, al-Maʿarrī continues to blame women for virtually every vice imaginable. Working from the general assertion that they bring about whatever is worst in life (L I.188.5), he proceeds to enumerate the particulars. Women are masters of temptation and authorities on seduction, who, not content with natural beauty, approach you with brightly colored makeup (188.7–8). They speak so as to flatter ears and wound hearts (188.9), and even before the pious, they are apt to step forward in the most tempting manner possible: so powerfully perfumed with ambergris around their mouths that their lips, even as they are closed, are like wine seals that break to reveal sweet, splendid cups of wine (188.13; 189.1–2). They desire husbands and finery but they curse when they must face life's misfortunes, and they are helpless in times of war (189.12). When shown love, they only chastise (191.5). When lived with intimately, they are refractory (191.10). Prideful and profligate, they disdain the best food they might be given, and they will exhaust with passion a man's wealth (191.11, 13).

There is no hope that women might be reformed by education or religion. Those secluded in prayer are still given to sin and seduction (192.1). Those made literate do evil in spite of—indeed because of—their learning (192.4). They benefit little from those who would give them right guidance if and when they go to seek such (192.5).

Remarks on women elsewhere in *Luzūm* largely merely reinforce, indeed in some cases fairly duplicate, the sum and substance of those just summarized. This is especially the case whenever the intent is to underscore the notion that women are above all else temptresses and seductresses and the prime suspects in sexual indiscretions. A few references might be enumerated for the sake of completeness. In L II.83.12, al-Maʿarrī says that women are like hyenas that are excited by lust. When they go forth intending to pray at the mosques, he declares in L II.315.7–9, in fact they fail to keep this intent. On pilgrimage to Mecca, they "throw burning coals" (i.e., make amorous, beckoning glances) whenever the eyes of would-be seducers are fixed upon them (II 418.8–9). When they go to a public bath to bathe, their real interests are in matters so shameful that, had Chosroes himself followed them, his crown and entire realm would have been dishonored (L I.208.2–3; i.e., in going to the public baths, women's real interests are in sexual indiscretions). Their special physical charms ("thin waists and well-rounded posteriors") make men oblivious to all that is virtuous (L I.153.3). In love, they are manifestly unfaithful (L I.186.13). As one specific example of the latter, al-Maʿarrī speaks of married Muslim women who go on the pilgrimage to Mecca without their husbands and in so doing leave the latters' "needs" unfulfilled (a sexual connotation is no doubt intended here; L I.356.14).

Neither the Prophet Muḥammad nor the Qur'ān has praised them for going on pilgrimage to Mecca, where they arrive with beckoning glances even before the gaze of seducers fall upon them. The home is the best place for young women to pray, should they desire as much, "so that their place of prayer always be concealed, and wherein, opinion has it, lies their best grave" (L 418.8–11; cf. L I.356, lines 13–15; the entire poem in which these lines are embedded is largely another diatribe against women, especially with regard to infidelity and sexual indiscretions). True, among free women there are those who as wives benefit their husbands (L I.357.13); and there are women who are estimable because they keep their charms under wrap and guard themselves against shame (L I.357.3). A man's first heaven *may* be his bride, but she must be the bride who is submissive, who agrees to please her husband (in which case, "if she offers up her ripe fruit, by all means it should be harvested"; L I.356.11).

In attempting to find an explanation for al-Maʿarrī's pronounced anti-feminist verses, undeniably extreme and bitter even for the time notwithstanding the deeply ingrained patriarchy, Zakī al-Maḥāsinī offered three suggestions. First, noting that during al-Maʿarrī's lifetime urban life under ʿAbbāsid rule was especially dissolute and debauched, and above all in Baghdad where al-Maʿarrī lived for two years, al-Maḥāsinī concluded that some women in fact made themselves open to the criticisms leveled against them by al-Maʿarrī. Second (and more obvious and compelling), al-Maḥāsinī argues that al-Maʿarrī's disparagement of women also must have been motivated by his truly sincere and deeply held belief that man should not marry and procreate. Women are disparaged because they are the child-bearing, life-giving force of human society par excellence. Third, adopting a Freudian inspired interpretation to *Luzūm*, al-Maḥāsinī argues for the likelihood of al-Maʿarrī's having harbored deep within himself the instinctive love and affection for women that prevails in most men, but it was a love and affection that at one time or another was rebuffed by a certain Umāmah/أمامة (whom al-Maḥāsinī identifies as al-Maʿarrī's beloved, in other words), so that the love became suppressed and—as is wont to happen in such instances—led to eruptions of the exact opposite nature.[102]

There could very well be some truth to al-Maḥāsinī's first suggestion, especially if city (and particularly Baghdadi) life in late ʿAbbāsid times was precisely as wanton as al-Maḥāsinī portrays it. Al-Maḥāsinī's third suggestion, although not as convincing as the first, might even have some truth to it, although arguing for the historical certainty of Umāmah (or an Umāmah-like figure) is problematic.[103] Furthermore, whether real or fictitious, she may have been merely a muse. In any event, one really needn't go beyond al-Maḥāsinī's second suggestion for having in hand the most plausible explanation for al-Maʿarrī's pronounced antifeminism. Al-Maʿarrī opposed marriage and procreation; he could hardly have spoken admiringly of women, who, although by no means solely responsible for propagating the human race, certainly are the most conspicuous and indispensable participants in the process inasmuch as it is they who carry, bear, and nurse children. In other words, al-Maʿarrī is extraordinarily harsh on women in *Luzūm* first and foremost because it is they more so than men who have come to symbolize human fertility and the life-giving and nurturing process. This becomes clearer still al-Maʿarrī's remark in II.261.13 that the best women for marrying are sterile women (although sterilization for men is a thought that crossed the poet's mind: that a man be castrated, L II.27.5 proclaims, is better for him than marrying even a fine free-born woman, not to mention a prostitute).

A second reason for al-Maʿarrī's opposition to the family—as if he needed one—is his low esteem for children. True, in many places in *Luzūm* where he makes mention of children, he speaks of them with remarkable compassion. For example, he considers them innocent victims of life's misfortunes. They are condemned to suffer not through any fault of their own, but simply because of their parents' having created them (an often-repeated view; e.g., L I.45.3–5; 168.7–12; 169.1–7; 253.2; 386.14; II.9.9 69.3–4; 199.13; 249.15; 250.1–7; 421.7–15). Lines 7–12 in *Luzūm* I.168 and 1–7 in *Luzūm* I. 169, addressed to a child whom al-Maʿarrī imagines as having died prematurely, are a particularly fine and sensitive example of this sentiment, especially in Nicholson's smooth rendering, and notwithstanding al-Maʿarrī's remarks elsewhere on the bliss and comfort of nonexistence.

O child of a tender mother—and surely Allah
Is able to bring to pass whatsoe'er He pleaseth—
Thou after thy death, destroyed by the hap most hateful,

Yet speakest and warnest us with a voice of wisdom.
"Unwilling" (thou sayst) "in this world I alighted
And lived; and how oft was medicined, how oft was potioned!
A year, month after month, I made by climbing—
And would I had never climbed on the new moon's ladder!
And when I was called away and my hour of weaning
Drew nigh, Death sought me out and I found no warden.
Life's hour I abandoned, empty, to other tenants,
And wretched I must have been had I still remained there.
I went forth pure, unsoiled: had my lease of living
Been long, I had soilure ta'en and had lost my pureness.
Oh, why dost thou weep? It may be that I am chosen
To dwell with the blessed souls in the state hereafter.
'Gainst evil the women charmed me, but when my day dawned,
It left me as though I ne'er had been charmed by charmers.
Suppose I had lived as long as the vulture, only
To meet Death at the last: I had either suffered
The poor man's wrong, oppressed without fear of Allah,
Or else I had been a ruler of men who feared me.
'Tis one of the boons my Lord hath bestowed upon me,
That hastily I departed and did not tarry."[104]

أيا طفلَ الشفيقةِ إن ربي   على ما شاءَ مِن أمرٍ مُقيتُ
تكلَّمُ بعد موتِكَ بٱعتبارٍ   وقد أوْدَى بِكِ النبأُ المَقيتُ
تقولُ حَللْتُ عاجلتي بكُرْهي   فعِشتُ وكم لُدِدْتُ وكم سُقيتُ
رقِيتُ الحَوْلَ شهراً بعد شهرٍ   فليتي في الأَهلّةِ ما رقيتُ
فلمّا صِيحَ بي ودنا فِطامي   تيمَّني الحِمامُ فما وُقيتُ
تركتُ الدارَ خاليةً لغيري   ولو طال المَقامُ بها شَقيتُ
نقيتُ فما دِنستُ ولو تمادتْ   حياةٌ بي دَنِستُ فما نَقيتُ
وما يُدريكِ باكيَتي عساني   لسُكْنَى الفوز في الأُخرى ٱنتُقيتُ
رَقَتْني الراقياتُ وحَمَّ يومي   فغادرني كأَني ما رُقِيتُ
هَبِيني عشتُ عُمرَ النسرِ فيها   وكان الموتُ آخر ما لَقيتُ
فقيراً فاستُضِمْتُ بلا ٱتِّقاءٍ   لربي أو أميراً فاتُّقِيتُ
ومِن صُنْعِ المليكِ إليَّ أنّي   تَعَجَّلتُ الرحيلَ فما بَقيتُ

But notwithstanding the occasional compassionate moments similar to the one just evinced, unmistakable in *Luzūm* is al-Maʿarrī's conviction that just as children suffer an abominable wrong from their parents, parents suffer from their children (L I.253.2). Children are apt to renounce their parents and treat them harshly, even though their parents may be kind to them (L I.69.6–7). They will accuse their parents of being cowardly and miserly (L I.253.2). They are likely to be of no practical use (L II.86.8). They complain of their maladies and misfortunes and thereby rob their parents of sleep (L II.421. 12–14). They are selfish, wasteful, ungrateful of parental affection and unconcerned about their parents when they are in poor health (L II.397.13–15; 388.1–15). They very often end up being enemies of not only their own parents, but also their siblings (L II.289.12; 98.2). In short, al-Maʿarrī quite unironically submits that children are a burden and nuisance to their parents and society as a whole. Notwithstanding their original innocence, they are just as prone to commit evil as adults, which of course in any event they eventually become—God willing.

The verses in *Luzūm* II.397.13–16; 398.1–12 best illustrate this mindset, inasmuch as it is one of the more concentrated pieces of its kind. At the same time, taken in conjunction with al-Maʿarrī's various and sundry trenchant remarks on women, the poem vividly reveals the third reason we have cited for al-Maʿarrī's being so hostile to the conventional human family: as he sees it, on balance, family life is neither harmonious and loving nor beneficial.

When the father leaves a portion remaining of his progeny,
he's disturbed that he dies while his wealth and finery endure;
for how often it is that parents have a wasteful child
who will reward them with avarice for their having sired him;
who keeps from them, begrudgingly, the least bit of food
while for his sake they travel and traverse even the desert.
Such a child deems a cow's two calves the worth of his parents,
but to them the two calves of Ursa Minor are not his worth.
Such a child faults his parents for excessive love for him,
yet they must censure him for his show of hatred toward them.
He'll do evil and not equate his parents with his sandal strap,
yet they'll equate him with the lights that come out at night.
He'll cast angry and haughty glances towards his parents—
as if in days gone by their love for him is what destroyed him.

He sleeps whenever they are laid low with illness, and yet
when he has a complaint, their eyes remain untouched by sleep.
If they claim taking pains for love for him, they can be believed;
what they're accused of doing to win his love, they will accept.
His acting dishonestly with them is a trifle to him,
yet how often they gave him advice carefully sifted!
They'd be happy were he spared the grave his entire life
or that they make their descent to it before he does.
Were he to signal to them, with but a blink of the eye,
that they hasten their departure from life, they would do so.
In his honor they'd love that he be shod with the star Suha
though the soles of their feet wear the prickles of the palm tree.
He damns what his parents have done for him, so misled is he;
and yet how good and beautiful are what they have done for him.
In their view he's like the sharp sword before the enemy,
like their war lance that they fasten between leg and stirrup.
And yet he prefers someone else for his cherished secret;
this person, not his parents, will pass it on from him.

إذا النسلُ أشواهُ الأَبُ اهتاج انَّـه   يَموتُ ويَبْقى مالهُ وخُلاهُ
فَكم ولَدٍ للوالدين مُضيّعٍ   يُجازيهما بُخلاً بما نَجَلاهُ
طوَى عنهما القوتَ الزهيدَ نفاسةً   وجرَّاه سارَا الحَزْنَ وارتحلَاهُ
يَرَى فَرقدَيْ وحشيَّةٍ بدَليهما   وما فرقدا مسراهُما بَدَلاهُ
ولامَهُما عن فرطِ حبِّهما لهُ   وفي بُغْضِهِ إياهُما عَذَلاهُ
أَساءَ فلم يَعْدِلْهُما بشراكِهِ   وكانا بأَنوارِ الدُّجى عدلاهُ
يُعيرُهما طَرْفاً من الغيظِ شافناً   كأَنهما فيما مضى تَبَلاهُ
ينامُ إذا ما أُدنفا وإذا سرى   لهُ الشكْوُ باتَ الغُمْضُ ما ٱكتحلاهُ
إن ادَّعيا في وُدِّهِ الجُهْدَ صُدِّقا   وما اتُّهِما فيه فينتحلاَهُ
يَغُشُّهما في الأَمرِ هانَ وطالما   أَفاآ عليه النصحَ وٱنتخلاهُ
يسرُّهما أن يَهْجُرَ الريمَ دَهرَهُ   وأنَّهما من قبلِهِ نَزلاَهُ
ولو بمُشارِ العينِ يُوحِي إِليهما   لوشْكِ ٱعتزالِ العيشِ لاَٱعتزلاَهُ
يَودّانِ إكراماً لو ٱنتعَلَ السُّها   وأَن حُذِيَا السلّاءَ وٱنتعلاهُ
يَذُمُّ لفرطِ الغيّ ما فعلا به   وأحسِنْ وأجمِلْ بالذي فعلاهُ
يعدّانهِ كالصارِمِ العَضِبِ في العِدَى   بظنّهما والذابلِ ٱعتقلاهُ
ويُؤْثرُ بالسرّ الكنينِ سِواهُما   فينقلُهُ عنهُ وما نقلاهُ

Al-Maʿarrī singles out for condemnation two aspects of family life associated especially with Islamic society as configured during his time: polygamous marriages and the harem system. With reference to both (for all intents and purposes), in *Luzūm* II.84.1–2, he wishes that God might destroy the good fortune of princes who impregnate their female slaves and then either cast them off while they are still pregnant or sell the children once they are born. In II.346.5, he remarks that the women who are the deprived in society are those who are treated as common property (*mushāʿāt*/كبيك) and left to bear bastard children.[105] Taking more than one wife is a great mistake (L II.159.9–10), the wrong course to take in life (II.91.11).[106] The practice is especially unvirtuous if done merely for the sake of the enhancement of pleasure (L I.281.6).

In the last section of this chapter, there will be further occasion to note that al-Maʿarrī not infrequently recorded remarks in *Luzūm* that on the surface seem incongruous with some of his above-mentioned dismissive opinions on women, children, procreation, and the conventional family. He demands from children that they honor their parents, for example. Also, occasionally, he refers to the bearing of children as a virtue. These should probably not be construed as serious reservations or misgivings about all that is said or implied to the contrary. It is likelier that they are intended merely to take some of the hard edge off of al-Maʿarrī's otherwise consistently radical, hostile (to most), repugnant views on women, children, procreation, and the family; in order to *suggest* that he may be somewhat conflicted, not quite the absolute anti-feminist, anti-social, and anti-family man whom he certainly gives every indication of being. These more normative sentiments or ideas were also probably expressed with the realization that few men and women would be likely to accept *Luzūm*'s bitter and cynical views on women and the family and adjust their lives accordingly. Al-Maʿarrī could be quite sober. He was also a moralist, and, notwithstanding his cynicism, hardly an advocate of free choice in terms of sexual mores. He no doubt anticipated that despite what *he* sincerely may have believed about the nature of men and women and the family, most of humankind would go on living more "normal" lives—go on marrying, procreating, and raising children, in other words—and in that case it would be best that they be inspired to live in accordance with the injunctions or opinions that lie within some of the more normative frameworks (for his time and place) with respect to marriage, procreation, and the family.

The final conclusion to be drawn here? The *Luzūm's* highly critical and unpleasant depiction of the more conventional family, inclusive of children as well as women, is essentially the one that should be associated with al-Maʿarrī's sociology (so to speak). The comparatively radical views on celibacy and sexual abstinence are the crowning tenet of that sociology. Could al-Maʿarrī's will have been done, the human race would have ceased to regenerate itself.

Society in General

Al-Maʿarrī's views in *Luzūm* on men and women in general as they typically interact with one another as social animals amount to a long litany of vices and foibles. A brief but fair summation yields a dim prognosis for any hope of amelioration of the human condition. Men and women are not really protective of one another (I 229.9; II.74.8). On the contrary; they mistreat and behave unjustly and callously toward one another (I.95.12, 96.1; 110.5; 388.6; II.103.9; 316.12–13). Al-Maʿarrī observes a humanity prone to murder and slaughter and callously leaving the dead as carrion for wild hyenas (I.387.16). In support of their wars, humans are willing to cause the spilling of much blood and the sacrifice of loved ones to death in battle (I.124.9). There is little hope that there will be an end to the wars. Humanity is habituated to aggression and blood feuds (II.169.4–6) with "killed bodies offered up to hyenas; the destruction of one state so as to replace it with another; such is our fate for one cause after another" (قتلى يطرحون لأمّ عمرو/ ومهلكُ دولةٍ وقيامُ أخرى/ كذاك الدهرُ أمر بعد أمر; L I.387.16; 388.1). Fraud and deceit are everywhere (L II.57.12; 11.9). When people are trusted, they don't live up to their words; if they have power, they act unjustly; if they don't have power, they will steal it (L II.11.10).

Humanity is selfish and self-serving. The well-off will not share what good fortune they might have with the hard-pressed (I.61.8), tolerating great economic inequality among peoples (I.64.1; 263.11) and allowing many to go without such basic necessities as footwear, clothing, and food (I.157.7; II.345.9–10). Humans suppress (I.158.8) and oppress one another

(II.316.12–13) to the extent that all people in the final analysis are no more than slaves to others (II.266.8). There is also genuine institutionalized (and legally condoned) slavery and, to make matters worse, cruel treatment of slaves (I.144.8; II.141.5–6). Even animals are subjected to cruel treatment (I.120.6; 156.11–12; 206.8–10; II. 141.5–6; 416.1–2).

Humans are so destructive that throughout their history they have managed to demolish one nation after another (I.388.1). Greedy (II.322.15), vain (II.370.1), luxury-loving (I.129.5–6), and enraptured with the present world to the point of being love-sick over it (I.85.4; 120.9; 174.5), they covet wealth (II.130.6) and live only for the pursuit of fine food and clothing (I.77.4). They compete for status in life (I.156.9), pursuing all that is trivial (I.437.9) and obeying and following only the rich and privileged (II.399.12). People will lie in order to acquire wealth (II.121.8). Even in death, they attempt to beautify themselves ostentatiously (i.e., with linen shrouds and perfumes; II.370.1–2). Shameful, momentary pleasures are what they seek rather than what is eternal and truly good (I.405.15; 406.1).

Humans are overwhelmed and enslaved by their passions (I.99.11; 117.5). Thus it is that, among other things, they are adulterers (I.373.1) who are not only easily seduced (I.124.13; 125.1–3) but also quite unashamed at being unchaste (I.377.5–6). The pleasures of food and sex dominate their lives (I.57.2). Men will consent to marry even base slaves (II.418.15–16), and they are quick to partake in the evil of wine drinking (I.144.2–4; I.387.16), especially to wash away their sorrow over the awareness of mortality (I.229.8–12). They are neither sincere (I.100.2; 135.7) nor humble (I.52.9) nor chivalrous (I.52.9) nor noble (I.120.5) nor faithful in love (I.120.4; II.90.4). Nor are they repentant (I.92.8), God-fearing (II.426.10) creatures who can be helpful (II.96.8–9), generous (II.9.8–9), truthful (I.69.4; 124.8; II.243.8), and, last but hardly least, tolerant of religious diversity (II.82.3–4). (Because of the perceived religious intolerance, in L.II.134, in a poem consisting of only a couplet [lines 6–7], al-Maʿarrī may be suggesting that it would *not* be *his* choice that Muslims proclaim in writing their testament of faith [الشهادة], i.e., not be so quick and self-satisfied to proclaim the faith.) Humans are treacherous (II.372.5), obscene (I.78.5), hypocritical (I.437.9), boastful (I.437.9), slanderous (I.120.5), impudent (I.251.13), and quarrelsome (II.83.13).

Finally, humans are supremely gullible, naive. They fall for the preposterous (II.122.4). From time immemorial, they have followed heretical sects that take them from the truth (I.105.13). They attentively respond to every and any religious propagandist (I.233.3–4; cf. here also the remark of al-Maʿarrī in L I.233.3–4 [quoted supra], where he says, "Were a wolf in the woods to say 'I am sent with a religion, by way of my Lord!' Some would reply 'Yes! Indeed you have!'").

Most of *Luzūm*'s negative views on human society at large are put forward with no specific references to Muslims, Jews, or Christians, Arabs, Persians, Indians, Byzantines, or whatever other races or nationalities with whom al-Maʿarrī might have been familiar and/or interacted. The referents "they," "them," "humankind," "people," or "community" (and so forth) predominate in this context. To that extent, al-Maʿarrī's extreme social criticism can and should be taken as applying to all men and women and all societies everywhere. However, there are sentiments or thoughts unquestionably aimed at those holding the faith into which he was born, leaving no doubt as to just how defiantly critical al-Maʿarrī was of his own immediate society in particular. There was occasion to see some of these sentiments and thoughts in the preceding sections of this chapter. A few more might be added here. Again, they are in reference to average, rank-and-file believers. (What al-Maʿarrī has to say about certain notable functionaries or office holders or figures of historical renown will be dealt with shortly.)

All these believers are lustful and eager to plunder for money (L I.407.16; 408.2). They do not honor their inheritance laws and stipulations (L II.286.2–4), and they do not truly work for their sustenance but instead hope that sustenance might come their way by virtue of their placing complete trust in God (i.e., *al-tawakkul*/التوكُّل; L II.99.4). As for the prevalent acceptance of divine predeterminism in Islam, al-Maʿarrī cynically notes that this is resorted to as an excuse for one's sinning (L I.327.12). The testament of faith by which a Muslim proclaims his confessional allegiance (i.e., the *shahādah*/الشهادة), he declares, is given only for the hope of monetary profit (L II.60.4). The Shīʿī imāms are perfectly aware that their missionaries are out and about for the sake of monetary gain. In *Luzūm* I.426.4, mosques are brazenly described as at times centers of merry making not unlike what goes on in taverns; in

Luzūm I.185.4–6, mosques are characterized as meeting places for the seditious. Al-Maʿarrī concedes that many Muslims know many verses of the Qur'ān, but at the same time, he charges that few of these individuals seriously heed what they read from their scripture (L I.324.11; II. 393.12). The entire Islamic *ummah* he sees as preoccupied with quarreling over the Sunnī-Shīʿite split (L I.425.15) despite the fact that those in the former camp (he submits) have no sound reason for making judgments against those in the latter (i.e., *ruffāḍ*/رُفّاض and *nuṣṣāb*/نُصّاب; L I.129.12, in connection with which see see the Dār Ṣādir edition of *Luzūm*, vol. 1, p. 154, fn. 2).

Further underscoring *Luzūm*'s relentless and frank criticism of first and foremost al-Maʿarrī's own immediate society and confessional community are the criticisms of his ethnic counterparts—the Arabs. Al-Maʿarrī regards people of Arab stock as being no better than any other people. In reference to the Arabs par excellence—which is to say the Hashemites and the Quraysh—he composed, for example, the following verses:

Let not the person of Hashemite origin
boast at the expense of a man who is non-Arab.

لا يفخرنَّ الهاشميُّ   على امرىءٍ من آلِ بَربر

(L I.421.9)

People will one day ask "What is Quraysh and Mecca?"
Just as people have said "What is Jadīs? And Ṭasm?"

سيسألُ ناسٌ ما قُريشٌ ومكّةٌ   كما قال ناسٌ ما جَديسٌ وما طَسْمُ

(L II.251.4)[107]

In L II.51.7, al-Maʿarrī boasts that he does not consider himself "a Qurayshite."[108] With Arabs and/or Muslims especially in mind are several citations just mentioned above under al-Maʿarrī's critical remarks on humankind in general; for example, the reference to blood-feuds; one of the references to human's being cruel to animals (viz., L I.120.6; the remark that people are not content to eat simply sheep or camel livers, but also desire to eat even lizard livers, is an allusion to the ancient Bedouin

Arab habit of eating lizards); the observation that people are so vain that even when dead they seek beautification with perfume and the burial shroud; and the observation that men allow themselves to marry base slaves (another obvious reference to his condemnation of polygamy and the harem system that were sanctioned by Islam).

Paradoxically, however, one of the reasons al-Maʿarrī gives for deprecating the Arabs in particular and prophesying their demise is that they lost their racial purity. Noting the willingness on their part to marry non-Arabs indiscriminately (see, e.g., L I.186.3; and II.435.8–11), not to mention slaves of base origin, he sees the resulting mixture of Arab with non-Arab blood as responsible for producing bad qualities among the Arabs (L II.435. 8–11).[109] (Not the least of these qualities, argues al-Maʿarrī incidentally, is that the Arabs by his time no longer knew how to express themselves properly in their own language; see L II.335.4, in a poem that bemoans the eclipse of both the Umayyad *and* the ʿAbbāsid caliphates, with ominous and eerily resonant lines on the virtual collapse of both Syria and Iraq).

Although al-Maʿarrī can freely condemn the Arabs for having become boorish peasants (L II.65.2–6), an implication of *Luzūm* is that the Arabs would have remained good, noble, and strong (or at least less morally reprehensible, less ignoble, likelier to have preserved their empires) had they remained racially pure.

Various Typically Influential Individuals in al-Ma'arrī's Society

The *Luzūm*'s comments in this area cover a wide range of individuals, such as princes, kings, tribal chiefs or rulers, astronomers, theologians, and litterateurs. The attention given each class or group is highly uneven. Some receive only a line or two of thought; others get slightly more; and others get much more. In order to review these components of al-Maʿarrī's society as he saw it, it would be most efficient to approach them within the framework of two broad, although hardly mutually exclusive, categories into which they might be said to fall: people of state (i.e., kings, princes, ministers, or similar such individuals invested with political power) and the intelligentsia or learned class (whether lay or bound up more particularly with the study and observation of religion).

People of State

Al-Maʿarrī was extremely censorious of the statespeople of his day, often openly, almost prosaically; hence just as much a radical contrarian politically as he is religiously. Subscribing essentially to the notion that power corrupts (L II.11.9–10; 403.3; I.285.1), he spoke frankly of misdeeds committed by the various officials around him who are empowered to one extent or another to govern him and others but while promoting the general well-being of society. Leaders of states in general allow the *Sharī'ah* to be abrogated, he argued in L I.238.4–6 (here of course assuming the posture of a good Muslim with respect to the value of the religious law; but leaving that aside, his point is that the potentates of his day had little genuine interest in maintaining the religious law). Statesmen are not truly protective of their domains (L II.402.11). Moreover, they allow the general populace to go through life mired in stupidity while simultaneously fleecing them for all they are worth (L I.425.4–6). Their rule over others comes about in the first place only because they are so arrogant as to presume that they deserve to be masters over others (L I.86.3). In truth, they are oppressors (L I.387.6), killing their own as though slaughtering sheep while all the while making a show of undertaking public works and defending the security of the state. They are all sinking in ignominy. How anyone might want to envy or emulate them is inexplicable.

ضمّكُمُ جنسٌ وأزرى بكمْ قِنْسٌ وأَنتمْ في دُجا تخبِطونْ
حَفرْتُمُ صَخْراً وأَنبَطتُمُ ماءً فهَلا العِلْمَ تستَنبِطونْ
بَعْضُكُمُ يَقْتُلُ بَعْضاً كأنْ جُوزيتُمُ عن غَنَمٍ تَعْبِطونْ
رابَطتُمُ الثغرَ بأفراسِكُمْ وفَوقَكُم في العَقْلِ ما تَرْبِطونْ
لم تُرْزَقوا خيراً ولم تَعدَموا شَرّاً فما بالُكُمُ تَهبطونْ
ظَنَّ آرتقاءً بكمْ جاهِلٌ وكلُّكُم في صَبَبٍ تَهبطونْ

(L II.392.4–9)

You are united by sort but base by origin;
you are all thrashing about in the dark.
You have hewed out stone, and found water;
so why haven't you discovered knowledge?
You are killing one another as if you were

recompensed for the slaughter of fatted sheep.
You have fastened down the borders with troops;
but up above, in your minds, what do you fix?
You aren't blessed with good, and you don't lack evil.
How can it be, therefore, that you are envied?
An ignoramus deems you elevated;
whereas all of you downhill are headed.

It is only for the sake of amassing wealth that the heads and notables of state govern (L I.283.13). They are quite prepared to legislate approvingly all that is evil (L II.80.1). In their basic character, they are no less ignoble than the average person. They are duplicitous (L I.71.5), ignorant (L I.215.1; 238.4), niggardly, and selfish (L I.238.5). They are addicted to the pleasures of wine, food, and sex (L II.134.8–12; also II.392.11: لم تَقْتَنوا مَجْداً وأصبَحتُمُ / قِنَّ فروجٍ لكمُمْ أو بطونْ, which translates "You have not achieved grandeur / you have become slaves either to the vulva or your own stomachs"; this is the closing line to the poem in which the lines from L II.392.4–9 [translated above] are embedded; an example of a shorter poem where al-Maʿarrī stays on course and where the invective that he desires to heap on his target is scarcely compromised or muddled by the requirements of rhyme).

Becoming more specific in his denunciation of people of state, al-Maʿarrī took dead aim at viziers, magistrates, princes, and kings. Viziers are criminals (L I.389.12). Magistrates are unjust and erring (L II.134.6; 323.3). They are as arbitrary in their rulings as games of chance (L II.323.3). Princes are promiscuous and obscene tyrants who abandon the welfare and best interests of the common people, instead oppressing and duping them (L II.270.16; I.263.2; II.84.1; I.55.6–7). As for kings, al-Maʿarrī rails against their preoccupation with collecting taxes (L I.218.6), plundering for wealth (L I.218.7), enslaving people (L II.320.2), and womanizing and reveling in drink and music (L I.218.6; I.369.13; II.343.10). They are especially despicable because of their perceived need always to be going to war (L I.212.4–5, which reads أَغْنَى الأَنام تقيٌّ في ذرى جبلٍ / يرضَى القليلَ ويأبى الوشي والتاجا / وأفقر الناس في دنياهُمُ مَلِكٌ / يُضْحي إلى اللجب الجرار محتاجا or "The richest man is the God-fearing in his mountain retreat, satisfied with little and shunning finery and crown. Whereas the poorest of men is the king among them, who is in need of a large and tumultuous army").

Striking the same pacifist note, al-Maʿarrī concludes that kings really accomplish nothing with their armed forces (L II.277.11). They are glorified because of their dignity, but what they truly deserve is to be rebuked for their crimes (L I.322.10).

The scattered descriptions that al-Maʿarrī gave in *Luzūm* of the overall state affairs in his community—social, economic, and political—speak to the corrupt, greedy, oppressive, and frivolous nature of those at the helm. He made mention of a polity rife with civil discord (L I.119.8; 148.8) and war (L II.268.1), a polity where there are executions (L II.94.5), hunger (L II.335.7), confusion (L I.142–6), ignorance (L II.156.3), and sorrow (L II.90.6–7). He found fraud pandemic (L II.156.1). Regimes became well-known for the bad or ugly things that they accomplished (L I.173.2). Political rot was rampant. And it rose to the top.

وإذا الرئاسةُ لم تُعَنْ بسياسةٍ عقليةٍ خطئ الصوابَ السائسُ

(L II.21.4)

When leadership is not aided with a policy,
and one rational, policymakers are in error.

هل آنَ للقيدِ أن تُفَكَّهْ إنَّ قبيحَ الفعالِ حِكَّهْ
بكلِّ أَرضٍ أَميرُ سوءٍ يضرِبُ للناسِ شَرَّ سِكَّهْ
قد كثر الغِشُّ وٱستعانتْ بهِ الأَشدَّاءُ والأرِكهْ
. . . .
فخلِّهِمْ والذي أرادوا وحُلَّ بالقدسِ أو بمكَّهْ
صكَّهُمُ الدهرُ صَكَّ أَعمى تكتُبُ أيدي الفَناءِ صَكَّهْ
قد ثَرَّبَتْ يَثْرِبُ عليهمْ وبكَّت المسلمينَ بَكَّهْ

(L II.155.13–14; 156.1–2, 5–7)[110]

Has the time come for the chains to be broken?
For the miscreant has become like the mange.
In every land there's a prince of evil,
minting for people the most evil coin.
Fraud abounds; weak *and* strong resort to it.

. . . .
Leave them, therefore, and whatever they want,
whether you live in Jerusalem or Mecca.
Fate has stricken them with a blind slap
whose deed is writ by the hands of death.
Medina has already found fault with them,
and Mecca has lamented the Muslims.

It's safe to assume that al-Maʿarrī did not intend to absolve any part of the greater Islamic *ummah* of his day. But he makes the comprehensiveness of the perceived decay explicit in several poems where he mentions by name certain provinces of the Islamic commonwealth. A few of the more revealing examples follow.

Our whole state is damnable, with no place to reside,
whether you halt in the wet lands or in the dry.
The Ḥijāz has been made inaccessible to virtues;
Tihāmah is no more than a mine of accusations.
Syria is ill-omened and Yemen without good fortune;
While Medina is now finding fault with acumen.

كلُّ البلادِ ذميمٌ لا مُقامَ به　　وإن حللتَ ديارَ الوَبلِ والرِهَمِ
أنَّ الحجازَ عن الخيراتِ محتجِزٌ　　وما تِهامةُ إلّا مَعْدنُ التُّهَمِ
والشّامُ شُؤْمٌ وليس اليُمْنُ في يمنٍ　　ويَثربُ الآن تثريبٌ على الفهمِ

(L II.301.4–6)

As for the Ḥijāz, residing there's not desired.
It's enveloped in five volcanic deserts.
And in Syria there burns the fuel of war
ignited by people who've girded up their loins.
In Iraq, meanwhile, is a lightning bolt that sheds blood,
a thunder clap that bespeaks the advent of evil.
Yet the end of time shall be as the beginning, just as
the rear in a line of verse can evoke the fore.
So get me prepared, O reviled mother earth;
perhaps I'll follow my friends and thus be finished.

أَمّا الحجازُ فما يُرجى المقامُ به   لأَنَّه بالحرار الخَمْسِ مُحتَجزُ
والشامُ فيه وَقودُ الحربِ مشتعلٌ   يَشُبُّهُ القوم شُدَّتْ منهم الحُجَزُ
وبالعراقِ وميضٌ يستهلُّ دماً   وراعدٌ بلقاءِ الشرِّ يرتجزُ
وآخرُ الدهرِ يُلفَى مثلَ أَوَّلَهُ   والصدرُ يأْتي على مقدارهِ العَجُزُ
فجهّزيني لحاك اللهُ والدةً   عَلّيَ أتبعُ أصحابي فأنتجزُ

(L I.431.4–7)

It's sad enough that the righteous have departed wholesale,
and *we* are the inhabitants of the world in their wake.
Both Iraq and Syria have been nought for a long time;
there is no one there has authority over the realm.
Humankind is ruled by devils empowered with authority.
In every city there's a devil among those who rule,
one who ignores the hunger of the people, all of them;
although *he* remains full-bellied and drinks his wine.
Pedigree is now dubious; the Byzantine's speech is like
that of Arabs while the Arabs of Ṭā' are unintelligible.
The Kilāb of Syria defy those who contest them;
it's as if in warfare their lances have become ropes.
When will there arise a leader to gain benefit for us,
so that justice be known in mountains as well as valleys?
Pray wherever you want. The realm is still an eyesore.
All of it is like the camel's putrid slop-hole.

يكفيك حُزناً ذهابُ الصالحينَ معاً   ونحنُ بعدَهمُ في الأرضِ قُطّانُ
إنّ العراقَ وإنّ الشامَ مُذ زَمنٍ   صِفرانِ ما بهما للمَلكِ سلطانُ
ساسَ الأنام شياطينٌ مُسلَّطةٌ في   كلِّ مِصرٍ من الواليِنَ شيْطانُ
من ليس يَحْفلُ خمْصَ الناسِ كلهم   إن باتَ يشرَبُ خمراً وَهْوَ مبْطانُ
تشابَهَ النجرُ فالروميّ منطقُهُ   كمنطق العُربِ والطائيُّ مِرطانُ
أَمّا كلابٌ فأعْيا من يغالبهمُ   كأَنَّ أرماحهم في الحربِ أَشطانُ
متى يقوم إمامٌ يستفيدُ لنا   فتعرفَ العدلَ أَجبالٌ وغيطانُ
صلّوا بحيثُ أردتمْ فألبلادُ قذًى   كأنّما كلُّها للإبلِ أعطانُ

(L II.335.4–11)[111]

Al-Maʿarrī underscored that the Quraysh Arabs were not spared internal bickering (L I.119.8–12) and rivalries (L II.277.9). He alleged that they were responsible, ultimately, for the killing of ʿAlī's son Ḥusayn (L I.261.5).[112] The suggestion is that through this deed the Quraysh Arabs played a prominent role in fostering the Sunnī-Shīʿite split in Islam, thereby keeping the greater Islamic community forever seriously divided against itself.

All Islamdom al-Maʿarrī accused of alienating non-Muslims through the implementation of the *jizyah*/الجزية, the head tax on non-Muslims living under Islamic jurisdiction. Were it not for this institution, Christians (for example) would be more likely to accept Islam (L II.78.11–12).

In his fault finding with respect to his own immediate polity and confessional community, al-Maʿarrī minced no words in laying the blame *primarily* on his own. Occasionally, however, he alleges extraneous influences as one of the root causes for the malaise. Just as he can occasionally attribute the general rottenness that he felt plagued his society to his perception that by his time the Arabs were no longer purely Arab, from time to time he attributed some of the rottenness of the political rule to the fact that it was no longer dominated by ethnic Arabs, but, rather, by ruling groups or dynasties of non-Arab stock. This tendency is apparent in the last poem quoted above. It is even more obvious in L II.316.3–5, where in verses addressed to the deceased caliph al-Manṣūr specific reference is made to the Daylamites, the tribal grouping of Iranian stock who wrested rule of Baghdad from the ʿAbbāsids in 945 A.D., and to the famed early ʿAbbāsid propagandist Abū Muslim.

Were al-Manṣūr resurrected he'd shout out:
"O city of peace! Do not rest in peace!
Banū Hāshim now live in the desert,
the realm ceded to the Daylamites.
Had I known their end would be like this,
I would not have killed Abū Muslim."

لو بُعثَ المنصورُ نادى أيا   مدينةَ التسليمِ لا تسْلمي
قد سكنَ القفرَ بنُو هاشمٍ   وانتقلَ المُلكُ إلى الديلمِ
لو كنتَ أدري أن عُقباهُمُ   لذاكَ لم أَقْتُلْ أبا مُسلمِ

(L II.316.3–5)

Al-Maʿarrī did not completely absolve the average citizen from bearing some of the responsibility for the abysmal state of the state. In L II.412.5, he accused the entire Islamic body politic of being without good sense. In L II.399.6–12,[113] he spoke of the ingratitude, rebelliousness, suspicion, and hypocrisy with which the ruled are wont to greet even a kind, generous, and just ruler:

قد ينصفُ القومَ في الأشياء سيدُهم ولو أطاقوا له ريباً لرابُوهُ
لم يقدروا إن يلاقوه بسيئةٍ من الكلام فلَمَّا غابَ عابُوهُ
تحدثوا بمخازيه مُكتمةً وقابلوه بإجلالٍ وهابُوهُ
وكم أرادوا لَهُ كيداً بيومِ ردًى مِن الزمانِ ولكن ما أَصابوهُ
أَكْدى فلامُوهُ لما قَلَّ نائلُهُ ولو حبا الوفرَ زاروهُ ونابُوهُ
صبراً قليلاً فإنَّ الموتَ آخِذُهُ وما يُخَلَّفُ لا صقرٌ ولا بُوهُ
لبَّى الغَنِيَّ بنو حَوَّاءَ من طَمَعٍ ولو دعاهم فقيرٌ ما أَجابُوهُ

The people's sovereign might be just with them on matters,
but if they could still suspect him, they would suspect him.
They are not up to speaking ill of him in his presence;
in his absence, however, they do find fault with him,
speaking about his shameful acts that are kept concealed.
When they meet him it is with awe and reverence.
How they long for his demise, and since long ago,
although they haven't been able to achieve it.
He gives little. They reproach him when his favor is scant.
Were he to give amply they'd visit him time and again.
Only scant patience is required, for death will take him;
with nothing to be left behind, neither hawk nor owl.
Humans heed the call of the rich due to greediness.
If the poor were to summon them, they wouldn't respond.

At the same time, the *Luzūm* occasionally cautions the ruled that those invested with the power to rule, even to rule supremely, can be beneficial to the ruled, and particularly for the sake of defense of the realm and avoidance of chaos and disorder:

Your sovereign is like fire: useful if moderate
although burning and damaging when gone astray.

سلطانُكَ النارُ إن تَعْدِلْ فنافعةٌ   وإن تَجُرْ فلها ضيرٌ وإحراقُ
(L II.121.11)

Fear kings and oblige them their due obedience,
for the king is like water-giving rain to the land.
If they're unjust they still have a usefulness for life;
often they protect you with foot soldiers and cavalry.
Were acts of tyranny and injustice not to be found
among the Persian and Ghassānid rulers of old?
Horses run off to pasture when left to act freely.
Only painful bridle and halter can restrain them.

واخشَ الملوكَ وياسرْها بطاعتِها   فالمَلْكُ للأرضِ مثلُ الماطرِ الساني
إن يظلمُوا فلهُمْ نَفْعٌ يُعاشُ به   وكم حَمَوْكَ برَجْلٍ أو بفرسانِ
هل خَلتْ قبلُ مِن جَوْرٍ ومَظْلَمَةٍ   أربابُ فارسَ أو أربابُ غسّانِ
خيلٌ إذا سُوِّمَتْ سامتْ وما حُبِسَتْ   إلا بلُجْمٍ تُعَنِّيها وأرسانِ
(L II.371.1–4)

Perhaps the occasional verses of the sort represented by the last few citations were expressed partially to soften extreme antiauthoritarian views. But given al-Maʿarrī's low estimation of the average person's ability to lead a good and orderly righteous life (to which indeed the last line refers by way of implied analogy), the sentiment behind such verses cannot be dismissed as totally disingenuous. Al-Maʿarrī was not an unreserved populist nor an anarchist.

In at least two places in *Luzūm,* he remarked that rulers ultimately must be considered as the servants (even "paid employees"—quite literally) of those over whom they rule:

Living on is wearisome, for I know many a nation
whose princes commanded what is not in its interests.
They wronged their subjects and permitted their deception.
Thus, they neglected their welfare, yet they were their hirelings.

مُلَّ المُقامُ فَكم أعاشرُ أُمَّةً　　أَمَرت بغيرِ صلاحها أمراؤُها
ظلموا الرعيَّةَ وٱستجازوا كيدَها　　فَعَدَوْا مصالحَها وهم أُجراؤُها

(L I.55.5–6)

When we examine matters, they become clear to us:
the prince of the people is the people's servant.

إذا ما تبيَّنّا الأُمورَ تكشَّفَتْ　　لنا وأميرُ القومِ للقومِ خادمُ

(L II.260.9)

The political inclinations expressed here, especially given the *Luzūm*'s generally scathing criticism of rulers and the overall typical state of affairs (social, economic, political) for the ruled, prompted Nicholson to remark that al-Maʿarrī anticipated an important principle of modern democratic theory.[114] To al-Maḥāsinī, the verse suggested that politically al-Maʿarrī can be compared to the revolutionary thinkers who helped orchestrate the French Revolution and the downfall of Louis XIV.[115] The latter claim is likely to strike many as considerable exaggeration, inasmuch as al-Maʿarrī's antiestablishment views—although as ʿAbd al-Qādir Zaydān has rightly observed,[116] "a direct attack on kings, princes, and governors with respect to their governing styles and manner as well as their personal morals" (لقد هاجم أبو العلاء الملوك والأمراء والحكام بطريقة مباشرة في سلوكهم وأساليبهم في الحكم وأخلاقهم الشخصية)—were essentially no more than a starting point for sociopolitical and economic reform, and often expressed merely as negative epigrams or aphorisms at that. For example, L II.23.7–8, a couplet on rulers, constitutes an independent poem in its entirety. Two lines and full stop.

يَسوسُونَ الأُمورَ بغيرِ عقلٍ　　فينفُذُ حُكْمُهُم[117] ويقالُ ساسَهْ
فأُفٍّ من الحياةِ وأُفَّ مني　　ومن زمنٍ رئاستهُ خساسَهْ

They govern affairs without use of reason;
their rule is executed and said "to govern."
So fie on life. And fie on me as well
and on a time whose leadership is vile.

No really detailed, constructive scheme emerges from all the negative broadsides. There is a call (explicit or implicit) for the end of many things (e.g., poverty, oppression, class differences and inequalities, discrimination) without concrete suggestions as to how, exactly, they are to be ended and what are to be the new beginnings, the replacements for a thoroughly transformed (revolutionized?) society. As Ṭāhā Ḥusayn noted (rather apologetically) in his *Ma'a Abī al-'Alā' fī Sijnih,*[118] for all of his concerns for poverty and inequality and classicism, "Abū al-'Alā' is not a practical reformer. He is merely a poet and thinker and critic who sees evil and therefore points it out"/ولكن أبا العلاء ليس صاحب إصلاح عملي وإنما هو مفكر شاعر ناقد يرى الشر فيدل عليه. Although very much intended in al-Ma'arrī's assault on the ancient regimes—still bearing in mind al-Maḥāsinī's having felt compelled to make a comparison to the thinkers who orchestrated the French Revolution—is the clerical class and for the alleged economic as well as ideological stranglehold that they were perceived to have had on the community of believers.

بالخُلْفِ قام عمودُ الدين طائفةٌ　　　تبني الصروحَ وأخرى تحفر القُلُبا
(L.I.105.7)

Disparity is what grounds the pillar of religion.
One group thereof builds palaces; another digs wells.

Because of his acknowledgment of (1) the injustice and/or discrimination that the Shī'ah and Carmathians and Zanj rebels gave voice to and (2) the great inequality in the distribution of wealth within the Islamic commonwealth ("Zayd's wealth is due to 'Amr's poverty"—غنى زيد يكون لفقر عمرو; L II.351.1), which provoked the Carmathians and the Zanj rebels especially, al-Ma'arrī was seen by Ṭāhā Ḥusayn as being of "socialist" (اشتراكي) persuasion in terms of anger over the injustice of unequal distribution of wealth and class divisions into rich and poor, even though he remained merely "philosophical" in life orientation [i.e., not an activist] with respect to his socialist views (اشتراكي الرأي فلسفي السيرة), as evidenced by his reclusiveness, his avoidance of any significant participation in the ordinary workaday life of the society surrounding him.[119]

Perhaps the "socialist" rubric is also an exaggeration. What can't be denied, however, even allowing for genuineness in the observation that sovereigns *can* be beneficial to their subjects, is that al-Maʿarrī demanded of society's rulers and leaders that they be more humane, just, responsible, and mindful of the needs and interests of the *common* weal, the *common* subjects because it is the ruled whom the rulers are supposed to serve first and foremost *here on earth.* In this life, regardless of whether there is an afterlife of the sort vouched for by revelation, better stewardship of state and society overrides punctilious concern for the letter of the law with respect to religion.

When will there arise a leader to gain benefit for us,
so that justice be known in mountains as well as valleys?

متى يقوم إمامٌ يستفيد لنا   فتعرفَ العدلَ أجبالٌ وغيط

(L II.335.11)

Nothing in the sky and on the horizon
looms higher than a plea of one ill-treated.

لا شيءَ في الجوِّ وآفاقِهِ   أصعد من دعوةِ مظلومِ

(L II.317.10)

Al-Maʿarrī's political views, if not revolutionary, socialist, or democratic in the fullest, strictest sense of the words, are certainly populist, antiroyalist, and anticlerical; and, for all that, if nothing more, quite extraordinarily radical for an eleventh-century denizen of the Arabic Islamic world. ʿAbd al-Qādir Zaydān reminds us[120] that even the certifiably knowledgeable Arab (or culturally Arabized) disciples of the politics of Aristotle and Plato, who continued the conversation on the art and science of politics with their own time and place in mind, were manifestly less comprehensive and expansive than their Greek masters. Why? "Because just to converse on Islamic governance was tantamount to placing restrictions on the authority of the caliphs, to diminishing their power, to setting down conditions that would make many of the caliphs undeserving of the caliphate."[121] That is to say (in so many words), the certifiably knowledgeable Arab (or culturally Arabized) disciples of the politics of Aristotle and Plato were intimidated. The esteemed al-Fārābī may have *preferred* a philosopher as the supreme ruler of his virtuous city, *but with allowance* for a ruler *not* among the ranks of the philosophers so long as this ruler had a philosopher as an advisor—this as a way "to conceal a type of flattery or acceptance of the form of rule at that time, with display of respect for the rule of the caliph or the governor or the prince in the Islamic state."[122]

In instances such as the verses in L II.266.12–14 (where the "they" in all likelihood refers to the Muslim community in general)

لو يُتركونَ وهذا اللبَّ ما قبلوا　　　مَيْناً يُقالُ ولكن شالَتْ الجِذَمُ
أتَوْهُمُ بأحاديثٍ وقيلَ لهم　　　قولُوا صَدَقْتُمْ[123] وإلا أُروِيَ الخَذِمُ
وأَرهبتهُمْ جُفونٌ مِلْؤُها نُوَبٌ　　　وأَرغبتهُمْ جِفانٌ للنَّدَى رُذُمُ

Had they been left alone with their reason, they'd have disapproved
any lie that was uttered; however, the whips were raised.
Aḥādīth were brought before them, and they were told to say
"you speak the truth"; either that or swords would have been
  bloodied.
They were terrified by sword scabbards brimming with affliction,
while bowls of bounteous generosity enticed them.

Zaydān sees al-Maʿarrī as having addressed a type of "ideological terrorism" (الإرهاب الفكري) that was firmly entrenched in the Islamic commonwealth by the tenth and eleventh centuries CE.[124]

Al-Maʿarrī was a recluse. Al-Fārābī was as well, and "Whether he [al-Fārābī] was in Aleppo in the midst of the Ḥamdānid rulers or in Baghdad under the rule of the Turks, he created for himself and whatever students gathered around him a sanctuary where he could advance his own research and learning . . . and nothing else in his life concerned him; only his own learning. As for anything above and beyond that in the realm of the various sides to politics and its vices, in the realm of the affairs and desires of the world, these al-Fārābī paid no attention to."[125] Al-Maʿarrī was undeniably more blunt, and thus arguably more fearless, in his criticism of the body politic of his day. Perhaps he was supremely confident that only *the real* philosopher, the *faylasūf*/الفيلسوف, put his life in danger for free thinking: فَكَمْ سَلِمَ الجهولُ المنايا / وعوجل بالحِمامِ الفيلسوفُ ("Though it is often that the foolish are spared the fate of death, the philosopher is quick to meet his" [L II.103.1]). With respect to the risk of being reviled or berated, al-Maʿarrī seemed quite prepared to pay the piper.

I have spoken a clear truth; so go ahead,
pardon whoever tells the truth or rebuke.

نطقتُ حقّاً[126] نيّراً فأعذري　　　من نَطَقَ النَّيِّرَ أو لومي

(L II.317.6)

Learned Class

Rounding out al-Maʿarrī's views in *Luzūm* on society at large are his remarks on specific members of the learned classes of his day. In this area of concern it may be said that he focuses on two broad groups of people: those who through their education and training essentially seek to uphold and promote the principles of Islam (i.e., religion-oriented scholars and functionaries, "clerics" if you will) and those who pursue intellectual disciplines of a basically secular nature (e.g., *adab*), whom one might call the lay intelligentsia.

With respect to the former group, al-Maʿarrī explicitly or implicitly refers to, inter alia, experts in jurisprudence (*fuqahā'*/فقهاء), *ḥadīth* scholars (*muḥaddithūn*/محدثون), judges (*quḍāh*/قضاة), speculative theologians (*mutakallimūn*/متكلمون), Qur'ān reciters (*qurrā'*/قراء), preachers or moral sermonizers (*khuṭabā'*/خطباء; *wu''āẓ*/وعاظ), prayer leaders (*a'imah*/أئمة), religiously learned or pious elders in a general sense (*shuyūkh*/شيوخ), and leaders of specific religious sects or orientations and their missionaries (*a'imah; du'āh*/دعاة). This constitutes a fairly extensive referencing of the learned class. It is a good indication of the breadth of al-Maʿarrī's sociopolitical and religious commentary in *Luzūm*, even if the epigrammatic approach prevails. (The same very expansive awareness of sociopolitical and religious developments, but with even greater specificity with respect to personal names, is of course in evidence in parts of his *Epistle of Forgiveness.*)

All the aforementioned persons are subjected to rebuke or scorn in *Luzūm*, in what amounts to a sweeping indictment of the pillars of a typical Arab Islamic society during al-Maʿarrī's day. The *fuqahā'*, for example, are branded as falsifiers who denominate as "science" absurdities that they teach (L II.263.1–2). The Qur'ān serves them only as a crutch to justify their errors (L II.172.6). They acquire no real knowledge of religion (L II. 419.1). Their concluding that something is legally permissible does not guarantee that the believer who listens to and obeys them is going to escape being apprehended (L I.432.8).

The *muḥaddithūn,* by the very technique through which they seek to verify what they relate, and thus justify their credibility and esteem (i.e., the use of the *isnād* or chain of identifiable authorities on which their tradition reports are based, going back to the Prophet Muḥammad himself), reveal that what they pronounce must necessarily be unreasonable, that is, can't be confirmed by the rational mind (L II.346.9–10); what is the need for the *isnād* if what is being related is so transparently true; so obvious, self-evident, and reasonable? The *muḥaddithūn* indulge in fabrications (Lz II. 87.3; II.196.2–3). Moreover, they are inconsistent (L II.179.9–10).

The *mutakallimūn* are described as given to bombastic rhetoric that only weakens one's intellect. Their field of learning, like that of the *fuqahā'*, is really not a science at all. It has no hard and fast first principles (L I.249.5). Lashing out at Muʿtazilite theologians in particular, al-Maʿarrī calls them "galled" in religion (L II.172.5). In a very rare display of specificity in the *Luzūm*, he accuses Ibn al-Muʿallam[127] of being "a jester" (هازل) (L II.172.5), and he argues that Muʿtazilite disputatious works like *al-Mughnī*/المغني (by ʿAbd al-Jabbār al-Qāḍī)[128] and *al-'Umad*[129] are motivated by the Muʿtazilite desire to rival others for worldly preeminence (L I.249.4). L I.131.5 advises not to pay heed to Abū al-Hudhayl al-ʿAllāf,[130] and in L II.172.4, al-Maʿarrī wonders out loud who is really more sinful, the Qāḍī of Rayy (most likely a reference to ʿAbd al-Jabbār, as Nicholson has pointed out)[131] or a poet who writes erotic verse. Saying that he took no sides in the Muʿtazilite rivalry with what came to be the more normative (i.e., Ashʿarite, presumably) tendency in the theological debates of the day, but, instead, held both orientations equally irrelevant, al-Maʿarrī accused al-Bāqillānī[132] of being even more of a jester than Ibn al-Muʿallam (L II.172.5). He dismissed Ibn Kullāb[133] in the same terms used to dismiss Abū al-Hudhayl al-ʿAllāf (L I.131.5).

The *quḍāh* are excoriated in L II.297.5. In this verse, al-Maʿarrī remarked that every man who finds himself a judge renders verdicts like those of Sodom, Sodom in Arabic (*sadūm*) referring to both the notorious biblical city and its evil judge.[134] This, however, is one of the relatively few unfavorable references to the *quḍāh* in *Luzūm*. In at least one passage (L II.347.4–5), they are spoken of as genuine seekers of justice who are unappreciated by the people and beleaguered by complainers.[135]

Qur'ān reciters are accused of plying their trade either purely for money (L II.172.7) or in order to make a pretense of piety (L I.56.9). Sermonizers or preachers are called adulterers whose religion is only a ruse (see, e.g., L I.366.15; L II.196.11). They lie when they mount the *minbar* (pulpit) to speak to the faithful who have gathered for prayer (L II.90.1). The distinct manner of speaking that they affect (i.e., *saj'* or rhymed prose) does not conceal their "nonsense" (L II.90.1).

Completing his denunciation of Islamic functionaries, al-Maʿarrī equated prayer leaders with some of the revelers in taverns (L I.81.10). They have less wisdom than cooing pigeons (L I. 136. 2–4). They are less beneficial to their listeners than a Christian priest (L II. 93. 6).[136] Revered religious elders (*shuyūkh*) are not really God-fearing, upright, and pious, and they carry their prayer beads only for ostentation (L I.230. 2; 5–6). The leaders of religious sects send out their special missionaries (*du'āh*) simply to make money (L I.94.4). The missionaries themselves owe their success in winning people over to their cause to deception or fear mongering (L II.10–11).

As for the lay intelligentsia of whom al-Maʿarrī spoke in *Luzūm*, they are not nearly as well represented as religious scholars and functionaries. Only poets, men of letters in general *(banū al-adab*), astrologers/astronomers, and philosophers are shown any remarkable concern; of these, astrologers/astronomers receive by far the greatest share of al-Maʿarrī's attention.

In several short passages (L II.48.9; 49.1; 51.2–4; 97.7; 284. 1–5; 312.4–6; 415.4–9), and one long one (L II.269.3–12; 270.1–8), al-Maʿarrī described astronomers essentially as shameful quacks whose predictions or readings of the stars are absolutely meaningless (most of the above passages just referenced have been translated by Nicholson in "The Meditations," pp. 111–13). In L II.51.3, they are equated with soothsayers (*mutakahhinūn*/متكهنون) and wizards (*mu'azzimūn*/معزمون). In L II.312.4–6 and II.269, regret is expressed that the astronomers are not ostracized.

People of letters in the broadest sense are damned in L I.137.5. Al-Maʿarrī found them to be led astray and seduced by their own rhetorical flourishes, which are comparable to "the buzzing of flies." The rest of the poem from which this remark is taken is directed toward poets. Al-Maʿarrī accused them of being plagiarizers, insincere flatterers, and more harmful to their friends than enemies. He remarked that he was content to leave their disreputable and nonproductive craft to others. Touching upon poets again in L I.56.1; 55.7, he called them evil money mongers. In L I.243.8, he submitted that poetry deserved to fare badly even though the dull products it turned out manage to fare well. The connoisseurs of verse were guilty of bad speech (L I.243.9). In all these instances, al-Maʿarrī undoubtedly meant to criticize the type of versifying that he criticized in his introduction to the *Luzūm* and *Saqṭ al-Zand.*

The critique of philosophers in *Luzūm* is very brief. It includes most noticeably the allegation that, despite all of their philosophizing, the philosophers could not alter the fact that humans come to naught in their lives (i.e., life leads to no more than inevitable [and final] death (L II.74.1–2). But al-Maʿarrī also accused them of lying in everything they say about God, in their denying resurrection, and in their assertion that humankind does not really know who Adam is (by which al-Maʿarrī apparently meant that the philosophers of his day denied the normative Islamic version of humankind's coming to be; that is, God is the ultimate creator of the first human being, along with the entire world, merely by His fiat that the world, the universe and all that is in it, "be") (L I.327.18; 328.1).

Al-Maʿarrī had more in common with the philosophers than he cared to admit in *Luzūm*. It is hard to imagine the attack on them—such as it is—as being sincere. It is no more than Maʿarrian doublespeak. He was clearly inclined to the philosophers' life orientation and intellectual bent, decidedly anathema to most theologians (*mutakallimūn*) of the day (even the more rationally inclined) not to mention the jurisprudents (*fuqahā'*), the Qur'ān commentators (*mufassirūn*), the *ḥadīth* scholars, and the scholars and promoters of the religious "sciences" in general (i.e., the *'ulamā'*). That in the *Luzūm* he protests too little over the philosophers (the number of critical utterances pales in comparison to the frequency of the opprobrium heaped on the other learned segments of his society, especially the pious, religiously oriented ones) is in itself quite revealing. Unlike with the case of the theologians, al-Maʿarrī mentions none of the philosophers by name, not even al-Fārābī who, although he died in Damascus in 950 CE, between 940 and 950 at intervals lived and carried on his scholarly research and teaching in Aleppo.

In any event, al-Maʿarrī is a rationalist ("There is no imām other than *'aql* [reason]") whose major objective in *Luzūm* was to conduct a free and critical inquiry into the nature of things, to turn over in his mind and interrogate many of the principles that as *naql* (revelation) underlay the wisdom and/or understanding of reality that prevailed in the Islamic *ummah* of his day. More particularly with respect to certain tenets, it has already been observed that like the more influential philosophers of his era, such as Ibn Sīnā, al-Maʿarrī cannot be said to have seriously believed in the full, normative Islamic doctrine of resurrection (including most notably a resurrection of body as well as soul and a life in a Hereafter). Like al-Rāzī—to cite another influential philosopher who flourished a century or so before al-Maʿarrī's maturation—he speaks of humans as deriving and ascending from eternal matter, an implicit denial of the revelation-based story of Adam (a denial that al-Maʿarrī also makes explicit, as will be observed in the next part of this chapter). His entire metaphysics, as will be seen shortly, although more implicit than explicit, is redolent of the overarching system attributed to al-Rāzī by his adversaries (or evident in his own words in the few of his writings that are extant).

L I.328.2 made a point of emphasizing that everything that the philosophers of the day related about God was a lie transmitted by the Jews; in other words, the Jews were responsible for all the wrong things the philosophers were professing about God; the philosophers merely repeated these teachings. It is difficult to imagine that al-Maʿarrī seriously submitted to this viewpoint. He deemed Jewish scripture and law,

Judaism in broad terms (he gives few specificities; for the most part he speaks only in broad generalities) only slightly more unconvincing and misleading than Islam or Christianity in terms of a worldview or life orientation; which is to say, only slightly more responsible—if at all—for the woes of humanity that he enumerated. It is likelier that the real purpose of L I.328.2 was simply an attempt to absolve the philosophers (and their like) for introducing the tradition of rationalism and free inquiry in Islam; although admittedly this raises the question as to why he spared the Christians, Persians, Indians, or—last but not least—Greeks, whose philosophical and theological legacy he must have known to be the true foundation stone for the more reason-based trajectories in Arab Islamic *kalām* and *falsafah*. In any event, the Jews are rarely singled out in *Luzūm* for any particular scorn. In fact, in L II.93.4, the line just before the brazen observation that "the Christian priest is better for you than a Muslim who gives the sermon in the congregational mosque," al-Maʿarrī remarks (adding insult to injury), "Your Christian deacon hasn't oppressed with his decrees, and the Jew among you is not greedy" (وما جار شمّاسُك في حكمِهِ ولا يهوديُّكَ بالطامع).

Part IV. Humankind and the Totality of Being: Al-Maʿarrī's Perception of the Make-Up and Dynamics of the Universe

A less well-developed but nonetheless highly intriguing dimension to al-Maʿarrī's thoughts in *Luzūm* is an articulation of the elements or forces that underlie the whole of being or creation—his physics and metaphysics, so to speak. Several of the references in preceding chapters to what al-Maʿarrī says about the nature of God and humankind have offered a foreshadowing of what some of these forces or elements are. There follows below a fuller exposition, with a consideration of possible ramifications and what they add to the breadth and depth of the more philosophical moments in *Luzūm*.

As a starting point here, it can be said that al-Maʿarrī envisioned all creation as being made up of the four natural elements fire, water, earth, and air, with these four elements being eternal. This idea is advanced in the following lines of *Luzūm*:

Creation comes from four brought together: fire, water, earth,
and air.

الخَلقُ من أربعٍ مجمَّعةٍ   نارٍ وماءٍ وتُربةٍ وهوَا

(L II.424.4)

We are returned to our origins, for every living thing
has affiliation with the four eternal [elements].

نُرَدُّ[137] إلى الأُصولِ وكلُّ حيٍّ   له في الأربعِ القُدُمِ انتسابُ

(L I.91.6)

With respect to the human body, al-Maʿarrī sees earth/earthly matter as having an especially important role in relation to the other eternal elements. He emphasizes that a human's corporeal form can be considered as ultimately having originated in, and ineluctably destined to return to, eternal dust, soil, or earthly matter.

People are one genus, no one distinguished from another.
And the origin of all bodies can be traced back to dust.

والناسُ جِنسٌ ما تميَّز واحدٌ   كلُّ الجسومِ إلى التراب تَنَسُّبُ

(L I.94.6)

I consider men as exhalations and inhalations of the soil,
appearing before us but then taken back, returned to the earth.

أرى الناسَ أنفاسَ الترابِ فظاهرٌ   إلينا ومردودٌ إلى الأرضِ راجعُ

(L II.77.11)

The body, no doubt, is earthlike.

والجسمُ لا شكَّ أرضيٌّ . . .[138]

Although dust, our bodies are filled with alarm
when their departure turns them from their kinfolk.
They are frightened when sensing return to their earth
although the earth is their immediate origin.

ثُرابُ جسومُنا وهي الترابُ   إذا وَلّى عن الآلِ اْغترابُ
تراعُ إذا تُحَسُّ إلى ثراها   إيَاباً وَهْوَ منصبُها القُرابُ

(L I.90.1–2)

If my body of dust has dust as its final return,
of what good fortune is it to me that I be wealthy?

إذا كان جسمي من ترابٍ مآلهُ   إليهِ فما حَظِّي بأنِّي مُثْرِبُ

(L I.83.4)

I swear my body will remain in misfortune
until it returns to the eternal element.
And when I return to that, my bones will become
dust that will decompose throughout the epochs.

آليتُ لا ينفكُّ جسميَ في أذًى   حتى يعودَ إلى قديمِ العنصُرِ
وإذا رجعتُ إليهِ صارت أَعْظُمي   تُرْباً تهافتُ في طوالِ الأَعصُرِ

(L I.398.6–7)

If a body dies, then this earth will contain it;
if a spirit leaves it, it's in the celestial sphere.

إن ماتَ جسمٌ فهذي الأَرضُ تَخْزِنُهُ   وإن نأَت عنهُ روحٌ فَهْيَ بالفَلَكِ

(L II.158.11)

An added feature of al-Maʿarrī's four eternal elements—and especially the earth or earthly matter—is that they are clean or unblemished; that is, in and of themselves, they do not contain the seeds of a human being's corruption or moral depravity, and, furthermore, when the human being is reduced again to earthly matter, he/she is returned to a state of pristine purity, to pure, simple matter.

> Our elements are pure, without any doubt;
> so woe unto bodies that have been sullied!
>
> عناصرُنا طواهرُ غيرَ شَكٍّ　　فيا أَسفا لأَجسامٍ نَجِسْنَهْ
>
> (L II.351.6)

> Our bodies will return to the earth,
> when we rejoin the clean element.
>
> تعودُ إلى الأَرضِ أَجسادُنا　　وتَلحَقُ بالعُنصُرِ الطاهرِ
>
> (L I.419.11)

> O body of man, what has befallen you,
> you having origins in a good element?
> You're now bad: your four elements combined
> in you and you then ridiculed life in me.
> So do not be upset when death calls out
> as debility sets in, "Come! Let us go!"
> You'll become pure again upon the return
> to your origin, just like the falling rain.
>
> أَيا جسَدَ المرءِ ماذا دهاكَ　　وقد كنتَ من عُنْصُرٍ طيّبِ
> تخبَّثْتَ إِذْ جُمِعَتْ أَربعٌ　　لديكَ وأَضحكتَ في الحيِّ بي
> فلا تجْزعنَّ إِذا ما الحِمامُ　　صاحَ بوفْدِ الضنا هيَّ بي
> تصيرُ طَهوراً إِذا ما رجعْتَ　　إِلى الأَصْلِ كالمطرِ الصيِّبِ
>
> (L I.148.3–6)

Al-Maʿarrī's belief in the eternity of the four natural elements implies a denial of the normative Islamic teaching of God's having created the world in time and *ex nihilo,* out of absolutely nothing. It would seem that a corollary to the belief in the eternity of the four natural elements is a rejection of normative Islam's rigid monism, that is, the doctrine that the Creator God is the One and only Eternal to Whom alone all living things, all being, owe their existence by virtue of His creative act, His fiat "Be!" when there was nothing other than He. At the very least, there seems to be the presupposition (if not articulated suggestion) of an eternal material substratum co-eternal with the Creator and out of which He fashions or brings about all creation as humans know it. The material substratum is inert. It is the initially passive, inactive, insensate stuff out of which a human body is given form by an outside active (i.e., creative but in the sense of informing) agent.

Not infrequently in *Luzūm*, especially where mention is made of the stars, al-Maʿarrī flatly disavows a belief in the eternity of the world and hence all that this implies theologically:

My guarantee is that everything will perish—
except He who does not enter into guarantee.
I don't fancy Arcturus, or Spica Virginis,
in their creation not becoming decrepit.

ضمانِي أَن سينفدُ كلُّ شيءٍ   سِوَى من ليس يدخُلُ في الضمانِ
وما خِلْتُ السماك ولا أَخاهُ   على خلْقيهما لا يَهرَمانِ

(L II.380.7–8)

These stars have born witness to King Tubbaʿa
and subjects of Ḥimyar or Qudum who've departed.
Their stations are like the tower here on earth;
if its lifespan becomes long it collapses.

هذِي نجومٌ شاهدتْ تُبَّعاً   ومَن مضى مِنِ حميَرٍ أَو قُدُمْ
بُروجُها كالبُرجِ في الأَرضِ إن   طالَ مَداهُ في العُصورِ آنهدمْ

(L II.325.1–2)

My belief is not the eternity of the stars,
nor my school of thought the eternity of the world.

وليس آعتقادي خلُودَ النجوم   ولا مذهبي قِدَمَ العالِمِ

(L II.320.11)

There *could* be an extinguishing of the sun, burning
since the time of ʿĀd and whose fire the Sovereign lit.
If its red glow vanishes over the passing of time
it's not impossible that the firmament be razed.

يجوزُ أن تُطْفأَ الشمسُ التي وقدَتْ   من عهد عادٍ وأَذْكى نارَها المَلِكُ
فإن خبَتْ في طوالِ الدهرِ حُمرَتُها   فلا محالةَ من أَن يُنقَضَ الفَلَكُ

(L II.145.7–8)

What are we, and what are the countless creatures of the world,
to a power just part of which swallows the celestial spheres?

ما نحنُ أَم ما بَرايا عالمٍ كُثُرٍ   في قُدْرَةٍ بعضُها الأفلاكَ يبتلعُ

(L II.82.1)

Are matters that are invisible knowable—
to stars that rise with the setting of the sun?
These stars are not eternal, not to my mind.
By my life! Rather they are created in time.
Had God Who created the Pleiades so ordered,
they'd have continually fallen in the dark gloom.

فهل علمتْ بغيبٍ من أُمورٍ   نجومٌ للمغيبِ مُعَرِّداتُ
وليست بالقدائم في ضميري   لعمرُكَ بل حوادثُ مُوجداتُ
فلو أَمر الذي خَلَقَ الثرايا[139]   تهاوتْ للدجى متسرِّداتُ

(L I.166.9; 167.2–3)

God's dominion is too great for poetry or prose
or for reports that you relate by way of tradition.
This sun will grow dim in it until such time
that it ends up being like a counterfeit coin.

يَجِلُّ المُلْكُ عن نظمٍ بأَثْرٍ   وعن خَبرٍ تحدّثهُ بأَثْرٍ
وتضْؤُلُ فيه هذي الشمس حتى   تعودَ كأَنَّها دينار عثْرٍ

(L I.389.14–15)

The greatest gift of time is a but a bequeathal of gifts,
for which time, after giving to you, extends the robber's hand.
I can only imagine it as dispatching a calamity
that will unfasten the Pleiades from the dark night skies.

أَجلُّ هباتِ الدهرِ تَرْكُ المواهبِ   يَمدُّ لِما أعطاكَ راحةَ ناهبِ
وما خِلْتهُ إلا سيبعَثُ حادثاً   يحلُّ الثرايا عن جَبِين الغَياهبِ

(L I.123.9;11)

I don't think that the fates will overlook the vast sky's stars.
They'll seize Aquila, Virgo, Arcturus, Spica Virginis.
They've sought out all that's alive in space's east as well as west.

وما أَظُنُّ المنايا   تَخْطُو كواكبَ جِرْبهْ
ستأْخذُ النسر والغَفْـــــــرَ والسماكَ وتِربَهْ
فَتَّشْنَ عن كلِّ حي[140]   شرقَ الفضاءِ وغَرْبَهْ

(L I.116.14; 117.1–2)

To the rising stars there's going to be an ending
in which they'll wither away as flowers wither.

ويكونُ للزُهْرِ الطوالعِ منتهًى   يَذوينَ فيهِ كما ذوى النُوّارُ

(L I.337.11)

Notwithstanding all the above, there are several lines in *Luzūm* more or less to the opposite effect; the following, for example:

How often have the Pleiades and Ursa Minor
been seen by tribes who end up in their own soil?
People have come and gone, time after time;
yet the stars are left behind just as you see them.

وكم رأَتْ الفراقدَ[141] والثريَّا   قبائلُ[142] ثم أضحتْ في ثراها
تقضّى الناس حيلاً بعد حيل[143]   وخُلِّفتْ النجومُ كما تراها

(L II.415.12–13)

You cannot delineate the birth time of the sun.
Reason tells us that it's eternally pre-existent.

ومولدُ هذي الشمسِ أعياكَ حدُّهُ   وخبَّرَ لبٌّ أنه متقادمُ

(L II.261.4)

Praise be their Creator! I do not profess that
the stars will fade away over the passing of time.

سبحانَ خالقهنَّ لست أقو   لُ الشهبُ كابيةٌ مع الدهرِ

(L I.415.6)

They've claimed the heavenly spheres will encounter decay;
but if that's true the unclean is the equal of the clean.

وقد زعَموا الأفلاكَ يُدْركُها البِلَى   فإنْ كان حقّاً فالنجاسةُ كالطهرِ

(L I.372.11)

We shall pass away just as our forefathers did,
while time will endure just as you see it:
a luminous day and a compelling night;
one star falling away, another to be seen.

نَزولُ كما زالَ أجدادنا   ويبقى الزمانُ على ما ترى
نهارٌ يضيءُ وليلٌ يُجييُ[144]   ونجمٌ يغورُ ونجمٌ يُرا

(L I.76.12–13)

The last cluster of cited passages should probably be understood as what al-Maʿarrī really espoused, with the contradictions intended to provide at least a semblance of camouflage for belief in the eternity of the natural elements (i.e., as matter) and hence the eternity of being/the universe, a belief that because of the theological implications is extraordinarily anathema with respect to normative Islamic doctrine. A contrarian within the *ummah* might not shirk from baldly labeling peoples' leaders satyromaniacs and embezzlers (وهَمُّ زعيمِهم إنهاب مالٍ / حرامِ النهب

(أو إجلال فَرْج), from calling public officials single-minded rapacious tax collectors and alleging that kings are preoccupied with wine and music (وشانُ مُلوكهم عزفٌ وهزفٌ / وأصحاب الأمورِ جباةُ خرَج) (L I.218.5–7). But with respect to pronouncing an unequivocal belief in an eternal (i.e., uncreated) universe, even a reclusive poet in a small provincial city would have to think twice—*appear* conflicted at the very least.

In the many lines where al-Maʿarrī suggests in so many words that the stars fade out (i.e., perish in terms of burning out), there is not necessarily a contradiction because he could have meant thereby that the stars could still be considered as eternal for all intents and purposes. A plausible explanation for how this may have been the case was given by Ṭāhā Ḥusayn very early in the modern era of study of al-Maʿarrī. Ḥusayn, after noting al-Maʿarrī's many denials of the eternity of the stars and conceding that these may have been delivered to hide the poet's real belief from the general public, goes on to say:

> or else he [al-Maʿarrī] believed [with respect to the stars] in the type of eternity from which he excluded the idea of eternity proper; i.e., they [the stars] are not eternal and everlasting in and of themselves even though they have been eternal in time. That is to say, the basic foundation which Abū al-ʿAlā' assumed for his physical philosophy required him logically to assert for the stars some sort of eternity. He affirmed the eternity of matter, time, and space; thus, if the stars are matter, they are undoubtedly eternal. The widest possible reading of him [with respect to his denial of the eternity of the stars] is that he only denied their being eternal in form and movement, so that it is as though he sees them the way he sees [all] material existents, whose visible forms vary whereas their matter in and of itself is eternal and everlasting.[145]

Ḥusayn's last point—that is, that al-Maʿarrī could have held the stars to be eternal in the sense that as matter, at least, they always were and always will be, even though at some moment in time they lose their distinctive movements and shapes (forms)—becomes especially plausible in light of the several passages in *Luzūm* quoted above where al-Maʿarrī implies that individuated human bodies, too, cease to exist as we know them yet never cease to exist as raw, indestructible matter; the human species never ceases to exist as raw primal matter. At bottom, humankind is an unbroken material chain, an eternally repeated sequence of matter that takes on human form that is eventually broken down into raw or primal terrestrial matter only to be reconstituted as (human) form again—and so on *ad infinitum* inasmuch as time and space as well as matter are infinite.

There is an eternal recurrence (above and beyond the eternal perdurance of time and space) operative in this respect; and, moreover, perhaps not merely an eternal recurrence of the sort whereby a totally new body appears with a totally new soul, or whereby—along the lines of Indian or Platonic/neo-Platonic teachings on the cyclical re-emergence of the individuated soul—a new body appears with a soul that has transmigrated and reincarnated and is released, thanks to the study of philosophy, from being attached to body and thereby being compelled to endure body's endless repeated cycle of birth, life, death. Eternal recurrence *of the individuated human being*, that is, its never-ending recurrence exactly as it is, might be the purport of L II.374.12 (ما أعودُ إلى الدنيا وقد زعموا / أنَّ الزمانَ بمثلي سوف يحكيني: "I won't return to this world; but they've claimed that time will replicate me"), although there does not appear to be any elaboration on this idea by way of any similar such statements by al-Maʿarrī.

Without suggesting a necessary correlation or influence, it is worth noting in this context a passage from the neo-Platonic commentary of Simplicius (d. around 560 CE) that is paraphrasing parts of the *Physics* of Eudemus (d. around 300 BC), namely, the following:

> Some people accept and some people deny that time repeats itself. Repetition is understood in different senses. One kind of repetition may be in the natural order of things, like repetition of summers and winters and other seasons, when a new one comes after another has disappeared; to this order of things belong the movements of the heavenly bodies and the phenomena produced by them, such as solstices and equinoxes, which are produced by the movement of the Sun.
>
> But if we are to believe the Pythagoreans, there is another kind of repetition in quantity, in which the same things exist a number of

> times. That means that I shall talk to you and sit exactly like this and I shall have in my hand the same stick, and everything will be the same as it is now. This makes it possible to suppose that there exists no difference in time, because if movements (of heavenly bodies) and many other things are the same, what occurred before and what will occur afterwards are also the same. This applies also to their number, which is always the same. Everything is the same and therefore time is the same.[146]

Another meaning al-Maʿarrī may have in mind when, on the one hand, he affirms the eternity of the stars, but then, on the other hand, argues for the exact opposite, is that the stars are eternal *a parte ante* but not *a parte post.* This distinction between pre-eternity (i.e., sempiternity, eternity without beginning; in the Arabic *azal*/أزل) and posteternity or eternity "after the fact" (in the Arabic *qidam*/قدم) was made by Islamic philosophers and theologians;[147] al-Maʿarrī was aware of it as well. "God is Sempiternal"/أمّا الله فأَزليّ he remarked in *al-Fuṣūl wa al-Ghāyāt*,[148] in a passage that overall is quite enigmatic and on the surface flippantly parodic; although a passage shortly thereafter, even if at first perhaps parodic with respect to cadence and rhyme—إنَّ اللهَ هو المَلِكُ، لا يَهْلِكُ ولكِنْ فأَعتصِمْ يُهْلِكُ، والفَلَكُ بَعْضُ ما يمْلِكُ—eventually is perfectly pious in sentiment (بِرَبِّ الشَّمسِ والقمرِ، ومُنْشِئِ الشَجَرِ والثَّمَرِ، ومالِكِ القِلَّةِ والأَمَرِ، من أَفعالِ الغُمْرِ والغَمَرِ) and fleshes out what an orthodox notion of a sempiternal creator God entails, namely, a Creator eternal both before as well as after His creation of heaven and earth, and eternally sustaining all being.

In both his affirmation and denial of the stars' eternity, al-Maʿarrī never uses the word *azal* in *Luzūm* but instead *qidam*, the adjective of which (*qadīm*) he also attributes to God when intending "eternal." In *al-Fuṣūl wa al-Ghāyāt,* he uses *azalī* when intending God's eternity, as just noted (أَمّا الله فأزليّ). His being aware of the distinction between *qadīm* and *azalī* makes inconceivable that he would have posited the perpetuity of the raw (earthly) matter of human bodies but not the perpetuity of the matter of celestial bodies *a parte ante* (i.e., as being *azalī*). Al-Baṭalyūsī[149] takes L II.254.8,9 as meaning that the world according to al-Maʿarrī is *not* أزليّ *(azalī).* L II.254.8,9 reads as follows:

أراك حَسبْتَ النجمَ ليس بواعظٍ لبيباً وخِلْتَ البدرَ لا يتكلَّمُ
بَلَى فد أتانا أَنَّ ما كانَ زائلٌ ولكننا في عالم ليس يَعْلَمُ

I see that you don't reckon the star as a wise preacher,
and you imagine that the full moon does not speak.
Of course not! It has come to us that what is, ceases—
though we live in a world that is undiscerning.

The second line is clear with respect to the transitory nature of the world. How al-Baṭalyūsī connects it logically to the first seems rather enigmatic, although once that connection is made in his mind, his argument is not baseless (assuming that he is equating *qidam* with *azalī,* which seems to be the case):

آثار الصنعة والحدوث والمشهادة. . . دالّة . . . من اعتبرها على أن العالم ليس بأزلي لأن الأزلي لا تقارنها الأعراض ولا تختلف به الأحوال وكل ما ليس بأزلي ولا موصوف بالقدم فجائز عليه الزوال والعدم.

The signs of the creation and happenings in time, and observed phenomena . . . are proof —for the one who has taken them into consideration—that the world is not sempieternal. Because accidentals do not adhere to the sempieternal, and it does not have differing states. And everything that is neither sempieternal nor describable as being eternal admits of ceasing to be, of becoming non-existent.

Khalīfāt,[150] in what logically flows from his conviction that al-Maʿarrī unequivocally posited the (sempi)eternity of the One Creator God Who created the world in time, taking at face values lines in the *Luzūm* such as II.266.10 (that he quotes): وعالمٌ ظلَّ فيه القولُ مختلفاً / ومُحْدثٌ هو من ربٍّ له القِدَمُ ("There is a world, about which doctrines remain different; but it is created, in time by an Eternal Lord"), and also taking into considerations three verses attributed to al-Maʿarrī by al-Baṭalyūsī (but not found in any printed or manuscript versions of the *Luzūm* or *Saqṭ al-Zand*), namely,

يا ليتَ شعري وما ليتَ بنافعة   ماذا وراءك أَو ما أنت يا فلكُ
كم خاضَ في أمرك الأقوام وٱجتهدوا   قِدَمَ فَما أَوضحوا حقاً ولا تركوا
وقال إنّك طبع خامس نفر   عمري لقد زعموا بطلاً وقد أَفَكوا

Would that I knew—and what would be of some advantage—:
What is beyond you, or what are you, O firmament?
How often people have dealt with and labored over you!
An old affair, but they've not clarified or bequeathed a truth.
A certain group has said that you're a fifth element.
By my life! They have alleged a falsehood, told a lie.

thus goes on to conclude that the Aristotelean Fifth Element as well as the plenum that denotes that the universe is infinite were rejected by al-Maʿarrī (although he did accept the notion of the void); the body or mass of the world (جرم العالم) is finite; there is nothing "beyond" it (although this obviously involves a contradiction).

On the basis of all this, in addition to what he believes is a figurative (مجازي) use of the word قديم/"eternal" when in the *Luzūm* al-Maʿarrī uses it to describe the world and its components—a figurative sense that Khalīfāt maintains Ṭāhā Ḥusayn overlooked—Khalīfāt dismisses in one fell swoop the contention that al-Maʿarrī posited the eternity of anything—for example, matter, space, time, the world—other than God. (But Khalīfāt in "Mītāfīzīqā al-ʿUlū wa al-Ṭabīʿah" does not address al-Maʿarrī's contradictions, especially if heretical views are in the balance, and regardless of the phenomenon of dissimulation in writing.)

Zaydān[151] sees al-Maʿarrī in the *Luzūm* as unequivocally positing eternal matter (and thus eternal time and space as well, and thus per force the rejection of the doctrine of the creation of the world in time *ex nihilo* [out of nothing]: الحدوث من العدم). Aside from the probability of dissimulation, with any references to time that might cause confusion, al-Maʿarrī had in mind ordinary measurable time that is calculated on the basis of the movement of the celestial spheres—according to Zaydān.

The two forces or elements that might next be mentioned as major constituents in al-Maʿarrī's perception of the totality of being are time and space. As indicated by the long quote from Ṭāhā Ḥusayn just cited above, and pursuant to his and the present study's (and others such as Zaydān's, Bikrī's, al-Maḥāsinī's, al-ʿAlawī's, Farrūkh's) approach to al-Maʿarrī's contradictions or prevarications or ostensibly fuzzy figurative language, the weight of the evidence in *Luzūm* leans heavily toward al-Maʿarrī's having held both time and space to be eternal, with no beginning (eternal *a parte post*) and no end (eternal *a parte ante)*, like the natural elements.

With respect to time, the following citations are noteworthy:

Throughout life the two youths that are day and night
are both going and coming with evil,
like two enemies who don't know fate of death;
so how can you suppose that they pass away?
. . . .
Whenever my personage becomes free from them,
they will never be uninhabited or vacant.
. . . .
They have passed the ages as constituted,
being neither diminished nor increased
. . . .
moving forward quickly with man, not tiring,
two swords of God not glancing off their victims.

وما فتىَ الفَتَيانِ الحياةَ   يروحانِ بالشر أو يغْدوانِ
عدوّانِ ما شَعَرا بالحمامِ   فكيف تَظُنُّهما يعدوانِ
إذا ما خَلا شَبَحي منهُما   فَما يقفِرانِ ولا يَخْلُوانِ
كما خلقا غبرا في العصورِ   لا يرخصانِ ولا يغلوانِ
مُغِذّانِ بالناسِ لا يَلغُبانِ   وسيفانِ للهِ لا ينبُوانِ

(L II.389.2-3, 8, 11, 14)

If time grew senile it would be an old man,
obliged to suffer dotage and palsy.
But it has been sound and free of disease,
its body not having any paralysis
If the stars were to say, "We are a group
older than it is," they would be lying.

إن خَرِف الدهرُ فَهْوَ شيخٌ　　يُحَقُّ بالهِثْرِ والزمانَهْ
أضحَى سليماً بغيرِ داءٍ　　لم تَبدُ في شخصِهِ ضمانَهْ
إن قالتِ الشهبُ نحن رهطٌ　　أَقدَمُ منهُ فهنَّ مانَهْ

(L II.347.7–9)

As for time, it consists of uninterrupted moments.
Alas, Sa'd! Are you aware of those swallowed by it?

أَمّا الزمانُ فأَوقاتٌ مواصَلَةٌ　　يا سعدُ وَيحَكَ هل أحسسْتَ مَن بُلَعْ

(L II.81.7)

Were Gabriel to fly for the remainder of his life,
fleeing time, even then he would not exit it.

ولو طارَ جبريلٌ بَقيَّةَ عُمرِهِ　　عن الدهرِ ما ٱستطاعَ الخروجَ من الدهرِ

(L I.372.10)

Time is eternal though human communities expire.
And it's invalid to affirm a reported lie.

والدهرُ يقدُمُ والمعاشر تنقضى　　والعجزُ تصديقٌ بمينٍ يُخْبَرُ

(L I.327.17)

Wake up! Wake up, O you who have been seduced!
Your religions are a deceit of the ancients.
They wished to amass this world's vanities, and they did.
Then they died though the *sunnah* of the wicked perdured.
They'd say that the time for death of time itself has arrived,
that nothing remained of the days save a last dying breath.
They lied; they knew nothing about time's expiration.
So do not listen to the lying conjecturers.

أَفيقوا أَفيقوا يا غواةُ فإنّما　　دياناتكم مكرٌ من القدماءِ
أَرادوا بها جمعَ الحُطامِ فأَدركوا　　وبادوا ودامت[152] سُنَّةُ اللؤَماءِ
يقولونَ إنّ الدهرَ قد حان موتُهُ　　ولم يبقَ في الأَيامِ غير ذماءِ
وقد كذبوا ما يعرفونَ ٱنقضاءَه　　فلا تسمعوا من كاذبِ الزُعماءِ

(L I.64.7–10)

There's an Eternal Creator, no doubt about this,
and a time eternally passing over man.

خالقٌ لا يُشَكُّ فيهِ قديمٌ   وزمانٌ على الأنامِ تقادَمْ

(L II.326.14)

I believe in a time that is eternal, endless;
So praise be to God the Awakener, the Perfect.

أرى زمناً تقادمَ غيرَ فانٍ   فسبحان المهيمن ذي الكمالِ

(L II.227.15)

We shall pass away just as our forefathers did,
while time will endure just as you see it:
a luminous day and a compelling night;
one star falling away, another to be seen.

نَزولُ كما زالَ أَجداُدنا   ويبقى الزمانُ على ما ترى
نهارٌ يضيءُ وليلٌ يُجيئُ   ونجمٌ يغورُ ونجمٌ يُرا

(L I.76.12–13)

As for the birth of the sun, fixing it is impossible
when reason has informed us that it's eternal.
The shortest moment of time has beneath it a whole world,
and even day and night's steeds lag behind moments of time.
Once they pass, they never return, though following in their wake
are equivalents as time proceeds with a past and future.
What vanishes of it once vanished doesn't come back,
yet nothing exists without constantly renewed time.

ومولد هذي الشمس أَعياكَ حدُّهُ   وخبَّرَ لبٌّ أَنَّهُ متقادمُ
وأَيْسرُ كونٍ[153] تحتَهُ كلُّ عالمٍ   ولا تُدرِكُ الأَكوانَ جُردٌ صلادِمُ
إذا هيَ مرَّتْ لم تَعْدو وورآءَها   نظائرُ والأوقاتُ ماضٍ وقادمُ
فما آلَ منها بعد غاب غائبٌ   ولا يَعدمُ الحينَ المجدَّدَ عادمُ

(L II.261.4–7)

Contemplating space, al-Maʿarri's more consequential remarks include the following:

As for space, it has permanence; it does not vanish.
It's your time that passes that is without permanence.

أمّا المكانُ فثابتٌ لا ينطوي   ولكنْ زمانُكَ ذاهبٌ لا يثْبتُ

(L I.169.8)

Can man run away from the domain of his Lord,
to exit from a heaven that's His? And from an earth?[154]

وهل يأبْقُ الإنسانُ من مُلكِ ربّهِ   فيخرجُ من أَرْضٍ لهُ وسمآءِ

(L I.63.8)

Al-Maʿarrī nowhere contradicts his contention that space is eternal and infinite, and while he occasionally speaks of time as being neither fixed nor permanent (L I.169.8), as being "passed out of existence" by God the Eternal (L II.373.6), or as being transitory and fleeting (L II.232.12; 256.10; 354.13), his point in these instances seems quite clearly to be that time obviously has a measurable and finite component—the days and nights[155] that can be thought of as coming and going and therefore beginning and ending (i.e., having finitude)—and an immeasurable and infinite component—eternal duration, without beginning (sempiternal) as well as without end.

In further defining space and time, al-Maʿarrī says that both are "vessels" (ظرفان/*ẓarfān*)[156] (L II.354.13; 368.3) that "hold every sentient thing, but they have no perceptible color or dimension" (أحرزا كلَّ مُدْرِكٍ / وما لهما لونٌ يُحَسُّ ولا حَجْمُ) (L II.252.6); the latter remark being further proof of his believing both to be infinite. Time conceived in this way—that is, in its immeasurable and eternal aspect as contrasted to its measurable and finite one—is especially important in his thinking:

Day and night are vessels for things, of which eludes
them little yet all that they do does not cramp them.

وعاآنِ للأَشياءِ ما شذَّ عنهُما   قليلٌ ولا ضاقا بما شَمِلاهُ

(L II.397.7)

The hours of time are the vessels of temporal events.
The contents appear only after the covers are lifted.

السـاعُ آنيةُ الحوادثِ ما حَوَتْ　　　لم يبْدُ إلا بعدَ كشفِ غطائِها

(L I.67.3)

The *Luzūm*'s other noteworthy remarks on time in this framework include the following verses (the first selection of which has as the referent for "these two" two camels, as metaphor for day and night):

If a man dies or is overtaken by a killing, these two
do not make him die—in my view—nor do *they* kill him.
A power has loaded this human race onto them,
which they wouldn't bear were it not for God's might.

فإن ماتَ أَو غاداهُ قتلٌ فماهما　　　أَماتَاهُ في حكمي ولا قَتَلاهُ
يدٌ حملَتْ هذا الأَنامَ عليهما　　　ولو لا يمينُ اللهِ ما ٱحتملاهُ

(L II.397.5–6)

God has fashioned for nations and their people
two vessels: a time that elapses and space.
Time eternal doesn't know what comes to be in it;
so how can it be reproached for what has been?
The body of the living is worn out by movement;
It's thus exhausted, and yet it's wary of stasis.
. . . .
We laugh and we cry, but all is imposed by fate;
it is not time that causes us to laugh and cry.
We complain about time, but it has brought no crime.
Were it able to speak, it would complain about us.

واللهُ صيَّر للبلادِ وأَهلِها　　　ظَرْفَينِ وقتاً ذاهباً ومكانا
والدهرُ لا يدري بمَنْ هو كائنٌ　　　فيه فكيف يُلامُ فيما كانا
. . . .
والحيُّ تخْلقُ جسمَهُ حركاتُها　　　فيكلُّ وهو يُحاذرُ الإسكانا
. . . .

نبكي ونضحَكُ والقضاءُ مُسَلَّطٌ ما الدهرُ أضحكَنا ولا أبكانا
نشكوُ الزمانَ وما أتى بجناية ولو أستطاع تكلماً لشكانا

(L II.354.13,14; 16, 17; 355.1)

When it's said that "time has destroyed" something, then no more is intended than *the God of time* and time is His servant.

إذا قيلَ غالَ الدهرُ شيئاً فإنّما يُرادُ إلهُ الدهرِ والدهرُ خادمُ

(L II.261.3)

Time is not aware of what exists in it.
Why then is it disparaged in poems?

والدهرُ لم يشعرْ بما هو كائنٌ فيه فكيفَ يُذَمُّ في الأَشْعارِ

(L I.413.15)

Time's nights do not have the sense of a living thing
so as to include awareness of being fast or slow.

ليست لياليه محسَّةَ كائنٍ وُصِفتْ بسرعتها ولا إبطائِها

(L I.67.5)

Time has no reason, according to my belief.
So how can it be blamed if it yields an offense?

ولا عقلَ للدهرِ فيما أرى فكيف يُعاتَبُ إن أذنبَ

(L I.118.11)

In many of these references to time, and particularly where the Arabic *al-dahr*/الدهر is used (as opposed to *al-zaman*/الزمن or *al-awqāt*/الأوقات, for example), inexorable fate (otherwise *al-qaḍā'*/القضاء—for example) is virtually synonymous. In either case, concept is given essential substance. Time (or more accurately Eternal Time) and Fate—regardless of which is meant—are hypostatizations. *Al-Dahr* as "fate" is also understood as fate in the sense that the universe perdures and events unfold strictly according to their own laws (laws in the sense of natural processes); that is, without a divine plan (divine determinism) divinely maintained at every passing moment. Al-Maʿarrī is not an occasionalist by any stretch of the imagination.

In much of this there is the distinct ring of Mazdeanism and Zervanism as well as the more commonly recognized philosophizing of the quasi-Gnostic, neo-Platonic Abū Bakr Zakariyyā' al-Rāzī (d. ca. 923–32 CE).

> The Mazdean cosmogony tells us that time has two essential aspects: the Time without shore, without origin (*Zervan-i akanarak*), eternal Time; and limited time or "the time of long domination" (*Zervan-i deran√ xvatai*), the Αιων [aeon] in the strict sense, although eternal Time also tends to assume this name. Eternal Time is the paradigm, the model of limited time that was made in its image.[157]

> In *The Book of Celestial Wisdom*, Zervan appears as a sovereign of inalienable sovereignty. He is exempt from old age, pain, and death, and it is with his approval that Ohrmazd (Ahura Mazda) forms his own Light, this Creation, the Archangels, and the celestial Wisdom. And in this book, the figure of Destiny—Fatum (*baksh*)—shines through the figure of Zervan.[158]

> For my part [the speaker is Abū Bakr Zakariyyā' al-Rāzī, defending his views on time against Abū Ḥātim al-Rāzī, a Fāṭimid Ismāʿīlī Shīʿite thinker and missionary (dāʿī/داعي)], I profess this: Time implies absolute Time (*zaman muṭlaq*) and a limited time (*zaman maḥṣūr*). Absolute Time is eternal Duration (*mudda, dahr*): this is the time that is eternally in movement and never halts. Limited time is that which exists through the movements of the celestial spheres, the course of the sun and the heavenly bodies.[159]

After demurring on the issue of "historical filiation" with respect to Abū Bakr Zakariyyā''s philosophy, Corbin goes on to add

> But we may say this much: in its terminology, Rhazes' distinction between an absolute Time and a limited time presents a direct and lateral correspondence with the two fundamental aspects of time

> in the Mazdean cosmogony. The relation seems to have been suggested as early as the eleventh century [CE] by Ibn Hazm . . . in his critical history of religions. On the other hand, as the historian Biruni remarked, the doctrine of Rhazes borrowed from Neoplatonism in so far as it distinguished between (1) the Time (*Zaman*, Χρονος) with which number is concerned and corresponds to the definition of Aristotle; (2) Duration (*Mudda*), analogous to διαστασις της ζωης, τη, the distance that dis-tends the life of the soul . . . and finally (3), the aeon (*dahr*), the time of the eternal intelligible world. Actually, the last two aspects tend to fuse into one.[160]

The eleventh-century Iranian Ismāʿīlī Shīʿite philosopher Nāṣir-i Khusraw (who was not only a contemporary of al-Maʿarrī but also visited him in Maʿarrat al-Nuʿmān on his way to Cairo) made the distinction between *zaman* and *dahr* in the following terms:

> Time is eternity measured by the movements of the heavens, whose name is day, night, month, year. Eternity is Time not measured, having neither beginning nor end. It is the Time of Duration without end, absolute Duration.[161]

Zervan as substance was also personified (as a celestial being) in Mazdean thought, and, moreover, regarded as the supreme godhead and Creator ("Zervan, eternal Time, is a sovereign; he is Wisdom-Daena; Zervan is Destiny; Zervan is Light and Glory"; "Before anything existed, the heavens or earth or any creation . . . Zervan existed. And from the outset the name Zervan holds a twofold meaning: that of Destiny . . . and that other meaning . . . of celestial Glory or Light (*xvarr*), the keystone of Mazdean theosophy."[162]

For both Zervanites and Ismāʿīlī Shīʿites, time is cyclical. Within Absolute or Eternal Time, measurable or limited instances of time occur in successive definable cycles but do not simply end; they return to their origin, Absolute or Eternal Time.

There are no notions of successive cycles in al-Maʿarrī's thoughts on time. His measured time is linear, it ends, and, moreover, and more significant, along with absolute or eternal time—notwithstanding the fact that eternal time eternally perdures—it does not necessarily lead to, that is, culminate in, anything, for example, salvation or bodily resurrection or (least of all) illuminating and comforting epiphanies (even if the translocation of spirit is allowed for). In contrast, the eschatology involved with Eternal Time for Zervanism (and Mazdeanism generally) includes *frashokart* or the world being transfigured as a renewed creation made excellent. For Ismāʿīlī Shīʿites, seven millennia during which is transmitted the esoteric teaching of the seven imāms culminate in one final Grand Cycle of years concluded by Resurrection. And in the eternal death and rebirth of the cosmos according to the Upanishads and the Bhagavad Gita, the human soul, at least, can achieve release from *karma* and "attains mystical eternity that is union with Krishna. . . returning to this final resting place, the soul enters into immortal bliss and is not reborn."[163]

In his *Risālat al-Ghufrān*, al-Maʿarrī has some additional noteworthy (and more extended, and also in prose) observations on time, responding to his interlocutor for whom the epistle was designated, and who finds it improper that the poet al-Mutanabbī should have lodged a complaint against time inasmuch as it is only the motion of the heavenly spheres and therefore devoid of sense (intellect). Irrespective of possible filiations, here, too, if nothing else the observations underscore the enormous importance of the topics of cosmogony and theodicy in Islamic intellectual (i.e., religio-philosophical) circles and the considerable extent to which al-Maʿarrī was interested. The observations are also remarkable for some likely disingenuousness (e.g., al-Maʿarrī's comments on belief or disbelief in Time as Creator).

> As for his [al-Mutanabbī's] complaint to time about time's people, he followed in that respect the practice of the ancients. Speech damning time was so extensive [among them] that there came down [in a *ḥadīth* narration]: "Do not revile time, for surely God is time." The purport of this remark was well known, as was the fact that the inner significance is not the same as the outer; for none of the prophets—upon whom be peace—was of the habit of believing that time is the Creator or the One to be worshipped. It has come down [in the Qur'ān] "nothing but time can destroy us." Someone's saying "time is the motion of the spheres" is a pronouncement with no basis in reality. In Sibawayh's *Kitāb,* there is what indicates that

for him time is the passing of day and night. This has been associated with him in this interpretation of time as the movement of the spheres. I have defined time with a definition for which it would have been fitting to have had precedent—although I never heard it. The definition is that one says "time is a thing the smallest part from which encircles all perceptible objects." In this respect, time is something contrary to space, for the smallest part of the latter cannot encircle a thing the way vessels encircle. Whereas for the smallest unit of time [*al-kawn*/الكون], there is no avoiding the fact of its holding fast to every thing, whether scant or abundant. As for those who have said "nothing but time destroys us" and the like, not one among them has been alleged to have thereby taken up making sacrificial offerings to the celestial bodies, or claiming that the celestial bodies are rational, although that is something that some communities bequeath to others time after time.[164]

أما شكيته أهل الزمان إليه فإنهُ سلك في ذلك منهاجَ المتقدمينَ وقد كَثُرَ المقالُ في ذمّ الدهر حتى جاء [في الحديث]: لاتسبُّوا الدهر فإن الله الدهرُ. وقد عُرِفَ معنى هذا الكلام وأنّ باطِنَهُ ليس كظاهره إذ كان الأنبياءُ عليهم السلامُ لم يذهب أحد إلى أنّ الدهرهو الخالق ولا المعبود. وقد جاء [في الكتاب الكريم]: وما يُهلِكُنا إلّا الدهر. وقول بعض الناس الزمان حركة الفلك لفظ لا حقيقة له. وفي كتاب سيبَوَيْهِ ما يدلّ على أن الزمان عنده مُضيُّ الليل والنهار.وقد تُعُلّقَ عليه في هذي العبارة. وقد حددْتهُ حدّاً ما أجدَرَه أن يكون قد سُبِقَ إليه إلّا أني لم أسمعه وهو أن يُقال الزمان شيء أقلُّ جزءٍ منه لا يمكن أن يشتمل على جميع المدرَكاتِ وهو في ذلك ضد المكان لأنّ أقلَّ جزءٍ منه لا يمكن أن يشتمل على شيءٍ كما تشتملُ عليه الظروف فأما الكونُ فلا بدَّ من تَشَبُّثِهِ بما قلَّ وكَثُرَ والذين قالوا وما يهلكنا إلّا الدهر وغير ذلك من المقال ... لن يُدَّعَ أنَّ أحداً منهم كان يُقَرّبُ للأفلاك القَرَابين ولا يزعمُ أنها تَعْقِلُ وإنما ذلك شيءٌ يَتَوارثُه الأُمَمُ في زمانٍ بعد زمان.

From all of this, duly noted by him, Nicholson insightfully summed up al-Maʿarrī's thoughts on absolute or eternal time in the following terms:

Time, being independent of the revolution of the celestial spheres, does not affect the course of events, which (indirectly, at any rate) is determined by the ever-changing position of the planets relatively to one another. Time brings nothing to pass; it is, so to speak, the

> neutral, unconscious atmosphere of all action and suffering. Man sins, by freewill or by fate: Time cannot sin, and therefore ought not to be reviled.[165]

> Time is not a conscious agent which can be described as moving quickly or slowly: it is the passive environment in which events appear.[166]

In the estimation of Khalīfāt,[167] time in al-Maʿarrī's thought may also be seen as perpetual movement, perpetual flux, a continuum of constant uninterrupted becoming although the becoming "movement" is the movement of being/existence from one stage to another, into new shapes or compositions, as in the "movement" of plants as they grow from seed to sprout to mature tree in blossom, or humans "moving" from fertilized ovum to newborn to child and adolescent and eventually reproducing (and thus the repetition of the "movement" ad infinitum). It is the perpetual flow (flux) of Heraclitus. The movement is not linear spatial movement from place to place. But it *is* within time and space—which are in any event *mental* categories or concepts by which things are arranged in human conscientiousness. The movement does not require the Aristotelean mover (who himself is unmoved) because "the movement of things is established in the type of composition that God gives the world with its creation" (فإن حركة الأشياء تتأسس على نوعية التركيب الذي أعطاه الله للعالم عند تكوينه). The awareness of becoming (which is change in motion in the sense of progressing) is a qualitative (as opposed to quantitative) awareness. One cannot be conscious of quantitative changes except when the changes take on a qualitative nature.

One final set of remarks in *Luzūm* on the nature of time begs pondering.

> Light, our thoughts tell us, is a temporal creation.
> And the Primordial Principle is Dark Time.
>
> والنورُ[168] في حُكْمِ الخواطر مُحْدَثٌ　　　والأوَّليُّ هو الزمانُ المظلمُ
>
> (L II.270.13)

> Thinking perceives that light has been created in time,
> that the origin of fixed bits of time is their darkness.

يرى الفكرُ أَنَّ النورَ في الدهرِ مُحْدَثٌ   وما عُنْصُرُ الأَوقاتِ إلا حُلوكُها

(L II.144.9)

Just as evil is an original thing in humans,
light is created in time and in darkness.

وكأنّ الشرَّ أصلٌ فيهِمُ   وكذا النورُ حديثٌ في الظُّلَمِ

(L II.323.10)

It is not entirely clear what al-Maʿarrī intends here. The paucity of remarks of this nature leaves little to work with. However, a number of possibilities come to mind, constituting what may be described as the poet's attempt at constructing his own rudimentary metaphysics of light bound up with his cosmogony. First of all, he may be referring again to his belief that there are two types of time, the eternal—and which he now equates with darkness—and the finite or measurable—which he now equates with light. Second, having posited an eternal and infinite time that is not defined in terms of the motion of the heavenly spheres or celestial bodies, he could be suggesting that one must inevitably posit a type of existence or Being that was prior to the stars (stars as form as opposed to raw matter) and hence is light, inasmuch as the stars are the source of light, imbued with it. Yet because this type of existence or Being is still thought of as "in" time (in the sense of being prior to the stars coming into formation), yet lightless (because the light comes with the stars coming into formation), it has to be thought of as Dark Time, and as that which is the oldest of all things.[169] Third, al-Maʿarrī may have embraced a dualistic cosmogony bound up with (1) light and darkness, somewhat akin to that of the Mazdeans (Zoroastrians) in which good is identified with light (and Ohrmazd) and bad with darkness (and Ahriman) and (2) the belief that all being is essentially an interplay or (more accurately) internecine struggle between these two forever diametrically opposed forces. Unlike Zoroastrian cosmogony, however, al-Maʿarrī would have envisioned Light/Good as issuing from Darkness/Evil and hence being subsequent to it in time; not *vice versa*.[170]

Supporting the thesis that al-Maʿarrī may have embraced a dualistic cosmology is the fact that a pronounced dualism (more specifically of opposites in tension or of counterintuitive realities) undergirds all the

Luzūm: man and God, man and woman, life and death, free will and determinism, body and soul, revelation and reason, good and evil; to cite some of the more transparent and ubiquitous examples. Gnostic as well as Mazdean cosmology may have had an influence in this respect.

With respect to primordial Darkness, there is also the possibility of the ancient Greek influence. "In ancient Greek cosmogonies. . . usually Darkness of Chaos begets Light or Day through a complex, arbitrary and sometimes awesome procedure."[171]

The Planets

In the passage from his "The Meditations of Maʿarrī" just cited above, Nicholson was accurate in his observations about the role of the planets in al-Maʿarrī's concept of the universe (a role foreshadowed earlier in this study). The planets are thus another important factor in what Ṭāhā Ḥusayn refers to as al-Maʿarrī's "physical" philosophy. They are no less significant than the four natural elements, time, and space. As al-Maʿarrī himself says, in an attempt to reduce all creation/the universe to its lowest common components, and, in quasi-Pythagorean (as well as Gnostic) fashion, with a concern for numbers that they represent (four natural elements; seven planets; twelve zodiacal stations):

These human bodies are barren dust,
so our boasting and mirth are stupid.
A body derived from four is supervised
by seven properly arranged in twelve.

هذه الأجسامُ تربٌ هامدٌ　　فمن الجهلِ ٱفتخارٌ وأَشَرْ
جسدٌ من أَربعٍ تلْحظها　　سبعةٌ راتبةٌ في اثني عَشَرْ

(L I.422.4–5)

I see four giving support to seven—
and these latter residing in twelve.

أرى أربعاً آرَزَتْ[172] سبعةً　　وتلك نوازلُ في اثني عشرْ

(L I.426.10)

Which is to say, it is al-Maʿarrī's view that "in their coming together and splitting up, the [natural] elements are obedient to the influence of the motion of the stars."[173]

In this respect, Nicholson was also correct in noting that "as to the influence of the stars, [al-Maʿarrī] shares the belief which prevailed among his contemporaries."[174] To be more precise in this particular context, one might add that al-Maʿarrī is especially redolent of the Muslim neo-Platonists, who also believed that the process whereby elements combine, revert back to their original separate identities, and then recombine (and hence generate and sustain being), is subject to the motion of the heavenly bodies, at least as ultimate physical cause in the chain of cause and effect.[175] However, unlike neo-Platonists, al-Maʿarrī seemed to hold that the planets and other celestial bodies have neither soul nor intellect. He questioned this view (rhetorically and ironically), caustically satirized it, or denied it altogether. With regard to the stars having intellect, he added with acerbic humor that surely they've lost it (as far he is concerned) if in fact they ever had it.

The higher world, in the view of some communities,
is like the lower one here: it can both sense and know.
Thus, some men have alleged about its planets
that they have intellects and are able to speak.
So then: are the stars like us in their religions?
Unable to agree and thus Jews or Muslims?
Perhaps a celestial Mecca is like Mecca on earth,
and by her the peaks of Naḍād, Yadhbul, and Yalamlam?

العالمُ العالي برأي معاشرٍ   كالعالم الهاوي يُحِسُّ ويعلمُ
وزعمَتْ رجالٌ أنَّ سيَّاراتِهِ   تَسِقُ العقولَ وأنَّها تتكلَّمُ
فهل الكواكبُ مثلُنا في دينها   لا يتفقنَ فهائدٌ أو مسلمُ
ولعلَّ مكةَ في السماءِ كمكة   وبها نضادِ ويَذْبُلٌ ويَلمْلَمُ

(L II.270.9–12)

If it's true that the luminous stars are sentient,
what do you deny them of love and marriage?
Perhaps Canopus, who is the stallion among the stars,

has married a daughter of Arcturus—and paid the dowry.
People say that stars above us proceed as proceed
human beings on earth, secretly or in the open.
So I wish I knew: Are they terrified of death?
Bowing piously in prayer at night or noon?

وإنْ صحَّ أَنْ النيّراتِ مُحِسَّةٌ   فماذا نكرتُـمْ من وِدادٍ ومن صِهْرِ
لعلَّ سهيلاً وهو فحلُ كواكبٍ   تزوَّجَ بنتاً للسِمّاكِ على مَهْرِ
يقولونَ تأْتي فوقَنا مثلُ ما أتى   بنو الأرضِ في حال السِرارِ أو الجهرِ
فَيا ليتَ شِعري هل تُراعُ من الردى   وتركعُ نسكاً بالعشاء وبالظهرِ

(L I. 372.13–16)

Are the shooting stars of night dead or are they sentient?
Without intellect? Or ingrained with both sense and intellect?

أَمَيِّتَةٌ شُهْبُ الدجى أَم مُحِسِّةٌ   ولا عقلَ أم في آلِها الحسُّ والعقلُ

(L II.171.2)

Do the rising moons possess intellect,
so that they know when they are eclipsed?
Do they hear or see or suffer distress?
Do they smell? Have the sense of taste?

فهل لطوالعِ الأقمارِ عَقْلٌ   فتعلَمَ حين يُدْرِكُها الخُسوفُ
أَتسمعُ أو تعاينُ أو تعاني   بلآءً أو تَذَوَّقُ أو تَسوفُ

(L II.102.12–13)

Glory be their Creator. I do not profess that
the stars will fade away over the passing of time.
No. But I do wonder, are they endowed with reason
by which they can discern the dirty from the clean?

سبحانَ خالقهنَّ لستُ أُقو   لُ الشهبَ كابيةٌ مع الدهرِ
لا بل أُفكِّرُ هل رُزِقْنَ حجًى   نجساً يَمزْن به من الطُهرِ

(L I.415.6–7)

Have stars that sink to the place where they set
learned anything about matters unseen?
. . . .
It has been claimed that they have intellects
(may the decrees of God be confirmed!);
that some have speech; and that among them too
are enviers and envied just like us.

فهل عَلِمَتْ بغيبٍ من أُمورٍ   نجومٌ للمغيبِ مُعَرِّداتُ
. . . .
وقد زعموا بأَنَّ لها عقولاً   وأَقضيةُ المليكِ مؤَكدَّاتُ
وأَنَّ لبعضها لفظاً وفيها   حواسدُ مثلنا ومُحسَّداتُ

(L I.166.9; 167.8–9)

Some men have said, "The intellects of the stars are ample."
If that were true, we'd respond, "Senility has touched them."

قالتْ رجالٌ عقولُ الشُهْبِ وافرةٌ   لو صَحَّ ذلك قُلْنا مَسَّها خَرَفُ

(L II.97.6)

In denying that the stars have intellect or soul, al-Maʿarrī distances himself from the neo-Platonists, who in their doctrine of eternal emanation as an explanation for the origin of the universe speak of a "soul of the outermost heaven" and a series of intellects that in essence generate and dominate the workings of the spheres of the universe and, ultimately, life here on earth.[176] It would seem that al-Maʿarrī attributes to the stars a purely natural (i.e., physical/mechanistic) *modus operandi* and influence, not one that emanates from either will or intelligence. It has as its cause none other than natural forces, the presence of which disseminates both in the stars as well as other entities of the observable world.[177]

In close proximity to many of his remarks on time, space, the celestial bodies, and the four natural elements, al-Maʿarrī in the *Luzūm* spoke of God as an additional and most important element to be incorporated into his understanding of the origin and functioning of the universe. Proceeding from his often expressed view of Him as Eternal and Omnipotent Creator, he could —and did—suggest that time, space, the stars, and the natural elements are all ultimately subject to His power and owe their existence to His fiat, so that whatever powers of causality they have are at best secondary.

If a man dies or is overtaken by a killing, day and night
do not make him die—in my view—nor do *they* kill him.
A power has loaded this human race onto them,
which they wouldn't bear were it not for God's might.

فإِنْ ماتَ أَو غاداهُ قتلٌ فماهما　　أَماتاهُ في حكمي ولا قَتَلاهُ
يدٌ حملَتْ هذا الأَنام عليهما　　ولو لا يمينُ اللهِ ما ٱحتملاهُ

(L II.397.5–6)

The shortest unit of time is the occurring moment
arranged by God's rule to vanish in other moments.

وأَقْصَرُ الوقتِ كونٌ ثم ينظِمُهُ　　حكْمُ القديمِ فيفنيهِ بأَكوانِ

(L II.373.6)

When it's said that "time has destroyed" something, then no more
is intended than *the God of time* and time is His servant.

إذا قيل غال الدهرُ شيئاً فإنما　　يرادُ إلهُ الدهرِ والدهرُ خادمُ

(L II.261.3)

The props of our world are the natures of four elements
made to stand as supports to Him who is above us.
And God has fashioned for nations and their people
two vessels: a time that elapses, and space.

أَركانُ دنيانا غرائزُ أَربعٍ　　جُعِلَتْ لمن هو فوقنا أَركانا
والله صيَّرَ للبلادِ وأَهلِها　　ظَرفَيْن وقتاً ذاهباً ومكانا

(L II.354.12–13)

A creation has consoled humans with grace,
ascribed to the Almighty by experts in such.

He is a king Who has fashioned the heavens,
with the moon unto Him like the nimble soldier.

صَنْعَةٌ عَزَّت الأنامَ بلطفٍ   وعَزَتْها إلى القديرِ العوازي
مَلِكٌ أَنشأَ السمواتِ فالبد   رُ لديه في صورة الجِلوازِ

(L I.435.14–15)

They say, "There's a creation that comes from seven planets."
Although it really comes only from the Lord of the stars.
When these mounted escorts stir raising clouds of dust,
it's their Mover who causes this to come into view.

يقولونَ صُنْعٌ من كواكب سبعةٍ   ما هو إلا من زعيم الكواكبِ
إذا رفعتْ تلك المواكبُ قَسطلاً   فرافِعُهُ للعين مُجْري المواكبِ[178]

(L I.122.7; 123.1)

Don't you realize that the stars in their orbits move
by the power of a sovereign who is unmoved?[179]

أَما ترى الشُهبَ في أَفلاكِها ٱنتقلت   بقدرةٍ من مليكٍ غير منتقلِ

(L II.219.13)

Let Him who in His omnipotence has fashioned forms
dissolve them; for He is the Lord of time and eternity.
The smallest atom becomes but a slave unto Him,
as the sun and moon are counted among His servants.

وخلِّ من صوَّر الأشباحَ مقتدراً   يحلُّها فَهْوَ ربُّ الدهرِ والقِدَمِ
وتصبحُ الذَّرَّةُ الصغرَى له أَمَةً   والشمسُ والبدرُ معدودَيْنِ في الخَدَمِ

(L II.301.8–9)

Four elements from the Lord's creation put us together;
transcending these—as dominion is God's—is a fifth.

ويجْمَعُنا من صَنْعَةِ الربِّ أَربعٌ   ومن فوقِها والملك للهِ خامسُ

(L II.6.8)

These views are inconsistent with *Luzūm*'s views on the eternity of matter, time, and space, which imply that God is only coeternal with them and that their role in the origin and duration of the universe is virtually as indispensable as His. But there is no reason not to believe that what one has here are examples of the sort of irony and paradox so typical of *Luzūm* as a whole. A short poem (II.179.1–3; the importance of which did not escape the attention of Nicholson[180] or, as already observed in this study,[181] al-ʿAlawī) states rather unequivocally that the notion of God the Creator being beyond or outside of space and time—that is, as being prior to them, and furthermore separated from them—is absurd in al-Maʿarrī's mind (which position alone prompted al-ʿAlawī to pronounce the poet an atheist):

You have said, "We have a wise Creator."
"True," we have responded. "We say the same."
You claim He transcends space and time; do say then
that this is talk that has something concealed in it
whose gist is that on this point we're brainless.

قُلتُمْ لنا خالقٌ حكيمٌ   قلْنا صدقتُم كذا نقولُ
زعمتمُوهُ بلا مكانٍ   ولا زمانٍ ألا فقولوا
هذا كلامٌ له خَبيٌّ   معناه ليست لنا عقولُ

Exactly how, then, does God fit into al-Maʿarrī's cosmogony (setting aside for the moment the possibility that he was actually an atheist)? What is God's precise relationship to time, space, and matter in the origin and sustenance of the universe, and in what way can he be spoken of as Creator?

In the first place, it would seem that He is simply one of four conditions or entities—the others being space, time, and the four natural elements or matter—all of which must be postulated in order to explain the coming-to-be and duration of the universe and all that is in it.

Second, since all four of these conditions are eternal, if God is spoken of as eternal, He is not the One Eternal. Co-existing with Him in eternity are space, time, and the four elements, including most important of all indestructible raw matter.

Third, although one is on less solid ground here because of a lack of detail and elaboration, it would seem that al-Maʿarrī envisions God's role as Creator (again setting aside for the moment the possibility that al-Maʿarrī was an atheist) as an extremely limited or restricted one. For one thing, He is a necessary but not a sufficient cause for creation (one of the ramifications of which is that God is not perfect, omnipotent). Furthermore, once the world as we know it came to be, His role was not to intervene perpetually through His Will or Power to guarantee that the world endures or goes on functioning. He *might* be a First Cause or Prime Mover (notwithstanding Khalīfāt's rejection of this notion),[182] but even if that were conceded, He has His secondary causes and movers that in and of themselves maintain or superintend the dynamics of the existing world, namely, space, time, matter, and the stars and planets, all or which in turn interact according to their own (i.e., intrinsic) eternal laws (and not by way of the interaction of atoms whose every movement and configuration, not to mention existence and duration from one moment to the next, is due to God's creative and perpetual sustaining powers). And of course, following this logic, God can't be said to create—whatever the modality of His creation—out of nothing.

A fourth and final point that might be added here (still momentarily setting aside the possibility of atheism) is one that emerges not so much from the lines quoted above with respect to creation, but from several others. This point is that Omnipotent Creator God must be seen as having tolerated or overseen, if not actually undertaken Himself, a creation of the world at random and in the fullest sense of the word: one that was without careful attention and was haphazard, aimless, ateleological.

Understandably, this point is not particularly explicit in *Luzūm*; but clearly it seems to be the deeper and broader intent of the lines beneath, not to mention as well the *Luzūm*'s many lines that express a general bitterness over the world's palpable misfortunes, cruelties, and absurdities:

A sphere appears as if time amuses itself with it.
Mighty is Guardian God since He made it a sphere.

بدَتْ كُرَةٌ كأَنَّ الوقتَ لاهٍ　　بها عزَّ المهيمنُ إذ كراها

(L II.417.6)

I think of my time, in both its being and its corruption,
as a baby who with earth's soil is toying and dawdling.

أَظُنُّ زماني كونَهُ وفسادهُ   وليداً بِتربِ الأَرضِ يلهو ويعبَثُ

(L I.199.7)

We hope from God generosity after want,
light after darkness in all of our affairs.
To Him are the kingdoms. The proofs have appeared—
to those who think—on banners as well as flags.
Good fortune without effort, nay, all that God bestows,
is like the drawing of lots by gamblers in games of chance.

نرجو من الله رحباً إِثْرَ ضَيِّقَةٍ   من الأُمورِ ونوراً بعد إظلامِ
له الممالكُ قد بانتْ دلائلُها   للمفكّرينَ براياتٍ وأَعلامِ
والحظُّ عن[183] غير سَعْي بل[184] مواهبُهُ   كأَنَّها ضَرْبٌ أَيسارٍ بأَزلامِ

(L II.307.8–10)

If you are told "Fear God your Lord," then say "Yes, to be sure.
The seven planets appear like child's play in the dirt."

إذا قيلَ لك ٱخشَ اللـ   ـهَ مولاكَ فقلْ آرا
كأَنَّ الأَنجمَ السبعـ   ـةَ في لُعبةِ بُقّارا

(L I.71.6–7)

The many lines in *Luzūm* where al-Maʿarrī speaks of the futility of life and wonders why he and others were created in the first place suggest the very same idea of creation as frivolous and purposeless. Together with the verses just quoted, they argue for taking as supremely ironic his remark that God is far above playing or busying himself with trivial things (L I.203.3).

Nicholson in his discussion of al-Maʿarrī's cosmogony emphasized the obvious traces of the metaphysics of Abū Bakr Zakariyyā' al-Rāzī.[185] This is one of the more meaningful, very specific comparisons that might be made between al-Maʿarrī and other thinkers of the heritage within which he worked. Like al-Maʿarrī, al-Rāzī (at least according to those—although mostly adversaries—who quote him on these topics) also spoke of space, time, matter, and God the Creator (Demiurge/*al-Bāri'*/البارى) as co-eternal principles that account for and explain our universe: creation comes about when the Creator gives form to previously formless matter which, because it is eternal and in need of a place in which to exist, desires a place to exist; which in turn also presupposes the need for an eternal space, a Creator, and an eternal time in which creation can occur. Al-Rāzī furthermore spoke of a definite distinction between measurable or finite time and immeasurable or infinite time; and the latter he conceived of as preceding, and being entirely independent of, measurable time, the creation of the world, and the movement of the stars and heavens. He made a distinction between universal and particular space and posited that the former is entirely detached from body, allowing—and indeed arguing for—the existence of a void. Al-Maʿarrī speaks similarly when on the one hand he mentions the impossibility of one's escaping space and time (as already observed, in his thought even God cannot be conceived of as beyond space and time, in the sense that both are coterminus with Him), while on the other hand (e.g., in *Risālat al-Ghufrān,* as already noted), he makes note of a space that can be divided up and boundaried into progressively smaller units associated with bodies.

> Time is a thing the smallest part from which encircles all perceptible objects. In this respect it is something contrary to space, for the smallest part of the latter cannot encircle a thing the way vessels do [i.e., cannot encircle—contain—all perceptible objects].

Although al-Rāzī like al-Maʿarrī was not a believer in the creation of the world *ex nihilo*, he was at the same time not a subscriber to the emanationist doctrine of the neo-Platonists; and he also conceived of God's creation as having come at random.[186]

Therefore, it is likely that al-Maʿarrī was influenced by al-Rāzī either directly or indirectly and that separately (i.e., not as formal disciple explicitly committed to upholding the legacy of his master), he strove to articulate a metaphysics that he intended to be virtually the same if laid out in greater detail (and with greater clarity) with respect to the technical terms of the *falsafah*. The shared disregard for—indeed rejection of—prophecy and prophets also suggests a connection. Although in that respect, Ibn al-Rāwandī's views must have exercised an influence (notwithstanding al-Maʿarrī's immoderate denunciation of him in *Risālat al-Ghufrān,* only to be expected given al-Rāwandī's by-then notoriety as an arch-heretic who was against prophecy and revelation). Mere coincidence in all these matters cannot be ruled out, but it seems highly unlikely, especially with respect to al-Rāzī, given his enormous resonance in Islamic thought in his lifetime and for centuries beyond.

In any event, it needs to be pointed out how al-Maʿarrī may be said to differ from al-Rāzī. Al-Rāzī has a fifth eternal principle of existence or being, the universal soul.

> According to him, the Soul, which was originally living, was nonetheless impetuous and foolish. Becoming enamored of matter, it sought to be united to it and to endow it with form so that it might partake of bodily pleasures. In view of the recalcitrance of matter and its resistance to the in-forming activity of the Soul, however, God was compelled to come to its assistance and create this world, with its material forms, in order to enable the Soul to satisfy its vile urge to partake of material pleasures for a while. In the same manner, God created man and imparted Reason to him from "the essence of His divinity" so that Reason might eventually rouse the Soul from its earthly slumber in man's body and remind it of its genuine destiny as a citizen of the higher (intelligible) world and of its duty to seek that world through the study of philosophy. To the extent that the Soul becomes addicted to this study it will be able to achieve its salvation and regain the intelligible world, whereby it will be released, as the old Pythagoreans put it, from the "wheel of birth." Such individual souls as have not been purified by the study of philosophy, however, will continue to linger in this world until they discover the therapeutic virtue of philosophy and turn toward the intelligible world. When this ultimate goal has been reached, and the human Soul, guided by Reason, has been restored to its true abode, this "lower world" will cease, and matter, which had been forcibly chained to form, will return to its original condition of absolute formlessness and purity.[187]

Soul for al-Maʿarrī is certainly vile once it is joined to body, and he sometimes suggests (in Platonic fashion) that it existed prior to being joined to body and will survive it after death and journey to a heavenly or celestial abode. But otherwise his remarks on the soul have little in common with those of al-Rāzī as sketched above, particularly as concerns metempsychosis and the soteriology bound up with it. For al-Maʿarrī, the use of reason or intellect can mitigate folly and unhappiness (and worse) here on earth; but it is not a panacea, and it hardly lead's to salvation of the soul in a celestial pleroma-like abode of comforting intelligibles or beatific vision.

Al-Rāzī's God is specifically thought of as *al-Bāri'*/البارى or the Arabic equivalent of the Demiurge, albeit the Platonic-inspired supreme creative being, not that of the Gnostics, that is, the subordinate being whose creative act is the source of evil in the cosmos and thus deserving of condemnation and vilification. Al-Maʿarrī speaks of a creator God (الخالق) but not of the Demiurge/البارى; although given the embrace of the Rāzian five eternal principles and the relationship therein of soul to matter and form, al-Maʿarrī when inclined to think about the possibility of a Creator God, like al-Rāzī may in fact have envisioned God less the *creator* of creation (in the sense of directly giving form to things) than the *enabler* (i.e., allowing/approving that soul join with matter and give form to it, which in turn allows for the generation of the entire universe).

Another elucidating comparison that might be made between al-Maʿarrī's cosmogony and that of other early Islamicate thinkers is the one between it and that of the *dahriyyah*/الدهرية or "materialists." It is not always easy to ascertain to whom, precisely, this appellation applies or does not apply, since it could be used rather loosely in the standard chronicles, but it would seem to include first and foremost those who (1) believe in the eternity of time (i.e., *dahr*/الدهر taken as time in the absolute, eternal time that is not measured in terms of years or days or hours) and the eternity of coterminus matter; and (2) explain all that transpires in the world in natural or physical/mechanistic terms, as phenomena resulting from natural laws (e.g., cause and effect), including those behind the movements of the heavenly spheres, which explains why *al-dahriyyah* is sometimes used, for good reason, as shorthand for *ilḥād* (إلحاد) or atheism.[188] What we have examined above of al-Maʿarrī's cosmogony strongly suggests that he was of the same persuasion. Especially relevant in this regard are his remarks to the effect that coming-to-be, being, and ceasing-to-be with respect to all existing things may be thought of as no more than simply a continually reoccurring, mechanistic process of the composition and decomposition of matter and the four natural elements.

As corollaries to their teaching of the eternity of time and matter, and to their naturalistic/mechanistic view of phenomena in the world, atheism as well as the repudiation of the postulates of revealed religion (e.g., divinely revealed laws, a future life, and divine retribution) were doctrines espoused by most of the *dahriyyah.*[189] Because of the latter, it is also useful to think of affinities between al-Maʿarrī and the *dahriyyah.* As for the former—that is, the atheism—one might be inclined to take it as the basis for expressing some hesitation in categorically declaring al-Maʿarrī as a follower of the *dahriyyah.* There is no *conclusive* evidence that he expressed a flat denial God's existence regardless of what he thought about His essence or nature or role as Creator (although concerning these there is arguably an agnosticism in evidence if not misotheism as well). However, some of the *dahriyyah* apparently conceded the existence of God while denying Him any significant role in creation by attributing the origin of the world to "the random concurrence of atoms whirling about in space."[190] If one were to read in place of "the random concurrence of atoms whirling about in space" the words "the random concurrence of the four elements or matter," this notion would not be an unlikely possibility for some of what al-Maʿarrī intended with his remarks pertaining to God, time, space, and the four elements and their role relative to one another in the process of creation; for example, that God exists—for whatever reasons or purposes—but the origin, duration, and happenings of the world, of the universe, are attributable to principles or forces not predicated of Him or His essence or His being. In sum, the bracketing of al-Maʿarrī with the *dahriyyah,* even if a direct link can't be established, and even if he is not to be regarded as an atheist, has considerable validity and is of help heuristically.

The many lines from *Luzūm* that have been quoted in this section of chapter 4 nearly exhaust al-Maʿarrī's remarks of significance on his views of the cosmos. An additional cluster, however, should not be overlooked before bringing the section to a close, especially since these have not failed to catch the attention of previous discreet studies (e.g., Nicholson's, Ḥusayn's, Zaydān's).

Whenever I become laid flat in the womb of the earth,
I will then be free of my maladies and diseases.
Perform your ablutions with my dust: perhaps doing so
after my extinction will accommodate my desires.
And if by God's decree I am made into pottery
to serve in ritual cleansing I'll be grateful and happy.
Substances are brought together by an amazing power—
then separated so that they become like accidents.

إذا غدوْتُ ببطنِ الأَرضِ مضطجعاً   فثمَّ أَفقدُ أَوصابي وأَمراضي
تَيَمّمُوا بتُرابي علَّ فعلكُمُ   بعد الهمودِ يوافيني بأَغراضي
وإِنْ جُعلْتُ بحكمِ اللهِ في خَزَفٍ   يقضي الطهورَ فإني شاكرٌ راضي
جواهرٌ أَلَّفَتْها قُدْرَةٌ عجبٌ   وزايلَتْها فصارت مثلَ أَعراض

(L II.61.2–5)

Adam is not, for those who believe in reason, one;
rather, according to logic he is multiple Adams.

وما آدمٌ في مذهبِ العقلِ واحداً   ولكنَّه عندَ القياسِ أَوادِمُ

(L II.261.9)

There's an Eternal Creator, no doubt about this;
and also a time eternally passing over man.
It's feasible that the Adam of all of this
was preceded by one Adam after another.

خالقٌ لا يُشَكُّ فيهِ قديمٌ   وزمانٌ على الأَنامِ تقادَمْ
جائزٌ أن يكونَ آدمُ هذا   قبلهُ آدمٌ على إثْرِ آدمْ

(L II.326.15)

At first glance, it appears that in the first passage quoted above, al-Maʿarrī might be subscribing to a contingent metaphysics that by his time came to be associated with Muslim theologians whose speculations on such issues—if not entirely pleasing to religious scholars who eschewed speculation altogether and relied on strict constructions of revelation (without asking "How" or "Why" where conundrums arose)—were at least less discomforting than the musings of the *falāsifah* (philosophers).

> The cardinal tenet of this metaphysics was that everything in the world (defined as everything other than God) consisted of two distinct elements, atoms (or indivisible particles) and accidents (*a'rāḍ*) . . . The most important characteristic of those accidents . . . was their perishable nature. The Mutakallims, as a whole, held that accidents do not endure for two moments.[191]

Consequently, the Mutakallims (المتكلّمون) also argued that the existence of things from one moment to another, not to mention their coming-to-be in the first place, depended upon the direct and constant intervention of God's power. Things continue to exist, in their view, only so long as God continues to create in them the accidents that cause them to exist.[192] Similarly, the atoms in which the accidents inhere are continually created by God and only endure by virtue of the accident of duration created in them by God.[193]

Nicholson took al-Maʿarrī to mean in the passage just quoted about "accidents" that "bodies consist of eternal and indestructible substances (elements) which, insofar as they are subject to combination and decomposition, thereby *assume* [the present study's emphasis] the form of accidents."[194] That is to say, Nicholson understood al-Maʿarrī as meaning that elements or substances (or atoms), unlike what the *mutakallimūn* hold, are eternal, although because they are susceptible of being compounded and then decompounded or returned to their simplest state, they may be said to become *like* (the key word in this passage) accidents, which are momentary and susceptible of being annihilated. Ṭāhā Ḥusayn interpreted this passage in essentially the same way; that is, as indicating that matter or substance endures eternally despite its taking on various (compound) forms and then returning to its (simple) origin over the course of time.[195]

I concur with Ḥusayn and Nicholson on this point, not only because of the *mithl*/مثل (like), but also because of what al-Maʿarrī says elsewhere in *Luzūm* in confirmation of the doctrine of the eternity of matter.[196]

In the remaining passages just cited above, al-Maʿarrī draws a conclusion to his postulation of the eternity of time, the natural elements, and the world as a whole. Since he holds time, the world, and the natural elements (of which humans are basically constituted) to be eternal, he must hold, too, that humankind is eternal; hence there was never an Adam in the sense of an original lone progenitor of the entire human race beyond whom the chain of human being cannot be traced back.[197] That is to say, since there has always been time, world, and matter, one can speak of an infinite regress with respect to humans in the sense of an eternally recurring series of human beings[198]—although one can only imagine here that al-Maʿarrī considers the human being's pre-eternal being not as a corporeal being (a proto-Adam fully formed as a human being as we know it) but, rather, formless, that is, the four elements (and especially earth-matter as an eternal material substratum) in their simple, uncompounded state. It is in this sense, it seems, that he utters L II.169.10–11:

If what the philosopher says is true, then my time
has never been free from me and never will be.
I'm split up one moment but recombined another;
like me in their states are the lotus and the palm tree.

إذا كان ما قال الحكيمُ فما خَلا　　زمانيَ منّي منذُ كان ولا يَخْلُو
أُفرّقُ طَوْراً ثمَّ أُجمعُ تارةً　　ومِثليَ في حالاته السِدْرُ والنخلُ

and L II.145.9–10, where "the realm"/المُلْك would seem to be a reference to the eternal material substratum:

Humans have passed on. But for my knowing their state
I'd say like the poet Zuhayr "Which way did they go
in the realm from which they've neither moved nor exited?"
And thus how can my belief be that they've expired?

مضى الأَنامُ فَلوْ لا عِلمُ حالهمْ[199]　　لقلتُ قولَ زُهيرٍ أَيّةً سلكوا
في المُلْكِ لم يخرجوا عنه ولا ٱنتقلوا　　منه فكيف ٱعتقادي أَنَّهُمْ هلكوا

On the basis of this and similar such sentiments in the *Luzūm* with respect to matter and eternity, Ṭāhā Ḥusayn in his *Tajdīd Dhikrā Abī al-'Alā' al-Ma'arrī*[200] unequivocally proclaimed al-Maʿarrī a materialist, although without resort to the often confusing term دهري/*dahrī*: يرى أبو العلاء رأي الفلاسفة في أن الأجسام تأتلف من مادة قديمة خالدة وصور تختلف عليها وله في إثبات ذلك كلام كثير في اللزوميات ("Abū al-ʿAlā' held the view of the [Greek influenced Muslim] philosophers in terms of bodies being composed of eternal and everlasting matter the forms of which differ. There are many statements to this effect in the *Luzūm*.")

Ḥusayn may or may not have been aware of it (it is hard to imagine he was not, given the great controversy over the topic), but the radical materialism of Shibli Shumayyil (1850–1917) was inspired by the thought of al-Maʿarrī and that of Darwin and German materialists such as Büchner. (By 1884 Shumayyil had translated into Arabic a summary of Ludwig Büchner's commentaries on Charles Darwin.) Moreover, Jamāl al-Dīn al-Afghānī's *The Truth about the Naturalists and Their School* appeared in a celebrated 1886 Arabic translation (from an Urdu translation based on the Persian original, *Ḥaqīqat-i Madhhab-i Nicharī va Bayān Ḥāl Nicharīyān*) as رسالة في إبطال مذهب الدهريين وبيان مفاسدهم وإثبات أن الدين أساس المدنية والكفر فساد العمران (*A Treatise on the Corruption of the Materialists' School, and Proof That Religion Is the Origin of Civilization and Unbelief the Source of Civilizational Decline*, soon commonly referred to as simply *A Refutation of the Materialists* [الرد على الدهريين]). In connecting materialism to ancient Greece and from there to other places in the world (and for "materialism" using the Arabic word الدهرية, which he took to mean the same thing as the "naturalism" referred to in the Persian original title of الرد على الدهريين), al-Afghānī also saw materialistic dimensions to al-Maʿarrī's thought.[201] More recently, ʿAbd al-Qādir Zaydān,[202] although acknowledging the accurateness of Ṭāhā Ḥusayn's interpretation overall, particularly in the sense that "matter taking on different forms is matter's way of taking on new life after corruption, meaning that life is an alternation between generation and corruption, as Aristotle held"—فاختلاف الصور على هذه المادة هو ميلاد جديد لها بعد فسادها. بمعنى أن الحياة مراوحة بين كون وفساد كما قال بذلك أرسطو—expressed the opinion that nonetheless al-Maʿarrī did not explicitly accept the philosophers' (Greek as well as Greek-inspired Muslims, especially al-Fārābī, Ibn Sīnā, and Ibn Miskawayh and the Brethren of Purity) view of the evolution of humans in a manner connected to plant or animal life (وكما رفض أبو العلاء دور القوى

الفلكية في نشأة الانسان والحياة في عمومها فقد أنكر أن تكون أصول الانسان لها صلة ما بالنبات (أو الحيوان).

Zaydān[202] draws this conclusion—after citing and taking as genuine (i.e., sincere) L II.261.9 ("Adam is not one . . . he is multiple Adams") and L II.326.15 ("It's feasible that the Adam of all this was preceded by one Adam after another")—on the basis of the following half-playful (and only *half*-playful) lines that also occur in *Luzūm*:

They say "Adam was furry; humans are like truffles."
Man *has been* ignorant but he has not been furry.

قالوا آدمُ مثلُ أَوْبَرَ والورى   كبناتِه جَهِلَ امرُؤٌ ما أوْبَرُ

(L I.328.1)

A certain people say (yet I don't believe it)
"A son of Adam is the same as a weasel.
People have never known who Adam's father is;
he is, rather, what is called 'eternal time.'"
This is narrated by one people to another,
based on one transcribed page after another.

قال قومٌ ولا أدينُ بما قا   لوه إنَّ ابن آدمٍ كابن عِرْسِ
جَهِلَ الناسُ ماأبوهُ على الدهـــــرِ   ولكنَّه مُسَمًّى بِحَرْسِ
في حديثٍ رواهُ قومٌ لقومٍ   رَهْنَ طِرْسٍ مُسْتَنْسَخٍ بعد طِرْسِ

(L II.43.11–13)

Ḥusayn[203] takes the disavowal in the first line of the latter citation as quintessential Maʿarrian dissimulation (which makes the interrogation—so to speak—represented by L I.328.1 virtually irrelevant; in fact, Ḥusayn makes no reference to it [that I am aware of]).

It is difficult not to agree with Ḥusayn. For those familiar with the entire *Luzūm* (if not *al-Fusūl wa al-Ghāyāt* and *Risālat al-Ghufrān* as well), the dissimulation is so thinly veiled (i.e., clichéd, clumsily formulaic) as to be slightly comical (which may in fact also have been intended).

This does not necessarily make al-Maʿarrī as a materialist a Darwinian in the sense that "life consists of the product of a single cell that undergoes evolution," and man is something other than the progeny of man (which interpretations are manifestly untenable for Zaydān;[204] they were never explicitly taken up by Ḥusayn within the context of his discussion of the last-cited verses from the *Luzūm*). However, clearly, al-Maʿarrī, in his own inimitable fashion—outrageously, half tongue in cheek—was endorsing (for the most part) and extending the conversation of the Greek "naturalists" and evolutionists (going as far back as Thales and Anaximander) with respect to their concept of the origin of life, as filtered most notably by Miskawayh and the Ikhwān al-Ṣafā', al-Fārābī, and Ibn Sīnā.[205] With respect to creation and Adam and the origin of life, al-Maʿarrī was not a revelationist, regardless of the "Abrahamic" version of revelation. (This is wonderfully understated by Zaydān's observation that ويبدو أن أبا العلاء لم يكن مستريحا للمعنى الحرفي للنص الديني ["It appears that Abū al-ʿAlā' was not at ease with the literal meaning of religious text."][206]).

Zaydān reminds us that al-Maʿarrī, even before his musings on life in the *Luzūm,* declared in the poem that opens *Saqṭ al-Zand* (in a line where the antecedent to "it" is "God's command" or أمر الله, spoken of in the immediately preceding line) والذي حارت البرية فيه حيوانٌ مستحدَثٌ من جماد ("What bewilders humankind about it is the fact of a living creature originating from an inorganic inanimate body"). Continuing in that vein, Zaydān adds that Ismāʿīl Maẓhar, the translator into Arabic of Darwin's *The Origin of the Species,* remarked in the introduction to his translation that, after the age of the discovery of the human cell, it would be Darwin who would provide the answer to the following question: كيف نشأت الحياة في تلك الصورة البسيطة ومن أين هبط السر الرهيب سر الحياة الذي جعل من المادة الجامدة كائناً حيّا ("How did life in that simple form evolve; and whence came down the awesome secret, i.e., the secret of life, which has made living beings from inorganic inanimate matter?").[207]

Part V. Humankind as It Ought to Be: Al-Maʿarrī's Ethics in the *Luzūm*

Through many apothegms and moralizing commands and prohibitions, al-Maʿarrī wove into the fabric of *Luzūm* a rather comprehensive vision of what a human being's standard of conduct should be with respect to self, fellow human beings, God, the world, and creation at large. To tie this into the note struck at the beginning of this chapter and into the general orientation of the present study as a whole, the expressions and sentiments along these lines represent one final way in which *Luzūm* may be thought of as a work that above all else pivots around humankind.

Few would question that the most striking feature of this aspect of al-Maʿarrī's thought is the promotion of a severe, and at times rather unusual if not almost unique, asceticism and flight from what most societies would consider normal social intercourse. Both of these dimensions are most astonishingly and unforgettably exemplified by the *Luzūm*'s unremitting advocacy of celibacy, sexual abstinence, and the end of procreation. Additional embracements of self-abnegation and self-imposed social marginalization are on the whole considerably less unusual as far as ascetic, quietistic philosophies go, and thus less shocking and notoriously memorable in and of themselves, although al-Maʿarrī's whole enterprise along these lines represents advocating a radical reconstruction of a well-established social order.

Al-Maʿarrī admonishes his readers to live completely cut off from their fellow human beings (L I.63.1; 66.1; 95.12; 96.1; 132.9; 175.8; 420.4; L II.143.6; 154.15; 176.10; 316.1). Humankind should be content to live with all but the bare necessities of life. For al-Maʿarrī, that meant only a thin cover of simple cloth for protection against summer's heat (L I.293.7); a coarse piece of plain cloth for protection against winter's cold (L I.293.7); and a diet consisting only of plants or products derived therefrom, such as grain and olive oil (L I.293.4; II.99.5; 264.11; 185.15). Fish (L I.232.7), milk (L I.232.8), eggs (L I.232.9), honey (L I.232.10; II.99.5), meat (L I.232.7; II.264.11), and wine (L I.96.9; 125.4–11; 126.1–3; 144.2–5; 380.12; II.299.1) are all to be avoided. Household items of personal luxury (e.g., drinking goblets of gold or silver; L I.293.6), ornamentation (L I.212.4), expensive and fanciful clothing (L I.123.10; 405.14), hair dye (L II.421.9), and even the linen shrouds and embalming ointments or perfumes for the dead are needless superfluities and should be forsaken. One should leave the world precisely as one came into it: naked (L II.370.1–3). One ought not to pass the days of his life seeking amusements (L II.390.14) or mundane pleasures (L I.103.1; 172.2; 186.1). There should be no accumulation of wealth or property (L I.123.10; 145.1; L II.78.7; 394.4).

The call for abstaining from eating meat, fish, or fowl is on the grounds that animals (the existence of which as part of creation must be considered as decreed by God; L I.120.6–7) no less than humans should be spared suffering pain; surely a good and merciful God could not wish this for them. If Almighty God has decreed and fashioned all living things, it is He who ought to determine when their life spans end, not humans. Humans ought not to spill blood under any circumstance (لا تُحدِثْ القطعَ في كفٍّ ولا قَدَمٍ / ولا تعرّضْ مدى الدنيا لسفكِ دم / وخلّ من صوّرالأشباحَ مقتدراً / يَحُلُّها فهو ربّ الدهرِ والقِدَم) (L II.301.7–8), even out of hunger. To shed blood in order to acquire food is vile (فإنّ من أقبحِ الأشياءِ يفعلُهُ / شاكي المجاعة يكفيك أدْماً يوماً أن يُريقَ دما) (L II.284.11). This causes pain to a living soul (سليطٌ ما أُريقَ لهُ / دمٌ ولا مسَّ روحاً إذ جرى ألَمُ) (L II.264.11–12). As for abstention from milk, honey, and eggs, the principal justification is that indulging in these items amounts to expropriating what is not rightfully one's to take; that is, consuming these products is a violation of nature, theft from the rightful owners, and, moreover, the infliction of harm on the animals that produce them: milk is for the young of lactating animals, to be drunk by them; honey is for the bees themselves to consume; eggs are the means by which egg-laying animals propagate the species (see in this context L I.206.8; 209.8–10; 232.6–11; II.99.5; 105.1–3; 169.7; 373.8; 383.13–14).

When he was seventy-five, L I.232.6–11 brought al-Maʿarrī to the attention of the chief missionary of the Fāṭimid (Ismāʿīlī) Shīʿite community and state, Hibat Allāh ibn Mūsā (al-Mu'ayyad fī al-Dīn), then stationed at the academy in Cairo founded by al-Ḥākim bi-Amr Allāh. Acknowledging his awareness that al-Maʿarrī's "ascetic practice" (التزهُّد) included "abstention from all luxurious food, drink, and clothing . . . , refusing to suffer [his] body to be the grave of animals, to taste their milk, or to turn into food any of the creatures whose generation and breeding give pleasure to the sources of them," Hibat Allāh, addressing al-Maʿarrī directly, intoned "your practice implies the belief that pain inflicted on animals will be avenged, and represents the extreme of asceticism." He continued:

> What is your ground for abstaining from meat, milk, and all other animal products, as though they are unlawful?
>
> . . . .
>
> [M]an utilizes the animals for a variety of purposes, and were it not for that, the creation of animals would be purposeless. Hence your refusing to use what is created for you, and ordained on your account, destroys the harmony of nature. Your purpose in abstaining from meat must be either compassion for the animals, which makes you disprove of doing them violence, in which case you have no right to be kinder to them than their Creator; . . . we see before us various beasts and birds of prey, created by God in forms . . . involving the tearing of animals and devouring of them. This fact being well established in creation, mankind may well be excused for eating meat. . . . Or, secondly, you may regard the shedding of the blood of animals as an unwise ordinance, in which case your objection will fall on your Creator.[208]

Al-Maʿarrī's written response includes the argument that inasmuch as "the Prophets tell us that Almighty God is merciful and loving," so if "He be loving towards mankind, assuredly He will be tender to other classes of living beings which are sensitive to the least pain";[209] that is, surely God Himself does not will that animals suffer pain.

Al-Maʿarrī also tells his distinguished interlocutor that there were health benefits to his having been a vegan (i.e., his obtaining and maintaining good health, p. 319; an assertion he makes in L II.359.4 as well). In any event, he protested, he was too poor to afford "animal food,"[210] "God Almighty" having "condemned" him "to privation."[211] At least one line in *Luzūm* (II.353.2) echoes the feeling of privation irrespective of personal desires (ولم أعْرِضْ عن اللذات إلا / لأنَّ خيارها عنّي خَنَسْنَهْ) : "I shunned pleasures only because they themselves didn't give me any choice." The primary reference here, of course, is to the obstacles he faced in life because of his blindness and the shame he felt because of a pockmarked body:

> I see myself imprisoned in three ways
> (thus, don't ask me about terrible news):

I'm without sight and confined to home,
and my soul exists in a sick body.
(L I.201.2–3)

أراني في الثلاثة من سجوني   فلا تسألْ عن الخبر النبيثِ
لفقدي ناظري ولزومِ بيتي   وكون النفس في الجسد الخبيثِ

The remark of L II.353.2 ("I shunned pleasures only because they themselves didn't give me any choice") is belied by the immediately preceding line "I subdued my difficult aspirations because they were like headstrong horses out to pasture" (ورُضْتُ صعاب آمالي / فكانت خيولاً في مراتِعها شَمسْنَهْ) which is more typical of the *Luzūm*. The truth of the matter with respect to the self-abnegation probably lies somewhere in between. Like virtually any other type of personality, the extreme ascetic can be born rather than made, although in al-Maʿarrī's case it is difficult to deny the likely significance of euthenics as well as eugenics (and in equal measure). L II.196.8–9 speaks of a dissociation from society born not out of a particular act of hatred that occurred but, rather, because of a natural disposition having made it appealing ("as destiny would have it"). At the same time, this was an evolutionary process. In his written response to Hibat Allāh ibn Mūsā concerning the latter's queries on vegetarianism, al-Maʿarrī said that it was in the thirtieth year of his life when he decided to become a vegan.[212]

Another rationale for al-Maʿarrī's embrace of withdrawal from society comes to mind more readily than his physical infirmities. Inasmuch as humans are irredeemably evil—corrupt, murderous, cruel, dishonest, selfish, and so on—avoiding them as much as possible is by extension of logic all the better. Seclusion protects one from base human habits (slander, libel, swindle, contempt, callous exploitation) that normal social interaction can't guard against (L I.95.11–12; 96.1; L II.66.5, 6). Having few companions diminishes the chances of one's being involved in misdeeds (L 63.1–2). Obscurity fends off affliction and misfortune, envy and calumny (L II.240.6; I 277.3). Living alone, one can do no wrong to others nor be wronged by them (L II.316.1). Isolation brings the greatest repose (L I.176.11), a cure for the sickness that adheres to society (L I.50.8). Faith and reason are contaminated by proximity to fellow humans (L I.50.8), who laugh as long as they are presented with lies but assault you if you tell the truth (L II.270.8).

This impoverished isolation and seclusion (interestingly enough, referred to by al-Maʿarrī himself as a kind of death [L II.118.6], giving further cause to believe that although he rejected suicide proper he sought ways to approximate it [as previously discussed]) must be accompanied by a curbing of the soul's wicked impulses and desires and a placid resignation to life's vicissitudes. (The moral philosopher Miskawayh [d. 1030 CE] spoke of a remarkably similar life orientation as "voluntary death."[213]) The soul must be rebuked whenever it is intemperate (L II.59.3; 323.8). It has to be broken and made malleable before it can be forced into inclining to the good, like the gold and silver that are transformed from their raw state so that they become jewelry (L I.429.15–16). If misfortune assaults a person, he or she should endure it with patience and dignity (L I.223.4). No great concern should be showed to misfortune (L I.350.1). If fate allows that a person be granted what he or she hopes for or would welcome, he or she should show no delight (L I.105.8). There should be no rejoicing over a surplus of good fortune just as there should be no despair over a paucity (L I.209.4). One should not express remorse over how events transpire in the world (L I.84.13). There should be no regard for anxieties (L I.399.9), no covetousness for lofty aspirations (L I.397.9), no heed to heartfelt emotions (L II.211.3), and no preoccupation with where one's daily sustenance will come from (L I.429.10). Reflections on what has been, or what may be, are to be swept from one's mind. One is to live only for the moment, with mute forbearance, patience, and self-contentment, irrespective of what life delivers up (L I.120.12; 406.10; 423.2; L II.57.7; 94.10–11; 275.8; 274.7; 289.4; 294.14).

While waiting in such fashion for the fate of death—which should be accepted with the same resigned impassivity reserved for every over major turn of events in life—men and women ought to strive to do good. This is enjoined time and again in *Luzūm* and with utmost seriousness of purpose (L I.142.3; 174.8; 266.13; 422.10; L II.87.5; 90.3; 154.13; 249.1; 264.5; 266.11; 323.5; 342.1–2). Notwithstanding al-Maʿarrī's criticism of revealed religion, of the masters of religious disciplines, and of the whole socio-intellectual edifice that ensued from revealed religions, and regardless of his cynicism, pessimism, deterministic moments, and even strong suggestions of misanthropy, misogyny and misotheism, in *Luzūm* he is neither morally ambivalent nor a moral relativist. He lets neither his cynicism nor his epistemological nihilism go that far. At the very least, he says in L I.431.9–11, although humans may not know what for certain is the good, they can apprehend and avoid doing evil.

The *Luzūm* praises the good as the most virtuous thing a human being can believe in, regardless of his or her religious affiliation (II.323.5). One's particular faith is of no great relevance in this regard. The good is something that is not denied by any religious denomination (L I.266.13).

Strictly speaking, the good in the abstract is not defined in *Luzūm*. There is hardly a careful, prolonged, theoretical scrutiny of it. But al-Ma'arrī leaves little doubt that for him it consists basically of the precept "Do unto others as you would have them do unto you," which in fact is recapitulated nearly verbatim in the first hemistich of L II.87.7: وَأفعَلْ بِغيرِكَ ما تختارُ (The second hemistich of this verse has وأسْمِعِ الناسَ ما تهواه يفعلهُ مِسْمَعَهُ /"And have them hear what they would choose [i.e., like] to hear.") The subsequent and concluding line of the short poem from which these hemistichs are taken has the less charitable cautionary advice that "Most of the human race are like wolves that you might befriend; if they detect any weakness in you, that prompts their cravings" (وأكثرُ الإنسِ مثلُ الذئبِ تصحبهُ / إذا تبيَّنَ منكَ الضعفَ أطمَعَهُ). Man is wolf to man.

Fleshed out in greater detail over the course of the entire *Luzūm*, the command in II.87.7, al-Ma'arrī's great moral imperative, can be said to encompass above all else kindness, generosity, compassion, tolerance, honesty, humility, forgiveness, chaste and reserved speech, and, last but hardly least, a supreme reverence for the lives of all living creatures in the world. All of these qualities of character that most people would want exhibited toward them al-Ma'arrī in the *Luzūm* enjoins to be upheld.

More specifically still, human beings ought to help their fellow human beings and without boasting about their efforts in this regard (L I.266.4). The human heart must be swept of hatred and envy (L I.248.5), even if this means enduring the hostility of an enemy, for it is to be hoped that the enemy will eventually become a loving friend (L II.150.4). If the true friend occasionally acts harshly, that friend must not be shown wrath (L II.322.9). He or she as well as all other people should be pardoned for misdeeds or sins that they may commit (L I.96.2; 364.1; L II.388.12–14).

One should be a person of few words according to al-Maʿarrī; but when one does speak, one ought to be concise, eloquent (L I.431.10), and sincere (L II.53.4). One ought to be truthful (L I.111.7), open, and genuine (L I.80.1). One should not degrade the lowly (L I.75.2), be reproachful (L I.80.1), make purely formulaic oaths (L II.98.5), or indulge in slander and insolence (L II.289.7; 390.3). As a rule, one should stay clear of making promises, but if one does make them, one must strive to honor them (L I.431.9).

Obviously, ideally there would be little routine socializing in al-Maʿarrī's world of taciturn ascetic recluses, *his* virtuous city. Goodness is bound up with seclusion, introversion, otherworldliness; it is almost inseparable from them. Nonetheless, al-Maʿarrī expounds some basic rules of sociability in *Luzūm,* again perhaps as another concession to reality and pragmatism. He specifies that should one be in a position to receive a guest or visitor, one should receive that guest or visitor with open arms. The guest or visitor should be met with a smile and shown hospitality (L I.75.1). Even in lean times, nourishment should be gladly provided (L I.175.7).

This same liberality and magnanimity is to be extended to all human beings regardless of whether they are visitors or members of one's family. None of an individual's brothers or sisters in society at large should be found to be in need of whatever riches an individual may have, argues al-Maʿarrī in *Luzūm* I.64.13; 65.1–2. Wealth is not to be hoarded, neither in one's lifetime nor after as a bequeathal. While a person is alive, his or her wealth should be distributed among or spent on the needy (L II.253.2; 87.6). Wealth may be passed on to one's heirs upon one's death (L II.78.7) but with the intent that it be disbursed among, shared with, humankind at large, especially the needy (see again L II.87.6 and II.253.2). Wealth only adds to one's anxieties (L II.260.10), and in any event wealth hoarded serves no meaningful purpose (II.253.2). If all Muslims paid their *zakāh* taxes, no one would hear complaints of poverty or deprivation, and certainly there would be no starvation (L II.345.9–10). Real wealth is the pious life of the abstemious; it brings the greatest happiness (L I.212.3–5). Life and material possessions are ephemeral. "What do you want of a domicile that you don't own, one in which you stay briefly but then depart from?" (وما تريدُ بدارٍ لستَ مالكَها / تقيمُ فيها قليلاً ثمّ تنطلقُ; L II.121.2)

Although al-Maʿarrī clearly intended to cast aspersions on, indeed subvert, the revealed religions of his age, and to suggest that their followers, for all of their punctilious submission to proscribed dogmas and rituals, were no more enlightened or spiritually privileged than all others, his vision of how humankind ought to live had no place for religious persecution or bigotry. All faiths may be equally (or nearly equally) grounded in unsubstantiated, unverifiable claims and—worse—all too often shaped and superintended by insincere, unenlightened, self-aggrandizing custodians (i.e., clerics). But al-Maʿarrī implores that people of all faiths be dealt with justly and honorably (L II.407.11–13; 308.6). Regardless of their fierce differences, for which they are sometimes quite prepared to go to war even, as human beings they all need to be considered as equals (L I.193.10).

Concerning these wars (i.e., the sectarian) and war in general, implicitly, al-Maʿarrī denounces them. His notion of the good must be said to include pacifism, nonviolence, and peaceful coexistence. In L I. 264.10–11, he wonders aloud why humankind brings about death on the battlefield when life is so short to begin with, when through wars parents lose their cherished children. More significantly, as already observed, L II.301.7 contains the declaration that a human being ought never spill a drop of blood for all of his life. In the correspondence with Hibat Allāh, al-Maʿarrī in speaking of pain and suffering, which he insists "all living beings" be spared, adds, "Ofttimes, too, have I seen a couple of armies, each of them professing a distinct cult, meeting in battle, and thousands falling on each side. For which theory does this make? Even study does not make it clear."[214]

In consonance with the *Luzūm*'s special dietary prescriptions for humankind, the injunction proscribing the spilling of blood is meant to include the slaughter of any animals the flesh of which might be used for human consumption (see, e.g., L I.206.8–10; 209.10; L II.264.11–12; 284.10–11). Moreover, all animals should be kept from any type of discomfort and suffering, according to al-Maʿarrī's ethics. He appeals to humans not to hasten the deaths of their beasts of burden (i.e., through overworking) (L I.206.8) nor to beat them (L I.143.10; 144.1). Something as relatively unglamorous as searching out an old camel that has gone astray is to be considered an act of grace (L II.278.5). Humans should not disturb birds or bees or lactating animals with the view of gathering the edibles or potables that they produce (L I.232.8–11; II.169.7; 373.8).

With the expressed wish in *Luzūm* that not a single living being in the world, animal or human, be harmed, we have al-Maʿarrī's compassion carried to its furthest extent. Within this context worth underscoring are his pleas to his readers that they be especially protective of the less fortunate members of society. From among them, the old, the physically challenged, orphans, and the enslaved are singled out, for example. The old, in their tattered clothes and walking with the aid of staffs, and with their bodies too weak to endure the extremes of heat and cold, need to be shown mercy (I.269.3–7). The blind should be taken by the hand in order to be properly guided; the deaf should be made to comprehend what they cannot hear (L II.278.4). Orphans should be protected from injury, hardship, and violence and also awarded their proper share of bequeathals (L II.415.15). Slaves are to be forgiven their shortcomings and whatever mistakes they may make (L I.376.12–13; L II.155.8). Female as well as male slaves are to be kept in a desirable condition, urges al-Maʿarrī in L II.310.12. Somewhat unexpectedly, nowhere in *Luzūm* is there the suggestion that slaves should be emancipated and slavery as an institution be abolished. One might reasonably suppose that al-Maʿarrī had no objection to such a proposition, but that he himself nowhere suggests something of the kind is strikingly incongruous within the broader, very effusive humanitarian contours of *Luzūm*.

Notwithstanding its doctrine of self-annihilation through an end to procreation, the *Luzūm* demands that children already in existence not be scorned in their sport or mirth nor shown so little regard as to have evil attributed to them. The children of today might some day be seen as their nations' dignitaries (II.308.3–4). Nonetheless, children are not to be excused from doing what is right because of youthful immaturity. They should be guided to what is right or proper even by means of corporal punishment (L II.305.3).

Reference has already been made to al-Maʿarrī's commonly recognized misogynistic views. Women in his estimation are hardly the equal of men in terms of rights and privileges and social standing and thus on the whole not to be treated so magnanimously. Women are for marrying for the sake of their protection (L I.216.9; II.288.8) and to prevent them from scandalizing family patriarchs (see, for example, L II.288.7–8). An allusion in II.288.8 to the story of the refractory daughters of one Hammām ibn Marrah is intended to make clear, in the unlikely event that there be any doubt, the type of scandal that al-Maʿarrī especially had in mind. The story of Hammām is provided by Zand in a detailed and quite graphic gloss. (A greatly truncated and bowdlerized version is provided by the Dār Ṣādir edition of the *Luzūmiyyāt.*) Nothing protects the honor of a virgin like having her married off (L I.194.6–7).

The best wives are sterile, reads L II.261.13, a rather startling and dark statement, even for al-Maʿarrī; although it does not seem to have been repeated elsewhere. The opinion is hardly cleverly oblique because of erudite word plays or the demands of the rhyme scheme: إذا شئت يوماً وصلةً بقرينةٍ / فخيرُ نساء العالمين عقيمُها ("If you wish to take a wife one day/the best woman in the world is the sterile woman"). But a similar sentiment with respect to male sterility is expressed in L II.289.10: أرى وَلَدَ الفَتَى عِبءً عَلَيْه / لقد سَعِدَ الذي أمسى عقيماً: "A man's offspring is a burden upon him./ Happy indeed is the man who becomes sterile."

Women should eschew jewelry and finery and attention to a fetching physical appearance, and, instead, emulate the sartorial simplicity of pious and modest women performing the pilgrimage to Mecca (L I.198.4–6). A man's wife ought to seek God-fearing piety (التقى) as an adornment; this is more resplendent than the wearing of pearls or cut jewels (L I.293.12). Women should not be taught reading and writing, nor praised if they somehow learn such, but instead trained in domestic chores (e.g., spinning and weaving) (L I.62.9; 192.3–4; II.199.5). Contact with men should be prevented as much as possible. Certainly, women should avoid going to the public baths, for example (L II.288.5–6). When they entertain thoughts of marriage, they should be kept from being in the presence of men (L I.192.12). Their learning recitations from the Qur'ān is acceptable; but the shorter the recitations, the better (L I.62.10), and the instructors should be elderly women rather than men, unless the men are well past the prime of their youth (L I.192.7–11). Women, even those veiled, are resolute and deliberately seductive temptresses who corrupt the morals of society and sap its strength (see, e.g., L I.188.1–13; 189.1–14;

here al-Maʿarrī manages to make quite titillating, and at considerable length, some of the very actions and behavior he purports to find abhorrent, although admittedly in some rather learned Arabic).

On the other hand, people—all people (al-Maʿarrī's emphasis: فإنَّ الناسَ كلَّهُم سواءٌ)—are equal, notwithstanding the wars that erupt among them; and thus, with respect to at least one of his less caustic observations on women, he enjoins that regardless of their religion, they be treated with equity and honor: وساوِ لَديكَ أترابَ النصارى / وعيناً من يهودَ ومُسْلِماتِ / ومَن جاورتَ مِن خُنُفٍ وسِرْبٍ / صوابئَ فليبِنَّ مُكَرَّماتِ (L 1.193.8–9).

In a similarly less caustic vein toward women, and again notwithstanding the *Luzūm*'s core doctrine of self-extinction through an end to procreation, wives especially (or the virtuous ones, we can assume al-Maʿarrī meant) are to be protected according to L I.216.9. Husbands ought to remain faithful to them for all of their lives, regardless of their loss of beauty as they grow old; and they should not exchange them for more voluptuous younger brides (L I.111.4–6). Contrary to what is legally permissible in Islam, al-Maʿarrī proclaims that women should not be shared in polygamous marriages (L I.194.1–2; 281.6–7). Nor should they be taken as brides when they are far younger than their spouses; for in that eventuality they will have no sincere interest in their prospective mates in and of themselves, but instead only covet the marriage dowries that Islam prescribes for them (L II.300.3–6). Their being married off while still "soft and sweet" adolescents and much younger than their husbands can only lead to "abominations" (L I.193.11–12). Mothers are to be treated with justice, kindness, and respect; as are fathers; but mothers are more deserving of this reverence because it is they who give birth to children, carry them during pregnancy, and nurse them when they are infants (II.278.4–8; 370.12). If wives give birth to and nurse children, they can be considered as having bestowed upon their spouses a true benefit or grace (*faḍl*/فضل) (L II.370.13)—yes, a contradiction, but scarcely if ever repeated.

Al-Maʿarrī's basic ethical benchmark of doing unto others what it would be hoped that they do unto you he extends to the political arena, notwithstanding his reclusiveness and his endorsement of withdrawal from the *polis*. Rulers are exhorted to be just (L II.113.6) in their judgments or decisions, not oppress (L II.219.7). As heads of state, they should behave such that all of their actions are deemed beautiful ones (L II.181.8). They should be humble and accessible to people (L II.113.10–11), offer hope to their subjects rather than remove it (L II.113.9), and remain content not to live sumptuously (L II.113.12; 374.10). In consonance with his opposition to war, al-Maʿarrī commands that there be no conquest of one regime or state by another: فلا تشهرَنْ سيفاً لتطلبَ دولةً ("Do not draw a sword demanding a state"; L I.204.11). On the other hand, should it so happen that there is conquest of one people by another, at the very least the vanquished should not be treated any differently from the victorious, and the latter certainly should not rejoice in their conquest (L II.238.1).

We might imagine these precepts too are concessions to reality as well. In keeping with his ideal of total withdrawal from the normal course of events in the world, and having this carried to its logical end (which in fact was the case with him), what al-Maʿarrī really advocated in the *Luzūm* approaches political quietism. That is to say, في ملته وأعتقاده (according to *his* faith and belief, to borrow a phrase of his in a poem in *Saqṭ al-Zand* where he expounds upon some of his world views), there should be no participation in government. "I forbid you to take up government" (أنهاك أن تليَ الحكومةَ), al-Maʿarrī proclaims to his readers in L I.293.8. On the heels of this he adds the following:

> Forget about princeship or taking up in city
> a whip that you regard as the warrior's sword.
> These affairs I detest for relatives and friends.
> So, you choose: either cheapen yourself or do good.
> (L I.293.9–10)

وذَرِ الإمارةَ وٱتخاذَكَ دِرَّةً   في المصرِ تحسبُها حُسامَ المُنْجِدِ
تلك الأمورُ كرهتُها لأَقاربِ   وأَصادقٍ فٱبخل بنفسكَ أَوْ جُدِ[215]

Al-Maʿarrī's plea to his readers that they not rule or in similar fashion assume the lead over others is repeated in at least two additional locations in *Luzūm* (i.e., I.285.1 and I.286.6–8). It is likely this spirit is what led him to say that the garb of the Christian monk is better than the garb of the king (L I.123.10), that the lowliest person in the world is the king who goes forth feeling the need for amassing a huge army (L I.212.5), and that one should not seek to be associated with political authorities or leaders (رؤساء) (L I.63.1).

Whenever it is invoked in *Luzūm*, the ascetic ideal of al-Maʿarrī to which reference has been made so frequently over the preceding pages of this study is usually expressed in the Arabic by derivatives of the roots ن س ك or ز ه د. Both of these roots have connotations of devoutness, piety, and godliness in addition to those of abstention from, renunciation of, and hatred for all things worldly. And indeed reverential fear of God (i.e., *taqwā*/تقوى; often also synonymous with piety) is urged and praised frequently in *Luzūm* (see, e.g., I.68.5; 176.2; 207.4; 212.4; 293.12; II.89.9; 143.2; 152.2; 213.2; 249.1), if the fulfillment of religiously driven cult practices or the belief in religious postulates (Islamic or other) are not. This fact cannot be denied. To many this may suggest that the asceticism and world-flight advocated by al-Maʿarrī, and hence indeed his whole notion of the good or exemplary life, must have had a serious formal religious component to it; more specifically, in the sense of containing a theosophy, for example, or a theocracy; or at the very least a certain theo-centrism (a point that this study has already conceded *may* have been the case). All of such would certainly be the case if one is to take al-Maʿarrī's numerous calls for *taqwā*/تقوى (God-fearing piety) as being sincere and heartfelt and virtually synonymous with إيمان (faith/belief in God).

However, to the extent that any or all of such *may* have been involved in al-Maʿarrī's thought, it must have amounted to little more than acknowledging and placidly resigning oneself to an abstract transcendent God's will or power as the ultimate force behind the natural processes and forces of life—the secondary causes in the natural or physical world—inclusive of the favorable as well as unfavorable events that one assigns to "fortune." The brand of asceticism that al-Maʿarrī enjoins upon humankind is essentially bare of piety in the sense of institutionalized ritualized prayer, warm and intimate God-directed meditation, and similar such devotional duties or orientations. It offers no epiphanies in terms of a better understanding of God and making more sense out of humankind and the world. Where *taqwā*/تقوى is invoked there is more fear or dread involved than there is loving reverence. Nowhere in *Luzūm* is there the suggestion that through the ascetic practices that al-Maʿarrī advocates humankind can reach even a higher state of intuitive spiritual awareness (e.g., gnosis or *dhawq*/ذوق) or emotion, let alone the glorious (re)union of the soul with the Divine, ideas that in addition to the need for fear and awe of God are commonly associated with the more religiously inspired varieties of asceticism and world withdrawal, including especially *taṣawwuf*/تصوّف, of which al-Maʿarrī could be particularly scornful and dismissive. In L. II.384.10–14, for example, he has the following to say about the adepts of *taṣawwuf* (especially the "wandering dervish" sorts), indulging in some rather tortuous (and virtually inimitable) word plays (above all with "wool" with the meaning of *ṣūf*/صوف), word plays that are brimming with sarcasm including a reference to his own *taqwā:*

We are cotton types whereas you are Sufis;
but with my cotton alone I've enough adornment.
You enter the belly of lands, and back country too.
But vulva and your own bellies are your real concern.
My Creator has protected me and thus I've lived
(were it not for fear of Him I'd say "Don't protect me").
My body is a tatter that gets sewn into the earth.
Therefore, go sew me in, O Tailor of the world.

نحنُ قُطنيَّةٌ وصوفيَّةٌ أنـــــــتم فقطْني مِن التجمُّل قُطْني[216]
تَقطعونَ البلادَ بطناً وظَهْراً إنَّما سعيُكُمْ لِفرجٍ وبطْنِ
حاطَني خالِقي فعشتُ ولَوْلا خوفُهُ قلتُ ليتَهُ لم يَحُطْني
جسدي خِرْقَةٌ تُخاطُ إلى الأَر ضِ فيا خائطَ العوالِمِ خِطْني

(L II.384.10–13)

In keeping with his advocacy of total flight from normal social intercourse, his rejection of revelation and hence the religious systems derived thereof, and his conviction that the human mind can know very little about God and other such suprasensables, al-Maʿarrī wants his ascetics to be distinctly *areligious* to the extent that they are not to concern themselves with religion's cult practices, higher doctrines and dogmas, and schisms. Similarly, his ascetics are to avoid not only the officials, proselytizers, and interpreters of religion, but also even the common practitioners. People are encouraged not to befriend prayer leaders or those who sermonize in mosques (L I.293.8). Associating with the religiously dutiful or listening to one who advances the cause of a particular denomination are not ways by which one can learn how to guard against doing evil (L I.210.7–8). The true or ideal ascetic should remain enraptured in silence when others become versatile or skilled in what they profess (L I.74.2). *He or she should be God-fearing but not advance any claims with respect to God* (L II.395.4; فراقبوا اللهَ ولا تزعُمُنْ). (Immediately following this line is the cautionary فكَّر يزدانُ على غِرَّةٍ / فصِيغَ مِن تفكيرِهِ أهرُمُنْ / "Yazdān [Ahura-Mazda, the source of good in Mazdeanism/Zoroastrianism] thought unawares; thus from his thought was formed Ahriman [the source of evil].")

Whosoever lays claim to religion is to be treated as being untruthful (L II.214.13). The one who performs the obligatory fasts and prayers in Islam is to be regarded as being no less likely than his or her contrary to succumb to what is false and absurd (L II.214.11–12). Regardless of a professed formal or institutionalized religion ("Whether you pray toward Mecca or speak as a Magian"), all that you should really be concerned with is the good ("the good is the best you can believe in") (L II.314.4). And this has nothing to do with, ipso facto, religious practices such as fasting, praying, or wearing the special garb of a mystic (L I.285.11–12). Virtue is good, and virtue is its own reward. Finally, and most important, when a person strives for the ascetic's life,[217]—which the *Luzūm* unequivocally argues is the best course of action that a person can take in the world—al-Maʿarrī adds in L II.239.6 (lest there be any doubt) that the striving should be driven by reason (عن عقل).

Al-Maʿarrī endorses an intellectually (as opposed to religiously) inspired and directed asceticism; a rather sober, dry-eyed embrace of this type of life orientation on largely rational grounds and with many quite practical worldly (even bodily) benefits, as opposed to an impassioned emotional endorsement impelled by an inner urge or longing that seems to need satisfaction or fulfillment, and that promises primarily ethereal, spiritual rewards (e.g., peace and happiness) in a nether world with a beatific vision. Dhū al-Nūn al-Miṣrī (d. 859 CE) "the prototype of the moderate mystic,"[218] taught that "fellowship with God" was the goal of the mystic, what other prominent theoreticians (e.g., al-Bisṭāmī, al-Junayd, al-Ḥallāj) of *zuhd* and *taṣawwuf* in the ninth and tenth centuries of the Common Era were to refer to as virtual spiritual or psychological (re)union with God and as such eternal perdurance through

Him. Al-Maʿarrī had no such aim. His asceticism is more akin to that of the Yogi of Hinduism, *sans* the notion of Being beyond space and time, which as we have seen he could not conceive of. "The aim of the Yogi sage is not union with God, but rather the isolation of the Soul and the realization of an eternal mode of being outside space and time. This 'isolation' amounts . . . to the destruction of particular existence, which is the ultimate goal of Samkhia-Yoga as indeed of all Hinduism."[219] In more severe forms of this type of thinking, Soul/Self and a Transcendent Absolute Who can be personalized are essentially effaced or annihilated; "a somewhat negative and hollow" relationship in the words of Majid Fahkri,[220] but which may be said to apply to al-Maʿarrī's *zuhd/tanassuk.*

Finally, al-Maʿarrī is a moral rationalist and empiricist. Questions of good or evil in life are to be resolved here on earth and by human reason, especially as employed in sense perception, observation. Everything that the mind shows to be in disaccord with reason (or conscience; the Arabic word used here is *ḥijan*/حجى) is bad, reprehensible, evil (قبيح) (L I.227.12).

In no place in *Luzūm* does al-Maʿarrī suggest that his vision of life as it ought to be lived not be embraced as anything less than an ultimate truth, an ideal to be diligently sought after with single-minded resolve. But in several places, he does seem to indicate that such a life orientation should not be embraced or pursued to the extent that it jeopardizes a person's life or safety. Among these passages, aside from those making reference to the caution that he said he himself exercised in preaching and practicing his beliefs, are the various lines that admonish silence or reticence in matters of faith, especially when in the presence of others advancing differing religious persuasions, and, more germane still, L II.303.6, where al-Maʿarrī in effect adds an important proviso to all of his pleas for honesty, sincerity, and truthfulness: *all of such is fine insofar as it doesn't lead to a person's being harmed or damaged*—in which case a person should deceive or mislead (a classic instance of justifiable *taqiyyah*/تقية as understood by Shīʿite doctrine). Perhaps also in a similar vein is L II.303.11, where al-Maʿarrī exhorts, "Prepare for each age that which is in accordance with it" (أعدِدْ لكُلِّ زَمَنٍ ما يشاكلُه), and the more enigmatic L I.422.1 and L II.378.1 where the reader is advised to rebuff evil with evil and not repay it with good. L I.422.1 and L II.378.1 are the only instances in *Luzūm* of any real vindictiveness being suggested on al-Maʿarrī's part, "an eye for eye and tooth for tooth" inclination. An additional possible understanding of this line is that the wise person should not totally turn the other cheek when confronted with evil *if* such a course of action aids and abets an enemy who could do a person serious harm. Inasmuch as the first hemistich of L II.378.1—ولا تَكُ جازياً بالخير شرًّا ("Don't reward evil with good")—has as the second hemistich وإنْ أنا خُنْتُ في سببٍ فَخُنِّي ("If I betray you in anything, then go ahead and betray me"), the meaning here may be more personal and self-referential; that is, for the entire verse of L I.378.1, along the lines of something like "If ever *I* were to betray you (and do something so uncharacteristic of me as an act of harm, which in principle I deplore), then in that (highly unlikely) event you may go ahead and betray me in kind, rather than repay the evil with good."

Real-life submissions to pragmatism would have amounted to compromises of course, but as ʿAbd al-Qādir Zaydān has insightfully stressed, al-Maʿarrī in the final analysis was interested in metaphysical freedom[221] more than anything else; which is to say real freedom, the highest form of freedom: freedom of mind, heart, and soul (conscience).[222]

The life orientation that al-Maʿarrī advocated in *Luzūm* he in the very same work claims by and large to have followed himself. In this sense, the poetry of *Luzūm* is largely and remarkably autobiographical and expansively confessional, another feature of the work setting it apart from the more mainstream trends in premodern Arabic poetry. *Luzūm* gives a fairly personal portrait of its author as a man. To the extent that al-Maʿarrī hoped others would follow his example, that portrait adds invaluably to our understanding of what he envisioned as the ideal or proper life for humanity at large, as idealistic or utopian as that may be.

Al-Maʿarrī claims, for example, that he generously gave to the poor from whatever he was blessed with in the way of sustenance and money (L I.156.2–3). He has recorded in L I.233.1 that he renounced the eating of all the types of food he asked others not to eat. He subsisted on very little (more specifically, on vegetables only), he alleged in L II.383.14; in fact, he often went hungry according to L I.117.9–10. He wore only white cotton clothing (L II.337.11; cf. the recently cited L II.284.10–14, first hemistich), and he shod himself in wood rather than leather (L II.51.10), apparently in order to save animals from slaughter for the use of their hides.[223] He boasts that he never stretched out his hand for anything (L I.286.13) and that whenever fate did not allow him his daily bread, he made no attempt to alter that fact (L II.402.10).

It is amply attested to (in the historical and bio-bibliographical sources, for example) that al-Maʿarrī did not marry, to which fact he also has many references in *Luzūm.* There is little need to recite these. There is hardly any contention over this fact. Notwithstanding al-Maḥāsinī's speculations about Umāmah, no one has never suggested that al-Maḥāsinī's boast of life-long celibacy was a false claim designed to conceal a reality that he wished to keep under wraps. Further examples of the extent to which he says he practiced withdrawal from normal social intercourse are to be found in his boasts that he cut himself off from friends as well as adversaries (L II.430.8) and generally kept at a distance from most people (L I.50.8), a claim that is not disputed in any of the standard premodern biographical sketches.

Because he was known to have had students, and furthermore readers and an amanuensis, he could not have been the absolute recluse he pretends he was. On the other hand, he claims he never engaged another person willingly (L II.139.4). (Perhaps the teaching to desiring students was regarded as a call to duty that he felt compelled to answer. The *Luzūm* makes no explicit mention of his teaching students, or of his teaching in broader terms, as opposed to his offering his advice or thoughts to people in general.)

In this self-imposed isolation (just one of the prisons to which Ḥusayn refers and assesses psychologically in his *Ma'a Abī al-'Alā' fī Sijnih*; another prison being—above and beyond the more obvious loss of sight—the self-imposed complicated formal structuring of the *Luzūm* as well as *al-Fuṣūl wa al-Ghāyāt*), following no religious path or sect other than that of "shunning the human race" (L I.123.13)—but for all that proclaiming his genuine compassion for the sufferings of his fellow human beings (L II.4.8)—al-Maʿarrī records that he faced the world at large, cosmos as well as mundus, with as much indifference as possible. He declares that he "broke" his soul until it became submissive (L II.59.3); suppressed his hopes and aspirations as well as griefs (L II.352.13; 353.1); and made himself resigned to whatever fate or God's decree (القضاء) brought him, "like a supple branch that could be bent and then straightened with equal ease" (L II.388.1–2). Contending that he never asked fate and time to spare him their difficulties (L I.130.1), he says he tolerated pain, distress, and misfortune with patient forbearance (L I.430.12; 85.2; a celebrated Qur'ānic virtue that no doubt allowed him some sympathy and redemption in the eyes of coreligionists). It was with this quality, he says, that he also found his worth in an age that he characterized as cheap or tawdry (L I.132.2). Of the past as well as the future, he claims he was totally oblivious (L II.280.14). He lived to at least endure the moment if he could not enjoy it. Although he said he longed for what he considered the good because he was cognizant of it, he adds that he did not grieve over why the good does not endure but instead is most ephemeral (L II.301.10).

Especially in the ascetic component of al-Maʿarrī's notion of how ideally humankind ought to live, including the advocacy of celibacy and the end to procreation, but also in the disapproval of taking the life of or otherwise harming any living being, von Kremer perhaps more remarkably than any other early, groundbreaking scholar of the *Luzūm* perceived and underscored specific striking similarities to Indian thought, both in its broad overarching configuration and the Jain strand in particular. So struck was von Kremer of this fact that, in the opening sentence of the very third paragraph of his pioneering monograph on *Luzūm,* he stated without a hint of equivocation, "Abulʿalâ ist wirklich in seiner Gesinnung ein indischer Ascet."

This parallelism in both its general and specific applications should not be denied; although it should only be looked upon as a useful way of better understanding and appreciating certain key aspects of al-Maʿarrī's thought, and not as necessarily implying that al-Maʿarrī was a crypto-Jain, or that whatever similarities there are between his thought and Jainism and Indian thought in general, he must have expropriated from the latter.[224] Von Kremer was right to point out that al-Maʿarrī's vegetarianism and, closely bound up with it, his finding loathsome the spilling of any blood or the killing any living being bear the clear stamp of Indian thought and practice generally speaking.[225] Al-Maʿarrī's plea, nay, demand, for a cessation in procreation, especially in the context of his own justification for abstaining from such, as expressed in the line وأرحتُ أولادي فَهُمْ في نعمةِ العدَمِ التي فضلَتْ نَعيمَ العاجل ("To my children I have given real peace. They are in the bliss of nonexistence that is preferable to the happiness of this world"; L II.236.4), may also be seen, à la von Kremer, as a call for achieving an approximation of nirvana.[226] More significantly in this vein, von Kremer pointed out that the proscription of eating honey is peculiarly Jainist[227] and that at one time in their history, Jains who aspired to the highest degree of holiness were encouraged to renounce all food, even to the point of death by starvation.[228]

Picking up on the connection between al-Maʿarrī and the Jains made by von Kremer, Nicholson in his study of *Luzūm* pointed out that "the rules for Jaina ascetics include celibacy."[229] Quoting from an at-the-time recent survey of Jainism, he demonstrated quite indisputably that "when we come to [al-Maʿarrī's] ethical discipline, we shall find that in the main it tallies with the ethics of Jainism":

> The first stage of a Jain layman's life is that of intelligent and well-reasoned faith in Jainism; and the second is when he takes a vow not to destroy any kind of life, not to lie, not to use another's property without his consent, to be chaste, to limit his necessaries, to worship daily, and to give charity in the way of knowledge, comfort and food. And these virtues are summed up in one word: *ahiṃsā* (not-hurting). "Hurt no one" is not merely a negative precept. It embraces active service also; for if you can help another and do not—your neighbour and brother—surely you hurt him.[230]

At the same time, however, it ought to be pointed out that "in ancient Greek religion, rejection of meat appeared particularly among the Orphics, a mystical, vegetarian cult . . . Among Jewish-Christian circles and Gnostic movements, various regulations regarding the use of vegetarian food were established. . . . Christian authors write of [the Manicheans'] ruthless and unrelenting fasting, and between their own monks and the Manicheans, only the Syrian ascetical virtuosos could offer competition in the practice of asceticism."[231] Moreover, although mention of fasting in the Qur'ān is restricted to that of the month of Ramadan, "yet ascetic forces among Christians in Syria and Mesopotamia, vigorous and conspicuous, were able to exercise their influence and were assimilated by Islam in the ascetic movement known as *zuhd* (self-denial) and later in that of Sufsim . . . that arose in the 8th century and incorporated ascetic ideals and methods."[232] By the second to third century of the Islamic Era, "the conception of *zuhd,* deepened from Ḥasan al-Baṣrī to Dārānī, became fixed: renunciation not only of dress, lodging, and pleasant food but also of women."[233] As al-Maḥāsinī underscored quite some time ago, that there is anything original about al-Maʿarrī's asceticism, something completely without precedent for his time and place, needs to be dismissed.[234] Eventually, the Islamic principle of *tawakkul* (putting one's life entirely in God's hands, believing and trusting in His plan for humankind) became inextricably linked to *zuhd* (and thus also *taṣawwuf).* A type of secular *tawakkul* may be said to be quite evident in al-Maʿarrī's *zuhd*; that is, submission (resignation) to the laws of nature, the natural observable physical processes that seem to govern all life and especially matter.

D.S. Margoliouth emphasized that al-Maʿarrī "tells us [in his correspondence with Hibat Allāh ibn Mūsā] his asceticism began in his 30th year—not after his return from Baghdad, as had seemed probable. Syrian does not seem a likely place for Jaina doctrines to have been reached, and yet before the journey to Baghdad Abu 'l-ʿAlā would seem not to have gone outside its limits."[235]

On that count, Margoliouth is justified in being skeptical about al-Maʿarrī's having been aware of Jain teachings. But doubting the awareness on the grounds that "if it were true, as Von Kremer and others supposed, that Abu 'l-ʿAlā was imitating the practice of the Jainas in his ascetic regime, we might expect some reference in these letters to the Indian doctrines, which, however, is not to be found"[236] is another matter. This is precisely the type of self-incriminating specificity that al-Maʿarrī may have been reluctant to reveal because of the decidedly extreme and (to the vast majority of Muslims) heterodox asceticism that, even without a self-proclaimed connection to 'foreign' (i.e., non-Islamic) influences, would have been likely to provoke hostile suspicions, as indeed they did with Hibat Allāh ibn Mūsā.

Al-Maʿarrī's appeal for emotional imperturbability in the face of God's will or the fates of time (or, more likely, the laws of nature, the natural observable physical processes that seem to govern all life and especially matter) may like his asceticism also have been autochthonous. There is a strong Qur'ānic precedent for the teaching, reinforced as well by *aḥādīth* reports and the praxis as well as theory of various mystics and mystical orders in Islam. But here, too, if only for the sake of enhancing understanding and appreciation, and no more, it is hard to refrain from drawing an elucidating parallel to the thought of others that progressed within a different civilizational base and at a different time.

Specifically, this tendency in al-Maʿarrī's thought almost immediately calls to mind the doctrines for which Epicureanism and Roman Stoicism are best remembered: *ataraxia* or tranquility of mind, in the case of the former, and *apathia*, "best translated by the word equanimity rather than indifference,"[237] in the case of the latter. In a very real sense al-Maʿarrī's patient forbearance, his *ṣabr*/صبر, which is at the same time bound up with a kind of secular *tawakkul,* may be seen as an Arab-Islamic equivalent of *ataraxia* and *apathia* (as equanimity) combined. Certainly, no one can say that al-Maʿarrī's Syria was not a likely place for Epicureanism or Stoic doctrine to have reached.[238]

To turn back to and reflect some more upon al-Maʿarrī's ethical prescriptions as a whole, it can easily be seen how those bound up with the mortification of the flesh, the renunciation of worldly ambition and possessions, and the complete abstention from conventional social intercourse and relationships, might be considered—to borrow Nicholson's words—al-Maʿarrī's "revenge upon a world which rejected him"[239] (although as the other side of this coin one might want to ponder the proposition that "It's not our ideas that make us optimists or pessimists; our optimism or pessimism of either physiological or pathological origin makes our ideas"[240]). Al-Maʿarrī did lose his sight shortly after his birth, so at a very early age he was afflicted with a physical handicap that obviously denied him many joys, including the freedom to move about easily and more easily pursue whatsoever vocation he may have wished. In L I.303.3–4, not to mention one of his many epistles, he acknowledges that it was with great sadness, and totally against his best wishes, that he left Baghdad after his two-year sojourn there to return to his native Maʿarrat al-Nuʿmān in Syria.[241] In L II.352.15;353.1, as we have previously observed, he said that men were wrong to call him a (true) ascetic; he avoided gratification of the senses only because the best of the gratifications were not forthcoming to him.

All that is on the one hand. On the other hand, for the most part, in *Luzūm* al-Maʿarrī's asceticism and his ethical precepts are argued for and advanced in terms that have little to do with his own personal, immediate socio-economic obstacles or with a temperamental quirk. They are justified in terms that are basically logical extensions of the totality of his thought as he wondered about himself and the world that he knew around him. They are corollaries derived from higher truths representing first principles, standards of conduct that were reasonable and sensible to al-Maʿarrī in light of his overarching understanding of things, and to be followed instead of any alternatives not because the alternatives are necessarily unobtainable but because al-Maʿarrī's reasoned observation led him to conclude that the standards of conduct he advanced were truly better than the alternatives, for all humankind as well as for himself. Thus, a person is to live alone and secluded because in this way he or she avoids being harmed by the base habits of society at large (L II.66.5–6), diminishes the likelihood that he or she will be wronged (L II.316.1), and diminishes the likelihood that he or she will do wrong or evil (L I.63.1). People should be content to live with little because fate does not always allow them all that they might want (L I.207.9). Such is life. There is no point in our becoming rich or accumulating wealth and property when our ultimate end is death and a return unto dust (L I.83.4; 145.1; 160.5–6) and because the poorer one is, the fewer the anxieties or worries one has (L II.260.10). If by chance one finds one's self with a surplus of wealth, one should distribute it to the needy; otherwise it is unproductive or useless (L II.253.2–3). Moreover, if everyone shared his or her wealth, there would be neither poverty nor hunger (L II.345.9–10). A man should not marry and produce children because by doing so he is only inflicting upon other humans the misery that awaits him in the world (L I.349.9–10).[242] People should shun religion and the religious inasmuch as religions are based on false human constructs; its practitioners are mostly hypocrites who, for all of their professed religiosity, are no less inclined to sinning and doing evil than all others:

> Muslims have not forsaken their evil;
> nor have Jews returned to repenting;
> nor Christians triumphed for their religion.
> They all provide me with testimony to that.

ما أسلم المسلمونَ شَرَّهُمْ   ولا يهودٌ لتوبةٍ هادوا
ولا النصارى لدينهم نصروا   وكلُّهم لي بذاك أشهادُ

(L I.268.3–4)

A person should be content with what God or the fates/nature send, exercise patience in the face of life's vicissitudes, because humankind is largely powerless to change these realities. What the fates or God arrange or what is determined by inexorable processes in nature are decisive and unalterable (L I.84.13; 423.2; II.289.4). Humans should not eat meat because this involves killing and inflicting pain (L II.264.11). A person should not gather honey, milk, and eggs for consumption because these products were not meant for humans but rather for the use of the creatures that produce them (L II.106.9; 169.7; II.373.8; 438). Wine should not be drunk because it destroys one's reasoning powers (L I.380.12; 125.4–11) and induces all kinds of immoral, reckless behavior (L I.144.5–9; 126.1–3). Food as a whole should be lightly indulged in for therapeutic reasons: a person is both healthier and wiser when eating less (L II.383.14; 359.4; in the latter citation, al-Maʿarrī remarks that by abstaining from food, he had no reason to fear diseases, and in particular dropsy (هبن); in an interesting passage on sustenance in *al-Fuṣūl wa al-Ghāyāt*,[243] al-Maʿarrī says that the food of the sound and healthy person is merely that which staves off hunger [مَذهب السّغب]). Last, and most important, in general, al-Maʿarrī advocates the type of life he does because in his understanding this leads not only to good or virtue but also to more peace of mind or equanimity. It is the more equanimous (or in al-Maʿarrī's angle on the world, less aggrieved or distressed) person who shuns humanity at large and leaves the world with no children (L I.212.3; II.215.13); who is poor and without concern for either material possessions or being punctilious in religious matters (L II.260.10); who is at peace with himself/herself (L II.271–8; II.367.2–3); who lives self-composed (L II.71.7–10); and who does not attempt to make of things what cannot possibly be made of them (L II.80.9). (In Jainism, incidentally, "liberation becomes possible only when all passions have been exterminated"; similarly, for Buddhism "suffering lies in causal relation with desires."[244]) It is also the happier person (or, to be more precise, least perturbed; the attainment of happiness being inconceivable) who, following al-Maʿarrī's lead, does good (L II.266.11; 341.11–12). Virtue and doing good are rewarding in and of themselves.

There are many more lines from *Luzūm* similar to those just cited, lines that explicitly link al-Maʿarrī's asceticism and ethics in the main to other aspects of his thought, so that they more or less follow as (in his eyes) reasonable deductions from first principles. Regardless, the reader of the present study should be able to see quite readily how, in its broadest terms, implicitly al-Maʿarrī's vision of life as it should be lived can be logically derived from the totality of his thought and is even the culmination of that thought. That thought as a whole exclusive of the ethical dimension may be said to amount to the discovery that a human being confronts a number of situations or realities that make his/her existence a most confused and tormented experience. The human soul is always at war with reason in its greed and lust and inclination to do evil; fellow human beings, and society at large are cruel, greedy, wanton, violent, hypocritical, and ignorant. The fates (i.e., life's vicissitudes) and God are overwhelming, inscrutable, capricious, unfair. The universe is majestic and enduring but likewise overwhelming and revealing no grand purpose to life nor certitudes by which one might seek right guidance or higher wisdom. Formal, institutionalized religions are fallible and misleading, primarily because of clerics who have constructed and promoted them, and at other levels all too often practiced by duplicitous, unenlightened self-seekers and reprobates. Death is not followed by bodily resurrection. Life is is painful and in the end scarcely more than a rough road unto death and extinction. The intellect, despite all of its estimable power and its superiority to received opinions (= revelation) that are encrusted with blind confirmation, cannot give sure answers to some of life's most vexing questions: Why creation? What is the purpose? Why evil? Why suffering? Where does the human soul go after death, if in fact it survives? What is God's real nature, if in fact we can conceive of Him and embrace His existence?

All of this al-Maʿarrī sees as afflicting humankind always and everywhere and as making human life unbearably perplexing, anxiety-ridden, and painful. Thus, he beckons the individual human being to shun society, to look forward to his or her own extinction, and to look forward to—and even help bring about—the extinction of all humankind by the avoidance of procreation. Until one's own death and that of humanity at large, one should curb the soul's desires and inclinations to do evil; be content to live without possessions or wealth, with only enough clothing and nourishment to keep one's self alive; perhaps live in awe of a Creator God's dreadful power but otherwise eschew formal, institutionalized religion and instead take reason as a guide throughout life; do the good whenever possible, which translates basically into not harming any living soul and behaving toward others as one would hope that they behave towards one's self; and resign one's self to life's vicissitudes with peaceful and quiet forbearance.

In this way—and only this way—can a human being hope to be reasonably released from trouble and distress so long as she/he is on the face of the earth. Life is a disease. In these courses of action is to be found the cure to the disease so long as one is alive.

So much for how one can draw, and how al-Maʿarrī himself draws, a more or less logical, rational connection between his asceticism and ethics in the main, on the one hand, and, on the other hand, the additional dimensions of his thought. The fact remains that his asceticism and ethics *are* an integral part of that thought. Of greater significance is realizing and appreciating the extent to which they change the tone or character of *Luzūm* entirely.

Although admittedly often in rather peculiar ways, al-Maʿarrī's ethics, his commands and prohibitions in *Luzūm* that represent his ideal of the exemplary life, were intended to offer humans hope, whereas for the most part the rest of his thought in the *Luzūm* offers despair. His commands and prohibitions were intended to offer humans a modicum of contentment (in peaceful resignation and lack of pain), whereas for the most part the rest of his thought offers sorrow. His commands and prohibitions were intended to offer humans serenity, whereas for the most part the rest of his thought offers fear and anxiety. His commands and prohibitions were intended to show humankind a this-worldly exit from life's labyrinth of evil, injustice, uncertainty, and suffering, whereas for the most part in the rest of his thought he speaks to men and women of being imprisoned in that labyrinth, while vividly and jarringly describing it to them.

In their own often peculiar ways, al-Maʿarrī's ethics give his thought a positive humanitarian and moralistic component that otherwise is largely absent. His urging humankind to stop reproducing seems to belie that, seems almost oxymoronic, as does his recommendation that men and women shun their fellow men and women and live as recluses (with the women, unmarried as well as married, under the confining guardianship of males). But until such time as these extreme courses of action are fully and universally realized, or in the event that they cannot be, and regardless of whatever obstacles that various organized, institutionalized religions might present, al-Maʿarrī urged upon humankind the pursuit of peace instead of the pursuit of war; peaceful and respectful coexistence instead of hate and enmity; charity instead of selfish and violent self-aggrandizement; kindness instead of cruelty; tolerance instead of bigotry; sobriety and chasteness instead of inebriation and licentiousness; a more equitable distribution of wealth instead of maintaining societies of haves and have nots; and justice (especially for the ruled) instead of tyranny and oppression.

As paradoxical (or perhaps oxymoronic) as it might seem, even his call for a cessation to procreation is advocated by and large for humane reasons, much like the rationale for euthanasia, for example.

Finally, al-Maʿarrī's ethical prescriptions give his thought a sense of completion and resolution that otherwise are hard to discern. Without them, his thought largely destroys values and beliefs without replacing them with others, calls everything into question without providing any answers, and reminds humanity of its problems and difficulties without offering some suggestions as to how to solve or overcome them.

To repeat, all of this is admittedly manifested in ways so peculiar to most (and inchoate to begin with) that it is likely to go largely unnoticed, by devout Muslims in particular but also by most other readers of the *Luzūm*. For others as well as for devout Muslims, al-Maʿarrī's vision of life as it should be lived involves the debunking of certain beliefs, values, practices, and institutions long held sacrosanct and worthy of emulation. But the more positive side to the *Luzūm* cannot and should not be denied. Hence, to counter an opinion of al-Maʿarrī made long ago, but one to which probably many would be inclined to subscribe even today, the present study proposes that it is not quite fair or accurate to say that al-Maʿarrī "grumble[s] generally at political conditions, the opinions of the orthodox multitude, and the scientific assertions of the learned without being able himself to advance anything positive. . . . He can analyse, but he does not hit upon any synthesis, and his learning bears no fruit."[245] Nor is it quite fair to suggest that "he establishes nothing, at the level of either language or meaning."[246] Fairer and closer to the truth is to suggest that al-Maʿarrī hits upon a strange synthesis, albeit a synthesis; his learning does bear fruit, albeit a fruit that most are apt to find bitter and unpalatable for the most part. The synthesis that DeBoer found lacking was left for readers to construct but not because of an innate absolute inability on al-Maʿarrī's part to see synthesis and more obviously, more transparently present it. The reluctance to synthesize was part of the jesting, "the game" or "sport" (à la Ṭāhā Ḥusayn)[247] that al-Maʿarrī indulged in while composing the *Luzūm* over decades, alternating between clarity and obfuscation, coherence and incoherence, the sublime and the tedious and uninspired, all in order to keep his readers/interlocutors off guard.

For those who feel that they simply cannot tolerate al-Maʿarrī's thought in *Luzūm* because of real or apparent heresies and blasphemies, feel they must actively refute and denounce it even, this last observation is not likely to have much resonance. However, it is of significance for those who want simply a better understanding of al-Maʿarrī, whether they can countenance his thought or not. The full and proper understanding of al-Maʿarrī's thought in *Luzūm* should not deny that that thought often disparages humankind, revealed religion, life, and creation; that it is often un- and anti-Islamic, anti-social, anti-establishment; even blasphemous and unedifying—as this study and others describe it—in its conception of God; in truth pronouncedly agnostic if not atheistic or—which may be worse for many—even misotheistic. But a full and proper understanding of al-Maʿarrī's thought in *Luzūm* should also be prepared to concede that at bottom that thought did not really intend evil. And it did not intend or wish for immorality, disorder, confusion, and misery. In its own unconventional way, it strove for just the opposite. Al-Maʿarrī's thought did not aim to harm humankind but to heal and save it, though popular consensus may regard the cure worse than the diseases that it is supposed to eradicate, especially with regard to the call for self-extinction.

The palpably urgent and sober moral sentiment that resonates throughout the *Luzūm,* the overriding ethical imperative, the humanism that lay behind the irreligion and skepticism, may arguably be seen as al-Maʿarrī's crowning achievement in the work, notwithstanding the significance of the social, religious, and political criticism, the physical and metaphysical probings, the theology, the new poetic art being advanced, and so forth. In this respect, the *Luzūm*, despite whatever "nonconformist" precepts emerge as logical corollaries to first principles, very much typifies a larger natural progression to be associated with Islamicate thought: the advancement of ethical guidelines and doctrines, of a genuine overarching humanism, stretching back to the Qur'ān and including the books of *fiqh*/فقه, *ḥadīth*/حديث, *taṣawwuf*/تصوف, *adab*/أدب, and, finally, what in due course became a discipline in its own right among the more philosophically influenced in their writings/discourses, *'ilm al-akhlāq*/علم الأخلاق (ethics). The true Islamicate philosophers (i.e., the genuine heirs of *falsafah*), as well as those thinkers greatly influenced by the scientific rigor, depth, and breadth of these philosophers, took up general theoretical considerations as well as the matter-of-fact enumeration and/or repetition of practical rules of conduct. There was a Greco/Roman influence on this strand of *falsafah,* but in any event, to one degree or another in the premodern period, it may be seen as extending from at least the ninth-century (e.g., in a work such as the Baghdad-based al-Kindī's *Art of Dispelling Sorrow*) through to some of the works of the tenth-century Syrian-based al-Fārābī (e.g., *The Intellect, The Virtuous City, The Attainment of Happiness*), the tenth-century Persian- and Iraqi-based al-Rāzī (e.g., and especially, his *Spiritual Physic*), the eleventh-century, Persian-based Ibn Sīnā (e.g., his *The Book of Politics, The Book of Salvation*, and *The Book of Healing*), the eleventh-century peripatetic (Ṭūs, Nishapur, Baghdad, Damascus, Jerusalem) al-Ghazzālī (e.g., *Revitalization of the Sciences of Religion*) and Baghdad-based ethicist Ibn Miskawayh (e.g., his *The Improvement of Morals*) and the thirteenth-century Persian-based Nāṣir al-Dīn Ṭūsī's *Ethics.* The culmination of the process may be said to have been achieved by Ibn Miskawayh's *The Improvement of Morals* and Ṭūsī's *Ethics,* where the focus is specifically ethics, the scientific rigor and systematizing much in evidence, and the Greek influences most transparent and self-conscious. Miskawayh's *The Improvement of Morals* has been regarded by F. E. Peters as "the first systematic rethinking of a humanistic ethic since the Stoics left off that task in the second Christian century."[248]

Especially with regard to theoretical categories and taken as a whole, the *Luzūm* as an *adab*-framed ethical work may not have the breadth or depth (not to mention the more immediately obvious cohesiveness) of works such as those just mentioned. However, as an ethical work, it is a noteworthy—albeit maverick—part of the ambitious continuum that these works represent.

NOTES

Chapter One

1. The brief biography that follows is based primarily on the information gathered from the following sources: Henri Laoust's "La vie et la philosophie d'Abū'l-ʿAlā' al-Maʿarrī," *Bulletin d'études orientales* 10 (1944–45), pp. 119–57; D. S. Margoliouth's *The Letters of Abu 'l-'Alā, Anecdota Oxoniensa Semitic Series*, part X (Oxford: Clarendon, 1898); Pieter Smoor's "al-Maʿarrī" (*The Encyclopaedia of Islam,* second edition; hereafter *EI2*) *Kings and Bedouins in the Palace of Aleppo as Reflected in Ma'arrī's Works* (University of Manchester, 1985); تعريف القدماء بأبي العلاء المعري *Ta'rīf al-Qudamā' bi-Abī al-'Alā' al-Ma'arrī* (*Al-Ma'arrī as Presented by the Pre-Moderns*), ed. Ṭāhā Ḥusayn et al. (Cairo: Dār al-Kutub al-Miṣriyyah, 1944); and تجديد ذكرى أبي العلاء (*Tajdīd Dhikrā Abī al-'Alā'*) (*Recommemorating Abū al-'Alā'*) by Ṭāhā Ḥusayn (Seventh Edition, Cairo: Dār al-Maʿārif, 1968). Smoor gives every indication of having thoroughly and critically canvassed most of the major biographical monographs, sketches, and anecdotes about Abū al-ʿAlā', both modern and premodern and including especially the premodern Arabic materials contained in history-oriented chronicles or narratives. Most of the definitive premodern Arabic-language materials have been conveniently compiled under one cover, namely, *Ta'rīf al-Qudamā' bi-Abī al-'Alā'*. Among these, of special importance is a relatively longer treatise by Ibn al-ʿAdīm, viz. *al-Inṣāf wa al-Taḥarrī fī Daf' al-Ẓulm wa al-Tajarrī 'an Abī al-'Alā' al-Ma'arrī*/الإنصاف والتحري في دفع الظلم والتجري عن أبي العلاء المعري (*Fairness and Selection of the Best, in Driving Away from Abū al-'Alā' al-Ma'arrī Injustice and Recklessness*). Ṭāhā Ḥusayn drew extensively on the premodern Arabic chronicles and narratives in the biographical portions (i.e., chapters 1 and 2) of *Tajdīd Dhikrā Abī al-'Alā'*. Twenty five years after publishing the first edition of his *Tajdīd Dhikrā Abī al-'Alā'*, Ṭāhā Ḥusayn in revisiting the thought

of Abū al-ʿAlāʾ (*Ma'a Abī al-'Alā' fī Sijnih*/ مع أبي العلاء في سجنه/ *With Abū al-'Alā' in His Prison*) (Cairo: Dār al-Maʿārif, 1939) declared that he would not attempt a new biographical sketch of the man because, he said, although between 1914 and 1939 a few books or epistles of his previously not available had turned up, "they add nothing to what we already know about his life" (p. 21). Ṭāhā Ḥusayn's account of al-Maʿarrī's life as presented in *Tajdīd Dhikrā Abī al-'Alā'* remains fairly canonical to this day. Similar although hardly identical, and thus of some interest because of some occasional different points of emphasis or extrapolation, are the brief biographies contained in the studies of Zakī al-Maḥāsinī, ʿAṭā Bakrī, *'Abd* al-Qādir Zaydān, and Hādī al-ʿAlawī. The most exhaustive listing of works with reference to al-Maʿarrī, biographical or otherwise, modern or premodern, superficially anecdotal or more substantive, up through the first half of the twentieth century, can be found in the 309-page annotated bibliographical study by Moustapha Saleh, "Abū'l-ʿAlāʾ al-Maʿarrī, Bibliographie critique,"*Bulletin d'études orientales* XXII (1969), XXIII (1970). This work is especially valuable for revealing where (and the extent to which) there is repetition (which in fact is frequent) or merely relatively brief anecdotes or passing remarks.

2. Nāṣir-i Khusraw (394–453 Islamic Era, 1002–61 Common Era), سفرنامه / *Safarnāmeh* (*Book of Travels*), as cited in *Ta'rīf al-Qudamā'*, 581–82.

3. Ibn Baṭṭūṭah, *Tuḥfat al-Nuẓẓār fī Gharā'ib al-Amṣār wa 'Ajā'ib al-Asfār*/ تحفة النظار في غرائب الأمصار وعجائب الأسفار (*The Prized Possession of the Viewer of Cities' Peculiarities and Travels' Curiosities*), more commonly referred to as رحلة ابن بطوطة (*The Travels of Ibn Baṭṭūṭah*), as cited in *Ta'rīf al-Qudamā'*, p. 597.

4. According to the classical Arab geographers; see D. S. Margoliouth, *Letters*, xii, n. 3.

5. Cited by D. S. Margoliouth, *Letters*, xii, n. 3.

6. D. S. Margoliouth, *Letters*, p. 43.

7. D. S. Margoliouth's translation, in *Letters*, p. 8; from the Arabic:

فهي كشهري ربيع سُمّيا مع الشهور في أوائل الدهور فصارتا بعد الجمد إلى الومد . . .
ولو لا جفاء التربة والأحجار عن التخلق بأخلاق الجار لأصبحت ساحتها للتأدب مختاره
والفصاحة من عن أهلها ممتاره.

8. D. S. Margoliouth's translation, in *Letters*, 61–62; from the Arabic:

ولو لا القاضي أبو جعفر لكان مثله بقدوم هذه الناحية مثل النسر الذي هو من ملوك الطير
وعظمائها تتصل من أوصاله رائحة المسك يهبط على نبيلة جِدّ وَبيلة وهذه جمل من صفة

المعرة هي ضد ما قال الله عز وجل مثل الجنة ... اسمها طِيرَة وعند الله ترجى الخيرة. المورد بها محتبس وظاهرترابها في الصيف يبس ليس لها ماء جار ولاتغرس بها غرائب الأشجار.

9. D. S. Margoliouth's translation, in *Letters*, p. 67; from the Arabic:

ونشأت في بلد لا عالم فيه وإنما تشبث النامية بالجواز

10. *Inbāh al-Ruwāh 'alā Anbāh al-Nuḥāh*/إنباه الرواة على أنباه النحاة

وكان الطلبة إذا قصدوه أنفقوا على أنفسهم من موجودهم ولم يكن له من السعة ما يبرّهم به وأهل اليسار من أهل المعرة يُعرفون بالبخل فكان رحمه الله يتأوّه من ذلك ويعتذر إلى قاصديه.

11. *Al-Inṣāf wa al-Taḥarrī*, cited in *Ta'rīf al-Qudamā'*, p. 477.

12. *Al-Inṣāf wa al-Taḥarrī*, cited in *Ta'rīf al-Qudamā'*, p. 488.

13. Ibn al-ʿAdīm, *Al-Inṣāf wa al-Taḥarrī*, cited in *Taʿrīf al-Qudamā'*, pp. 488–90. For a concise "modern" overview of this early chapter in Arab/Islamic history, and particularly the role of Abū ʿUbaydah Ibn al-Jarrāḥ, one might consult Philip Hitti, *History of the Arabs* (Tenth Edition, London: Macmillan, 1970), 147–54 (although the Tanūkh are not mentioned in these pages, brief but insightful observations on them do appear on pp. 65, 81, and 360; those on p. 360 point out that the ʿAbbāsid caliph al-Mahdī [775–85 CE], reflecting a greater sense of urgency with respect to having subject populations convert to Islam, felt compelled in particular to order five thousand Christian Tanūkh of Aleppo to embrace Islam en masse). If only in passing, it is quite remarkable in this context to compare the account of Ibn al-ʿAdīm—the medieval Arab Muslim chronicler—on conversion (particularly with respect to Syria) with the account of Philip Hitti—the modern Arab Christian historian. Hitti, quoting Balādhurī's *Futūḥ al-Buldān*/فتوح البلدان (*The Conquest of Nations*), draws attention to a most considerate, charitable Khālid ibn al-Walīd, celebrated conqueror of Damascus. Khālid promises security—for "lives, property, and churches"—to the Damascenes. "So long as they pay the poll tax, nothing but good should befall them." In the same vein, Hitti quotes as "representative of the sentiments cherished by the native Syrians towards the new conquerors" the following line from Balādhurī, allegedly spoken by the population of Ḥimṣ: "We like your rule and justice far better than the state of oppression and tyranny under which we have been living." (The tyranny and oppression would have been with reference to the Byzantines.) Ibn al-ʿAdīm's account of the early conversion of Tanūkh goes as follows:

When ʿUmar [Ibn al-Khaṭṭāb]—God be pleased with him—came to Syria, the Tanūkh came forward to him. He said to them "I shall not be content with you unless you become Muslims. It is either that or the sword." He gave them two years (to comply). Then he imposed upon them what was imposed upon non-Muslim subjects in the way of the poll tax (الجزية). The Tanūkh refused this. "Take the money from us in the name of the voluntary contribution of alms (الصدقة), but not in the name of the poll tax," they said. ʿUmar refused this. But then he consented to take the money in the name of the land tax (الخراج). Some of the Tanūkh complied with this.

فلما سار عمر رضي الله عنه إلى الشام قدموا عليه فقال: ما أقنع منكم إلا بالدخول في الإسلام أو السيف، وأمهلهم سنتين. ثم أنه ألزمهم ما يلزم أهل الذمة من الجزية فأبوا عليه وقالوا خذ المال منّا على اسم الصدقة دون اسم الجزية فأبى عمر ثم أجابهم إلى أن يأخذها على اسم الخراج فاستجاب له قوم منهم.

14. Ibn al-ʿAdīm, *al-Inṣāf wa al-Taḥarrī*, in *Taʿrīf al-Qudamāʾ*, p. 490; see the poem of praise by Abū Bakr Aḥmad ibn Muḥammad al-Ṣanawbarī.

15. An example of a short descriptive piece on a candle and its light is provided by Ibn al-ʿAdīm, *al-Inṣāf wa al-Taḥarrī*, in *Taʿrīf al-Qudamāʾ*, pp. 490–91.

16. وكان . . . فاضلا أديبا لغويا شاعرا; Ibn al-ʿAdīm, *al-Inṣāf wa al-Taḥarrī*, in *Taʿrīf al-Qudamāʾ*, p. 492.

17. Ibn al-ʿAdīm, *al-Inṣāf wa al-Taḥarrī*, in *Taʿrīf al-Qudamāʾ*, p. 499:

وكان رئيس المعرة وكبيرها والمقدم بها وولّى القضاء بها بعد أبيه

18. Ibn al-ʿAdīm, *al-Inṣāf wa al-Taḥarrī*, in *Taʿrīf al-Qudamāʾ*, p. 499.

19. *Al-Inṣāf wa al-Taḥarrī*, in *Taʿrīf al-Qudamāʾ*, p. 511.

20. Letters VII, XVII, XVIII, and XX, in D. S. Margoliouth, *Letters*.

21. XXX in the collection edited and translated by Margoliouth.

22. VII in D. S. Margoliouth's collection.

23. D. S. Margoliouth, *Letters*, pp. 35–36.

24. Beirut: Dār Ṣādir, 1963, p. 46. The poem with the canonical pre-modern commentaries by al-Baṭalyūsī (البطليوسي), al-Tibrīzī (التبريزي), and al-Khwārazmī (الخوارزمي) can be found in *Shurūḥ Saqṭ al-Zand* (شروح سقط الزند) (*The Explications of Saqṭ al-Zand*), ed. by Ṭāhā Ḥusayn et al., in five volumes (Cairo: Dār al-Maʿārif, 1964), pp. 1685–91.

25. Beirut: Dār Ṣādir, 1963, p. 39.

26. See pp. 13–18 of the Beirut Dār Ṣādir edition.

27. XXIV in the D. S. Margoliouth collection, p. 67.

28. "And he named himself 'the hostage of two prison houses,' meaning his vision and his home"; وسمّى نفسه رهن المحبسين يعني منزله وبصره; *Mir'āh al-Zaman*/مرآة الزمن (*The Mirror of Time*); cited in *Ta'rīf al-Qudamā'*, p. 144.

29. Al-ʿAbbās al-Makkī, *Nuzhat al-Jalīs*/نزهة الجليس (*The Promenade of the Sitting Companion*), in *Ta'rīf al-Qudamā'*, p. 353.

30. According to al-Suyūṭī, *Bughyat al-Wu'āh*/بغية الوعاة (*The Objective of the Sagacious*), cited in *Ta'rīf al-Qudamā'*, p. 322.

31. Al-Dhahabī, *Tārīkh al-Islām*, cited in *Ta'rīf al-Qudamā'*, p. 191.

32. Ibn al-ʿAdīm, *al-Inṣāf wa al-Taḥarrī*, cited in *Ta'rīf al-Qudamā'*, p. 514.

33. *Tārīkh al-Islām*, cited in *Ta'rīf al-Qudamā'*, p. 191.

34. For example: al-Dhahabī, Ibn al-Wardī, al-Suyūṭī, Ibn al-ʿAdīm; see the sections under their names in *Ta'rīf al-Qudamā'*.

35. *Inbāh al-Ruwāh*, cited in *Ta'rīf al-Qudamā'*, p. 30.

36. In *Taʿrīf al-Qudamā'*, pp. 30–31; the relevant Arabic with respect to the monastery at Latakia is as follows:

> فاجتاز باللاذقية ونزل دير الفاروس وكان به راهب يشدو شيئا من علوم الأوائل فسمع منه
> أبو العلاء كلاما من أوائل أقوال الفلاسفة

37. For al-Dhahabī, see *Ta'rīf al-Qudamā'*, p. 190; for al-Ṣafadī and al-ʿAbbāsī, see *Ta'rīf al-Qudamā'*, p. 288 and p. 337 respectively.

38. *Al-Inṣāf wa al-Taḥarrī*, cited in *Ta'rīf al-Qudamā'*, p. 555.

39. D. S. Margoliouth, *Letters*, xvii.

40. D. S. Margoliouth, *Letters*, p. 32, in the Arabic section for the Arabic text of the letter; see VII for the English translation (p. 40).

41. See D. S. Margoliouth, *Letters*, p. 44, for his English translation of the Arabic text that appears on pp. 34–35 of the Arabic section.

42. *Inbāh al-Ruwāh*, in *Ta'rīf al-Qudamā'*, p. 31. Al-Dhahabī has a similar entry, reprinted in D. S. Margoliouth, *Letters*, Arabic text p. 129, although the "officials" in Aleppo (نواب حلب) who raise objections to the income from the endowment become the "prince" or "governor" of Aleppo (أمير حلب). Margoliouth notes that the information "is not free from difficulty; for the governor of Haleb at this time is not dependent on Baghdad, but on Cairo"; but—more importantly—he hastens to add, and quite reasonably, that "We may . . . believe that the loss of this pension was the reason for the poet's quitting Maʿarrah, without supposing that he went to Baghdad to recover it. His letters and poems say nothing about the pensions; but it is clear from

them that he went to Baghdad with the idea of staying there permanently"; see *Letters*, xx–xxi. Perhaps Margoliouth's "may" needs to be italicized. The loss of a pension, even if that did occur, does not necessarily mean that it was the reason for al-Maʿarrī's having left Maʿarrat al-Nuʿmān and striking out for Baghdad.

43. *Inbāh al-Ruwāh*, in *Ta'rīf al-Qudamā'*, p. 30.

44. *Al-Inṣāf wa al-Taḥarrī*, in *Ta'rīf al-Qudamā'*, p. 514.

45. *Al-Inṣāf wa al-Taḥarrī*, in *Ta'rīf al-Qudamā'*, p. 534–34. The poem eulogizing Abū Aḥmad Mūsā is in *Saqṭ al-Zand* (Beirut Dār Ṣādir edition, p. 31).

46. The overview in this paragraph inclusive of the citations draw from Joel Kraemer, *Humanism in the Renaissance of Islam* (Second Revised Edition. E. J. Brill: Leiden, 1993), pp. 55–57.

47. Mafizullah Kabir, *The Buwayhid Dynasty of Baghdad* (Calcutta: Iran Society, 1964), p. 181.

48. D. S. Margoliouth, *Letters*, p. 52, for the Arabic.

49. D. S. Margoliouth, *Letters*, pp. 58–59.

50. Mafizullah Kabir, *The Buwayhid Dynasty of Baghdad*, p. 181. The line in question, followed by Kabir's translation, is as follows:

وغنت لنا في دار سابور قينة　　من الورق مطراب الأصائل مهياب

There appeared to us in the House of Sābūr a songstress,
made of silver, gay in the evening and excited.

51. Letter VII in D. S. Margoliouth, *Letters*, pp. 37–38. The quotations here are either from proverbs or verses of poetry by other poets.

52. D. S. Margoliouth, *Letters,* p. 40.

53. D. S. Margoliouth, *Letters*, p. 44.

54. Cited by Ibn al-ʿAdīm, *al-Inṣāf wa al-Taḥarrī*, in *Ta'rīf al-Qudamā'*, p. 542.

55. Al-Dhahabī, *Tārīkh al-Islām* (*The History of Islam*), cited in *Ta'rīf al-Qudamā'*, p. 196.

56. D. S. Margoliouth, *Letters*, xxviii.

57. Yāqūt al-Ḥamawī reports the incident in his *Irshād al-Arīb ilā Ma'rifat al-Adīb*/إرشاد الأريب إلى معرفة الأديب (*The Guide of the Intelligent to the Knowledge of the Literate*), cited in *Ta'rīf al-Qudamā'*, p. 76. D. S. Margoliouth's account is in *Letters*, xxviii.

58. Letter VII in D. S. Margoliouth, *Letters*, p. 42.

59. Letter VIII in D. S. Margoliouth, *Letters*, p. 43.

60. D. S. Margoliouth, *Letters*, xxxix.

61. III in D. S. Margoliouth's *Letters.*

62. See XIX in D. S. Margoliouth's *Letters,* and n. 4, p. 58 with the reference to Ibn Khallikān.

63. XXIV in D. S. Margoliouth's *Letters.*

64. *Kings and Bedouins*, passim.

65. نشوار المحاضرة وأخبار المذاكرة (*Lecturing's Rumination and Tales of Recollection*) was translated by D. S. Marogoliouth (with the title of *The Table Talk of a Mesopotamian Judge*).

66. *Apud* Pieter Smoor; *Kings and Bedouins*, p. 99.

67. Pieter Smoor, *Kings and Bedouins*, p. 99, 15, n. 35.

68. Pieter Smoor, *Kings and Bedouins*, p. 96.

69. Pieter Smoor, *Kings and Bedouins*, pp. 96–97; *EI2*, "al-Maʿarrī"; and *Journal of Arabic Literature* 12 (1981), 50–51.

70. For details of the incident based on the standard premodern historical-biographical sources, as well as on al-Maʿarrī's own references (in verses of *Luzūm Mā Lā Yalzam*) to his mediation with Ṣāliḥ, see Pieter Smoor, *Kings and Bedouins*, pp. 144–159; and also Ṭāhā Ḥusayn, *Tajdīd Dhikrā Abī al-'Alā'*, pp. 57).

71. Ibn al-ʿAdīm *apud* Pieter Smoor, *Kings and Bedouins*, p. 66.

72. Pieter Smoor, *Kings and Bedouins*, passim.

73. The correspondence in Arabic with accompanying English translation by D.S Margoliouth are in the *Journal of the Royal Asiatic Society* (April, 1902), pp. 289–332.

74. Ibn al-Qifṭī, *Inbāh al-Ruwāh*, in *Ta'rīf al-Qudamā'*, p. 63; *apud* Pieter Smoor, *EI2*, "al-Maʿarrī."

75. For a brief description of the conventions of style to which letters in Arabic were supposed to conform in al-Maʿarrī's time, see D. S. Margoliouth, *Letters*, xli–xliii. Margoliouth notes that above all else letters were expected to employ rhyme, highly pedantic language, and frequent proverbs and idiomatic expressions; "and those compositions which were intended not only to convey a message of immediate importance, but to have permanent literary value, had a tendency to get more and more obscure" (xli). The standards for the "epistolary style" were allegedly set by Abū Ghālib ʿAbd al-Ḥamīd, secretary to the last Umayyad caliph, Marwān (xli).

76. Wiesbaden: Harrassowitz Verlag, 2013. Peltz's study, especially with the massive glossary that comprises part 2, provides among other things a valuable semantic mapping and topical layout of coordinates for the recurring features

of al-Maʿarrī's thoughts, sentiments, and figures of speech as expressed in *al-Fuṣūl wa al-Ghāyāt.*

77. *Zajr al-Nābiḥ* by Amjad al-Ṭarabulsī (Damascus, 1965); and *Mulqā al-Sabīl* by Ḥasan Ḥusnī ʿAbd al-Wahhāb (Damascus, 1912).

78. Although these are not without interest; see e.g., S. M. Stern's, "Some Noteworthy Manuscripts of the Poems of Abū al-ʿAlā' al-Maʿarrī," *Oriens* 7 (1954); I. Krackovskiy's *Abū al-'Alā' al-Ma'arrī, Mulqā al-Sabīl*, Petrograd (1915).

79. P. 28, Beirut Edition [n.d.].

80. *Al-Inṣāf wa al-Taḥarrī,* cited in *Ta'rīf al-Qudamā'*, p. 527.

81. Cairo: The Egyptian Book Organization.

82. Cited in *Ta'rīf al-Qudamā'*, p. 527.

83. Cited in *Ta'rīf al-Qudamā'*, p. 8; reading—as one recension of this observation has it subsequent to al-Bākharzī—الجناية for الحيانة; see *Ta'rīf al-Qudamā'*, p. 8, n. 3; for "and hastened . . . as the ass hastens to the Ṣilliyānah plant," see Lane's *Lexicon,* part 2, p. 394, where this is given as a proverbial expression for "one who boldly ventures upon taking a false oath"; the literal meaning of جذّ being "to cut" or "cut off" a thing or object.

84. See *Ta'rīf al-Qudamā'*, p. 527.

85. Cairo, 11th edition: Dār al-Maʿārif, 1971.

86. See p. 201.

87. *Ma'a Abī al-'Alā' fī Sijnih,* pp. 197–200.

88. *Ma'a Abī al-'Alā' fī Sijnih,* p. 231.

89. The emphasis is that of the present study.

90. *Cambridge History of Arab Literature*, ed. Julia Ashtiany, T.M. Johnston, et al. (Cambridge University Press, 1990), p. 74.

91. "Der 'Koran' des Abū'l-ʿAlā'"; in *Berichtung über die Verhandlung ders Sächsishcen Akademie der Wissenschaften Leipzig, Phil.-Hist.* Kl. no. 94 (1942), vol. 2.

92. "Some Fragments of the *Mu'āradat al-Qur'ān* Attributed to Ibn al-Muqaffaʿ," *Studia Arabica and Islamica,* ed. Widad al-Qadi (Beirut, 1981), p. 153, and Addendum, p. 11.

93. P. 158, p. 160.

94. Peltz's *Der Koran des Abū l-'Alā'* does not fail to underscore—already in al-Maʿarrī's lifetime (e.g., and most remarkably, the testimony by Nāṣir-i Khusraw) but especially in the ensuing centuries—the presence of bio-bibliographical sources in Arabic that mention the possibility of a parodic intent (to one degree or another) lying behind composing *al-Fuṣūl*

wa al-Ghāyāt. "No source overlooks the charge (Vorwurf) that the *Fuṣūl* are a parody (eine Parodie) of the Koran." Peltz is translating عارض as "to parody" as opposed to "imitate"; see 2.3.5 (pp. 20–21) and 2.3.6 (21–22) for his discussion. (I gratefully acknowledge the assistance of Nicholas Reynolds [assistant professor of German, Trinity University, San Antonio, Texas] for some of the takeaways in the perusal of *Der Koran des Abū l-'Alā'*.)

95. Ameen Rihani (Amīn Rīḥānī), *The Luzumiyat of Abu'l-Ala* (New York: James T. White, 1918), p. 22.

96. *Risālat al-Ṣāhil wa al-Shājiḥ*, Dār al-Ma'ārif, Cairo, 1975.

97. See his "Enigmatic Allusion and Double Meaning in al-Ma'arrī's Newly-Discovered Letter of a Horse and a Mule," *Journal of Arabic Literature* 12 (1981), 13 (1982), and also the relevant portion of his "al-Ma'arrī," *EI2*.

98. R. A. Nicholson, *The Risālatu'l-Ghufrān* (JRAS, Art. 25) 1900, p. 639.

99. NYU Press, 2013, 2014.

100. Ameen Rihani, *The Luzumiyat of Abu'l-Ala* (New York: James T. White, 1918), p. 22.

101. See the *Journal of the Royal Asiatic Society*; for 1900, pp. 637–720; and for 1902, pp. 75–101, 337–62, 813–47.

102. See Palascio's once fairly celebrated *La Escatología musulmana en la Divina Comedia* (Madrid, 1919); English tr. *Islam and the Divine Comedy* by Harold Sutherland (London: Frank Cass, 1968).

103. *Risālat al-Ghufrān* (Cairo, 1954).

104. *Saqṭ al-Zand* (William Penn College, 1972).

105. Manchester: University of Manchester, 1985.

106. *Sitzungsberichte der Philosophischen-Historischen Classe der Akademie der Wissenschaften* (Vienna), 17, no. 5, pp. 1–108.

107. 'Azīz Effendī Zand (Cairo: al-Maḥrūsah Press).

108. His trials and tribulations as an argumentative and intellectually audacious student, even as a teenager and especially at al-Azhar (at which he enrolled at age 12), are of course the leitmotif of his autobiography *al-Ayyām* (*The Days*).

109. Cambridge: Cambridge University Press, 1907.

110. Cambridge: Cambridge University Press, 1921.

111. *Bulletin d'études orientales*, x, pp. 119–57.

112. Second Edition. Beirut: al-Kashshāf Press, 1948.

113. Second Edition. Cairo: Anglo-Egyptian Bookstore, 1970.

114. Beirut: Dār al-Ma'ārif, 1963.

115. Beirut: Maktabat al-Ḥayāh, 1980.

116. *Majallat Dirāsāt* (The University of Jordan) 12, no. 3 (1985).

117. *Majallat Dirāsāt (*n.d.).

118. Cairo: Al-Hay'ah al-Miṣriyyah al-'Āmmah li al-Kitāb, 1986.

119. Second Edition. Damascus: Al-Mada, 2007.

120. *A History of Islamic Philosophy* (New York: Columbia University, 1970), p. 11.

121. Oxford: Oneworld Publications, *Beginners Guide* series, pp. 44–46.

122. One of the problems with the doctrinal (or, if you will, religio-philosophical orientation) labels, although admittedly it is virtually impossible to ignore them entirely.

123. *Ibn Khaldun's Philosophy of History* (Chicago: University of Chicago Press, 1964), p. 11. Another compelling reason for taking this approach, notwithstanding the difficulties involved in reading al-Ma'arri's works, lies in the fact that we are fortunate to have a relatively sizable body of his works, in *his* words and in their original format, as opposed to relatively few fragments and fragments that (few or many) are reported by commentators/biographers, a situation which, as Sarah Stroumsa has pointed out (in *Freethinkers of Medieval Islam: Ibn al-Rāwandī, Abū Bakr al-Rāzī, and Their Impact on Islamic Thought* [Leiden: Brill, 1999, p.17]) with respect to others in the history of Islamic thought, makes interpretation even more speculative than normal and furthermore can allow for objections on the basis of "Aussagen über Aussagen," i.e., information two-, three-, or even four-times removed. Stroumsa had in mind Ibn al-Rāwandī especially, and (although to a lesser extent) also Abū Bakr al-Rāzī, who are the focii of *Freethinkers of Medieval Islam*; but adds (ibid.) that "practically everything written on ninth-century Islamic theology" is based on fragmentary material filtered through commentators/biographers (and of course not necessarily fair and balanced ones).

124. "The Meditations of Ma'arrí," *Studies in Islamic Poetry* (Cambridge: Cambridge University Press, 1921), p. 44.

125. See "The Meditations of Ma'arrí," p. 51.

126. To that end, the translations of verses from the *Luzūm* that are by the author of this study do not attempt the exceptionally fluid renderings or transpositions of the sort represented by Nicholson or Rihani or more recently Paul Smith in *Al-Ma'arri, Life and Poems* and *The Book of al-Ma'arri* (Campbells Creek Victoria Australia: New Humanities Books, 2014, 2015), where cadence (i.e., meters) and rhymes (or near rhymes) are employed. The translations of the present study aim primarily for capturing

meaning. Thus, on the one hand, they have the style of plain prose and may admittedly be comparatively wooden at times. On the other hand, as Bahman Solati in *The Wine Goblet of Ḥāfeẓ* (New York: Peter Lang, 201), xix has written about translation, "the primary aim of the translator of poetry should be to present the original as accurately as possible with respect to meaning, even if this means sacrificing at times (or entirely) the replication of meters and rhyme." Even Nicholson speaks of achieving only a "shadowy resemblance" in trying to "imitate the original meters" of the *Luzūm* and concludes that "more than that we dare not hope for: even when transplanted by skillful hands they lose the best of their beauty and never become quite acclimatised" ("The Meditations," p. 55). Rihani (*The Luzumiyat*, p. 16) had the following to say about his selections "first rendered" into English:

> There being no affinity between the Arabic and the English, their standards of art and beauty widely differ, and in the process of transformation the outer garment at times must necessarily be doffed. I have always adhered to the spirit.

In the same passage from which this quotation comes, Rihani also makes mention of a "native imagery" that can be "too clannish or grotesque" (and that he tried to avoid in his renederings/transformations).

With respect to translation in general, Nabokov held that "the clumsiest literal translation is a thousand times more useful than the prettiest paraphrase"; *apud* Jiyang Fan, "Buried Words" (*The New Yorker*, January 15, 2018), p. 62.

Chapter Two

*The principal sources consulted for the first section of chapter 2 includes the following: Carl Brockelmann, *History of the Islamic Peoples* (New York: Capricorn Books, 1960); *The Encylopaedia of Islam* (Leiden: E. J. Brill); Philip Hitti, *History of the Arabs* (London: Macmillan, Tenth Edition, 1970); Marshall G. S. Hodgson, *The Venture of Islam* (Chicago: University of Chicago, 1974); P. M. Holt, Ann K. S. Lambton, and Bernard Lewis, *The Cambridge History of Islam* (Vol. 1; Cambridge: University Press, 1970); Albert Hourani, *A History of the Arab People* (New York: Warner Books, 1991); Mafizullah Kabir, *The Buwayhid Dynasty of Baghdad* (Calcutta: Iran Society, 1964); Ira Lapidus, *A History of Islamic Societies* (Cambridge:

University Press: 2002); *Shorter Encyclopaedia of Islam* (Ithaca: Cornell University Press, 1965); Pieter Smoor, *Kings and Bedouins in the Palace of Aleppo as Reflected in Ma'arrī's Works* (University of Manchester, 1985); Suhayl Zakkar, *The Emirate of Aleppo 1004–1094* (Beirut: Dār al-Amānah, 1971); 'Abd al-Qādir Zaydān, *Qaḍāyā al-'Aṣr fī Adab Abī al-'Alā'* (Cairo: al-Hay'ah al-Miṣriyyah li al-Kitāb, 1986); and Ṭāhā Ḥusayn, *Tajdīd Dhikrā Abī al-'Alā'* (Cairo, 7th Edition: Dār al-Ma'ārif, 1968). All of the above works draw on primary sources; in several significant instances (e.g., *The Encylopaeida of Islam, History of the Arabs, The Buwayhid Dynasty of Baghdad, The Emirate of Aleppo 1004–1094, Kings and Bedouins in the Palace of Aleppo as Reflected in Ma'arrī's Works*) most exhaustively in terms of detail and specific historical chronicles consulted.

The narrative that follows in the first section of chapter 2 of the present study admittedly stands squarely on the shoulders of the narratives of the aforementioned sources. It does not pretend otherwise. To that end, it largely dispenses with end notes preceded by tags such as "according to" or "see."

In the course of their studies on al-Ma'arrī, and drawing on primary sources, Ṭāhā Ḥusayn (*Tajdīd Dhikrā Abī al-'Alā'*), Nicholson ("The Meditations of Ma'arrí," chapter 2 of his *Studies in Islamic Poetry*), and, not to mention more obviously Pieter Smoor (*Kings and Bedouins*), all give adequate illustrations of some of the more consequential social, political, and economic tensions and turmoil in tenth- and eleventh-century Islamic societies. Mafizullah Kabir's *The Buwayhid Dynasty of Baghdad* contains much material of a similar nature as it applies particularly to the city of Baghdad and its environs. Citing from the year-by-year historical reports of Ibn Taghrībardī (i.e., *al-Nujūm al-Zāhirah*), Nicholson, for example (idem, pp. 98–99), draws attention to specific civil wars, famines, pestilence, and inflation in wheat and bread prices. "Prevailing anarchy" and "social and economic disorders of the gravest kind" were his impressions of the period (p. 98). Citing the historian ('Abd al-Laṭīf) al-Baghdadī, Ḥusayn paints an especially gruesome picture of a "universal famine" that led to cannibalizing living as well as dead corpses and the eating of dogs (idem, p. 67). Smoor concentrates on the specifics (e.g., identifiable personal and place names, dates, and historical events) of what can be learned from al-Ma'arrī himself—not always an easy task, and for that reason alone Smoor's *Kings and Bedouins* is a remarkable undertaking. Political, social, and religious tensions, not to mention armed conflict, are highlighted by Smoor. Kabir's work is especially revealing for a ground-level view of a major urban center disintegrating at certain levels, including that of Sunnī-Shīʿite peaceful coexistence (if not mutual love and affection). Redolent of Kabir's work in terms of detail, but with a different geographical setting—fortuitously one that is even more central to the life and times of al-Maʿarrī—is Suhayl Zakkar's *The Emirate of Aleppo 1004–1094*. The political upheavals (i.e, battles, sieges, shifting alliances) occasioned by the struggle for supremacy among the Mirdāsids, Fāṭimids, and Byzantines dominate Zakkar's narrative, but the narrative also contains many valuable insights on ethnic and religious strife, including not only the inter-Muslim but also the Christian-Muslim (for which see especially pp. 235–64). Speaking of northern Syria, Zakkar's assessment (p. 239) is that "perpetual [Muslim and Christian] religious strife gave this region and its inhabitants special attributes and made its impression." Marshall G. S. Hodgson's early chapters in *The Order of Assassins* (The Hague: Mouton, 1955) give the grand overview of the confrontation of (Fāṭimid) Ismāʿīlī Shīʿism with (Seljūk) Sunnism in the eleventh century CE. Drawing on primary as well as secondary source materials, he speaks of a period of declining prosperity and jettisoning of civic institutions; even a reconfiguration, in cities, of previously inherited more open and cohesive urban spaces, this in order that more discreet, walled-off and compartmentalized urban quarters could result.

1. As Albert Hourani has underscored with respect to "political unity" during the time of the ʿAbbāsids, one must not exaggerate; "Even when the ʿAbbāsid caliph's power was at its height, his effective rule was limited. It existed mainly in the cities and the productive areas around them; there were distant regions of mountain and steppe which were virtually unsubdued" (*A History of the Arab Peoples* [New York, Warner Books, 1991], p. 38).

2. *EI2*, p. 861.

3. For details, see Suhayl Zakkar, *The Emirate of Aleppo*, p. 56, where Zakkar cites several primary sources (more specifically, premodern historical chronicles).

4. Suhayl Zakkar, *The Emirate of Aleppo*, p. 129; for more details on the man and his times, see the same work passim but especially chapter 3.

5. Ibn al-ʿAdīm, *Zubdat al-Ḥalab min Tārīkh Ḥalab*/زبدة الحلب من تاريخ حلب (*The Cream at the Top in the History of Aleppo*), *apud* Smoor, *Kings and Bedouins*, p. 204.

6. Suhayl Zakkar, *The Emirate of Aleppo*, p. 144.

7. Suhayl Zakkar, *The Emirate of Aleppo*, p. 83, citing several primary sources (the premodern historical chronicles).

8. Suhayl Zakkar, *The Emirate of Aleppo*, p. 41; p. 81 (citing several of the premodern historical chronicles).

9. Suhayl Zakkar, *The Emirate of Aleppo*, p. 58 (citing several of the premodern historical chronicles).

10. See Smoor, *Kings and Bedouins*, p. 5; and Suhayl Zakkar, *The Emirate of Aleppo*, p. 60, where several of the standard premodern historical chronicles are cited.

11. As cited by Ibn al-'Adīm, *Bughyat al-Ṭalab fī Tārīkh Ḥalab*/ بغية الطلب في تاريخ حلب (*The Objective of Study of the History of Aleppo*), *apud* Suhayl Zakkar, *The Emirate of Aleppo*, p. 236.

12. *Safar-Nameh* (*The Book of Travel*) (Arabic tr. al-Khashshāb [Cairo: 1945]), pp. 10–11, *apud* Suhayl Zakkar, *The Emirate of Aleppo*, p. 236.

13. Ibn al-'Adīm, *Zubdat al-Ḥalab min Tārīkh Ḥalab*, *apud* Suhayl Zakkar, *The Emirate of Aleppo*, p. 173.

14. *Apud* Suhayl Zakkar, *The Emirate of Aleppo*, p. 241, where several of the standard premodern chronicles are cited.

15. *The Emirate of Aleppo*, pp. 243–45, based on several of the standard premodern chronicles; the quotation with respect to the proliferation of taverns and brothels appears on p. 245.

16. See Suhayl Zakkar, *The Emirate of Aleppo*, pp. 245–49 for his overview of these events based on several of the standard medieval Arabic chronicles.

17. Suhayl Zakkar, *The Emirate of Aleppo*, p. 254 (citing several of the standard medieval Arabic chronicles).

18. Mafizullah Kabir, *The Buwayhid Dynasty of Baghdad*, p. 68.

19. Ibn al-Jawzī, *al-Muntaẓam fī Tārīkh al-Mulūk wa al-Umam* (*The Compendium on the History of Kings and Nations*) (Hyderbad Edition, 1938–43); Ibn al-Athīr, *Chronicon* (Leyden, 1851–76), IX, p. 233; *apud* Mafizullah Kabir, *The Buwayhid Dynasty of Baghdad* , p. 99.

20. Demitri Gutas, *Greek Thought, Arabic Culture* (London: Routledge, 1998), p. 13.

21. Demitri Gutas, *Greek Thought, Arabic Culture,* p. 1.

22. Demitri Gutas, *Greek Thought, Arabic Culture*, p. 137; Joel L. Kraemer, *Humanism in the Renaissance of Islam* (Leiden: E. J. Brill, 1992), p. xxii.

23. For more detailed accounts, with focii on the above-mentioned remarkable savants as examples of the spirit of the age and the means by which learning was commonly advanced before the advent of the *madrasah* in the Islamicate commonwealth, Joel L. Kraemer's *Humanism in the Renaissance of Islam* is excellent.

24. See his "Ḳarmaṭians," *SEI* (*Shorter Encyclopaedia of Islam*), p. 218.

25. Massignon, "Ḳarmaṭians," *SEI,* p. 218.

26. Massignon, "Ḳarmaṭians," *SEI,* p. 219.

27. Massignon, "Ḳarmaṭians," *SEI,* p. 219.

28. *Wikipedia.*

29. "Ḳarmaṭians," *SEI,* p. 222.

30. *SEI,* p. 456.

31. Abdulhamit Sinanoglu, Nusayrilerin Inanc Dunyasi ve Quetzal Kitabi. Istanbul: Esra Yayilari, 1977; *apud* "Simeon's Article and Papers," *Elements of Nusayri Theology*, thestlitepapers.bogspot.com/2007/04/elements—of.

32. Philip Hitti, *History of the Arabs*, pp. 462–63.

33. Philip Hitti, *History of the Arabs*, p. 515.

34. Philip Hitti, *History of Arabs*, p. 524.

35. Cambridge: University Press, paperback edition, 1969, p. 324.

36. What follows is essentially derivative, following in the footsteps of others who have undertaken the more thorough, detailed, and discreet studies. The intent is merely to allow for a better visualization of the larger picture within which the present study can be framed.

37. Marshall G.S. Hodgson, *The Venture of Islam*, vol. 1 (Chicago: University of Chicago Press, 1974), p. 235.

38. There is the argument that competing dynastic seats of power and authority can actually "stimulate and encourage cultural developments"; see *Cambridge History of Arabic Literature: Abbasid Belles-Lettres*, ed. Julia Ashtiany, T. M. Johnstone, et al. (Cambridge University Press, 1990), p. 15; precisely the argument that Ṭāhā Ḥusayn made in his PhD dissertation in 1914, and specifically with respect to the break-up of the larger Islamicate commonwealth during the ʿAbbāsid caliphate (*Tajdīd Dhikrā Abī al-'Alā'*, p. 38).

39. *EI2*, p. 20.

40. *EI2*, p. 20.

41. *Cambridge History of Arabic Literature: Abbasid Belles-Lettres*, ed. Julia Ashtiany, T. M. Johnstone, et al. (Cambridge University Press, 1990), p. 15.

42. "Contacts between Islamic Legal History and Literary Theory: The Case of *Majāz*"; draft of a paper (subsequently submitted for publication); p. 1.

43. Heinrichs; op cit., p. 2. The *kalām*-master [*mutakallim*/متكلم] according to this schematization could be subsumed under religious scholar; although, speaking of compartmentalization, with very special connotation; a *faqīh* (scholar of the law) is one thing and a *mutakallim* something else, as shall

be made clear shortly. The *faqīr*-mystic might otherwise be thought of as *mutaṣawwif* /متصوف or *ṣūfī*/صوفي (*taṣawwuf*-master or practitioner).

44. More exhaustive overviews that include the wider range of activities and leading lights, even if there are no discernible overt connections to al-Maʿarrī, are presented by Ṭāhā Ḥusayn's and ʿAbd al-Qādir Zaydān's studies of al-Maʿarrī, respectively *Tajdīd Dhikrā Abī al-ʿAlā al-Maʿarrī* and *Qaḍāyā al-ʿAṣr fī Adab Abī al-ʿAlā' al-Maʿarrī.* Of similar such surveys of Arab-Islamic learning in the premodern era there is no shortage, but one in English that is especially accessible and yet scholarly is part 1 of Ilse Lichtenstadter's *Introduction to Classical Arabic Literature* (New York: Schocken Books, 1976), which takes into consideration discipline-specific prose writing—e.g., historical, geographical, legal, scientific texts—as well as merely *adab.*

45. "Alexandria was the most important center for the study of Greek philosophy and theology in the seventh century, but by no means the only one. In Syria and Iraq Greek was studied as early as the fourth century at Antioch, Ḥarrān, Edessa, and Qinnesrīn in northern Syria, and at Nisibis and Ras'aina in upper Iraq. Some of these centers were still flourishing when the Arab armies marched into Syria and Iraq. The study of Greek had been cultivated chiefly as a means of giving Syriac-speaking scholars . . . access to Greek theological texts emanating chiefly from Alexandria"; Majid Fakhry, *A History of Islamic Philosophy* (Columbia: University Press, 1970), p. 13.

"According to al-Shahrastānī, the early theological discussions [among Muslim scholars] on 'fundamental beliefs' (*uṣūl*) during the latter part of the seventh century were vitiated by by dialectical elements derived from the 'books of the (Greek) philosophers'. . . . Moreover, a Christian influence appears to have been at work during the early period at Damascus, where contact between Muslim and Christian theologians may be presumed to have been frequent, as evidenced by an extant tract purporting to summarize a discussion on free will and related subjects between a Christian and Saracen. This work is attributed to Theodore Abū Curra (d. 826), Bishop of Ḥarrān and disciple of St. John of Damascus (d. ca. 748), the last great theologian of the Eastern Church" (Majid Fakhry, *A History of Islamic Philosophy,* p. 58).

46. The *mutakallimūn* by the ninth century CE were facing not only the challenges of the theology or theodicy of non-Muslims—e.g., and most notably, eastern Christians—but also "the rationalist portrayal of the universe as a whole" as represented especially by the masters of *falsafah* (Hodgson, *The Venture of Islam*, vol. 1, p. 437).

47. Marshall Hodgson, *The Venture of Islam*, vol. 1, pp. 437–38.

48. Cambridge, MA: Harvard University Press, 1976.

49. Ibn Khaldun, *al-Muqaddimah*, as cited by Wolfson, *The Philosophy of the Kalam*, p. 4; it is at this point that Wolfson found it imperative to underscore the important distinction between the *mutakallim* and the *faqīh* or master of *fiqh*/فقه: "Thus Kalam means theology in contradistinction to Fiqh, which means jurisprudence."

50. Majid Fakhry, *A History of Islamic Philosophy*, p. 62, citing, *among others,* al-Shahrastānī in his *Kitāb al-Milal wa al-Niḥal*/كتاب الملل و النحل and al-ʿAsharī in his *Maqālāt*/مقالات. The heated debates over free will (in this historical and religio-political framework, *al-qadar*/ القدر) as opposed to predeterminism (الجبر), both within the Islamic community and between Muslim and Christian thinkers (particularly in Damascus), can be traced back at least as far as the late seventh and early eighth centuries CE, to the views of the Damascenes Maʿbad al-Juhānī/معبد الجهاني (d. 699) and Ghaylān al-Dimashqī/غيلان الدمشقي (d. 743) as well as the more celebrated and influential early Basrite theologian and ascetic Ḥasan al-Baṣrī/حسن البصري (d. 728). Greek philosophical teachings as well as responses to Christian theology may have influenced the proponents of *al-qadar* or *al-Qadariyyah.* Wāṣil ibn ʿAṭā'/واصل بن عطاء (d. 748) of Basra, a student of Ḥasan al-Baṣrī, was among *al-qadariyyah*, and furthermore commonly referred to as the founder of the Muʿtazilah (Majid Fakhry, *A Short Introduction to Islamic Philosophy, Theology, and Mysticism* [Oxford:Oneworld, 1997], pp.14–15). Jahm ibn Ṣafwān's adherence to complete and absolute predeterminism was defended on the grounds that only the Creator God has the power to create any and all actions, the actions that we attribute to humans or nature are only figurative associations. "Thus we say: 'The tree bore fruit, the water flowed, the stone moved and the sun rose and set,' without any implication of free will or choice. The same is true of humans, whose actions are thoroughly determined by God. . . ." (Fakhry, idem, p. 15; the quotation is from al-Shahrastānī, *Kitāb al-Milal wa al-Niḥal*). Maʿbad and Ghaylān were put to death by the authorities; the Umayyad caliphs at the time regarded the doctrine of free will as a threat to their rule; predeterminism was endorsed by the caliphs because it allowed them to absolve themselves of misrule and abuses on the grounds that all things in life are a matter of fate.

51. Theories of atomism among the *mutakallimūn* were not restricted to the Muʿtazilah only. "Atomism had become firmly established in theological circles by the middle of the ninth century [CE]" (Majid Fakhry, *A History of Islamic Philosophy,* p. 239).

52. Majid Fakhry, *Islamic Occasionalism* (London: George Allen and Unwin Brothers Limited, 1958), p. 29.

53. *Islamic Occasionalism*, p. 13. It is the Basrite branch of the Muʿtazilah, not the Baghdadi, that is especially associated with the atomism of the likes of Abū al-Hudhayl/أبو الهذيل. In any event, "despite this and other philosophical divergences, the two . . . branches were in agreement on two fundamental principles which are essential ingredients of any genuine moral theory: namely, that in the domain of *willing*, individuals are free or capable of choice, and in the domain of outward action or *doing* (*fi'l*), they are capable of carrying out their freely chosen designs" (Majid Fakhry, *A Short Introduction to Islamic Philosophy, Theology, and Mysticism*, p. 17).

54. Majid Fakhry notes that al-Ashʿarī in his *Istiḥsān al-Khawḍ fī 'Ilm al-Kalām*/استحسان الخوض في علم الكلام (*The Vindication of Absorbing the Science of Kalām*) "approves the use of logical deduction (*qiyās*) on the ground that the Prophet himself had practiced it" and furthermore holds that "it is the duty of every 'reasonable Muslim' to refer in such matters 'to the body of principles, consecrated by reason, sense-experience, or common sense,' as well as the explicit pronouncements of the Qur'ān and Ḥadīth" (*A Short Introduction to Islamic Philosophy, Theology, and Mysticism*, pp. 64–65). The quotations within the quotation are from *Istiḥsān al-Khawḍ fī 'Ilm al-Kalām*, and taken from R. J. McCarthy, *The Theology of al-Ash'arī* (Beirut: Imprimerie Catholique, 1953), p. 95.

55. *Al-Ibānah*/الإبانة; as cited by Majid Fakhry, *A Short Introduction to Islamic Philosophy, Theology and Mysticism*, p. 233.

56. See *The Muslim Creed* (London: Frank Cass, 1965), pp. 92–93.

57. See Majid Fakhry, *A History of Islamic Philosophy*, p. 231; see also his *A Short Introduction to Islamic Philosophy, Theology, and Mysticism*, p. 65, and A. J. Wensinck, op. cit., pp. 90–93.

58. Wensinck, idem, p. 86.

59. Wensinck, idem, p. 91; the quotation is from *al-Ibānah*. On the important question of how to understand God's attributes as predicated of Him in the Qur'ān, al-Ashʿarī, contra the Muʿtazilah, argued that the attributes were *not* identical to His essence although they may be said to subsist in it but in a manner that human reason can't grasp, which is where the *bi-lā kayfa* defense comes into play. As represented by the *faqīh* Mālik ibn Anas/مالك بن أنس with respect to the Qur'ānic passage where mention is made of God's sitting on a throne, this notion is expressed as follows: "The sitting is well known, its modality is unknown; believing it is an obligation and questioning it is a heresy (*bid'ah*)"; Majid Fakhry, *A Short Introduction to Islamic Philosophy, Theology, and Mysticism*, p. 65; the quotation of Mālik is taken from al-Shahrastānī, *al-Milal wa al-Niḥal*.

60. Wensinck, *The Muslim Creed*, p. 88. The *somewhat* less agnostic approach to the anthropomorphisms in the Qur'ān, at a stage in al-Ash'arī's life prior to the writing of *al-Ibānah*, is the "no nothingism" with respect to the modality of God's attributes (as opposed to denying them altogether). According to a report about this earlier stage in his life, al-Ash'arī with respect to God's attributes proclaimed that God indeed has hands and a face, just as He has knowledge and power, for example. But, al-Ash'arī added, drawing upon the formula in wide circulation among those who wanted to affirm God's oneness as mentioned in the Qur'ān while at the same time not suggesting that He can be compared to human from, it has to be said that He has hands and a face unlike other hands and faces, just as His knowledge and power are unlike other knowledges and powers; see Wolfson, *The Philosophy of the Kalam,* p. 38, where the author also points out that al-Ash'arī himself assents to the *bi-lā kayfa* ("without asking how") approach to the anthropomorphisms of the Qur'ān, which is what is at play here. The more extreme negative conceptualization of God's attributes, as assigned to the Mu'tazlites (or at at least the more extreme elements thereof with respect to this question) by al-Ash'arī himself, and against whom he was offering his own understanding, runs as follows:

> Allah is one, without equal, hearing, seeing; He is not body, nor object, nor volume, nor form, nor flesh, nor blood, nor substance, nor accidens . . . No place encompasses Him, no time passes Him. . . He cannot be described by any description which can be applied to creatures, in so far as they are created . . . Nothing of what occurs to any mind or can be conceived by phantasy resembles Him (*al-Maqālāt*, cited by Wensinck, *The Muslim Creed*, pp. 72–73).

Cf. al-Shahrastānī's account (*Kitāb al-Milal wa al-Niḥal*):

> The common belief of the sect of the Mu'tazilites is, that Allah is eternal and that eternity is the most peculiar description of His essence. They absolutely reject all other eternal qualities, saying: It is by virtue of His essence that He has knowledge, power and life; not because they are eternal qualities or ideas inherent if Him. For if the qualities should partake of His eternity . . . they would partake of His divinity. . . . (Cited by Wensinck, *The Muslim Creed*, p. 75).

61. *EI2*, p. 769

62. F. E. Peters, *Allah's Commonwealth* (New York: Simon and Schuster, 1973), pp. 429–30.

63. S. H. Nasr, *Islamic Life and Thought* (London: George Allen & Unwin, 1981), p. 64.

64. Majid Fakhry, *A History of Islamic Philosophy*, p. 33.

65. F. E. Peters, *Allah's Commonwealth*, p. 430.

66. F. E. Peters, *Allah's Commonwealth*, p. 432.

67. F. E. Peters, *Allah's Commonwealth*, p. 432.

68. Majid Fakhry, *A History of Islamic Philosophy*, p. 85.

69. Majid Fakhry, *A History of Islamic Philosophy*, p. 104.

70. Majid Fakhry, *A History of Islamic Philosophy*, p. 90.

71. Majid Fakhry, *A History of Islamic Philosophy*, pp. 90–92.

72. George N. Atiyeh, Al-Kindī, *The Philosopher of the Arabs* (Rawalpindi: Islamic Research Institute, 1966), p. 52. Atiyeh points out that the theory of creation out of nothing is essentially a Christian one (as opposed to pagan Greek) based on the Old Testament: "The Greeks as a whole never thought of creation as being out of nothing. *Ex nihilo nihil fit* was a deeply embedded theory in their culture. Whether it was Aristotle, Plato or Plotinus they all maintain that creation was a making of one thing out of another either through movement, formation or emanation. Christianity was responsible for bringing to maturity the idea of *creatio ex nihilo*, already found in the Old Testament" (idem, p. 50).

73. Majid Fakhry, *A History of Islamic Philosophy*, p. 95; the resemblance to al-Ashʿarī's theory on free will or human agency is quite remarkable.

74. Majid Fakhry, *A Short Introduction to Islamic Philosophy, Theology and Mysticism*, p. 27.

75. Majid Fakhry, *A History of Islamic Philosophy*, p. 102.

76. Majid Fakhry, *A History of Islamic Philosophy*, p. 110.

77. F. E. Peters, *Allah's Commonwealth*, p. 440.

78. See the discussions of Majid Fakhry, *A History of Islamic Philosophy*, pp. 115–24; and F. E. Peters, *Allah's Commonwealth*, pp. 440–45.

79. Majid Fakhry, *A History of Islamic Philosophy*, pp. 119–20.

80. Majid Fakhry, *A History of Islamic Philosophy*, p. 120.

81. *Allah's Commonwealth*, p. 445. Al-Bīrūnī, the notable eleventh-century (d. 1048) astronomer and historian of Indian (i.e., Hindu) thought, attributed to al-Rāzī two specific, pointedly hostile treatises on prophecy: *On the Repudiation of Prophecy* and *On the Devices of False Prophets*; see Fakhry, *A History of Islamic Philosophy*, p. 124, citing Paul Kraus, *Épître de Beruni* (Paris, 1936), p. 20. It is, however, primarily from criticisms of al-Rāzī by Abū Ḥātim al-Rāzī/أبو حاتم الرازي (d. 933) and Nāṣir-i Khusraw/ناصر خسرو (d. 1088 CE) that his decidedly un-Islamic metaphysics is known

(Fakhry, ibid.). Fakhry suggests that al-Rāzī may have been influenced by "Indian religious doctrines . . . especially in his concepts of space and time and the atomic composition of bodies" (Fakhry, *A Short Introduction to Islamic Philosophy, Theology and Mysticism*, p. 10).

82. *Allah's Commonwealth*, p. 443.

83. Majid Fakhry, *A History of Islamic Philosophy*, p. 142.

84. Majid Fakhry, *A History of Islamic Philosophy*, p. 146.

85. F. E. Peters, *Allah's Commonwealth*, p. 629.

86. See Majid Fakhry, *A History of Islamic Philosophy,* p. 174.

87. Majid Fakhry, *A History of Islamic Philosophy*, p. 162.

88. Majid Fakhry, *A History of Islamic Philosophy*, p. 187, citing a statement from the *Epistles* (رسائل) of the Ikhwān (Beirut, 1957); IV, p. 42.

89. Ḥasan al-Baṣrī, *apud* A. J. Arberry, *Sufism* (New York: Harper & Row, 1950), p. 34.

90. Al-Junayd, *apud* Arberry, *Sufism*, p. 58.

91. Annemarie Schimmel, *Mystical Dimensions of Islam* (Chapel Hill: University of North Carolina Press, 1975), p. 57.

92. A. J. Arberry, *Sufism*, p. 58.

93. A. J. Arberry, *Sufism*, p. 58.

94. F. E. Peters, *Allah's Commonwealth*, p. 424.

95. Dhū al-Nūn al-Miṣrī, *apud* Schimmel, *Mystical Dimensions of Islam*, p. 43.

96. *Apud* Schimmel, *Mystical Dimensions of Islam*, p. 199.

97. F. E. Peters, *Allah's Commonwealth*, p. 553.

98. Cited in A. J. Arberry, *Sufism*, p. 60.

99. F. E. Peters, *Allah's Commonwealth*, p. 564; and Schimmel, *Mystical Dimensions of Islam,* p. 242.

100. A. J. Arberry, *Sufism*, p. 73.

101. See F. E. Peters, *Allah's Commonwealth*, p. 565.

102. Ilse Lichtenstadter, *Introduction to Classical Arabic Literature* (New York: Schocken Books, 1976), p. 74.

103. Mālik ibn Anas's approach to jurisprudence emphasized a consensus that relies on the early scholars of Medina who established *sunnah* based on reports of the descendants of the close associates of Prophet Muḥammad during his lifetime. Abū Ḥanīfah allowed for *ra'y* and *istiḥsān*. Aḥmad ibn Ḥanbal rejected *ra'y* and *istiḥsān*, not to mention *qiyās*, as valid foundations or principles for rendering legal judgments. Only the Qur'ān and the *sunnah* could be accepted. For the brief but clear and serviceable overview, see Lichtenstadter, op. cit., pp. 71–75, which concludes with the

most helpful observation that "though not entirely identical, [*sharī'ah* and *fiqh*] are not strictly distinguished in actual use and are often employed interchangeably. However, one may say that *fiqh*, on the whole, designates the theory of law, jurisprudence, whereas *sharī'ah* is used largely for its practice, jurisdiction."

104. Marshall G. S. Hodgson, *The Venture of Islam,* vol. 1, p. 378. "The special mood of devotion" of course is the special reverence for, and unswerving loyalty to, 'Alī and the acknowledged imāms descending from him. "For the Shī'īs, it was not sufficient for the law to be an autonomous corps of authoritative norms which the community as a whole would maintain against any given ruler. Its continuity must be ensured, as in Muḥammad's time, through the presence of an authoritative spokesman for the divine will—a true imām. 'Alid loyalism offered just that" (Hodgson, idem, p. 372).

105. *Allah's Commonwealth*, pp. 579–80.

106. *Allah's Commonwealth*, p. 579. The Ḥusaynid line of imāms refers to those descending from 'Alī's son al-Ḥusayn, who is regarded as the third imām after 'Alī and al-Ḥasan, al-Ḥusayn's brother. The mother of both al-Ḥasan and al-Ḥusayn was Fāṭimah, daughter of the Prophet Muḥammad.

107. R. A. Nicholson, *A Literary History of the Arabs* (Cambridge: University Press, 1969), p. 136.

108. R. A. Nicholson, *A Literary History of the Arabs*, p. 136.

109. R. A. Nicholson, *A Literary History of the Arabs* p. 240.

110. F. E. Peters, *Allah's Commonwealth*, p. 400.

111. R. A. Nicholson, *A Literary History of the Arabs,* p. 289.

112. A. J. Arberry in *Arabic Poetry* (Cambridge: University Press, 1965), pp. 21–26, gives a longer list with specific examples, at the same time pointing out that he enumerates "the principle ones only"; "detailed lists . . . run to great length."

113. R. A. Nicholson, *A Literary History of the Arabs,* p. 291.

114. R. A. Nicholson, *A Literary History of the Arabs*, p. 299.

115. *History of the Arabs* (London: Macmillan St. Martin's, Tenth Edition, 1970) p. 458. 1935 CE was the one-thousandth anniversary of his death according to the Islamic calendar. The occasion was commemorated in several Arabic-speaking countries.

116. Nicholson, *A Literary History of the Arabs*, p. 311, citing Dieterici, *Mutanabbi und Seifuddaula aus der Edelperle des Tsaâlibi* (Leipzig, 1847), pp. 49–74. Al-Tha'ālibī (*apud* Nicholson, idem, p. 309) could also find fault with al-Mutanabbī in no uncertain terms. Al-Tha'ālibī was one of a trio of influential post-Jāhilī, post-Umayyad critics (the other two being Ibn

Rāshiq/ابن راشق [d. 1070] and Ibn Qutaybah/ابن قتيبة [died end of ninth century CE]) who argued the merits of the "old" poets (i.e., pre-Islamic) compared to the "new" (i.e., poets born in the Islamic and especially ʿAbbāsid eras). Ibn Rāshiq, like al-Thaʿālibī, was inclined to concede superiority to the "new." Ibn Qutaybah was less categorical and also less chronologically determined in his critique. In a remarkably clear-headed and insightful statement on modernity and classicism (regardless of time and place), he wrote, "I have not regarded any ancient with veneration on account of his antiquity nor any modern with contempt on account of his being modern, but I have taken an impartial view of both sides, giving every one his due. . . . God . . . did not restrict learning and poetry and rhetoric to a particular age nor appropriate them to a particular class, but has always distributed them in common amongst His servants, and has caused everything old to be new in its own day and every classic work to be an upstart on its first appearance" (from his *Kitāb al-Shi'r wa al-Shu'arā'*/كتاب الشعر و الشعراء [*The Book of Poetry and Poets*], ed. De Geoje, p. 5, ll. 5–15; *apud* R. A. Nicholson, *A Literary History of the Arabs*, p. 287).

117. F. E. Peters, *Allah's Commonwealth,* p. 406.

118. Ignaz Goldziher, *Alte und Neue Poesie im Urtheile der Arabischen Kritiker, in his Abhandlung zur Arabischen Philologie*, Part I; *apud* R. A. Nicholson, *A Literary History of the Arabs*, p. 289 and 285, note 1.

119. F. E Peters, *Allah's Commonwealth*, p. 410.

120. Ṭāhā Ḥusayn, *Tajdīd Dhikrā Abī al-'Alā'*, p. 90.

121. *EI2*, "Bayān," pp. 114–15.

122. *Apud* Charles Pellat, *The Life and Works of Jāḥiẓ* (Berkeley: University of California Press, 1969), p. 47.

123. Ṭāhā Ḥusayn *Tajdīd Dhikrā Abī al-'Alā',* p. 92.

124. "Iʿjāz," *Wikipedia.*

Chapter Three

1. In the present study, hereafter commonly referred to as "the *Luzūm*" or merely "*Luzūm*." In many English language sources, the work is also referred to as "*al-Luzūmiyyāt*" or "the *Luzūmiyyāt*."

2. This is the reading of the "Leyden" (Leiden) manuscript version of the *Luzūm* (Cod. Or. 100, p. 1); ʿAzīz Effendī Zand/عزيز أفندي زند, ed., *al-Luzūmiyyāt aw Luzūm Mā Lā Yalzam* /اللزوميات أو لزوم ما لا يلزم (two vols., Cairo: Al-Maḥrūsah, 1891, 1895), has أوراق (papers).

Here and elsewhere in this study, Zand's edition of *Luzūm* is used for basic citation purposes. References to it henceforward will be incorporated into the text and include line numbers as well as page and volume numbers. For citation purposes, *Luzūm* will be indicated simply as L, not italicized. Volume I of L, therefore, will look as follows when referenced for citation purposes: L I. Volume II will be indicated by L II. Page number will follow volume number, and line number will follow page number.

The Leyden manuscript is cited in this study only when its wording varies from Zand's for the passages of *Luzūm* that are quoted. In such a case, its reading is given preference to Zand's and the latter's indicated in an endnote. The (photographed copy of) the Leyden manuscript is numbered in pages rather than foliated, so page numbers are used when referring to it. It has not been deemed necessary to give line numbers.

This procedure is admittedly cumbersome and somewhat distracting, but there is good cause for adopting it. On the one hand, Zand's published typescript version of *Luzūm* is more accessible and readable than the Leyden handwritten manuscript version. Zand's version also contains footnotes for vocabulary and/or Zand's commentary/interpretation. On the other hand, the Leyden manuscript is perhaps the most reliable recension we have of *Luzūm* (see S. J. Stern, "Some Noteworthy Manuscripts of the Poems of Abū'l-ʿAlā' al-Maʿarrī," *Oriens* [Leyden] 7 [1954], pp. 322–47). Preference should be given to its wording where it differs from Zand's. There is no commentary in the Leyden manuscript. Zand's footnotes for vocabulary and commentary/interpretation are not necessarily reliable—they may be taken as somewhat or even extremely speculative—but they offer vastly more food for thought than the more accessible Beirut (Dār Ṣāḍir, 1961) edition of *Luzūm Mā Lā Yalzam*.

3. Leyden ms., p. l; L I.9.5 has الدنيا (the world).

4. Leyden ms., p. l; L I.9.5 has عبثت (to play or sport with).

5. Leyden ms., p. l; L I.9.5 has الأوّل (the first).

6. Leyden ms., p. l; L I.9.8 has وإنما وضعت ("And I have put down in writing only") preceding أشياء .

7. Alfred von Kremer, "Ueber die philosophischen Gedichte des Abu'l-ʿalâ Maʿarry," *Sitzungsberichte der Philosophisch-Historischen Classe der Akademie der Wissenschaften* (Vienna) 117, no. 6 (1888), pp. 13–14.

8. Made in the introduction to his *Saqṭ al-Zand* (Beirut: Dār Ṣādir, 1963), p. 5.; which is remarkably similar to his introduction to *Luzūm Mā Lā Yalzam,* indicating that even with the poems of *Saqṭ al-Zand*, on the whole quite transparently representing a different trajectory in his poetry, he was determined to craft a new type of poetry.

9. What al-Maʿarrī says verbatim here is: "To al-Aṣmaʿī [the ninth century CE editor, philologist, and critic of poetry] there has been attributed an utterance the meaning of which is that poetry is one of the gates of falsehood [or vanity]" (ويروى عن الأصمعي كلام معناه أن الشعر باب من أبواب الباطل).

10. In the Arabic, الكَذِب.

11. R. A. Nicholson, "The Meditations of Maʿarrí," in his *Studies in Islamic Poetry* (Cambridge: Cambridge University Press, 1921), pp. 50–51. Yohanan Friedmann, "Literary and Cultural Aspects of the *Luzūmiyyāt*," *Studia Orientalia Memoriae D.H. Baneth Dedicata* (Jerusalem: Magnes, Hebrew University, 1979), pp. 347 ff., has also noted that aspect of al-Maʿarrī's introduction to *Luzūm* that stands as an *apologia* (and defense) for a new *ars poetica*; and he maintains that "the very existence [in *Luzūm*] of an introduction in which the poet declares his moral and literary creed is unique in the history of Arabic poetry" (p. 348). And yet the introduction to *Saqṭ al-Zand*—the poems of which al-Maʿarrī has suggested that he composed first, before the poems of the *Luzūmiyyāt*—must be seen as quite unique too, for similar reasons. Al-Maʿarrī (*apud* Ḥusayn, *Tajdīd Dhikrā Abī al-ʿAlāʾ*, pp. 180–81) alleged that the poems of *Saqṭ al-Zand* were composed "in the days of his youth," although Ḥusayn has dated some of the poems (based on historical references) to the years after the return from Baghdad. One of these poems was written when al-Maʿarrī was 50 years old. Ḥusayn concludes that most of the poems in *Saqṭ al-Zand* were composed before al-Maʿarrī's poems of middle and advanced age, and this explains the remark that they were poems from "his youth" (ibid.).

In their treatment of al-Maʿarrī's introductory remarks to *Luzūm* that pertain to lying or falsehood in Arabic poetry, both Friedmann ("Literary and Cultural Aspects," p. 349) and especially Nicholson ("The Meditations," p. 50; see also his remark on "Moslem [*sic*] Theory" regarding poets, p. 44) tend to give the impression that "lying" or "falsehood" was a universally acclaimed and accepted practice in medieval Arabic poetry. But this was not the case. There were critics who championed it and those who argued against it; see Vicente Cantarino, *Arabic Poetics in the Golden Age* (Leiden: E. J. Brill, 1975), pp. 34ff. Further, neither Friedmann nor Nicholson emphasized that for at least some medieval Arabic critics of poetry, lying or falsehood in poetry was not conceived of as simply a matter of deliberately falsifying statements with the intent to deceive, but, rather, a matter of using hyperbole or describing things with attributes that transcend the commonplace and possible, this for the purpose of achieving the *true* aim of poetry, namely, before anything else, beautiful speech; see Cantarino,

Arabic Poetics, pp. 35–37. Thus, too, Nicholson and Friedmann did not emphasize the point that although there is obviously a strong moral dimension to al-Maʿarrī's remark to the effect that he does not lie in his poems in *Luzūm*, and this *moral* dimension is obviously at the heart of the "unique" literary "creed," there also seems to be intended an aesthetic dimension involving diction itself; namely, like some other medieval Arab critics of poetry, al-Maʿarrī may have felt that poetry that shows good artistic taste avoids hyperbole and exaggeration and *exclusively* striving after beautiful speech or the *bon mot*. Although on balance in the *Luzūm*, especially in the longer poems, hyperbole and exaggeration (in the meaning of straining for the *bon mot* and demonstration of mastery of *badī'*/بديع ornamentation and linguistic erudition, i.e., foregrounding sound and imagery even at the expense of sense) easily equals unadorned directness and transparency.

In his study on the *rubā'iyyāt* (quatrains) in the Persian tradition (more specifically in the eleventh and twelfth centuries CE), Peter Avery felt that "the rise of the *ruba'i* coincided with revulsion from lengthy and highly artificial panegyrics and narrative poems in a single rhyme. . . . Its force lay in the capacity to make a short and telling statement. . . ." (Peter Avery and John Heath-Stubbs, *The Ruba'iyat of Omar Khayyam* [Middlesex, England: Penguin, 1983], p. 10). Avery noted as well that the Qur'ān exegete and philologist al-Zamakhsharī (d. 1141 CE) alleged that Omar Khayyam ('Umar Khayyām) was "acquainted with the Arabic stanzas of . . . Al-Ma'arri" (the words in quotation are Avery's *apud* an article published in 1948 by one Badī'uz-Zaman Firuzanfar; duly cited by Avery, idem, pp. 24–25). Avery himself found that "the imagery and sentiments of [al-Maʿarrī's] epigrammatical verses are strikingly like the *ruba'is* which have come down to us under Khayyam's name"; and that "E. G. Browne (*Literary History of Persia*, vol. II, London, 1906, and Cambridge, 1956, p. 292) saw the resemblance between al-Maʿarrī's verses and the *rubā'īs* long before Professor Firuzanfar discovered al-Zamakhsharī's reference to Khayyam and his acquaintance with the Arabic sceptic" (ibid.).

Ameen Rihani in his *The Luzumiyat of Abu'l-Ala* (subtitled, significantly, *Selected from his Luzum ma la Yalzam and suct uz-Zand and first rendered into English*), presented English language versions of what Rihani refers to as "quatrains . . . culled from three Volumes of his [al-Maʿarrī's] poems, as far as possible, in the logical order of the sequence of thought" (p. 16). Although occasionally al-Maʿarrī in *Luzūm* (but not *Saqṭ al-Zand*) composed poems as short as two lines (which would yield four hemistichs, although a rhyme scheme not of "aaba" but of the standard rhyming only of the end of each stich or full line of verse), the "quatrains" to which Rihani refers are his own "renderings" based on two verses that more typically he separated from longer (to one degree or another) poems by al-Maʿarrī. Rihani in other words *superimposed* the quatrain form on these "culled" lines (in the Arabic, two full verses with the end rhyme only), by having each hemistich a line of verse and the entire resulting one-stanza poem exhibit the "aaba" rhyme scheme of the quintessential Persian quatrain.

Rihani (idem, p. 30) remarked that "Omar wrote poetry in Arabic too. My learned friend, Isa Iskandar Maluf of Zehleh . . . showed me some quatrains . . . in an old Arabic Ms. which bear a striking resemblance to some of Abu'l-Ala's both in thought and style." Rihani was convinced that Khayyam was "an imitator or a disciple" of al-Maʿarrī. "The birth of the first poet and the death of second are not very far apart. . . . To be sure, the skepticism and pessimism of Omar are to a great extent imported from Ma'arrah" (idem, p. 22). ʿUmar Farrūkh (*Ḥakīm al-Maʿarrah*) was convinced that Omar Khayyam read al-Maʿarrī's poetry, was influenced by al-Maʿarrī's pessimism and skepticism with respect to received opinions of revealed, scriptured religion, and in his quatrains *self-consciously* recapitulated some of al-Maʿarrī's thoughts. In terms of the influence and the similarities in "philosophies," see pp. 115–20 of Farrūkh's study.

12. Nicholson's estimate; "The Meditations," p. 53.

13. On the order of consonants أ ، ب ، ت (and so forth, following the order of the Arabic alphabet, until al-Maʿarrī concludes with ياء). With the exception of أ, each consonant bears in turn the vowel sound "u" (long or short), the vowel sound "a" (long or short), the vowel sound "i" (long or short), and no vowel (i.e., *sukūn*/سكون or the symbol of vowlessness), and always in that order. This explains Friedmann's remark that the *Luzūm* "consists of 113 chapters" ("Literary and Cultural Aspects," p. 351). What he calls "chapters" are none other than a representation of this ordering of consonants and vowels; i.e., they are not chapters in the more conventional sense wherein a topic or subject heading is given. They simply announce the rhyme scheme. (The editors of the Beirut edition of the *Luzūm* provided short titles to all poems. The title is typically a reference to a main idea or theme or turn of phrase regarded as especially remarkable). Friedmann (ibid.) has observed that within the various so-called chapters of *Luzūm*, the poems are arranged according to meter following the order established by the early Arab grammarian and theoretician of metrics al-Khalīl.

14. Namely, *al-sinād*/السناد, *al-iqwā'*/الإقواء, *al-ikfā'*/الإكفاء, *al-īṭā'*/الإيطاء, concerning which see W. Wright, *Grammar of the Arabic Language* (Cambridge:

Cambridge University Press, 1967), vol. II, pp. 356–57. That al-Ma'arrī avoids these for the most part is this study's general impression; the study does not claim to have kept a record of possible "violations" of, or taking liberty with, the standardized rules of prosody.

15. The translation and text of this poem are taken from A. J. Arberry, *Arabic Poetry* (Cambridge: University Press, 1965), pp. 126–27.

16. Translation and text taken from Arberry, *Arabic Poetry*, pp. 40–41. The poem is by 'Umar ibn Abī Rabī'ah (643–719 CE).

17. Leyden ms., p. 41; L I.153.5 has عَتَب, which Zand translates as women.

18. Leyden ms., p. 140; L II.36.1 has قَنْس (origin).

19. Leyden ms., p. 140; L II.36.2 has هِمَّتُه (his high-mindedness).

20. Leyden ms., p. 140; L II.36.2 has جِنْس (genus).

21. Leyden ms, p. 140, L II.36.2 has جِنْس.

22. Leyden ms., p. 108; L I.377.1 has وإِنْ (and if).

23. "Literary and Cultural Aspects of the *Luzūmiyyāt*," p. 351.

24. And especially in the *qāfiyah murdafah*/قافية مردفة poems where the *u* vowel sound and the *i* vowel sound are not allowed to alternate, as Friedmann rightfully observes; "This change in the rules of versification is a great improvement upon the artistic form of the poem concerned: it intensifies the impression of acoustic uniformity even more than the addition of a second rhyming consonant" ("Literary and Cultural Aspects," p. 351).

25. As al-Ma'arrī proudly, and rightfully, proclaims in his introduction to *Luzūm* (see L I .31.6–9), few Arab poets prior to him enriched their rhymes the way he did; and if they did, they did so very infrequently. It does not seem that any major poet after al-Ma'arrī attempted to rhyme in the manner that he did in *Luzūm*; or if there was an attempt, certainly it was not to the same extreme. Less surprisingly, no poet self-consciously attempted to recapitulate and advance the trajectories of al-Ma'arrī's thinking, excluding (as per Rihani and Farrūkh, for example) the possibility of Omar Khayyam in his quatrains.

26. Nicholson, "The Meditations," p. 45; Ṭāhā Ḥusayn, *Ma'a Abī al-'Alā' fī Sijnih* (eleventh edition, Cairo: Dār al-Ma'ārif , n.d.), pp. 101ff.

27. Leyden ms., p. 190; L II.202.16 has an extra و and preceding the لا; i.e., وولا.

28. Leyden ms., p. 45; L I.170.1 has تَخِيبُ (from the verb خاب, meaning to fail or miscarry).

29. Leyden ms., p. 45; L I.170.3 has تَخِيبُ.

30. Leyden ms., p. 45; L I.171.1 has طماعَاتُها (their avidities or greedy desires), which is metrically impossible.

31. Leyden ms., p. 45; L I.171.4 has *yukhālifu al-ayyāma*/يُخالِفُ الأيام ("Making different the days [is . . .]").

32. Leyden ms., p. 45; L I.171.11 has سَلَبَتْ (from the verb سَلَبَ, meaning to wrest or to snatch).

33. Leyden ms., p. 46; L I.172.10 has هُلَعاتُها, meaning virtually the same thing as هَلِعاتُها.

34. Leyden ms., p. 46; L I.172.13 has تَوُدَّةُ, a misspelling.

35. Leyden ms., p 30; L I.254.7 has مَخْبُو with ء suppressed.

36. Leyden ms., p. 29; L I.181.2 has العَقْلُ (the mind or intellect).

37. Leyden ms., p. 122; L I.415.6 has كابِيَةٌ (extinguished; dimmed).

38. Leyden ms., p. 157; L II.94.7 has لِأَمْرٍ لنا (at an order from us).

39. Philip Wheelwright, "Philosophy and Poetry," *Princeton Encyclopedia of Poetry and Poetics*, 1974 ed., p. 615. Cf. Sari Nusseibeh's remarks on poetry in the Introduction to his *The Story of Reason in Islam* (Stanford: University Press, 2017), p. 6:

> It may seem surprising to find mention of poetry right at the the beginning of a story about reason. Yet poetry is key. . . . As the natural and immediate medium of creativity and imagination, poetry is a progenitor of reason. Breaking free from elementary elocutionary forms, it invokes a world invisible to the untrained eye yet immanent to the event or object described. . . . Approaching these newly revealed horizons of sense, reason grows bold, makes exploratory steps, and begins to search for order as yet undiscerned. Beginning to stir, over time, it comes to make fuller and better sense of what poetry has described.

40. Which is not to say that the "poeticity" of *Luzūm* is to be seen always as a shortcoming when we evaluate *Luzūm* as a philosophical work. Far from it. Again, for the most part, the philosophy of *Luzūm* consists of "new insights into values, relationships, and significant possibilities" that (1) are revealed in the poet's use of poetry's full linguistic resources, and (2) can be fairly restated *only* within the poems that express them. The *Luzūm*'s poetic nature is an integral and indispensable part of its philosophical nature and enriches and deepens the latter.

This same symbiosis, by the way, also keeps the poems of *Luzūm* from being artistically inferior philosophical poetry. "A [philosophical] poem whose meaningful utterances were confined strictly to general propositions in their abstract character would be little more than a didactic tract" (Wheelwright, "Philosophy and Poetry," p. 615).

Stefan Sperl's chapter on al-Maʿarrī in his *Mannerism in Arabic Poetry* (paperback edition, Cambridge: Cambridge University Press, 2004, pp. 97–154) focuses on the more technical side to poems from the *Luzūmiyyāt,* as the title as well as subtitle of his work (*A Structural Analysis of Selected Texts [3rd Century AH/9th Century AD-5th Century AH/11th Century AD]*) indicate. ʿAbd Allāh al-Ṭayyib also addresses more the poeticity of al-Maʿarrī than the thoughts or philosophy ("Abū al-ʿAlā' al-Maʿarrī as a poet: an aesthetic appreciation," SOAS, PhD thesis, London, 1950).

Sperl has a rather severe indictment of the philosophical dimension to the poems of the *Luzūmiyyāt*, as though the observations of someone like Wheelwright are unconvincing, adding that there seems to be a consensus about this issue:

> There is now general agreement that, contrary to older opinion, the *Luzūmiyyāt* are not philosophical poems. No philosophical problem is treated *per se* in any detail, and all of the multitude of subjects touched upon . . . are reducible to a few basic principles that make no claim to philosophical originality. (p. 99)

Apropos of Wheelwright's understanding of how a philosophy may be expressed in literary forms other than prosaic didactic tracts, additional thoughts worth considering lie in the observations of Eknath Easwaran (*The Bhagavad Gita* [Tomales, CA: Nilgiri, 1985] pp. 9, 30), bearing in mind first and foremost that the *gita* is a song (although with respect to the *Luzūm*, the point being made here is not an attempt to argue for any equivalency in terms of philosophical breadth and depth, or for that matter in artistry):

> The Upanishads are not systematic philosophy; they are more like ecstatic slide shows . . . vivid, disjointed. . . . If they seem to embrace contradictions, that is because they do not try to smooth over the seams of these experiences.

The Gita does not present a system of philosophy.

41. Majid Fakhry, *A History of Islamic Philosophy* (New York: Columbia University Press, 1970), p. 11.

42. Ṭāhā Ḥusayn, *Tajdīd Dhikrā Abī al-'Alā'* (Cairo, 8th edition: Dār al-Maʿārif, 1976), pp. 243–45.

43. For von Kremer, see "Ueber die philosophischen Gedichte," pp. 12–13; for Nicholson, "The Meditations," p. 151.

44. At this point, it is important to note that in his *Zajr al-Nābiḥ* زجر النابح (ed. Amjad al-Ṭarābulsī/أمجد الطرابلسي [Damascus: Al-Hāshimī, 1965]),

al-Maʿarrī denies, in effect, that his supposedly unorthodox or antireligious statements in *Luzūm* are unorthodox or antireligious at all. Citing particular lines from *Luzūm* for which he was attacked by adversaries, he in essence alleges that these lines only *appear* objectionable—when in fact they are not—because those who take objection to them have not properly understood his figurative speech (i.e., his ellipses, his deliberate use of words which may be taken in several significations, and other such characteristics of his writing style). He also defends some seemingly unorthodox (or otherwise offensive) remarks in *Luzūm* by not infrequently citing lines from the Qur'ān and *ḥadīth* and *tafsīr* (تفسير) literature that (he alleges) can be seen as being in consonance with those remarks.

In what we have of *Zajr al-Nābiḥ* (only fragments of the work have been retrieved, gleaned from the marginalia of a ms. of *Luzūm*), al-Maʿarrī generally makes somewhat of an arguable case for himself; but just barely. In the end, he is not especially convincing. He shows no remorse, for example, nor gives any justification, for his being so opaque and thus open to misinterpretation in lines of *Luzūm* that he claims (in so many words) are meant to be perfectly in keeping with the normative ethos of his time and immediate society (i.e., Muslim). Anyone who reads *Zajr al-Nābiḥ* will likely come away from it with the strong impression that this is a classic example where one doth protest too much to be taken seriously.

The existence of the work, incidentally, would seem most definitely to indicate that the contradictory religious statements in *Luzūm* were not due to a change in al-Maʿarrī's mind over the course of time; more specifically, a change from embracing nonconforming views to embracing conforming ones. It would also seem to provide additional—and perhaps the best?—cause for rejecting the suggestion that perhaps al-Maʿarrī really intended *neither* his pro-Islamic *nor* his anti-Islamic remarks in *Luzūm* (cf. the comments supra with respect to being deliberately frivolous on one side of the equation—the heterodox, heretical, and irreligious—playing devil's advocate for mere sport).

45. Muhsin Mahdi, *Ibn Khaldun's Philosophy of History* (Chicago: University of Chicago Press, 1964), pp. 72–73; Leo Strauss, *Persecution and the Art of Writing* (Glencoe, IL: The Free Press, 1952), pp. 9–10, 17–18, 32–33; L. Massignon, "Zindīḳ," *SEI*, p. 659.

Concerning the threat of persecution faced by al-Maʿarrī and other thinkers or poets of the medieval Islamic community, it cannot be denied that that threat was a real one. However, one can legitimately wonder just how great the threat actually was from time to time. During the reign of caliph Mahdī, in 783 CE, the poets (!) Bashshār ibn Burd/بشار بن برد and Ṣāliḥ ibn ʿAbd al-Quddūs/

صالح بن عبد القدوس were put to death for reputedly heretical statements (concerning the details surrounding the execution of Ṣāliḥ and Bashshār, see, e.g., Nicholson, *Literary History,* pp. 373–47). On the other hand, philosophers as anathematic, indeed heretical, as the renowned al-Fārābī and Abū Bakr al-Rāzī/ابو بكر الرازي, for example, both of whom flourished slightly before al-Maʿarrī was born, escaped the fate that befell Bashshār ibn Burd and Ṣāliḥ ibn ʿAbd al-Quddūs. They died natural deaths. Moreover, al-Maʿarrī himself died a natural death, and he does not seem to have been greatly harassed (even though apparently badgered with interrogations or threatening allegations) in his lifetime, despite the fact that some of his contemporaries did not fail to notice beneath the dissimulation—or precisely because of it—the serious and seriously intended antireligious, antiprophesy strain to his thought, with even atheism (الإلحاد) sometimes alleged; see, for example, the correspondence between al-Maʿarrī and Dāʿī al-Duʿāh initiated by the latter, *Bayna Abī al-'Alā' al-Ma'arrī wa Dā'ī al-Du'āh*/بين أبي العلاء المعري وداعي الاال الدعاة, ed. Muḥibb al-Dīn al-Khaṭīb (Cairo, 1930), passim, but especially p. 33ff.; and the historical and bio-bibliographical chronicles by al-Bākharzī/الباخرزي (*Dumyat al-Qaṣr*/ دمية القصر (*The Statue of the Palace*), ed. Muḥammad Rāghib al-Ṭabbākh [Aleppo, 1930], pp. 50–52); by al-Khaṭīb al-Baghdādī/الخطيب البغدادي (*Tārīkh Baghdād*/تاريخ بغداد (*The History of Baghdad*) [Cairo, 1931], vol. 4, pp. 240–41); and by Sibṭ ibn al-Jawzī (سبط أبن الجوزي), also quoting several others of similar persuasion, in his *Mir'āh al-Zaman*/ مرآة الزمن (*The Mirror of the Times*) (*apud* Ṭāhā Ḥusayn, Ibrāhīm al-Abyārī, *et al., Ta'rīf al-Qudamā'*, p. 144 ff), and in his *Talbīs Iblīs*/ تلبيس ابليس (*The Delusion of the Devil*) p. 69, (*apud* Bakrī, *al-Fikr al-Dīnī*, p. 77, although with the edition of تلبيس ابليس not indicated). Abū al-Wafā' ibn 'Aqīl, according to Sibṭ ibn al-Jawzī (*apud* Ṭāhā Ḥusayn, Ibrāhīm al-Abyārī, *et al., Ta'rīf al-Qudamā'*, p.144 ff.), remarked that al-Maʿarrī repented of his كفر/*kufr* (disbelief) and apologized for the fact that it was according to the inner esoteric meaning of his verse that he was a Muslim. “There is neither intelligence nor religion [behind this],” continues Abū al-Wafā', referring to al-Maʿarrī; “because he made a show of disbelief while alleging that secretly he was a Muslim. This was the opposite of the cases with the الزنادقة/*al-zanādiqah* and hypocrites. They made a show of [their] Islam while keeping secret their disbelief. Was al-Maʿarrī living in the lands of disbelievers so that he needed recourse to this [approach of his with respect to keeping his Muslim identity a secret]?”

ثمّ اعتذر بأن لقوله باطنا وأنّه مسلم في الباطن. فلا عقل ولا دين؛ لأنّه تظاهر بالكفر وزعم أنّه مسلم في الباطن. وهكذا عكس قضايا المنافقين والزنادقة فإنهم تظاهروا بالاسلام وأبطنوا الكفر. فهل كان في بلاد الكفر حتّى يحتاج إلى هذا؟

While not denying al-Ma'arrī's dissimulation (*al-Fikr al-Dīnī,* pp. 81ff.), Bakrī persuasively argues that a number of other factors were also very instrumental in preventing his suffering any serious harm (دون أن يصاب بأذى أو مكروه), such as his reclusiveness, his kind and decent nature and high moral standards, and, finally, the fact that rule over Syria during the time after his return from Baghdad was being contested by the Fāṭimids and the Mirdāsids, with the former attaching little importance to normative Sunnī Muslim principles (indeed, as a Shī'ite dynasty under al-Ḥākim bi-Amr Allāh, aspiring to a new belief system contradicting much in Sunnī Islam) and the latter as a Bedouin dynasty being less concerned with matters intellectual and religious than simply holding on to its rule and authority (idem, p. 81).

46. For his general argument about heterodox thinkers needing to write obliquely, see Strauss, *Persecution*, pp. 22–25, 32–37.

47. Moustapha Saleh/مصطفى صالح, "Abū'l-'Alā' al-Ma'arrī: bibliographie critique." *Bulletin d'études orientales* (Damascus: Institut français), Part 1, Tome 22 (1969), pp. 152, 161, 176 (quoting al-Sam'ānī, *al-Ansāb*/الأنساب; al-Qifṭī, *Inbāh al-Ruwāh'alā 'alā Anbāh al-Nuḥāh*; and Ibn al-'Adīm, *Kitāb al-Inṣāf wa al-Taḥarrī fī Daf' al-Ẓulm wa al-Tajarrī 'an Abī al-'Alā' al-Ma'arrī*).

48. "Literary and Cultural Aspects," p. 351.

49. Hamori, *On the Art of Medieval Arabic Literature* (Princeton: Princeton University Press, 1974), p. 58; al-Ma'arrī, *Risālat al-Ghufrān,* ed. Bint al-Shāṭi' (Cairo: Dār al-Ma'ārif, 1969), pp. 432–34; R. A. Nicholson, *A Literary History of the Arabs* (Cambridge: Cambridge University Press, 1969), p. 373.

50. Peter Avery and John Heath-Stubbs, *The Ruba'iyat of Omar Khayyam*, p. 114.

51. Aristotle felt that diverting attention from the message to the medium is an inherent characteristic of all metrical discourse. G. M. A. Grube, tr., *Aristotle on Poetry and Style* (New York: Liberal Arts Press, 1958), p. 82.

52. Nicholson, "The Meditations," p. 53.

53. See, for example, Saleh, "Abū'l-'Alā' al-Ma'arrī," part 2, tome XII (1970), pp. 204, 208, 239, 271.

Chapter Four

1. "El hombre de carne y hueso, el que nace, sufre, y muere—sobre todo, muere—; el que come, y bebe, y juega, y duerme, y piensa, y quiere. . . ."; Miguel de Unamuno, *Del sentimiento trágico de la vida*, in *Unamuno: sus*

mejores paginas, ed. Philip Metzidakis (Englewood Cliffs, NJ: Prentice Hall, 1966), p. 110.

2. Sometimes also referred to as simply أربع (four), a good example of how vague or elliptical al-Maʿarrī can be even with some of his more important technical terms; see, e.g., L I.91.2; 422.5; L II.98.11.

3. Leyden ms., p. 132; this line is missing in Zand's edition of *Luzūm.*

4. As it was also for al-Ghazzālī; see, for example, his الرسالة اللدنية *al-Risālat al-Laduniyyah,* trans. Margaret Smith, *Journal of the Royal Asiatic Society* (April, 1938), p. 193.

5. Also frequently referred to, and with no apparent distinction, as *rūḥ* (روح); see, e.g., L I.283.11; 287.4; L II.366.9; 421.3. For a concise helpful overview of the distinction between *rūḥ* and *nafs* sometimes made by Islamic theologians and the masters of *ḥadīth* reports, one might consult Yvonne Yazbeck Haddad and Jane Idleman Smith, *The Islamic Understanding of Death and Resurrection* (Albany: State University of New York Press, 1981), pp. 17–20.

6. Because he took the soul as being a simple and "imperceptible" (or "subtle") "thing" (or "substance"), and nowhere refers to it as a body in terms that might be reserved for the human body (e.g., *jism*/جسم), it would seem that al-Maʿarrī accepted Aristotelian and neo-Platonic derived theories of the soul's nature insofar as its incorporeality (and thus immateriality) is concerned (as pointed out, for example, by Ṭāhā Ḥusayn, *Tajdīd Dhikrā Abī al-ʿAlā',* p. 266). These are theories that eventually found a lasting foothold in Islamic philosophy (as early as al-Kindī at the very least); for a brief but informative overview see, e.g., E. E. Calverley, "Nafs," *SEI,* pp. 434–35. But the position on the nature of the soul that al-Maʿarrī is advancing here is not the one that has dominated Islamic religio-philosophical thought (ibid.).

7. Leyden ms., p. 256; this line is missing in Zand's edition of *Luzūm.* The first religio-philosophical position in the line (i.e., that which appears in the first hemistich), might be a reference to the doctrine of the transmigration of the soul, although this is by no means clear. What al-Maʿarrī means by *arḍ*/ أرض here is somewhat puzzling. The second religio-philosophical position (i.e., that in the second hemistich), by implication in any event, might also be a reference to transmigration, although it is more likely to be a link to the neo-Platonic, emanationist theory on the origin of the human soul—inclusive of the very important concept of the Universal Soul—so widely embraced by medieval Islamic philosophers and mystics. Al-Maʿarrī did seem to have in mind that there is individuated soul and also Universal Soul from which individuated soul is derived or dispersed. The words *kharrat ilayhi min maʿālīhā*/

خرت عليه من معاليها are reminiscent of *habaṭat ilayka min al-maḥall al-arfa' warqā' dhāt ta'azzuz wa-tamannu'*/ هبطت إليك من المحلّ الأرفع ورقاء ذات تعزّز وتمنّع ("A noble and proud dove [i.e., the soul] has fallen unto you from the Higher Abode"). This is the opening line of Ibn Sīnā's famous ode to the soul, which speaks of the soul as falling from its original heavenly home and becoming a sad and suffering captive of the human body until it once again returns to its heavenly home, its true dwelling place; see *Dīwān Ibn Sīnā*, ed. Nūr al-Dīn ʿAbd al-Qādir and Henri Jahier (Algiers: Libraire Ferrais, 1960), pp. 31–35.

8. Calverley, "Nafs," *SEI*, p. 435.

9. Notwithstanding its brevity, the poem under discussion here might rightfully be considered a Maʿarrīan counterpart to Ibn Sīnā's poem addressed to the soul. Dogmatically it resembles the poem in certain key areas. It is also one of al-Maʿarrī's more unified, transparently coherent, and sustained efforts in *Luzūm* (even for the shorter poems) on something of religio-philosophical import. Below is Nicholson's admirable English poetic interpretation of L II.22.7–11, replete with rhymes and a cadence that emulates the original (from Nicholson, "The Meditations," p. 179)

O spirit, how long will thou with pleasure wear
this body? Fling it off, 'tis worn threadbare.
If thou hast chosen to lodge thus all these years,
Thine is the blame—and smiles oft end in tears.
Or if the fault was Fate's, then thou art blind,
As water feels no barrier, though confined.
Wert thou not there, to sin it ne'er had stirred,
But would have lain like earth without a word.
The lamp of mind neglecting, thou dost stray,
Although in Reason's light thou has a God-given ray.

Beneath in its entirety is E. G. Browne's version of Ibn Sīnā's Arabic poem on the soul (from Browne, *A Literary History of Persia*, vol. II [Cambridge: Cambridge University Press, 1956], pp. 110–11). The poem is certainly more ambitious, majestic, and philosophically developed than al-Maʿarrī's of L II.22.7–11, but otherwise not greatly debased by being bracketed with it. The whole poem is repeated here, despite the length, to give a sense of the higher level of intellectual composition in Arabic that al-Maʿarrī (1) must have been aware of and (2) aspired to (and on a more consistent level) as both a poet and thinker in *Luzūm;* meaning, among other things, that special idiom as well as message become as much of a concern as the medium.

It descended upon thee from out of the regions above,
That exalted, ineffable, glorious, heavenly Dove.
'Twas concealed from the eyes of all those who
its nature would ken,
Yet it wears not a veil, and is ever apparent to
men.
Unwilling it sought thee and joined thee, and
yet, though it grieve,
It is like to be still more unwilling thy body
to leave.
It resisted and struggled, and would not be tamed
in haste,
Yet it joined thee, and slowly grew used to this
desolate waste,
Till, forgotten at length, as I ween, were its
haunts and its troth
In the heavenly gardens and groves, which to
leave it was loath.
Until, when it entered the D of its downward
Descent,
And to earth, to the C of its centre, unwillingly
went,
The eye (I) of Infirmity smote it, and lo, it
was hurled
Midst the sign-posts and ruined abodes of this
desolate world.
It weeps, when it thinks of its home and the peace
it possessed,
With tears welling forth from its eyes without
pausing or rest,
And with plaintive mourning it broodeth like
one bereft
O'er such trace of its home as the fourfold
winds have left.
Thick nets detain it, and strong is the cage
whereby
It is held from seeking the lofty and spacious
sky.

Until, when the hour of its homeward flight
draws near,
And 'tis time for it to return to its ampler
sphere,
It carols with joy, for the veil is raised, and
it spies
Such things as cannot be witnessed by waking eyes.
On a lofty height doth it warble its songs of
praise
(For even the lowliest being doth knowledge raise).
And so it returneth, aware of all hidden things
In the universe, while no stain to its garment
clings.
Now why from its perch on high was it cast like
this
To the lowest Nadir's gloomy and drear abyss?
Was it God who cast it forth for some purpose wise?
Concealed from the keenest seeker's inquiring eyes?
Then is its descent a discipline wise but stern,
That the things that it hath not heard it thus may
learn.
So 'tis she whom Fate doth plunder, until her star
Setteth at length in a place from its rising far,
Like a gleam of lightning which over the meadows
shone,
And, as though it ne'er had been, in a moment is
gone.

Al-Maʿarrī has left no indication that he was even aware of Ibn Sīnā, let alone directly or indirectly influenced by him, although the two were roughly contemporaries (al-Maʿarrī was born seven years before Ibn Sīnā's birth; he outlived him by twenty years). The latter was such a towering figure, however, even in his day, that it would be almost inconceivable that al-Maʿarrī was not aware of his name as well as some of the more important dimensions to his psychology (whether these reached him indirectly through secondary sources or directly through primary sources). Ṭāhā Ḥusayn was convinced that Ibn Sīnā and al-Maʿarrī, even if they never met, undoubtedly knew of each other and each other's writings and views (*Tajdīd Dhikrā Abī al-'Alā',* p. 76).

10. See, e.g., *Avicenna's Psychology*, trans. Fazlur Rahman (London: Oxford University Press, 1952), pp. 56–58.

11. Haddad and Smith, *Death and Resurrection*, p. 12.

12. Even this was less important than affirming bodily resurrection; see Haddad and Smith, op cit., p. 12.

13. See his *Psychology*, trans. Rahman, chapters 9 and 11, passim.

14. Nicholson ("The Meditations," p. 179) observes the following (although his listing is by no means exhaustive):

> The idea that the spirit corrupts and wears out the body is expressed in the following passages [of *Luzūm*]: "Does my spirit blame my body, which never ceased to serve it until it (the body) became too weak? And yet my spirit laid upon it amazing burdens, now one by one, now two at a time. The state of Man is contrary to that of trees, for they (being void of spirit) bear fruit, whilst he commits sin" [L I.78.1–3]. "The spirit's dwelling in the body makes it (the body) diseased, and its departure restores it (the body) to health. The body, when it returns to earth, does not feel the winds that sweep away its dust in the grave" [L II.421.3–4]. "If a spirit dwelt in the mountains of the earth neither Naḍādi nor Irāb would be everlasting" [L I.91.3].

Aware of this aspect of al-Maʿarrī's psychology, too, Ṭāhā Ḥusayn (*Tajdīd Dhikrā Abī al-'Alā'* p. 267) insightfully points out that here al-Maʿarrī differs from the Platonists; "For Plato considers that the soul is good, and that the body and matter are the real source of evil, whereas Abū al-ʿAlā' thinks the opposite: it is the body that is good and the soul that is evil."

فأن أفلاطونَ يرى أن الروح خيراً وأن الجسم والمادة هما مصدر الشر وأما أبو العلاء فيرى العكس من ذلك أن الخير هو الجسمُ وأن الشرير هو الروح.

Thus as well, in this teaching, al-Maʿarrī differs from (1) Arab neo-Platonism (cf., e.g., the aspects of the psychology of al-Kindī and al-Fārābī as paraphrased [respectively] on pp. 102–103 and 145–46 of Fakhry's *Islamic Philosophy*), and, (2) Avicenna's psychology as expressed in his poem on the soul (supra, n. 9).

15. Al-Maʿarrī's depiction of the human soul as both beautiful and commanding to do evil has a Qur'ānic basis (79:40; 22:53) and his remark that the soul is man's greatest enemy is recapitulated both in *ḥadīth* literature (see Annemarie Schimmel, *Mystical Dimensions of Islam* (Chapel Hill: University of North Carolina Press, 1975), p. 112) and the Islamic Divine Law or

Sharī'ah (according, e.g., to al-Ghazzālī; *al-Risālat al-Laduniyyah*, trans. by Margaret Smith, p. 195). These positions became critical articles of faith for Islamic mysticism. The Islamic mystic's path toward God and spiritual purification must begin with the admission that the soul commands to do evil, is lustful, and is man's worst enemy and hence must be struggled against (Schimmel, ibid.).

However, unlike Qur'ān 75:2 and 89:27 and the Islamic mystics (Schimmel, ibid.), al-Maʿarrī does not advance the notion that the soul in addition to commanding to do evil can also be "blaming" (*lawwāmah*/لوّامة)—i.e., serving to prevent man from doing evil—or "at peace" (*muṭma'innah*/مطمئنة)—i.e., in a purified state removed of all vices. For al-Maʿarrī, for all intents and purposes, *nafs*/نفس appears always to be evil, or at least always inclined/attracted to evil. Unlike the Arab neo-Platonists (see, e.g., Avicenna's *Psychology*, trans. Rahman, pp. 24 ff; Fakhry, *Islamic Philosophy*, pp. 38–39; *Rasā'il Ikhwān al-Ṣafā'*/رسائل إخوان الصفاء [Beirut: Dār Ṣādir, 1957], vol. II, p. 387 ff.), al-Maʿarrī makes no mention of the human soul having three divisions or levels or faculties, the vegetative, animal (or carnal), and human (or rational), with evil arising essentially only at the lower levels (i.e., the vegetative and animal). (This latter teaching is also what the Islamic mystics have in mind when advocating a struggle against the *nafs*, which for them equals the lower animal soul, the base instincts and passions. See Schimmel, *Mystical Dimensions*, ibid.; and al-Ghazzālī, *al-Risālat al-Laduniyyah,* trans. Smith, p. 195. The "lower self" or "animal soul" is also how, according to al-Ghazzālī [ibid.], the *Sharī'ah* interprets *nafs* in its declaration that one's greatest enemy is one's *nafs*.) It would appear that for al-Maʿarrī, *nafs*/نفس is in no way divisible. It is also wholly evil; or, more precisely, on the whole and as a whole, inclined to evil. Rationality is not a faculty or function of the soul but of the mind or intellect (*al-'aql*/العقل).

16. Otherwise, al-Maʿarrī implies no physical nexus between soul and intellect. That is to say, unlike the influential Muslim Aristotelians on this topic (see, e.g., al-Fārābī, *The Letter Concerning the Intellect*, trans. Arthur Hyman in *Philosophy in the Middle Ages*, ed. Arthur Hyman and James J. Walsh [New York: Harper Row, 1967], p. 215), al-Maʿarrī does not speak of *'aql* or the human mind (or intellect) as though it is a part or faculty or function of the soul. His language suggests that *al-'aql* is organically separate from *nafs*.

17. Leyden ms., p. 224; Zand has *fī al-ṭab' majbūl*/في الطبع مجبول instead of *fī al-arḍ maṭbū'* /في الأرض مطبوع but giving essentially the same meaning.

18. Fakhry, *Islamic Philosophy*, pp. 61–62; quote from al-Shahrastānī, *al-Milal*, pp. 59 ff.

19. Fakhry, *Islamic Philosophy*, p. 229.

20. Fakhry, *Islamic Philosophy*, p. 230.

21. Fakhry, *Islamic Philosophy*, pp. 58, 61–63

22. These are the focus of chapter 6 of this study.

23. Ḥusayn (*Tajdīd Dhikrā Abī al-'Alā',* p. 263), takes this last line of L II.79.7–9 as being ironic; i.e., we should understand it as signifying that al-Maʿarrī *did* believe in divine predeterminism, *and* to the extent that he did not hold man censurable for sinning or wrongdoings; but he was prevented from espousing this belief because of the fear of public opinion (*not* because of piety).

On the basis of this as well as other instances in *Luzūm* of what Ḥusayn considered as clear endorsements of a belief in divine predeterminism (he said he counted over 200 examples; idem, p. 262), Ḥusayn was inclined to take al-Maʿarrī as in fact firmly believing in divine predeterminism; idem, pp. 262–63, 265.

To me, the frequent, earnest moralizing in *Luzūm* does not seem to support Ḥusayn's interpretation of L II.79.9, not to mention his overall assessment of al-Maʿarrī and divine predeterminism; this notwithstanding his documentation of over 200 instances in *Luzūm* of a strong leaning toward a rigid belief in predeterminism. Moreover, Ḥusayn (rather inexplicably) failed to take into consideration L I.351.1 and L II.358.9, where al-Maʿarrī says, respectively: "If they ask me about my school of thought, it's fear of God/ I affirm neither free will (*ṭawq*/طوق) nor predeterminism (*jabr*/جبر)"; "Don't live as a determinist (*mujbar*/مجبر) or as a believer in free will (*qadarī*/قدريّ); strive for an intermediary position between the two."

Nicholson ("The Meditations," p. 147) interpreted L II.79.9 as Ḥusayn did, although unlike the latter correctly went on to observe (idem, p. 162; but without supportive citations), that al-Maʿarrī sometimes "keeps clear of" absolute determinism in *Luzūm,* and that he possesses a "moral rationalism" (which this study takes to mean, among other things, the opposite of a moral determinism, and thus humans should not forsake thinking about the virtuous life and how to effect it on the basis that it simply could not be realized because a divine predetermination may have ruled otherwise).

Von Kremer ("Ueber die philosophischen Gedichte," p. 20) discussed al-Maʿarrī's views on free will and determinism only very briefly and superficially. However, he, too, concluded that al-Maʿarrī should not be seen as a thoroughgoing upholder of divine predeterminism, a position more or less mirrored in the more recent Arabic language sources consulted for the present study

24. *An Introduction to Arabic Poetics* (Austin: University of Texas, 1990), p. 65.

25. For example, L II.78.2–3:

Your moments in time are light-giving candles,
so rush after them until they are snuffed out.
The soul's annihilated with repeated breaths
as a fire's flames extinguish its radiant light.

دولاتكم شمعات يُستضاءُ بها　　فبادروها إلى أن تُطفأ الشَمَعُ
والنفس تفنى بأَنفاسٍ مُكرَّرةٍ　　وساطعُ النارِ تخبي نورَهُ اللُّمَعُ

And also L I.83.2:

I see a live coal in the body that death snuffs out.
But for as long as I live it continues to blaze.

أَرى قبسا في الجسم يطفئها الردى　　وما دمتُ حياً فهو ذا يتلهّبُ

And also L II.432.14:

Advancing over the earth are souls that arrive
having been created from souls that have perished.

In each of these citations, al-Maʿarrī could very well mean something considerably less than the notion that the soul dies or perishes; e.g., only the life-providing or animating force that the soul provides to body is ultimately severed from the body (i.e., ceases to exist in body), although the soul itself does not expire. Also, as deliberately indicated in our translations, L II.78.3 and L II.432.14 contain undeniable ambiguities in key places. A comparatively clear, straightforward admission by al-Maʿarrī of the possibility that the soul might perish when and as the body does, seems to be contained in L I.103.7–8:

If my intellect escorts the soul after her departure
with death, how fitting that you see such a strange marvel.
And if my soul goes into the vast atmosphere, perishing
as my body perishes in my grave, then how terrible.

إِن يَصْحب الروحَ عقلي بعد مَظْعَنها　　للموت عني فأجدِرْ أن ترى عَجَبا
وإن مضتْ في الهواءِ الرحبِ هالكةً　　هَلاَكَ جسمي في تُرْبي فَوَا شَجَبا

L I.243.5–6 reads:

وشخصي وروحي مثل طفل وأُمّهِ   لتلك بهذا من يَدِ الرب عاقدُ
يموتانِ مثلَ الناظرَيْنِ توارَدا   فلا هو مفقودٌ ولا هي فاقدُ

The lines came to the attention of Nicholson ("The Meditations," p. 179). He translated as "My body and spirit are like a child and its mother: they are tied, that is, by the hand of the Lord. They die simultaneously, and neither is the body lost (to the spirit) nor does spirit lose (the body)," adding in a note that the literal meaning of the Arabic from which he derived "they die simultaneously" (مثل الناظرين تواردا) is "like the two eyes which converge (on the subject of vision)."

This is one of the rare instances in the *Luzūm* where quite clearly soul and body are said *to die* and where there is added in the same breath words that can be taken to mean that a dead body and a dead soul have a second life (in the form of a resurrected human body, in tandem with soul). It is probably an instance of dissimulation with respect to the body not being lost to soul (in resurrection); not likely to fool given the fact that the view in L I.243.5–6 is scarcely repeated.

L I.185.11–12, wherein al-Maʿarrī speaks of the soul at the time of the body's death, seems to intend conferring some credibility to the argument that the soul perishes with the body:

The soul is earthly [i.e., earth-bound] in the view of one faction;
according to another it ascends through the heavens,
proceeding in the form of the body it occupied
either to an abode of bliss or one of miseries.

والروح أرضيةٌ في رأي طائفةٍ   وعند قومٍ تَرَقَّى في السمواتِ
تمضي على هيئةِ الشخص الذي سكنتْ   فيه إلى دار نُعمى أو شقاواتِ

26. Following the Leyden ms., p. 120; Zand has ناوى

27. Haddad and Smith, op cit., pp. 56–57; Fakhry, pp. 260–61.

28. Al-Ghazzālī, *Tahāfut al-Falāsifah*/تهافت الفلاسفة, trans. Sabih Ahmad Kamali (Lahore: Pakistan Philosophical Congress 1963), chapter 10, passim.

29. For example, the Ikhwān al-Ṣafā' (*Rasā'il*/رسائل vol. III, pp. 7, 79) and Abū Bakr al-Rāzī, *Opera Philosophica*, ed. Paul Kraus (Cairo, 1939), pp. 381ff.

30. Haddad and Smith, p. 59.

31. The Nuṣayrī sect, over the centuries since its inception especially strong in and around Aleppo, has been and remains rather well-known for the belief in wide-ranging forms of transmigration. See L. Massignon, "Nuṣairī," *SEI*, p. 455.

32. Nicholson ("The Meditations," p. 183) helpfully pointed out that what al-Maʿarrī must have had in mind with the reference to the instance of *maskh/* مسخ witnessed by the Jew was the Qur'ānic account (2:65) of the Jews being ordered by God to turn into apes. This was as punishment for their not keeping the Sabbath. A fuller version of the narrative is found in Qur'ān 7: 163–166.

L I.239.1–3 need further amplification at the level of taking نسخ as transmigration of souls. The point seems to be this: نسخ cannot be dismissed; and مسخ once occurred (according to our—i.e., the Muslims'—Holy Scripture), so why should it be denied now? Some have even gone so far as to posit رسخ.

This in all likelihood is largely tongue-in-cheek, intended as a rather insulting imprecation. At the same time, however, al-Maʿarrī in invoking several controversial doctrines, while seemingly at least half-serious about them, bestows upon them, as well as (in the eyes of his more "orthodox" co-religionists) anything similar, considerable notoriety as topics worthy of serious discussion.

33. Leyden ms., p. 63;

34. Leyden ms., p. 63, has *al-'aks*/العكس (the opposite). This wording would seem to suggest the meaning "the opposite [of man's soul translocating/reincarnating in animals]"—i.e., animals' souls translocating/reincarnating in man.

35. The present study slightly disagrees here with both Nicholson and Ḥusayn. The former ("The Meditations," p. 182) has written: "Maʿarrí rejects the doctrine of metempsychosis and even derides it." The latter's opinion in the matter is the following: "It is clear that Abū al-ʿAlā''s reasoning did not endorse metempsychosis, so he rejected it and renounced it"/ الظاهر أن عقل أبي العلاء لم يؤيد التنسخ فرفضها وأعرض عنه (*Tajdīd Dhikrā Abī al-'Alā',* p. 268).

Ḥusayn adduced as evidence for his conclusion only L II.171.7–8. Nicholson referenced L II.171.7–8; L II.166.14–16; and L II.239.1–3, but he did not allow for the ambiguity of نسخ in L II.239.1, translating it only as "abrogation."

More recent insightful Arabic language source materials devoted to al-Maʿarrī and consulted for the present study, while taking al-Maʿarrī at his word when he derides and rejects the notion of the translocation of the human soul involving in-dwelling in other bodies (e.g., mineral or vegetal or human or animal), do allow that al-Maʿarrī's views on the human soul suggest that translocation of the human soul to a higher, transcendent, spiritual (i.e., immaterial) realm (transmigration in the strictest sense of the word and not metempsychosis) is possible or even inexorable. Zaydān and Khalīfāt, for example, and as already indicated, are of this persuasion.

36. "Al-Jawānib al-Mītāfīzīqiyyah li al-Nafs wa Naẓariyyat al-Ma'rifah li Abī al-'Alā' al-Ma'arrī," pp. 54–60.

37. قضايا العصر في أدب أبي العلاء المعري (*Qaḍāyā al-'Aṣr fī Adab Abī al-'Alā' al-Ma'arrī* (Cairo: الهيئة المصرية العامة للكتاب / The Egyptian General Book Organization, 1986), pp. 176–204.

38. *Qaḍāyā al-'Aṣr,* p. 134.

39. "The Meditations," pp. 59–95.

40. Leyden ms., p. 94; Zand has *kulluna*/كلُنا

41. Adonis, *Arabic Poetics*, p. 67.

42. Albert Camus, *The Myth of Sisyphus*, trans. Justin O'Brien, Penguin Books (reprint; Middlesex, England: Penguin Books, 1977), p. 11.

43. Although in his *Risālat al-Ghufrān* (ed. Bint al-Shāṭi', pp. 395–96) al-Ma'arrī does acknowledge having given suicide serious thought:

> And I am amazed at a group's assisting one another with something which is neither the good nor the pious and which has no sure proof of validity. And then skilled craftsmen polish it or repair [it]. I [once] nearly joined, without sorrow or repentance, the community of nonbeing. But I fear going to [God] the All Powerful without having put my palm trees in good order by means of fecundating them. [I.e., I fear going to God before bringing to fruition my doings here on earth?] It was told to one of the philosophers, "So-and-so showed gentleness of manner until he killed himself, not having been able to bear what he wrestled with in this world [literally, "in the empty abode"], having hated that he pursue the marvels of iniquities, and having desired moving to the resting places of bliss." [To this] the philosopher then said words whose significance is the following: "That young man in the prime of his life committed an error; to him and his mother bereavement is deserved. Why did he not show steadfastness in the face of time's vicissitudes until the One who puts to the test test him with Divine Fate? [That is, why did he not wait until God determined for him his proper time to die?] For he does not know to what he advances, and to every house there is destruction." Were it not for the wisdom of God (His power is manifest), and the fact that He has restrained man from [going to] death, by means of the fear of anxiety and of vanishing, everyone whose wrath has been furious, and whose pruning knife has become dull from what is struck [by it], would desire that cups of death be filled for him. And yet it is God Who knows what He will grant as recompense.

وإني لأَعْجَبُ من تَمالُؤِ جماعة، على أمر لَيَس بالحسنِ ولا الطاعةِ ، ولا ثَبَتَ له يقين ، فَيَشُوقُهُ الصَّنَعُ أَو يَقينُ قد كِدتُ أَلحَقُ برهطِ العَدَمِ ، مِن غيرِ الأَسفِ ولا النَّدم ، ولكنما أرهبُ قدومي على الجَبَّار ، ولم أُصلحْ نَخلي بإبار. وقيلَ لبَعضِ الحُكماءِ : إنَّ فُلاناً تَلطف حتى قَتَلَ نَفْسهُ ولم يُطِقْ في الدار الخاليةِ عَفْسه ، وكره أَن يُمارس بدائعَ الشُّرور ، وأَحبَّ النُّقلَةَ إلى مَنازلِ السُّرور. فقال الحكيمُ قولاً معناهُ: أَخطأ ذلك الشابُّ المقتبل ، لَهُ ولِلأُمِّه يُحَقُّ الهَبلُ ، هَلا صَبَرَ على صُروفِ الزَّمان ، حتى يَمْنوَ لهُ القَدَرَ مانٍ؟ فإِنَّهُ لا يَشعُر علام يقدمُ ، ولكلِّ بيتٍ هَدَم. ولولا حِكمةُ اللهِ جَلَّت قُدْرتُه ، وأَنَّهُ حَجَزَ الرَّجُلَ عن المَوتِ ، بالخَوفِ مِن العَلزِ والفَوْتِ ، لَرَغِبَ كلٌّ من احتَدَمَ غَضَبُه ، وكَلَّ عن ضَريبةِ مِقْضَبه ، أن تُتْرَعَ له الموت كؤوسٌ ، والله للعالم بما يَؤُوسُ.

The existence of this passage lends further credibility to the conclusion supra that al-Maʿarrī sincerely contemplated suicide. As does the fact that he was familiar with the Phaedon.

Surprisingly, the full significance of the passage if not the passage itself seems to have escaped the attention of nearly all of al-Maʿarrī's major commentators, biographers, and interpreters (and especially the premoderns); as has also the notion that al-Maʿarrī's philosophy as expressed elsewhere—e.g., and most notably, in *Luzūm*—has suicidal implications if not explicit endorsements of the act; although it has been correctly underscored by Nicholson ("The Meditations," p. 85), von Kremer ("Ueber die philosophischen Gedichte," p. 83), and others, including the more recent interpreters of al-Maʿarrī consulted for this study (for the Arabic is quite clear) that in L I.260.4–6 al-Maʿarrī refers rather admiringly (as opposed to matter-of-factly) to pious Indians who commit suicide by self-immolation. Nicholson (idem, p. 109) also interpreted several verses in *Luzūm* (I.295.7–8; II.123.1ff; 130.11) as endorsements of "anaethesia to relieve him [al-Maʿarrī] of the pain of life"; although Nicholson's finding al-Maʿarrī's longing to be dead matter (i.e., something inorganic; *al-jamād*/الجماد) and insensate, like a rock, this so as to be free of pain and suffering, is not exactly "anaesthesia"; even though one can well imagine al-Maʿarrī endorsing it, not to mention (more likely still) euthanasia.

Nicholson became aware of the long Arabic passage just quoted above through his ground-breaking overview of *Risālat al-Ghufrān* for *The Journal of the Royal Asiatic Society* (part I, 1900; parts II and III, 1902), and quite rightly understood the passage as a clear reference to suicide; in the table of contents of part II of his study of *Risālat al-Ghufrān*, p. 80, he titled the passage "A philosopher condemns suicide." In a footnote he translates the words فقد كدت ألحق برهط العدم من غير الأسف ولا الندم ولكنما أرهب قدومي على الجبار

ولم أصلح نخلي بإبار as "Presently I shall join the dead, without regret or repentance. Yet I fear to approach the Omnipotent before I have duly seen to the grafting of my palm trees (sown in order that I may reap)."

In an unpublished paper titled "The Last Crossroad: Absurdity, Death, and Hope (?) in the Thought of Abū al-ʻAlā' al-Maʻarrī," I discussed al-Maʻarrī's suggested contemplation of suicide within the context of Albert Camus' philosophy of the absurd. I concluded (among other things) that with respect to al-Maʻarrī, inasmuch as he rejected suicide proper (i.e., bodily suicide), the most important questions that arise over the topic are: (1) why the rejection?, and (2) but did he not commit what Camus labeled "philosophical suicide" (i.e., rejecting the absurd, not acknowledging it, by embracing transcendent religious articles of faith, a higher reality to supersede or explain away the absurd)? I argued (in so many words) that, notwithstanding the *possibility* of a "leap of faith" with al-Maʻarrī, at least to the extent of an inchoate deism or theism (if not an irreproachable belief in God and Islam) and the hedging of bets with respect to Divine Reward and Punishment in a hereafter, the preponderance of evidence suggests that a Camusian (i.e., disapproving) understanding of a "leap of faith" (i.e., a leap *to* faith, or back to faith after doubt and despair) cannot be taken seriously: al-Maʻarrī fully acknowledged the absurd, the meaningless in life and the world, and he revolted against it with his lifelong commitment to contrarian, dissident, and transgressive thinking with respect to God and religion. Sisyphus had his rock; al-Maʻarrī had his.

At least one Arabic-language author of the modern era for whom al-Maʻarrī's remark in *Risālat al-Ghufrān* (in the Bint al-Shāṭi' edition on pp. 395–96) had similar such resonance and significance is ʻAbd al-Qādir Zaydān; see his *Qaḍāyā al-'Aṣr fī Adab Abī al-'Alā' al-Ma'arrī*/قضايا العصر في أدب أبي العلاء المعري (*The Issues of the Age in the Literature of Abū al-'Alā' al-Ma'arrī*) (Cairo: The Egyptian General Book Organization, 1986), pp. 108–16, which contains a very thoughtful and informed discussion. I was not made aware of *Qaḍāyā al-'Aṣr* until several years after my presentation of "The Last Crossroad: Absurdity, Death, and Hope (?) in the Thought of Abū al-ʻAlā' al-Maʻarrī."

Zaydān also cites a line from al-Maʻarrī's *al-Fuṣūl wa al-Ghāyāt*/الفصول والغايات that is similar in tone and meaning to his implied contemplation of suicide in *Risālat al-Ghufrān* with the words قد كِدتُ ألحَقُ برهطِ العَدَمِ ، مِن غير الأسفِ ولا النَّدمِ ولكنما أرهبُ قدومي على الجَبَّار ، ولم أُصلحْ نَخلي بإبار.

The line in question from *al-Fuṣūl wa al-Ghāyāt* reads as follows:

لو أمنتُ التابعة لجازَ أن أُمْسِكَ عن الطعام والشراب حتى أخلُصَ من ضَنْكِ الحياة ولكن أرهبُ غوائل السبيل.

"Had I felt safe about the attendant consequences, it would have been possible for me to refrain from eating and drinking until being rid of the wretchedness of life; but I fear the dangers of this way" (*al-Fuṣūl wa al-Ghāyāt*, ed. Muḥammad Ḥasan Zanātī/محمد حسن زناتي [Cairo: The Egyptian General Book Organization, 1977], p. 429).

Zaydān concurs that al-Maʿarrī rejected not only bodily but also philosophical suicide; لم ينتحر أبو العلاء بالجسد لقد هم ولكنه لم يفعل وأغلب الظن أنه لم ينتحر فلسفيا أيضا لقد ظل أبو العلاء في حالة من التساؤل الذي لم ينته إلا بوفاته ("Abū al-ʿAlā' did not commit bodily suicide; he gave it some thought but did not do it. One must presume that he did not commit philosophical suicide either, for he remained in a state of constantly questioning things, which did not end until his death"). In other words, and to connect more transparently to the Camusian discourse, al-Maʿarrī's "state of constant questioning" can be seen as a lifelong "state of revolt."

Nicholson's al-Maʿarrī (not to mention Ḥusayn's and von Kremer's and most assuredly many others') takes the leap of faith. He acknowledges the existence of a transcendent Being/Existence/Universe superintended by God (even if he wonders about the wisdom behind how life and creation unfold). In other words, he commits philosophical suicide (although hardly thought of in these terms by Nicholson) but rejects suicide proper.

Al-Maḥāsinī (*Abū al-'Alā Nāqid al-Mujtama'*, p. 22) reminds us that Ibn al-Habāriyyah as cited by Sibṭ ibn al-Jawzī alleged that al-Maʿarrī actually *did* commit suicide in order to escape "the trap" that Dāʿī al-Duʿāh set for him (presumably in the questions he posed to him that led to the exchange on vegetarianism). But Ibn al-Habāriyyah is the only chronicler of al-Maʿarrī—al-Maḥāsinī quickly points out—who made this allegation; the main reason for which al-Maḥāsinī dismisses it as spurious, but also because "suicide was characteristic of the Romans but not Muslims and Arabs."

44. Franz Rosenthal, "On Suicide in Islam," *Journal of the American Oriental Society* 66 (1946), p. 243.

45. Rosenthal, idem, p. 250.

46. The observation was Nietzsche's; see *Beyond Good and Evil,* trans. Walter Kaufmann, Vintage Books (New York: Random House, 1966), p. 91); italics mine.

47. Von Kremer, "Ueber die philosophichen Gedichte," p. 12. Curiously, von Kremer himself was not willing to admit this possibility, inexplicably excluding al-Maʿarrī's orthodox declaration that God is a truth or reality from his other orthodox remarks that he (von Kremer) was quick to hold (and rightly so) as insincere. Von Kremer took al-Maʿarrī to be a firm monotheist if only that; i.e., he did not affiliate with any organized religion ("Der Dichter ist entschiedener Monotheist, aber nicht mehr"); ibid. Nicholson, too, was unjustifiably quick and decisive to conclude that al-Maʿarrī sincerely believed in God: "Maʿarrí . . . believes in a Creator, whom he identifies with Allah. He emphatically repudiates atheism" ("The Meditations," p. 158). "Partly on rational grounds and partly, perhaps, by instinct Maʿarrí believed in the existence of a divine Creator" (idem, p. 164). The instinct that Nicholson speaks of—which this study understands as simply inherited opinion, or what a modern Muslim religious thinker (Ismāʿīl Maẓhar,"Maʿa al-ʿAqqād," *Fī al-Naqd al-Adabī* [Beirut: Maktabat al-Ḥayāh] 1965, p. 23) has labeled as "that with which reason is familiar" (ألفة العقل) with respect to God's existence—is more in evidence than any attempt at an explicit rational proof (e.g., cosmological or teleological).

I thank Ralph M. Coury (professor emeritus of history, Fairfield University) for bringing to my attention Maẓhar's article "Maʿa al-ʿAqqād," portions of which I translated for chapter 5 of *Sceptics of Islam*, ed. Ralph M. Coury (London: I.B. Tauris, 2018).

Ṭāhā Ḥusayn in his *Maʻa Abī al-ʻAlāʼ fī Sijnih* (pp. 44–45) said that on rational grounds al-Maʿarrī in *Luzūm* (e.g., I.186.9: أثبت لي خالقاً حكيماً / ولستُ من معشر نفاة) held and held without any manifested doubts that the world has a Creator God and that He is wise (أن أبا العلاء قد هداه عقله إلى أن لهذا العالم خالقاً وإلى أن هذا الخالق حكيم لا يشكّ في ذلك أو على الأقل لا يظهر فيه شكّاً), adding that by his count the *Luzūm* is "full of" poems acknowledging the existence of the Creator God (تمتلئ به اللزوميات) and that in them al-Maʿarrī speaks of the wise Creator God with complete and clear sincerity and credibility, even though he admittedly can't understand the wisdom of God's ways: (وهو إذا تحدث عن هذا الخالق الحكيم تحدث عنه في لهجة صادقة يظهر فيها الأخلاص واضحاً جليّاً ولكنه عاجز عن فهم هذه الحكمة).

Nowhere in *Luzūm* are there explicit rational arguments attempted for *proving* the existence of God, although that should hardly be expected.

Ḥusayn regards *al-Fuṣūl wa al-Ghāyāt* as a sincere expression of God-fearing piety and God-centered devotion and praise, al-Maʿarrī's own stated purpose for composing the work. "And he does praise God; there is no doubt about that. I know of no one who who has praised God to the extent that

Abū al-ʿAlāʾ has" (*Ma'a Abī al-'Alā' fī Sijnih*, p. 199). However, al-Maʿarrī "believes in God but at the same time he believes in his own reason. His belief in God moves him to love and security and confidence—at times—but also—at other times—to fear and anxiety and despair. His belief in reason moves him to doubt and denial on occasions although on other occasions to belief and certainty. He wavers in *al-Fuṣūl wa al-Ghāyāt* just as he does in the *Luzūmiyyāt*, but he affirms irrefutably two things, the existence of God (وجود الله) and the use of reason and reason alone as being the only way to prevent the disconnection between man and God" (idem, p. 200).

Regardless, even more so than in his *Tajdīd Dhikrā Abī al-'Alā'*, and with the benefit of an additional twenty-five years during which to revisit and reflect anew on the topic, Ḥusayn in his *Ma'a Abī al-'Alā' fī Sijnih* emphasized the remarkable transgressiveness in al-Maʿarrī's thinking with respect to received opinions about God, religion, revelation, resurrection, and so on, transgressiveness quite literally deserving of the attribute "revolutionary."

> Muslims had never known anyone like him with regard to the intellectual freedom that he permitted himself, a freedom that no Muslim enjoys even in this modern era, the era of constitutionalism and representative democracy . . . [He was] free in his opinions and in his thinking, in what he envisioned and imagined to himself and to the population at large, in the convictions that he reached and the school of thought that he summoned people to . . . [T]his man who moved beyond freedom to the point of revolution . . . had freed himself from the bonds of religion and society, and from the natural order of things as well" (*Ma'a Abī al-'Alā' fī Sijnih*, pp. 130–31).

However, although what Ḥusayn regards as al-Maʿarrī's "vainglorious" faith in the power of reason (p. 48; he uses the word الكبرياء in this context; surely he had in mind hubris; he studied Greek and Latin and the classics) is what led him to unprecedented skepticism (his real flaw) within the context of Islamicate thought, this vainglory never led him to "the impudent rebellion" (التمرد الوقح) that can be found in many other radical rationalists (p. 176); even though it is the mind that burdens itself with analysis and explanations that can fathom the defiant pride of the atheist's mind, which is the mind that does not believe in God, does not acknowledge His existence and His wisdom (pp. 174–75). "It is the mind that believes in God, and establishes His Justice and Wisdom, that oppresses itself if it rebels (إن تمرّد), and tyrannizes itself if it gets ensnared in denial and repudiation" (p. 175).

In other words, Ḥusayn's al-Maʿarrī, notwithstanding his excessive faith in reason, which could take him to extremes in skepticism, outright denials or repudiations of certain received opinions about revealed religion (and above all Islam), had enough awareness of reason's limitations not to take his questions, speculations, and doubts with respect to God (particularly His Wisdom) to the point of the conviction of the atheist, although the atheist's convictions were not completely enigmatic. As exemplified by L I.349.14–18; II.1–2, al-Maʿarrī's moments of hubris would be checked; and, in the final analysis, the day would be carried by his soul's humble resignation, by its assent, and not by recalcitrance and revolution or at least not revolution against God: al-Maʿarrī's revolt is against humans (*Ma'a Abī al-'Alā' fī Sijnih*, pp. 177–178). The Maʿarrīan revolt that Ḥusayn speaks of, more specifically, that he acknowledges, is thus decidedly not Camusian; cf. in this regard note 43 of this chapter.

At the same time, Ḥusayn rightly draws attention to the fact that al-Maʿarrī's materialism can seem to approach Epicurean materialism "in the broadest and at the same time most subtle" meaning of the word (p. 212), by which he obviously means, and later spells out himself (p. 227; فالأبيقوريون كما هو معروف ماديون لا يعترفون بقدرة الإله على شيء من الخلق), the Lucretian doctrine on nature and the universe: "[T]he world has been made by nature through the spontaneous, random, and purposeless congregation and coalescence of atoms whose suddenly formed combinations could serve on each occasion as the starting-point of substantial fabrics—earth and sea and sky and the races of living creatures. . . . Nature is free and uncontrolled by proud masters and runs the universe without the aid of gods" (*On the Nature of the Universe* [Middlesex, England: Penguin Books, 1976], pp. 90–91). Ḥusayn (*Ma'a Abī al-'Alā' fī Sijnih*, p. 226) believed that al-Maʿarrī consciously borrowed from Epicurean thought. (For his full discussion of the connection, see pp. 212–31, passim).

Al-ʿAlawī (*Abū al-'Alā' al-Ma'arrī*, e.g., pp. 20–21) takes al-Maʿarrī as being *inclined* to denying God's existence (يميل المعري إلى إنكار وجود الإله) at times (تارة) but at other times conceding His existence but impugning His justice and wisdom. There are three lines of poetry in *Luzūm* that al-ʿAlawī interprets as being clearly a denial of God's existence (at least as transcendent Creator God as understood by Islam). The lines are in L I.179.1–3:

قلتم لنا خالق حكيم   قلنا صدقتم كذا نقولُ
زعمتموهُ بلا مكان   ولا زمان ألا تقولوا
هذا كلامٌ له خَبيٌّ   معناه ليست لنا عقول

You have said, "We have a wise Creator."
"True," we have responded. "We say the same."
You claim He transcends space and time; do say then
that this is talk that has something concealed in it
whose gist is that on this point we're brainless.

Al-ʿAlawī believes that in here denying the possibility (because reason can't conceive) of the Creator God's transcendence in the sense of His being beyond space and time, and thus outside the world, al-Maʿarrī is positing that He—if we are to assume His existence—must be within the world. But within the context of the entire notion of Creator God this presupposes that He encompasses matter (inasmuch as He would exist necessarily *in* the material world) and indeed the entire material world, of which time and place (space) are components. In other words, God "in" the world is merely one of the existents "in" the world, which invalidates the notion of the Godhead as the source of creation that is distinct from the world and prior to it spatially and temporally (al-ʿAlawī, idem, p. 21).

Khalīfāt (in his "Mītāfīzīqā *al-'Ulū wa al-Ṭabī'ah*," p. 60) takes al-Maʿarrī at face value when he states in the *Luzūm* that there is no doubt that God the Creator is a reality/truth. By logical extension, therefore, atheism (specifically denying God's existence) for Khalīfāt's Maʿarrī must necessarily be seen as simply a denial of a truth, falsifying a reality. Although relying to a considerable extent on the skilled, cerebral, and sympathetic commentary on the *Luzūm* by Ibn al-Sīd al-Baṭalyūsī, Khalīfāt proposes (implicitly at least) that al-Maʿarrī's "proof" or argument for God's existence is that there is an obvious (i.e., empirically verifiable) creation, so there must be a creating agent, and the creating agent is either "in time" and thus requiring an infinite chain of creating agents also "in time" or is not "in time" (i.e., is eternal); and the infinite chain is an impossibility. Al-Maʿarrī in L II.266.100 (if not elsewhere as well) admittedly pronounces that the world (العالم) is created, and created in time, but by God Who is eternal (ومُحدَثٌ هو من ربٍّ له القِدمُ)—as Khalīfāt underscores. But elsewhere, as will be elaborated upon later in this study, this position is not without considerable contradictions.

Bakrī (*al-Fikr al-Dīnī*, p. 138; following which are his supportive citations selected from the *Luzūm*) takes al-Maʿarrī as a firm believer in God although skeptical or completely dismissive with respect to many of "the other pillars of religion" (وقد آمن المعري بالله إيمان وثوق وإن هو شك أو أنكر العديد من أركان الدين الأخرى).

Bakrī furthermore argues that al-Ma'arrī attempted a rational argument for God's existence, namely, on the principle of cause and effect: the celestial bodies are in movement in orbit by virtue of an underlying reason and thus there can be no doubt about a mover (Bakrī's argument is based on the line in *Luzūm* that reads فلكٌ يدورُ بحكمة ولهُ بلا ريبٍ مديرُ. Bakrī does not take into consideration the three lines of poetry in *Luzūm* that al-'Alawī interprets as being clearly a denial of God's existence.)

Zaydān's al-Ma'arrī established for himself in rational fashion—as opposed to blindly accepting commonly held teachings—knowledge of the One Wise Omnipotent Creator God (*Qaḍāyā al-'Aṣr*, pp. 140–46).

48. As already remarked, it is quite unwarranted to assume that al-Ma'arrī seriously intended to take his belief in divine predeterminism as far as suggested in the last-quoted line. Therefore, the point that he really wished to make there may be that, if he did accept a divine predeterminism so thorough as to ascribe all acts, unjust ones included, to God, he would have yet another reason for disbelieving in God's justice. At the same time, the line no doubt was also meant to pique the clerics and other religious thinkers (e.g., the Mu'tazilite-inspired) in al-Ma'arrī's society, reminding them of the seemingly irresolvable problem that they faced in trying to reconcile the idea of an all-powerful God (Who by virtue of His omnipotence must needs superintend evil as well as good in the world) with the idea of a totally just God.

49. The translation follows Zand's understanding of حطم; which Lane's *Lexicon* (part 2, p. 594) provides as well.

50. Admittedly—although hardly surprisingly—none of the quotations just given prove beyond a shadow of a doubt the thrust of the argument being advanced here. راعي المنايا in L II.267.8, for example, could very well mean "the shepherd that is fate" (see Wright, *A Grammar of the Arabic Language*, II, p. 231ff.). للمنايا سائق in L II.266.6 could mean "a driver that is the fates." Still, the point made is quite justifiable especially in light of the discussion and citations that follow).

51. "The Meditations," p. 163.

52. Actually, Ḍirār ibn 'Amr/ضرار بن عمرو (d. around 800 or 820 CE), a master of debate in theological dogma (i.e., *kalām*) and whose particular orientation (*madhhab*/مذهب) therein was very eclectic, seems to have been the real inventor of the concept of *kasb*/كسب; but *kasb* was accepted by al-Ash'arī and his followers and then became one of the most distinctive features of their orientation in theological debates; see W. M. Watt, *The Formative Period of Islamic Thought* (Edinburgh: Edinburgh University Press, 1973), pp. 189–93.

53. "The Meditations," p. 163.

54. Al-Ashʿarī himself mentions a sizable number of individuals or groups who subscribed to *kasb* before his day; see Watt, *The Formative Period,* pp. 193–94; "Altogether the conception had played an important part in Islamic thought before it was taken over by al-Ashʿarī and the Ashʿarites"; idem, p. 194.

55. "The Meditations," p. 163.

56. Consider W. Mongtomery Watt's remarkably insightful and nuanced explanation of it:

> It may help the modern reader to appreciate the formula of "creation by God and 'acquisition' by man" if he regards the aspect of creation as the influence of all the natural forces involved. These include those belonging to the agent's body as an entity obeying physical and chemical laws. Thus the shooting of an arrow presupposes and involves a man's ability to stand or kneel and to flex his arm muscles, and also the normal behavior of the materials of the bow, of the air and of the object hit. Gravity and light also play a part. In Muslim eyes all this is the province of God as creator; man's share in the act, or his "acquisition" of it, is whatever is left. Even from a modern scientific viewpoint man does not make or bring into existence any of the objects or forces involved, though in daily life the ordinary man or woman takes them for granted; when everything of this sort has been set aside as not belonging to the essential human act, what is left—the inner decision—is very little. (*Islamic Philosophy and Theology*, Edinburgh: the University Press, 1962, p. 87)

57. It is worth noting here—speaking of the Muʿtazilites—that had al-Maʿarrī wanted to appear more convincing about maintaining God's justice in an unjust world, one might reasonably expect an approval, one way or another, of the famed Muʿtazilite position with respect to this perennially knotty theological problem. Like the doctrine of *kasb*, said position could hardly have been unknown to al-Maʿarrī given its currency in learned circles even during his lifetime. Second, it is a much less rarified, and therefore more powerful and persuasive, vindication of God's justice; and, although its terse, straightforward assertion that man has free will might have seemed as a gross oversimplification to al-Maʿarrī, he certainly would have welcomed the main point that the Muʿtazilites thereby hoped to advance: that *humans* determine their moral (or immoral) course of behavior (whichever the case may be) and are responsible for it. Third, since a pro-Muʿtazilite leaning in this respect would have been considered nonnormative, it would have given

the alert readers of *Luzūm* good reason for recognizing it as a serious article of belief in al-Maʻarrī's religious philosophy. However, al-Maʻarrī does not associate the teaching of free will specifically with Muʻtazilites. Nor does he in any way indicate an acceptance of the Muʻtazilites' zealous insistence, by way of referring to themselves as "the people of justice," on God's complete and absolute justness. Al-Maʻarrī actually speaks disapprovingly of the Muʻtazilites, although admittedly in very broad, nonspecific terms (to be cited in the next part of this chapter).

On the basis of all of these factors, as well as *Luzūm*'s quite transparent attempt to compromise quite seriously God's justice, it would not be farfetched to conclude that al-Maʻarrī deliberately intended to signal a desire *not* to be associated with most of the major Muʻtazilite views, including that of God's absolute justice (and also, Ṭāhā Ḥusayn believed, the notion that the Muslim who commits major sins will be condemned to the fires of Hell for all eternity; *Ma'a Abī al-'Alā' fī Sijnih*, p. 228). Al-Maʻarrī does strongly resemble the Muʻtazilites, however, when in *al-Fuṣūl wa al-Ghāyāt,* for example (*apud* Ḥusayn, *Ma'a Abī al-'Alā' fī Sijnih,* p. 228) he declares that he must deanthropomorphise God; he can't think of Him as having human attributes; as the Creator of human attributes, He must transcend them (كيف يوصف بشيء خالق الشيء). In the *Luzūm,* one can find verses expressing a similar understanding of God, all of which underscore what is expressed in the most condensed, austere, categorical form in I.363.9 where even becoming can't be predicated of God; God simply "is":

God is great; logical analogy doesn't apply to Him.
It can't be said of Him "He was" or "He became."

والله أكبر لا يدنو القياسُ لهُ   ولا يجوزُ عليهِ كانَ أو صارا

58. Nicholson did not seem to allow for the possibility, the propriety of which is just as questionable as his somewhat precipitous assumption that al-Maʻarrī is clearly a believer in God. Without adducing much additional supporting evidence, Nicholson surprisingly took al-Maʻarrī at his word when he simply declares that God is just while in fact frequently suggesting the opposite (and in graphic and jarring terms); see "The Meditations," pp. 162–63. Much of what al-Maʻarrī has to say on the topic is arguably, if not manifestly, ironic and even tongue-in-cheek, which would subvert what on the surface appears to be perfectly innocuous. (This study holds that the same case might be made, and even more emphatically, and certainly more emphatically than what Ṭāhā Ḥusayn allows for, with respect to passages in

al-Fuṣūl wa al-Ghāyāt that are in "glorification" of God—i.e., as per what the full title of this work promised.)

59. "Mītāfīzīqā al-ʿUlū wa al-Ṭabīʿah," pp. 72–73.

60. As it stands, the second sentence of this line seems to be a non sequitur (of which, on the surface at least, without consideration of a subtext, there is no shortage in *Luzūm*). Perhaps what is intended by way of implication is something like "so guard against causing discontent by abstaining from any attempts to understand God, [this] for the sake of your people [i.e., friends and family] here on earth." As such, it follows a premise on which it is based, and, furthermore, is perfectly consistent with a major pronouncement of *Luzūm*: although God exists, is a reality, His nature and His ways and His wisdom are unfathomable. He is conceivable but not really knowable with respect to His nature. Zaydān had a similar understanding when this verse was the object of his attention in *Qaḍāyā al-'Aṣr* (p. 142). The Divine Essence is beyond humans' intellectual grasp, especially when by way of intellect humans are guided to the realization of God's oneness; thus, humans eschew descriptions or comparisons or definitions. Bakrī's understanding is almost identical when he cites the verse (in *al-Fikr al-Dīnī*, p. 140). But Ḥusayn (*Tajdīd Dhikrā Abī al-'Alā'*, p. 254) when citing L II.69.7 allows (in so many words) for the meaning of "As for God, He is a matter you do not know [i.e., cannot verify]; so beware of the scorn of your people here on earth"; i.e., since you can not (and furthermore do not) acknowledge the existence of God, you should be prepared to guard against the popular resentment that this belief is going to provoke. Cf. note 61.

61. Ḥusayn remarked in *Tajdīd Dhikrā Abī al-'Alā'* that, from all outward appearances in L II.69.7 (أمّا الإلهُ فأمر لستَ مدركَه / فاْحذَرْ لجيلك فوقَ الأرض إسخاطا) al-Maʿarrī certainly gives the *impression* (my italics) that he cannot acknowledge the existence of God. Ḥusayn also allowed that perhaps in actuality this was al-Maʿarrī's conviction and the passages in *Luzūm* reflecting the contrary are manifestations of *taqiyyah*/تقية. Ḥusayn went on to opine, however, that "the spirit" of al-Maʿarrī in his day-to-day living, and in all of his prose and poetic works, contradicts this tendency; so that all we should finally infer concerning the possible ramifications of L II.69.7 is that

> [Al-Maʿarrī] professes ignorance with respect to the true nature (*kunh*/كُنْه) and essence (*ḥaqīqah*/حقيقة) of God; he is incapable of giving Him a logical definition (تحديد منطقي); and he cannot make clear to humankind His quiddity (*māhiyyah*/ماهية). [All of] this he fears to utter or announce openly because the masses of ordinary people are incapable

> of grasping its import and distinguishing between the person who doesn't know God and the person who doesn't know His essence (*ḥaqīqah*/حقيقة). (*Tajdīd Dhikrā Abī al-'Alā'*, pp. 354–55)

In *Tajdīd Dhikrā Abī al-'Alā'*, therefore, Ḥusayn, like von Kremer and Nicholson in their pivotal studies, took al-Maʿarrī to be a believer in God; i.e., not an atheist; although obviously Ḥusayn was not as hasty in reaching this conclusion as were von Kremer and Nicholson, but quite understandably so given his awareness of L II.69.7 and his appreciation of its full ramifications.

A quarter of a century later in *Ma'a Abī al-'Alā' fī Sijnih,* Ḥusayn also affirmed al-Maʿarrī's belief in God; but not before an even more arduous process, especially when al-Maʿarrī's questioning the wisdom of God was revisited and when there was the discussion of the dimensions of the *Luzūm* that suggest a very plausible self-conscious connection to Epicurean (Lucretian) materialism.

62. "*The Meditations*," p. 43.

63. This, of course, is what is really intended by *furqān*/فرقان in this line; the substitution is hardly an instance of clever dissimulation, especially when in L I.358.4–5, for example, one finds: فلا يَغُرَّنْكَ من قرّائنا زُمَرٌ يتلونَ في الظُّلَمِ الفُرقانَ والزُّمَرا ("Do not be deceived by a group of our reciters declaiming in the dark *al-Furqān* and *al-Zumar*"). *Al-Furqān* and *al-Zumar* are chapters in the Qur'ān.

64. Cf. al-Maʿarrī's views on religion as expressed in his *Risālat al-Ghufrān*, ed. Bint al-Shāṭi', p. 464:

> Worship of God (*al-ta'alluh*/التألّه) is something to be found in human instincts (*mawjūd fī al-gharā'iz*/موجود في الغرائز). It is considered one of the strongly fortified refuges therein. Growing up, a child takes what he hears from adults. This remains with the child as time goes by, to the very end. Thus those who live in [Christianity's] monastic cells, as well as the pious worshippers in the mosques, take what they believe in in the manner of transcribing what a reporter reports without distinguishing between the true and the false of the one who is doing the expounding. Had some of these people found their families to be adherents of Mazdeanism, they would have emerged as followers of Mazdeanism. Had their families been Sabians, they would have become associates of the Sabians and exactly the same as they.

> والتألّه موجود في الغرائز يُحْسبُ من الألجاء الحرائز ويلْقَنُ الطِّفْلُ الناشئُ ما سَمِعَهُ من الأكابرِ فيلبَثُ معه في الدهر الغابر والذين يسَكُنونَ في الصوامعِ والمتعبِّدون في الجوامِع

يأخذونَ ما هم عليه كنقلِ الخَبرِ عن المُخبر لا يُمَيّزون الصدق عن الكذبِ لدى المُعبّر فلو
أَنَّ بعضَهم أَلْفى الأُسرَةَ من المَجوسِ لخَرجَ مجوسيًّا أو من الصابِئةِ لأَصبحَ لهم قرِيناً سِيًّا.

Nicholson's overview of this passage can be found in his *al-Ghufrān,* part 2, p. 351. He translates التأله as "piety."

Among other things, one needs to note well that in the first line of this passage, and also in L I.252.1 (previously cited and discussed), al-Maʿarrī seems to be underscoring that he finds theism in particular just as irrational (in the sense of being without a convincing rational explanation; it is an instinct buttressed by unthinking tradition) as religion in the broadest sense of the word. This gives further cause to wonder about the real sincerity of the belief in God suggested elsewhere in al-Maʿarrī's corpus of writing. Nicholson's statement that "partly, perhaps, by instinct Maʿarrí believed in the existence of a divine Creator" (see note 47) probably derives from the above-quoted passage from *Risālat al-Ghufrān.*

65. The Arabic wording just given for this verse is following the Leyden ms., p. 28. Zand has المكتين instead of المكتان and شفتان instead of شفتين, yielding "My sins have not cleansed either Mecca or Medina, although I have two lips that have sucked dry the teats of life."

Although al-Maʿarrī had a legally permissible excuse for not having performed the pilgrimage—being blind he had a physical disability that could have made the trip too difficult to bear, and thus allow him a dispensation—he never invokes it in *Luzūm*. He makes absolutely no attempt, in other words, to conceal his nonendorsement (often barbed) of pilgrimage to Mecca on the basis of religio-philosophical objections first and foremost. As Ḥusayn notes (*Ma'a Abī al-'Alā' fī Sijnih*, pp. 168–69), the lack of endorsement for the pilgrimage is especially conspicuous in the poem in *Luzūm* in which al-Maʿarrī *does* enjoin paying of *zakāh*/زكاة, praying the five obligatory prayers in Islam, and fasting during Ramadan (L II.349.4–6).

66. The point here, it seems, is not that worshippers are to be avoided merely because they are less than religiously clean and pure, but also because they are motivated to congregate by a herd instinct rather than by reasoned reflection that leads to a sincere and genuine rational affirmation of faith.

67. Here as in L II.177.7, al-Maʿarrī avoids using Qur'ān/قرآن when making critical reference to the Islamic holy scripture, choosing instead the epithet *furqān*/فرقان (the proof).

68. P. 168.

69. See B. Shriek, "*Isrā',*" *SEI.* The present study is inclined to allow for the possibility that L II.289.6 is another somewhat circumspect questioning

of Muḥammad's prophecy (in agreement with Ḥusayn's *Tajdīd Dhikrā Abī al-'Alā'* p. 270):

> I don't profess that shooting stars once upon a time
> were made missles for Muḥammad's prophetic mission.

ولستُ أقولُ إنَّ الشهبَ يوماً   لبعثِ محمّدٍ جُعِلَتْ رُجوما

Admittedly, one might argue that here al-Maʿarrī is denying less the belief in Muḥammad's prophecy than the belief in the occurrence of supernatural celestial phenomena connected with the prophecy. Yet this would still leave the line rather blasphemous. A denial of "stars made as missiles" is a clear refutation of an evidentiary miracle, an event mentioned in Qur'ān 67:5. Ḥusayn (ibid.) takes L I.397.12 as also signifying a denial by al-Maʿarrī of Muḥammad's having been bestowed his prophetic office. The line reads as follows:

> Muḥammad, although he was informed, complained
> during his meal time of his aorta being severed.

ومحمدٌ وهو المنبّأُ يشتكي   لمكانِ أكلتِهِ آنقطاعَ الأَبْهَرُ

The reference in this verse is to an incident that took place at the Arabian town of Khaybar. After Muḥammad with his band of followers seized the town in 7 CE, he was given a meal there prepared by one Zaynab bint al-Ḥārith. Zaynab was a local. Upset at the misfortune that had befallen her town and its inhabitants, she gave Muḥammad a poisoned piece of lamb to eat. Muḥammad chewed the piece but did not swallow it. Remarking that it was poisoned, he spit it out. When Zaynab was then asked by Muḥammad why she poisoned his meat, she replied, "I said to myself, if he is a king I shall ease myself of him and if he is a prophet he will be informed [of what I have done]." Muḥammad did not punish Zaynab bint al-Ḥārith. However, later, when stricken with the illness that was to lead to his death, he was reported to have said that he was suffering from a deadly pain that resulted from what he had eaten at Khaybar. See Ibn Isḥāq, *The Life of Muhammad*, trans. A. Guillaume (offset printed ed., Karachi: Pakistan Branch of the Oxford University Press, n.d.), pp. 515–16.

Ḥusayn does not indicate why he takes L I.397.12 to be a denial of Muḥammad's prophecy. Perhaps he took the inner significance of this passage as being that, at Khaybar in 7 CE, Muḥammad, despite having been "informed" (*munabba'*/منبّأ) by virtue of his being a prophet (i.e., *nabī*/نبي; the word play here needs to be appreciated) of the plot to kill him, nevertheless eventually fell victim to the plot and thus failed to meet Zaynab bint al-Ḥārith's criterion for prophethood. That is to say, having eventually died from the poisoning at Khaybar, Muḥammad was merely a king. The line that precedes L I.397.12, however, would seem to indicate that al-Maʿarrī only intends (or *primarily* intends) to emphasize that Muḥammad, like all mortals, was subject to the cruel and unpredictable fates. L I.397.11 reads as follows:

Disaster overtakes man when he does not fear;
so marvel at the adversities of the fates.

والمرءُ يغشاهُ الأذى من حيثُ لا　　يخشاهُ فأعجبْ من صروفِ الأدهُرِ

70. *Al-Fikr al-Dīnī*, p. 141.

71. For the latter verses, for line 1 on p. 140, following the Leyden ms. (which has وجِبِلَّةُ الناسِ الفسادُ فضَلَّ من يسمو بحكمته إلى تهذيبها) and not Zand's فظَلَّ for the verb at the end of the first hemistich; yielding "The nature of humans is corrupt; thus the one who aspires to set them right with his wisdom is misguided" instead of the significantly different "The nature of humans is corrupt; thus the one who aspires to set them right with his wisdom is persistent."

72. Laws based on religious revelation/law; all of them (الشرائعُ كُلُّها), says al-Maʿarrī, are uncritical reiterations of received opinions (خَبَرٌ يُقَلَّدُ) that don't stand up to logical scrutiny (لم يَقِسْه قائسُ) and in the midst of which reason (العقل) can only wonder in amazement (يَعْجَب). If you pursue religion, it is destroyed by thinking that plots against good conscience (ومتى ركبتَ الى الديانة غالَها فكرٌ / على حسن الضمير دسائسُ). And how can the religious-minded bestow authority when the objectives of even the most venerable and noble in society are base? (أنّى ينالُ أخو الديانةِ سودداً / ومآربُ الرجل الشريفِ خسائسُ). Accordingly, it is irrelevant what faith one professes, whether Mazdeanism, Islam, Christianity, or Judaism. The practitioners of all of these faiths represent falsehoods (رسائس). All are prisoners of their own evil. Thus speaks al-Maʿarrī in an equal-opportunity deprecation of revealed religion that has few ambiguities or enigmatic allusions:

ومتى ركبتَ إلى الديانة غالَها　　فكرٌ على حسْن الضمير دسائسُ
والعقلُ يَعْجَبُ والشرائعُ كُلُّها　　خَبَرٌ يُقَلَّدُ لم يَقِسْه قائسُ
مُتمجّسونَ ومُسلمونَ ومَعْشَرٌ　　متنصّرونَ وهائدونَ رسائسُ
وبيوتُ نيارانٍ تزارُ تعبُّداً　　ومساجدٌ معمورَةٌ وكنائسُ
فالصابئونَ يعظمونَ كواكباً　　وطباعُ كُلٍّ في الشرورِ حبائسُ
أنّى ينالُ أخو الديانةِ سودداً　　ومآربُ الرجلِ الشريفِ خسائسُ

(L II.20–21; 13–15, 1–3)

The poem from which these lines are taken concludes with وإذا الرئاسةُ لم تُعَنْ بسياسةٍ / عقليةٍ خَطئَ الصوابَ السائسُ ("When leadership is not aided with a policy, and one rational, policymakers are in error"). The leadership intended first and foremost may be the heads of state—governors, princes, ministers, or caliphs—and not clerics (e.g., the *'ulamā'*). However, religious leadership is probably also intended, for which the logical conclusion with respect to religion is that it essentially self-destructs (*al-naql*/النقل would need to cede to *al-'aql*/العقل). Either that or it continues to keep the adherents captives in the dark. It is remarkable to recall that the issue of the stultifying effect of تقليد was of extra special concern to, and central in the writings of, the pivotal Egyptian reform-minded theologian Muḥammad ʿAbduh writing in the 19th century (CE), over 800 years after the death of al-Maʿarrī.

Al-Maʿarrī is alleged to have composed the following although the lines cannot be found in any of his extant works (Saleh; *Abū-l-'Alā'*, part 2, tome XXIII, p. 158):

Don't regard what the prophets say as true,
but as false talk they put down on paper.
People once enjoyed a life of comfort;
then prophets brought the absurd, and spoiled it.

Ṭāhā Ḥusayn cites the Arabic in *Ma'a Abī al-'Alā' fī Sijnih* (p. 149) but without indicating a source:

ولا تحسَبْ مقال الرّسْل حقاً وَلَكنْ قَوْلُ زور سَطَّروُه
وكانَ الناسُ في عيش رَغد فَجاءوا بالمحال فَكدَّروُه

Referring to these as well as other verses (which in fact *are* to be found in *Luzūm*) as evidence, Ḥusayn in *Ma'a Abī al-'Alā' fī Sijnih* (p. 46) submits rather enigmatically that "God did not lead al-Maʿarrī to belief in prophecies. He did not believe in them. But neither did he completely reject them, because he asked himself from time to time 'Who knows? Perhaps there is some truth to some of these prophecies, and maybe some of what they have brought to us is correct. And woe unto me if what they have brought is correct!'"

In his study of what has been recovered from *al-Fuṣūl wa al-Ghāyāt* to date, Ḥusayn found that therein al-Maʿarrī made mention of the Prophet Muḥammad on more than twenty occasions, although only incidentally, and with a view either of merely quoting a word or two that the Prophet spoke or that were attributed to him, or of having some particular linguistic documentation by way of one *ḥadīth* or another. "If he [al-Maʿarrī] mentions the

Prophet, he praises him and asks that God bless him; but says no more than this" (*Ma'a Abī al-'Alā' fī Sijnih,* p. 200).

73. It is probably Muslim's *Ṣaḥīḥ* and not Bukhārī's that he had in mind (see L I.209. n.1); although the distinction in this instance does not seem to be of great importance.

74. The blanket condemnation of religious laws (*al-shurū'/*الشروع or *al-sharā'i'/*الشرائع) in the last three citations, although not emphasized by von Kremer or Nicholson, must be seen as constituting one of the most blatantly contra-Islam aspects of al-Ma'arrī's thought in *Luzūm*. One need only think of, e.g., Sayyed Hossein Nasr's remarks concerning the Islamic Divine Law in his *Ideas and Realities of Islam* (Boston: Beacon Press, 1975), p. 93: "The *Sharī'ah* is the Divine Law by virtue of accepting which a person becomes a Muslim. Only he who accepts the injunctions of the *Sharī'ah* as binding upon him is a Muslim although he may not be able to realize all of its teachings or follow all of its commands in life"; and p. 107: "Islam is not technically speaking a theocracy but a nomacracy, that is a society ruled by a Divine Law"; and p. 117: "Every man must accept the *Sharī'ah* in order to be a Muslim."

75. *Tajdīd Dhikrā Abī al-'Alā',* p. 271.

76. *Abū al-'Alā' Nāqid al-Mujtama'/*أبو العلاء ناقد المجتمع (Beirut: Dār al-Ma'ārif), 1963, p. 18–20.

77. *Abū al-'Alā' al-Ma'arrī wa Qaḍāyā al-'Aṣr,* especially pp. 75–91 but also 68–73, 127–37, 177–203, 225–26.

78. *Freethinkers* (1999).

79. Fakhry, *Islamic Philosophy*, p. 114; the hostile sources to which he refers include al-Khayyāṭ/الخياط, upon whose *Kitāb al-Intiṣār*/كتاب الأنتصار, ed. Albert Nader (Beirut: Catholic Press, 1957, pp. 11–12) he largely bases his brief notice on Ibn al-Rāwandī.

80. Fakhry, *Islamic Philosophy,* p. 124, based on al-Rāzī, *Opera Philosophica*, ed. Kraus, p. 295. For a more detailed and nuanced overview, in English, of al-Rāzī's metaphysics and rejection of revelation and prophecy, one might consult the summation of *Opera Philosophica* (ed. Kraus, pp. 291–316) by Marshall G. S. Hodgson in his *The Venture of Islam*, vol. I (Chicago: University of Chicago Press, 1974), pp. 431–33, or Paul Walker's "Al-Razi (Rhazes)," http://www.muslimphilosophy.com/ei2/razi.htm.

81. Ed. Bint as-Shāṭi', pp. 469–76, 495. Nicholson's partial translation of *Risālat al-Ghufrān,* part II, pp. 355ff., included the reference to Ibn al-Rāwandī along with the scathing denunciation.

82. Al-Ma'arrī's circumspection in the last citation shouldn't be overlooked. What he says precisely is *wa amsaktu lammā 'aẓẓamū al-ghāra wa-khumm*/وأمسكتُ لمّا عظّموا الغار وخمّ ("I remained indifferent when they [the referent is *ma'āshir*, i.e., groups of men or people; communities] glorified the cave and *khumm*"). Zand rightly points out in a gloss to his edition of *Luzūm* (II.279) that *khumm* should be taken as a metonym for Shī'ism and *al-ghār* as a metonym for Sunnism. (Al-Ma'arrī himself makes this clear in L I.412.15). *Khumm* refers to (the incident of) *ghadīr khumm*, i.e., Muḥammad's saying, "Of whom I am the patron, so too is 'Alī," which is the pronouncement the Shī'ites interpret as meaning that Muḥammad named 'Alī to be his immediate successor as leader of the Islamic community (see, e.g., L. Veccia Vaglieri, "*ghadīr khumm*," *EI2*). Hence the equation *khumm*=Shī'ites. *Al-ghār* (the cave) is the *al-ghār* of Qur'ān 9:40; i.e., the place where Muḥammad hid from his persecutors while making the *hijrah* from Medina to Mecca. According to tradition, accompanying Muḥammad on the *hijrah* and hiding with him in the cave was Abū Bakr (see, e.g., W. Montgomery Watt, "Abū Bakr," *EI2*), the "second of two" (*thāni thnayn*/ثاني اثنين) mentioned in Qur'ān 9:40, and who, after Muḥammad's death, became first caliph in Islam. Hence the *al-ghār*/الغار=Sunnīs equation. Those who glorified the cave as opposed to *ghadīr khumm* would have been those who believed especially in the legitimacy of Abū Bakr's caliphate and Abū Bakr's unique relationship to Muḥammad; those who are Sunnī Muslims, in other words.

Von Kremer ("Ueber die philosophischen Gedichte," p. 60, n. l) seems to have missed this point. He took *al-ghār* /الغار to be an allusion to a Shī'ite-inspired story concerning Muḥammad ibn al-Ḥanafiyyah/محمد بن الحنفية. According to this story, Muḥammad ibn al-Ḥanafiyyah, the seventh-century imām of the Kaysāniyyah (الكيسانية) Shī'ites, never died; but, rather, lived in occultation in a mountain ravine (see C. van Arendonk, "*Kaisānīya*," *Shorter Encyclopaedia of Islam*).

There is another possible signification to *al-ghār*/الغار. It might very well be a metonym for the Prophet Muḥammad, because Muḥammad was the principal character in the incident related in Qur'ān 9:40. In this case, the idea behind al-Ma'arrī's remark "I remained indifferent when they glorified the cave and Khumm" would be that he remained indifferent when his co-religionists praised either 'Alī or the Prophet Muḥammad; i.e., neither deserved praise in terms of being super humans, having special powers of intellection, as far as al-Ma'arrī was concerned. This would conform perfectly with al-Ma'arrī's utterance that every mind is a prophet, and there should be no imām other than reason.

83. Referred to in the singular as *naṣīb shārin*/نصيب شارٍ. Although this seems to be a clear reference to the Khārijite (الخوارج) Muslims (see, e.g., Lane's *Lexicon*, vol. 8 under *n-ṣ-b*/نصب), both Nicholson ("The Meditations," p. 103) and von Kremer ("Ueber die philosophischen Gedichte," p. 59, n. 2) take it as indicating unorthodox extremists in general.

84. Specifically, for spreading stories about the Jinn/الجنّ; although ordinarily they are associated with a literal interpretation of anthropomorphic traditions in the history of Islamic religious thought (see "*Ḥashwiyyah*," *EI2*).

85. Al-Maʿarrī has more to say about the Carmathians and their beliefs than the other religio-philosophical orientations or movements that he touches upon. He is eager to portray them as being completely beyond the pale of Islam. He accuses them of dualistic tendencies; of permitting incestuous marriages; of allowing their women to be violated by adulterers; of attaching no importance to the Qur'ān ; of paying no concern to the Ramadan fast and the obligatory prayers; and of discouraging people from going to the mosques (L I.182.3–9; 183.1–8; 297.6–11; 384.3–7). There is little if any cause to doubt the damning of the first three alleged improprieties. The opprobrium elsewhere must be seen as largely feigned. In none of these citations are the Carmathians as a group mentioned by name, although it is clear that they are in fact intended. The eponymous leader himself, al-Qarmaṭī (القرمطي), is named in L I.65.10 as "the Carmathian at al-Aḥsā'." The context is the rather remarkable poem in which al-Maʿarrī dismisses all chiliastic orientations, imāmī-Shīʿī included (more specifically, Ismāʿīlī, given the reference to the "legislating imām" or إمام ناطق):

يا ملوكَ البلادِ فُزْتمْ بِنَسْءِ الـ   عُمْرِ والجورُ شأنكم في النَّساءِ
مالَكم لا ترَوْنَ طُرْقَ المعالي   قد يزورُ الهيجاءَ زيرُ نِساءِ
يرتجي الناسُ أن يقومَ إمامٌ   ناطقٌ في الكتيبة الخرساءِ
كَذِبَ الظَّنُّ لا إمامَ سِوى العقـ   لِ مشيراً في صُبْحِهِ والمساءِ
فإذا ما أطعتَهُ جلب الرحمة   عند المسيرِ والإرساءِ
إنما هذه المذاهبُ أسبا   بٌ لجذْبِ الدنيا إلى الرؤَساء
غَرَضُ القومِ مُتْعةٌ لا يَرِقُّو   نَ لدمع الشَّماءِ والخنساءِ
كالذي قامَ يجمعُ الزنج بالبصـ   رة والقرمطيِّ بالأحساءِ
فأنفردْ ما آستطعتَ فالقائلُ الصا   دقُ يُضحي ثِقْلاً على الجُلساءِ

O kings of countries, you have prolonged your lives,
but tyranny is your concern in the prolongation.
What's wrong with you that you don't see the high road?
Even the womanizer might go to battle!
People expect a legislating imām to rise

from amidst the ranks of the silent army.
A false belief. There's no imām other than reason,
giving guidance in the morning as well as at night.
Whenever you obey it it will bring mercy,
and to both the moving as well as the still.
Only these religious sects are what cause the world
to be made attractive for the heads of states.
The goal of people is pleasure; they've no pity;
whether for the tears of the fine-faced or the coarse,
as with him who united the slaves in Basra,
and with the Carmathian at al-Aḥsā'.
Withdraw, then, for as long as you possibly can;
the veracious is a burden to his companions.

For Nicholson's more mellifluous, rhymed rendition of parts of this poem, see his "The Meditations," p. 102, (109). For a brief but very precise and crystal clear overview of how precisely the *nāṭiq*/ناطق features in the world view of the Ismā'īlī Shī'ites, Philip Hitti, *History of the Arabs*, pp. 442–43, is still remarkably serviceable, although the topic discussed with more detail and elaboration can be found in many of the more recent religio-historical or philosophical studies of Islam as well as in *The Encylopaedia of Islam*.

In *Luzūm* I.384.3–7 the Ismā'īlīs are referred to as the sect having an affiliation either with al-Qaddāḥ/القداح (i.e., 'Abdullah ibn Maymūn al-Qaddāḥ/عبد الله بن ميمون القداح, the alleged founder of Ismā'īlism in its most basic configuration) or Hajar/هجر (i.e., the city in the al-Aḥsā'/الأحساء province of Saudi Arabia, which was the main geographical center of Carmathian power during its zenith). In L I.297.6–11, the Carmathians are referred to as *'uṣbah hajariyyah*/عصبة هجرية ("a Hajarite gang"). In L I.182.3–9; 183.1–8, they are denominated *rahṭ musallim*/رهط مسلم ("Musallim's group"), the explanation of which is hard to account for. Von Kremer bypasses the problem altogether ("Ueber die philosophischen Gedichte," p. 62). Nicholson translates the phrase as "partisans of [one like] Musaylimah," taking Musallim as an abbreviation for Musaylimah, the rather notorious would-be prophet of Arabia. He argues that there is a precedent for this form of writing Musaylimah's name, and that furthermore the beliefs discussed in L I. 182.3–9; 183.1–8 resemble those espoused by Musaylimah ("The Meditations," p. 104, n. 2). F. Buhl in his "Musailima" (*Shorter Encyclopaedia of Islam*) wrote that according to one source who gives "a picture of [Musaylimah] which is in the main correct," Musaylimah believed in the obligatory prayers (although reducing them to three per day instead of five), he did not permit the drinking of wine, and he preached sexual moderation, forbidding marital intercourse after the birth of a son. That the poem of L I.182.3–9; 183.1–8 is meant to describe the Carmathians is very clear, for it mentions their ʿAlid sympathies (182.9) and their belief that their imām would appear at the time of the conjunction of the planets (Jupiter and Saturn) (183.8), a belief with which they were especially associated (de Goeje, *Mémoires sur les Carmathes du Bahrain et les Fatimides* [Leiden, 1886], p. 196 ff.; cited by von Kremer, "Ueber die philosophischen Gedichte," p. 62). Furthermore, as von Kremer discovered (idem, p. 63), L I.182.3 ff. is remarkably similar in content to a poem, clearly directed against the Carmathians, by a South Arabian poet whom de Goeje quoted in his *Mémoires sur les Carmathes du Bahrain et des Fatimides* (Arabic text of the poem on p. 226; French translation on pp. 160–61).

Concerning the Carmathian belief that their imām would come with the conjunction of Saturn and Jupiter: in L I.183.7 al-Maʿarrī ridiculed this by noting that when the conjunction did appear, the imām did not. Al-Jannābī is cursed by name in *Risālat al-Ghufrān* (*apud* Nicholson, *Risālat al-Ghufrān*, Part II, p. 344), particularly for his theft of the black cornerstone of the Kaʿbah.

86. See M. G. S. Hodgson, "Bāṭiniyya," *EI2*.

87. Ever the grammarian and philologist, al-Maʿarrī notes in L I.104.8 that if the mystics of Islam had really derived their name from the Arabic for sincerity or purity, they would have been called *ṣafwiyyah*/صفوية. Elsewhere he asserts that they attempted to connect their name with the verb *ṣafā*/صفا, meaning pure or sincere, rather than with the noun *ṣūf*/صوف, meaning wool (which according to most accounts is the real origin of their name) because they were not happy merely to be associated with the latter (L I.101.9).

88. Nicholson ("The Meditations," p. 194) thinks al-Maʿarrī meant to be critical only of Sufis of bad character for in L I.104.11, after having referred to them as "one of Iblis' armies" two lines previous to this, he says, "and I mean by this only the one among you who is dissolute, for the pious one [or piety] triumphs if you vie with him [or it]" (ولستُ أعني بهذا غير فاجركم إنَّ التقيَّ إذا زاحمتَه غَلَبَ). Nicholson then goes on to say (p. 194):

> That a free-thinker should speak of mystics with admiration and respect will not surprise those who remember how often extremes meet. Free-thought and mysticism converge from opposite sides to strike at orthodoxy. Ṣúfís, who regard forms of creed and ritual as *relatively* true and therefore as obstacles to the attainment of essential truth, have something in common with *zindíqs* like Maʿarrí, who "acknowledge neither

prophet nor sacred book" [the quotation is from al-Maʿarrī's *Risālat al-Ghufrān* and is al-Maʿarrī's definition of *zandaqah*/زندقة] nor any law that is not sanctioned by the inner light of reason.

The present study is inclined to take L I.104.11 as yet another example of a remark by al-Maʿarrī intended to give merely the appearance of supporting what many in the Muslim community may have been inclined to uphold by the mid to late eleventh century (CE). It is the *Luzūm*'s only favorable reference to the mystics of Islam, and, as Nicholson himself admitted, "[al-Maʿarrī] had nothing of the mystical spirit." Thus, the present study maintains that Nicholson may have been somewhat off the mark in suggesting that al-Maʿarrī seriously intended to speak of some mystics with "admiration and respect," notwithstanding his and their common disregard for orthodox creeds and rituals.

Speaking of the mystical "spirit" that is lacking in al-Maʿarrī: among other things it most noticeably includes a palpable lack of love for the Divine, and a sense that the Divine is hardly immanent and lovable to begin with. He is utterly transcendent, aloof, inscrutable. His omnipotence is terrifying. There may be much to fear and find awesome but little to love.

Nonetheless, astonishingly, Ameen Rihani recalls his visiting a "distinguished Sufi" in Damascus who "quoted from the Luzumiyat to show that the poet-philosopher of Maʿarrah was a true Sufi." Rihani's distinguished contact went on to say that al-Maʿarrī was "like a dervish dancing in sheer bewilderment; a holy man, indeed, melting in tears before the distorted image of the Divinity. . . . The ecstatic negations of Abu'l-Ala can only be translated in terms of the Sufi's creed. . . . in his bewilderment, *heirat*, he was as deeply intoxicated as Ibn ul-Fareed. If others have symbolized the Divinity in wine, he symbolized it in Reason." (*The Luzumiyat of Abu'l-Ala*, p. 17)

As Rihani quips after this recollection, he was quite aware of "zealous Moslem scholars who see in Abu'l-Ala an adversary too strong to be allowed to enlist with the enemy. They will keep him, as one of the "Pillars of the Faith," at any cost" (idem, p. 18). This, too, may be seen as one of the factors explaining how al-Maʿarrī was spared any form of truly severe persecution.

89. He does not omit Mazdeanism (Zorastrianism) from his denunciation of revealed religions, but aside from L I.398.11 (already cited supra) and L II.201.5, where he considers its followers "led astray" (*muḍallalah*/مضللة), he makes few other really critical references to it in *Luzūm*.

90. His argument against Jesus Christ's divinity, contained in the last poem cited, is basically this: if Jesus Christ was really the son of God, then

why did God abandon him when he was crucified? Inasmuch as al-Maʿarrī accepted the crucifixion of Jesus Christ, albeit as proof that al-Maʿarrī could not have been the son of God, it is worth calling to mind Nicholson's having noted ("The Meditations," p. 170, n. 2) that for this reason he is in disagreement not only with Christianity but also with orthodox Islam, the latter not believing that Jesus Christ's crucifixion ever took place.

91. Leyden ms., p. 136; Zand I.23.1 has للقوم (for the people).

92. دينهم للملك is according to Leyden ms, p. 136; Zand I.23.1 has لجميع الناس (for all of the people).

93. "The Meditations," pp. 172–73.

94. "The Meditations," p. 172.

95. Such as those, apparently, of some of the pious-minded transcribers of *Luzūm*. As already noted, Zand's edition of L II.23.1 reads *wa innamā ja'alū li al-qawm ma'kalatan wa-ṣayyarū li-jamī' al-nās nāmūs*/وإنما جعلوا للقوم مأكلةً وصيّروا لجميعِ الناسِ ناموسَ which, with the substitution of للقوم for الرحمان and of لجميعِ الناسِ for دينهم للملك, makes "net" just as likely a translation of ناموس as "law," allowing the reader's equating "they" to "some people" slightly more likely.

The Oxford ms. version of L I.23.1 has also been ignored somewhere down the line (e.g., by Zand as well the Dār Ṣādir editors); it reads precisely the same as that of the Leyden ms. (see Nicholson, "The Meditations," p. 172).

96. "The Meditations," p. 196.

97. As already observed, and to be seen even more so in the parts of this chapter that follow, in thought and in deed, al-Maʿarrī was so independent, peculiar, and nonconforming for his time and place that sui generis (even as a "free thinker") may be the only words that in a nutshell accurately describe him—religiously, philosophically, politically, morally, or in whatever manner one is speaking. Thus, it would be useful to one day have a summary correction, one by one, of Maʿarrīan commentators (medieval or modern) who have quite erroneously tried to place the man exclusively within one religious tradition or persuasion or sect or another. Such a correction can't be accomplished here and now; it would be too long a task and in any event is beyond the scope of this study. On the other hand, space does allow, by way of example, for corrections to a couple of modern-era attempts—one by Henri Laoust and the other by ʿUmar Farrūkh—to link al-Maʿarrī categorically to one particular religious or religio-philosophical sect or another as a self-conscious, systematic, and dedicated follower. These should be singled out not so much because they are necessarily more flagrantly off the mark than similar such efforts, but because they come from the pens of men who

researched al-Maʿarrī and Islamic thought especially carefully and hence are bound to be taken as authoritative.

Laoust, in the conclusion to his generally excellent article "La vie et la philosophie d'Abū-l-'Alā' al-Ma'arrī," states in reference to al-Maʿarrī that

> Les critiques fort vives que nous l'avons vu adresser au qarmatisme, comme à l'ismaélisme tempéré et officiel des Fatimides, ainsi qu'à des sectes dériveés, comme celle des Ḥākimīya [i.e., the Druze], ne nous autorisent certes pas à le ranger dans l'une d'entre elles.

Up to here Laoust's conclusion is fine. But then he continues with the remark:

> Mais, par son amertume métaphysique, son relativisme religieux, son rationalisme à tendances gnostiques, le caractère particulierement accusé de son ascetisme, l'inspiration humanitaire, égalitaire et internationaliste de sa morale, le symbolisme de toute sa pensée, son désir de chercher, au delà des manifestations ritualistes de la religion, leur signification morale profonde, il est certain qu'Abū-l-'Alā' a éte influencé par quelques-unes des idées maîtresses que l'on retrouver à l'origine du mouvement philosophico-religioux des Bāṭinīya.

To the extent that al-Maʿarrī's thought in *Luzūm* is *somewhat* esoteric at times—in the sense of quasisecretive or cryptic, with the suppressed analogies lying beneath metaphor and symbol and word plays and contradictions (etc.)—it *may* have been influenced, directly or indirectly, by one or another of the Bāṭinī sects that in general were noted for their practicing secret propaganda for their causes (see M. G. S. Hodgson, "Bāṭiniyyah," *EI2*). To the extent that al-Maʿarrī's thought very often calls into question or even repudiates the conventional, exoteric (i.e., mainstream or more normative) religio-philosophical wisdom of his day, it *may* have been inspired by the Bāṭinī (more precisely, Ismāʿīlī-Carmathian) practice of *tashkīk* or the attempt to win over converts to the cause by first instilling thorough doubt in recruits before going on to teach them the "real" (i.e., deeper, interiorized) meaning of things (on *tashkīk* see, for example, Massignon, "Ḳarmaṭians," *SEI*; Massignon saw in al-Maʿarrī's skepticism and querying an evocation of *tashkīk*; Laoust ["La vie et la philosophie d'Abū-l-'Alā' al-Ma'arrī," pp. 128, 137] is of like mind). And as will become clearer by the end of the present study, it seems almost certain that al-Maʿarrī, like the Bāṭinīs (in the sense of esotericists generally), hoped to advance a world view "which seemed to go beneath the superficial differences among the quarreling religious communities with their incompatible dogmatic claims, to reach a profounder common truth" (Hodgson, "Bāṭiniyyah").

However, to conclude that al-Maʻarrī's "metaphysical bitterness, religious relativism, rationalism with gnostic tendencies, pronounced asceticism," and so on must have been "for certain" because of Bāṭinī influences is considerable interpretative overreach. Why must one think of his esotericism, his search for a common truth which is more profound than the conflicting dogmatic claims of various religions, and his evocation of *tashkīk,* as unquestionably originating in Bāṭinī circles? They may have; but then again, they may not have.

Another obvious problem with Laoust's ascribing a definite Bāṭinī influence to al-Maʻarrī's thought, even though Laoust may not have intended it, is that the connection inevitably leads to images of a close al-Maʻarrī/Shīʻite association (inasmuch as the term Bāṭinī is usually applied to various Shīʻite groups) or to images of al-Maʻarrī being an advocate of the principle of *ta'wīl*/تأويل (the allegorical interpretation of the Qur'ān, the purpose of which is revealing the text's inner—which is to say truer—meaning), because the acceptance and advocacy of *ta'wīl* was what the Bāṭinī movement most fundamentally was all about. Both of these images should not be allowed currency. In general, al-Ma'arrī gives every indication of being no less hostile to Shīʻites than he was to Sunnīs, and his scant regard for the authority (or even authenticity) of divine revelation would have rendered rather irrelevant to him any type of "interpretation" of the Qur'ān, allegorical or otherwise. Ṭāhā Ḥusayn said that he was inspired to revisit *Luzūm Mā Lā Yalzam* in preparing his *Ma'a Abī al-'Alā' fī Sijnih* in part because of Massignon's telling him that he (Massignon) felt that al-Maʻarrī was influenced by the Ismāʻīlīs. Ḥusayn's level-headed (and very early) verdict on the matter was that al-Maʻarrī took from various religio-philosophical "schools of thought" (*madhāhib*/مذاهب) only what was "closest to his own way of thinking" (أدناها من مزاجه), but he remained highly eclectic, idiosyncratic, and independent. One might wish to suppose, Ḥusayn submits with some credibility, an influence by the Shīʻites, the leader of the Zanj Revolt, and the Carmathians to the extent of al-Maʻarrī's having felt that the world was filled with tyranny, poverty, injustice, and oppression, which he attributed to sociopolitical (e.g., class) and economic reasons. But (continues Ḥusayn) it would be incorrect to say that al-Maʻarrī was laying the groundwork for a coherent plan to end the injustice, and that he lay in wait for an imām or was responding to an established imām on the ground. "Abū al-ʻAlā' is not an Ismāʻīli or a Carmathian or a Shīʻite more generally speaking. He believes that the earth is filled with injustice, but he has no hope that the injustice can be eliminated by way of the leader of the Zanj Revolt in Basra, the leader of the Carmathians in al-Aḥsā', or the living Fāṭimid imāms in Cairo, or the imām awaited by those various communities that await concealed imāms" (*Ma'a Abī al-'Alā' fī Sijnih*; pp. 186–187).

A more recent and comprehensive rejection of the notion that al-Maʿarrī's name should be bracketed with the Ismāʿīlī or Carmathians can be found in Bakrī's *al-Fikr al-Dīnī* (pp. 161–80). The decisive factors for Bakrī are al-Maʿarrī's denial of ʿAlī's divinity (فالحق يحلف ما عليٌّ عنده إلّا كقنبر) and his rejection of every belief system that arises by way of revelation and his enjoining reason instead: أما أبو العلاء فيرفض كل إيمان وارد عن طريق النقل يفرض على العقل فرضاً (Bakrī, p. 173). This rejection would ipso facto include *strict* formal allegiance to a "fraternity" such as Ikhwān al-Ṣafā' (The Brethren of Purity) even though their eclectic, ecumenical principles in pursuit of knowledge (العلم) in all likelihood would have appealed to al-Maʿarrī:

> Our Brethren—may God the Almighty support them—must not have one science outweigh in value another, or avoid any one particular book, or to cling fanatically to one sect or another. Because our views, our sect, are wholly engaged in all schools of thought, and bring together all of the sciences.
>
> ينبغي لإخواننا أيدهم الله تعالى أن لا يعادلوا علماً من العلوم أو يهجروا كتاباً من الكتب ولا يتعصبوا على مذهب من المذاهب لأن رأينا ومذهبنا يستغرق المذاهب كلها ويجمع العلوم جميعها . . .

(From one of the epistles of the Ikhwān al-Ṣafā' cited by Bakrī, p. 96)

In al-Maʿarrī's *Saqṭ al-Zand* (Beirut, p. 240) there is a line that references a personal affection for the Ikhwān:

> كم بلدةٍ فارقتها ومعاشرٍ يُذْرُونَ من أسفٍ عليَّ دُمُوعا
> وإذا أضاعتْني الخُطوبُ فلنْ أرى لِودادِ إخوان الصفاءِ مُضِيعا

> I've left many a country, and communities too,
> that cause tears of sorrow to pour down my face.
> But if circumstances forsake me, I'll never see
> my affection for the Brethren forsaking me.

Certainly, the morals and principles of the Ikhwān would have been swirling in the intellectual circles of Baghdad when al-Maʿarrī visited the city.

As for the attempt by ʿUmar Farrūkh decisively to link al-Maʿarrī to a particular religion or religio-philosophical sect—again associated with Shīʿism—it entails his very strong implication that al-Maʿarrī adopted certain ideas from the Druze community; specifically, (1) opposition to revealed religions; (2) a denial of the divine nature of revelation; (3) a criticism of the inheritance laws of Islam as they apply to females (in L II.81.1, where al-Maʿarrī basically says mothers do not get a fair share of bequeathals—i.e., they are allowed only a one-sixth share); (4) assigning more importance to the performance of a good deed than to the strict upholding of religious statutes or ordinances; (5) the belief that Adam was not one, but was preceded by many other Adams (for which see part 4 of this chapter), and (6) the belief that there is no imām other than reason (*Ḥakīm al-Ma'arrah* [2nd ed.; Beirut: Al-Kashshaf Press,1948], pp. 111–14).

Farrūkh does not give solid evidence for all or any of these ideas being specifically and exclusively of Druze origin. (Farrūkh's contention that al-Maʿarrī's belief in no imām other than reason derives from the Druze veneration of the *'uqqāl*/عقال [sing. *'aqīl*/عقيل] or "sages," who are initiated into the higher truths of the faith, seems especially farfetched or forced.) It is difficult to regard the ideas as enumerated by Farrūkh as having a *specific and exclusively* Druze origin (see, for example, M. G. S. Hodgson, "Durūz," *EI2*; or Philip K. Hitti, *The Origins of the Druze People and Religion* [New York: Columbia University Press, 1928]), also still serviceable for a good overview notwithstanding many more recent studies).

To be fair to Farrūkh's study, it also points out how al-Maʿarrī's thought *contradicts* Druze doctrines, especially his views on transmigration or metempsychosis (historically, the Druze seem to have accepted wholeheartedly both transmigration and metempsychosis), and his disdainful and oppressive views toward women (for which see the next part of this chapter) (historically, the Druze on the whole have accorded great respect and considerable freedom for women). It was right for Farrūkh to be interested in exploring the possibility of a close link between al-Maʿarrī and the Druze. As he pointed out, the sect arose around 1017 CE, well before al-Maʿarrī died and during his maturer years; it eventually won most of its converts in the western stretches of greater Syria lying between Tiberius and Antioch; and, most significantly, most of the Syrian Tanūkh, the tribe from which al-Maʿarrī descended, were eventually to embrace the Druze faith.

Nonetheless, to reiterate, there is not good cause to imply *as strongly* as Farrūkh did that al-Maʿarrī took from the Druze the six ideas just enumerated above. (Even Farrūkh's sensibly cautious remarks on p. 114 of *Ḥakīm al-Ma'arrah*, "we have no positive proof that al-Maʿarrī embraced the Druze faith" eventually leads to a subordinate clause to the effect of "although on the other hand, we have much evidence that he was.")

98. This he suggests elsewhere, too, e.g., L I.158.11; 159.1–2; II.36.4; and religion in general he predicts will die out with time (L II.211.10 [as opposed to being abrogated; a completely different matter, bound up, for example, with Shīʿism]; 427.6); if, al-Maʿarrī hastens to add, it (religion) is not already dead—arguably one of the meanings of L I.276.2: والدينُ متجرُ ميّتٍ فلذاك لا / تلفيهِ في الأحياءِ إلا كاسداً ("Religion is the merchandise of one who is dead; thus you find it only selling poorly with the living").

99. *Freethinkers*, p. 5.

100. Stroumsa, *Freethinkers*, p. 6.

101. al-Maḥāsinī, *Abū al-'Alā'*, p. 26.

102. al-Maḥāsinī, *Abū al-'Alā'*, pp. 26–27, 46–54. Pages 46–54 contain the complete details of al-Maḥāsinī's Freudian analysis of al-Maʿarrī. I have given only the main thrust of the argument he advances.

103. Seriously mitigating against it is the fact that we have no hard proof that al-Maʿarrī was the victim of unrequited love. Al-Maḥāsinī's certainty seems to rest on the basis of one poem by al-Maʿarrī in *Saqṭ al-Zand,* a poem in which al-Maʿarrī mentions his love for Umāmah and how she caused him repeated discomfort (*Abū al-'Alā'*, p. 49; the poem in question is cited therein; in the Dār Ṣādir edition of *Saqṭ al-Zand*, the poem appears on p. 223). As far as the present study can determine, al-Maʿarrī makes no other mention of this Umāmah (and certainly not in *Luzūm*). It is difficult to concur, therefore, especially on the basis of merely the one poem, that al-Maʿarrī really loved such a woman or that she actually existed at all.

Nonetheless, it interesting to note in passing how uncannily al-Maʿarrī's overall personality conforms to that which is typical of someone (according to Freudians) who suppresses his sexual desires or instincts. Al-Maḥāsinī (*Abū al-'Alā'*, p. 47) cites Freud (*Three Experiments Concerning the Theory of Sexual Instinct* [Paris, 1932], p. 177) as saying "We must consider the suppression of the sexual instinct as one of the causes of psychological sublimation" (*al-'ulū al-nafsī* in al-Maḥāsinī's Arabic). Al-Maḥāsinī then reminds us that Freudians maintain that people who experience psychological sublimation (*ahl al-'ulū*) characteristically (1) embrace an ascetic way of life, (2) shun humanity at large, and (3) develop a deep enthusiasm for literature and the arts (here al-Maḥāsinī is citing an article on Freud in *The Encyclopedia of the Twentieth Century* [in French], volume II, p. 638).

104. "The Meditations," pp. 62–63.

105. The reference here could also be to prostitutes and the evil consequences of prostitution, rather than to harem slaves and the evil consequences

of the harem system. Less likely an interpretation of L II.346.5 is Zand's. He thinks al-Maʿarrī means by *mushāʿāt* adulterous wives who are not faithful to their husbands (II.346.n.4). Ṭāhā Ḥusayn (*Tajdīd Dhikrā Abī al-ʿAlāʾ* p. 281) understands a line of poetry that he alleges to have been composed by al-Maʿarrī (وسيان من أُمه حرّةٌ / حَصانٌ ومن أمه زانية) ("The adulteress's child is equal to the child of a chaste free woman") as signifying that al-Maʿarrī for rational reasons (في حكم العقل) made no distinction between the offspring of adulteresses and the offspring of the chaste free-born woman. Ḥusayn understands as being similar in intent L I.339.3, ما ميّزَ الأطفالَ في أشباحها / للعينِ حِلّ ولادةٍ وعهارُ ("Children can't be distinguished outwardly by the eye as being from lawful birth or that of fornication"). He cites these lines (ibid.) as instances of the *Luzūm*'s affirming that "during some of the stages of his life al-Maʿarrī leaned towards having women treated as shared common property" (وفي اللزوميات ما يؤيّد ميلَ أبي العلاء في بعض أطواره إلى الاشتراكية في النساء). These lines alone hardly seem to indicate sharing women as common property (الاشتراكية في النساء). The present study has found no other lines even remotely suggesting such. With respect to al-Maʿarrī's misogyny, Ḥusayn (ibid.) remarked that al-Dhahabī saw Mazdakean origins.

106. Presumably because it amounts to man's repeating a course of action that is evil, sinful, and misery-laden. But al-Maʿarrī also suggests that he finds polygamous marriages—as practiced by Muslims at least—unfair to women because (1) they diminish the amount of inheritance money a man's first wife is to receive from him, and (2) they deny women the same sexual freedom that they allow men, amounting to a double standard with respect to morality and marriage. L II.91.9–10 reads:

A man takes as a bride, after one woman, three more;
saying to each "A fourth of my estate will suffice you."
He pleases her if she's content with bare sustenance;
but he stones her if *she's* drawn to another companion.

تزوَّجَ بَعدَ واحدَةٍ ثلاثاً   وقال لعِرْسِهِ يكفيكِ ربْعِي
فيُرضِيها إذا قَنِعَتْ بقُوتٍ   ويرجمها إذا مالتْ لتَبْعِ

107. These lines seem also to imply that in time Islam and the Islamic empire will suffer the same demise that other religions and states have suffered, a common theme of *Luzūm*. Religions, religious communities, and nations are subject to rise and fall, life and death, existence and extinction.

108. Here, too, it seems that it is Islam as much as Arabism from which al-Maʿarrī wants to distance himself.

109. He may have been opposed to interracial marriage in general. In L II.197.8, he remarks that the siring of whites by blacks is a "loathsome abomination."

110. This is following the Leyden ms. version, p. 92, which has تظاهر in line 3 instead of قد كثر and بكّة in line 7 instead of بكّت.

111. This is following the Leyden ms. version with فأَعْيَا مَن يُغالِبُهم in l. 6 instead of Zand's فأَغْنَى مِن ثعالبهم (and the wealthiest among their foxes); and يستفيد in l. 10 instead of يستقيد (asking permission to slay a killer on behalf of the killed; see Lane's *Lexicon*, Part 7, p. 324); and, finally, قذى in l. 11 instead of أذى (damage, pain, suffering).

112. In L II.108.5–6, however, al-Maʿarrī implies that the killing of Ḥusayn as well as of ʿAlī was an inevitable consequence of Muslims as a whole being inclined to go to war for the sake of their religion. The early battles of Uḥud and Badr, he says, set off a chain of events leading to Ḥusayn and ʿAlī's being killed; that is, one battle in the name of Islam simply led to others, eventually to include those that claimed the lives of the most renowned Shīʿite martyrs.

113. Taking "sovereign" in l.6 as the subject of the verb and "people" as object, in accordance with the Leyden ms., p. 130; the Zand redaction has just the opposite.

114. "The Meditations," p. 107.

115. *Abū al-'Alā'*, p. 57. With respect to al-Maḥāsinī's claim, it is interesting to note that often al-Maʿarrī did speak in *Luzūm* as though he was not averse to the idea of unjust rulers being overthrown (L I.288.4–6; 387.5; II.147.5). In L II.181.8, he advised would-be rulers to rule justly "because every ruler can be overthrown." This and similar lines are also made with the thought that in the end rulers like all other humans are mere mortals; good or bad, they are ultimately doomed—although not soon enough for the latter, and the former are few and far between—to see the downfall of their rule on earth; in the sense that no matter how powerful and durable, in the end they die, like everybody else (cf. L I.183.11; II.73.9–10; 74.1–3; 277.11). In *Luzūm* I.286.6, where al-Maʿarrī speaks to the issue of opposing or resisting rulers, he suggests that what he means by this is more or less passively resisting by way of nonparticipation in their rule; which is to say, refusing to join in the political process.

Finally, ever the pessimist, he had little reason to believe that the overthrowing of a bad ruler would necessarily usher in the reign of a good one. L II.270.10 says in effect that although rulers of any given moment may be tyrannical, it can be expected that those who replace them will be even more tyrannical.

116. *Qaḍāyā al-'Aṣr fī Adab Abī al-'Alā' al-Ma'arrī*, p. 255.

117. Following the Leyden ms. for حكمهم; Zand has أمرهم (their command).

118. P. 183.

119. *Ma'a Abī al-'Alā' fī Sijnih*, p. 184.

120. *Qaḍāyā al-'Aṣr fī Adab Abī al-'Alā' al-Ma'arrī*, pp. 245–46; citing Aḥmad Shalabī, *Politics and Economics in Islamic Thought*/السياسة والاقتصاد في التفكير الإسلامي (Cairo: Maktabat al-Nahḍah/مكتبة النهضة), p. 18.

121. Zaydān, ibid., quoting Aḥmad Shalabī.

122. Zaydān, idem, p. 247, quoting Ṭāhā Ḥusayn, *Ma'a Abī al-'Alā' fī Sijnih*, pp. 192–93.

123. This is the Leyden ms. wording; Zand has صدقنا (we have spoken the truth).

124. Zaydān,

125. Zaydān, ibid., citing Aḥmad Amīn, *Ẓuhr al-Islām*/ظهر الإسلام, part 1 (3rd edition), p. 96.

126. This is following the Leyden ms. recension; Zand has حيًا instead of حقًا and consequently understands the meaning as a more enigmatic "I have put a sash on a brilliant being, so go ahead and pardon who does as much or rebuke."

127. If this is the Ibn al-Muʿallam who is mentioned in Ibn al-Nadīm's *Kitāb al-Fihrist* (trans. Bayard Dodge [New York: Columbia University Press, 1970], p. 443), his full name is Abū 'Abdallah Muḥammad ibn Muḥammad ibn al-Nuʿmān ibn al-Muʿallam. He died 1023 CE in Baghdad, and he was a theologian of "the Imamiyah school of thought" (ibid.). Zand (L II.172, n. 3) identifies him simply as "a Muʿtazilite shaykh." ʿUmar Farrūkh (*Ḥakīm al-Ma'arrah*, p. 56, n. 5) calls him "a Shīʿite Muʿtazilite." He is not mentioned in W. M. Watt's very detailed account of the Muʿtazilites in his *The Formative Period of Islamic Thought*, nor is he included in Ibn al-Murtaḍā's equally thorough *Ṭabaqāt al-Mu'tazilah* (*The Classes of the Mu'tazilites*).

128. The prolific and influential Muʿtazilite scholar and writer during the twilight years of Muʿtazilite endeavors. He was chief *qāḍī* of Rayy after 978 CE and died in 1025 CE. *Al-Mughnī* is his major dogmatic work. For a concise overview of the life, times, and work of the man, one might consult S. M. Stern, "ʿAbd al-Djabbār b. Aḥmad," *EI2*. For one of the more recent concise yet discreet overviews of his importance to the Muʿtazilite "tradition," I highly recommend Sari Nusseibeh's *The Story of Reason* (passim).

129. This would certainly be a Muʿtazilite work if as Zand has it (L I. 249, n. 4) al-Maʿarrī had ʿAbd al-Jabbār's authorship in mind. Nicholson's "The Meditations" (p. 164, n. 2) emphasized that *al-'Umad* (along with *al-Mughnī*) is a very common title for "theological and other learned books" in Arabic.

130. One of the more important early Muʿtazilites (he died between 840 and 850 CE, in Baghdad); see Watt, *The Formative Period,* passim; and H. S. Nyberg, "Abu'l-Hudhayl al-ʿAllaf," *EI2*.

131. "The Meditations," p. 164, n. 2.

132. The Baghdadī *mutakallim* (d. 1013 CE) who played such an important role in advancing the cause of Ashʿarism as well as the discussion over the "miraculous" nature of the Qur'ān; for a brief overview, see R. J. McCarthy, "Al-Bāqillānī," *EI2*.

133. An important early *mutakallim* (d. around 854 CE). Some of his ideas attracted al-Ashʿarī and apparently were largely responsible for leading him away from his early embracement of Muʿtazilism; see Watt, *The Formative Period*, pp. 286–89, for a brief overview.

134. See L II.297. n.5.

135. Al-Maḥāsinī (*Abū al-'Alā'*, pp. 61–63) notes this relatively restrained denunciation of the *quḍāh.* He thinks the restraint is because al-Maʿarrī hailed from a family that produced a long and distinguished line of judges, and thus he was partial to this class of Islamic functionaries.

136. All things considered with respect to *Luzūm* and al-Maʿarrī generally, II.93.6 in all likelihood was meant not so much a defense of the Christian clergy (because of any innate superiority) as the casting of aspersions on the sincerity or integrity or probity of Muslim religious dignitaries (or, more precisely, the leaders of the congregational prayers). As previously emphasized, al-Maʿarrī looked askance at *all* revealed religions.

Zand in a commentary makes a case for reading the line so that it is not so pernicious to Muslims. (The most accessible printed edition of *Luzūm* [Dār Ṣādir: Beirut, 1961] passes over the line in complete silence with no glosses.) Zand preserves the wording and vocalization found in the Leyden ms. (p. 156): فالقسّ خير لكَ فيما أرى من مسلم يخطب في الجامع. However, while Zand admits that *al-qass*/القس could mean, as the present study has it (and also in accord with Nicholson's "Meditations," p. 196), "a Christian priest" (والذي يتبادر إلى ذهن القارئ هو أن المقصود بالقس أحد رؤساء الدين عند النصارة), he prefers taking it to mean "striving for livelihood," on the grounds that the meaning thus imparted to L II.93.6 ("and striving for livelihood is better for you, in my opinion, than a Muslim who preaches in the mosque") seems to be an obvious reference to a saying of the Prophet Muḥammad to the effect that certain otherwise unpardonable sins committed by a person can be atoned for by that person's going to great lengths to strive for his/her livelihood:

فيحتمل أن المراد بالقس راعي الإبل الذي لا يفارقها أو طلب الشيء وتتبعه يقال قسّ الشيء إذا طلبه وتتبعه وحينئذ فقوله يخطب صفة لمسلم فالمراد بالقس هنا طلب المعيشة وذلك أنفع ولا شك وقد ورد عنه (صلعم) إنّ من الذنوب ذنوباً لا يكفرها الصلاة ولا الصيام ولا الحج ولا العمرة ويكفرها الهموم أي الاهتمام في طلب المعيشة على أنّه سياتي لأبي العلاء وأدْين الناس من يسعى ويحترف.

(L II.93. n. 4)

Nicholson's "The Meditations" (p. 196, n. 1) found Zand's interpretive reading of L II.93.6 rather far-fetched. I concur. The reading with the extended gloss is worth noting as an example of how merely a challenging word or two, in only a line or two in the *Luzūm,* can sometimes lead to rather disproportionate efforts on the part of at least some editors/commentators to explain away in terms that are perfectly unremarkable, innocuous.

137. Leyden ms., p. 25; L I.91.6 has تُرَدُّ.

138. Leyden ms., p. 256; this line does not appear in Zand's edition of *Luzūm.*

139. Leyden ms., p. 44; L I.167.2 has البرايا (creatures; things that are created).

140. Leyden ms., p. 32; L I.117.2 has نفس (soul; individual).

141. Leyden ms., p. 257; L II.415.12 الفراقدُ, the vocalization making the word the subject of the verb رأت.

142. Leyden ms., p. 257; L II.415.12 has قبائلَ, the vocalization making the word the object of the verb instead of the subject.

143. Leyden ms., p. 257; L II.415.13 has جيل بعد جِيل (generation after generation).

144. Leyden ms., p. 16; Zand has يَجيء (comes).

145. *Tajdīd Dhikrā Abī al-'Alā',* p. 251.

146. P. D. Ouspensky, "A New Model of the Universe," chapter 11, "Eternal Recurrence and the Laws of Man," www.org.uk/library/book18/chap11 .html.

147. See al-Ghazzālī's (al-Ghazālī's) *Tahāfut al-Falāsifah*/تهافت الفلاسفة, trans. by Sabih Ahmad Kamali, Problems I and II; and Averroes' *Tahāfut al-Tahāfut*/تهافت التهافت, trans. by Simon Van Den Bergh (Oxford: Oxford University Press, 1954), vol. 1, The First and Second Discussion.

148. P. 473.

149. *Apud* Khalīfāt, "Mītāfīzīqā al-ʻUlū wa al-Ṭabīʻah," p. 60.

150. "Mītāfīzīqā al-ʻUlū wa al-Ṭabīʻah," pp. 80–81.

151. *Qaḍāyā al-'Aṣr*, pp. 148–49.

152. Leyden ms., p. 19; L I.64.8 has—not surprisingly—ماتت (died).

153. Here perhaps al-Maʿarrī's language is influenced by the vocabulary of the Islamic occasionalists. According to them, the whole universe consists of indivisible particles or atoms. When these particles or atoms combine, bodies arise; when they break up, bodies disintegrate. Corresponding to these bodily atoms are temporal atoms, so that time, too, consists of individual particles. In reference to the rise and dissolution of bodies, the occasionalists sometimes speak of the various *modi* (*akwān*/أكوان; sing. *kawn*/كون) of being rather than of generation and corruption. See Majid Fakhry, *Islamic Occasionalism* (London: George Allen and Unwin, 1958), pp. 26–27.

In light of this, Nicholson's translation of *kawn* in *Luzūm* II 261.5 as "atom of existence" (see "The Meditations," p. 157) is an especially good one and should not be strenuously objected to, but al-Maʿarrī himself seems to define the word more nearly as we have translated it when he says in L II.373.6 that "the shortest period of time is a *kawn*" (*wa-aqṣar al-waqt kawn*/وأقصر الوقت كون). His remark on *al-kawn* in *Risālat al-Ghufrān* (cited and translated above) also seems to be to this same effect.

Al-Maʿarrī, in a short segment (*faṣl*) in *al-Fuṣūl wa al-Ghāyāt*, p. 59, makes it quite clear that he knew what the "atomism" of his day essentially consisted of, using the Arabic technical term for atom (جزء لا يتجزّأ) or "a particle that cannot be broken up into another particle": "And 'the thing' is an atom; the waters of the ocean are divisible into atoms, as are also the sands of the earth and heavy rocks" (والشيء جزء لا يتجزّأ تقسم على ذلك مياه البحر ورمال الأرض وثقال الهضاب).

154. Like so many of the lines in the *Luzūm*, this one has many possible references, e.g., God's omnipotence, His complete sovereignty over everything on earth and in heaven, and humankind's utter subjection to Him. But like Ḥusayn in *Tajdīd Dhikrā Abī al-'Alā'* (p. 250), not to mention the authors of other works on al-Maʿarrī (e.g., Zaydān, *Qaḍāyā al-'Aṣr*, pp. 147–48), I also believe that space for al-Maʿarrī is infinite and eternal. With respect to space, he comes close to saying here what he says in I.372.9 (previously cited and translated) with respect to time.

155. Cf. Zaydān, *Qaḍāyā al-'Aṣr*, p. 149.

156. *Ẓarf*/ظرف as a grammatical concept is something that al-Maʿarrī is also playing with here; see, e.g., W. Wright, *Grammar*, vol. I, p. 124 and vol. II, p. 112.

157. Henri Corbin, *Cyclical Time and Ismaili Gnosis* (London: Kegan Paul, 1983), p. 3.

158. Corbin, idem, p. 14.

159. Abū Ḥātim al-Rāzī, *Kitāb A'lām al-Nubuwwah, apud* Corbin, idem, p. 31.

160. Idem, p. 32.

161. *Kitāb Zād al-Musāfirīn, apud* Corbin, idem, p. 33.

162. Corbin, idem, pp. 23, p. 15.

163. Eknath Easwaran, *The Bhagavad Gita* (Tomales, CA: Nilgiri, ninth printing, 1998), pp. 122–24.

164. *Risālat al-Ghufrān*, ed. Bint al-Shāṭi', pp. 426–28.

165. "The Meditations," p. 156.

166. "The Meditations," p. 59, n. l.

167. "Mītāfīzīqā al-ʿUlū wa al-Ṭabīʿah," pp. 80–87.

168. This in keeping with the Leyden ms., p. 109. Zand has النون (the letter "n" in Arabic; or, alternatively, large fish, sword blade, inkstand).

169. This is Ṭāhā Ḥusayn's explanation; see *Tajdīd Dhikrā Abī al-'Alā'*, p. 250.

170. Ninian Smart, "Zoroastrianism," *The Encyclopedia of Philosophy*, 1967, vol. 8, p. 381. The present study concurs with Ṭāhā Ḥusayn (*Tajdīd Dhikrā Abī al-'Alā'*, p. 250) that one should not go so far as to infer from al-Maʿarrī's somewhat mysterious and enigmatic reference to "dark time" in L II.270.13 that he was elevating it to the point that he felt it should be worshipped because it is prior to everything else, a position that Ḥusayn implies "some" interpreters of al-Maʿarrī have taken.

171. Preface, ix, *Light and Darkness in Ancient Greek Myth and Religion*, by editors Menelaos Christopoulus, Efimia D. Karakantza, and Olga Levaniouk (Lanham, Maryland: Lexington Books, 2010). This work encompasses a number of articles reflecting the centrality of primordial Darkness in ancient Greek thought.

172. Leyden ms., p. 67; L I.426.10 has أزرَت.

173. Ḥusayn, *Tajdīd Dhikrā Abī al-'Alā'*, p. 252.

174. "The Meditations," p. 151.

175. See, e.g., Fakhry, *Islamic Philosophy*, pp. 47, 159, 163.

176. Fakhry, *Islamic Philosophy*, pp. 137, 177.

177. Ḥusayn, *Tajdīd Dhikrā Abī al-'Alā'*, p. 252.

178. Leyden ms., p. 33, L I.123.1 has الكواكِبِ.

179. Ṭāhā Ḥusayn in his ground-breaking *Tajdīd Dhikrā Abī al-'Alā'* (p. 258) remarked that in this line al-Maʿarrī intended to express the Aristotelian concept of motion and God; i.e., he makes a distinction between two types of motion—(1) material, or movement from one area in space to

another over the course of two different moments in time, and (2) the type of motion which is defined as the potential passing into the actual—and he denies that the former may be attributed to God, but not the latter, since God is pure actuality or being or being and hence cannot be said not to have passed or moved from potentiality into actuality. In other words, al-Maʿarrī is saying (to follow Ḥusayn's line of argument) that God is at rest or unmoved in the sense that He does not move like a physical object from one place to another in measurable time, although He is not at rest or unmoved in the sense that He never became actual after being potential.

Ḥusayn further suggested that since Aristotle's pure actuality is tantamount to pure motion, and his God is the source of motion in the world only in the sense that He is in essence motion, al-Maʿarrī must have been of this opinion too; Ḥusayn adds that in this way Aristotle (and thus al-Maʿarrī) can be seen as overcoming certain anticipated objections or reservation's to his (Aristotle's) doctrine of God's being at rest (i.e., the unmoved mover) and his (Aristotle's) metaphysics as a whole; for example: (1) so how could the world have issued forth from Him as such, this issuance being undoubtedly a movement [in the more conventional sense—a physical movement from one place to another]; (2) from whence comes the undeniable motion of the world, since it cannot come from God inasmuch as He is motionless [the unmoved mover], and it cannot come from the world itself inasmuch as everything in the world is dependent upon God; and (3) what is the function and value of a motionless God in an eternal world, the latter [i.e., the eternity of the world] presupposing that either the world was not created by God or there is a plurality of necessary causes (which is an absurdity) (*Tajdīd Dhikrā Abī al-'Alā'*, pp. 257–58).

Concerning all of this, I think it is safe to say that in referring to God as *ghayr muntaqil*/غير منتقل, al-Maʿarrī no doubt meant to deny Him movement in the normal, commonly understood sense (i.e., as material motion from one point in place and time to another)—a rather gross, unsophisticated anthropomorphism totally inconsistent with al-Maʿarrī's level of thinking. (If nothing else, his God is so radically transcendent that, although He may be conceived of as existing, He is virtually unknowable and incomprehensible, one of the many conundrums al-Maʿarrī faces as a thinker raised and trained within the intellectual framework of Islam.)

However, to see the poet on the basis of this very same expression (غير منتقل) as also having been quite aware of the precise Aristotelian (*Metaphysics*) concept of motion in the sense of the potential becoming the actual could be a case of attributing to him a philosophical sophistication that may not be warranted, all things considered (notwithstanding al-Maʿarrī's obvious awareness of the general notion of the unmoved mover), which in turn makes moot the question of whether or not he conceived of God as pure act, hence pure motion, and hence indistinguishable from the motion of the universe and as such its cause or source. Although al-Maʿarrī's Creator God in *Luzūm* does not transcend space and time and hence the universe.

Certainly L II.219.13 should be seen as an example of al-Maʿarrī's wanting to underscore once more (if he is not to deny God's existence) God's complete incomparability to, and transcendence over, human nature if He is to be spoken of as the Creator of the world and the author of all that happens in it. That is to say, accepting Him as transcendent Creator God is tantamount to accepting that it is through His Will or Power that the planets in their spheres (and thus the universe as a whole) move, even though He cannot be said to have caused this movement by Himself moving (in the conventional sense). He is above this otherwise logical cause-and-effect relationship in the sense of He Himself having the attribute of moving (in the conventional sense; one cannot—assuming the rejection of crude anthropomorphisms—logically conceive of how God as unmoved mover makes the universe move).

Ḥusayn's having allowed for the possibility of a complete harmonization between the metaphysics and theology of Aristotle and the metaphysics and theology of al-Maʿarrī with respect to the notion of God as unmoved mover cannot be faulted; it is a real possibility. But, in unjustifiably concluding that the harmonization is *in actuality* the case, he did a not inconsiderable disservice. Perhaps it was wishful thinking, but in any event, he thereby gave al-Maʿarrī the appearance of having a logically coherent and convincing explanation for how God as Unmoved Mover and Eternal Creator can be said to be creator of an eternal universe and moreover a moving one, whereas what al-Maʿarrī really seemed to confess above all else in *Luzūm* is that exactly how the Abrahamic Creator God participates in the creation or movement of the world—and indeed how or why (i.e., for what ultimate aim [telos]) He does anything other than simply be (here there *is* an obvious Aristotelian dimension although al-Maʿarrī never brings into the equation thought thinking thoughts)—is a complete mystery to him and beyond the powers of his (and indeed all human) comprehension. This is where al-Maʿarrī is more Ashʿarian (not to mention latter-day) agnostic than Aristotelian *faylasūf.*

Khalīfāt, in his "Mītāfīzīqā al-ʿUlū wa al-Ṭabīʿah (passim)," although extremely thoughtful and informed, does not with respect to theology and theodicy (not to mention other matters) address dissimulation in al-Maʿarrī's writing, especially as it involves contradictions of apparent or undeniable contra-Islam heresies. Thus, he sees al-Maʿarrī as irrefutably having believed (but in a manner similar to the philosopher Ibn Sīnā, and not the theologians) in Creator God, One, Eternal (قديم) in essence (not in any framework of perceptible measured time, time perceived by the senses); and this meaning by its very definition (continues Khalīfāt) that (1) He is First, and (2) His Essence is not in need of any cause. His Essence is the requirement/necessity for being/existence. Of course Khalīfāt's al-Maʿarrī has God create the world out of absolutely nothing (in this sense in agreement with the Qur'ān and the theologians), with the act of creation being the manifestation of Omnipotence and also the beginning of causality and the other laws (processes) of the universe (nature) that (1) govern the universe (nature) in mechanistic fashion and (2) reflect Divine Will, so that movement in the world, change, and generation and corruption happen in a real sense in accordance to God's will, and only for as long as He wills. The mechanistic working of the world is what al-Maʿarrī means by "the fates" that he often seems to present as being capricious. There is no need for Aristotle's Prime Mover in al-Maʿarrī's thought; it is implicitly not embraced, in other words (according to Khalīfāt), because motion adheres in the type of composition that God bestows to things at the time of His creation of the world. There is an objective (telos/غاية) to God's creation, but man is not, and may never become, entirely aware of it.

As for the seemingly jarring, inscrutable, nonrational or counterintuitive binarisms that appear in al-Maʿarrī's thought, often as ineluctable "fate" or God's predetermined arranging of all matters in the world (including particulars as well as universals), Khalīfāt, on the basis of lines in the *Luzūm* such as "There is no doubt about the existence of God . . . and everything gravitates towards an intrinsic nature" (الله لا ريب فيه . . . وكل إلى طبع له جذب), believes that al-Maʿarrī was advancing the notion of the Heraclitean "unity of opposites" that explains all being, indeed without which there could be no being (e.g., there is no generation without corruption, no life without death).

I remain unpersuaded by most of this (especially that al-Maʿarrī actually believed in the Creator God of the Muslim theologians); instead being inclined to maintain that al-Maʿarrī's theology and ontology may have considered allowing for something closer to Aristotle's Prime Mover through whose agency all motion in the universe ensues, and thus, too, ad infinitum change, generation, and corruption (by way of matter taking on form as a natural process, a process adhering in the nature of matter to take on form in the presence of the other basic elements of nature). Or he (al-Maʿarrī) believed in something closer to al-Rāzī's Demiurge God who supervised, indeed by His will enabled, raw primordial matter's taking on form. Of course, al-Maʻarrī may not have believed in God at all; inasmuch as he had a very pronounced mechanistic materialistic view of the world in the sense that the only thing that truly exits, that can be established through human sense perception/observation and direct experience, is matter, its various forms, and its various functions or purposes.

Zaydān's al-Maʻarrī does not embrace *creatio ex nihilo* since he clearly posited the eternity of matter, space, and time. Further, although he is a mechanistic materialist possibly influenced by Anaximander's ateleological materialism that explains all life/existence (i.e., things come to be and cease to be in an infinite continuum so that becoming itself never ceases, but without a purpose other than the continuation of becoming ad infinitum), and although he was also influenced by Aristotle's notion of God as Prime Mover but certainly a believer in God ("there is no doubt in his (al-Maʻarrī's) belief in God"; *Qaḍāyā al-'Aṣr*, p. 49), it can't be said of him categorically that there was a difference between him and the Muslim theologians over the belief in God *as Wise Creator* (p. 147). He may have advanced some thoughts that conflicted with the thinking of some of the speculative theologians, and that agreed with the teachings of the Islamic philosophers, but these were merely speculation, not views that al-Maʻarrī held as certain truths (Zaydān, idem, p. 149).

I am also unconvinced by this line of thought (or, more to the point, its culmination in the notion that al-Maʻarrī basically embraced the belief in God as Wise Creator); but certainly it is more plausible than the thrust of Khalīfāt's argument(s) with respect to al-Maʻarrī's theology.

180. "The Meditations," p. 235.

181. Chapter 4, note 47, where the poem is also translated.

182. See note 179.

183. Leyden ms., p. 224; L II.307.10 has مِن (from).

184. Leyden ms., p. 224; L II.307.10 has مِن (from).

185. "The Meditations," p. 158.

186. Al-Rāzī's metaphysics is nicely summarized in English in Fakhry, *Islamic Philosophy,* pp. 46–47, 118–24, and also by Paul Walker, *Al-Rāzī (Rhazes)* at http://www.muslimphilosophy.com/ei2/razi.htm and Michael Ryan's "Al-Razi on Space and Time," an unpublished translation of a passage from Abū Ḥātim al-Rāzī's *A'lām al-Nubuwwah*/أعلام النبوة (*Signs of Prophecy*). Ryan's translation (pp. 17–20) contains Abū Bakr Zakariyyā' al-Rāzī's concept of how the world is essentially produced by a random motion.

187. Fakhry, *Islamic Philosophy*, pp. 119–120.

188. I. Goldziher, "*Dahrīya,*" *SEI*, p. 68. According to al-Ghazzālī's opinion, those who embraced الدهرية/*al-dahriyyah* were "an ancient faction

who renounced the Creator, Governor, Knower, and Almighty. They claimed the universe has always existed as it is without a creator, and that animals come from seed and seed from animals, and that this has always occurred and will occur forever. These are the atheists" (*apud* Marwa Elshakry, *Reading Darwin in Arabic 1860–1950* [Chicago: University of Chicago Press, 2013], p. 99). As Elshakry (idem, p. 121), reminds us, "[T]he term [*al-dahriyyah*] could be applied to Socrates, Plato and Aristotle as well as to Ibn Sīnā and al-Fārābī. Some [classical Muslim writers on the topic] referred specifically to atomists, others to Epicureanism, and in general to those who denied divine creation, reward and punishment, the existence of angels and demons."

189. I. Goldziher, "*Dahrīya*," *SEI*, p. 68.

190. I. Goldziher, "*Dahrīya*," *SEI*, p. 68.

191. Fakhry, *Islamic Philosophy*, pp. 68–69.

192. Fakhry, *Islamic Philosophy*, p. 70.

193. Fakhry, *Islamic Philosophy*, p. 243.

194. "The Meditations," p. 150.

195. *Tajdīd Dhikrā Abī al-'Alā' al-Ma'arrī*, p. 247.

196. L II.62.1, which reads in the Arabi *wa-jism al-mar' li al-a'rāḍ rab'* / *fa-hal zakkāhu tazkiyyat al-'urūḍ* (وجسم المرء للأعراض ربعٌ / فهل زكّاه تزكية العروض), might at first glance seem to be a contradiction to all of this. If we read أعراض here as meaning "accidents," we get in the first hemistich "and the body of man is an abode for accidents," a statement that we might want to compare to the thought of Ḍirār ibn ʿAmr.

> Ḍirār ibn ʿAmr, a contemporary of Wāṣil [ibn ʿAtā', the traditionally reputed founder of the Muʿtazilites] rejected the whole notion of atom (or substance) and reduced the body to an "aggregate of accidents which, once constituted, becomes the bearer (or substratum) of other accidents." (Fakhry, *Islamic Philosophy*, p. 68; citing al-Ashʿarī's *Maqālāt*/مقالات, pp. 305, 345)

But أعراض can also mean "manifestations of a disease," and the second hemistich of L II.62.1 and the *rab'*/رَبْعٌ (abode) *'urūḍ*/عروض (household goods) connection seem to indicate that indeed "manifestations of a disease" is how أعراض should be understood here. That is to say, the line in English in full should be taken as saying, "And the body of man is an abode for the manifestations of disease, but has he [i.e., man] cleansed it [the body full of disease] the way household goods are cleansed?" The question is rhetorical, of course.

197. Cf. Nicholson, “The Meditations,” pp. 157–58; and Ṭāhā Ḥusayn, *Tajdīd Dhikrā Abī al-'Alā' al-Ma'arrī*, p. 261.

198. Cf. Nicholson, “The Meditations,” pp. 149–50; and von Kremer, “Ueber die philosophischen Gedichte,” pp. 44–45.

199. Leyden ms, p. 272; L II.145.9 has حاكِمهم (their ruler).

200. P. 246.

201. See Marwa Elshakry, *Reading Darwin in Arabic, 1860–1950* (Chicago: University Press), pp. 99, 119–121, 124.

Professor Ralph M. Coury in his *Sceptics of Islam* (I. B. Tauris, 2018) brought to my attention both the Shumayyil/al-Maʿarrī link and the relevance of Elshakry's work notwithstanding its focus on modern materialism in Arabic writings.

202. *Qaḍāyā al-'Aṣr*, p. 228.

203. *Tajdīd Dhikrā Abī al-'Alā'*, p. 277.

204. *Qaḍāyā al-'Aṣr*, p. 230.

205. Zaydān, p. 126, citing Ismāʿīl Maẓhar, *Aṣl al-Anwā'*/أصل الأنواع (tr. of Charles Darwin's *Origin of the Species*) and Yūsuf Karam, تاريخ الفلسفة اليونانية/ *Tārīkh al-Falsafah al-Yūnāniyyah* (*The History of Greek Philosophy*).

206. Idem, p. 231.

207. Idem, p. 231. Writing in the fourteenth century (CE), Ibn Khaldūn had the following to say in the *al-Muqaddimah*/المقدّمة or introduction to his book of world history (*apud* the translation by Franz Rozenthal [Princeton University Press, Bollingen Series, 1967], pp. 74–75):

> The world with all created things in it has a certain order and solid construction . . .
>
> One should then look at the world of creation. It started out from the minerals and progressed, in an ingenious, gradual manner, to plants and animals. The last stage of minerals is connected with the first stage of plants, such as herbs and seedless plants. The last stage of plants, such as palms and vines, is connected with the first stage of animals, such as snails and shellfish which have only the power of touch. . . .
>
> The animal world then widens, its species become numerous, and, in a gradual process of creation, it finally leads to man, who is able to think and to reflect. The higher stage of man is reached from the world of the monkeys, in which both sagacity and perception are found, but which has not reached the stage of actual reflection and thinking. At this

> point we come to the first stage of man. This is as far as our (physical) observation extends.
>
> Now, in the various worlds we find manifold influences. . . . In the world of creation there are certain influences of the motions of growth and perception. All this is evidence of the fact that there is something that exercises an influence and is different from the bodily substances. This is something spiritual. It is connected with the created things. . . . This spiritual thing is the soul. . . .

Citing parts of the same passage in his *Understanding the Text*/مفهوم النص (Beirut: Arabic Cultural Center, 1996), p. 36, Naṣr Abū Zayd, for what above in Rozenthal's English appears as

> The animal world then widens, its species become numerous, and, in a gradual process of creation, it finally leads to man, who is able to think and reflect. The higher stage of man is reached from the world of the monkeys.

gives for the Arabic that he (Naṣr) cites

> واتسع عالم الحيوان وتعددت أنواعه وآنتهى في تدريج التكوين إلى الإنسان صاحب الفكر والروية ترتفع إليه من عالم القدرة الذي آجتمع فيه الحس والإدراك ولم ينته إلى الروية والفكر بالفعل.

The Arabic that Ṇaṣr cites does not allow for "the higher stage of man is reached from the world of monkeys." The Arabic in this segment of the above passage has عالم القدرة, which could indeed yield "the world of [God's] omnipotence" and certainly not "the world of monkeys." القِرَدة however is a plural for القِرْد, which indeed is a word meaning monkey or ape.

In al-Afghānī's estimation, in at least one verse of poetry "al-Maʿarrī's intentions were clear . . . He meant evolution, taking this concept from Arab scientists before him . . . who claimed that minerals transform into plants, plants into animals, and that the last of these three transformations and the highest link in the chain is man" (*apud* Elshakry, *Reading Darwin*, pp. 124–25; the quote is from an essay by al-Afghānī that appeared in 1884).

When all is said and done, it is difficult not to regard al-Maʿarrī as a materialist *and* evolutionist (although not necessarily to the extreme of the Khaldūnian variety—in Rosenthal's redaction of *al-Muqaddimah*—with respect to the rise and development of humans and their most immediate antecedent in the chain of living things). As al-Ghazzālī saw things, this would make al-Maʿarrī ipso facto an atheist. Pure and simple. And indeed, he may have been. But as a materialist and an evolutionist he could also have been an agnostic or—although much less likely—the type of evolutionist who had a "theistic view of evolution," one that advanced "faith in a benign, gradual evolution under divine Providence" (Elshakry, idem, p. 106, describing some of the late nineteenth-century Arab evolutionists who were critics of Shumayyil's theory of evolution, which included among other things the theory of spontaneous generation). The rub here for al-Maʿarrī would have been acknowledging a *benign* evolution under divine Providence.

George Harun (Shiblī Shumayyil, *Une Pensée evolutionniste Arabe à l'époque d'an-Nahḍa* [Beirut, 1985], p.150) has regarded Shumayyil as the first person in the history of Arabic thought who not only doubted religions and thus rejected them but also denied the existence of God and any type of spiritual philosophy; i.e., he was the first materialist in the history of Arabic thought who was also an atheist. (Shumayyil est donc le premier dans la pensée arabe à dépasser la négation des religions, le doute religieux, pour nier Dieu, la philosophie spiritualiste, et adopter celle de la matière.) Other materialists in the history of Arabic thought—i.e., those of *al-dahriyyah* persuasion—were such only in the sense that they may have simply embraced the eternity of matter or eternity of the world (i.e., without denying the existence of God). Even Ibn al-Rāwandī and al-Rāzī were probably deists (Probablement, ar-Rāwandī et ar-Rāzī furent des croyants à la manière des déistes et sans se servir des religions.) Al-Maʿarrī in Harun's estimation, at least in his *Une Pensée evolutionniste Arabe à l'époque d'an-Nahḍa* (p. 150), is merely a pessimist using his reason to criticize religion (Ar-Rāwandī et ar-Rāzī . . . ne furent même pas plus pessimistes qu'Abū l-ʿAlā' al-Maʿarrī. Celu-ci critiquait les religions au profit de la raison). In other words, notwithstanding his criticisms, al-Maʿarrī was not an atheist—according to Harun. Professor Emeritus Ralph M. Coury (History, Fairfield University) first brought Harun's work to my attention and graciously provided me with photocopies of relevant chapters.

208. "Abū'l-ʿAlā al-Maʿarrī's Correspondence on Vegetarianism," D. S. Margoliouth, *JRAS* (April 1902), pp. 316–17.

209. Margoliouth, idem, p. 318.

210. Margoliouth, idem, p. 320.

211. Margoliouth, idem, p. 317.

212. Margoliouth, idem, p. 319.

213. See Majid Fakhry, *A History of Islamic Philosophy*, p. 215.

214. Margoliouth, idem, p. 319.

215. Leyden ms., p. 43 for أوْ جُدْ; Zand has أوجُدْ, in what seems like a typographical error.

216. Leyden ms., p. 128, has قَطْنِي (lower portion of the loins), although in this instance that it is not قُطْنِي seems almost inconceivable.

217. Reading *al-nask*/النسك according to Leyden ms., p. 201, instead of *al-nasl*/النسل in Zand's L II.239, which would yield "procreation."

218. Majid Fakhry, *A History of Islamic Philosophy*, p. 267.

219. Zaehner, *Hindu and Muslim Mysticism, apud* Fakhry, ibid.

220. Fakhry, idem, p. 272.

221. *Qaḍāyā al-'Aṣr*, p. 111.

222. Idem, p. 117.

223. In L II.415.14, al-Maʿarrī says that the taking of furs or skins from animals is one of mankind's gravest deeds.

224. That he *could* have, especially by word of mouth during his two-year sojourn in Baghdad, is a real possibility (von Kremer, for example, held that during al-Maʿarrī's lifetime Jains were living in nearly all the port cities of the Persian Gulf as merchants and money-changers and that many Indians in general could have been led to Baghdad as a result of Maḥmūd of Ghazna's campaigns into India and spreading of Islam there; "Ueber die philosophischen Gedichte," p. 84). But that such was *actually* the case would be impossible to verify unless somewhere al-Maʿarrī himself admits as much (which, as far as far as the present study knows, he does not).

In any event, as Nicholson suggested ("The Meditations," p. 137), the establishment of this ideational borrowing would prove no more than al-Maʿarrī's desire and resolve to live according to beliefs or practices established and advocated by others; for which reason the present study is not overly preoccupied with the whole question of whence al-Maʿarrī's ascetic principles, at least not insofar as the chief concern lies with understanding al-Maʿarrī's thought rather than tracking down all of its possible sources (although admittedly finding possible sources can be illuminating with a thinker as elusive as al-Maʿarrī).

For the record, Nicholson thought that al-Maʿarrī "probably" derived his asceticism from the Indian variety thereof ("The Meditations," p. 137). Von Kremer went one step further and said he definitely did and, furthermore, seems to have studied under a Jain tutor or instructor ("Ueber die philosophischen Gedichte," pp. 83–84).

225. "Ueber die philosophischen Gedichte," p. 84.

226. "Es ist wie ein Welterlösungswahn, der ihm beherrscht, und zwar einer Erlösung im Wege des allgemeinen Nirvana; indem alles in dem

Nichtsein Ruhe findet" ("Ueber die philosophischen Gedichte," p. 43). Nirvana here is understood in the philosophical sense of the word, although as a term signifying a lifestyle involving asceticism it is also applicable to the discussion of possible Indian influences on al-Maʿarrī's thought; see, e.g., "The Meaning of Nirvana," Jay ram V, Hinduwebsite.com.

227. Von Kremer, "Ueber die philosophischen Gedichte," p. 83. In his autobiographical novel *The Days* (*al-Ayyām*), Ṭāhā Ḥusayn relates a story, traditionally told of al-Maʿarrī, that gives as an additional reason for his abstention from eating honey or treacle an unpleasant personal experience. According to the story, al-Maʿarrī, being blind, was not very adept at eating treacle or honey, which one day resulted in his appearing before his students with traces smeared on his chest. When notified of this by his students, al-Maʿarrī was embarrassed and ashamed. He feared that people would mistake him for a glutton. From that day onward he vowed never to eat treacle or honey again; (*al-Ayyām* [Cairo: Dār al-Maʿārif, 1971], pp. 20–21).

228. Von Kremer, "Ueber die philosophischen Gedichte," p. 16. Perhaps al-Maʿarrī also had this in mind when advocating a meager diet and praising going hungry. If so, this is further support for believing that he may have been searching for an "acceptable" suicide in his ethics, one not as obvious as the more violent varieties of taking one's life (and thus also not as manifestly in violation of the Qur'ān and the consensus of the legal [religious] scholars on the issue).

229. "The Meditations," p. 138, n. 1.

230. "The Meditations," pp. 137–38. The quote is from *Outlines of Jainism* by J. Jani, introduction, p. 23.

231. "The origins of asceticism," www.britannica.com/topic/asceticism.

232. "The origins of asceticism," www.britannica.com/topic/asceticism.

233. *SEI*, p. 661.

234. *Abū al-'Alā' Nāqid al-Mujtama'*, p. 21.

235. "Abū'l-'Alā al-Ma'arrī's Correspondence on Vegetarianism," pp. 291–92.

236. Idem, p. 291.

237. *Apatheia*, Wikipedia.

238. See, e.g., www.askelm.com/people/peo019.htm.

239. "The Meditations," p. 125. Al-Maḥāsinī with respect to all of the contours of al-Maʿarrī's asceticism extended his Freudian interpretation. He argued that al-Maʿarrī's sexually repressed personality, occasioned by being spurned by a beloved, explains every facet of his asceticism and not simply his renunciation of women (*Abū al-'Alā' Nāqid al-Mujtama'*, pp. 48–53; the

introduction to this work contains an emotive reflection—occasioned by a visit by al-Maḥāsinī to Maʿarrat al-Nuʿmān—on the beloved [Umāmah] and her connection to al-Maʿarrī as if her existence is a proven historical fact).

240. "No suelan se nuestras ideas las que nos hacen optimistas o pesimistas, sino que es nuestro optimismo o pesimismo, de origen fisiológico o patológico quizá, tanto el uno como el otro, el que hace nuestras ideas" (*Unamuno, Sus Mejores Páginas*; ed. Philip Metzidakis, p. 112). In other words, al-Maʿarrī may have been hardwired for his pessimism even without the affliction of blindness and the other setbacks in his life.

241. See Nicholson, "The Meditations," pp. 46–47, for the translation of the epistolary passage dealing with the departure from Baghdad, as well as for L II.303.3–4.

242. This is precisely why al-Maʿarrī says he did not marry and have children (L II.395.6–8).

243. P. 474.

244. "The origins of asceticism," www.britannica.com/topic/asceticism.

245. T. J. DeBoer, *The History of Philosophy in Islam*, trans. by Edward R. Jones (New York: Dover, 1967), p. 66.

246. Adonis, *An Introduction to Arabic Poetics*, p. 65.

247. Cf. Ṭāhā Ḥusayn, *Ma'a Abī al-'Alā' fī Sijnih*, 11th edition, p. 151.

248. *Allah's Commonwealth*, p. 543. The overview in the paragraph preceding the quotation also draws from Peters's *Allah's Commonwealth.*

PRINCIPLE WORKS CITED OR CONSULTED

ʿAbd al-Qādir, Ḥāmid. *Falsafat Abī al-'Alā'.* Cairo: Lajnat al-Bayān al-ʿArabī, 1950.

Abū Zayd, Naṣr Ḥāmid. *Mafhūm al-Naṣṣ*. 3rd Edition. Beirut: al-Markaz al-Thaqafī al-ʿArabī, 1996.

Adamson, Peter, and Richard C. Taylor. *The Cambridge Companion to Arabic Philosophy.* Cambridge: University Press, 2005.

Adonis. *An Introduction to Arab Poetics*. Austin: University of Texas Press, 1985.

al-ʿAlawī, Hādī. *Abū al-'Alā' al-Ma'arrī, al-Muntkhab min al- Luzūmiyyāt: Naqd al-Dawlah wa al-Dīn wa al-Nās*. 2nd Edition. Damascus: Al Mada, 2007.

Albert, Ethel M., Theodore C. Denise, and Sheldon P Peterfreund. *Great Traditions in Ethics.* New York: American Book Company, 1953.

Arberry, A. J. *Arabic Poetry*. Cambridge: Cambridge University Press, 1965.

———. *Aspects of Islamic Civilization.* Ann Arbor: University of Michigan Press, 1967.

———. *Reason and Revelation in Islam.* London: George Allen and Unwin, 1957.

———. *The Rubaiyat of Omar Khayyam.* London: Dent, 1972.

———. *Sufism.* New York: Harper Torchbooks, 1950.

Ashtiany, Julia; Johnston, T. M. et al. *The Cambridge History of Arabic Literature: Abassid Belles-Lettres.* Cambridge: Cambridge University Press, 1990.

Asin Palacios, Miguel. *Islam and the Divine Comedy.* Tr. and abridged by Harold Sutherland. London: Frank Cass, 1968.

Atiyeh, George N. *Al-Kindī: The Philosopher of the Arabs*. Rawalpindi: Islamic Research Institute, 1966.

Avery, Peter, and John Heath-Stubbs. *The Ruba'iyat of Omar Khayyam*. Middlesex, England: Penguin Books, 1983.

Aristotle. *Aristotle on Poetry and Style*. Tr. G. M. A. Grube. New York: Liberal Arts, 1958.

———. *The Philosophy of Aristotle*. Selections, translations by A. E. Wardman and J. L. Creed. Mentor Books. New York: New American Library, 1963.

Averroes. *Tahāfut al-Tahāfut*. Tr. Simon Van den Bergh. Oxford: Oxford University Press, 1954.

Avicenna (Ibn Sīnā). *Avicenna's Psychology*. Tr. Fazlur Rahman. London: Oxford University Press, 1952.

———. *Dīwān Ibn Sīnā*. Ed. Nūr al-Dīn 'Abd al-Qādir and Henry Jahier. Algiers: Libraire Ferrais, 1960.

———. "Healing: Metaphysics X." Tr. Michael Marmura. *Medieval Political Philosophy*, ed. Ralph Lerner and Muhsin Mahdi. Ithaca: Cornell University Press, 1963.

———. "On the Proof of Prophecies and the Interpretation of the Prophets' Symbols and Metaphors." Tr. Michael Marmura. *Medieval Political Philosophy*, ed. Ralph Lerner and Muhsin Mahdi. Ithaca: Cornell University Press, 1963.

Bakrī, 'Aṭā. *Al-Fikr al-Dīnī 'inda Abī al-'Alā' al-Ma'arrī*. Beirut: Maktabat al-Ḥayāh, 1980.

Bambrough, Renford. *The Philosophy of Aristotle*. New York: Mentor, 1963.

Bint al-Shāṭi' ('Ā'ishah 'Abd al-Raḥmān). *Ma'a Abī al-'Alā'*. Beirut: Dār al-Kitāb al-'Arabī, 1972.

Boer, T. J. de. *The History of Philosophy in Islam*. Tr. Edward R. Jones. New York: Dover, 1967.

Brockelmann, Carl. *History of the Islamic Peoples*. New York: Capricorn Books, 1960.

Brown, Jonathan A. C. *Misquoting Muhammad*. London: Oneworld, 2015.

Commins, Saxe, and Robert N. Linscott. *Man and Spirit: The Speculative Philosophers*. New York: Random House, 1947.

Camus, Albert. *The Myth of Sisyphus*. Tr. Justin O'Brien. Middlesex, England: Penguin Books, 1977.

Cantarino, Vicente. *Arabic Poetics in the Golden Age*. Leiden: E. J. Brill, 1975.

Corbin, Henri. *Cyclical Time and Ismaili Gnosis*. London: Kegan Paul International, 1983.

Coury, Ralph M., ed. *Sceptics of Islam: Revisionist Religion, Agnosticism and Disbelief in the Modern Arab World.* London: IB Tauris, 2018.

Ḍayf, Shawqī. *Al-Fann wa-Madhāhibuh fī al-Shi'r al-'Arabī.* 4th Edition. Cairo: Dār al-Maʿārif, 1960.

Durant, Will. *The Story of Philosophy*. New York: Simon and Schuster, 1961.

Edgerton, Franklin. *The Beginnings of Indian Philosophy*. Cambridge, Mass. Harvard University Press, 1965

Elshakry, Marwa. *Reading Darwin in Arabic, 1860–1950*. Chicago: University Press, 2013.

The Encylopaedia of Islam.

The Encyclopedia of Philosophy.

Ernst, Carl W. Sufism, *An Introduction to the Mystical Tradition of Islam*. Boston and London: Shambala Press, 2011

Fakhry, Majid. *A History of Islamic Philosophy*. New York: Columbia University Press, 1970.

———. *Islamic Occasionalism.* London: George Allen and Unwin Ltd., 1958.

———. *Islamic Philosophy*. Oxford: Oneworld Publications, 1997.

———. *A Short Introduction to Islamic Philosophy, Theology, and Mysticism.* Oxford: Oneworld Publications, 1997.

al-Fārābī. "The Attainment of Happiness." Tr. Muhsin Mahdi. *Medieval Political Philosophy.* Ed. Ralph Lerner and Muhsin Mahdi. Ithaca: Cornell University Press, 1963.

———. "The Letter Concerning the Intellect." Tr. Arthur Hyman. *Philosophy in the Middle Ages*. Ed. Arthur Hyman and James J. Walsh. New York: Harpur and Row, 1967.

———. "Plato's Laws." Tr. Muhsin Mahdi. *Medieval Political Philosophy.* Ed. Ralph Lerner and Muhsin Mahdi. Ithaca: Cornell University Press, 1963.

———. "The Political Regime." Tr. Fauzi M. Najjar. *Medieval Political Philosophy.* Ed. Ralph Lerner and Muhsin Mahdi. Ithaca: Cornell University Press, 1963.

Farhat-Holzman, Laina. *Strange Birds from Zoroaster's Nest*. Oneonta, NY: Oneonta Philosophy Studies, 2000.

Farrūkh, ʿUmar. *Ḥakīm al-Ma'arrah*. 2nd Ed. Beirut: al-Kashshāf Press, 1948.

Friedmann, Yohannan. "Literary and Cultural Aspects of the Luzūmiyyāt." Studia Orientalia Memoriae D.H. Baneth Dedicata. Jerusalem: The Magnes Press, the Hebrew University, 1979.

al-Ghazzālī (al-Ghazālī). *Al-Risālah al-Laduniyyah.* Tr. Margaret Smith. *Journal of the Royal Asiatic Society* (April, 1938), pp. 177–200.

———. *Tahāfut al-Falāsifah.* Tr. Sabih Ahmad Kamali. Lahore: Pakistan Philosophical Congfress, 1963.

Gibb, H. A. R. *Arabic Literature.* 2nd Edition. Oxford: Oxford University Press, 1963.

Goeje, M. J. de. *Mémoires sur les Carmathes du Bahrain et les Fatimides.* Leiden: E. J. Brill, 1886.

Gutas, Dimitri. *Greek Thought, Arabic Culture.* New York: Routledge, 1998.

Haddad, Yvonne Yazbeck, and Hane Idleman Smith. *The Islamic Understanding of Death and Resurrection.* Albany: State University of New York Press, 1981.

al-Ḥamd, Muḥammad ʿAbd al-Ḥamīd. *Al-Zandaqah wa al-Zanādiqah.* Damascus: Al-Ṭalīʿah al-Jadīdah, 1999.

Hamori, Andras. *On the Art of Medieval Arabic Literature.* Princeton: Princeton University Press, 1974.

Harun, George. Shibli Shumayyil. *Une pensée évolutionniste arabe a l'époque d'an-nahda.* Beirut, 1985.

Hava, J. G. *Al-Farā'id al-Durriyyah.* 3rd Edition. Beirut: Dār al- Mashriq, 1970.

Heinrichs, Wolfhart. *Arabische Dichtung und griechische Poetik.* Beirut: Orient-Institut der Deutschen Morgenländischen Gesellschaft, 1969.

———. "Contacts between Islamic Legal History and Literary Theory: The Case of *Majāz*" (unpublished version of an article).

Herman, Arthur. *The Cave and the Light.* New York: Random House, 2014.

Hitti, Philip. *History of the Arabs.* 10th Edition. London: Macmillan, 1970.

———. *The Origins of the Druze People and Religion.* New York: Columbia University Press, 1928.

Hodgson, Marshall G. S. *The Order of the Assassins.* The Hague: Mouton, 1955.

———. *The Venture of Islam.* Vols. I and II. Chicago: University of Chicago Press, 1974.

Holt, P. M., Ann K. S. Lambton, and Bernard Lewis. *The Cambridge History of Islam.* Vol. I. Cambridge: Cambridge University Press, 1970.

Hourani, Albert. *A History of the Arab People.* New York: Warner Books, 1991.

Ḥusayn, Ṭāhā. *Al-Ayyām.* 17th Edition. Cairo: Dār al-Maʿārif, 1971.

———. *Maʿa Abī al-ʿAlā' fī Sijnih.* 10th Edition. Cairo: Dār al-Maʿārif, n.d.

———. *Tajdīd Dhikrā Abī al-'Alā'*. 8th Edition. Cairo: Dār al- Maʻārif, 1976.

———. *Ta'rīf al-Qudamā' bi-Abī al-'Alā' al-Ma'arrī.* Ed. (along with others). Cairo: Dār al-Kutub al-Miṣriyyah, 1944.

Hyman, Arthur, and James Walsh, eds. *Philosophy in the Middle Ages*. New York: Harper and Row, 1967.

Ibn Isḥāq. *The Life of Muhammad.* Tr. A. Guillaume. Offset printed ed. Karachi: Pakistan Branch of the Oxford University Press, n.d.

Ibn Khaldūn. *The Muqaddimah.* Tr. Franz Rosenthal, ed. and abridged by N. J. Dawood. Princeton: Princeton University Press, Bollingen Series, 1967.

Ibn al-Nadīm. *Kitāb al-Fihrist*. Ed. and tr. Bayard Dodge. 2 vols. New York: Columbia University Press, 1970.

Jaini, Jagmanderlal. *Outlines of Jainism*. Cambridge: University Press, 1916.

James, William. *The Varieties of Religious Experience*. New York: Collier, 1961.

al-Jundī, Muḥammad Salīm. *Al-Jāmi' fī Akhbār Abī al-'Alā' al-Ma'arrī wa-Āthārih.* 3 vols. Damascus: Arab Academy of Science, 1962–1964.

Kabir, Mazifullah. *The Buwayhid Dynasty of Baghdad.* Calcutta: Iran Society, 1964.

Khalīfāt, Saḥbān. "al-Jawānib al-Mītāfīzīqiyyah li al-Nafs wa Naẓariyyat al-Maʻrifah ʻinda Abī al-ʻAlā' al-Maʻarrī." *Majallat Dirāsāt* (The University of Jordan) 12, no. 3, 1985.

al-Khaṭīb, Muḥibb al-Dīn. *Bayna Abī al-'Alā' wa-Dā'ī al-Du'āh.* Cairo (n.p.), 1930.

———. "Makānat al-ʻAql fī al-Falsafat al-Khulqiyyah ʻinda Abī al-ʻAlā' al-Maʻarrī."*Majallat Dirāsāt* (The University of Jordan) 12, no. 8, 1985.

———. "Mītāfīzīqā al-ʻUlū wa al-Ṭabīʻah fī Falsafat Abī al-ʻAlā' al-Maʻarrī." *Majallat Dirāsāt* (The University of Jordan), n.d.

Kraemer, Joel L. *Humanism in the Renaissance of Islam.* Leiden: E.J. Brill, 1992.

Kremer, Alfred von. *Kulturgeshichte des Oriens unter den Chalifen,* Vol. II. Reprint of the Vienna edition of 1875. Heidenheim: Scientia Verlag Aalen, 1996.

———. "Ueber die philosophischen Gedichte der Philosophisch- Historischen Classe der Akademie der Wissenschaften (Vienna), 17, no. 6 (1888), pp. 1–108.

Lane, Edward William. *An Arabic-English Lexicon.* Offset printed ed. Beirut: Libraire du Liban, 1968.

Lapidus, Ira. *A History of Islamic Societies*. Cambridge: University Press, 2002.

Laoust, Henri. "La vie et la philosophie d'Abū'l-ʿAlā' al- Maʿarrī." *Bulletin d'études orientales,* X (1944–45), pp. 119–157.

Levy, Reuben. *The Social Structure of Islam.* Cambridge: University Press, 1971.

Lichtenstadter, Isle. *Introduction to Classical Arabic Literature.* New York: Schocken Books, 1976.

Lucretius. *On the Nature of the Universe.* Tr. and introduced by R. E. Latham. Middlesex: Penguin Books, 1951.

al-Maʿarrī, Abū al-ʿAlā'. *Al-Fuṣūl wa al-Ghāyāt.* Ed. Maḥmūd Ḥasan Zanātī. Cairo: al-Hay'ah al-Miṣriyyah li-al-Kitāb, 1977.

———. *The Letters of Abu 'l-'Alā'.* Compiled, ed., and tr. D. S. Margoliouth. Anecdota Oxoniensa Semitic Series, Part X. Oxford: Clarendon. 1898.

———. *Luzūm Mā Lā Yalzam.* 2 vols. Beirut: Dār Ṣādir, 1961.

———. *Luzūm Mā Lā Yalzam.* Ed. ʿAzīz Effendi Zand. 2 vols. Cairo: al-Maḥrūsah Press, 1891, 1895.

———. *Luzūm Mā Lā Yalzam.* Ed. with a commentary by Ibrāhīm al-Abyārī. Part I. Cairo: Ministry of Education, 1959.

———. *Luzūm Mā Lā Yalzam.* Leyden University Library MS. OR 100.

———. *Risālat al-Ghufrān.* Ed. Bint al-Shāṭi'. Cairo: Dār al-Maʿārif, 1969.

———. *Risālat al-Ṣāhil wa al-Shājiḥ.* Ed. Bint al-Shāti' (ʿĀ'ishah ʿAbd al-Raḥmān). Cairo: Dār al-Maʿārif, 1975.

———. *Saqṭ al-Zand.* Beirut: Dār Ṣādir, 1963.

———. *Zajr al-Nābiḥ.* Ed. Amjad al-Ṭarābulsī. Damascus: Arabic Language Academy, 1965.

MacIntyre, Alasdair. *A Short History of Ethics.* New York: Macmillan, 1966.

al-Maḥāsinī, Zakī. *Abū al-'Alā' Nāqid al-Mujtama'.* Beirut: Dār al-Maʿārif, 1963.

Mahdi, Muhsin. *Ibn Khaldūn's Philosophy of History.* Phoenix Books. Chicago: University Press, 1964.

Margoliouth, D. S. "Abu'l-ʿAlā al-Maʿarrī's Correspondence on Vegetarianism." *Journal of the Royal Asiatic Society* (April 1902), pp. 289–332.

____ *The Letters of Abu 'l-'Alā.* Oxford: The Clarendon Press, 1898.

Mason, Herbert W., Ronald L. Nettler, and Jacques Waardenburg, eds. *Humaniora Islamica* Vol. I. The Hague: Mouton, 1974.

Maẓhar, Ismāʿīl. "Maʿa al-ʿAqqād, Naqd Kitābih *Allāh*" *Fī al-Naqd al-Adabī.* Beirut: Manshūrāt Dār Maktabat al-Ḥayāt, 1965.

Menocal. María Rosa. *The Arabic Role in Medieval Literary History.* Philadelphia: University of Pennsylvania Press, 1983.

Miskawayh. *The Refinement of Character.* Tr. Constantine K. Zurayk. Beirut: American University of Beirut Press, 1968.

More, Paul Elmer. *Platonism.* Princeton: University Press, 1926.

al-Mutanabbī. *Dīwān al-Mutanabbī.* Ed. with a commentary by ʿAbd al-Raḥmān al-Barqūqī. 2 vols. Beirut: Dār al-Kitāb al-ʿArabī, n.d.

———. *Poems of al-Mutanabbī.* Selected and ed. A. J. Arberry. Cambridge: Cambridge University Press, 1967.

Nusseibeh, Sari. *The Story of Reason in Islam.* Stanford: Stanford University Press, 2017.

Nasr, Seyyed Hussein. *The Heart of Islam.* New York: HarperOne, 2004.

———. *Ideas and Realities of Islam.* Boston: Beacon, 1975.

———. *Islamic Life and Thought.* London: George Allen & Unwin, 1981.

———. *Three Muslim Sages.* Cambridge: Harvard University Press, 1964.

Netton, I. R. *Muslim Neoplatonists.* London: George Allen & Unwin, 1982.

Nicholson, R. A. *A Literary History of the Arabs.* Cambridge: Cambridge University Press, 1969.

———. "The Meditations of Maʿarrī." *Studies in Islamic Poetry.* Cambridge: Cambridge University Press, 1921.

———. *The Mystics of Islam.* London: Routledge and Kegan Paul, 1966.

———. "The Risālatu'l-Ghufrān by Abū' l-'Alā al-Ma'arrī, summarized and partially translated." *Journal of the Royal Asiatic Society,* 1900 (Part 1) and 1902 (Part 2).

Nietzsche, Friedrich. *Beyond Good and Evil.* Tr. Walter Kaufman. New York: Random House, 1966.

O'Leary, De Lacy. *Arabic Thought and Its Place in History.* London: Routledge & Kegan Paul, 1968.

Peltz, Christian. *Der Koran des Abū l-'Alā': Teil 1: Materialien und Überlegungen zum K. Al-Fuṣūl wa-l-ġāyāt des al-Ma'arrī.* Wiesbaden: Harrosowitz, 2013.

Peters, F. F. *Allah's Commonwealth.* New York: Simon and Schuster, 1973.

Plato. *Great Dialogues of Plato.* Tr. W. H. D Rouse. Mentor Books. New York: New American Library, 1956.

———. *The Timaeus and the Critias.* Tr. Thomas Taylor. Princeton: Princeton University Press, 1944.

———. *The Timaeus and the Critias.* Tr. Robin Waterfield, introduction and noted by Andrew Gregory. Oxford: University Press, 2008.

Plotinus. *The Essence of Plotinus.* Based on translations by Stephen Mackenna. Compiled by Grace H. Turnbull. New York: Oxford University Press, 1934.

Rasā'il Ikhwān al-Ṣafā'. Beirut: Dār Ṣādir, 1957.

Rahman, Fazlur. *Islam.* New York: Anchor Books, 1968.

al-Rāzī, Abū Bakr (Muḥammad Zakariyyā'). *Opera Philosophica.* Ed. Paul Kraus. Cairo, 1939.

———. *The Spiritual Physick of Rhazes.* Tr. A. J. Arberry. London: Murray, 1950.

Rihani, Ameen. *The Luzumiyat of Abu'l-Ala Selected from his Luzum ma la Yalzam and Suct uz-Zand* and first rendered into English. New York: Jame T. White & Co., 1918.

Rosenthal, Franz. "On Suicide in Islam." *Journal of the American Oriental Society* 66 (1946), pp. 239–59.

Ryan, Michael. "Al-Rāzī on Space and Time." Unpublished paper, Harvard University, 1976.

Saleh, Moustapha. "Abū-l-ʿAlā', al-Maʿarrī: bibliographie critique." *Bulletin d'études orientales* 22 (1969), pp. 133–204; 23 (1970), pp. 197–309.

Salmon, George. *Le poete aveugle.* Paris: Charles Carrington, 1904.

Schact, Joseph. *The Legacy of Islam.* 2nd Edition. Oxford: University Press, 1979.

Schimmel, Anne Marie. *Islam.* Albany: SUNY Press, 1992.

———. *Mystical Dimensions of Islam.* Chapel Hill: North Carolina University Press, 1975.

Shorter Encyclopaedia of Islam.

Smith, T. V. *Philosophers Speak for Themselves.* Chicago: University of Chicago Press, 1934.

Smoor, Pieter. "Enigmatic Allusion and Double Meaning in al-Maʿarrī's Newly Discovered Letter of a Horse and a Mule." *Journal of Arabic Literature* 12 (1981), pp. 49–73; 13 (1982), pp. 23–52.

———. *Kings and Bedouins in the Palace of Aleppo as Reflected in Ma'arrī's Works.* Manchester: University of Manchester, 1985.

Sperl, Stefan. *Mannerism in Arabic Poetry.* Cambridge: University Press, 1989.

Stern, S. M. "Some Noteworthy Manuscripts of the Poems of Abū'l-ʿAlā' al-Maʿarrī." *Oriens* (Leyden) 7, no. 2, pp. 322–47.

———, Albert Hourani, and Vivian Brown. *Islamic Philosophy in the Classical Tradition.* Essays presented by his friends and pupils, to Richard Walzer. Columbia: South Carolina University Press, 1972.

Stroumsa, Sarah. *Freethinkers of Medieval Islam.* Leiden: Brill, 1999.

Strauss, Leo. *Persecution and the Art of Writing.* Glencoe, IL: Free Press, 1952.

Taymūr, Aḥmad. *al-'Alā' al-Ma'arrī.* 2nd Ed. Cairo: Anglo-Egyptian Bookstore, 1970.

Unamuno, Miguel de. "Del sentimiento trágico de la vida."

———. *Unamuno: sus mejors paginas.* Ed. Philip Metzidakis. Englewood Cliffs, NJ: Prentice Hall, 1966.

Underhill, Evelyn. *Mysticism*. New York: E. P. Dutton, 1961.

Van Ess, Josef. "Some Fragments of the *Mu'āraḍat al-Qur'ān* Attributed to Ibn al-Muqaffa'." *Studia Arabica and Islamica.* Festschrift for Ihsan Abbas. Beirut: 1981, pp. 151–63.

Walbridge, John. *The Wisdom of the Mystic East.* Albany: State University of New York Press, 2001.

Watt, Montgomery. *The Formative Period of Islamic Thought.* Edinburgh: Edinburgh University Press, 1973.

———. *Islamic Philosophy and Theology*. Edinburgh: Edinburgh University Press, 1962.

Wensinck, A. J. *The Muslim Creed.* London: Frank Cass, 1965.

Wheelwright, Philip. "Philosophy and Poetry." *Princeton Encyclopedia of Poetry and Poetics,* 1974.

Wolfson, Henry Austryn. *The Philosophy of the Kalam*. Cambridge: Harvard University Press, 1976.

Wright, William. *A Grammar of the Arabic Language.* 3rd ed. Cambridge: Cambridge University Press, 1967.

Zaehner, R. C. *Hindu and Muslim Mysticism.* New York: Schocken Books, 1969.

Zakkar, Suhayl. *The Emirate of Aleppo*. Beirut: Dār al-Amānah, 1971.

Zaydān, 'Abd al-Qādir. *Qaḍāyā al-'Aṣr fī Adab Abī al-'Alā' al-Ma'arrī.* Cairo: Al-Hay'ah al-Miṣriyyah al-'Āmmah li al-Kitāb, 1986.

INDEX

ʿAbbāsid caliphal court. *See* ʿAbbāsid court
ʿAbbāsid caliphal suzerainty, 48, 49, 51
ʿAbbāsid caliphate, 62
  authority, 91, 93
  Būyids and, 89
ʿAbbāsid caliphate era. *See* ʿAbbāsid era
ʿAbbāsid caliphs, 46, 48–50, 61, 64, 86. *See also specific caliphs*
  Aleppo and, 61
  Baghdad and, 39, 42, 43, 51, 54, 62, 68, 69, 72, 84–85
  Būyids and, 39, 45, 73, 75
  Carmathian insurgencies and, 48
  Jawhar al-Ṣiqillī and, 43
  power/authority, 12, 43, 45, 365n1
  as Sunnī, 43, 61
ʿAbbāsid court, 49, 93
ʿAbbāsid dynasty, 39, 64, 82, 86
  Baghdad and, 252–53, 268
  Fāṭimids and, 40, 90
  urban life during, 252
ʿAbbāsid era, 130
  poetry of the, 130–32, 134
ʿAbd al-Qādir Zaydān, 201, 235, 271, 273, 321
ʿAbd al-Salām al-Baṣrī, Abū Aḥmad (al-Wājikah), 14, 17, 22
ʿAbd Allāh Abū al-Hayjā', 48
abstractionism, 101
absurd, philosophy of the, 398n43
Abū ʿAbd Allāh al-Ḥusayn al-Shīʿī, 41
Abū ʿAbd Allāh Muḥammad, 81
Abū Abū Manṣūr Fūlād Sulṭān, 75
Abū Aḥmad al-Mūsawī/al-Sharīf al-Ṭāhir, 14
Abū al-Majd Muḥammad ibn ʿAbd Allāh (brother of al-Maʿarrī), 8
Abū ʿAlī al-Burjumī, 74–75
Abū ʿAlī ibn Ustādhurmuz, 71
Abū ʿAlī Musharrif al-Dawlah, 73–74
Abū Manṣūr, 16, 22
Abū Shujāʿ (Sulṭān al-Dawlah), 72, 73
Abū Ṭāhir Jalāl al-Dawlah, 74–75
Academy of Sābūr, 15–16, 22
acquisition. *See kasb*
Active Intellect, 111
adab (literature), 7, 126–35
  al-Maʿarrī and, 24, 96, 149, 352
  masters of, 96, 126–27, 149. *See also adīb*
  poetry and, 24, 127, 128
Adam, 248, 278, 279, 322
  evil instinct and, 187
  historicity, 278, 279, 320
  multiplicity, 318, 322, 423n97
  revelation and, 279, 323
adīb (master of *adab*), 96, 126–27, 133. *See also adab*: masters of
ʿAdīm, Ibn al-, 6, 11, 14, 25, 27–28, 355–56n13
ʿAḍud al-Dawlah, 45, 64, 66–69, 71, 77
adulterers, 259, 415n85, 425n105
adulterous wives, 425n105
agnosticism
  al-Maʿarrī's, 181, 221, 229, 317, 433n179, 439n207
  rationalism driving, 184
  types of, 181
aḥdāth (citizen-based militia), 55, 58, 59
ahl al-sunnah. See ritual piety: *Sharīʿah*-driven

Aḥmad ibn Abū Shujāʿ, 62–63
Aḥmad ibn Ḥanbal, Abū ʿAbd Allāh, 100, 102
ʿAjamī, Abū al-Ḥasan ʿAlī ibn Aḥmad al- (al-Ḍayf), 54
Akhṭal al-Taghlibī, al-, 129
al-Andalus. *See* Umayyads in Spain
al-ʿaql (mind/intellect), 391nn15–16. *See also* reason
al-naql, 97, 412n72
Alawites. *See* ʿAlids
Aleppo
  Christians of, 59–60
  governors of, 22, 24, 50–52, 54, 55, 59–61, 357n42
  history, 4, 5
  Maʿarrat al-Nuʿmān and, 3–5, 24, 53
  al-Maʿarrī in, 10–12
  al-Maʿarrī's relatives in, 8
  Mirdāsid dynasty and, 23, 24, 39, 51, 54, 56–59
  officials in, 357n42
  Seljūks and, 92
ʿAlī ibn Abī Ṭālib (cousin and son-in-law of Muḥammad), 83, 124–26. *See also* ʿAlids
  assassination of, 426n112
  belief in the divinity of, 83–84, 422n97
  descendants, 90, 124–26
  Fāṭimids and, 40, 45
  loyalty and allegiance to, 83, 124, 125, 237–38, 374n104
  Shīʿites and, 83, 124–26, 237, 414n82
  and succession to Muḥammad, 125, 414n82
ʿAlī ibn Abū al-Hayjāʾ ʿAbd Allāh ibn Ḥamdān ibn al-Ḥārith al-Taghlibī. *See* Sayf al-Dawlah
ʿAlī ibn Abū Shujāʿ Būyī, 61–62
ʿAlī ibn al-Ḥusayn al-Maghribī. *See* Qāsim, Abū al-
ʿAlid loyalism and loyalists, 24–25, 374n104, 417n85
ʿAlids, 13–15, 44, 68, 73, 74, 83
  Fāṭimids and, 40, 81
Allāh. *See* God
"animal" faculties, 114, 115
"animal soul," lower, 391n15
animal world, Creation and the, 437–38n207
animals, 326. *See also* vegetarianism
  cruelty to, 259, 261
  killing, 110, 209, 235, 325, 326, 331, 340–41
  reincarnation and souls of, 110, 199, 395n34
  speaking, 24, 30
  suffering, 325, 326, 331
  taking of furs or skins from, 340–41, 440n223
anthropomorphism and God, 101, 371n60, 406n57, 433n179
aqdār, 215. *See also al-dahr/al-dahriyyah*; fatalism; predeterminism
ʿaql, 182, 183, 279, 391n16. *See also* rational faculty; reason
Aristotelianism, 78, 104, 107
Aristotle, 103, 104, 385n51. *See also* Active Intellect
  metaphysics, 103, 104, 107, 110–11, 431–35n179
  notion of God as Prime Mover, 434–35n179
ascetic ideals, 336, 343–44
ascetic practices, 336–37
ascetic principles of al-Maʿarrī, 440n224
asceticism, 24–25, 118, 343, 344. *See also* celibacy; sexual abstinence
  Alfred von Kremer and, 342–44
  extreme, 325–27
  Freudians and, 424n103, 441n239
  Hibat Allāh on, 325–26
  nirvana and, 441n226
  practiced by al-Maʿarrī, 24–25, 325–26, 345, 441n239
  preached/promoted by al-Maʿarrī, 24–25, 324, 330, 336–39, 342–44, 347, 349, 421n97, 440n224
  R. A. Nicholson and, 343, 440n224
  religion, God, and, 336–39, 343, 344
  taṣawwuf and, 118
ascetics, 337–38
  Jaina, 343, 344

Ash'arī, Abū al-Ḥasan al-, 189
free will and, 218, 372n73
God and, 100–102, 370n59, 371n60
Henry Wolfson and, 371n60
influence, 103
kasb and, 101, 218, 404n52, 405n54
Majid Fakhry on, 369n50, 370n54
Mu'tazilah/Mu'tazilites and, 100–101, 370n59, 371n60, 428n133, 436n196
overview, 100–103
Qur'ān and, 100–102, 370n59, 371n60
Ash'ariyyah, al- (theological tendency), 100
'Āshūrā', 71
'Askarī, Ḥasan al-, 83, 125
'Atāhiyyah, Abū al-, 131
atheism, 38, 106, 312, 316–17. *See also* God: existence/non-existence and; naturalism
Al-'Alawī's al-Ma'arrī, 311, 401–2n47
Bakrī's al-Ma'arrī and, 402–3n47
Georges Haroun's al-Ma'arrī and, 439
Ḥusayn's al-Ma'arrī and, 399–401n47, 406–7n61
Khalīfāt's al-Ma'arrī and, 400–403n47
al-Ma'arrī and, 196, 221, 242, 311, 312, 316–17, 384n45, 400–403n47, 408n61, 435–36n188, 439n207
Nicholson's al-Ma'arrī and, 399
von Kremer's al-Ma'arrī and, 399n47
Zaydān's al-Ma'arrī and, 403n47
atheists, 436n188, 439n207
atomism, 99, 102, 430n153
mutakallimūn and, 99, 319, 369n51
Mu'tazilah/Mu'tazilites and, 99, 369n51, 370n53
Avery, Peter, 175, 378n11
Avicenna. *See* Ibn Sīnā
'Azīz al-Dawlah (Abū Shujā' Fātik ibn 'Abd Allāh al-Rūmī), 22–24, 54–55, 58
'Azīz Billah, al-, 21, 43–45, 52, 67, 68

Baghdad. *See also specific topics*
governors of, 39, 45–46, 48, 49, 51, 62, 66–75
al-Ma'arrī in, 13–14. *See also under* Ma'arrat al-Nu'mān
Saqṭ al-Zand and, 5, 13, 16, 377n11
Sunnīs in, 19, 65, 69, 71–74, 77
Baghdad branch of Mu'tazilah movement, 98
Bahā' al-Dawlah (Abū Naṣr Fīrūz Khwāshād), 15, 21, 70, 71
Bahrain, 65
Bakjūr, 21, 51–52
Bakrī, 'Aṭā, 35, 227, 242, 384n45, 403–4n47, 407n60, 422n97
baqā', 119–20
Bāqillānī, Basrite Abū Bakr al-, 102, 134, 135, 277
Basra, 64, 70
Basra/Basrite branch of Mu'tazilah movement, 98, 100, 370n53
Bāṭiniyyah, 420–21n97
Being, 107, 111, 114, 119, 120, 304, 339, 399n43. *See also* First Being
being/existence (*wujūd*), 107, 113, 119, 180–82, 188, 194, 219, 221, 236, 243, 245, 284, 296, 303, 304, 312, 315, 317, 319, 339, 348, 399–401, 402n47, 407, 409, 433–35, 439. *See also* metaphysics
blind poets, 12
blindness, 9–10
of al-Ma'arrī, 9–10, 12, 326–27, 409n65, 441n227
body, 107, 281–84, 387–88n9, 436n196. *See also* disease
as evil, 182
soul and, 108, 110, 289, 390n14, 393n25
death and, 112, 393–94n25
resurrection and, 114–15. *See also* resurrection
soul as captive of the body, 386–87n7
spirit and, 390n14
body politic, 269, 275
bon mot, 148, 378n11
Brethren of Purity/Sincere Brethren (Ikhwān al-Ṣafā'), 79, 105, 116–18, 422n97
Buwayhids. *See* Būyid dynasty/Buwayhid dynasty

Būyid dynasty/Buwayhid dynasty, 78, 90, 364
'Abbāsid caliphs and, 39, 45, 51
'Abbāsid dynasty and, 89
al-'Azīz and, 45
cultural vitality during, 77–78
end of, 75, 76, 92
governors and governorship, 39, 45–46, 48, 49, 51, 61–79
Mu'izz al-Dawlah and, 63, 64
overview, 61–79
royal building projects, 68–69, 77
Shī'ī and, 45, 61, 77, 90, 92, 126
Būyid palace complex (Dār al-Mamlakah), 68–70, 73, 74
Būyid princes, 21
Būyid suzerainty, 39, 46, 64, 67

Carmathians (Qarāmiṭah), 272, 417n85, 421–22n97
Abū al-Hayjā' and, 48
al-Aḥsā', 415–16n85
in Bahrain, 65
in Basra, 64, 70
Ḥamdān ibn Ḥamdūn and, 48
overview, 79–82
in Syria, 44, 48
celestial spheres/celestial bodies (heavenly spheres/heavenly bodies), 108, 111, 114, 116, 195, 217, 282, 285–87, 301, 302, 305, 306, 308
God and, 160, 185
motion of, 114, 289, 290, 292, 299, 301, 304, 306, 316, 404n47
time and, 302, 304
celibacy, 24, 209, 249, 258, 324, 342. *See also* procreation
cessation of life through, 209, 248
Jainism and, 343
al-Ma'arrī's boast of life-long, 341
rationale for, 249
certainty, absolute, 186, 192, 193
Chapters with End Rhymes and Imitation of Chapters and Verses (al-Ma'arrī), 27
Christianity, 7, 96, 280, 368n45, 408n64
creatio ex nihilo and, 372n72
free will and, 368n45, 369n50
al-Ma'arrī's criticism of, 239, 242, 247, 280, 419n90
Tanūkh and, 7
women and, 239
Christians, 343
of Aleppo, 59–60
Fāṭimid Caliphate and, 47–48
relations between Muslims and, 23, 60, 268, 365, 369n50
Syrian, 59, 60, 365n
cognition, 107, 109, 111, 112
cosmogony, 299, 304–5, 311, 313, 316–17
cosmology, principles of al-Rāzī's, 109
creatio ex nihilo, 106, 107, 109, 283, 372n72, 435n179
Creation, 292. *See also* Adam
natural elements, God, and, 178, 221, 280–81, 283–84, 308–9, 311
Crucifixion of Jesus, 419n90

al-dahr/al-dahriyyah, 216–17, 294, 295, 297, 298, 307, 309, 310, 316–17, 321, 322, 435n188, 439n207. *See also aqdār*; fatalism; fate; materialism; materialists; naturalism
time, eternity, and, 299, 300, 316. *See also* eternal time
al-zaman and, 298–300
Darwin, Charles, 321–23
Day of Judgment. *See* Judgment Day/Day of Judgment
death, 207. *See also* resurrection; suicide
praise of, 209, 210
as preferable to life, 208
soul, body, and, 393–94n25
deism and deists, 184, 244, 398n43, 439n207. *See also* Rāzī, Abū Bakr Muḥammad ibn Zakariyyā' al-; revelation: vs. reason
Demiurge God, 434n179
determinism. *See* free will; *al-Jabariyyah*; predeterminism
Dhahabī, al-, 10, 11, 357n42
Dhikrawayh al-Dindānī, 81

diet, al-Maʻarrī on, 324, 331, 441n228
Ḍirār ibn ʻAmr, 404n52, 436n196
disease
  evil and, 182, 192, 227
  freedom from, 293, 318, 390n14. *See also* death; suicide
  life as a, 203, 207–9, 349
  manifestations of, 436n196
  spirit and, 390n14
diseased soul, 182, 192
dissimulation, 170, 292, 322, 384n45
Divine Law, 199–200, 245, 390n15, 413n74. *See also Sharīʻah*
Dīwān al-Rasāʼil (*Collection of the Epistles*), 26, 31
dīwān/dawāwīn (poetry collections), 5, 8, 11, 25, 129, 131, 210. *See also Saqṭ al-Zand; specific poetry collections*
doing and willing, domains of, 370n53
Druze, 61, 82, 423n97
dualisms, 304–5

education
  levels of, 95
  of al-Maʻarrī, 10–11, 14, 15
ego, annihilation of, 119. *See also fanāʼ*
elements. *See* four elements; natural elements
emanationism
  neo-Platonic, 107, 308, 314, 386n7
  Plotinian, 104
emanations, 110, 111, 113, 114
Emirate of Aleppo 1004–1094, The (Zakkar), 365
empiricism, moral, 339
end rhymes, 156, 175
Epicureanism, 345
epistemological nihilism, 192, 231, 329
Epistle of Forgiveness, The (*Risālat al-Ghufrān*), 21, 25, 26, 31–34, 237, 276, 314
  Ibn al-Rāwandī and, 315
  al-Jannābī and, 417n85
  al-kawn and, 430n153
  quotes from, 396–99n43, 408n64, 415n85
  religion and, 408–9n64
  suicide and, 396–99n43
  time and, 301
Epistle of the Angels (*Risālat al-Malāʼikah*), 25–27
Epistle of the Horse and the Mule (*Risālat al-Ṣāhil wa al-Shājiḥ*), 22–25, 30, 201
eternal principles of cosmology, 109–10
eternal time, 109, 188, 216, 217, 294, 295, 297–304, 306, 307, 309, 314, 316, 317, 322
eternity
  of God, 290, 318, 371
  natural elements and, 221, 280–81, 283–84, 287, 293, 320
ether. *See* Fifth Element
ethics. *See* morality/ethics
Ethics (Ṭūsī), 352
eugenics, 327
euthenics, 327
evil, 187–90, 225, 247, 264–67, 339–40. *See also* good and evil
  children and, 255, 332
  God and, 215–19, 391n15
  human nature as, 144, 186–88, 190, 192, 201–2, 215–17, 225, 247, 327
  light, darkness, and, 304
  nafs as, 391n15
  and the Qurʼān, 225–26, 390n15
  religion and, 251, 337–38, 346
  and the soul, 182, 186, 192, 193, 348, 390n14
evolution and evolutionism, 321–23, 438–39n207
existence. *See* being/existence

faith, 159, 231, 241, 327–29, 391n15
  call to, 233
  leap of, 398–99n43
  the Muʻtazilah and articles of, 98
  testament of, 226, 259, 260
Fakhr al-Dawlah, 67, 69
Fakhr al-Mulk, Abū Ghālib ibn Khalaf, 21, 22, 71, 72
Fakhry, Majid, 368n45, 369–70n50–53, 373n81

Fakhry, Majid (*continued*)
on al-Ash'arī, 369n50, 370n54
on Ḍirār ibn 'Amr, 436n196
on al-Ma'arrī, 35–36, 169
falāsifah/faylasūf (Islamic philosophers), 28, 103, 105, 106, 275, 319. *See also* philosophers: Islamic
Fallāḥī, Abū Naṣr Ṣadaqah ibn Yūsuf al-, 22, 54
falsafah (philosophy), 105, 181, 280, 314, 352
Brethren of Purity and, 116–18
overview, 103–6
Platonism and, 110, 201
falsehoods, 172. *See also* "lying" and falsehood in poetry
discourse stripped of, 140, 142, 149
family, al-Ma'arrī on, 248–58
fanā', 119, 121
Fārābī, al-, 50, 104, 274, 384n45
Ibn Sīnā and, 113, 114
al-Ma'arrī and, 181, 197, 274, 279
metaphysics, 110–12
neo-Platonism and, 112, 114
overview, 110–13
Farrūkh, 423n97
fasting during Ramadan, 225, 343
fatalism, 161, 214, 215. *See also aqdār*; *al-dahr/al-dahriyyah*; fate; materialism; naturalism; predeterminism
fate, 298. *See also aqdār*; *al-dahr/al-dahriyyah*; materialism; naturalism; predeterminism
Fāṭimah, 40
Fāṭimid expeditions, 57–58
Fāṭimid suzerainty, 4, 21, 39, 42–44, 46
Fāṭimids
governors and, 21, 39, 42, 44–46, 52, 54, 55
overview, 40–48
faylasūf. *See falāsifah/faylasūf*
Fifth Element, 292
Firdawsi, 85
First Being, 107, 111, 113
First Cause, 110, 111, 113, 114, 246, 312
first philosophy, 103, 106, 107
defined, 107
food, 347
four elements, 283, 309
four humors, 178, 182
four natures/instincts (*arba' ṭabā'i'/gharā'iz arba'*), 178
free will, 161, 405n57
al-Ash'arī and, 218, 372n73
vs. determinism/predetermination, 96, 99, 101, 161, 189–92, 215, 218, 369n50, 392n23
God and, 99, 100, 161, 405n57
good and evil and, 99, 101, 161, 188–90, 193
Islam and, 96, 189–90
Mu'tazilah/Mu'tazilites and, 99–101, 190, 218, 405–6n57
reason and, 97, 99, 192
freedom, 340, 401n47
French Revolution, thinkers of the compared with al-Ma'arrī, 271, 272
Friedmann, Yohanan, 148, 174, 377n11, 379n13

gangs, 19, 60, 71, 74
generation, theory of, 99
Ghaznavids, 85
Ghazzālī, al-, 122, 197, 391n15, 435n188, 438n207
gnosis, 120, 121
Gnosticism, 120, 305, 316, 343, 421n97
God (Allāh), 101, 113, 212, 400n47. *See also* Being; First Cause; humankind and God; One; *specific topics*
anthropomorphism and, 101, 371n60, 406n57, 433n179
arguments for the existence of, 107
al-Ash'arī and, 100–102, 370n59, 371n60
attributes/characteristics, 100, 102, 121, 211, 370n59, 371n60, 406n57
existence/non-existence and, 107, 113, 188, 194, 219, 221, 319, 348, 399n43, 400–404n47, 407n60, 409n64, 433–35n179, 439n207

fear of. *See* piety
kasb and, 101, 217, 218
al-Ma'arrī's religious philosophy, humankind, and, 221–47
Mu'tazilites and, 371n60
nature of, 107–11, 407n60
oneness of, 98, 100, 116, 119, 211, 220, 221, 371n60, 407n60
praising, 9, 160, 166, 167, 239, 287, 295, 400–401n47
and the Qur'ān, 101
reason and, 97, 99–100, 116, 219, 220, 236, 348, 370n59, 400–403n47
understanding, 407n60
good and evil, 186, 187, 221, 264, 329, 339–40. *See also* evil
beyond, 221
body and soul and, 182, 390n14
distinction and discernment between, 99, 101, 188–90, 193, 236
free will and, 99, 101, 161, 188–91, 193, 216
God and, 100, 101, 188, 217, 219, 221, 236
reason and (discerning between), 186–89, 193, 219, 236, 329, 339, 348

Hādī, 'Alī al-, 83
Hajar, 416n85
ḥajj (pilgrimage to Mecca), 121, 223–24, 333, 409n65
Ḥajjāj, al-, 129
Ḥākim bi-Amr Allāh, al-, 22, 23, 44, 45, 47, 53, 54
Ḥamdān ibn Ḥamdūn, 48
Ḥamdān Qarmaṭ, 80–81
Ḥamdānid dynasty, 10, 63–68
Aleppo and, 4, 10, 12, 13, 44–45, 49, 51–53, 62
end of, 53
Mirdāsids and, 13, 51
Mosul and, 62, 64, 67
Nāṣir al-Dawlah and, 49, 62, 63
overview and history, 48–53
Syria and, 13, 21, 39
Ḥamdānid princes, 4, 10
harem system, 86, 257, 262, 425n105
Ḥasan, al-. *See* Nāṣir al-Dawlah
Ḥasan al-Aṣma'ī, al-, 44
Ḥasan al-Baṣrī, 119, 344, 369n50
Ḥasan 'Alī, Abū al-, 53
Ḥasan 'Alī ibn Aḥmad al-'Ajamī, Abū al-. *See* 'Ajamī, Abū al-Ḥasan 'Alī ibn Aḥmad al-
Hayjā', Abū al-, 48, 53
Heaven and Hell, 5–6, 31, 201, 229, 243. *See also* Paradise
heavenly spheres/heavenly bodies. *See* celestial spheres/celestial bodies
hegira. *See hijrah* from Medina to Mecca
Heinrichs, Wolfhart, 94, 95
Hellenism, 93–95, 97, 106
Hibat Allāh ibn Mūsā. *See* Mu'ayyad fī al-Dīn Abū Naṣr Hibat Allāh ibn Abī 'Imrān Mūsā
Ḥijāz, 266
hijrah from Medina to Mecca, 414n82
Holy Reason, 115. *See also* Reason
Hourani, Albert, 365n1
humankind and God: al-Ma'arrī's religious philosophy, 210–47
humankind and the totality of being: al-Ma'arrī's perception of make-up and dynamics of universe, 280–305
the planets, 305–23
humankind as it ought to be. *See under* morality/ethics
humankind interacting with humankind: al-Ma'arrī's social and political views in *Luzūm*, 247–48
the family, 248–58
influential individuals in al-Ma'arrī's society, 262
learned class, 275–80
people of state, 263–75
society in general, 258–62
Ḥusayn, Ṭāhā, 149, 170, 377n11
Ḥusayn ibn 'Alī, 69, 71
assassination of, 268, 426n112
Ḥusayn ibn Ḥamdān, 48

Iberian Peninsula. *See* Umayyads in Spain
Ibn al-Rāwandī, 236
ibn Ḥanbal, Aḥmad, 100–102, 373n103
ibn Miskawayh, Abū ʿAlī, 79, 328, 352
Ibn Sīnā (Avicenna), 85, 104, 105, 387n7
  on God, 113–15
  on Holy Reason/Intellection, 115
  al-Maʿarrī and, 181, 387–89n9
  metaphysics, 113–15
  psychology, 114
  on the soul, 113–15
Ikhwān al-Ṣafā'. *See* Brethren of Purity/ Sincere Brethren
ilḥād, 316, 384n45. *See also* atheism
Improvement of Morals, The (Miskawayh), 352
Incoherence of the Philosophers, The (al-Ghazzālī), 197. *See also* Ghazzālī, al-; philosophers
injustice, 218, 219, 272, 421n97
intellect. *See al-'aql*; cognition; rational faculty; reason
Intellection, 115
interracial marriage, 426n109
irredentism, 4, 92
Islamic Divine Law. *See* Divine Law; *Sharī'ah*
Ismāʿīl ibn Aḥmad, Sāmānī, 84
ʿIzz al-Dawlah (Bakhtiyār), 64–66

Jabariyyah, al-, 99. *See also* predeterminism
Jaʿfar al-Ṣādiq, 40, 41, 45, 80
Jāḥiẓ, al-, 133, 134
Jainism, 342–44
  ethics, 343
  renunciation and, 343, 347
Jains, Alfred von Kremer and, 342–44, 440n224
Jannābī, Abū Saʿīd al-Ḥasan al-, 81
Jannah. *See* Paradise
Jawhar al-Ṣiqillī, 42–44
Jazīrah, al-, 70
  rulers, 48–50, 65–67
Jesus Christ, 239–41, 418–19n90
  historicity, 228, 239
Jewish Messiah, 242
Jews, 47, 48, 59, 60, 241, 279, 280, 346
jinās, 131, 156–58
Judaism, 210, 241–42
  al-Maʿarrī's criticism of, 239, 241, 242, 279–80
judges, 277
Judgment Day/Day of Judgment, 150, 160, 196, 197, 201, 243
Junayd, Abū al-Qāsim al- (Junayd of Baghdad), 119
Jurjānī, ʿAbd al-Qādir al-, 134, 135
justice. *See also* injustice
  absolute, 98–99, 218, 406n57
  God's, 98–100, 106, 401–2n47, 405–6n57

Kabir, Mafizullah, 364–65
kalām, 95
  al-Ashʿarī and, 102
  God and, 98, 99
  Henry Wolfson on, 98, 369n49
  Luzūm and, 231, 280
  Muʿtazilah and, 98, 100
  overview, 96–103
kalām-master. *See mutakallim*
kasb, 218, 405n57
  al-Ashʿarī and, 101, 218, 404n52, 405n54
  Ḍirār ibn ʿAmr as inventor of the concept of, 404n52
  God and, 101, 217, 218
kawn, 430n153
Khālid ibn al-Walīd, 355n13
kharrat, 179–80
khumm, 414n82
Kindī, Abū Yūsuf Yaʿqūb al-, 105–9
knowledge, 109. *See also* cognition; reason

Laoust, Henri, 34, 419–21n97
Leyden manuscript, 215, 224, 375–76n2
life
  cessation of, 209, 248. *See also* procreation
  as a disease, 203, 207–9, 349. *See also* death; suicide
"lower self," 391n15
"lower world," 112, 315
Luzūm Mā Lā Yalzam (al-Maʿarrī). *See also specific topics*

contents, 139–42, 149
mundane elements, 149
overview and nature of, 139–40
topics of, 139, 140
transcending the contradictions and other challenging features of, 169–76
"lying" and falsehood in poetry, 141–42, 377n9, 377n11

Maʿarrat al-Nuʿmān, 3, 5, 8
Aleppo and, 3–5, 24, 53
Christians in, 60
description and characterization of, 3
geography, 3, 4
geopolitical importance, 4–5
history and warfare, 4, 13, 19, 24, 53, 57–58, 60
house of Sulaymān and, 6, 7
judges in, 7, 8
al-Maʿarrī on, 5, 6
al-Maʿarrī's departure to Baghdad from, 11–12, 358n42
al-Maʿarrī's return from Baghdad to, 5, 8–9, 13, 18, 20, 24, 27
Muslims in, 60
sociodemographics, 6
Maʿarrī, Abū al-ʿAlā' al-. *See also specific topics*
blindness, 9–10, 12, 326–27, 409n65, 441n227
childhood, 9
children and, 249
daily life, 20
death, 39
education, 10–11, 14, 15
epistles, 25. *See also specific epistles*
family and relatives, 7–9
father, 7–10
mother's death, 8–9, 13, 19–20
Majid Fakhry's characterizations of, 35, 169
meaning of his name, 172
perception of make-up and dynamics of universe. *See* humankind and the totality of being
personality, 274–75, 441n239
as philosopher, 28, 38, 105, 156, 181, 278, 432n179
praise and. *See* praise
as recluse, 274
religious philosophy. *See* humankind and God
smallpox, 9
social and political views. *See* humankind interacting with humankind
students, 22–23
Maḥāsinī, al-, 252–53, 272, 341, 344, 441n239
Mahdī, Ḥujjat Allāh al- (Muḥammad al-Mahdī), 125
Maḥmūd ibn Nāṣir, 46
Maḥmūd of Ghaznah, 72
Malik al-ʿAzīz, al-, 75
Manṣūr bi-Naṣr Allāh, al-, 42, 268
Manṣūr ibn Lu'lu', 53–54, 58, 60
Mardawīj ibn Ziyār, 61–62
Margoliouth, D. S., 12, 16, 18–20, 344, 357n42, 359n75
marriage, 148, 253, 333. *See also* polygamy
procreation and, 248, 249
materialism, 321. *See also* naturalism
Epicurean, 36, 235, 402n47, 408n61
al-Maʿarrī and, 36, 235, 316, 321, 322, 402n47, 408n61, 435n179, 438–39n207
materialists, 316, 321, 322, 439n207. *See also al-dahr/al-dahriyyah*
Mazdeanism (Zorostrianism), 222, 299–301, 304, 305, 408n64, 418n89
Mecca, 266, 306
history, 43, 130
Mesopotamia, 48, 49, 67, 81. *See also* Jazīrah, al-
metaphysics, 103. *See also* Rāzī, Abū Bakr Muḥammad ibn Zakariyyā' al-
of al-Fārābī, 110–12
of al-Maʿarrī, 313, 314, 318–19, 421n97, 431–35n179. See also humankind and the totality of being
of Aristotle, 103, 104, 107, 110–11, 431–35n179
first philosophy and, 106, 107

metaphysics (*continued*)
of Ibn Sīnā, 113–15
Mu'tazilah and, 99
reason and, 116, 220
taṣawwuf and, 120–21
mind. *See al-'aql*; reason
Mirdāsid dynasty, 44, 51, 57, 60, 89, 385n45
Aleppo and, 23, 24, 39, 51, 54, 56–59
Syria and, 13, 39, 57, 385n45
Miskawayh, Abū 'Alī ibn, 79, 328, 352
monorhyme, 130, 142, 143
moral admonitions, 29, 140, 190
moral rationalism, 339, 392n23
moral responsibility, 100, 101
moralism, 257
morality/ethics, 185–87, 191, 193, 227. *See also* ethics
Al-Ma'arri's Ethics in the *Luzūm*, and humankind as it ought to be, 323–52
fate and, 205, 216, 392n23
free will and, 191, 216
God and, 101, 189, 219, 243
The Improvement of Morals (Miskawayh), 352
poetry and, 38, 378n11
suicide and, 209–10, 441n228
women and, 250, 333
moralizing in *Luzūm*, 323, 392n23
Moses, 228, 240, 241
Mosul, Iraq, 49, 63, 66
governors of, 48, 49
Ḥamdānids in, 62, 64, 67
Nāṣir al-Dawlah (al-Ḥasan) and, 49, 62, 63
motion and God, 107, 431–33n179
Mu'ayyad al-Dawlah, 67–68
Mu'ayyad fī al-Dīn Abū Naṣr Hibat Allāh ibn Abī 'Imrān Mūsā, al-, 23–25, 54, 325–27, 331, 344
Muḥammad, Prophet
customs of. *See sunnah*
praise of, 165, 227, 242–43, 245, 412–13n72, 414n82
succession to, 40–41, 125, 414n82
Muḥammad al-Mahdī (Ḥujjat Allāh al-Mahdī), 125
Muḥammad ibn Nāṣir, 58
Muḥāsibī, Ḥārith al-, 120
Mu'izz al-Dawlah, Abū 'Ulwān Thimāl, 56
Mu'izz al-Dawlah, Aḥmad, 49, 63, 64, 69, 89
Mu'izz li-Dīn Allāh, al-, 42, 43
Mulqā al-Sabīl (al-Ma'arrī), 26
Murtaḍā, al-Sharīf al-, 13–14, 17, 18
mushā'āt, 257, 425n105
Musharrif al-Dawlah (Abū 'Alī), 21, 73, 74
mutakallimūn/mutakallim, 97–99, 104, 125, 276, 278
atomism and, 99, 319, 369n51
challenges faced by, 368n46
vs. *faqīh*/master of *fiqh*, 367n43, 369n49
God and, 97–99, 319
Mutanabbī, al-, 11, 18–19, 132, 301
Mu'tazilah/Mu'tazilites, 99, 369n50
abstractionism of, 101
Abū al-Ḥasan al-Ash'arī and, 100–101, 370n59, 371n60, 428n133, 436n196
al-Ash'arī and, 100–101, 370n59, 371n60, 428n133, 436n196
atomism and, 99, 369n51, 370n53
free will and, 99–101, 190, 218, 369n50, 405–6n57
God and, 98–101, 370n59
Jahm ibn Ṣafwān, *al-Jabariyyah*, and, 99, 369n50
principles associated with, 98–99
rationalism and, 100–101
reason and, 99, 370n59
right vs. wrong, good vs. evil, and, 99, 101
Wāṣil ibn 'Aṭā', *al-Qadariyyah*, and, 369n50

naql. *See* revelation
Nāṣir al-Dawlah (Abū Muḥammad al-Ḥasan ibn Abū al-Hayjā' 'Abd Allāh ibn Ḥamdān al-Taghlibī), 49–50, 62, 63, 65
Mosul and, 49, 62, 63
Nāṣir al-Dawlah al-Ḥamdānī, 46
Nāṣir-i Khusraw, 3, 59, 300
Nāṣir Shibl al-Dawlah (son of Ṣāliḥ ibn Mirdās), 56

naskh, 199
Naṣr ibn Aḥmad, 84
natural elements, 305, 306, 317
Creation, God, and, 178, 221, 280–81, 283–84, 308–9, 311
eternity and, 221, 280–81, 283–84, 287, 293, 320
naturalism, 108, 317, 321, 323. *See also al-dahr/al-dahriyyah*; materialism
nature, 402n47
Necessary Being, 113
neo-Platonism, 289, 299, 300, 314, 386nn6–7
al-Fārābī and, 112, 114
neo-Platonists, al-Ma'arrī contrasted with, 306, 308, 390n14, 391n15
Nicholson, R. A., 142, 149, 175, 377n11, 440n224
Alfred von Kremer and, 34, 35, 37, 38, 149, 156, 170
asceticism and, 343, 440n224
'Azīz Effendī Zand and, 428n129, 428–29n136
nihilistic epistemology, 192, 231, 329
nirvana, 343, 440n226
Niẓām al-Mulk, 14
nonexistence (*al-'adam*), 113, 208
bliss/comfort of, 249, 253–54, 342–43
nothingness, 107–8, 206, 208
Nuṣayrīs, 83, 198, 394n31
Nuṣayriyyah, al-. *See* 'Alids
Nusseibeh, Sari, 381n39, 427n128

Old Anatolian Turkish. *See* Seljūk Turks
Omar al-Khayyam and al-Ma'arrī, 32, 378–79n11. *See also* quatrains
One, the, 167, 213, 284, 291, 301, 404n47
al-Kindī and, 107
Plotinus's doctrine of, 104
oneness of God, 98, 100, 116, 119, 211, 220, 221, 371n60, 407n60

Paradise, 26, 31, 201. *See also* Heaven and Hell
Peters, F. E., 106, 110, 125–26, 352
philosophers, 47, 79, 104–6, 178, 274, 275, 278–80, 321
critique of, 197, 277–80
God and, 278, 279
Islamic, 104–7, 179, 197, 198, 290. *See also falāsifah/faylasūf*
Islamicate, 180, 352
knowledge and intelligence, 111
al-Ma'arrī as philosopher, 28, 38, 105, 156, 181, 278, 432n179
prophets and, 111–12, 115
resurrection and, 278
terminology and translations of the term, 32
philosophical suicide, 398–99n43
defined, 398n43
piety, 118, 183. *See also* ritual piety
claims and pretenses of, 238, 277
God-centered, 28
God-fearing, 173, 191, 223, 333, 336, 400n47
inducing, 223, 225
al-Ma'arrī's criticisms of, 162
Qur'ān and, 121, 277
taṣawwuf and, 118, 121–22
terminology, 336, 409n64
pilgrimage routes to Mecca, 68, 71, 81
pilgrimage to Mecca (*ḥajj*), 121, 223–24, 333, 409n65
Plato, 110, 390n14
Platonism, 97, 103–4, 109, 110, 200–201, 316
Platonists, 390n14
Plotinus, 104
poems of praise (*madḥ*), al-Ma'arrī and, 18, 21, 22, 30, 127–29, 131
poems/poetry (*shi'r*), 127–28. *See also specific topics*
collections. See dīwān/dawāwīn
"lying" and falsehood in, 141–42, 377n9, 377n11
qaṣīdah, 128–30, 133
political views of al-Ma'arrī. *See* humankind interacting with humankind
polygamy, 146, 257, 262, 334, 425n105
polymaths, 104
Porphyry, 104

"Praise be their Creator," 160, 287
"Praise be to God," 166, 167, 295
praise poems. *See* poems of praise
praising, al-Ma'arrī's
  death, 209, 210
  God, 154, 160, 166, 239, 287, 295, 400–401n47
  the good, 329
  the mind/intellect/reason/rationalism, 184, 192
  neither Shī'ites nor Sunnīs, 414n82
  others by name, 21
  piety, 336
  the Prophet Muḥammad, 165, 227, 242–43, 245, 412–13n72, 441n228
predeterminism, 188. *See also aqdār*; fatalism; fate; free will
  absolute, 99, 161, 369n50
  divine, 101, 190–92, 214–15, 260, 299, 392n23, 404n48
  kalām and, 98
prime matter, 116, 117
Prime Mover, God as, 246, 310, 434–35n179
Proclus, 104
procreation, 248, 249, 257–58
  avoidance/cessation of, 209, 248, 253, 324, 332, 334, 342, 348, 350
prophets/prophecy/prophethood, 47, 98, 106, 109–11, 114–15, 120, 165–66, 184, 227, 228, 235–37, 240–42, 244, 314–15, 410–11nn69, 410–12n72
prostitution, 424n105. *See also* harem system
punning, 156, 157

qadar, al-, 369n50
Qadariyyah, al-, 189–90, 369n50
Qaḍāyā al-'Aṣr, 407n60
Qādir, al-, 21
qāfiyah murdafah, 147, 148, 380n24
Qarāmiṭah. *See* Carmathians
Qāriḥ, Ibn al- ('Alī ibn Manṣūr al-Ḥalabī), 21, 31
qaṣīdah, 128–30, 133
Qāsim, Abū al- ('Alī ibn al-Ḥusayn al-Maghribī), 20–22
Qāsim, al-Ḥusayn ibn Rūḥ al-Nawbakhtī, Abū al-, 20–21
Qāsim 'Alī ibn Sabīkah, Abū al- (maternal uncle of al-Ma'arrī), 8, 13
qawm, 163–64
qidam, 290
Qifṭī, al-, 6, 11, 13
Qifṭī, Ibn al-, 6, 11, 13
Qirwash, 21
quatrains, 32, 378–79n11
Qur'ān/Kuran, 101
  al-Ash'arī and, 100–102, 370n59, 371n60
  piety and, 121, 277
  praise for, 243, 245
  reason and, 97
Qushayrī, Abū al-Qāsim al-, 121–22

Raba'ī, 'Alī ibn 'Īsā al-, 14
Rabī'ah al-'Adawiyyah, 119
Rāḍī, Al-Sharīf al-, 13–15, 17, 126, 133
Ramadan, 225, 343
rational faculty (of the soul), 108, 112, 114, 115. *See also 'aql*; Reason
rationalism, 100, 184, 192, 231, 279, 280. *See also* Mu'tazilah
  moral, 339, 392n23
rationality, 193, 228, 391n15. *See also* rational faculty; reason
Rāzī, Abū Bakr Muḥammad ibn Zakariyyā' al-, 236
  cosmology, 109–10, 313–14
  deism, 110, 236, 413n80, 439n207
  on God, 109–10, 236, 314–16, 434n179
  metaphysics, 109–10, 279, 299, 313–15, 372–73n81, 413n80, 435n186
  overview, 109–10
  Platonism, 110
  on the soul, 109–10, 179, 315, 316
  writings, 85, 109, 372n81
reason, 193, 206, 280, 307, 328, 338, 347, 401–2n47, 411n72, 418n88. *See also 'aql*; rational faculty; rationality; revelation: vs. reason
  Divine Law and, 200
  free agency and, 97, 99, 192

God and, 97, 99–100, 116, 219, 220, 236, 348, 370n59, 400–403n47
and (discerning between) good and evil, 186–89, 193, 219, 236, 329, 339, 348
and liberation, 231
limitations of, 185, 384, 402n47
metaphysics and, 116, 220
Mu'tazilah and, 99, 370n59
philosophy and, 118
poetry and, 381n39
politics, government, and, 271
the power of, 115, 184–85, 188, 192, 220, 228, 231–32, 236, 401n47
Qur'ān and, 97
(institutional/scripture-based) religion and, 221–22, 231–32, 234, 241, 348
and the soul, 116–17, 182, 193, 198–99, 206, 348
"There is no imām other than reason," 237, 279, 414n82, 416n85, 423n97
women, intellect, and, 250
Reason, 418n88
God and, 107, 110, 236, 315, 387n9
Soul and, 110, 115, 315
reincarnation, 289. *See also under* animals
religious devotion. *See* piety
resurrection, 166, 194, 229, 243, 279, 301, 394n25
God and, 160, 196–97, 201
Ibn Sīnā on, 114
Islam, the Qur'ān, and, 106, 114, 123, 196, 197, 201, 279
Judgment Day and, 150, 160, 196, 197, 201
philosophers and, 278, 279
revelation (*naql*), 97, 112, 121, 223, 229
Active Intellect and, 111–12, 115
Brethren of Purity and, 116
falāsifah/faylasūf (Islamic philosophers) and, 105–7, 110
Ibn al-Rāwandī and, 236
Ibn Sīnā and, 114–16
laws based on, 411n72
al-Ma'arrī's rejection of, 323, 337
philosophy and, 109, 117
and the Qur'ān, 105–7, 114, 122, 127, 230
al-Rāzī and, 110
vs. reason, 97, 109, 110, 184, 231–32, 236, 241–42. *See also* deism and deists
rhetorical questions, 166
rhyme (in Arabic), 141–49
rules of, 139, 142, 143, 145
rhymed prose (*saj'*), 25–26, 29–31, 133, 277
rhymes
enriched/supererogatory, 148, 380n25
in poems, 22
Rihani, Ameen, 30, 32, 156, 362–63n126, 378–79n11, 418n88
Risālat al-Ghufrān. *See Epistle of Forgiveness*
Risālat al-Malā'ikah. *See Epistle of the Angels*
Risālat al-Ṣāhil wa al-Shājiḥ. *See Epistle of the Horse and the Mule*
ritual piety, 95, 162. *See also* piety
Sharī'ah-driven, 122–26
rituals of Islam, 244
rubā'iyyāt, 378n11. *See also* quatrains
Rukn al-Dawlah, 64, 66, 67

Sābūr ibn Ardashīr, Abū Naṣr, 15–16, 22
Sa'd al-Dawlah (Abū al-Ma'ālī), 21, 51, 52, 67
Ṣaffārids, 84, 85
Sa'īd al Dawlah, 52, 53
Sa'īd ibn Ḥusayn/'Ubayd Allāh, 41–43
saj'. *See* rhymed prose
Ṣāliḥ ibn Mirdās (Asad al-Dawlah), 23, 44, 54–55, 59, 60
Sāmānids, 72, 84–85
Ṣamṣām al-Dawlah, Abū Kalījār Marzubān, 69, 72
Saqṭ al-Zand (*The Spark of the Fire Drill*), 18, 22, 30, 424n103
Abū al-'Alā' and, 26, 32
on al-Ma'arrī's homeland, 5
Baghdad and, 5, 13, 16, 377n11
commentaries on, 23, 33
compared with *Luzūm Mā Lā Yalzam*, 25, 32, 33, 323, 335, 376n8, 377–78n11
contents, 30–31
Ikhwān al-Ṣafā' and, 422n97
inspiration for, 5

Saqṭ al-Zand (*continued*)
introduction, 278, 376n8, 377n11
al-Maʿarrī's writing of, 5, 16, 25, 377n11
mother's death lamented in, 9
Pieter Smoor and, 23
poem eulogizing the father in, 9
poem of praise (*madḥ*), 21
poem that opens, 323
Ṭāhā Ḥusayn on, 377n11
Sayf al-Dawlah (ʿAlī), 10, 49–51, 53, 63, 65, 132
Sayyidat al-Mulk (First Lady of the Realm), 54
self, dying from. *See fanā'*
self-annihilation, 119, 332
Seljūk Turks, 43–46, 61, 62, 75, 76
Seljūks, 92–93
sexual abstinence, 209, 249, 258, 324. *See also* asceticism; celibacy; procreation
sexual behavior, 257, 258. *See also* harem system
sexual misconduct and abuse, 23, 60, 239, 415n85. *See also* adulterers
sexual repression and suppression, 424n103, 441n239
sexuality, 238, 259
al-Maʿarrī and, 239, 257, 258, 425n106, 441n239
women's, 250–52, 415n85, 425n106
shahādah. *See* faith: testament of
Sharaf al-Dawlah, 70
Sharīʿah, al- (religious law/"the way"), 95, 122, 413n74. *See also* Divine Law
shaykh al-dawlah (head/chief of state), 58
Shīʿites, 40. *See also* ʿAlids; Sunnīs: Shīʿites and; *specific topics*
al-Zaydiyyah, 82–83
Sicily, 41–43
Sitt al-Mulk. *See* Sayyidat al-Mulk
skepticism (of al-Maʿarrī), 197, 223, 231, 235, 244, 379n11
humanism behind, 351
"know-nothing," 181
rationalism driving, 184
reason and, 401–2n47
slave soldiers, 71
slavery, 259, 332
slaves, 257, 259, 262, 332
Smoor, Pieter, 23–24
social views of al-Maʿarrī. *See* humankind interacting with humankind
socio-intellectual currents and discourses in Islamicate community before and during the age of al-Maʿarrī, 88–96
soul, 108, 113–14. *See also* body: soul and; emanationism
al-Kindī on the nature of, 108
nature of the, 386n6
rational. See rational faculty
reason and the, 116–17, 182, 193, 198–99, 206, 348
Soul, 339. *See also* Universal Soul
first intellect and, 111
God and, 107, 109–10
Matter and, 109, 111
Reason and, 110, 115–17, 315
souls, virtuous vs. nonvirtuous, 112
Spain, Umayyads in, 43, 86–87
Spark of the Fire Drill, The. See Saqṭ al-Zand
Sperl, Stefan, 382n40
spirituality, 438–39n207
statespeople, 263–75
Stroumsa, Sarah, 246, 247, 362n123
suffering, 325, 326, 331, 347–49
of animals, 325, 326, 331
of children, 249, 253, 255
Sufism, 118–21, 238, 337, 390–91n15, 417–18n88
suicide, 210, 397n43, 441n228
"acceptable," 441n228
courage, cowardice, and, 209
Islam and, 208–9
al-Maʿarrī's consideration and sympathy to (the notion of), 208, 396–99n43
al-Maʿarrī's contemplation of, 208, 209, 397–98n43
al-Maʿarrī's reasons for refraining from, 209
al-Maʿarrī's rejection of, 328, 397–98n43
"A philosopher condemns suicide," 397n43

philosophical, 398–99n43
societal/communal, 209. *See also* celibacy
Zaydān and, 398–99n43
Sulaymān, house of, 6, 7
Sulṭān al-Dawlah. *See* Abū Shujā'
sunnah (customs of Muḥammad), 44, 120–24, 294, 373n103. *See also* ritual piety: *Sharī'ah*-driven
Sunnīs, 43, 60, 69, 84, 85, 124, 414n82. *See also* 'Abbāsid caliphs; Seljūk Turks
in Baghdad, 19, 65, 69, 71–74, 77
Shī'ites and
peaceful coexistence, 365
sectarian strife between, 19, 69, 71–74, 77
split between, 237, 261, 268. *See also* Muḥammad: succession to
Sunnism, 237–39, 414n82
Syria, 92, 266, 267, 368n45. *See also* Aleppo; Ma'arrat al-Nu'mān; Nāṣir al-Dawlah; Sayf al-Dawlah; *specific topics*
'Aḍud al-Dawlah in, 67
aḥdāth (citizen-based militia), 55, 58, 59
asceticism in, 343
Carmathians in, 44, 48
Fāṭimids and, 4, 21, 43, 44, 51, 55, 57, 65, 67, 91, 385n45
history, 4, 6, 12–13, 21, 44, 48–51, 55, 65
Mirdāsid dynasty and, 13, 39, 57, 385n45
Philip Hitti and, 355
Syrian Christians, 59, 60, 365n
Syrian Tanūkh, 356n13, 423n97

tail rhymes. *See* end rhymes
Tanūkh, 7, 59, 355–56n13
Syrian, 356n13, 423n97
taqiyyah, 170. *See also* dissimulation
taqwā (God-fearing piety), 336, 337
tarṣī', 131, 156, 157
taṣawwuf, 118–22, 337
piety and, 118, 121–22
tashkīk, 420–21n97
Tawḥīdī, Abū Ḥayyān al-, 79, 117–18, 133, 134
ṭibāq, 131, 156, 157

time, 285–304. *See also al-dahr/al-dahriyyah*; eternal time
absolute, 299–303, 316
fundamental aspects of, 299–300
God and, 301
reason and, 287, 295, 298
Torah, 242
Transoxiana, 84
truth, oneness of, 116. *See also* oneness of God
Ṭughril Bey, 46
Turkish soldiers/Turkish army, 44, 59, 71–76
Turks, 72

'Ubayd Allāh/Sa'īd ibn Ḥusayn, 41–43
'Umar Farrūkh (*Ḥakīm al-Ma'arrah*), 379n11, 419n97, 422n97, 427n127
Umayyad Caliphate, 129–30
Umayyad caliphs, 369n50
Umayyad dynasty, 86, 96
Umayyad governors, 132
Umayyads in Spain, 43, 86–87
Universal Soul, 315–16, 386n7. *See also* Soul
Upper Mesopotamia. *See* Jazīrah, al-
urban gangs. *See* gangs
urbanization and poetry, 130

Van Ess, Josef, 30
veganism, 325–27
vegetarianism, 24–25, 325–27, 340, 342, 343
virtue (*faḍl*), 188, 192–93, 338, 347
virtuous cities and city-states, 112–13, 274, 330
virtuous life, 188–90
von Kremer, Alfred, 35, 37, 211, 235, 246, 414n82, 416n85
on al-Ma'arrī, 38
on al-Ma'arrī's belief in God, 400n47, 407–8n61
on al-Ma'arrī's views on free will and determinism, 392n23
asceticism and, 342–44
Jains and, 342–44, 440n224
Luzūm Mā Lā Yalzam and, 33, 34, 141, 149, 156, 170, 177
R. A. Nicholson and, 34, 35, 37, 38, 149, 156, 170

willing and doing, domains of, 370n53
wisdom
  celestial, 299
  falsafah and, 105
  of God, 160, 188, 206, 213, 396n43, 400–402n47, 407n60, 408n61
  philosophical, 106, 112–13, 117
  prophetic, 106, 112–13
  Zervan and, 299, 300
Wolfson, Henry Austryn, 98, 369n49, 371n60
women, 146–48. *See also* marriage; polygamy; procreation
  adultery and, 415n85, 425n105
  Christianity and, 239
  and the Druze, 423n97
  education, 333
  interactions with men, 333
  al-Maʿarrī and, 223, 239, 249, 250, 253, 332–34, 349
  Muḥammad and, 242, 243
  pilgrimage to Mecca, 223, 251–52, 333
  translations of the term, 380n17
women poets, 128
wujūd (being/existence), 113, 401, 402–4n47. *See also* being/existence; metaphysics

Zajr al-Nābiḥ (al-Maʿarrī), 25, 26, 382–83n44
Zakkar, Suhayl, 60, 365
Zand, ʿAzīz Effendī, 375–76n2, 428n129, 428–29n136. *See also specific topics*
zandaqah, 418n88
Zanj Revolt in Basra, 81, 272, 421n97
Zayd ibn ʿAlī, 82
Zaydān, ʿAbd al-Qādir, 167, 235, 271, 272, 321, 407n60
  on "ideological terrorism," 274
  on al-Maʿarrī
    and Adam, 322
    and Creation, 292
    and evolution, 323
    and freedom, 340
    and God, 323, 404n47, 407n60
    and Greek philosophy, 201
    and life, 323
    and metaphysics, 292, 340, 435n179
    and politics, 273
    and the soul, 395n35
    and suicide, 398–99n43
Zaydiyyah Shīʿites, al-, 82–83
Zervan, 299, 300
Zervanism, 299
zindīq, 31
Zoroastrianism. *See* Mazdeanism

www.ingramcontent.com/pod-product-compliance
Lightning Source LLC
Chambersburg PA
CBHW020257240426
43673CB00039B/620
9781438479446